D1723811

German #MeToo

Women and Gender in German Studies

Series editor:

Elisabeth Krimmer (*University of California, Davis*)

German #MeToo

Rape Cultures and Resistance, 1770–2020

Edited by Elisabeth Krimmer
and Patricia Anne Simpson

CAMDEN HOUSE
Rochester, New York

First published 2022 by Camden House

Camden House is an imprint of Boydell & Brewer Inc.
668 Mt. Hope Avenue, Rochester, NY 14620, USA
and of Boydell & Brewer Limited
PO Box 9, Woodbridge, Suffolk IP12 3DF, UK
www.boydellandbrewer.com

ISBN: 978-1-64014-135-3

Library of Congress Cataloging-in-Publication Data

CIP data is available from the Library of Congress.

The publisher has no responsibility for the continued existence or accuracy of URLs for external or third-party internet websites referred to in this book and does not guarantee that any content on such websites is, or will remain, accurate or appropriate.

This publication is printed on acid-free paper.
Printed and bound by CPI Group (UK) Ltd, Croydon, CR0 4YY

Contents

Illustrations

Introduction

Elisabeth Krimmer and Patricia Anne Simpson

> *Ich, der ich immer gehört hatte, auf die Ohrfeige eines Mädchens*
> *gehöre ein derber Kuß, faßte sie bei den Ohren und küßte sie zu*
> *wiederholten Malen. Sie aber tat einen solchen durchdringenden*
> *Schrei, der mich selbst erschreckte.*
>
> —Goethe, "Der Neue Paris," *Dichtung und Wahrheit*, 1811[1]

> [I, who had always heard that a girl's slap should be followed by
> a rough kiss, took her by the ears and kissed her repeatedly. But
> she gave such a piercing scream that it startled even me.]

ON OCTOBER 5, 2017, Jodie Kantor and Megan Twohey of the *New York Times* published an article that detailed how, for decades, the movie producer Harvey Weinstein had paid off and thus silenced women who accused him of sexual harassment.[2] On October 15, the actress Alyssa Milano retweeted the suggestion of a friend: "If all the women who have been sexually harassed or assaulted wrote 'Me too.' as a status, we might give people a sense of the magnitude of the problem."[3] In the next twenty-four hours, twelve million Facebook posts responded to this invitation.[4] Through her tweet, Milano introduced to a mainstream audience a movement founded in 2006 by Tarana Burke in order to support young women of color who had experienced sexual abuse. In the weeks and months after Milano's tweet, #MeToo resonated around the globe, including in France as #BalanceTonPorc, in China as #RiceBunny, in Spain as #YoTambien, and as #ichauch in Germany, where the most

---

1 Johann Wolfgang von Goethe, *Dichtung und Wahrheit*, ed. Peter Sprengel, in vol. 16 of *Sämtliche Werke nach Epochen seines Schaffens*, ed. Karl Richter, Herbert G. Göpfert, Norbert Miller, Gerhard Sauder, and Edith Zehm (Munich: btb Verlag, 2006), 68.

2 https://www.nytimes.com/2017/10/05/us/harvey-weinstein-harassment-allegations.html.

3 https://twitter.com/alyssa_milano/status/919659438700670976?lang=en.

4 Karen Boyle, *#MeToo, Weinstein and Feminism* (Cham, Switzerland: Palgrave Macmillan, 2019), 3.

prominent cases involved accusations of sexual assault against the director Dieter Wedel and against Siegfried Mauser, the president of the Musikhochschule Munich.

The worldwide resonance of #MeToo drastically illustrates the ubiquity of sexual abuse and sexual violence and of the failure to acknowledge their impact publicly. It shows that there is a great need not only to hold perpetrators accountable but also to raise public consciousness. All too often, attention is directed exclusively to the victimization of white middle-class women, while neglecting the experiences of women from lower socioeconomic backgrounds, women of color, members of LGBTQ and immigrant communities, and also of men, including, but not limited to, the rape of male prison inmates.[5]

All too often, the fact that so many experience harassment and rape is seen as evidence that such forms of aggression are natural and inevitable. And yet, studies have shown that some cultures are rape-prone, whereas in others rape is relatively rare, and that "higher rape rates correlate with greater male dominance"[6] and pronounced hierarchical structures. Sexual violence is not a universal human constant. Rather, it is enabled and sustained by the social, political, cultural, and economic fabrics of specific societies. The crimes of individual perpetrators are embedded in what feminists have called "rape culture"—that is, discourses and practices that dehumanize and objectify women while measuring men against a toxic standard of high-octane masculinity;[7] that naturalize, normalize, or trivialize sexual violence; that "other" perpetrators by casting them as monsters and outliers; that politicize rape; and that promote euphemistic reinterpretations of rape as seduction, as the manifestation of an excess of passion or as a by-product of an "artistic temperament or standard business practice."[8] An analysis of such discourses and practices in German history and culture forms the subject of this edited volume. Throughout, we are interested not only in individual instances of misbehavior but also in structural conditions for sexual violence. Indeed, the assumption that representations of sexual violence cannot be divorced from the economic,

---

5   Bianca Fileborn and Rachel Loney-Howes, "Introduction: Mapping the Emergence of #MeToo," in *#MeToo and the Politics of Social Change*, ed. Bianca Fileborn and Rachel Loney-Howes (Cham, Switzerland: Palgrave Macmillan, 2019), 1–18, here 6 and 9.

6   Liz Kelly, *Surviving Sexual Violence* (Cambridge: Polity Press, 1988), 23, and Peggy Reeves Sanday, "Rape and the Silencing of the Feminine," in *Rape: An Historical and Social Enquiry*, ed. Sylvana Tomaselli and Roy Porter (Oxford: Blackwell, 1989), 84–101, here 84.

7   Joanne Bourke, *Rape: Sex, Violence, History* (London: Virago Press, 2007), 142.

8   Boyle, *#MeToo, Weinstein and Feminism*, 13.

legal, and political structures that sustain and indemnify such violence forms one of the central tenets of this book.

In order to lay the groundwork for the individual chapters, the following sections offer a deconstruction of the most common rape myths followed by a brief discussion of some of the most canonical representations of rape in Western civilization in general and German literature in particular. While the concepts, theories, and data presented in the first section are culled from the extensive scholarship on rape and are readily available elsewhere, they are included here because we believe that even readers who have some familiarity with the topic will benefit from a systematic overview of the often inaccurate and problematic perceptions of sexual violence in Western culture. The last section contrasts these literary fantasies of rape with historical realities of rape, focusing on large-scale occurrences of sexual violence, such as those that accompanied colonial conquest and wars but also on ideological and institutional continuities between specific instances of rape in civil society and historical occurrences of mass rapes in the context of warfare, colonialism, and genocide. In linking sexualized violence to specific historical and institutional contexts, we hope to shed light on the intricate nexus of sexuality and power that informs all discourses on rape and desire. Juxtaposing the discursive, historical, and representational dimensions of sexual violence[9] allows us to explore the continuities between them, showing how public discourses and literary texts are informed by and perpetuate rape myths even as they seek to deconstruct and challenge them. Throughout, it is our aim to reread the legacy of sexism and sexist cultural constructions through the lens of a contemporary sociopolitical movement, while challenging "dominant 'scripts' around sexual violence"[10] and emphasizing the importance of taking control over one's own story. Rape is not only "a dense transfer point for relations of power," as Sabine Sielke maintains,[11] but also a crime that does not exist without narrative. In analyzing the representation of sexualized violence, we must attend not only to the various silences and blind spots that undergird these narratives but also to the many discourses in which rape is detached from individual suffering and made to perform the work of ideology.

---

9   See Laura E. Tanner, *Intimate Violence: Reading Rape and Torture in Twentieth-Century Fiction* (Bloomington: Indiana University Press, 1994), 6.

10   Kaitlynn Mendes and Jessica Ringrose, "Digital Feminist Activism: #MeToo and the Everyday Experiences of Challenging Rape Culture," in Fileborn and Loney-Howes, *#MeToo*, 37–51, here 42

11   Sabine Sielke, *Reading Rape: The Rhetoric of Sexual Violence in American Literature and Culture 1790–1990* (Princeton, NJ: Princeton University Press, 2002), 2.

Rape Myths

Rape myths are social scripts that inform our thinking about the nexus of violence and sexuality.[12] They are entwined with cultural preconceptions about proper femininity and masculinity and laden with misogynistic prejudice and problematic assumptions about desire, lust, agency, and identity. In seeking to deconstruct the most prevalent rape myths, we seek to unravel the discursive web that subtends Western attitudes toward sexual violence and to set the stage for the investigations in the individual chapters.

One of the most persistent rape myths is the idea that no means yes. It is informed by a variety of sexist stereotypes, including the notion that standards of female modesty compel women to pretend to resist sex even when they want to consent. Thus, women are seen to be conflicted, torn between the id's raw desire and the superego's adherence to norms, whereas male sexuality is associated with a drive to dominate and conquer. Those who subscribe to such notions can refer to Sigmund Freud himself. In his *Psychopathology of Everyday Life* (1901), Freud discusses the possibility of a "sexuellen Attentats auf eine Frau, bei dem der Angriff des Mannes nicht durch die volle Muskelkraft des Weibes abgewehrt werden kann, weil ihm ein Teil der unbewußten Regungen der Angegriffenen fördern entgegenkommt" (sexual assault upon a woman, where the man's attack cannot be repelled by her full muscular strength because a portion of her unconscious impulses meets the attack with encouragement).[13] In Freud's male-authored rape fantasy, women secretly or unconsciously wish to be raped. Freud thus performs an ideological maneuver that, as Sielke points out, presents "female desire as an effect of male aggression,"[14] an assumption that, as Ellen Rooney notes, is itself based on an "eroticization

---

12 Sanyal criticizes the term "rape myths," arguing that a critique of rape myths remains beholden to the same paradigms while simply inverting all associated values. In contrast, we believe that such a critique is necessary because, as a culture, we have not moved beyond these myths. Moreover, a critique of rape myths does not simply imply that the opposite is necessarily true but rather serves to complicate our perception of sexualized violence. Mithu M. Sanyal, *Vergewaltigung* (Hamburg: Edition Nautilus, 2016), 40–41.

13 Sigmund Freud, *Die Psychopathologie des Alltagslebens (Über Vergessen, Versprechen, Vergreifen, Aberglaube und Irrtum)* (Berlin: S. Karger, 1912), 127; https://www.google.com/books/edition/The_Psychopathology_of_Everyday_Life/rs5s hiYhUawC?hl=en&gbpv=1&dq=a+sexual+assault+upon+a+woman,+where+the+man's+attack+cannot+be+repelled+by+her+full+muscular+strength+because+a+portion+of+her+unconscious+impulses+meets+the+attack+with+encouragement &pg=PA235&printsec=frontcover.

14 Sielke, *Reading Rape*, 46.

of dominance and submission."[15] In this view, a woman's claim that she was raped arises after the fact and is designed to protect her reputation of chastity or, conversely, to prevent that she is perceived as promiscuous or as an adulteress.[16] The "no means yes" mindset is further subtended by the sexist notion that women are fickle and ex post facto reinterpret as rape what was bad sex at the time. Thus, in the premodern era up until the eighteenth century, a pregnancy that resulted from coerced sex served to discredit claims of rape, since it was widely assumed that the female orgasm is a precondition of conception.[17] Misogynistic perceptions of this sort persist into the present, most recently in the notion of "legitimate rape" advocated by the late candidate for the United States Senate Todd Akin, who argued that if a woman is truly raped, her body automatically blocks pregnancy.[18] Such notions lend credence to the belief that "false accusations of rape are endemic" even though study after study has shown that false accusations are rare, hovering around 2 to 3 percent of all charges.[19]

Another rape myth involves the notion that rape is the province of male lowlifes who fail to secure sexual access to women in a nonviolent manner. This hypothesis was presented by Randy Thornhill, Nancy Wilmsen Thornhill, and Gerard Dizinno, who argued that "rape may be engaged in by men who are relatively unsuccessful in competition for the resources and status necessary to attract and reproduce successfully with desirable mates."[20] Such arguments are part of a larger endeavor to "other" rapists and present them as exceptional, while denying that persons who appear "normal" in other contexts could possibly be rapists.

---

15   Ellen Rooney, "A Little More than Persuading: Tess and the Subject of Sexual Violence," in *Rape and Representation*, ed. Lynn A. Higgins and Brenda R. Silver (New York: Columbia University Press, 1991), 87–114, here 99.

16   Brownmiller draws attention to "the assumption that a woman who has been raped by a man she knows is a woman 'who changed her mind afterward.'" Susan Brownmiller, *Against Our Will: Men, Women and Rape* (New York: Fawcett Books, 1975), 352.

17   Christine Künzel, *Vergewaltigungslektüren: Zur Codierung sexueller Gewalt in Literatur und Recht* (Frankfurt am Main: Campus, 2003), 34.

18   See John Eligan and Michael Schwirtz, "Senate Candidate Provokes Ire with 'Legitimate Rape' Comment," *New York Times*, August 19, 2012; https://www.nytimes.com/2012/08/20/us/politics/todd-akin-provokes-ire-with-legitimate-rape-comment.html.

19   Bourke, *Rape*, 28 and 393. Krakauer points to egregious methodological problems in studies that claim to prove the ubiquity of false rape claims. One such study, for example, used the opinions of police officers as proof that rape allegations were false. See Jon Krakauer, *Missoula: Rape and the Justice System in a College Town* (New York: Anchor Books, 2015), 116.

20   Randy Thornhill, Nancy Wilmsen Thornhill, and Gerard Dizinno, "The Biology of Rape," in *Rape: An Historical and Social Enquiry*, ed. Sylvana Tomaselli and Roy Porter (Oxford: Basil Blackwell, 1989), 102–21, here 103.

Thornhill, Thornhill, and Dizinno view rape as a form of maladaptive behavior exhibited by social misfits.

Conversely, they argue that "wealthy men who rape are apparently the exception, not the rule."[21] It stands to reason that, in light of the recent scandals revolving around Harvey Weinstein, Donald Trump, Bill O'Reilly, Roger Ailes, Louis C.K., Charlie Rose, Kevin Spacey, Bill Cosby, Brett Kavanaugh, Matt Lauer, and Dieter Wedel, to name just a few, the notion that rape is a poor man's crime can be laid to rest.[22] (The underlying assumption that rape is about a competition for successful reproduction has long been disproved.[23]) Similarly, rape has often been cast as a crime committed by male members of other races or ethnicities. One need only think of the deeply problematic history of justifying lynchings through fabricated accusations of rape or the instrumentalization of sexual assault in the context of the New Year's Eve celebration in Cologne in 2015/16. Shining a spotlight on nonnative perpetrators is a well-practiced discursive maneuver designed to "other" rapists while drawing attention away from the prevalence of sexual violence in the "native" culture.

Another widely accepted and deeply problematic rape myth concerns the idea that victims of rape have brought their fate on themselves through careless behavior. Such behavior can include going for a walk after dark, taking public transportation, accepting a ride home, or dressing "provocatively." Indeed, a woman's looks are frequently faulted for a man's behavior. As Gesa Dane puts it, "Tatwaffe ist das Aussehen der Frau" (the weapon is a woman's appearance).[24] Careless behavior can also refer to the consumption of alcohol, since, paradoxically, women who drink and are then raped are often considered more guilty than sober victims, whereas men who rape while inebriated are perceived as less guilty than nondrinking perpetrators.[25] Susan J. Brison points out that a focus on such "contributory" factors holds great appeal not only to perpetrators but also to victims of sexual assault because it allows them to trade feelings of guilt for a sense of safety. As Brison notes astutely, "It can be less painful to believe that you did something blameworthy than it is to think that

---

21 Thornhill, Thornhill, and Dizinno, "The Biology of Rape," 116.
22 See Bourke, *Rape*, 98.
23 Bourke notes that not all women who are raped are of childbearing age. Moreover, rapists often fail to ejaculate: Bourke, *Rape*, 115. Conversely, the concept of *Jus primae noctis*, that is, the legal right of a feudal overlord to have sex with a female subordinate on the latter's wedding night, suggests that, alongside rape as a weapon of the poor, there is also a tradition of rape as the prerogative of the powerful.
24 Gesa Dane, *"Zeter und Mordio": Vergewaltigung in Literatur und Recht* (Göttingen: Wallstein, 2005), 17.
25 Bourke, *Rape*, 57.

you live in a world where you can be attacked at any time."[26] Similarly, to bystanders, blaming the victim offers the false assurance that those who proceed with caution do not run the risk of rape. If we subscribe to these arguments, it follows that it is up to women to prevent rape by policing their own behavior and curtailing their freedom. And it is precisely such self-policing that prompted Susan Brownmiller to suggest that rape is "nothing more or less than a conscious process of intimidation by which all men keep all women in a state of fear."[27] While Brownmiller overstates her point by implicating all men in a deliberate effort to oppress women while eliding the possibility of male victimization, the pervasiveness of cultural normalizations of sexual violence should not be underestimated.

A related form of victim-blaming motivates the ongoing focus, in court proceedings but also in the public eye in general, on whether the victim resisted the attack or did so "sufficiently." In the public perception of rape as well as in its legal codification, the concept of resistance typically constitutes the tipping point between seduction and rape. Dane notes that German law used to differentiate between rapes outside of city boundaries and rape in cities.[28] This distinction was rooted in the idea that in densely populated areas one would hear the victim's screams. In other words, it is the responsibility of the victim to prove her innocence by putting up a fight, either verbally, through the infamous "Zeter und Mordio" (screaming bloody murder),[29] or physically, by fending off her attacker. Many nineteenth- and even twentieth-century legal scholars went so far as to argue that a woman who resists her attacker cannot be raped.[30] This calculus changed only if she was accosted by more than one man. The implications of this approach are dire, even more so since it is well documented that most victims of rape do not fight back either because they were socialized to respond to aggressive behavior with passivity or, more commonly, because they fear for their lives. Alice Sebold, a rape survivor and author of the memoir *Lucky* (1999), puts it succinctly: "Those who say they would rather fight to the death than be raped are fools."[31]

---

26   Susan J. Brison, *Aftermath: Violence and the Remaking of a Self* (Princeton, NJ: Princeton University Press, 2002), 13.

27   Brownmiller, *Against Our Will*, 15.

28   See also Brownmiller, who notes that "if a man raped a virgin within the walls of the city both shared the same fate of death by stoning, for the elders reasoned that if the girl had screamed, she would have been rescued": *Against Our Will*, 20.

29   Dane, *"Zeter und Mordio,"* 22.

30   Bourke, *Rape*, 25.

31   Alice Sebold, *Lucky* (New York: Scribner, 1999), 3. A similar form of victim-blaming affects women who experience domestic violence. Joel notes that here victims are held accountable for the abuse they suffered because they did not

Rape victims not only have to prove their innocence through forceful resistance; they also are often on trial for their sexual history preceding the rape. This attention to the victim's sexual activities preceding the rape has shaped notions of "respectability" and credibility, which, in turn, have informed legal practice for centuries. In legal codes of the eighteenth century, the expectation of sexual purity in a victim is stated explicitly. The "Codex Bavarici Criminalis" (1751), for example, decrees that only an honorable woman qualifies as a victim of rape, whereas a woman of ill repute has no case.[32] Brownmiller relates this attention to a victim's sexual history to the premodern notion of rape as a property crime that affects the financial interests of the victim's male relatives. In this view, the gravest form of rape is the rape of a virgin, since it constitutes "an embezzlement of his daughter's fair price on the market."[33] In this model, a woman who has engaged in any form of sexual activity before the rape has no claim to restitution unless her male relatives advocate on her behalf.

Among the most pernicious rape myths are those that spring from a fundamental misunderstanding of the conditions that make consent possible. Thus, Bourke points to a study of college men in the 1980s who had trouble understanding the difference between consensual and coerced sex. A shocking "39% of the students claimed that it was 'all right' to force sex if a girl was 'stoned' or drunk."[34] Similarly, studies show that some men readily admit to rape if it is not labeled as such; that is, if they are asked whether they ever forced a woman to have sex with them even though the woman said no. Moreover, it is not only men who fail to perceive forced sex as rape. Even "women may not necessarily define incidents of sexual violence as rape, incest or domestic violence."[35] Particularly women

leave or because they chose the wrong man to begin with. Antje Joel, *Prügel: Eine ganz gewöhnliche Geschichte häuslicher Gewalt* (Hamburg: Rowohlt Taschenbuch, 2020), 48. Joel cites a study that shows that 42 percent of all Germans believe that women's provocative behavior causes domestic violence; see Joel, *Prügel*, 191. Snyder points out that blaming women for not leaving is misguided, since partner violence tends to escalate when a battered spouse leaves: "as dangerous as it is in their homes, it is always far more dangerous to leave." Rachel Louise Snyder, *No Visible Bruises: What We Don't Know about Domestic Violence Can Kill Us* (New York: Bloomsbury, 2019), 25. To be clear, Snyder does not suggest that women should stay with abusive husbands but simply that leaving is likely to trigger of spike in violence.

32 Dane, *"Zeter und Mordio,"* 72.
33 Brownmiller, *Against Our Will*, 18.
34 Bourke, *Rape*, 45.
35 Kelly, *Surviving Sexual Violence*, 10. See also Estrich, who notes that "many women continue to believe that men can force you to have sex against your will and that it isn't rape so long as they know you and don't beat you nearly to death in the process." Susan Estrich, *Real Rape: How the Legal System Victimizes*

who were raped by friends or acquaintances have trouble identifying their experience as rape, and such rapes are also particularly likely to go unreported. To this day, a conviction for rape is much harder to come by if the victim knew the assailant. This is all the more troubling since the vast majority of rapes (70–80 percent) are committed by men who are acquainted with their victims.[36] Moreover, if the courts do concede that a woman was raped by an acquaintance or a husband, such rapes are frequently seen as less severe, even though studies suggest that "contrary to myth, wives . . . sustained more severe physical injuries than did other rape victims."[37] Indeed, marital rape is particularly likely to occur when a wife is being beaten by her husband.[38] One might add that the breach of trust inherent in "date rape" or "marital rape" inflicts its very own kind of emotional trauma that can prove to be even more insidious than that caused by stranger rape.[39] Feminist scholars have pointed out that the confusion of consensual sex and rape that informs these issues is unique to the crime of rape: "We don't think of theft as 'coerced gift-giving.' We don't think of murder as 'assisted suicide minus consent.'"[40] And yet, precisely such a confusion motivated the refusal to legislate against rape in marriage. German law, for example, did not recognize the rape of a wife by her husband until 1997.

The inability to perceive acquaintance rape as rape is not the only misapprehension that inflects the prosecution of this crime. Another concerns the credibility problem that distinguishes rape from other crimes. Jon Krakauer notes that "police routinely presume that victims of other crimes, such as burglaries, are telling the truth," whereas reports of rape are met with disbelief.[41] Here, the perception of the accusing party stands in a long tradition of misogynistic stereotypes that go back to Greek antiquity and invariably cast women as natural liars who seek to deceive and dissimulate. Tellingly, the word "testify" is etymologically connected to the Latin word *testis*, which signifies both testimony and testicle. In German, the same link between testimony and male procreativity is evident in the verb "zeugen."[42] Christine Künzel notes that in German courts female witnesses in rape trials are far more likely to be required

Women Who Say No (Cambridge, MA: Harvard University Press, 1987), 4. See also Krakauer, *Missoula*, 280.

36 Brison, *Aftermath*, 130; Ann J. Cahill, *Rethinking Rape* (Ithaca, NY: Cornell University Press, 2001), 21.

37 Bourke, *Rape*, 321.

38 Kelly, *Surviving Sexual Violence*, 53.

39 Christina Clemm, *AktenEinsicht: Geschichten von Frauen und Gewalt* (Munich: Antje Kunstmann, 2020), 35.

40 Brison, *Aftermath*, 6.

41 Krakauer, *Missoula*, 300.

42 Künzel, *Vergewaltigungslektüren*, 228 and 208.

to undergo a "Glaubwürdigkeitsbegutachtung" (evaluation of their credibility) than witnesses in other trials.[43] The credibility problem plays out in a variety of scenarios. Karen Boyle lays out a whole list of factors that can damage or strengthen a woman's credibility: "Women are more likely to be believed . . . if they are: either very young or very old; if they are assaulted by a stranger; if they suffer physical injury; if they are from the dominant ethnic group in the society (and if the perpetrator is not); if they are deemed sexually 'respectable' (a deeply classed and racialized notion); if they haven't been drinking or taking drugs."[44] Research also shows that a delay in reporting is often seen as a sign that the victim is lying or reinterpreting a consensual event even though such delays are the norm rather than the exception. Unsurprisingly, credibility issues create a double bind for women who have the courage to testify: a rape victim on the stand is perceived either "as traumatized, because sick (emotional, hysterical), and thus, not credible or as calm and reasonable, and thus clearly not traumatized, and so not credible."[45] Finally, men who are the victims of rape also face a credibility problem. Because sexual victimization is not compatible with standard notions of masculinity, the rape of men threatens to remain invisible.

As we survey the most prevalent rape myths, we would do well to bear in mind that these are not simply flawed intellectual constructs. Rather, rape myths have palpable real-world consequences, including an impact on sentencing standards. In the 2016 Stanford University rape case, *People v. Turner*, the defendant's father submitted a statement in which he argued for leniency, noting "that it is a steep price to pay for 20 minutes of action out of his 20 plus years of life."[46] Such compassion for the offender neglects to take into account that a return to a "normal" life remains out of reach for many victims. Brison, herself a survivor of a sexual assault and attempted murder, describes the long-term effects of rape on the victims, "who can lose years of their lives, the freedom to move about in the world without debilitating fear, and any hope of returning to the pleasures of life as they once knew it."[47] Sebold too emphasizes that she was forever changed by the experience of rape: "I share my life with my rapist. He is the husband to my fate."[48] Similarly, Annie Ernaux, in describing an experience that she did not understand was rape at the time and still cannot call "rape" at the time of writing, nonetheless

---

43   Künzel, *Vergewaltigungslektüren*, 218.
44   Boyle, *#MeToo, Weinstein and Feminism*, 80. See also Kelly, *Surviving Sexual Violence*, 36.
45   Brison, *Aftermath*, 71.
46   https://www.independent.co.uk/news/world/americas/stanford-rape-case-judge-explains-controversial-brock-turner-sentence-a7083406.html.
47   Brison, *Aftermath*, 10.
48   Sebold, *Lucky*, 51.

eloquently captures its effect on her as "a staggering imbalance between the influence those two nights with that man have had upon my life, and the nothingness of my presence in his."[49] To be sure, the effects of rape are highly individualized, and we must guard against imposing expectations of uniform traumatization. But we must also resist frameworks that teach us to minimize and even forget instances of sexual harassment and violence.

Taken together, the rape myths elucidated above shape everyday perceptions of the nexus of sexuality and violence. Rape myths determine how victims and perpetrators think about the crime of rape and how rape is conceptualized in legal and political frameworks. They are deeply embedded in our culture and form an inextricable part of our most cherished literary heritage. In fact, more often than not, our cultural heritage inculcates the denial, minimization, and erasure of sexual violence. And while we cannot suppress these stories, we can become attuned to their sexist undercurrents.

Western Civilization, a Rape Culture?

Rape is built into the cultural and historical fabric of Western civilization, and while our focus in this volume is on German-language culture, we cannot ignore the fact that German-language culture is itself profoundly influenced by the foundational texts of Western religion and mythology. As we aim to show in this section, this heritage, be it derived from the Bible, from Greek and Roman mythology, or from German baroque or classical literature, is preoccupied with sexualized forms of violence. Rape features prominently in literary texts ranging from Homer's *Iliad*, where Chryseis and Briseis are taken as prizes of war and Cassandra is raped by Ajax the Lesser during the sack of Troy, to Shakespeare's *Titus Andronicus* (1594) and from Samuel Richardson's *Clarissa* (1748) to Toni Morrison's *Beloved* (1987). In the figure of Potiphar's wife, the Bible tells the story of a woman who falsely cried rape, thus offering one of the first substantiations of the notion that fabricated accusations of rape are common. But the Bible also contains multiple stories of "real" rape, including the rape of Tamar by her half-brother Amnon in 2 Samuel 13 and the rape of Jacob's daughter Dinah by Shechem in Genesis. A deeply disturbing but foundational narrative of rape is portrayed in Judges 19, which tells the tale of an old man who hosts three guests: a male stranger, his concubine, and his servant. As they feast, "wicked men of the city" surround the house and demand that the host hand over the male guest: "Bring out the man who came to your house so we can have sex with

---

49 Annie Ernaux, *A Girl's Story*, trans. Alison L. Strayer (New York: Seven Stories Press, 2016), 96.

him." The host refuses but offers his own virgin daughter and the concubine instead. After a brief negotiation, the concubine is taken outside, and "they raped her and abused her throughout the night, and at dawn they let her go." The concubine does not survive the ordeal, but her corpse serves to unite competing tribes and ultimately to incite violence: "When he reached home, he took a knife and cut up his concubine, limb by limb, into twelve parts and sent them into all the areas of Israel. Everyone who saw it was saying to one another, 'Such a thing has never been seen or done, not since the day the Israelites came up out of Egypt. Just imagine! We must do something!'"[50] Judges 19 is paradigmatic in several ways. It establishes that women are available for rape, while men must remain impregnable. (As Brownmiller points out, "'Thou shalt not rape' was conspicuously missing from the Ten Commandments."[51]) Furthermore, by reinscribing the sacrificed female body into a political narrative, it also demonstrates that rape can be made to perform important symbolic work.

The legitimization of the rape of women that is evident in the story of the Levite also characterizes Greek mythology and the Roman mythology derived from it. Indeed, Greek gods and their Roman counterparts rape frequently and with impunity. Poseidon (Roman: Neptune), for example, raped Medusa in Athena's (Minerva's) temple. In a characteristic act of victim-blaming, Athena, who wanted to avenge the sacrilege, punished not Poseidon but Medusa by turning her into a monster. And Medusa is not Poseidon's only victim. The god of the sea also violated his sister Demeter while both were transformed into horses. Demeter's daughter Persephone (Proserpina) also fell victim to rape. She was abducted by Hades (Pluto), who took her to the underworld against her will. Like his brothers Poseidon and Hades, Zeus (Jupiter) too is a rapist: he violated Alcmene by assuming the shape of her husband; Danae by showering her in the form of rain; Leda by transforming into a swan; and Callisto while she slept, as is detailed in Ovid's *Metamorphosis*. Moreover, while the saying "Quod licet Iovi, non licet bovi" (What is permissible for Jupiter may not be permissible for a bull) suggests that the gods are subject to a different set of moral rules, rape was conceived as an equal-opportunity crime: both gods and mortals rape—though the gods more successfully evade punishment. Thus, the rape of Philomela by her brother-in-law Tereus, the king of Thrace, has become symptomatic for the silencing of rape victims: Tereus cut out Philomela's tongue after the assault to keep her from telling her story. Philomela, however, bested him by weaving her experience into a tapestry.

---

50 https://www.biblegateway.com/passage/?search=Judges%2019&version=NIV.

51 Brownmiller, *Against Our Will*, 19.

While rape features prominently in both Greek and Roman mythology, the politicization of rape that characterizes the Levite's story is particularly topical in Roman mythology. Porter notes that "rape played a crucial role in accounts and explanations of the rise and demise of cities."[52] The founding of Rome, for example, is linked to the rape of the Sabine women, who were abducted by force when the Romans' requests for marriageable women had been rejected. The nexus of rape, tyranny, and revolution is evident in the story of the Plebeian virgin Virginia. When the consul Appius Claudius desired her, her father, Verginius, stabbed her to prevent "a fate worse than death." Virginia's demise heralded the overthrow of the legislature. Similarly, in Livy's telling, the rape of Lucretia by Sextus Tarquinius motivated a rebellion that resulted in the end of the monarchy and the founding of the republic. Sextus Tarquinius coerced Lucretia to have sex with him by threatening to kill her and her slave and put the bodies next to each other, thus creating the appearance of a sexual relationship between them. The fact that Lucretia committed suicide after submitting to Sextus Tarquinius caused Augustine to cast aspersion on her chastity and credibility. In chapter 19 of *De civitate Dei* (The City of God), Augustine wonders, "If she was adulterous, why is she praised? If chaste, why was she put to death?" In a classic act of victim-blaming, Augustine suggests that Lucretia may have been "betrayed by the pleasure of the act, and gave some consent to Sextus, though so violently abusing her, and then was so affected with remorse, that she thought death alone could expiate her sin? Even though this were the case, she ought still to have held her hand from suicide, if she could with her false gods have accomplished a fruitful repentance. However, if such were the state of the case, and if it were false that there were two, but one only committed adultery; if the truth were that both were involved in it, one by open assault, the other by secret consent, then she did not kill an innocent woman."[53]

It should be clear by now that all our classic stories of rape are inextricably intertwined with rape myths. This holds true for the classical texts of Western civilization in general and of German literary history in particular. In the German canon, representations of rape are prevalent in medieval and in baroque literature. In the baroque period, rape would be referred to as "Notnunft," "Notzucht" or "Schändung"; the word "Vergewaltigung" became the standard term for rape in the early

52 Sylvana Tomaselli, "Introduction," in *Rape: An Historical and Social Enquiry*, ed. Sylvana Tomaselli and Roy Porter (Oxford: Basil Blackwell , 1989), 1–13, here 3.
53 Aurelius Augustine, Bishop of Hippo, *The City of God*, vol. 1 of *Works*, ed. and trans. Marcus Dods (Edinburgh: T & T Clark, 1871), 29.

twentieth century.[54] Works by baroque authors that feature rape include Georg Philipp Harsdörffer's "Die Genothzüchtigte" (The Rape Victim), published in his *Der grosse Schauplatz jämmerlicher Mordgeschichte* (1649; The Great Arena of Miserable Stories of Murder), Daniel Casper von Lohenstein's novel *Großmüthiger Feldherr Arminius* (1689; Magnanimous Commander Arminius), and Andreas Gryphius's *Catharina von Georgien* (1657). It is notable that one of the most frequently taught texts from this period, Hans Jakob Christoph von Grimmelshausen's novel about the Thirty Years' War, *Die Lebensbeschreibung der Erzbetrügerin und Landstörzerin Courasche* (circa 1669; The Autobiography of the Arch Cheater and Troublemaker Courage), features a brutal gang rape suffered by the title character; a crime that is ignored in much of the secondary literature on this canonical text:

> Die folgende Nacht logierten wir in einem Quartier, darin wenig zum besten war, allwo mich der Obristleut. zwang, zu Revanche seiner Schmach, wie er's nennete, seine viehische Begierden zu vollbringen, worbei doch (pfui der schändlichen Torheit) weder Lust noch Freud sein konnte, indem er mir anstatt der Küss', ob ich mich gleich nit sonderlich sperret, nur dichte Ohrfeigen gab. . . . Die zweite Nacht fanden sie Quartier, da der Bauer den Tisch deckte, da lude mein tapferer Held von Offizirn seines Gelichters zu Gast, die sich durch mich mit ihm verschwägern mußten, also daß meine sonst unersättliche fleischliche Begierden dermalen genugsam kontentiert wurden. Die dritte Nacht . . . gieng es mir gar nit besser, sondern viel ärger; dann nachdem ich dieselbe kümmerlich überstanden und alle diese Hengste sich müd gerammelt hatten (pfui, ich schämte mich's beinahe zu sagen, wann ich's dir, Simplicissime, nit zu Ehren und Gefallen täte), mußte ich auch vor der Herren Angesicht mich von den Knechten treffen lassen. Ich hatte bisher alles mit Geduld gelitten und gedacht, ich hätte es hiebevor verschuldet; aber da es hierzu kam, war mir's ein abscheulicher Greuel, also daß ich anfieng zu lamentieren, zu schmälen und Gott um Hülf und Rach anzurufen. Aber ich fande keine Barmherzigkeit bei diesen viehischen Unmenschen.[55]

> [The following night we lodged in a quarter in which little was well, where the lieutenant colonel forced me to fulfill his animal desires, to avenge his disgrace, as he called it, in which (ugh the shameful folly) there was neither pleasure nor joy since he gave me tight slaps

---

54   Dane, *"Zeter und Mordio,"* 35–36.

55   Hans Jakob Christoph von Grimmelshausen, *Die Lebensbeschreibung der Erzbetrügerin und Landstörzerin Courasche*, ed. Klaus Haberkamm and Günther Weydt (Stuttgart: Reclam, 1971), 57–58.

in the face instead of kisses, even though I did not defend myself much. . . . The second night they found quarters where the farmer set the table. Then my brave hero invited officers of his ilk to be guests, who through me had to become related to him, so that my otherwise insatiable carnal desires were sufficiently contented. The third night . . . I did not get off any easier, but much worse; then after I had survived it poorly and all these stallions were tired from going at it (ugh, I would almost be ashamed to say it if I didn't do it in your honor and pleasure, Simplicissime), I also had to let myself be hit by the servants in front of the gentlemen. I had suffered everything with patience and thought that I was to blame for it; but when this came about, it was an abominable horror to me, so that I began to lament, to cry and to call on God for help and revenge. But I found no mercy in these beastly monsters.]

If rape features prominently in seventeenth-century literature, it is even more central in the age of Enlightenment. The authors of the Storm and Stress movement exhibited a keen interest in various forms of sexual transgressions, including rape. Frequently, rape is represented obliquely through the crime of infanticide, as in Heinrich Leopold Wagner's play *Die Kindermörderin* (1776; The Child Murderess), in which the female protagonist's pregnancy is the result of a rape. Friedrich Schiller's *Verschwörung des Fiesco zu Genua* (1783; Fiesco's Conspiracy at Genoa) harks back to Roman mythology in its identification of tyranny and rape. Similarly, in his play *Die Räuber* (1782; The Robbers), Schiller uses the motif of rape to underline the nefarious character of the evil mastermind Franz and the villain Spiegelberg, who boasts about raping and impregnating nuns.

In his scandalous novel *Lucinde* (1797), Friedrich Schlegel portrays the protagonist Julius in his wild youth in the "Lehrjahre der Männlichkeit" (Apprenticeship of Masculinity). The frustrated, restless Julius seeks out an appealing girl he had known and rekindles the relationship. In his attempts to seduce the "Kind" (child), she begins to respond, "Aber in demselben Augenblick brach ein Strom von Tränen aus ihren Augen und die bitterste Verzweifelung entstellte ihr Gesicht" (But in the same instant, a stream of tears poured forth from her eyes and the most bitter despair contorted her face).[56] After coming to his senses, finding sympathy in himself, and comforting her, Julius flees the scene, "wo er den Blütenkranz der Unschuld hatte mutwillig zerreissen wollen" (43; where he had deliberately wanted to tear the wreath of innocence). Yet he later imagines her complicity in desire—in the practiced manner of "no means yes"—and nurtures resentment toward her.

---

56 Friedrich Schlegel, *Lucinde: Ein Roman* (Leipzig: Ullstein, 1930), 43.

Johann Wolfgang von Goethe portrayed an attempted rape in his epic poem *Hermann und Dorothea* (1782), and his poem "Heidenröslein" is widely interpreted as a representation of rape. The author who was most prolific in his representations of rape, however, was Heinrich von Kleist, who wrote several texts that revolve around a rape or attempted rape, including *Amphitryon* (1807), *Der zerbrochene Krug* (1808; The Broken Jug), "Die Marquise von O" (1808), *Penthesilea* (1808), and *Die Hermannsschlacht* (1808). Several of these texts are marked by a conflation of rape and seduction that informs interpretations of rape even today.[57]

For women authors of the eighteenth century, rape presented a much more difficult topic since female honor was defined as a function of sexual innocence, and such innocence was incompatible with knowledge of and thus with the representation of sexual matters. Even so, some of them, such as Sophie von La Roche, tackled the issue of rape. La Roche's *Geschichte des Fräuleins von Sternheim* (1771; The History of Lady Sophia Sternheim), for example, features an attempted rape, narrated by the would-be rapist: "Ich drang in sie, und sie sträubte sich so lange, bis Ungeduld und Begierde mir eingaben ihre Kleidung vom Hals an durchzureißen, um auch wider ihren Willen zu meinem Endzweck zu gelangen" (I pursued her and she resisted until impatience and desire prompted me to tear her clothing from the neck to achieve my end goal against her will).[58] While La Roche is an outlier in the eighteenth century, in the nineteenth century women writers began to identify rape as an important topic in the emergent women's movement. Marie von Ebner Eschenbach's stories "Der Erstgeborne" (The First-Born) and "Die Totenwacht" (1894; The Wake) highlight the long-term effects caused by the trauma of rape. And while Ebner Eschenbach focuses on the rape of unmarried women, Ida Hahn-Hahn dared to address the highly controversial topic of marital rape in her *Gräfin Faustine* (1841; The Countess Faustina). At the same time, rape continued to be an important topic in male-authored texts, such as Gerhard Hauptmann's drama *Rose Bernd* (1903).

---

57 Künzel notes that the reception history of the "Marquise von O" offers many examples of exculpatory strategies that deny or minimize the occurrence of rape: *Vergewaltigungslektüren*, 25–31. Cohn, for example, suggests that the marquise's "flight into unconsciousness appears as an instant reaction to salvage the purity of consciousness in the moment of emerging eros." Dorrit Cohn, "Kleist's Marquise von O: The Problem of Knowledge," *Monatshefte* 67, no. 2 (1975): 129–44, here 133. Künzel notes further that many critics assume the marquise is not trustworthy even though there is no textual evidence to support this claim: *Vergewaltigungslektüren*, 53.

58 Sophie von La Roche, *Geschichte des Fräuleins von Sternheim*, ed. Barbara Becker-Cantarino (Stuttgart: Reclam, 1983), 222.

Numerous twentieth-century texts portray rape both in civilian and in military contexts. Franz Fühmann deals with the topic of rape in his story "Amnon und Tamar" (1982). Claire Goll's novel *Ein Mensch ertrinkt* (1931; A Human Being Drowns) tells the story of a maid who is raped by the master of the house. Rape features particularly prominently in texts that deal with the Second World War, such as Christoph Hein's "Die Vergewaltigung" (1994; The Rape), Julia Franck's *Die Mittagsfrau* (2007; The Noon Woman; translated as *The Blind Side of the Heart*, 2009), and Jenny Erpenbeck's *Die Heimsuchung* (2008; Visitation). In Libuse Monikova's novel *Eine Schädigung* (1981; An Injury), the protagonist is raped by a policeman but manages to disarm him and fight back. The protagonist in Inka Parei's *Die Schattenboxerin* (1999; The Shadow-Boxing Woman) is raped on November 9, 1989, the night when the Berlin Wall fell. Slavenka Drakulić's *Als gäbe es mich nicht* (1999; As If I Didn't Exist) is based on interviews with women who were raped in the Bosnian war.

While these literary representations of rape are free to reimagine and reinterpret historical realities of sexual violence, they often take their cue from historic incidents of rape. Some of these texts are inspired by individual cases, such as legal cases of infanticide; others seek to come to terms with events that gave rise to mass rapes. The next section briefly outlines the most momentous periods of large-scale sexual violence in German history.

Realities of Rape in War and in the Home

While rape was prevalent at all times in German history, times of war frequently provide an arena in which soldiers can rape with impunity. As Sharon Frederick points out, "rape is almost risk free for soldiers."[59] Indeed, rapes have been part of almost every major military conflict: German soldiers raped Belgian women in the First World War, while Turkish soldiers raped Armenian women in the 1915 Armenian genocide. In the Second World War, German soldiers raped Russian women, and Russian soldiers raped German women, while Japanese soldiers raped Chinese women in Nanking and enslaved Korean women—euphemistically labeled "Comfort Women"—for sex. American soldiers raped Vietnamese women in the Vietnam War, and Pakistani soldiers raped Bengali women during the 1971 Bangladesh War for Independence. Serbs raped Bosnian women during the Yugoslav war and Hutus raped Tutsi women in the Rwandan genocide. This list could be extended to include violent conflicts in Guatemala, Indonesia, Congo, Peru, Liberia, Haiti, Sudan, Myanmar, El

---

59 Sharon Frederick and the Aware Committee on Rape, *Rape: Weapon of Terror* (River Edge, N.J.: Global Publishing, 2001), 88.

Salvador, East Timor, Kuwait, Cambodia, Afghanistan, Algeria, Somalia, Sierra Leone, and many others.

In the context of German history, two forms of mass rape frequently go unmentioned. The first concerns the rape of indigenous women by German colonizers in territories that now form parts of Burundi, Cameroon, the Central African Republic, Chad, Congo, Gabon, Ghana, Namibia, Nigeria, New Guinea, the Micronesian Islands, Rwanda, Tanzania, and Togo. In the colonial context, German men frequently raped native women at random or forced them to cohabit with them as sex slaves. In a speech in the Reichstag in 1910, the Social Democrat Georg Ledebour sharply criticized these crimes, noting how common it is that "sich die Weißen, während die männlichen Eingeborenen alle in Lohnarbeit sind, mit den Frauen der Eingeborenen 'amüsieren'" (white men "amuse" themselves with the women of the natives, while the male natives are busy with wage labor).[60] Such abusive behavior, informed by the same racism that made Black women available for rape during the era of American slavery,[61] was exhibited and condoned by white men of all ranks and social classes. In contrast, attempts to legitimize relationships of German colonizers with native women and, rarely, native men were strictly regulated and often forbidden altogether. In her excellent study *Herrenmenschen* (Male Masters), Martha Mamozai comments on the pervasiveness of sexual assault, brutal beatings, and even murder, documented in the 1918 British Blue Book, which highlighted such instances of abuse in order to prove the unsuitability of the Germans to the colonial enterprise. Mamozai singles out some of the worst offenders, such as the colonial official (*Gouverneursbeamte*) Leist in Cameroon, who was wont to fetch women from the local prison to satisfy his sexual needs. She also draws attention to the participation of scientists in the sexual degradation of native women. Thus, Friedrich von Fülleborn, the chief medical officer in German Southwest Africa, dedicated his time to studying the breasts of local women, while his colleague Gustav Fritsch published an anatomical study of the people of Southwest Africa with special sections on the breasts and clitorises of native women. In all this, German male colonizers enjoyed the support of their female compatriots, many of whom stood ready to defend every form of cruelty.[62]

Much like the German colonial empire, the Nazi war of conquest and the Holocaust provided numerous opportunities for sexual humiliation, sexual assault, rape, and sex slavery. Already upon entering a concentration

---

60   Cited in Martha Mamozai, *Herrenmenschen: Frauen im deutschen Kolonialismus* (Reinbek bei Hamburg: Rowohlt, 1982), 130; see also 128.

61   See Brownmiller, who notes that "legally the concept of raping a slave simply did not exist," *Against Our Will*, 162; see also 154.

62   See Mamozai, *Herrenmenschen*, 56, 60–61, 122, 191.

camp, women were forced to strip down and lost all right to privacy. During their time in a camp, female inmates were vulnerable to all forms of sexual abuse. Sonja M. Hedgepeth and Rochelle G. Saidel note that "Nazi guards could rape with impunity: if accused of *Rassenschande* (racial defilement), they could simply deny their actions."[63] In addition to the exploitation of the inmates' vulnerable situation by Nazi officers, soldiers, and guards, there were also institutionalized forms of sexual abuse. The concentration camps of Auschwitz, Buchenwald, Mauthausen, Dora-Mittelbau, and Dachau all had official brothels for which they recruited non-Jewish prisoners from the all-female Ravensbrück camp. These women were promised release after six months—a promise that, as Robert Sommer points out, was invariably broken.[64] The brothels were envisaged as a reward system designed to increase the productivity of a select group of male camp inmates and were open to non-Jewish prisoners only. Yehiel De-Nur's (Ka-Tzetnik) novella *House of Dolls* (1953) portrays such forms of sexual slavery in concentration camps, as does the German-Yugoslav coproduction, *Zeugin aus der Hölle* (1966; Witness out of Hell).

While camp inmates lived in constant fear of death, Jewish women who went into hiding to avoid the camps struggled to secure food and lodging, and some were forced to barter sex for a meal, for a roof over their heads, or to avert denunciation. Survivor memoirs, such as Marie Simon Jalowicz's *Untergetaucht: Eine junge Frau überlebt in Berlin 1940–45* (Gone to Ground: One Woman's Extraordinary Account of Survival in the Heart of Nazi Germany), published posthumously in 2014, illustrate the vulnerability of a Jewish woman in Germany. Jalowicz, one of the approximately fourteen hundred Jews who managed to elude their Nazi captors by hiding in wartime Berlin, was exposed to various forms of sexual assault. In no position to choose her helpers, she encountered several individuals who took advantage of her plight. She was not only raped repeatedly by the husbands of women who took her in but was forced to sell herself in exchange for protection.

While Jalowicz faced danger on the home front, the war in the East also provided ample opportunities for sexual violence. For example, during the German military's search for partisans, suspects were routinely forced to strip down.[65] Even mass executions were typically accompanied

---

63 Sonja M. Hedgepeth and Rochelle G. Saidel, "Introduction," in *Sexual Violence against Jewish Women during the Holocaust*, ed. Sonja M. Hedgepeth and Rochelle G. Saidel (Waltham, MA: Brandeis University Press, 2010), 1–10, here 9.

64 Robert Sommer, "Sexual Exploitation of Women in Nazi Concentration Camp Brothels," in Hedgepeth and Saidel, *Sexual Violence*, 45–60, here 45.

65 Regina Mühlhäuser, *Eroberungen: Sexuelle Gewalttaten und intime Beziehungen deutscher Soldaten in der Sowjetunion 1941–1945* (Hamburg: Hamburger Edition, 2010), 114.

by sexual humiliations. There is also ample evidence that German soldiers raped women or engaged in coerced prostitution as starving women traded sex for food, particularly in the Ukraine, where the supply situation was dire. All too often, such coerced sexual encounters were then reinterpreted as romantic relationships; for example, in the oft-repeated claim that Russian women welcomed German soldiers with open arms.[66] The Wehrmacht also ran its own brothels with local women, some of whom were likely forced into sexual slavery. The Nuremberg trials addressed several cases of brutal rape, including that of thirty-two female factory workers in Lemberg, who were raped and then murdered by German SS troops, and that of the village of Borodajewka, where all women and girls were raped by German troops. The German military authorities tended to ignore crimes of a sexual nature. If soldiers were convicted, the punishment was lenient. Whereas on the Western front rape could result in a prison sentence of several years, on the Eastern front rapists were rarely sentenced to more than a couple of months in prison.[67]

While the victimization of Russian women by German soldiers has received relatively little attention in the German media, the rape of several hundred thousand German women by Russian soldiers toward the end of the war featured prominently in public discourses.[68] It was politicized and instrumentalized in both national contexts. In the Russian press, the mass rapes were framed as just punishment for German crimes, whereas many German authors and journalists seized the opportunity to cast German women, and by extension the entire German nation, as victims of the Second World War. To this day, the topic of mass rapes in the context of the Second World War remains a fraught one, since it radically questions the all-too-common identification of victimization and innocence. After all, many women who were raped were supporters of or complicit in the National Socialist war and genocide.

While sexual violence is particularly prevalent during periods of warfare, rape continues to shape the structure of women's everyday lives, and

---

66 Mühlhäuser, *Eroberungen,* 7.

67 Mühlhäuser, *Eroberungen,* 74–75, 20, 146.

68 On the rape of German women by Russian soldiers, see Helke Sander and Barbara Johr, eds., *BeFreier und Befreite: Krieg, Vergewaltigung, Kinder* (Frankfurt am Main: Fischer, 2008); Atina Grossmann, "A Question of Silence: The Rape of German Women by Occupation Soldiers," in *West Germany under Construction: Politics, Society, and Culture in the Adenauer Era,* ed. Robert G. Moeller (Ann Arbor: University of Michigan Press, 1997), 33–51; Svenja Eichhorn and Philipp Kuwert, *Das Geheimnis unserer Großmütter: Eine empirische Studie über sexualisierte Kriegsgewalt um 1945* (Gießen: Psychosozial Verlag, 2011); Miriam Gebhardt, *Als die Soldaten kamen: Die Vergewaltigungen deutscher Frauen am Ende des Zweiten Weltkriegs* (Munich: Deutsche Verlags-Anstalt, 2015).

it remains "a crime disproportionately committed against women,"[69] as well as a crime that disproportionately affects young women: "Females between sixteen and twenty-four years old face a higher risk of being sexually assaulted than any other age group."[70] The World Health Organization classifies violence against women as a "major public health problem" and estimates that "worldwide, 1 in 3, or 35%, of women have experienced physical and/or sexual violence by an intimate partner or non-partner sexual violence."[71] In both Germany and the United States, the numbers are staggering. According to Biliter, "One out of every six American women has been the victim of an attempted or completed rape in her lifetime. Nine out of every 10 victims of rape are female."[72] The situation is no different in Germany. For the year 2018 alone, Christina Clemm, a lawyer and author of *AktenEinsicht* (Insight into Files), documents 114,393 cases of so-called *Partnerschaftsgewalt* (partner violence); 122 women who were murdered by ex-partners; 15,000 cases of child abuse in which 75 percent of the victims were female; 9,000 cases of rape and sexual assault; and 400 victims of sexual trafficking. Of the perpetrators of these crimes, 95 percent were male; 95 percent of the victims were female.[73] These numbers reflect only those crimes that were brought to the attention of the police. Analyses of discrepancies between reports to rape crisis centers and to the police suggest that in the United States up to 80 percent of all sexual assaults still go unreported.[74] Clemm estimates that in Germany up to 92 percent are never reported to the police.[75] Feminist scholars have argued convincingly that the low rate of reporting is connected to the low rate of conviction. Antje Joel cites a study in which only 6 out of 310 defendants served time.[76]

The cost of sexual assault and domestic violence to society is enormous. Indeed, one might even argue that domestic violence constitutes a form of mass murder that is all but invisible. While societies show great respect for military deaths, women (and men) who die in their own homes receive little attention. And yet, as Rachel Louise Snyder notes,

---

69   Ann J. Cahill, *Rethinking Rape* (Ithaca, NY: Cornell University Press, 2001), 109.

70   Krakauer, *Missoula*, 377.

71   https://www.who.int/news-room/fact-sheets/detail/violence-against-women.

72   Mary Biliter, "Consent: Breaking the Silence," in *#MeToo: Essays about How and Why This Happened, What It Means, and How to Make Sure It Never Happens Again*, ed. Lori Perkins (Riverdale, NY: Riverdale Avenue Books, 2020), 55–60, 59.

73   Clemm, *AktenEinsicht*, 7, 126 and 19.

74   See Krakauer, *Missoula*, xiv.

75   Clemm, *AktenEinsicht*, 19.

76   Joel, *Prügel*, 123.

the years 2000 to 2006 witnessed 10,600 domestic homicides in the United States, whereas 3,200 soldiers were killed in action.[77] In the year 2017, the number of German women killed by their partners exceeded the number of people killed in terrorist attacks in all of Europe: 147 versus 142.[78] Indeed, several scholars have pointed out that there is a direct link between domestic violence, mass shootings, and domestic terrorism. In 54 percent of mass shootings, an intimate partner is either the first victim or is among the victims.[79] Devin Patrick Kelley, for example, was convicted of domestic violence long before he killed twenty-six congregants in the Sutherland Springs Church in Texas. Omar Mateen beat his wife before he shot forty-nine people at the Pulse nightclub in Orlando. Adam Lanza killed his mother before he shot and killed twenty first-graders and six staff members at the Sandy Hook Elementary School in Connecticut.

This volume was written with these brutal facts in mind.

Chapter Overview

The contributions to this volume confront the representations and realities of rape culture from the eighteenth century to the present through the lens of the #MeToo movement. Although we have sought to cast a wide net, a single volume cannot possibly claim to address all aspects related to the nexus of sexuality and violence over the course of several centuries. We hope that German studies scholars will continue this important work.

The individual chapters included in this volume provide insights into representations and discourses of sexual violence while acknowledging social, political, and cultural differences and the important context of other intersecting discourses, such as those of gender, class, and race. While depictions of sexuality and violence are historically inflected, continuities emerge regarding power hierarchies and the policing of bodies marked as "other." Collectively, the arguments capture the durabilities of systemic, institutional sexism and its consequences, manifest as toxic masculinity, the commodification of the female body, and the constant reinscription of female desire as an attack on the sovereignty of the male body.

The contributions are divided into five sections: "Histories"; "Dialogues across Time"; "Sexual Violence, War, and Genocide"; "The

---

77   Snyder, *No Visible Bruises*, 6.

78   Joel, *Prügel*, 258. The same holds true for the United States: in 2013 alone, 895 American women were killed by their partners, whereas the number of Americans killed in terrorist attacks between 2006 and 2016 runs to 92; see Joel, *Prügel*, 259. According to Snyder, "137 women each and every day are killed by intimate partner or familial violence across the globe": *No Visible Bruises*, 5.

79   Joel, *Prügel*, 256.

Institutions of #MeToo"; and "#MeToo across Cultural and National Borders." While we are mindful of historical contexts and chronologies, representations and discourses of #MeToo-related topics defy readings that emphasize progress. The first section, "Histories," explores cultures of sexual violence in Enlightenment thinking, which remains foundational for current debates on gender, autonomy, and the body politic. While the #MeToo movement is a twenty-first-century phenomenon, an examination of Enlightenment values and discourses of self-determination and the supremacy of reason yields important insights into the relation of body and mind, the social nature of gender, and structures of gendered violence that continue to shape discursive and social environments today. Beginning with "Eighteenth-Century #MeToo: Rape Culture and Victim-Blaming in Heinrich Leopold Wagner's *Die Kindermörderin* (1776)," Lisa Wille focuses on violent sexuality, unwanted pregnancy, and the precarious position of women in this Storm and Stress work about infanticide. Wille argues that the opening act, which takes place in a brothel, involves a rape: the protagonist, Evchen, is victimized by Lieutenant von Gröningseck. Wille offers a close reading of the play but goes beyond the text to analyze trends in German studies scholarship about *Die Kindermörderin*. She shows that early interpretations regarded Evchen as a "seduced" woman; discussions of rape remained ancillary until the 1990s. In recent years, scholars have again displayed ambivalence, a concerning development that Wille interprets as victim-blaming. Thus, Wagner's text functions as a kaleidoscope that reflects historically changing attitudes toward sexual violence.

Patricia Anne Simpson's "#MeToo: Prostitution and the Syntax of Sexuality around 1800" engages the male representation of female desire and pleasure. Through the lens of #MeToo, she rereads three texts of Johann Wolfgang von Goethe: *Egmont* (1788), the "Witch's Kitchen" from the *Faust* fragment (1790), and "Der Gott und die Bajadere" (1797; The God and the Bayadere) to generate an alternative narrative to institutional histories about transactional sex and the sanctioning of desire through bourgeois domesticity. Simpson argues that, read in the context of contemporary language about prostitution, the three texts by Goethe foreground a contractual relationship to the sexualized female body. Goethe's Egmont casually condemns sexual violence against a "Dirne" (prostitute)—though he suggests that the violation is contingent on the victim's demonstrated innocence. In the *Faust* fragment, Goethe creates the witches' kitchen as a brothel. Finally, in "Der Gott und die Bajadere," he displaces male sexual desire, fear of contracting venereal disease, and the precarious innocence of bourgeois *Mädchen* (girls) onto the exoticized Indian legend of the prostitute who succumbs to the god who appears to her in disguise—interpreted as a variation of the Mary Magdalene story. Here, we see that as early as 1800, female sexuality provided a path to masculine redemption, predicated on the sacrifice of female desire. At this point, the tenacity of male models of female desire, the inevitable result of a phallogocentric modernity, must be acknowledged; it is attributable in no small part to the creation and re-creation of the image of a submissive victim as sexual prey. Here and elsewhere, the sexual victimization of women and the erasure of agential female desire are inextricably linked.

While the first section focuses on the various reverberations and echoes of eighteenth-century Enlightenment discourses and concepts up until the present, the second section, "Dialogues across Time," high-lights intertexual webs, showing how twentieth- and twenty-first-century authors take up, vary, and depart from rape discourses of the past. Melissa Sheedy's contribution explores resonances between early nineteenth- and twentieth-century rape cultures. In "'Immaculate' Conception, the 'Romance of Rape,' and #MeToo: Kleistian Echoes in Kerstin Hensel and Julia Franck," Sheedy reads the trope of unexpected birth using the tools of feminist narratology. She finds echoes of Heinrich von Kleist's novella about a marquise who searches for the father of her child—effectively, her rapist—in works of contemporary German fiction by authors Kerstin Hensel and Julia Franck. Hensel's 1999 novel *Gipshut* (Cap Rock) por-trays a young mother who does not understand the causal link between conception and birth. Similarly, Franck's novel *Die Mittagsfrau* (2007) depicts rape and unexpected motherhood, here within the context of warfare. Sheedy interprets Hensel's and Franck's protagonists as contem-porary marquise-figures who are subject to abuse both within and out-side the home and are precluded from seeking recourse by domestic and social structures of sexism, racism, and ableism. Ultimately, this chapter elucidates the connections among violence, gender, and power, making legible sinister patterns that link violence to ignorance and to the policing of female domesticity.

Deborah Janson's "Female Sacrifice, Sexual Assault, and Dehumani-zation: Bourgeois Tragedy, Horror, and the Making of *Jud Süß*" examines the themes of sexual abuse and female sacrifice across eighteenth-century bourgeois tragedy, the horror film, and anti-Semitic Nazi propaganda. Taking Gotthold Ephraim Lessing's *Miß Sara Sampson* (1755) and *Emilia Galotti* (1772) as her points of departure, Janson constructs an analyti-cal context in which Friedrich Murnau's film *Nosferatu, eine Symphonie des Grauens* (1922; *Nosferatu: A Symphony of Horror*) and Veit Harlan's Nazi propaganda film, *Jud Süß* (1940; Jew Süss) enter into a dialogue with bourgeois tragedy. Like their eighteenth-century model, both Murnau's and Harlan's films revolve around sexual abuse and female sacrifice to uphold the prevailing patriarchal order. Janson explores similarities among the dramas and the films, while acknowledging significant differences and modulations of class inequities, racism, and anti-Semitism. In so doing,

Janson demonstrates how the sexual abuse of women across these times and genres enables patriarchal and racist institutions to maintain their power over those they label inferior.

Sonja Boos's "'Na, wenn du mich erst fragst?': Reconsidering Affirmative Consent with Schnitzler, Schnitt, Habermas, and Rancière" departs from Arthur Schnitzler's play *Reigen* (*La Ronde* (1897–1900; La Ronde) as a basis for thinking through implications of gender, sex, power, inebriation, coercion, rape, violence, and consent—and their legacies. Schnitzler uses ellipsis to showcase the unperformable act of sexual intercourse onstage, but also, as Boos points out, to indicate at least one loss of consciousness in a series of sexual encounters between unequal partners. Bringing the concerns of #MeToo discourse to this literary work, Boos conducts an inquiry into the represented forms of ostensibly consensual sex. With this in mind, she fast-forwards to Corinna Schnitt's short film *Aus einer Welt* (2007; About a World), in which the director references drug-induced blackouts and the rape of an incapacitated victim from a female perspective. Set within a lush and idyllic landscape, the film radicalizes and simplifies the power relations of Schnitzler's play. Asserting men's systemic power in all matters of sexuality, it shows a dozen nude women who lie motionless and speechless as they are approached by a man who caresses and makes erotic overtures to one woman after another, at times tenderly, at other times more forcefully. A close reading locates the film's ellipses—of forgetting, of omission, of lack of consent—figuratively, in a meandering fissure in the Alpine meadow, and in its rhetorically purposeful editing style: repeated jump cuts figure as a "Filmriss" (literally, a tearing of the filmstrip, and metaphorically, a lapse of memory) and arguably also point toward a traumatic memory that cannot be processed into a coherent narrative. In a final section, Boos asks whether Jürgen Habermas's *Theory of Communicative Action* (1981) and his insistence on a consensual mode of discourse by which actors "mobilize the potential for rationality" could be productively used to articulate a new model of sexual consent by way of ordinary, rational, verbal and nonverbal language. Boos concludes with a comparison of Habermas and Rancière. While Habermas presents affirmative consent as a form of mutual conflict resolution through compromise, Jacques Rancière's concept of disagreement highlights how inequality forecloses consent.

The third section, "Sexual Violence, Warfare, and Genocide," investigates the nexus of sexual violence in the context of the First and Second World Wars and the Holocaust. It is interested in the continuities between instances of individual cases of rape in civil society and mass rapes in times of war, but also in how the dissolution of the rules of civilian society and the sanctioning of violence on a national scale specific to times of war set the latter apart. In "War of the Vulva: The Women of Otto Dix's *Lustmord* Series," Jessica Davis interprets six works created between 1920 and 1922 by the German artist and First World War veteran Dix (1891–1969), with a focus on his 1922 work *Der Lustmörder (Selbstbildnis)* (The Sexual Murderer [Self-Portrait]). As Davis points out, the series displays violence against women within intimate settings. Drawing from Dix's biography, print sources, and self-portraiture, Davis analyzes the psychological effects of post-traumatic stress disorder (PTSD) on Dix's postwar oeuvre. She departs from previous scholarship that focuses on the artist and instead reads these works through a #MeToo lens—concentrating on the victim(s) and the contempt the artist displays for the murdered women's sexuality. The victims represent the menace of the sexually self-possessed "New Woman" in the wake of the First World War. Davis's reassessment of Dix's visual imagery of the mutilated female nude attempts to deny power to the abuser and instead reinvests it in the victim.

Art Spiegelman's autobiographical graphic novel *Maus* (serialized 1980–91) epitomizes the Holocaust-centered comic book. The riveting result, told from the perspective of a survivor's son, casts Jews as mice, Nazis as cats, and Poles as pigs. Maureen Burdock's "Death to the Patriarchal Theater! Charlotte Salomon's Graphic Testimony" reaches back into the early twentieth century to examine the works of the German-Jewish artist Salomon (1917–43), who, unlike Spiegelman, experienced the Holocaust firsthand: she died in Auschwitz. In more than one thousand works that combine image and text, Salomon sketched her life while in French exile. In reframing the artist's work, traditionally displayed mostly as Holocaust art, Burdock examines several paintings and texts as evidence of the social and political violence inflicted on Salomon and her family. Based on close readings, Burdock argues that Salomon's *Leben? oder Theater?* (*Life? or Theatre?*) constitutes an early graphic memoir. Salomon bears witness to her love interests; the impact of her mother's, aunt's, and grandmother's suicides; and the depression among the women of her family, which, as Burdock speculates, could be attributable to intergenerational domestic abuse. Decades before the emergence of the graphic novel and graphic confession, Salomon illustrated the emotional truths of her life. They warrant revisiting in the era of #MeToo.

In the context of the #MeToo movement and an understanding of conflict-related sexual violence (CRSV), Katherine Stone focuses on the remembrance of wartime rape in postwar Germany. In "#MeToo and Wartime Rape: Looking Back and Moving Forward," she draws on the insights of memory studies to shed light on Ralf Rothmann's novel *Der Gott jenes Sommers* (2018; *The God of That Summer*, 2022), a work that explores sexual violence in 1945. With its reflection on sexual violence, the toxicity of military masculinity, and gender inequalities, this novel is "a memory narrative for the #MeToo age." Contextualized within a broader discussion of CRSV, Stone asks how conceptual shifts impact the cultural memory of wartime rape. Using the example of Rothmann's novel, Stone demonstrates the ways #MeToo enables readers to revisit sexual and gender relations during the Second World War toward a better understanding of the relevance of memory to contemporary activism.

The fourth section, "The Institutions of #MeToo," parses a number of institutional contexts that are of particular relevance for #MeToo discourses: the school, the family, the police, the labor market, and the theater. This section seeks to draw attention to the fact that sexual violence is impacted not only by its historical but also by its institutional context. The section opens with Niklas Straetker's "Boarding-School Novels around 1900: The Relation of Male Fear of Women to Male-Male Seduction and Sexual Abuse in Hesse, Musil, and Walser," which investigates gender-based power dynamics in boarding-school novels, a burgeoning genre at the turn of the twentieth century. As Straetker emphasizes, scenes of predominantly male-on-male sexual abuse and/ or seduction are pivotal in Hermann Hesse's *Unterm Rad* (1906; *The Prodigy*, 1957), Robert Musil's *Verwirrungen des Zöglings Törleß* (1906; *Young Törless*, 1955), and Robert Walser's *Jakob von Gunten* (1909; *Jakob von Gunten*, 1969). Straetker approaches these works not exclusively as examples of the "institutional novel" but, in the context of #MeToo, examines the sequestering of boys and young men from the world and from women. Straetker's analysis parses the recoding of agency and power—to inflict pain and commit violent acts—that inevitably undergirds institutional hierarchies. He observes that while the "female" functions as the instantiation of the dangers outside the institutions, the institutional repression of the corporeal leads to an overdetermination of sexuality that itself reproduces violence.

Anna Sator's "Breaking the Silence about Sexualized Violence in Lilly Axster's and Beate Teresa Hanika's Young Adult Fiction (YAF)" offers readings of contemporary novels that depart from the hegemonic imaginary of fantasy series, such as Harry Potter, the Twilight Saga, and A Song of Ice and Fire, that have come to dominate the lucrative youth market. Sator argues that sexuality plays an increasingly explicit role in YAF. She focuses on two novels that move past the depiction of adolescent sex as natural exploration. Further, she demonstrates that key contributions of the #MeToo movement, most prominently breaking the silence about sexualized violence and bringing it into the public sphere, have had an impact on YAF. Sator details empowering aspects of Beate Teresa Hanika's *Rotkäppchen muss weinen* (2009; Little Red Riding Hood Has to Cry) and Lilly Axster's *Die Stadt war nie wach* (2017; The City Was Never Awake), both award-winning novels. *Rotkäppchen* tells of two weeks in the life of Malvina, whose grandfather sexually assaults her. Through the first-person perspective of Malvina, Hanika illustrates the consequences of abuse for a victim whose parents do not believe her story. Similarly, Lilly Axster's third-person narration speaks to the psychosocial effects of abuse on a group of five friends. The story commences after the character Reza witnesses a sexual assault committed by a teacher. With an eye to questions of empowerment, Sator identifies the characters' efforts to overcome the silence surrounding sexualized violence and speak out, thus regaining their agency. The chapter explores the potential in YAF narratives to address topics of sexuality and abuse, potentially giving voice to the dialogue between texts and contexts.

Lisa Haegele's "Eine gigantische Vergewaltigung": Rape as Subject in Roger Fritz's *Mädchen mit Gewalt* (1970)" examines rape in two films associated with the New Munich Group. *Mädchen mit Gewalt* was released in English as *The Brutes* in 1970 and as *Cry Rape* in 1975. A West German low-budget B movie, it was directed by Roger Fritz, who, in addition to his work as an actor, producer, and journalist, was cofounder of the West German youth magazine *twen*. The last film in Fritz's so-called Mädchen-Trilogie (girl trilogy), *Mädchen mit Gewalt* revolves around the abduction and rape of a young woman named Alice in a quarry near Munich. As Haegele observes, the plot could be viewed as a misogynistic rape fantasy. She demonstrates, however, that the film exceeds the limits of the cinematic rape drama by highlighting the "secondary victimization" of the victim by the police and a patriarchal legal system. Her readings show how the film was influenced by the contemporary feminist movement that emerged in West Germany in the 1970s. The portrayal of the primary and secondary victimization of the female protagonist offsets the focus on the male perpetrators.

Aylin Bademsoy's "Elfriede Jelinek and Ingeborg Bachmann: Transformations of the Capitalist Patriarchy and Narrating Sexual Violence in the Twentieth Century" elaborates on female revenge fantasies. Informed by Marxist critic Roswitha Scholz's theory of value dissociation, Bademsoy constructs a framework for locating the relationship between capitalism's concept of value and woman's position in a capitalist system. Her analysis of Elfriede Jelinek's *Clara S.: A Musical Tragedy* (1988) and Ingeborg Bachmann's novel *Malina* (1971) brings the systematic repression of women and their creativity into dialogue with socially determined notions of value—with dramatically different outcomes. Jelinek's play depicts the artist Clara S. (loosely based on Clara Schumann), who commits mariticide, and concludes with the murder of the figures who embody the patriarchal order. Bachmann's *Malina* posits a triangular constellation of the "I" narrator; the male lover, Ivan, who embodies the criminal violence of the Nazi past; and Malina, who erases any trace of the "murder" of the narrator after she disappears into a crack in the wall. Both works, according to Bademsoy, indict the intentional failures of the patriarchal state and its institutions to assign women value. She argues that literary fantasies of vengeance in fact constitute responses to the material violence that victimizes not only women but any others not accorded sufficent value in the capitalist patriarchy.

In comparison with the reach and force of the social media outcry in the United States, the German response to #MeToo may seem tepid. The theater, however, especially those institutions with a track record of featuring contemporary social and political controversies, did respond in force. As Daniele Vecchiato demonstrates in "Staging Consent and Threatened Masculinity: The Debate on #MeToo in Contemporary German Theater," the Maxim Gorki Theater in Berlin offered the most pronounced response to the gender-based inequities seemingly intrinsic to the performing arts and entertainment industry. It opened the 2018–19 season with two original plays that explicitly thematize the movement. Vecchiato analyzes the performances of *Yes but No* by Yael Ronen, which premiered on the main stage on September 7, 2018; and *You Are Not the Hero of This Story* by Suna Gürler and Lucien Haug, which premiered on the theater's smaller stage the next day. Vecchiato, on the basis of these works, investigates the representation of gender conflict and sexual abuse—and foregrounds the normalization of harassment and abuse, both on and beyond the stage. His contribution looks specifically at the attempts in *Yes but No* and *You Are Not the Hero of This Story* to portray and harness the potentially transformative power of #MeToo toward staging a more equitable future.

The fifth section, "#MeToo across Cultural and National Borders," traces #MeToo discourses across cultural and national borderlines. Discussions of sexualized violence along racial and ethnic lines have often led to the instrumentalization of gendered discourses to support racist and xenophobic stereotypes. To counter such attempts, numerous #MeToo movements and activists have worked to overcome the divisions of race and class, while advocating for the end of male-dominated power structures that perpetuate rape culture, violence, abuse, and gender inequality. National contexts respond differently to the challenges of inclusion and visibility. In the German context, issues of gender and work, complicated by religion, make their way into popular culture and media with tropes of abused Turkish women, bound by German prejudice and toxic Turkish masculinity. In his "Patriarchy, Male Violence, and Disadvantaged Women: Representations of Muslims in the Crime Television Series *Tatort*," Sascha Gerhards looks at several episodes of the legendary German police procedural that thematize these tropes. The episodes predate the 2014 European "refugee crisis," which revived a debate about immigration and integration. One point of continuity, however, is the stereotypical representation of the predatory Muslim man and the objectified Muslim woman. Gerhards analyzes *Tatort* (Crime Scene) episodes "Wem Ehre gebührt" (2007; To Whom Honor Is Due), "Schatten der Angst" (2008; Shadow of Fear), and "Wacht am Rhein"

(2017; *Watch on the Rhine*) for their depiction of gender roles in Muslim communities, along with the response to such representations of Muslim life in the German media. His analysis shows that the media frequently project a negative image of Muslim culture while appealing to an audience that empathizes with the victimization of women.

Florian Gassner's "Fatih Akin's *Head On*: Challenging Mythologies of German Social Work in *Gegen die Wand* (2004)" offers a reading of the celebrated director's film about a Turkish German "girl gone wild." *Gegen die Wand* (Against the Wall) follows its German-Turkish protagonist Sibel as she attempts suicide to escape her oppressive family, arranges a marriage of convenience with the desperately unhappy Cahit, and retreats to Istanbul when Cahit is imprisoned for manslaughter. Sibel, who is committed to pursuing life and pleasure on her own terms, suffers and survives substance abuse, rape, and a knifing. Gassner argues that the film challenges the audience to look past what may initially seem like victim-blaming—Sibel is repeatedly warned that her behavior will be her downfall—and ultimately defies stereotypical expectations about Turkish men and women.

Kathrin Breuer's "Is a Prostitute Rapeable? Teresa Ruiz Rosas's Novel *Nada que declarer*" directs our focus onto international sex work, prostitution, and migration. The German-Peruvian author Teresa Ruiz Rosas's novel *Nada que declarar* (2013; Nothing to Declare) portrays a young heroine, Diana Postigo, who lives in abject poverty in the slums of Lima. There she succumbs to the seductive charms of Murat B., who lures her to Germany under false pretenses and forces her into prostitution. Displayed in a brothel window, Diana submits until she learns to tell her story and gains a new perspective on her life. Breuer's analysis brings in public debates about prostitution in Germany, where brothels are legal. Yet she observes the irony that this technical legality obscures human rights violations and, in the novel, keeps the protagonist's suffering invisible. Breuer analyzes the rhetoric and optics that enable Diana to recover her dignity and reclaim her body.

As this chapter summary shows, although rape myths remain prevalent in cultural artifacts, legal practice, and daily reality, much work has been done to challenge problematic assumptions about gender, power, the body, and the nature of male and female desire. While it is important to draw attention to problematic naturalizations and trivializations of rape and sexual assault, however, we should not forget that sexualized violence and the erasure of agential female desire are inextricably linked. A focus on sexual violence threatens to reduce women's sexual agency to the power "to consent or refuse (to be taken) rather than to desire or will (to take)."[80] In light of this reductive view of female sexuality, we

---

80 Rooney, "A Little More than Persuading," 93.

want to conclude by shining the spotlight on an issue that underlies many #MeToo-related debates but that exceeds the scope of this volume: the destigmatization of female desire and the problematization of the intricate link between female sexuality and shame. Indeed, while combating sexual violence is a matter of great urgency, there is an equally great need to deconstruct cultural myths of female desire along with the persistent association of female sexuality and shame.[81]

Like rape, the demonization of female desire has deep roots in Western civilization. Consider that the ultimate danger that Lessing's Emilia Galotti fears is not rape, but her own lust: "Gewalt! Gewalt! wer kann der Gewalt nicht trotzen? Was Gewalt heißt, ist nichts: Verführung ist die wahre Gewalt"[82] (Who cannot defy violence? What they call violence is nothing: seduction is true violence). It is no coincidence that the word "pudendum" is derived from the Latin word "pudere," to be ashamed. Over and over again, female desire is wed to shame. As Annie Ernaux writes, "I am endowed by shame's vast memory, more detailed and implacable than any other, a gift unique to shame."[83] One might claim that Ernaux's struggle to categorize what she experienced as rape is intimately related to the cultural effacement of female desire, which makes the difference between assault and consent illegible.[84] Tellingly, in her exploration of female desire in *Three Women* (2019), Lisa Taddeo writes about a conversation with her dying mother that motivated her to embark on her project. In this conversation, her mother passes on a piece of advice that she considers critical: "Don't let them see you happy. . . . If they see you happy, they will try to destroy you."[85] Both Taddeo's and Ernaux's books suggest that there is a link between the inability to perceive rape as such and the learned misrecognition of one's own desire. Thus, while we devote this volume to the analysis of sexual violence, we want to end with a call for scholarship that explores political discourses and cultural representations of female desire.

---

81 In fact, the German word "Scham" also designates the female genitalia. See Mithu M. Sanyal, *Vulva: Die Enthüllung des unsichtbaren Geschlechts* (Berlin: Klaus Wagenbach, 2009), 46.

82 Gotthold Ephraim Lessing, *Emilia Galotti: Ein Trauerspiel in fünf Aufzügen* (Berlin: Christian Friedrich Voß, 1772), 149.

83 Ernaux, *A Girl's Story*, 15.

84 On this, see also Sanyal, who points to the tendency to describe the vulva as "Loch, Leerstelle oder Nichts" (hole, void or nothing). Sanyal, *Vulva*, 8. Sanyal traces the lack of anatomical knowledge and accurate terminology of the female genitalia throughout history.

85 Lisa Taddeo, *Three Women* (New York: Avid Reader Press, 2019), 297.

Part I

Histories

1: Eighteenth-Century #MeToo: Rape Culture and Victim-Blaming in Heinrich Leopold Wagner's *Die Kindermörderin* (1776)

Lisa Wille

Tʜᴇ #MᴇTᴏᴏ ᴍᴏᴠᴇᴍᴇɴᴛ has given rise to a virulent international debate about sexualized violence, repressive power structures, and rape cultures.[1] The 2017 launch of this hashtag, which revived a phrase coined a decade earlier, dates back to a tweet by the American actress Alyssa Milano on the social media platform Twitter. Milano's tweet, which invited her followers to share their experiences of sexual harassment or violence, received an overwhelming response and kickstarted a movement. The fallout included publicized allegations leveled against the Hollywood producer Harvey Weinstein, who, despite his initial denial, eventually stood trial.

At first, #MeToo-related allegations were limited to figures in the public sphere, especially in film, sports, and politics, but soon they expanded into all social realms and across national borders. Millions of women around the world shared their experiences of sexualized violence in everyday life through #MeToo. The immense scale of these cumulative stories has shown the extent to which sexism remains omnipresent and normalized in society. Further, sexism not only exists in violent form, such as sexual assault and rape, but also encompasses structural discrimination and gender-based oppression. The German-language dictionary *Duden*, which is representative of common usage, defines "sexism" as the "Vorstellung, nach der ein Geschlecht dem anderen von

---

This essay is a slightly modified version of the chapter "Zwischen sozialer Repression und sozialisierter Gewalt: *Die Kindermörderin* (1776)" of my dissertation, *Zwischen Autonomie und Heteronomie: Bürgerliche Identitätsproblematik in Heinrich Leopold Wagners dramatischem Werk* (Würzburg: Königshausen & Neumann, 2021).

1   Cf. my contribution "Medien, Macht und #MeToo: Zum Kontext einer aktuellen Debatte," in *Männeraufbruch 2019: Das Jahrbuch für Männer in der Gegenwart*, ed. Boris von Heesen (Darmstadt: mensLit, 2018), 122–29.

Natur aus überlegen sei, und die [daher für gerechtfertigt gehaltene] Diskriminierung, Unterdrückung, Zurücksetzung, Benachteiligung von Menschen, besonders der Frauen,[2] aufgrund ihres Geschlechts"[3] (the notion that one sex is innately superior to the other; and the [therefore considered justifiable] discrimination, oppression, neglect, and disadvantaging of people, especially women, because of their sex). The idea of female inferiority, deeply rooted in cultural history, is not new but merely a reactualized version of a stereoytpe that reaches back across the ages.

While the #MeToo movement is a twenty-first-century phenomenon, a look at eighteenth-century German drama reveals an acute awareness of the tragedies surrounding gendered violence. Heinrich Leopold Wagner's (1747–79) bourgeois tragedy *Die Kindermörderin* (1776; *The Child Murderess*), one of the most important dramas of the Sturm und Drang movement, mercilessly stages sexual violence, unwanted pregnancy, familial and social constraints, and the precarious position of women and their reasons for commiting infanticide. The opening act features a key scene that takes place in a brothel. From the very beginning, the question of whether Evchen, who commits infanticide, was raped by Lieutenant von Gröningseck or merely seduced is central to the interpretation and significance of the entire drama. The evidence provided by the text indicates rape. This finding, however, remains controversial. Traditionally, German studies scholarship about *Die Kindermörderin* has considered Evchen a seduced woman—with the possibility of rape a secondary focus. A different research perspective emerged in the 1990s, emphasizing that a rape has been committed. Since then, however, research has once again displayed ambivalence, questioning the occurrence of rape in the text. These recent readings seek to restabilize myths of feminity; for example, of the sexually willing but coy woman. In the era of #MeToo, this change of direction is particularly troublesome.

Gender polarization in literary texts of the eighteenth century (and beyond) now represents an important area of German studies research. While this approach is of historical import, it is even more urgent that we ask, with a view to 2017 (and beyond), whether and to what extent eighteenth-century literature constitutes a discursive framework for our society today. In other words, do eighteenth-century gender discourses shape current collective ideas about gender? As early as 1776, Wagner's *Kindermörderin* reveals the sexual objectification of women, repressive structures of violence, and male disposition over the female body—topics that form the core of the #MeToo movement and affect our society today. In this sense, reading *Die Kindermörderin* today calls for a dialogue with

---

2   Sexual and gender preference should be added to this list.
3   "Sexismus," Duden online, accessed November 3, 2020, https://www.duden.de/rechtschreibung/Sexismus.

the #MeToo movement that makes cultural-discursive correspondences and transformations between the eighteenth and twenty-first centuries transparent. This brings up questions related to the social relevance of literature but also to the emergence and manifestation of gender alterity. After all, gender is still the central category of identity construction: it organizes both individual biographies and social, cultural, and political institutions and structures. And yet, there is still little public recognition of the constructedness of the category of gender—and of the power and hierarchies inscribed therein. A quick glance at the entertainment industry confirms this. Every day, we are fed prescriptive patterns of gendered behavior and normative value judgments, cementing stereotypical concepts of masculinity and femininity. In the literature of previous centuries and in film and television, the sexual objectification of women is omnipresent and is consequently perceived and internalized as normal. Gender categories inform the distribution of power in our society.[4] In order to elucidate the links between gender and power, the first section of this chapter examines Wagner's crucial "brothel scene" in detail. Then I turn to the scholarly debate about whether Evchen, Wagner's female protagonist, was raped or seduced—the latter underscoring her potential complicity. Finally, I explore the backlash in literary scholarship that retreats from the interpretation of rape, instead suggesting Evchen's complicity, and link these critical endeavors to the potential impact of eighteenth-century models of rape culture and victim-blaming on the contemporary #MeToo debate.

The Brothel Scene: Between Rape Culture and Male Power

The first act of *Die Kindermörderin* begins in medias res: hours after midnight, Lieutenant von Gröningseck and his companion, the bourgeois Frau Humbrecht and her daughter, Evchen, return to the "*Wirthshaus zum gelben Kreutz*" (KM, 5;[5] "*Yellow Cross, an inn,*" 57) after a carnival ball to have breakfast. Von Gröningseck knows that the inn is a brothel but deceives the women: when Frau Humbrecht asks him with slight

---

4   Cf. Wille, "Medien, Macht und #MeToo," 124.

5   Heinrich Leopold Wagner, *Die Kindermörderin: Ein Trauerspiel; Im Anhang: Auszüge aus der Bearbeitung von K. G. Lessing (1777) und der Umarbeitung von H. L. Wagner (1779) sowie Dokumente zur Wirkungsgeschichte*, ed. Jörg-Ulrich Fechner (Stuttgart: Reclam, 1997), cited in the text as KM with page number. English from Heinrich Leopold Wagner, *The Childmurderess*, trans. Betty Senk Waterhouse, in *Sturm und Drang: "The Soldiers," "The Childmurderess," "Storm and Stress," and "The Robbers,"* ed. Alan C. Leidner (New York: Continuum, 1992), 55–122. My insertions are in brackets and labeled "L.W."

skepticism whether they are in a "honetten Haus" (KM, 6; "respectable establishment," 58), he replies, "So soll mich der Teufel lebendig zerreißen, Frau Humbrecht! wenn hier nicht täglich alles, was beau monde heißt, zusammenkommt" (KM, 6; May the devil tear me alive, Frau Humbrecht, if everybody of the *beau monde* [fashionable world] doesn't come here daily," 58). The brothel functions as a site where normative bourgeois standards of behavior can be transgressed; it also represents a dangerous and forbidden space for members of the bourgeoisie, particularly for women.

The audience quickly realizes that von Gröningseck pursues a nefarious plan and is sexually interested in Evchen. He flirts with both mother and daughter, but his fantasies of sexual submission are reserved exclusively for Evchen's young body. On the symbolic level, the motif of unmasking anticipates the impending sexual act: when the trio arrive at the brothel, they wear their carnival costumes, their bodies veiled. Von Gröningseck has donned a wolf's coat, the women dominos—that is, black coats worn at Venetian carnivals. While Mrs. Humbrecht and von Gröningseck take off their masks and robes themselves, the latter removes Evchen's mask (cf. KM, 5; 57). Matthias Luserke-Jaqui associates the unmasking with a symbolic renunciation of normative (and gender-specific) standards of behavior.[6] But the mask also symbolizes changing identities. In the brothel, where social boundaries are crossed, the figures set aside their civilized identities along with their masks. Mrs. Humbrecht and von Gröningseck do so intentionally and actively, whereas Evchen remains passive.

Along with her mother, Evchen accepted the invitation of the lieutenant, who has been a paying guest in the Humbrecht family home for over a month, even though both mother and daughter are aware that they are acting against the will of the husband and father, Metzger Humbrecht, who is currently away on business. The mother fails utterly in her responsibility to protect Evchen's virtue. While Evchen is reserved in her behavior, the mother flirts with the lieutenant. In an aside, she says, "Er ist zum Fressen der kleine Narr!" (KM, 7; "I could just eat him up, the little fool," 59). Frau Humbrecht is portrayed as stupid, naive,[7] and frivolous; she remains oblivious to von Gröningseck's escalating mockery. The mother's simplicity is revealed when she addresses von Gröningseck with "Herr Hauptmann!" ("Captain!"), and he corrects her; he is not yet one. She then unmasks herself anew by calling him "Herr Major." At

---

6   Cf. Matthias Luserke-Jaqui, *Medea: Studien zur Kulturgeschichte der Literatur* (Tübingen: Francke, 2002), 136. Luserke-Jaqui's book contains an entire chapter on Wagner's *Kindermörderin*: 131–46.

7   See Georg Stanitzek, *Blödigkeit: Beschreibungen des Individuums im 18. Jahrhundert* (Tübingen: De Gruyter, 1989).

this point, Evchen intervenes: "Ey, Mutter, . . . Major ist ja noch mehr als Hauptmann, sie weiß ja gar nichts" (KM, 5; "Oh, Mother . . . Major is higher than captain, you really don't know anything," 57). Clearly, Evchen is more discreet, although she too is amused and intoxicated by the experience of her first ball (cf. KM, 12–13).

From the beginning, the drama stages a failure of communication. Evchen is initially unable to decode the sexual allusions exchanged between von Gröningseck and her mother. When Evchen states that she would not enjoy merely watching ballroom dancing and not dancing herself, von Gröningseck comments: "Du machst lieber selbst mit, nicht wahr?" (KM, 10; "You'd rather get in on the fun, is that it?" 61), and Evchen answers "*unschuldig*" (KM, 10; "*innocently*," 61): "Ja!" (KM, 10; "Yes!" 61). Mrs. Humbrecht's laughter at this language game signals her understanding of the sexual implications. The stage directions read, "*sich recht auszulachen bückt sie sich vorwärts an des Lieutenants Brust, das Gesicht von Evchen abgekehrt: Er spielt ihr am Halsband, sie drückt ihm die Hand, und küßt sie*" (KM, 10; "*laughs so hard she leans forward onto the lieutenant's chest; her face is turned away from Evchen. He plays with Frau Humbrecht's necklace; she presses his hand and kisses it,*" 61–62). Her comment, "das hat sie nicht verstanden: müssen ihr ihre Dummheit nicht übel auslegen" (KM, 10–11; "She didn't understand you. You mustn't misinterpret her naiveté," 62), highlights the contrast between the innocent Evchen and the sexually experienced Mrs. Humbrecht and von Gröningseck, who are united in their depravity. Here the difficulty of decoding becomes clear. As an unmarried young woman, Evchen is excluded from the discursive field of sexuality; at the same time, as an embodiment of innocence and virtue, she is highly sexualized for von Gröningseck. His allusions and choice of topics of conversation become increasingly objectionable; he alludes to the mother's wedding night and deflowering—thus anticipating his design on Evchen (cf. KM, 7; 59).

Von Gröningseck's character is diametrically opposed to Evchen's; his lifestyle is excessive, his behavior overbearing and self-confident. The embodiment of the careless social life of an officer, he knows how to enjoy himself, also in a sexual sense. French idioms display his affiliation with the nobility. Von Gröningseck takes possession of the female body in a completely self-evident and self-satisfied way. His terms of endearment for Evchen, such as "Kleine" (KM, 5; "little one," 57), "mein Kind" (KM, 5; "my child," 57) and "Närrchen" (KM, 16; "my little fool," 65), linguistically infantilize her and reinforce her inferiority. His increasingly aggressive power and sense of entitlement to the female body are first revealed when the light goes out as he knocks over the table and candlestick (cf. KM, 6; 58). When Evchen hands him the fallen candlestick, he reaches past it and *grabs* her. She comments in shock, "Ey hier! sie greifen ja dran vorbei—pfuy—" (KM, 6; "Here, for heaven's sake! You're reaching right past it. Honestely!" 58) and then, "*[sich] die Hände am Schnupftuch abwischend*" (KM, 6; "*wiping her hands on her handkerchief,*" 58) complains, "ey da hab ich mir die Hände am Inschlitt [= Kerzentalg, L.W.] beschmiert. (*Wirft dem Lieutenant heimlich einen drohenden Blick zu: er lächelt)*" (KM, 6–7; "Lord, now my hands are all covered with tallow. (*secretly throws a threatening look at von Gröningseck; he smiles),*" 58). The scene is full of ambiguities that oscillate between symbols of the Enlightenment (light) and sexuality. When the candle goes out, the light of enlightenment is extinguished with it. Both the reality of the brothel and its symbolism function as the "Other" of normalized society; in the brothel, sexuality and desire dominate. The first act, and this scene in particular, are permeated with sexual symbols. The candle is a phallic symbol, the candle wax that splatters on Evchen ejaculate; this scene symbolically initiates the rape. The handkerchief, which traditionally symbolizes shame and with which Evchen wipes her hand, serves here as an attempt to undo the "defilement" that has just occured.

While I read the candle wax as an anticipation of the impending rape, Yvonne Alefeld claims that it signals consent: "Diese haptische Plastizität zieht Evchen an, die sich die Hände—eindeutig genug—mit Kerzentalg beschmiert, wonach sie vergnügt lacht"[8] (This haptic plasticity appeals to Evchen, who—clearly enough—smears her hands with tallow, and afterward laughs happily). Alefeld argues against a one-sided notion of guilt that casts the man as perpetrator and Evchen as victim,[9] but she fails to recognize that Evchen laughs not in the context of this "scene of defilement" but rather later, when she rebukes von Gröningseck and glances at him in a threatening manner (cf. KM, 7; 58).

When the mother and Evchen go into the next room to take off their coats, the landlady, Marianel, joins them, and von Gröningseck strikes up a conversation with her. The two know each other, since von Gröningseck has often used Marianel's services as a prostitute. In this scene, his intention is revealed: he wants to incapacitate Mrs. Humbrecht with a sleeping powder in order to have intercourse with Evchen. In exchange for payment, Marianel becomes his accomplice charged with the preparation of the sleeping draft (cf. KM; 8; 60). All the while, von Gröningseck makes no secret of his disregard for her ("Halts Maul! und thu was ich dir sagte," KM, 9; "Shut up and do what I tell you!" 60). When she

---

8   Yvonne-Patricia Alefeld, "Texte und Affekte: Zur Inszenierung der Leidenschaften in Heinrich Leopold Wagners *Die Kindermörderin*," in *Von der Liebe und anderen schrecklichen Dingen: Festschrift für Hans-Georg Pott*, ed. Yvonne-Patricia Alefeld (Bielefeld: Aisthesis, 2007), 163–88, here 172.

9   Cf. Alefeld, "Texte und Affekte," 172n27. In contrast, Luserke-Jaqui argues that in this scene, von Gröningseck attacks the female body and marks it as possession: *Medea*, 133.

wants to caress him, he pushes her away, because "wenn der Soldat Eyerweck [= Brötchen, L.W.] hat, frißt er kein Kommißbrod" (KM, 8; "When a soldier has a breakfast roll to eat, he doesn't need army bread," 60). In the third act, during a conversation with his fellow officer von Hasenpoth, von Gröningseck refers to certain women as our "Spielwerk" (KM, 34; "games," 81) who otherwise "zu gar nichts nütze sind" (KM, 34; "wouldn't be good for anything," 81).

Through the figures of von Gröningseck and Marianel, the play highlights asymmetrical power structures. The relation between the lowest social class, represented by the prostitute Marianel, and the ostensibly noble Lieutenant von Gröningseck is characterized by a coarse, disrespectful manner of interaction (cf. KM, 8–9; 60–61). But they are bound by their shared understanding of transactional sexuality. In this way, both von Gröningseck's and Marianel's values are incongruent with bourgeois norms of behavior.[10] It is significant that von Gröningseck does not reflect or acknowledge his deviation from the norm. Rather, he reproaches Marianel, whom he has just paid to help him with his malicious plan: "Einer Hur ist niemals zu trauen" (KM, 9; "A whore is never to be trusted," 60). In contrast, Marianel's aphoristic answer, "keinem Schelmen auch nicht, und wenn keine Hurenbuben wären; so gäbs lauter brave Mädels" (KM, 9; "Nor a whore's trick. If there weren't any of your sort around, there would be nothing but good girls," 60), not only points to hegemonic conditions but also describes the sociological and sociopsychological connections that undergird this power differential, as Bengt A. Sørensen explains.[11] Matthias Luserke characterizes Marianel as an emotionally and economically dependent, disenfranchised woman on the fringes of society,[12] whereas von Gröningseck partakes of all the privileges reserved for a noble officer. Officers are accountable only to their superiors; they enjoy a greater freedom of action than the bourgeoisie, also and especially with regard to their sexual behavior. Tellingly, this central formula of this drama's epistemology is exposed by a marginalized, lower-class figure: if men did not behave like von Gröningseck, both Evchen and Marianel would remain virtuous. His male hubris evokes the contemporary notion of toxic, hegemonic masculinity, on both an individual and societal scale.

Von Gröningseck's hegemonic masculinity becomes increasingly evident when the mother and Evchen return, now without dominoes. Here, the text showcases the sexual objectification of a young woman. Clearly,

---

10   Cf. Bengt A. Sørensen, *Herrschaft und Zärtlichkeit: Der Patriarchalismus und das Drama im 18. Jahrhundert* (Munich: C. H. Beck, 1984), 140.

11   Cf. Sørensen, *Herrschaft und Zärtlichkeit*, 140.

12   Matthias Luserke, *Sturm und Drang: Autoren–Texte–Themen* (Stuttgart: Reclam, 2010), 234.

the lieutenant's primary concern is the female body: "Ma chere, das ist recht, das ist schön, sehr schön!—le diable m'emporte—siehst so recht appetitlich aus! so dünn und leicht angezogen!—bist auf mein Ehr recht hübsch gewachsen, so schlank! alles so markirt!—" (KM, 9; "Yes, *ma chère* [= my dear], that's right. That's lovely, lovely! *Le diable m'emporte* [= the devil takes me, L.W.], you do look appetizing! Such sheer, light clothing! On my honor, you have grown into a beauty. So thin, everything standing out so much," 61). The text emphasizes the contrast between Evchen's unwilling but young body and the mother's aging one, both of which stand in the way of male wish fulfillment.[13] Indeed, the sexual marginalization of the mother owing to her age is evident. When Mrs. Humbrecht asks von Gröningseck, "wie seh denn *ich* aus?" (KM 9; "how do *I* look?" 61), he answers, "*ohne sie anzusehn*" ("*without looking at her*"): "Superb, superb! das Neglische steht ihnen recht gut" (KM, 9; "Superb! Superb! The gown flatters you," 60). The older female body does not even warrant a glance; only the young woman holds his interest: "Wie göttlich schön dir das derangirte Haar läßt, mein Liebchen! kann mich nicht satt an dir sehn: die Zöpfe so flott!—" (KM, 9–10; "How divinely beautiful your disarrayed hair makes you, my darling! I can't gaze upon you enough," 61). Importantly, the standardization, idealization, and objectification of the young female body that is on display in this eighteenth-century text is not fundamentally different from similar dynamics in our society today; for example, in advertising or high-circulation magazines.

In Wagner's play, von Gröningseck's sense of entitlement over the female body grows increasingly audacious. His actions are active and targeted right from the start. He kisses Evchen and leads her—his arm around her body—to the table, where he sits down next to her (cf. KM, 10; 61). Both the officer's speech and body language signal control not only over Evchen's but over every female body.[14] Thus, he also "*packt . . . ihre Mutter um den Leib, und stellt sie zwischen seine Beine*" (KM, 10; "*seizes Frau Humbrecht and sets her between his legs,*" 61). Similarly, when Mrs. Humbrecht wants to leave, he "*faßt sie um den Hals*" (KM, 62; "takes her by the neck," 12) with the words, "Aufbrechen? jetzt schon? rappelt dirs Weibchen?" (KM, 12; "Leaving? Already? Are you out of your mind, little lady?" 62). Later, trying to persuade her to drink, he grabs the mother's neck with one hand and holds the glass to her mouth with the other to make sure that she drinks it all up ("das Restchen noch," KM, 15). Evchen, too, is urged to drink the punch: "Frisch Evchen! nicht so geleppert [= zaghaft getrunken, L.W.], das Glas muß aus: (*Evchen leerts.*) So bist brav! sollst auch ein Mäulchen [= Küßchen, L.W.] haben!—*(küßt sie)*" (KM, 12; "Come on, Evchen! Don't sip it like

---

13 Cf. Luserke-Jaqui, *Medea*, 136.
14 Cf. Luserke, *Sturm und Drang*, 234.

that. The glass must be drained. (*Evchen finishes her glass*) Well done! For that you get a kiss (*kisses her*)," 63).

As Evchen and her mother are degraded from subject to object and von Gröningseck asserts power of disposition over the female body, a literal *dehumanization* of women takes place. It is precisely this constellation of pervasive, ubiquitous, and normalized sexual objectification and assault that is captured in the term "rape culture". In the play, rape culture is connected to masculinity and military socialization and extended from a description of an individual case of rape to an indictment of socially accepted violence against women. Von Gröningseck exemplifies this collectively internalized male entitlement over the female body. He is more than just an irresponsible seducer; rather, his male privilege is constituted in part via his access to the female body. Nagla El-Dandoush notes that an officer is characterized by loyalty, obedience, and discipline, but only vis-à-vis the institution of the military.[15] At the same time, as both El-Dandoush and Katrin Heyer point out, von Gröningseck's socialization in the military, and in the homosocial officers' union, carries over into his sexual behavior: his detailed planning to become intimate with Evchen resembles a military campaign:

> Frauen werden generell oft mit Festungen gleichgesetzt, die es zu *erobern*, *erstürmen* und zu *besiegen* gilt. Der Sieg des Mannes, der erlangte sexuelle Verkehr, ist immer die Niederlage der Frau. Die Schuld für die Niederlage, sei sie nun freiwillig erfolgt oder gewaltsam, liegt immer bei der Frau, denn sie *lässt* sich erobern, bestürmen, vergewaltigen. Die von ihr verlangte Passivität wird nun zu ihrem Schuldeingeständnis.[16]

> [Women are often equated with fortresses that have to be *stormed*, *conquered*, and *defeated*. The victory of the man, the obtained sexual intercourse, is always the defeat of the woman. The guilt for the defeat, regardless of whether it happened volutarily or violently, is always the woman's because she *allows* herself to be conquered, stormed, raped. Thus the passivity demanded of her becomes her admission of guilt.]

The conversation between von Gröningseck and von Hasenpoth in the third act makes clear that, for officers, sexual objectification unfolds as

---

15   Nagla El-Dandoush, *Leidenschaft und Vernunft im Drama des Sturm und Drang: Dramatische als soziale Rollen* (Würzburg: Königshauen & Neumann, 2004), 178.

16   Katrin Heyer, *Sexuelle Obsessionen: Die Darstellung der Geschlechterverhältnisse in ausgewählten Dramen von Goethe bis Büchner* (Marburg: Tectum, 2005), 41.

a ritual dehumanization of women; it is a normalized part of everyday life and serves to confirm male identity. Von Gröningseck instrumentalizes the female body for his needs without taking into account human integrity or the consequences of his actions. Evchen's lack of experience makes her helpless against his aggression and positions her as inferior to him. She does not know what punch is (cf. KM, 13; 63), and this was her first ball. When her mother, after drinking the poisoned punch, falls asleep on von Gröningseck's chest, Evchen "*springt ganz erschrocken und besorgt auf, schüttelt ihre Mutter*" (KM, 15; "*leaps up, frightened and tries to rouse her mother*," 65). She asks, "Mutter! was fehlt ihr:—hört sie? hört sie nicht?—Guter Himmel! wenn sie nur nicht krank wird!" (KM, 15; "Mother! What's the matter with you? Can you hear me? God in heaven! I hope she's not ill!" 65). She is deeply concerned and cannot tell if her mother has passed out ("in Ohnmacht"; KM, 15) or is dead ("gar tod"; KM, 15). The catastrophe begins.[17]

Evchen—Seduced or Raped?

Von Gröningseck offers some comforting words ("der Punsch hats gethan—sie ist ihn nicht gewohnt," KM, 15; "The punch did it. She's not used to it," 65) and together they carry the mother to bed. Von Gröningseck "*setzt sich neben die Mutter, zieht Evchen nach sich*" (KM, 15–16; "*sits down next to Frau Humbrecht, draws Evchen to him*," 65) and appeases her: "Sey doch kein Kind, ma chere! was ists denn weiter?" (KM, 16; "Don't be a child, *ma chère*! Nothing else is going to happen," 65). Thereupon he "*sieht ihr starr unter die Augen*" (KM, 16; "*gazes at her fixedly*," 65) and asks: "Bist du mir gut Evchen?" (KM, 16; "Do you still like me, Evchen?" 65). This question can be interpreted as an invitation to sexual intercourse.[18] But Evchen does not follow suit: "ums Himmelswillen sehn sie mich nicht so an; ich kanns nicht ausstehn" (KM, 16; "For heaven's sake, don't look at me like that. I can't stand it," 65). The lieutenant ignores this rejection; his subsequent "warum denn nicht, Närrchen?" (KM, 16; "Why can't you, my little fool?" 65) is a purely rhetorical act, already accompanied by physical overtures: he "*küßt ihr mit vieler Hitze die Hand, und sieht ihr bey jedem Kuß wieder starr in die Augen*" (KM, 16; "*kisses her hand passionately, looking deeper and deeper*

---

17 Today, von Gröningseck's calculated alcoholisation of Evchen and her mother, the knock-out drug in the form of a sleeping pill, and the subsequent rape of Evchen would constitute as "date rape" and would be punishable by law. Cf. John A. McCarthy, "Abermals 'Sektionsberichte des Lasters': Bilaterale Reformvorstellungen in Literatur und Recht um 1800," *Internationales Archiv für Sozialgeschichte der deutschen Literatur* 31, no. 2 (2006): 100–130, here 111.

18 Cf. Heyer, *Sexuelle Obsessionen*, 42.

into her eyes with each kiss," 65). Christine Künzel posits that the gaze bears masculine connotations: it objectifies, fixates, and serves as a metaphor for the potential power or even violence that can be converted into action at any moment.[19] In other words, the gaze implies action. Von Gröningseck tries to fixate Evchen with a steady gaze.[20] Just before the rape, his gaze moves from the eyes to the body, when he sees "her staring *below* the eyes." Here, male power of control over women is explicitly represented by the male gaze. *Die Kindermörderin* positions von Gröningseck's gaze as an instrument of power and moves to make its dire effect transparent. Evchen's answer, "darum!—ich will nicht—" (KM, 16; "That's why! I won't!" 65), is clear and explicit. Her gestures also signal a fundamental rejection: von Gröningseck wants to hug and kiss her ("*will sie umarmen und küssen,*" KM, 16), but she struggles, breaks free, and runs to the chamber ("*sträubt sich, reißt sich los, und läuft der Kammer zu*" KM, 16).

Evchen's linguistic and physical rejection remains ineffective. The young woman recognizes this when she calls out: "Mutter! Mutter ich bin verlohren" (KM, 16; "Mother! Mother! I am lost!" 66), while attempting to escape. Interestingly, Heinz-Dieter Weber does not interpret her behavior as an escape but as consent to sexual intercourse. According to Weber, Evchen could have run outside, not into the chamber, if she had wanted to. Weber underscores this problematic interpretation with the statement that she had long since fallen for him ("sie war ihm längst verfallen").[21] In contrast, Heyer recognizes Evchen's panic and concludes that her escape into the chamber does not signal consent or an invitation.[22] Gesa Dane also argues that Evchen's rejection is clear and compelling and should not be understood as a titillating scenario of seduction.[23] Von Gröningseck preempts any further attempt to escape: "Du sollst mir doch nicht entlaufen!" (KM, 16; "You shouldn't run away from me!" 66). He rushes after her and slams the chamber door; from the next room "*Getös*" (KM, 16; "*Pandemonium offstage,*" 66) can be heard. Meanwhile, the old landlady and Marianel appear onstage but pretend not to hear anything, and little by little it grows quiet (cf. KM, 16; 66).

---

19   Cf. Christine Künzel, "Johann [*sic*] Heinrich Leopold Wagners *Die Kindermörderin*: Geschlechterkodierung und Geschlechtskritik im Sturm und Drang," in *Sturm und Drang: Epoche—Autoren—Werke*, ed. Matthias Buschmeier and Kai Kauffmann (Darmstadt: WBG, 2013), 203–19, here 210.

20   Cf. Luserke-Jaqui, *Medea*, 137.

21   Heinz-Dieter Weber, "Kindsmord als tragische Handlung," *Der Deutschunterricht* 28, no. 2 (1976): 75–97, here 91.

22   Cf. Heyer, *Sexuelle Obsessionen*, 43.

23   Cf. Gesa Dane, *"Zeter und Mordio": Vergewaltigung in Literatur und Recht* (Göttingen: V&R, 2005), 226.

Only a few moments later, Evchen returns, sobbing. The stage direction specifies: she rushes out of the next room and falls on her mother's chest (*"stürzt wieder aus dem Nebenzimmer heraus . . . fällt schluchzend ihrer Mutter auf die Brust,"* KM, 17). Crying, she announces what was done to her: "—Mutter! Rabenmutter! schlaf,—schlaf ewig!—deine Tochter ist zur Hure gemacht" (KM, 17; "Mother! Cruel Mother! Sleep, sleep forever. Your daughter is a whore!" 66). Everything indicates that Evchen was the victim of a sexual assault. Heyer states unequivocally that Evchen is the victim of a malicious rape. Any other word would be a euphemism.[24] Günter Saße also acknowledges that there is no hint of consent.[25] In the final act, Evchen will say that she was "verführt, übertöpelt" (KM, 78; "seduced, deceived," 116). Luserke-Jaqui reads these later statements as evidence of her submission to the male power to define social reality.[26] Crucially, Wagner himself, in his critical objection to Karl Gotthelf Lessing's trivializing treatment in the *Frankfurter gelehrte Anzeigen* in 1777, explicates his intent. By no means, he writes, "giebt sie vor, sie wär übertölpelt worden" (does she state she was duped); rather, "sie [ist] es wirklich"[27] (she really was).

From the moment of the rape Evchen expects draconian punishments. The loss of her virtue sets in motion the mechanisms of social norms and sanctions, and she fears their brutal effects on her. Along with her virginity, a bourgeois woman loses her honor, her most important and often sole asset. The only way to restore her reputation is to marry the rapist. If she cannot, the woman and her family fall victim to stigmatization. When Evchen cannot calm down, von Gröningseck appeals to her reason, now addressing her formally as "Sie" (you): "So wollen sie denn gar nicht Raison annehmen, Mademoiselle?—wollen sich selbst fürs Teufels Gewalt prostituiren?—alle Welt wissen lassen, was jetzt unter uns ist?" (KM, 17; "Have you taken leave of your senses, Mademoiselle? Do you want to be a prostitute? To let the whole world know what's happened between us?" 66). Thereupon Evchen straightens up, but covers her face with a handkerchief and tries to chase him away: "—Fort, fort! Henkersknecht!—Teufel in Engelgestalt!" (KM, 17; "Go! Go, tormentor! Devil in angel's clothing!" 66). This gesture of turning away and hiding one's face traditionally expresses feelings of shame or sadness.[28] Evchen's juxtaposition of angel and devil alludes to Samuel Richardson's

---

24 Cf. Heyer, *Sexuelle Obsessionen*, 45.

25 Günter Saße, *Die Ordnung der Gefühle: Das Drama der Liebesheirat im 18. Jahrhundert* (Darmstadt: WBG, 1996), 216.

26 Luserke-Jaqui, *Medea*, 139.

27 *Frankfurter gelehrte Anzeigen 1777*, 100–108; reprinted in Fechter, *Heinrich Leopold Wagner*, 142.

28 Cf. Dane, *"Zeter und Mordio,"* 227.

Clarissa (1748), whose female protagonist, Clarissa, is also forced to have sexual intercourse. Von Gröningseck confirms this intertextual link when he comments cynically,[29] "Sie haben Romanen gelesen, wies scheint?— Ewig schade wärs ja, wenn sie nicht selbst eine Heldin geworden wären" (KM, 17; "You've been reading novels, I presume? It would be an eternal shame if you weren't a heroine yourself," 66). Here, Richardson's novel stands symbolically for the prototypical sentimental love story with its sensitive "heroine." It was commonly assumed that women derived their ideas of love from these novels. In the age of Enlightenment, however, reading also served as a source of education and information for women.[30] Thus, for bourgeois girls, reading not only fed a thirst for romance but also promised knowledge about the world in general and about male and female options for action in particular. And yet, for Evchen, the fundamental aspirations of the Enlightenment remained unattainable.

Von Gröningseck's attempts to appease Evchen are completely inappropriate: "Ums Himmelswillen, so komm doch zu dir!—du bist ja nicht die erste.—" (KM, 17; "For heaven's sake, pull yourself together! You certainly aren't the first," 67). This trivializing strategy of justification confirms that male control over the female body is collectively anchored. According to Heyer, this short sentence reveals what the lieutenant thinks of Evchen's value as a human being.[31] Evchen completes his sentence: "Die du zu Fall gebracht hast?—bin ichs nicht—nicht die erste? o sag mirs noch *einmal*" (KM, 17; "That you've ruined? I'm not . . . not the first? Oh, say that just once more," 67). Heyer interprets Evchen's statement as a desperate attempt to assert her individuality: If she were the first, the only one for von Grönigseck, then she would have occupied a unique position in his life. But, as it is, she is not the first nor the only one. She has become a thing, an object of his desires, unlike von Gröningseck, who, as Heyer argues, is always conceived as an autonomous subject.[32]

To appease Evchen, von Gröningseck revises his statement: Evchen is not the first to become a woman (in the sense of being deflowered) before she was married (cf. KM, 17; 67). Now expanding his statement, the lieutenant proclaims, repeats, and reaffirms his promise of marriage: "Von dem jetzigen Augenblick an bist du die Meinige; ich schwurs schon in der Kammer. . . . In fünf Monaten bin ich majorenn, dann führ ich dich an Altar, erkenne dich öffentlich für die Meine" (KM, 17; "From this moment on, you are mine. I made this oath already in the

---

29   Cf. Dane, *"Zeter und Mordio,"* 227.

30   Cf. Linda Simonis, "Aufklärung," in *Metzler Lexikon: Gender Studies / Geschlechterforschung,* ed. Renate Kroll (Stuttgart: Metzler, 2002), 26–27, here 27.

31   Cf. Heyer, *Sexuelle Obsessionen,* 34.

32   Cf. Heyer, *Sexuelle Obsessionen,* 35.

bedchamber. . . . In five months I shall be of age. I shall lead you to the altar then and proclaim you publicly to be mine," 67).

This moral turn "vom Saulus zum Paulus" (from Saul to Paul)[33] is utterly surprising and unmotivated. Saße argues that it is a result of dramaturgical considerations rather than psychological consistency.[34] Evchen responds with fear and skepticism: "Darf ich dir trauen, nach dem, was vorgefallen?—Doch ja! ich muß" (KM, 17; "How can I trust you after what's happened? But of course I must," 67). Evchen realizes that she has no choice but to trust that von Gröningseck will keep his promise of marriage, since, as a deflowered woman, she cannot sink any lower. The prospect of marriage is Evchen's only chance to improve her social (and familial) reputation. In this emergency situation, Evchen tries to bind von Gröningseck to his promise: "Stehn sie auf und hören sie meine Bedingung an.—Fünf Monat, sagten sie? gut! so lang will ich mich zwingen, mir Gewalt anthun, daß man meine Schande mir nicht auf der Stirne lesen soll" (KM, 18; "Get up and hear my conditions! Five months, you said! Good! That's how long I'll choke back every emotion: No one will learn of my disgrace from my face," 67).

In Evchen's response, we can detect no confession of love, no joy, and no excitement about the promise of marriage, even though some scholars read her reluctant consent as a sign of love.[35] In contrast, I argue that her words confirm that she knows she was violated and recognizes the promised marriage as an acknowledgment of the damage done to her. Characteristically, Evchen's speech consists almost exclusively of questions or exclamations, all of which articulate her vacillation between uncertainty (questions) and determination (exclamations). Dane notes that the loss of virtue and thus honor makes Evchen vulnerable and further increases the social gap between her and von Grönigseck.[36]

After von Gröningseck confirms his offer of marriage, the stage directions specify that Evchen kisses him but immediately tears herself away (cf. 67; KM 18; "*küßt ihn, reißt sich aber, sobald er sie wieder geküßt, gleich los*"). She then proclaims,

> so sey dieser Kuß der Trauring, den wir einander auf die Eh geben.—
> Aber von nun an, bis der Pfarrer sein Amen! gesagt, von nun an—
> hören sie ja wohl, was ich sage—unterstehn sie sich nicht, mir nur
> den Finger zu küssen;—sonst halt ich sie für einen Meineidigen,
> der mich als eine Gefallene ansieht, der er keine Ehrerbietung mehr
> schuldig ist, der er mitspielen kann, wie er will:—und so bald ich das

---

33   Cf. Luserke, *Sturm und Drang*, 235.

34   Cf. Saße, *Ordnung der Gefühle*, 218.

35   See especially my analysis of Alefeld and Meyer-Sickendiek in the following section.

36   Dane, *"Zeter und Mordio,"* 228.

merke, so entdeck ich Vater oder Mutter—es gilt gleich, wer?—dem ersten dem besten alles was vorgegangen, und sollten sie mich mit Füßen zu Staub treten!—Haben sie mich verstanden?—warum so versteinert, mein Herr?—wundert sies, was ich gesagt habe?—jetzt lassen sie den Kutscher rufen. (KM, 18)

[May these kisses be the rings that we exchange in promise of our marriage. But from now on, until the minister says, "Amen," from now on—listen to what I am saying—do not be so bold as to even kiss my finger. Else I shall hold you to be a perjurer, who sees me as a fallen woman to whom he owes no respect, whom he can play with as he wants. As soon as I sense this, I shall reveal the whole story to Father or Mother. It doesn't matter which one, right? To whomever, I'll tell everything that happened, even if they should trample me to dust! Do you understand? Why so silent, sir? Are you surprised at what I said? Now go call the coachman!" 67]

Clearly, the kiss that Evchen resists does not signal love, as has been suggested. Rather, it symbolizes the nonexistent "Trauring" (betrothal ring) that seals the engagement and binds von Gröningseck to his marriage vow.

Evchen faces an existential crisis, a conflict between despair and social pressure; and, as Saße observes, she struggles to find the correct response, violating either her personal sense of honor or her reputation. On the one hand, as Saße explains, she needs to keep her distance from her rapist to regain a sense of control and integrity. On the other hand, she needs to accept his offer of marriage in order to restore her reputation.[37] These ambivalent, divergent of points of view become clear in the following dialogue:

v. Gröningseck.	Ich bewundre sie, Evchen!—in diesem Ton—
Evchen.	Spricht beleidigte Tugend:—muß so sprechen:—Jetzt hängt es von ihnen ab zu zeigen; ob sie wahr geredet haben.
v. Gröningseck (will auf sie loß.)	Engelskind!—
Evchen (tritt zurück.)	Schimpfst du mich, Verräther?—kannst du Engel sagen, ohne an die Gefallne zu denken? gefallen durch dich!—. (KM, 18)

[*von Gröningseck*:	You astonish me, Evchen! This tone!
Evchen:	Offended virtue speaks. It must speak so. Now everything depends on you to prove that you have spoken the truth.
von Gröningseck (about to embrace her):	Angelic child!

---

37 Cf. Saße, *Ordnung der Gefühle*, 218.

> *Evchen (draws back):* Are you insulting me, betrayer? Can you
> say "angel" without thinking of the fallen ones?
> Brought down by you! 67–68]

Here, Evchen takes control of the situation and rises to moral greatness. Her virtuous demeanor causes von Gröningseck to idealize her, perceiving her, as Anke Bennholdt-Thomsen and Alfredo Guzzoni suggest, as an angel and goddess, an object of admiration rather than a real woman who was victimized by him.[38] Evchen's transformation from passive victim to agent is motivated by a balancing act, as she straddles the need to shield her reputation and the extremely limited options for self-determined action open to her. To Evchen, female autonomy is possible only within the narrrowly circumscribed confines of male discourse. At the same time, the text affirms Evchen's moral development, since it motivates von Gröningseck's transformation. Once again, a text recycles the motif of woman's moral superiority.

Euphemistic Legitimation Strategies: The Backlash in Current Scholarship

Literary interpretations of the "chamber scene" in Wagner's *Die Kindermörderin* variously speak of seduction, rape, and the elimination of ambiguity. The sexual intercourse takes place offstage. Nevertheless, the circumstantial evidence provided by the text clearly indicates a rape. And yet, this interpretation has not endured. An metaanalysis of German studies scholarship on the *Kindermörderin* paints a problematic picture, as both older and newer publications continue to reassemble patriarchal masculinity. Significantly, research has traditionally seen Evchen as a woman who was "seduced" or as a "seduced innocent."[39] To some, the

---

38 Anke Bennholdt-Thomsen and Alfredo Guzzoni, *Der "Asoziale" in der Literatur um 1800* (Königstein im Taunus: Athenäum, 1979), 95.

39 Cf. Erich Schmidt, *Heinrich Leopold Wagner: Goethes Jugendgenosse; Nebst neuen Briefen und Gedichten von Wagner und Lenz* (Jena: Ed. Frommann, 1875), 62; Jörg-Ulrich Fechner, "Nachwort," in *Heinrich Leopold Wagner*, 163–74, here 168; Walter Hinck, "Metamorphosen eines Wiegenliedes: H. L. Wagner, Heine, G. Hauptmann, Toller, Brecht," in *Zeiten und Formen in Sprache und Dichtung: Festschrift für Fritz Tschirch zum 70. Geburtstag*, ed. Karl-Heinz Schirmer and Bernhard Sowinski (Cologne: Böhlau, 1972), 290–306, here 295; Gerhard Kaiser, *Aufklärung, Empfindsamkeit, Sturm und Drang* (Tübingen: Francke, 2007 [1976]), 234; Heinz-Dieter Weber, "Kindsmord als tragische Handlung," *Der Deutschunterricht* 28, no. 2 (1976): 75–97, here 91; Jörg-Ulrich Fechner, "Leidenschafts- und Charakterdarstellungen im Drama (Gerstenberg, Leisewitz, Klinger, Wagner)," in *Sturm und Drang*, ed. Walter Hinck (Frankfurt am Main: Athenäum, 1978), 175–91, here 187; Walter Hinck, "Produktive Rezeption

scene qualifies as a "brutale Verführung"[40] (brutal seduction). Wolfgang Wittkowski chooses the highly disturbing wording "freundschaftlich vergewaltigt"[41] (raped in a friendly way). Barbara Mabee claims that Evchen used the sexual act to express her desire for freedom,[42] a statement that can only be classified as a misguided euphemism. Conversely, von Gröningseck is perceived as a "Verführer"[43] (seducer), "bedenkenloser Verführer"[44] (unscrupulous seducer), or "Überwinder"[45] (conqueror). In contrast, in the 1990s,[46] scholars attest the occurrence of rape.[47] Yet

heute: Am Beispiel der sozialen Dramatik von Jakob Michael Reinhold Lenz und Heinrich Leopold Wagner," in Hinck, *Sturm und Drang*, 257–69, here 264; Dieter Kafitz, *Grundzüge einer Geschichte des deutschen Dramas von Lessing bis zum Naturalismus*, 2 vols. (Königstein im Taunus: Athenäum, 1982), 98; Georg Pilz, *Deutsche Kindesmord-Tragödien: Wagner, Goethe, Hebbel, Hauptmann* (Munich: Oldenbourg, 1982), 18; John Whiton, "Faith and the Devil in H. L. Wagner's *Die Kindermörderin*," *Lessing Yearbook* 16 (1984): 221–28, here 222; Barbara Mabee, "Die Kindesmörderin in den Fesseln der bürgerlichen Moral: Wagners Evchen und Goethes Gretchen," *Women in German Yearbook* 3 (1986): 29–45, here 35; Peter Bekes, *Theater als Provokation: Gerhart Hauptmann, "Die Ratten"; Heinrich Leopold Wagner, "Die Kindermörderin"* (Stuttgart: Klett, 1989), 18; Klaus Kastner, *Literatur und Wandel im Rechtsdenken* (Stuttgart: Boorberg, 1993), 26; Jung Kwon Lee, "Geschlechterdifferenz und Mutterschaft im bürgerlichen Trauerspiel von Lessing bis Hebbel: Kulturwissenschaftliche Analysen" (PhD diss., Trier University, 2012), 264, accessed November 5, 2020, https://ubt.opus.hbz-nrw.de/opus45-ubtr/frontdoor/deliver/index/docId/479/file/PDF_Endfass._der_Diss._v._J.K.L._09_03_2013_Publi.pdf.

40   Jürgen Haupt, "*Die Kindermörderin*: Ein bürgerliches Trauerspiel vom 18. Jahrhundert bis zur Gegenwart," *Orbis Litterarum* 32 (1977): 285–301, here 286.

41   Wolfgang Wittkowski, "Plädoyer für die Dramen Heinrich Leopold Wagners," *Literaturwissenschaftliches Jahrbuch* 35 (1994): 151–80, here 151.

42   Mabee, "Die Kindesmörderin," 35.

43   Examples include Dieter Mayer, "Heinrich Leopold Wagners Trauerspiel *Die Kindermörderin* und die Dramentheorie des Louis Sébastien Mercier," *literatur für leser* 2 (1981): 79–92, here 89; and Kaiser, *Aufklärung, Empfindsamkeit*, 230.

44   Karl S. Guthke, *Das deutsche bürgerliche Trauerspiel* (Stuttgart: J. B. Metzler, 2006 [1972]), 106.

45   Wittkowski, "Plädoyer," 151.

46   Huyssen spoke of a rape as early as 1980, but a fruitful research discussion did not emerge until the 1990s. Andreas Huyssen, *Drama des Sturm und Drang: Kommentar zu einer Epoche* (Munich: Winkler, 1980), 174.

47   Cf. among others, Martha Kaarsberg Wallach, "Emilia und ihre Schwestern: Das seltsame Verschwinden der Mutter und die geopferte Tochter," in *Mütter—Töchter—Frauen: Weiblichkeitsbilder in der Literatur*, ed. Helga Kraft and Elke Liebs (Stuttgart: Metzler, 1993), 53–72, here 63; Saße, *Ordnung der Gefühle*, 206; Luserke, *Sturm und Drang*, 234; John A. McCarthy, "'Ein

recent research has once again begun to call the rape into question, while downplaying von Gröningseck's crime. Here, the focus is on Evchen's complicity, on strategies of female self-staging (*Selbstinszenierungen*), and on her supposed confession of guilt. *Die Kindermörderin* clearly portrays male entitlement over the female body, but some scholars continue to maintain that this dominance has no impact on the interpretation of the play and thus fail to reflect on the consequences of sexualized violence. These regressive interpretations themselves exemplify the extent of male power of disposition over the female body and thus point to a paradigm that remains rooted in our cultural memory and persists in society today. In the following, I discuss the most recent regressive research chronologically and in detail.

According to Alefeld (2007),[48] the chamber scene cannot be read as rape since it unfolds in the patriarchally coded world of the eighteenth century. Citing Anke Meyer-Knees, Alefeld refers to the contemporary notion that a woman cannot become pregnant through rape since the fertilization and implantation of an egg cell is not possible without an orgasm.[49] To be sure, this idea was widespread in the eighteenth century.

Verbrechen, wozu man gezwungen wird, ist kein Verbrechen mehr': Zur Spannung zwischen Rechtspflege und Aufklärungsmoral im 18. Jahrhundert," *Das achtzehnte Jahrhundert* 20, no. 1 (1996): 22–44, here 36; Anne-Britt Gerecke, "*Die Kindermörderin, ein Trauerspiel: Leipzig 1776*," in *Dramenlexikon des 18. Jahrhunderts*, ed. Heide Hollmer and Albert Meier (Munich: C. H. Beck, 2001), 312–15, here 313; Michael Ott, *Das ungeschriebene Gesetz: Ehre und Geschlechterdifferenz in der deutschen Literatur um 1800* (Freiburg im Breisgau: Rombach, 2001), 205; Luserke-Jaqui, *Medea*, 138; Ursula Hassel, *Familie als Drama* (Bielefeld: Aisthesis, 2002), 64; Franziska Schößler, *Einführung in das bürgerliche Trauerspiel und das soziale Drama* (Darmstadt: WBG, 2003), 58; Theo Elm, *Das soziale Drama: Von Lenz bis Kroetz* (Stuttgart: Reclam, 2004), 70; Hannes Fricke, *Das hört nicht auf: Trauma, Literatur und Empathie* (Göttingen: Wallstein, 2004), 171; Heyer, *Sexuelle Obsessionen*, 40; Martina Schönenborn, *Tugend und Autonomie: Die literarische Modellierung der Tochterfigur im Trauerspiel des 18. Jahrhunderts* (Göttingen: Wallstein, 2004), 188; Dane, *"Zeter und Mordio,"* 225; Matthias Luserke-Jaqui, "*Die Kindermörderin* (Wagner)," in *Handbuch Sturm und Drang*, ed. Matthias Luserke-Jaqui in collaboration with Vanessa Geuen and Lisa Wille (Berlin: De Gruyter, 2017), 328–38, here 331; Gaby Pailer, "Medeas neue Masken: Dramatische Aktualisierungen zwischen femme forte und zärtlicher Tochter in Heinrich Leopold Wagners *Die Reue nach der That* (1775) und *Die Kindermörderin* (1776)," in *Heinrich Leopold Wagner: Neue Studien zu seinem Werk*, ed. Matthias Luserke-Jaqui and Lisa Wille (Würzburg: Königshausen & Neumann, 2020), 81–102, here 92.

48 Alefeld, "Texte und Affekte," 174.

49 Cf. Anke Meyer-Knees, *Verführung und sexuelle Gewalt: Untersuchung zum medizinischen und juristischen Diskurs im 18. Jahrhundert* (Tübingen: Staufenburg-Verlag, 1992), 53.

Immanuel Kant, for example, states that "die natürliche Zeugung . . . ohne Sinnenlust beider Teile nicht geschehen kann" ("Natural generation can't occur without sensual pleasure on both sides"),[50] and Jean-Jacques Rousseau postulates, "Der freieste und süßeste aller Akte läßt keine wirkliche Gewalt zu, Natur und Vernunft widersetzen sich ihr" ("The freest and sweetest of all acts does not admit of real violence. Nature and reason oppose it").[51] According to Alefeld, a reading of *Die Kindermörderin* must take this historical context into account. Consequently, Alefeld disagrees with Luserke-Jaqui, who considers the idea that Evchen was complicit a "groteske Fehldeutung"[52] (grotesque misinterpretation). To Alefeld, *Die Kindermörderin* stages the "Erfüllung des Liebestriebes"[53] (fulfillment of the love drive). She fails to recognize that the infanticide debate in the 1770s forms an inextricable part of the historical contexts she references and offers incontrovertible proof that numerous women unintentionally conceived children.

In 1843, over half a century later, Søren Kierkegaard wrote in his *Tagebuch des Verführers*: "Denn des Weibes Wesen ist eine Hingabe, deren Form Widerstand ist" ("It is the common resistance of womanliness, for woman's essence is a devotedness that takes the form of resistance").[54] This statement echoes similar sentiments in Rousseau's work: "Ob nun das Menschenweibchen die Begierden des Mannes teilt oder nicht und sie befriedigen will oder nicht, es stößt ihn immer zurück und wehrt sich, aber nicht immer mit der gleichen Kraft und folglich nicht mit dem gleichen Erfolg. Damit der Angreifer siegreich sei, muß der Angegriffene es geschehen lassen oder befehlen." ("Whether the human female shares man's desires or not and wants to satisfy them or not, she repulses him and always with the same force or, consequently, with the same success. For the attacker to be victorious, the one who is attacked must permit

---

50   Immanuel Kant, *Die Religion innerhalb der Grenzen der bloßen Vernunft*, in *Werke in zwölf Bänden*, ed. Wilhelm Weischedel, vol. 8 (Frankfurt am Main: Suhrkamp, 1968), 736; Kant, *Religion within the Limits of Bare Reason*, trans. Jonathan Bennett 2017, 44n1, accessed May 5, 2021, https://www.earlymoderntexts.com/assets/pdfs/kant1793.pdf.

51   Jean-Jacques Rousseau, *Emile oder Über die Erziehung*, ed. Martin Rang, trans. Eleonore Sckommodau (Stuttgart: Reclam, 1963), 723; Rousseau, *Emile; or, On Education*, trans. and ed. Christopher Kelly and Allan Bloom (Hanover, NH: University Press of New England, 2010), 359.

52   Luserke-Jaqui, *Medea*, 138.

53   Alefeld, "Texte und Affekte," 166.

54   Søren Kierkegaard, *Das Tagebuch des Verführers: Entweder/Oder*, part 1, vol. 2 (Cologne: Hegner, 1979), 419; Søren Kierkegaard, *The Seducer's Diary*, ed. and trans. Howard V. Hong and Edna H. Hong, foreword by John Updike (Princeton, NJ: Princeton University Press, 2013), 121.

or arrange it.")[55] Referencing contemporary discourses such as these along with Evchen's eager consumption of novels, Alefeld posits that Evchen's strategy to reject von Gröningseck's advances verbally originates in Richardson's popular novels. Evchen acts according to the "Pamela model,"[56] exemplified in Richardson's novels.

In the eighteenth century, love, marriage, and sexuality are seen as a unit; at the same time, the discourse of virtue demands that women should enter marriage untouched. Alefeld cites Niklas Luhmann, who postulates that "die [weibliche, L.W.] Verweigerung jeder geschlechtsbetonten Beziehung vor der Ehe auch als sanfter Druck oder als taktischer Zug in Richtung auf die Eheschließung begriffen werden [kann]"[57] (the [female] refusal of any sexually connoted premarital relationship [can] also be understood as gentle pressure or as tactical pull toward marriage). For Alefeld, this applies to Evchen, as she confesses to von Gröningseck in the fourth act: "ich liebte sie, so wie ich sie kennen lernte, jetzt kann ichs ihnen sagen—sonst hätten sie mich nicht so schwach gefunden" (KM, 51; "I loved you from the moment I met you. Now I can say it to you. Otherwise you would not have found me to be so weak," 94). Turning this admission against Evchen and a reading that detects rape, *Die Kindermörderin* is received as a tragedy of love and Evchen as a victim of seduction, not rape. Dane quite rightly counters that being in love and being raped need neither exclude nor contradict each other, since an emotional relationship does not change the fact that the sexual act was forced.[58]

For Alefeld, Evchen's behavior after the "Sündenfall" (original sin) is motivated by an awareness that she has deviated from the *Pamela* plot and has thus failed to secure the "virtue rewarded" prize that guarantees social advancement and social security.[59] The underlying assumption here is that Evchen "blitzschnell" (lightning-fast) changed her behavior after the chamber scene and, in the manner of Richardson's *Clarissa*, forced a promise of marriage from von Gröningseck. Alefeld argues that Evchen's raving fits are not authentic but rather staged on the basis of literary models. Ultimately, however, Evchen's "Leben in der Fiktion entlarvt sich als Phantasma"[60] (life in fiction is revealed to be a phantasm).

According to Alefeld, Richardson's novels provide the textual references that shape Evchen's behavior; that is, the semantics of love were

55 Rousseau, *Emile oder Über die Erziehung*, 723; *Emile; or, On Education*, 533.

56 Alefeld, "Texte und Affekte," 175.

57 Niklas Luhmann, *Liebe als Passion: Zur Codierung von Intimität* (Frankfurt am Main: Suhrkamp, 1994), 159; cited in Alefeld, "Texte und Affekte," 175.

58 Cf. Dane, *"Zeter und Mordio,"* 231.

59 Alefeld, "Texte und Affekte," 175.

60 Alefeld, "Texte und Affekte," 177 and 184.

transmitted intertextually in the eighteenth century. Significantly, Dane also detects intertextual references to Richardson's *Clarissa*, but, unlike Alefeld, she does not deny but, rather, confirms the legitimacy of the rape thesis. Alefeld's observations regarding the traditional semantics of love and the enormous influence of the associated communication models are interesting. Her reading of Evchen, however, is one-sided: the facts of violence and rape are simply negated or ignored. Alefeld's interpretation not only encourages victim-blaming, as Evchen's "fits of rage" are perceived as staged, but reproduces a problematic association of rape with a woman's desire for love, thus casting love as an essential constituent of female identity.

Künzel (2013), citing historical concepts of virtue and femininity, also hesitates to read the stage directions as a confirmation of rape,[61] even though Luserke emphasizes that they are quite literal.[62] Künzel notes that the vague term "Getös," which refers to noise in the chamber, does not indicate rape, since there are no cries for help.[63] Here, Künzel ignores the fact that a rape is not necessarily accompanied by cries for help: the victim may be unconscious, paralyzed with fear, or silenced. Künzel further suggests that von Gröningseck's proclamation that he has made an offer of marriage immediately upon exiting the chamber (cf. KM, 17; 67) suggests that Evchen consented to intercourse in the hope of becoming his wife. Much like Alefeld, albeit with a different nuance, Künzel reactivates the narrative of consent in view of the prospect of social advancement through marriage. If this were the case, however, why would Evchen then rush out of the chamber distraught and disconsolate? Künzel does not answer this question and instead references the aforementioned rape discourse in the Enlightenment that cannot imagine a form of sexual violence in which the victim is blameless, especially in light of the supposed impossibility of pregnancy without orgasm. Künzel herself admits that seduction is a problematic concept since it implies guilt or complicity on the part of the victim. Even so, she concludes that the chamber scene is ambiguous and concedes that Evchen may only have pretended to resist in order to maintain a semblance of virtue,[64] thus reproducing one of the longest-lasting gender clichés. In contrast, I argue that the scenes do not support the interpretation that Evchen only pretended to offer resistance.

Hyunseon Lee (2013) also offers a simplistic interpretation that affirms the narrative of unhappy love. She concedes the possibility of rape

---

61 Künzel, "Johann Heinrich Leopold Wagners *Die Kindermörderin*," 211.

62 Cf. Luserke, *Sturm und Drang*, 234.

63 Cf. Künzel, "Johann Heinrich Leopold Wagners *Die Kindermörderin*," 211.

64 Künzel, "Johann Heinrich Leopold Wagners *Die Kindermörderin*," 211 and 209.

but adds that Wagner's text leaves open the possibility that Evchen was "verführt und dann vergewaltigt"[65] (seduced then raped), noting that Evchen went out with von Gröningseck, fell in love with him, and wanted to marry him in spite of the experience in the brothel. She concludes that Evchen killed the child out of disappointed love and because she believed herself abandoned. Although Lee examines the gender dynamics of the drama and speaks of female absence,[66] she concludes against all evidence that Evchen acted out of disappointed love. Thus, she affirms the gendered definition of women as inherently identified with the realm of love, while disregarding the social determinants that limit Evchen's options.

Drawing on Saße, Burkhard Meyer-Sickendiek (2016) labels the sexual intercourse in the first act as undoubtedly a rape ("zweifellos eine Vergewaltigung")[67] but then proceeds to ignore evidence of sexual violence. He reads Evchen's blushing as a confession of guilt ("Schuldgeständnis"), citing the importance of concepts of shame in this period.[68] Here, he refers to Rousseau's claim in the fourth book of *Emile* that shame is a sign of sexual experience: "Wer errötet, ist schon schuldig; die wahre Unschuld kennt keine Scham" ("Whoever blushes is already guilty. True innocence is ashamed of nothing").[69] Along the same lines, Meyer-Sickendiek speaks of Evchen's confession both to herself and to von Gröningseck. This, to Meyer-Sickendiek, turns Evchen into a variant of Emilia Galotti, transforming the innocent, blushing girl into a guilty woman who is willing to "sin." According to this reading, Wagner rejected the shy virtue of a *Miss Sara Sampson* (1755). Rather, here, shame signals guilt, not virtue.[70] Curiously, Meyer-Sickendiek initially assumes that a rape occurred but then pivots; he implies that Evchen was flirting and actually wanted sexual intercourse. This shift exemplifies victim-blaming par excellence.

To summarize, research on Wagner's *Die Kindermörderin* remains problematic; it is also highly pertinent to topics highlighted by the #MeToo debate, such as accusations of complicity leveled at victims of sexual violence. Such legitimizations of rape veil the extent and effects of sexual violence. Indeed, these works might even be said to reproduce

---

65 Hyunseon Lee, "Vor Gericht: Kindsmord im Sturm und Drang und Heinrich Leopold Wagners Drama *Die Kindermörderin* (1776)," in *Mörderinnen: Künstlerische und mediale Inszenierungen weiblicher Verbrechen*, ed. Hyunseon Lee and Isabel Maurer Queipo (Bielefeld: transcript, 2013), 89–109, here 103.

66 Lee, *Vor Gericht*, 101.

67 Burkhard Meyer-Sickendiek, *Zärtlichkeit: Höfische Galanterie als Ursprung der bürgerlichen Empfindsamkeit* (Paderborn: Fink, 2016), 367.

68 Meyer-Sickendiek, *Zärtlichkeit*, 371 and 365.

69 Rousseau, *Emile oder Über die Erziehung*, 450; *Emile; or, On Education*, 368.

70 Meyer-Sickendiek, *Zärtlichkeit*, 371.

such violence in frighteningly unreflective ways. In addition, critical readings of Wagner remind us of literature's important contribution to social debates. Evchen exemplifies the suffering of many rape victims whose personal integrity is damaged not only by rape but by the legitimation of rape in the context of a rape culture that blames victims. Regressive research perspectives are rooted in interpretive strategies that refuse to acknowledge the consequences of male power over the female body as represented in *Die Kindermörderin*. To this day, the patriarchal order subtends a concept of violence that legitimates male possession of things and persons. Gender-specific sexual violence remains socially legitimized and culturally anchored.

When Evchen states *expressis verbis,* "Ich will nicht" (KM, 16), her "no" is to be read as "no means no." As such, it stands in a tradition that links Wagner's drama to the debate about the revised versions of §§177 and 179 in the German Criminal Code, which were implemented on November 10, 2016, as part of the new criminal law on sexual offences. This reform, which is anchored in the principle "Nein heißt Nein" (no means no), is intended to strengthen the protection of sexual self-determination. The alliance *No means No* was initiated by the German Women's Council, which consists of women's and human rights organizations and numerous other supporters and was the focus of much public attention in the run-up to the 2016 amendment of the law.[71] In this context, #MeToo and #NeinheißtNein stand in a reciprocal relationship to each other and were linked in public discussions. In direct opposition to these developments, Alefeld questions the sincerity of Evchen's "Ich will nicht" and characterizes it as "trotzig[ ]" (defiant) and "leere Rhetorik" (empty rhetoric).[72]

To be sure, #MeToo, its mediality, and the biographies that are negotiated, is itself a historical phenomenon. Even so, it helps us recognize how firmly and deeply male entitlement is anchored in cultural memory and in our literary canon. It is our responsibility as scholars to critically challenge not only literary texts but also problematic readings of these texts, such as those relating to *Die Kindermörderin*. Indeed, challenging such interpretations constitutes one of the most importants tasks in the humanities: as Anja Heise-von der Lippe and Russell West-Pavlov (2018) explain, the real core competence of the humanities lies in this gray area of implied knowledge and ambiguity, which they consider highly relevant

71   Cf. "Neinheißtnein," UN Women Deutschland: Für die Rechte von Frauen, accessed November 7, 2020, https://www.unwomen.de/ueber-uns/vergangene-kampagnen/neinheisstnein.html.

72   Alefeld, "Texte und Affekte," 174.

in our contemporary society of multiple crises.[73] It is important to examine critical statements about literature because it is the core responsibility of the humanities to complicate precisely that which at first glance appears to be simple. The humanities disrupt norms, change contexts, and make visible what remains invisible in a "normal" context.[74] Thus, literary studies achieves its social potential above all by making past and present power structures transparent. This is especially true in view of current political developments that elevate the ideologies of right-wing populists amid a resurgent conservative culture that collides with the values of social diversity, sexual self-determination, and gender justice.

73   Anja Heise-von der Lippe and Russell West-Pavlov, "Literaturwissenschaften in der Krise: Einleitung," in *Literaturwissenschaften in der Krise: Zur Rolle und Relevanz literarischer Praktiken in globalen Krisenzeiten,* ed. Anja Heise-von der Lippe and Russell West-Pavlov (Tübingen: Narr Francke Attempto, 2018), 9–26, here 18.

74   Dorothee Kimmich, "'Nach der Krise ist vor der Krise': Vom Überleben in, mit und durch die Krise," in Heise-von der Lippe and West-Pavlov, *Literaturwissenschaften in der Krise,* 29–40, here 37–38.

2: #MeToo: Prostitution and the Syntax of Sexuality around 1800

Patricia Anne Simpson

THE #MeToo MOVEMENTS assumed specific national and regional characteristics while they circulated globally. In Germany, few powerful men fell from prominence owing to allegations and proof of sexual harassment and predation. #MeToo did, however, reframe a debate about systemic sexism that revived and expanded the agenda of twentieth-century feminism. Still underexamined is the transhistorical normalization of the female body as object of a predatory, prurient gaze and the site of sexual violence as spectacle. In *Sexuality, State, and Civil Society in Germany, 1700–1815* (1996), Isabel V. Hull elaborates the "sexual system" of Germany as its leaders negotiate the transition from absolutism to the modern state, with a focus on "the patterned ways in which sexual behavior is shaped and given meaning through institutions."[1] Specifically, she marks a semantic shift in the meaning of *Dirne* (prostitute), a transformation from the eighteenth-century model of the innocent victim seduced by a male villain to the prostitute, indicative of a nineteenth-century revision in which the man becomes the victim of the promiscuous, sexually incontinent woman.[2] Hull's argument underscores the exclusion of women from civil society. Though objectively true, this thesis is open to criticism, as James Van Horn Melton's intervention reveals.[3] He notes in Hull's work the absence of women writers, salon hosts, and works about intellectual politics and practices that interrogate gendered exclusions. Moreover, as I argue, the issues of female desire and pleasure—and their regulation—elude these analyses. Indeed, there are few narratives in Western modernity that acknowledge female sexuality without relegating

---

1   Isabel V. Hull, *Sexuality, State, and Civil Society in Germany, 1700–1815* (Ithaca, NY: Cornell University Press, 1996), 1.

2   Hull, *Sexuality*, 404.

3   See James Van Horn Melton's review of Hull's book in the *American Historical Review* 102, no. 5 (December 1997): 1509–10, https://doi.org/10.1086/ahr/102.5.1509. He writes, "Oddly, it never occurs to the author to ask what German women of the period thought of early civil society and its sexual norms" (1509).

it to the realm of innocent purity, sanctioned and contractual reproductivity, or prostitution—that is, transactional sex, for whatever reason, subject to civic regulation. In this chapter, I examine the representation of female sexuality and its syntactical place in a range of texts that do not so much challenge Hull's analysis as capture post-Enlightenment obsessions with women as sexually active yet innocent victims. First, I examine the construction of female submissiveness and victimhood. With reference to two engravings, the Prussian legal code, and Immanuel Kant's moral justification of marriage, I explore three texts by Johann Wolfgang von Goethe to demonstrate how female desire around 1800 is coded as sacrificial or transactional. Finally, the displacement of seduction, prostitution, and possible violence is mapped onto distant topographies, away from the public gaze.

In several late-eighteenth-century works, writers and intellectuals debate the institutionalization of sexuality through both marriage (conventional) and prostitution (transactional) in ways that have attracted scholarly attention, with a focus on homosociality, triangular constellations, and male desire.[4] For centuries and across continents, the hegemony of heteronormative sexuality has privileged male desire, naturalizing any other expression of body sovereignty as aberrant. In a contemporary context, the editors of *Yes Means Yes!* (2008; new edition, 2019) take an aggressively positive stance, decidedly "for a world where we are each of us sovereign over our own bodies, free to say yes and no to whatever we like without shame, blame, or violence."[5] The editions of this anthology, categorized by many as pop feminism, span the pre- and post-#MeToo era, with Jessica Valenti's *Full Frontal Feminism*[6]—she is the founder of feminista.com—making the leap from the blogosphere to the printed page and paving the way for a generation of activists to advocate for their own interests. These works effect change, as several

---

4   See Roman Graf, "The Homosexual, the Prostitute, and the Castrato: Closet Performances by J. M. R. Lenz," in *Outing Goethe and His Age*, ed. Alice A. Kuzniar (Stanford, CA: Stanford University Press, 1996), 77–93; on the range of desires in Goethe's work, see, for example, W. Daniel Wilson, "'Höhere Begattung,' 'höhere Schönheit': Goethe's Homoerotic Poem 'Selige Sehnsucht,'" *Goethe Yearbook* 20 (2013): 117–32. See also Robert Tobin, *Warm Brothers: Queer Theory and the Age of Goethe* (Philadelphia: University of Pennsylvania Press, 2001). Tobin's contribution to the field of sexuality and German studies also encompasses female same-sex desire.

5   Jaclyn Friedman and Jessica Valenti, "Introduction," in *Yes Means Yes: Visions of Female Sexual Power & a World without Rape*, ed. Jaclyn Friedman and Jessica Valenti, 2nd ed. (New York: Seal Press, 2019), 5–11, here 7.

6   Jessica Valenti, *Full Frontal Feminism: A Young Woman's Guide to Why Feminism Matters* (Emeryville, CA: Seal Press, 2007).

states implemented "yes means yes" laws. From the realm of popular culture, in other words, insistence on finding a nonjudgmental way to talk about female desire steadily gains a volubility that may lead to an intersection with second-wave feminist claims to equality, but with the representation of plural, intersectional sexual identities. Yet the paradigm of sex as something men do to women and of female sexuality as commodified—to be given within patriarchal structures or sold in systems of exchange constructed by Western masculinity—has a long history and a ubiquitious present.

With insights and methodologies gleaned from contemporary #MeToo movements, I propose a reading of Goethe's *Egmont* (1788), the "Witch's Kitchen" from the *Faust* fragment (1790), and his "Der Gott und die Bajadere" (1797; The God and the Bayadere) to generate an alternative narrative to institutional history. The hypothetical soldiers' brothel posited in Jakob Michael Reinhold Lenz's *Die Soldaten* (1776; The Soldiers) in some ways anticipates and obviates the nineteenth-century moral panic about women's bodies. The three texts by Goethe in the context of contemporary language about prostitution foreground a contractual relationship to the sexualized female body. Goethe's Egmont casually condemns sexual violence against a "Dirne"—though recognizing that the violation is contingent on the victim's demonstrated innocence. In the *Faust* fragment, Goethe creates the witches' kitchen as a brothel. And in "Der Gott und die Bajadere," he displaces male sexual desire, fear of contracting venereal disease, and the precarious innocence of bourgeois *Mädchen* (girls) onto the exoticized Indian legend of the prostitute who succumbs to love for the god in disguise. Female sexuality already provides a path to masculine redemption around 1800, predicated on the sacrifice of female desire and the tragic death of the beloved. Reading literature around 1800 through the lens of the #MeToo movement has consequences; it may seem anachronistic to capture the political force of a modern-day social movement and apply it to the works of a literary icon. Admittedly, I am interested in rhetorical constructs, literary figures, and cultural tropes. Nonetheless, I contend that the #MeToo movement allows us to reframe a discipline that has normalized rape culture, marginalized narratives of male dominance, and sustained a model of art, beauty, and entertainment based on access to a particular ideal of the female body. This paradigm obtains for eighteenth-century literature as well as for the social, political, and economic structures that galvanized the #MeToo movement through twenty-first-century social media. At this point, the tenacity of male models of female desire, the inevitability of a phallogocentric modernity, must be acknowledged; attributable in no small part to the creation and re-creation of the image of a submissive victim as sexual prey.

#MeToo ca. 1800:
"Sie ist die Erste nicht" (She is not the first)

The ever-striving Faust embodies the predatory male, rhetorically under the influence of devilish desire. Goethe's Faust constructs a moral universe in which the consequences of his predation are deferred. In the Gretchen figure, Goethe incarnates moral ambivalence, rhetorically equating her desire for pleasure with an innocent articulation of goodness.[7] Taming female sexuality necessitates transactional relationships between gendered social and institutional codes. Mephistopheles's true but brutally dismissive comment: "Trüber Tag. Feld," "Sie ist die Erste nicht" (line15; "Dreary Day. A Field," "She is not the first," 126),[8] which elicits a tirade from the culpable Faust about his satanic companion's inhumanity, serves as an eighteenth-century prequel to the twenty-first-century hashtag movement. While feminist scholars have for decades raised questions about unquestioned devotion to literary works by "great men" who achieved fame through erasing their female interlocutors and partners, the hegemony of masculine gendered desire and its entitlements has yet to be shaken. The #MeToo movements caused funnel-like winds around the reputations of powerful men and, in doing so, exerted an impact on feminism in the twenty-first century, particularly in the coalescence of theory and activism. With reference to Goethe, a robust canon of feminist scholarship emerged around a reading of the "Ewig Weibliche," the "eternal feminine" in the final act of *Faust II*, which has variously been read as redemptive, delusional, or ironic.[9] The #MeToo emendation of feminism

---

7   On this process, see Patricia Anne Simpson, "Gretchen's Ghosts: Goethe, Adorno, and the Literature of Refuge," in *Goethe's Ghosts: Reading and the Persistence of Literature*, ed. Simon Richter and Richard Block (Rochester, NY: Camden House, 2013), 168–85.

8   References to Goethe's *Faust* in the original are taken from the Hamburger Ausgabe, ed. Erich Trunz (Munich: Beck, 1982), vol. 3. Translations are from *Faust*, trans. Walter Arndt, ed. Cyrus Hamlin (New York: Norton, 2011). Other translations, unless noted, are my own.

9   See Barbara Becker-Cantarino, "Goethe and Gender," in *The Cambridge Companion to Goethe*, ed. Lesley Sharpe (Cambridge: Cambridge University Press, 2002), 179–92, for an overview. For an endorsement of the emancipatory moment, see Katharina Mommsen, "Goethe as a Precursor of Women's Emancipation," in *Goethe Proceedings: Essays Commemorating the Goethe Sesquicentennial at the University of California, Davis*, ed. Clifford A. Bernd, Timothy J. Lulofs, and H. Günther Nerjes, Studies in German Literature, Linguistics, and Culture, vol. 1 (Rochester, NY: Camden House, 1984), 51–65; also Gail K. Hart, "Das Ewig-Weibliche Nasführet Dich: Feminine Leadership in Goethe's *Faust* and Sacher-Masoch's *Venus*," in *Interpreting Goethe's Faust Today*, ed. Jane K. Brown, Meredith Lee, and Thomas Saine (Rochester, NY: Camden House, 1994), 112–22.

insists on holding famous men accountable not only for their workplace behavior but for their private lives. At the center of controversy is the intractable connection between power and masculinity. At its core, this model of power accounts for the question of female agency; in particular, the agency of desire. Goethe, in his works and his life, displayed contradictions, indulged or repressed desires, and inscribed these inconsistencies into the production of literature. Goethe's articulations of female desire cluster around the question of pleasure and its regulation.

A rich scholarly archive addresses Goethe's spectrum of female figures; additionally, his relationships with women also receive considerable attention. Images of *Weiblichkeit* (femininity) are subject to scrutiny in a collective effort to reconstruct and understand gendered identities in transition from the early modern period to modernity, characterized by heteronormative hegemony. In her *Hexen—Huren—Heldenweiber: Bilder des Weiblichen in Erzähltexten über den Dreißigjährigen Krieg* (Witches—Whores—Heroic Women: Images of the Feminine in Narrative Texts about the Thirty Years' War), Waltraud Maierhofer attempts to fill the lacunae in representations of femininity in the Thirty Years' War and the literature about women in war written in the ensuing three centuries.[10] Barbara Becker-Cantarino has written extensively on Goethe and gender through a wider lens, highlighting the range of desires articulated in his work and underscored in his real-life encounters. A youthful search for fulfillment in plural senses of the word stalls and falters, owing in no small part to anxiety about contracting the "French disease" (syphilis) through sexual contact. The expansive horizons he encountered in Weimar for sexual, creative, and intellectual exploration belie its provinciality and peripheral placement. Many readers approach his prose as they would a roman à clef, hoping to identify the women behind Lotte, Iphigenie, or the unnamed lover of the "Roman Elegies" (1795). From Helena in *Faust II* to Leonora in *Torquato Tasso* (1790), his feminine rhetorical constructs inspired works of art capable of appealing to popular tastes, even to the modification of gendered traits. Here, the series of Wilhelm von Kaulbach features prominently.[11] That Goethe recognizes female desire as agentic is evident in the tragic figure of Gretchen; beyond her inscription into colloquial German (*Gretchenfrage* [Gretchen question]), her justification of pleasure by defining it in an ethical framework is nothing short of radical—and commensurately self-punished. Gretchen's lonely despair at the spinning wheel expresses desire from her perspective; and the retribution

---

10   Waltraud Maierhofer, *Hexen—Huren—Heldenweiber: Bilder des Weiblichen in Erzähltexten über den Dreißigjährigen Krieg* (Cologne: Böhlau, 2005).

11   See, for example, George Henry Lewes, *Goethe's Female Characters: From the Original Drawings of William Kaulbach* (London: Frederick Bruckmann, 1867).

she anticipates ("Am Brunnen"; At the fountain) culminates in incarceration for child murder. She famously refuses to escape but, rather, accepts her fate. Still, she insists, "Doch—alles was dazu mich trieb / Gott! war so gut! Ach war so lieb!" (But everything that drove me to do it / God! Was so good! Oh, it was so lovely!). Admittedly, the male author projects his model of female desire onto this figure, who nonetheless exerted considerable influence through cultural reproductions and interpretations of *Faust I* in a century of opera repertoires, among other media. Rarely, it must be noted, is female desire transitive—that is, rarely does it take an object. In those exceptional cases, its expression is bent to European social conventions and moral orders. While Goethe and his works engage female sexuality and desire, they equivocate. The equivocal moments in the three texts selected for closer examination in this chapter indicate intimate connections between sexual desire and social codes, especially in the representation of prostitution.

Either/Or: Wife/Whore

Eighteenth-century European institutions grappled with legislating desire, skewed toward protecting noble men and punishing wayward woman. In England, the Marriage Act of 1753 effectively abolished the protection of verbal consensual partnerships between men and women that served as marriage without ceremony. Scholar Eve Tavor Bannet writes, "All traditional 'bargains of cohabitation,' all the old local marriage rites, all seductions, abductions and clandestine marriages—and indeed, all intercourse outside the state of marriage as demarcated by the Act—now made a woman a whore and her children bastards."[12] In France, the promise of marriage persisted, underwritten by the ability to purchase letters of legitimacy in order, for example, to integrate a child born outside of marriage into a family[13] or, in other cases, to compensate a bourgeois father for a "ruined" daughter. Prior to 1800, regional laws governed how violated women were supposed to act.[14] In his *Denkschrift* (memorandum)

---

12   Eve Tavor Bannet, "The Marriage Act of 1753: 'A Most Cruel Law for the Fair Sex,'" *Eighteenth Century Studies* 30, no. 3 (Spring 1997): 233–54, here 234.

13   See Matthew Gerber, "On the Contested Margins of the Family: Bastardy and Legitimation by Royal Rescript in Eighteenth-Century France," in *Family, Gender, and Law in Early Modern France*, ed. Suzanne Desan and Jeffrey Merrick (University Park: Penn State University Press, 2009), 223–64, here 243.

14   See Alfred Lefleur, *Concessionirte Prostitution und die Bedingungen ihrer Zulässigkeit, ein Beitrag zur Lösung der Bordell-Frage*, 2nd ed. (Berlin: Expedition der Deutschen Gasthaus-Zeitung, 1878). Lefleur sketches a brief historical overview of pertinent laws in Bavaria, though his primary interest centers on fin-de-siècle Berlin.

about regulating or zoning prostitution in late nineteenth-century Berlin, Alfred Lefleur outlines a variety of brutal punishments for men guilty of rape in the medieval and early modern periods. He additionally comments on the barbarity of capital punishment for women who murder their children, a circumstance with which Goethe was familiar as a civil servant and a poet. Lefleur describes the "Barbarei" of dunking, which persisted into the eighteenth century: "Noch im J. 1734 ward in Sachsen eine Kindesmörderin ertränkt, zu welcher man einen Hund, eine Katze und eine Schlange in den Sack gethan"[15] (Even in the year 1734, in Saxony a female child murderer was drowned; a dog, a cat, and a snake were put in the sack with her). Indeed, the consequences of unsanctioned, non-institutional love, desire, or attraction inflict damage measured not only socially but economically. The value of female desire exists only in prostitution. Even though transactional sex is performance based, the male construction of female desire often conflates economic need with sexual agency, attributing nefarious aims to women sex workers. We see evidence of this economy in contemporary visual arts as well.

Eighteenth-century Europe, with its generalized performance of reason, the rights of man, and later, revolutionary impulses, enacts a catastrophic displacement of humanity and sovereignty of the person, disenfranchising all nonwhite, nonmale, non-Cartesian bodies. The contortions of logic to proclaim political freedom of the individual while enslaving Africans in the Americas, for example, required vigilant renegotiating of racial identities, as Susan Buck-Morss has thematized in *Hegel, Haiti and Universal History*.[16] In terms of gender discourse, even those writers and intellectuals who devoted their attention to the rights of women do not necessarily confront issues of sexual pleasure.[17] Karen Harvey, in a historiographic review of gender and sexuality studies of the long eighteenth century (primarily in England), cogently traces the influence of Thomas Lacquer's highly influential *Making Sex: Body and Gender from the Greeks to Freud* (1990) and the pivotal role of eighteenth-century medical discourse in shifting away from "one-sex thinking" (e.g., male

---

15 Lefleur, *Concessionirte Prostitution*, 29. Other historical documents indicate that Frederick the Great abolished the practice of dunking/drowning child murderesses. See *Friedrich der Große: Versuch eines historischen Gemähldes*, vol. 2 (Weimar: Hoffmann, 1786), 67.

16 Susan Buck-Morss, *Hegel, Haiti, and Universal History* (Pittsburgh: University of Pittsburgh Press, 2009).

17 Prominent examples include Theodor von Hippel, "Über die Ehe" (1774) and "Über die bürgerliche Verbesserung der Weiber" (1792); Mary Wollstonecraft, *A Vindication of the Rights of Women: With Strictures on Political and Moral Subjects* (1792); and the works of Olympe de Gouges (1748–93), who advocated for women's rights in France; see, for example, Hippel and others in German-speaking Europe.

and female bodies differ by degree).[18] In concluding, she cautions gender historians about relying too heavily on a medical model at the expense of cultural constructions of sexuality. Adopting one model, she writes, "tends to eclipse the way in which different areas of life—work, domestic arrangements, reproduction, pleasure—are subject to distinct forces for change and persistence."[19] One persistent force evident in both cultural and medical discourse is a dominant model for female desire and pleasure that filters through a male optic, legible especially in the visual arts.

William Hogarth's series *A Harlot's Progress* (1732), for example, engages the optics of a female sexual allegory. In particular, the second engraving (the originals no longer extant) not only displays the transactional success of Moll, the country girl whose beauty leads her into prostitution and decline in London; it critiques the attributes of excess, here visualized as cosmopolitan acquisitiveness (fig. 2.1). The prostitute's patron is portrayed as a prosperous, unattractive Jewish merchant; she keeps a West Indian page and owns a monkey. The grammar of desire in this representation places Moll in a syntax of exotic acquisitions that can be purchased and kept—until they deteriorate. Male desire, thus displaced, goes on display, but deferred away from the sphere of the home and fatherland to highlight aspects of the private and public availability of sexualized objects, acquired across oceans, imported, exploited; and in the case of Moll, incarcerated, punished, and pocked. Closer to Goethe's time and cultural territory, the illustrated *Taschenbuch für Grabennymphen* (Paperback for Graben Nymphs) by Joseph Richter (1749–1813) depicts everyday prostitution in Vienna. Published in 1787, this work presents itself as a well-intended, tongue-in-cheek manual for prostitutes who ply their wares in the capital, though the satire also takes aim at the clients and moralizing hypocrites. The table of contents, for example, lists a section with tips for the *Nymphen* on holy days.[20] The how-to volume provides useful maxims for each month of the year. The image (fig. 2.2) introduces August, with its dog-day heat and the potentially negative effect of cold baths on business. An authorial, narrative voice advises the

---

18   Karen Harvey, "The Century of Sex? Gender, Bodies, and Sexuality in the Long Eighteenth Century," *Historical Journal* 45, no. 4 (2002): 899–916, here 901.

19   Harvey, "Century of Sex?," 916.

20   [Joseph Richter,] *Taschenbuch für Grabennymphen auf das Jahr 1787* (s.l., s.n. [Vienna: Wucherer], 1787), 84 pages, 12 engravings. Published anonymously. Wienbibliothek im Rathaus, Druckschriftensammlung, Signatur Secr-A 761, here 84. The book was reprinted in 1910, 1982, and 1986, according to the website of the Vienna Library, https://www.wienbibliothek.at/bestaende-sammlungen/objekte-monats/objekte-monats-2016/objekt-monats-september-2016-joseph-richters. *Grabennymphen* is a joking euphemism for the streetwalkers who worked that turf.

Figure 2.1. William Hogarth, *Harlot's Progress*, plate 2: 12 3/8 x 14 13/16 in. (31.4 x 37.7 cm) sheet: 13 3/8 x 15 7/8 in. (33.9 x 40.4 cm). Etching and engraving, Metropolitan Museum of Art.

Nymphen to hit the streets in the evening and pay particular attention to the "Limonadehütten" (lemonade stands).[21] Meanwhile, the illustration highlights the competition. According to a note on the copperplates, two Grabennymphen fight over a prosperous mama's boy, practically ripping him apart as they grab each other by the hair.[22] This gendered, public confrontation belongs to the cityscape, portraying the sex trade in an open, commercial thoroughfare.[23] The illustration of two prostitutes fighting in the street, possibly a dispute over payment, epitomizes the private made public.[24] The same year this work was published, a light opera, *Les promesses de marriage*, libretto by Jean-Baptiste Desforges

---

21 On the "Limonadehütten," see https://www.a-wgm.at/bestaende. The stand, in the 1780s, was a locale for social gathering that served ices where open-air concerts took place on the Graben. Richter advises that the lemonade stands are, for the nymphs, "ihr bester Anstand" (your best chance for propriety), 25.

22 Richter, *Taschenbuch für Grabennymphen*, 81.

23 Richter, *Taschenbuch für Grabennymphen*, 24–26.

24 "Eingeschränkte Rechte für bestimmte redaktionelle Kunden in Deutschland. Prostitution: Illustration aus dem *Taschenbuch für Grabennymphen*"

Figure 2.2. Joseph Richter, *Taschenbuch für Grabennymphen auf das Jahr 1787*, "Streitende Dirnen"—Stich, Eighteenth Century. Photo by ullstein bild/ullstein bild via Getty Images.

(1746–1806), music by Henri-Montan Berten (1767–1844), premiered in Paris.[25] The focus on sexual cultures in eighteenth-century urban centers, particularly when publicly visible, causes a moral panic that cries out for intercession, and I return to this point below.[26] The artistic commentary on the state of relationships intersects with the legal values of sexual exchange, regulated by damage and reparations.

The local histories about exchanging money for virginity—or in some cases, a sullied reputation that precludes respectable marriage—returns us to the Goethe circle. Lenz, for example, was engaged as a mediator between Friedrich Georg von Kleist (1751–1800) and Susanna Cliophe Fibich (1754–1820), the seduced daughter of a Strasburg jeweler; his task was to negotiate the *promesse de mariage*, an agreement between the nobleman and her father for damages.[27] Laws and statutes determined the monetary value of individual women. Historical documents, foremost among them §999 of the 1794 *Preußischen Allgemeinen Landrechts* (Prussian General Laws), help frame and situate the analysis. This paragraph established that "liederliche Weibspersonen" (loose women) must go to state-sanctioned whorehouses. It further defined them as women "welche mit ihrem Körper ein Gewerbe betreiben" (who conduct business transactions with their bodies). Reflected in then-contemporary philosophy, the corporate approach to the transacted female body sequesters it from marriage; love and sexual love or desire and enjoyment (*Genuß*) pass through categories of reason, morality, and right.

Positioned between a philosophy of right and moral law, Immanuel Kant's ethical stance on sanctioned, transactional sex has exerted considerable influence on subsequent discussions of plural sexualities. In his lectures on ethics (1780), Kant defined the rights of marriage beyond the exchange of access to reproductive organs. He prefaces this inflection with strong condemnation of prostitution. In elaborating the regulation of sexual relationships, based on a concept of (male?) body sovereignty in contractual exchange, Kant scorns the satisfaction of mere inclinations (*Neigungen*). Thus he rules out prostitution on moral grounds: "Diese Art der Befriedigung der Geschlechtsneigung ist *vaga libido*, wo man aus Interesse die Neigungen des anderen befriedigt" (208; "This way of satisfying sexuality is prostitution, in which one satisfies the inclinations

---

(Limited Rights for Specific Editorial Clients in Germany. Prostitution: Illustration from the Paperback for Graben Nymphs).

25 Alexandre Choron, *Dictionnaire historique des musiciens, artistes et amateurs: Morts ou vivans* (Paris: Chimot, 1817), 73.

26 Lefleur, *Concessionirte Prostitution*, 35. He quotes paragraph 1000 of the *Preußischen Allgemeinen Landrechts* that restricts bordellos to large, populous cities.

27 Julia Freytag, Inge Stephan, and Hans-Gerd Winter, eds., *J. M. R. Lenz Handbuch* (Berlin: De Gruyter, 2017), Zeittafel, 612.

of others for gain"[28]). Though Kant notes that both sexes are capable of this behavior, signaling a tacit acknowledgment of libido in both sexes, his further stipulations about marriage reveal unequal rights: "Das Matrimonium bedeutet einen Vertrag zweier Personen, wo sie sich wechselseitig gleiche Rechte restituieren und die Bedingungen einge- hen, daß ein jeder seine ganze Person dem anderen übergibt, so daß ein jeder ein völliges Recht auf die ganze Person des anderen hat. Nun läßt es sich durch die Vernunft einsehen, wie ein *commercium sexuale* ohne Erniedrigung der Menschheit oder Verletzung der Moralität möglich sei" (210; "Matrimony is an agreement between two persons by which they grant each other equal reciprocal rights, each of them undertaking to sur- render the whole of their person to the other with a complete right of disposal over it. We can now apprehend by reason how a sexual union is possible without degrading humanity and breaking the moral laws"[29]). The definition excludes the possibility of rape within marriage, demon- strating, among other things, the need for a sustained reexamination of rape culture. Though Kant notes that both sexes are capable of immoral exchange, his transition from moral to civic law obliterates any notion of equality. Unsurprisingly, Kant is concerned with regulating masculine desire and the sovereignty of the male body: a man who can compart- mentalize his existence by indulging appetite and seeking only sexual sat- isfaction would render his person a thing; in the objectification lies the moral violation. Moral objections notwithstanding, the law intervenes in the reality of prostitution. By 1794, related discourses of male sexual violence against women and legalized prostitution saturate the culture of German-speaking states; literary responses align particular virtues of masculinity within a post-Enlightenment sexual logic, inscribed onto a European geography of desire.

Centuries of precedent institutionalized and accommodated male desire as agency. That paradigm relegates female desire to a realm of tena- cious tropes. Judeo-Christian cultures produce culpable women: from Eve's temptation of Adam to the allegorical Whore of Babylon, to the redeemable Mary Magdalene and the exalted Virgin, through the com- promised bourgeois daughter to femmes fatales and *femmes fragiles* of the

---

28 Immanuel Kant, "Von den Pflichten gegen den Körper in Ansehung der Geschlechtsneigung," in *Eine Vorlesung Kants über Ethik* (*Philosophia Practica Universalis una cum Ethica*), ed. Paul Menzer (Berlin: Pan Verlag Rolf Heise, 1924), 204–12, here 208.

29 "Kant on Sex, Marriage, Concubines, Prostitutes, and Incest," comp. Stephen Hicks from lecture notes of Kant's 1775–80 courses, in Immanuel Kant, *Lectures on Ethics*, trans. Louis Infield (New York: Harper & Row, 1963), 162–68, https://www.stephenhicks.org/2016/12/14/kant-on-sex-marriage-con cubines-prostitutes-and-incest/.

fin-de-siècle,[30] women desiring knowledge or pleasure threaten power structures, always already transgressing; female figures demonstrating a will to subordination, piety, and/or maternal destiny prove worthy of salvation. These divergent trajectories of male and female desire produce intransigent heteronormativity. Michel Foucault famously locates heteronormative sexual codes of post-nineteenth-century humans among the "'other Victorians.'"[31] By comparison to the Victorian era, its predecessors evinced greater tolerance: "Codes regulating the coarse, the obscene, and the indecent were quite lax compared to those of the nineteenth century."[32] Foucault engages the legacy of Sigmund Freud on sexuality and recovers histories from the silence surrounding discourses and practices of desire beyond socioeconomic sanction and regulation. Not until Jacques Lacan is female sexuality reconsidered; subsequent critiques and corrections go beyond the scope of this chapter. Among the articulations of early nineteenth-century female desire, we see the extremes of Heinrich von Kleist's *Penthesilea* (1808), in which the Amazon warrior desires passion that can only be expressed as madness. Later, in Georg Büchner's *Woyzeck* (1879), Marie, a reincarnation in some ways of Gretchen's innocence, laced with beauty beyond her status, studies the *Tambourmajor* (drum major) through a lusty female gaze. This, too, ends badly. The Goethean texts here under consideration follow the trajectory from the innocent, the complicit, to the exoticized female, paired with male sexual agents from predatory soldiers to an overreaching scholar and a god in search of sexual prey.

Damages

Goethe's *Egmont*, set in the Low Countries and embroiled in the power politics of the Spanish crown and religious rivalries, intersects the gender politics of the #MeToo movement at multiple points. First, the regent, Margarete von Parma, sister to Charles V, displays acute awareness of her limitations as a female ruler. Too lenient toward the generals, too receptive to tolerance, respected among the citizens, who at worst accuse her of trafficking too thickly with the priests, Margarete lacks an army to enforce her will. Egmont too, though agreeing with the characterization of the regent as "trefflich" (good), irritates her. In her dialogue with Machiavell,

---

30 Female tropes of the late nineteenth century and their relationship to the image of the prostitute are treated in an important volume. See Christiane Schönfeld, *Commodities of Desire: The Prostitute in Modern German Literature* (Rochester, NY: Camden House, 2001).

31 Michel Foucault, *The History of Sexuality*, vol. 1: *An Introduction*, trans. Robert Hurley (New York: Pantheon, 1978), 4. He is citing Steven Marcus.

32 Foucault, *History of Sexuality*, 3.

she insists, "Er nimmt das Ernstliche scherzhaft" (WA 1,7: 191, lines 6–7; "He turns serious things into a joke").[33] Machiavell, in turn, in dialogue with William of Orange, dismisses her power: "Sie ist ein Weib . . . und die möchten immer gern daß sich alles unter ihr sanftes Joch gelassen schmiegte, daß jeder Herkules die Löwenhaut ablegte und . . . daß, weil sie friedlich gesinnt sind, die Gärung, die ein Volk ergreift, der Sturm, den mächtige Nebenbuhler gegen einander erregen, sich durch ein freundlich Wort beilegen ließe, und die widrigsten Elemente sich zu ihren Füßen in sanfter Eintracht vereinigten" (WA 1,7: 222 lines 17–25; "She is a woman . . . and women always wish that everyone will meekly creep under their gentle yoke, that every Hercules will doff his lion's skin and . . . that, because they desire peace, the ferment that seizes a people, the tempest that powerful rivals raise among themselves, can be soothed by a kind word, and that the most hostile elements will lie down together at their feet in gentle concord," 66). On the basis of her sex, she relies on the power of gentle persuasion, rather than action; feminine agency and cajoling should, in his estimate, hold no sway.[34] In contrast, Machiavell passes judgments with stunning ease that both acknowledge gender difference and sustain the status quo. The power of the regent protects her person from direct assault. Betrayal and intrigue, backed up with an army, unseat Margarete. Egmont's interactions with minor characters illuminate his engaging and charismatic persona.

In the affairs of state, sexual politics center not only the banter about the gender of the regent but also determine the fate of the marginalized. In the second act, after these minor characters and the regent offer radically different views of Egmont, he appears at the residence with his secretary ready to do business. Essentially, sexual politics, both public and private, dominate the discussion. When Egmont orders the *Secretär* to be punctual while he himself takes the liberty of detaining others, a sign of negligence, the Secretär displays his annoyance, and Egmont jokes: "Dona Elvira wird auf mich böse werden wenn sie hört daß ich dich aufgehalten habe" (WA 1, 7: 213, lines 25–26; "Donna Elvira will be angry with me when she hears that I've kept you," 62). In other words, Egmont understands that the secretary has an assignation with a lady in the castle. Returning to matters of state, the secretary reports that a soldier from Captain Breda's company wants to marry, but Breda objects,

33   Johann Wolfgang von Goethe, *Egmont,* trans. Michael Hamburger, in *The Essential Goethe,* ed. Matthew Bell (Princeton, NJ: Princeton University Press, 2016), 41–106, here 50.

34   Egmont's teasing dialogue with Klärchen, in which he denigrates her appearance and masculine features—specifically, some facial hair—has received considerable scholarly attention. See Matthew Head, *Sovereign Feminine: Music and Gender in Eighteenth-Century Germany* (Berkeley: University of California Press, 2013), 207.

fearing a loss of discipline. According to the Secretär: "Es sind so viele Weiber bei dem Haufen, schreibt er, daß, wenn wir ausziehen, es keinem Soldatenmarsch, sondern einem Zigeunergeschleppe ähnlich sehen wird" (WA 1, 7: 215 lines 5–8; "There are so many women hanging around the regiment, he writes, that when we're on the march it looks less like a body of soldiers than a troop of gipsies," 62–63). Egmont, however, refuses to refuse: he will not deny the soldiers their *Spaß* (WA 1, 7: 215 line 14; "amusement," 63). The next case, the secretary continues, involves two of his own people, Seter and Hart: they "haben einem Mädel, einer Wirtstochter, übel mitgespielt. Sie kriegten sie allein, und die Dirne konnte sich ihrer nicht erwehren" (WA 1, 7: 215 lines 16–18; "have behaved abominably toward a girl, an inn-keeper's daughter. They caught her when she was alone, and the girl had no means of defending herself," 63). The translation sidesteps the issue of the "Dirne," simply employing the more generic "girl." Though some insist the use of "Dirne" did not connote prostitute, the restraint in diction, "übel mitgespielt" ("behaved abominably"), for example, is unmistakably euphemistic. Her focus on the figure of Klärchen, Marie-Luise Waldeck writes, "Incidentally, Goethe is of course using *Dirne* in the above quotation in its original meaning of 'maiden' or 'girl' with no suggestion of the meaning that this term acquired later."[35] She offers other examples from Friedrich Schiller and contemporary usage, including Goethe's own notes about Klärchen. The Goethean texts, however, leverage the semantic shift that Hull identifies. In this case, the victim of soldierly abuse needs a hashtag.

My interest in the nameless, peripheral figure is motivated precisely by her marginal status. A nearly scholastic form of reasoning ensues. The scene of the crime, reported so dispassionately in the secretary's teichoskopic delivery, is thus: two probably inebriated soldiers get the innkeeper's daughter alone, so that she cannot escape. In effect, the secretary reports a kidnapping and rape with two perpetrators. This scene, however, is less about the victim; rather, it highlights Egmont's sense of gender justice— contingent upon her character: "Wenn es ein ehrlich Mädchen ist, und sie haben Gewalt gebraucht, so soll er sie drei Tage hintereinander mit Ruten streichen lassen, und wenn sie etwas besitzen, soll er so viel davon einziehen, daß dem Mädchen eine Ausstattung gereicht werden kann" (WA 1, 7: 215 lines 19–23; "If she's an honest girl, and they used force, they are to be birched for three days in succession, and if they have any possessions, Captain Breda [their superior, PAS] is to confiscate enough of them to make provision for the girl"). The physical punishment he orders for the perpetrators depends on an if/then proposition: her honesty plus

---

35   Marie-Luise Waldeck, "Klärchen: An Examination of Her Role in Goethe's *Egmont,*" *Publications of the English Goethe Society* 35, no. 1 (1965): 68–91, DOI :10.1080/09593683.1965.11785727.

their violence equals three days of flogging. Another logical conclusion follows: if they have property, the girl will be provided for (possibly in the form of a dowry). Both pronouncements require investigation beyond the scope of the drama, and the report then turns to the urgent topic of religious protest. The victim, the *Mädel* (girl), however, once violated, becomes a Dirne. Hull observes the transition in meaning: Goethe may be the force driving the change. Damage done, the downward descent of the victim on the periphery of Goethe's historical, tragic love story disappears from view. Moreover, the judge dispensing justice, though popular among the occupied, serves a colonial power. In the larger political power context, Egmont subjects his men to imperial injunction to respect the rights of the colonized.

Interlude in the *Hexenküche*

Faust: Ein Fragment, published in 1790, differs from the *Urfaust* (the earliest known form of the drama) in several ways: the most salient is the addition of the *Hexenküche* (witch's kitchen). The juxtaposition of Faust's conjuring of the *Erdgeist* (Earth Spirit), his negotiation with Mephistopheles, and the pranks that precede the visit to the witch's kitchen with the desire to shed thirty years from his body and possess the womanly ideal reflected in the mirror parallels the decline of reason and the rise of explicitly sexual desire. In his collected lectures on Goethe and philosophy from the early twentieth century, Thomas Davidson characterizes the witch's kitchen as a locus of articulated desires: "The witch's kitchen is the natural home of that vice which corrupts man's fleshly passion, house of prostitution, with all the degrading influences, in the shape of literature, art, jugglery, gambling, etc., that naturally belong to it. . . . the witch is simply the corrupt woman . . . the figure in the mirror is corrupt art."[36] All sources of pleasure, sensual and otherwise, are stirred into the cauldron here. The #MeToo moment calls for a reexamination of Davidson's view of the Faustian brothel, composed of magic, art, play, an old woman, and a beautiful image of ideal womanhood. For these are the components of supposed seduction, a formula for the constant replication of the gender paradigm that blames women for tempting men.

Faust and Mephistopheles, the former presumably under the malignant influence of the latter (and the potion), trade places, but only in some regards. Some note that Mephistopheles becomes more reasonable as Faust becomes more reckless and impassioned. The ambivalence in their power hierarchy—who is subordinate to whom—does not change. In fact, the voice of Mephistopheles speaks from a moral high ground. If

---

36 Thomas Davidson, *The Philosophy of Goethe's Faust*, ed. Charles M. Bakewell (Boston: Ginn, 1906), 38.

the definition of prostitution hinges on the adjective "liederlich" (loose) modifying the noun "Weibsperson" (woman), Goethe disrupts that language. First, Faust disparages age, when he himself seeks youth. When they enter the scene, he asks in a pique: "Verlang' ich Rath von einem alten Weibe?" (line 2340; "Do I seek counsel from some [old woman]?").[37] The price of admission and concern about money; the antics of the animals are familiar; as is the preparation of the potion and its consumption. Additionally, Faust falling for his own image as an idealization of female beauty invokes legend and myth beyond the scope of this essay. The abrupt shift to the street, the encounter with Gretchen, and the demonic conscience still have the capacity to surprise. Mephistopheles, insisting he has no power over the "unschuldig Ding" (line 2624; "right innocent young lass"), elicits a curt: "Ist über vierzehn Jahr doch alt" (line 2627; "She's over fourteen, after all").[38] At this point, Mephistopheles calls Faust a "Hans Liederlich" (line 2628; "loose Lothario"), insinuating that the scholar on the prowl shares the status of a prostituted woman. The agentic beverage aside, male desire, unchecked and uncompensated, can only be predatory. Goethe, who tries on a variety of erotic personae and explores multiple sexualities in his work, here depicts the man known for eternal striving as one who lusts for a younger woman of lower status. And he gets away with it.

The God and the Sex Slave

According to Adelung's dictionary, the *Bajadere* is an "*indische Tänzerin, zugl. Freudenmädchen; sozial den Parias vergleichbar*" (Indian dancer, also prostitute; socially comparable to pariahs).[39] Goethe took inspiration for his poem "Der Gott und die Bajadere," later set famously to music by Franz Schubert, from a volume about travels to India and China. The displacement of desire onto distant locales characterizes much of Goethe's ambivalence about sex. The eroticism of the "Roman Elegies" and *Venetian Epigrams* (1795) celebrates mutual desire and passion, albeit

---

37 "Old woman" is my more literal modification of the Arndt translation, which reads "skirted quack."

38 Fourteen is the age of confirmation, after which, according to historical sources, many working-class children were considered self-sufficient and capable of supporting themselves.

39 Further: "Denn du [*Brahma*] hast den B-n | Eine Göttin selbst erhoben 3,9 Paria Gebet 21 [1823] 412,100,5 Die drei Paria [1824] *geläutert u erhöht durch die Liebesvereinigung mit dem Gott u den freiwilligen, nur der rechtmäßigen Gattin vorbehaltenen Opfertod im Ged 'Der Gott u die Bajadere.'*" Marie Erxleben, "Bajadere," *Goethe-Wörterbuch*, http://woerterbuchnetz.de/cgi-bin/WBNetz/wbgui_py?sigle=GWB&sigle =GWB&mode=Vernetzung&hitlist=&patternlist=&lemid=JB00150#XJB00150.

through a male optic. His 1810 poem "Das Tagebuch" (The Diary)[40] repudiates aspects of attaining sexual fulfillment at the expense of a young female, perhaps evident of a mature restraint. Hans Vaget recounts the problematic publication history owing to the subject matter, of which he writes: "*The Diary* unfolds a carefully organized narrative that centres on the failure of an older man in a sexual encounter with a young woman."[41] *The Divan* (1819), not to mention peculiar chemistries of the *Elective Affinities* (1809), reveal Goethe's scrupulous attention to—even obsession with—the details of propriety and transgression when sex acts are involved. Goethe takes sex stories from "exotic" cultural contexts to express desire against the grain of bourgeois sensibilities and rigid social structures. One biographical moment exposes this aspect of his creativity. When "Der Gott und die Bajadere" was published, it appeared with Carl Friedrich Zelter's accompanying music.[42] In a diary entry from 6 June 1797, as Marie Erxleben documents, "[*Marianne Willemer sang*] 'Der Gott und die B.' Goethe wollte dies anfangs nicht . . . daß es fast ihre eigene Geschichte sei—so daß er gesagt, sie soll es nimmer singen" ([*Marianne Willemer sang*] "The God and the B." At first Goethe did not want her to . . . that it was almost her own story—so that he said she should never sing it).[43] The expression of female desire in the poem cuts through much of the static and stigma surrounding unsanctioned heterosexual attraction. That said, Goethe redirects male sexual agency into colonial conquest.

In "Der Gott und die Bajadere," Goethe directly confronts the stigma of prostitution in India but performs a lyrical deus ex machina to reverse the trajectory from fallen to recuperated woman. Mahadeva, one of the many names for Shiva, visits the humble quarters of a bayadere, who is keenly aware of her inferiority. Her painted cheeks, grace, and profession lure the god in human form into her "Liebe Haus" (line 19; house of love).[44] The myths of gods fulfilling desire by assuming human form abound. Here, Goethe elaborates on Shiva's sixth descent to earth; he resurrects the prostitute: "Der Göttliche lächelt; er siehet mit Freuden /

40 See Johann Wolfgang von Goethe, *Erotic Poems*, trans. David Luke, introd. Hans Vaget (Oxford: Oxford University Press, 1999), 99–117.

41 Hans Vaget, "Introduction: The Poet as Liberator; Goethe's Priapean Project," in Goethe, *Erotic Poems*, ix–xlvi, here xxxvi.

42 According to the Hyperion label, "It was written in 1797 and published in Schiller's *Musenalmanach* for 1798 with Zelter's melody as part of the supplement provided in a pocket at the back of the book," https://www.hyperion-records.co.uk/dw.asp?dc=W1928_GBAJY9402406.

43 Erxleben, "Bajadere."

44 Johann Wolfgang von Goethe, "Der Gott und die Bajadere," in *Gedichte*, vol. 1 of the Hamburger Ausgabe, ed. Erich Trunz (Munich: Beck, 1981), 273–76. References to this poem will appear as line numbers in parentheses.

Durch tiefes Verderben ein menschliches Herz" (lines 32–33: "The God holds back laughter, with pleasure he knows / Within form so corrupted, a human heartbeat").[45] The complete surrender of the bayadere, of her body, heart, and ultimately her life, construct a narrative of salvation.

Throughout that construction, the titillation of the bayadere's skills captivates the reader as well. She is enslaved, completely at the will of the god in human form. Her professional submission leads to love: "Und er fordert Sklavendienste; / Immer heitrer wird sie nur, / Und des Mädchens frühe Künste / Werden nach und nach Natur" ("And he plays at domination / Always shows she her good cheer, / And the maiden's simulation / Bit by bit becomes sincere").[46] The Malinofsky translation blurs the severity of the original, which could be rendered: "And he demands the services of a slave." The seduction only heightens the demands; the god escalates the intensity of physical response, with intent: "Aber, sie schärfer und schärfer zu prüfen, / Wählet der Kenner der Höhen und Tiefen / Lust und Entsetzen und grimmige Pein" ("But that she might now more keenly be tested, / He tries her next, all before both have rested, / With dark lustful pressures, and pains most unkind"). With the tyrannical indifference of Zeus torturing Prometheus, the god self-awarely pushes the bayadere to a breaking point. Central to the story is the bayadere's complete capitulation.

Goethe does acknowledge female desire in this poem through the deconstruction of sex for pay as the condition of prostitution. The text also invokes a series of myths about gods assuming human or animal form, from the bull in the rape of Europa; to the desire for Alcmene, Amphytrion's wife and mother of the demigod Heracles; to Leda and the swan. In the ballad, Goethe wrests the Hindu god, the Indian dance girl (*bayadere* derives from the Portuguese, via French, thus Europeanized in transit), and the *sati* from cultural context, forcing them into a Western bourgeois marriage constellation. The reader has to search for the moment of the bayadere's brokenness in desire; the natural sincerity undergirding the performance of the seduction:

Und das Mädchen steht gefangen,
Und sie weint zum erstenmal,
Sinkt zu seinen Füßen nieder,
Nicht um Wollust noch Gewinst,
Ach! und die gelenken Glieder,
Sie versagen allen Dienst. (lines 47–52)

---

45 The translation is by Leon Malinofsky (2011), The LiederNet Archive, https://www.lieder.net /lieder/get_text.html?TextId=74030.

46 The Malinofsky prioritizes the demands of performance, emphasizing rhyme and rhythm for the Schubert *Lied*.

[She became his captive wholly,
And her tears began to rain;
Falls she weeping down before him
Not for pleasure, nor for gains,
Oh! and every supple limb,
Now is still, and so remains.][47]

Only the repudiation of her "services" signals complete submission. From the moment she awakens to find the young man dead, she assumes the role of spouse. She defies the "chorus" of mourners who would forbid her ritual sacrifice of dying on the funeral pyre, *sati*, sometimes written *suttee*: "Nur die Gattin folgt dem Gatten" (line 84; "Just the wife her husband follows").[48] And she ascends: "Unsterbliche heben verlorene Kinder / Mit feurigen Armen zum Himmel empor" (lines 97–99; "The immortals raise lost children / With fiery arms up to heaven").[49] The final lines resonate with the act of redemption yet evoke the flames of desire simultaneously. Goethe gets it both ways. The bayadere's arts of seduction are "naturalized" by love. G. W. F. Hegel cites Goethe's poem as an example of the apologue in the *Lectures on Aesthetics* (1835); he compares the trope to Mary Magdalene in the Christian context. Hegel writes, "Die Bajadere zeigt dieselbe Demut, die gleiche Stärke des Liebens und Glaubens, der Gott stellt sie auf die Probe, die sie vollständig besteht, so daß es nun zur Erhebung und Versöhnung kommt"[50] ("The Bayadere exemplifies the same humility, a like strength of love and faith; God puts her to the proof, an ordeal she completely sustains, and her exaltation and reconciliation follows").[51] Goethe restores the bayadere to the German canon, both as a sacrificed bride and a woman saved by love. Ultimately, these articulations thematize male models of female desire.

Goethe was not alone in thematizing the sati for the German (Christian) reader. The work of his contemporary, Karoline von Günderrode (1780–1806), though unpublished in her lifetime, invites comparison.

---

47 Malinofsky translation.
48 Malinofsky translation.
49 My translation. Malinofsky translates the stanza: "But the Godling never tarried, / Rose up from the pyre strong: / Rising from the flames he carried / His dear loved one right along. / The Gods in their Heaven are pleased with repentance; / Immortal ones lost children spare from their sentence, / And raise them from fire to where they belong."
50 G. W. F. Hegel, *Vorlesungen über die Ästhetik I–III*, in *Werke in 20 Bänden*, vol. 13, ed. Eva Moldenhauer and Karl Markus Michel (Frankfurt am Main: Suhrkamp, 1986), I:504.
51 G. W. F Hegel, *The Philosophy of Fine Art*, trans. F. P. B. Ostmason (London: Bell, 1920), 4 vols., https://www.gutenberg.org/files/55445/55445-h/55445-h.htm.

Her suicide contributed to the shelving of "Die Malabarischen Witwen" (The Malabar Widows), intended for publication in the volume *Melete* under the pseudonym J. C. B. Mohr. Stephanie Galasso compares the representation of sati in Günderrode's poem to her "Adonis Todtenfeyer," eschewing for good reasons Goethe's "Bajadere." With a keen eye for the formal sonnet, Galasso reads the Günderrode poem against the assumption that the self-immolating ritual death underscores the poet's romanticized philosophy of love. Moreover, her identification of the colonial moments in the production and consumption of the poem's portrayal of sati illuminates a connection to Goethe's enterprise. Galasso observes that Günderrode "exoticizes the women and effectively repeats some of the gestures of colonial 'eyewitness' accounts."[52] In her comparative argument, Galasso does reference the Goethe poem, favorably comparing his rendition of the bayadere to Günderrode's while acknowledging the romanticization he, too, undergoes: his bayadere "is at least rendered as an individual figure in the poem,"[53] in contrast to the former's collective widow and undifferentiated emotional world. The profession of desiring men for money and rendering of the bayadere as a prostitute to the gods does not factor in Galasso's analysis, as it does in mine. The sexualization of death occurs both in Goethe and in Günderrode: "Nicht Trennung ferner solchem Bunde droht, / Denn die vorhin entzweiten Liebesflammen / In einer schlagen brünstig sie zusammen" (Such a bond cannot be threatened by separation, / For the flames of love, previously parted / Set fire fervently together in one).[54] Both Goethe and Günderrode, I would claim, participate in colonial appropriation of the sati, though apparently toward different ends and with different means. Yet both exploit the moment of death in flames to make a metaphor of sex and posit a conflagration as the only possible consequence of female desire fulfilled.

Conclusion

In the early nineteenth century, attitudes toward prostitution began to change, though selectively at best. In one example, Percy Bysse Shelley (1792–1822) counters the Kantian exclusion of prostitution on moral grounds with an acknowledgment of double standards and consequences

---

52 Stephanie Galasso, "Form and Contention: Sati as Custom in Günderrode's 'Die Malabarischen Witwen,'" *Goethe Yearbook* 24 (2017): 197–220, here 199.

53 Galasso, "Form and Contention," 208.

54 Karoline von Günderrode, "Die Malabarischen Witwen" (1922), BYU Scholars Archive, Sophie: Poetry, no. 500, https://scholarsarchive.byu.edu/sophpm_poetry/500.

of female desire. In "Queen Mab" (1813), his philosophical poem with notes, Shelley addresses precisely this point: "Prostitution is the legitimate offspring of marriage and its accompanying errors. Women, for no other crime than having followed the dictates of a natural appetite, are driven with fury from the comforts and sympathies of society."[55] One may wonder if the natural appetite includes hunger as well. The justification of sexual desire as natural remains a matter of debate for centuries, extending to designate gendered sex practices as "natural" or "unnatural." In the #MeToo era, real women break the silence around the clandestine sexual abuse, harrassment, and violence perpetrated by powerful men. My retrospective reading of three texts by Goethe in the cultural context around 1800 recapitulates several important points: a female leader, empowered by family relations, who is denigrated by men who did not get her job and forced to succumb to the use of brute force; a nameless rape victim who, although the perpetrators are punished, remains silent; a poet praised for telling the story of a prostitute who dies for love—not the self-empowering Stormy Daniels, by any means, but in context the bayadere undergoes a transformation that speaks volumes about the portrayal of female desire. The locus of transacted sex is subject to regulation; such legal interventions obviate the need to acknowledge or countenance the possibility of female desire. Paragraph 999 of the *Preußischen Allgemeinen Landrechts* provides for collectives of "loose women." Paragraph 1000 and subsequent statutes qualify that existence: "Dergleichen öffentliche Häuser sind nur in großen, volkreichen Städten und nicht anders als in abgelegenen und von öffentlichen Wegen und Straßen entfernteren Orten zu dulden" (Public houses of this kind are to be tolerated only in large, populous cities and nowhere else but in remote and distanced places away from public paths and streets). The secluded scene of the rape in *Egmont*, the bewitched domestic kitchen in *Faust*, and the bedchamber of the bayadere remain sequestered from public view. The colonizing male gaze wanders to India—or Italy, or the alley—for sexual fulfillment. When detected, prevailing sexual syntax differentiates male and female agency: male sexuality transitive and female desire intransitive. From the eighteenth-century stage to twenty-first-century social media platforms, we continue to lack a language and a public space for female desire.

---

55   Percy Bysshe Shelley, *The Poems of Shelley*, vol. 1: *1804–1817*, ed. Geoffrey Matthews and Kelvin Everest (New York: Routledge, 2014), 371.

Part II

Dialogues across Time

3: "Immaculate" Conception, the "Romance of Rape," and #MeToo: Kleistian Echoes in Kerstin Hensel and Julia Franck

Melissa Ann Sheedy

THE INFAMOUS "KLEISTIAN DASH" that marks the murky encounter of a young woman and her ostensible savior in Heinrich von Kleist's 1808 novella "Die Marquise von O. . ." (1808)[1] conceals a moment of extreme import for the protagonist and her story. The text's narrative puzzle obliges the reader to return to the punctuation mark as the likely scene of the marquise's rape, and it plays with themes of consent and awareness to cast her position of purity in doubt. Kleist's nineteenth-century tale of sexual abuse and punishment continues to resonate today, especially in light of the recent wave of digital feminist activism and the #MeToo movement. Whereas Kleist's famous dashes often serve to indicate an event *un*narrated or a truth unspoken,[2] the hashtag symbol signals the explicit intent to communicate. This communication afforded by the hashtag takes place via a large-scale digital platform that allows users to "tag" content, linking social media messages and posts under a single thematic umbrella. The #MeToo movement originated in 2006, after activist Tarana Burke used the phrase "Me Too" to empower and amplify the voices of survivors of sexual assault, especially women of color. Following actor Alyssa Milano's revitalization of the term in 2017, it became a

---

1   Heinrich von Kleist, "Die Marquise von O. . .," in *Sämtliche Erzählungen und andere Prosa*, ed. Helmut Sembdner (Stuttgart: Reclam, 2007), 116–63. All translations of "Marquise" are from "The Marquise of O—," in *The Marquise of O— and Other Stories*, trans. David Luke and Nigel Reeves (London: Penguin, 2004), 68–113. In-text citations will not include the author's last name unless the source of the quote is otherwise ambiguous.

2   While Kleist's charged dash in "Marquise" is perhaps his best known, the author's penchant for the punctuation mark can be seen elsewhere; for example, in "Das Erdbeben in Chile" (1807). Capitalizing on the tension between that which is said and that which is unsaid, Kleist's dashes represent a realm of possibility not explicitly stated.

worldwide phenomenon.[3] At once an emblem of solidarity, support, and visibility, the phrase "#MeToo," like Kleist's dashes, heralds a story that had remained untold, while endowing survivors with the power to tell—or not to tell.[4] For Kleist's marquise, the struggle to articulate a truth she herself only partially understands is made all the more difficult by the fact that she is simply not believed. It is this particular burden—the unnecessary extension of suffering that follows the original assault—that resonates with Kleist's readers today and recalls the #MeToo movement's emphasis on the perspectives and experiences of survivors.

Kleist's tale of a mysteriously expectant mother finds an ironic echo in two works of contemporary German fiction: Kerstin Hensel's *Gipshut* (1999; Cap Rock)[5] and Julia Franck's *Die Mittagsfrau* (2007).[6] The reimagined marquise figures in these texts are subject to abuse both within and outside the home, and they are precluded from seeking recourse by domestic and social structures of sexism, racism, and ableism. While both texts predate #MeToo and thus cannot be said to engage with it overtly, each can nevertheless be read in dialogue with the discourses that the movement brings to light, particularly the culturally normalized reinscription of rape into the structures of marriage and domesticity. Hensel's and Franck's stories of assault end without justice for the survivor, thus revealing the widespread patterns of sexual violence at the core of patriarchal society, paradigms of brutality that the #MeToo movement seeks to deconstruct. In each of the three texts, the victims bear not only the burden of assault itself and its enduring trauma but also the blame for its occurrence. The thematization of innocence, purity, and penance reveals the disproportionate hardships facing female survivors of violence, whereas the male aggressors largely go unpunished. Drawing on feminist

---

3　Alyssa Evans, "#MeToo: A Study on Sexual Assault as Reported in *The New York Times*," *Occam's Razor* 8, no. 3 (2018): 11.

4　The #MeToo Movement is certainly not without its weaknesses, having recently drawn criticism for its failure to fully take the experiences of women of color into account, particularly in light of the disproportionate threats that many women of color, transgender people, and disabled women face by going public with their stories. See Evans, "#MeToo," 12. In her 2018 TED Talk "Me Too Is a Movement, Not a Moment," Burke herself stated: "We have moved so far away from the origins of this movement that started a decade ago, or even the intentions of the hashtag that started just a year ago, that sometimes, the MeToo movement that I hear some people talk about is unrecognizable to me." See Tarana Burke, "Me Too Is a Movement, Not a Moment," filmed November 2018 in Palm Springs, TED video, 16:07.

5　Kerstin Hensel, *Gipshut* (Leipzig: Gustav Kiepenheuer, 1999).

6　Julia Franck, *Die Mittagsfrau* (Frankfurt am Main: Fischer, 2007). All translations of *Mittagsfrau* are from *The Blindness of the Heart*, trans. Anthea Bell (New York: Grove Press, 2009).

narratology and Walter Burkert's "Maiden's Tragedy,"[7] this chapter examines Hensel's and Franck's engagements with "immaculate" conceptions, sexual abuse, and motherhood, and it analyzes their deconstruction of romanticized and normalized rape upheld in the male-authored "Marquise." Capitalizing on the connections between violence, gender, and power, these contemporary authors draw on nineteenth-century literary discourses, with specific reference to Kleist's novella, to breathe new life into the familiar "Maiden's Tragedy" pattern.

Crime and Punishment in Kleist's "Die Marquise von O. . ."

Kleist's "Die Marquise von O. . ." takes place during the Napoleonic Wars in Italy and centers on the eponymous marquise, a widowed mother of two who finds herself inexplicably pregnant. The text opens in memorable fashion with a newspaper advertisement placed by the marquise entreating the father of her unborn child to come forward, for she has been cast out by her family and is prepared to marry the man who answers her summons. Some weeks earlier, a mysterious "Count F" had rescued the marquise from a group of Russian soldiers. He led her from the fray, "wo sie auch völlig bewußtlos niedersank. Hier—traf er, da bald darauf ihre erschrockenen Frauen erschienen, Anstalten, einen Arzt zu rufen; versicherte, indem er sich den Hut aufsetzte, daß sie sich bald erholen würde; und kehrte in den Kampf zurück" (118; "[where] she collapsed in a dead faint. Then—the officer instructed the Marquise's frightened servants, who presently arrived, to send for a doctor; he assured them that she would soon recover, replaced his hat, and returned to the fighting," "The Marquise," 70). When the count later comes forward to declare himself the father, bewildered readers must retrace their steps and center on that incongruous dash to conclude that the count must be the perpetrator.[8] Despite all obstacles, the count and the marquise marry and attain their happy ending, forcing the reader to attempt to reconcile the opposing forces of rape and love.[9] Given the count's likely guilt, the reader is left to question the morality of a story in which rape leads to a happy marriage. If the count is indeed the culprit, how is it permissible that he escapes unpunished and in fact receives for his actions the marquise's

---

7   Walter Burkert, *Creation of the Sacred: Tracks of Biology in Early Religions* (Cambridge, MA: Harvard University Press, 1996), 69.

8   For a detailed analysis of this scene and its legal and moral implications, see Gesa Dane, *"Zeter und Mordio": Vergewaltigung in Literatur und Recht* (Göttingen: Wallstein, 2005), 235–56.

9   Armine Kotin Mortimer, "The Devious Second Story in Kleist's Die Marquise von O. . . ," *German Quarterly* 63, no. 7 (1994): 293.

hand? While the questions of *how* and *why* receive no clear answers, what remains evident is the marquise's vulnerability both within and outside of the home: her rescue at the hands of a dashing count comes at a violent price, and the family is quick to enact its own punishment for her perceived misdeeds.

Despite the relative neatness of the text's conclusion, Kleist does not content himself with one mystery but rather lets his reader glimpse another: a disturbingly intimate scene between father and daughter that takes place after he accepts her innocence. Focalized through the mother's perspective as she watches through the doorway, the scene oscillates between moments of romantic and paternal love: "[Sie] sah nun—und das Herz quoll ihr vor Freuden empor: die Tochter still, mit zurückgebeugtem Nacken, die Augen fest geschlossen, in des Vaters Armen liegen; indessen dieser, auf dem Lehnstuhl sitzend, lange, heiße und lechzende Küsse, das große Auge voll glänzender Tränen, auf ihren Mund drückte: gerade wie ein Verliebter!" (157; "She saw a sight that made her heart leap with joy: her daughter, with her head thrown right back and her eyes tightly shut, was lying quietly in her father's arms, while the latter, with tears glistening in his wide-open eyes, sat in the armchair, pressing long, ardent, avid kisses on to her mouth, just like a lover!" "The Marquise," 107). Strikingly detailed, this moment of reconciliation borders on the grotesque as the colonel holds his daughter on his lap and caresses her. In addition to providing yet another potentially weighty dash,[10] the narrative itself seems to revel in contradictory prose: The "himmelfroh[e] Versöhnung" (157; "blissful scene of reconciliation," "The Marquise," 107) witnessed by the mother seems an incongruous descriptor for a scene marked by "lechzende Küsse" (ardent kisses) from a man acting "wie ein Verliebter" (157; "like a lover," "The Marquise," 107). At dinner that evening, to which the Marquise and her father arrive "wie Brautleute" (157; "like a pair of betrothed lovers," "The Marquise," 108), the colonel alternates between cheer and visible despondency, and he plays continuously with his daughter's hand ("The Marquise," 157). To account for the uneasiness these passages provoke in the reader, Mortimer suggests

---

10   See Mortimer, "Devious," and Thomas Dutoit, "Rape, Crypt and Fantasm: Kleist's 'Marquise of O. . . ,'" *Mosaic: An Interdisciplinary Critical Journal* 27, no. 3 (September 1994): 45–64. Both Mortimer and Dutoit connect the structural function of Kleist's dashes to thematic undercurrents and emotional upheavals. Mortimer links the occurrence of dashes to "breath-taking" events, "acute moments of transgression and interdiction, where the text recoils from its own monstrosity and shuts up in horror" (299). Mortimer describes the dashes throughout the text as "repercussions" of the unspoken moment of trauma (299), echoes that parallel the marquise's relentless suffering. Similarly, Dutoit writes that the abundance of dashes "correlates stylistically with the problems of trauma, paternity and fantasy" (46).

that the episode serves as a narrative replacement for the love scene that would have occurred had the marquise's earlier encounter been consensual: "In grotesquely magnified detail, it is the scene that would have happened if there had been an agreed-to love act between the count and the marquise."[11] Kleist's narrator is careful not to give too much away, and yet the scene as an explicit analogy to the dash is enough to throw the count's claimed paternity into doubt and casts the marquise's own father as a potential new suspect. The question of true perpetrator aside, the narrative's instantiation of a romantic tableau between father and daughter reveals a household that conceals its own abuse.[12]

Almost as an afterthought, the text presents yet another possible culprit: the hunter Leopardo. To trick the marquise into admitting guilt, her mother falsely claims that Leopardo had responded to the newspaper advertisement. When the marquise accepts this explanation, her mother rejoices at this "proof" of innocence, for had her daughter expressed any doubt in response to this made-up tale, her misgivings would have contradicted her claims of ignorance. At first merely a figment of her mother's ruse, Leopardo nevertheless becomes suspicious in the eyes of the reader when the marquise recalls an afternoon nap that she had taken some time ago: "Ich war einst in der Mittagshitze eingeschlummert, und sah ihn von meinem Diwan gehen, als ich erwachte!" (153; "It did once happen that I had fallen asleep in the mid-day heat, on my divan, and when I woke up I saw him walking away from it!" "The Marquise," 103). Following this revelation, Leopardo is not mentioned again, but the marquise's recollection of his presence near her place of repose is telling. Despite the lack of detail, the very possibility of another suspect highlights the marquise's vulnerability within her own home, an exposure to potential violence in the private sphere that parallels the dangers on the public stage as a woman in a time of warfare. Moreover, the sheer number of paternal candidates not only exposes the heteronormativity of these incidents of threatened and realized violence but also reveals a suggestion on the author's part of the marquise's inherent promiscuity—a form of victim-blaming that interrogates *her* actions and motivations, rather than those of her aggressor(s).

Through its emphasis on perdition and redemption, the marquise's story is reminiscent of the so-called Maiden's Tragedy, a centuries-old narrative paradigm that delineates five specific stations of a female heroine's story. According to Burkert, these stages include leaving home, a

---

11 Mortimer, "Devious," 300.

12 For a discussion of the marquise's marginalized position as a widow who has returned to her father's house, see Christina Künzel, *Vergewaltigungslektüren: Zur Codierung sexueller Gewalt in Literatur und Recht* (Frankfurt am Main: Campus, 2003), 37.

period of isolation, a catastrophe associated with a first (violent) sexual encounter, a period of suffering, and salvation through the birth of a child, usually male.[13] This tradition, evident in so-called female fairy tales, links narrative conventions with biological stimuli,[14] as the heroine's progression reflects the domestic and maternal roles reinforced in both tales and society.[15] Within this embedded narrative path, real and threatened violence are a necessary impetus that leads heroines such as Rapunzel and Sleeping Beauty[16] to their happy endings. For the marquise, this happy ending comes at a price: the experience of sexual violence at the hands of her future husband. According to Burkert, this third stage of the Maiden's Tragedy is undoubtedly a scene of rape: "The catastrophe that upsets the idyll [is] normally caused by the intrusion of a male, . . . who violates the girl and leaves her pregnant."[17] This codified chapter of sexual violence corresponds to the motif of "romantic rape," which Betsy Bauman-Martin describes as a "deeply entrenched literary theme that impacts all Western literary forms [and] which depicts the sexual exploitation of a woman but presents [it] as acceptable, or even enjoyable, to the woman."[18] The marquise's implied pleasure in her own abuse seems to be supported by her condition: in many Western scientific discourses in the eighteenth and nineteenth centuries, pregnancy and assault were in fact mutually exclusive, because a woman's sexual pleasure was considered to be a prerequisite for conception.[19] Moreover, within this paradigm of

13   Burkert, *Creation*, 71.

14   Burkert, *Creation*, 71.

15   See Melissa Sheedy, "Feminine Paradigms and Fairy-Tale Transformations in the Works of Kerstin Hensel: The Political Implications of Telling a Tale," in *Protest and Refusal: New Trends in German Literature since 1989*, ed. Hans Adler and Sonja E. Klocke (Paderborn: Wilhelm Fink, 2019), 172.

16   Both Grimm tales also serve as archetypes of the romanticization of rape. In earlier versions of "Rapunzel," the young protagonist finds herself pregnant with no knowledge of how this came to be. She asks why her clothes have become so tight, an innocent question that informs both her captor and the reader that the girl has had more than one visitor in her tower. Similarly, earlier versions of "Sleeping Beauty" thematize the rape of a comatose woman, and like "Rapunzel," nevertheless conclude with a wedding celebration and happy ending.

17   Burkert, *Creation*, 71.

18   Bauman-Martin, "Mary and the Marquise: Reading the Annunciation in the Romantic Rape Tradition," in *Sacred Tropes: Tanakh, New Testament, and Qur'an as Literature and Culture*, ed. Roberta Sterman Sabbath (Boston: Brill, 2009), 217.

19   Künzel, *Vergewaltigungslektüren*, 33. This implied connection between pleasure in the sexual act and pregnancy is also echoed in twenty-first-century anti-abortion discourses in the United States, perhaps most infamously in Republican Senate candidate Todd Akin's 2012 statement that conception cannot result from rape: "If it is a legitimate rape, the female body has ways to try to shut that whole

"romantic rape," the woman's experiences and perspective are appropriated by the male narrator,[20] who in the marquise's case declares a state of fairy tale–like happiness for her and her bridegroom.[21]

The marquise's wedding to the count nevertheless resolves the catastrophe of "romantic rape" by lending legitimacy to the child and restoring her innocence in the eyes of her father. No longer proof of sin, her newborn son represents a sort of "immaculate conception," for the marquise's proven lack of awareness and connection to the sexual act has rendered her nearly divine.[22] In contrast, the count himself, beyond his own guilty conscience, is never satisfactorily penalized or called to answer for his misdeeds, whereas the marquise is disproportionately punished for her pregnancy—and perceived promiscuity—on account of her gender alone.

Unexpected Motherhood in Hensel's *Gipshut*

Kleist's familiar—and indeed biblical—themes of seemingly immaculate conception and unexpected maternity are picked up anew by East German author Hensel in *Gipshut*, which draws on fairy-tale discourses of innocence and motherhood. *Gipshut* traces parallel stories that take place before and after the fall of the Berlin Wall. As the novel opens in the German Democratic Republic in 1950, teenager Veronika Dankschön, an orphan of the Second World War and apprentice at a trading firm, finds herself drawn to the nearby Siethener Lake. Overcome by pain and nausea, Veronika does not realize that she is pregnant; but an unseen force compels her toward the water, where she gives birth to a son. Veronika draws on instinct rather than knowledge to pull the child out of the water and keep him warm: "Sie wußte nicht, was sie tat; aber sie wußte, was sie tun mußte" (*Gipshut*, 21; She did not know what she was doing, but she

---

thing down." Lori Moore, "Rep. Todd Akin: The Statement and the Reaction," *New York Times*, August 20, 2012, https://www.nytimes.com/2012/08/21/us/politics/rep-todd-akin-legitimate-rape-statement-and-reaction.html.

20   Bauman-Martin, "Mary," 217.

21   Kleist himself undermines this reading with the remark: "Eine ganze Reihe von jungen Russen folgte" (163; "A whole series of young Russians now followed the first," "The Marquise," 113). A simultaneous suggestion of either more children *or* more Russian lovers, Kleist's quip points once again to the marquise's supposed promiscuity.

22   The links between "Marquise" and biblical discourses of Mary are manifold. As Bauman-Martin points out in her discussion of the encounter between Mary and the angel Gabriel in Luke 1, "Parallels with the annunciation should be obvious: the Marquise is frightened, she considers the Count an 'angel,' the resulting situation is one of illegitimate pregnancy, and the sexual act is not described." Bauman-Martin, "Mary," 230.

knew what she had to do).[23] Veronika's connections to the socialist state, which she does not understand, and to a community that marginalizes her are tenuous, but her strong intuition indicates a close bond between herself and nature, embodied in the text by the mysterious Siethener Lake.

Like the marquise, Veronika is ill equipped to understand the cause of her condition; but whereas Kleist's heroine at the very least intuits the involvement of a man, Veronika's remarkable naivety makes it impossible for her to see the connections between childbirth and sex. In her case, conception almost certainly took place during an incident of sexual violence that occurred nine months ago. Kleist's nineteenth-century dash effectively—and coyly—conceals what Hensel thematizes directly: her narrative interweaves images of the birth scene with Veronika's disjointed memories of a nonconsensual sexual encounter, disguised as a game, with an older colleague:

> Veronika Dankschön krallte die Fingernägel in das Holz des Bootsrandes.
> "Ich zeig dir das Baustofflager," hatte Gabelstapler-Jochen gesagt.
> Der Schmerz bohrte sich vom Rücken in den Unterleib. Sie war mit ihm auf den Gabelstapler gestiegen. Wenn sie die Luft anhielt und schreiend ausstieß, verteilte sich der Schmerz auf den Körper. Jochen hatte den Richtungshebel gezogen und den Schalter gedrückt. Ein Fisch glitt unter Veronika hin. (*Gipshut*, 20)

> [Veronika Dankschön dug her fingernails into the wood of the boat's edge. "I'll show you the builder's yard," said Forklift-Jochen. The pain bored from her back into her abdomen. She had climbed up onto the forklift with him. When she held her breath and let it out with a scream, the pain spread across her body. Jochen pulled the directional lever and pushed the switch. A fish glided underneath Veronika.]

Unlike the punctuative intrusion of Kleist's dashes, Hensel's text smoothly merges images of past and present. The two timelines are initially separated through paragraph breaks, but the narrative abandons these interruptions in favor of a fluid relay of sentences, forcing the reader to rely on visual cues, such as the fish or the forklift. In both texts, narrative strategies tell their own story. Kleist's simple dash signals a violent intervention in the story, an example of what Bauman-Martin describes as the "textual-sexual hole" marking the literary trope of "romantic rape."[24] In contrast, Hensel's passage oscillates between violent cause and effect to trouble the boundary between Veronika *remembering* and *experiencing*,

---

23 All translations of *Gipshut* are my own.
24 Bauman-Martin, "Mary," 217.

obscuring the progression of events and reinforcing the cyclical nature of trauma.

Despite the narrative's interlocking structure that correlates each stage of labor with the events of the assault, Veronika fails to connect the child's unexpected appearance with her earlier liaison. Her good-natured ignorance stands in contrast to the narrator's dryly ironic tone and the deliberately structured narrative sequence of cause and effect that is so apparent for the reader. In an echo of classic fairy-tale diction, Hensel writes, "Ein wenig wunderte sich das Mädchen freilich schon, denn was mit ihr geschehen war, konnte sie sich nicht erklären. Soviel verstand sie: sie war Mutter geworden" (*Gipshut*, 22; The girl certainly marveled a bit, because she could not explain to herself what had happened to her. She understood this much: she had become a mother). Indeed, like Veronika's experiences of motherhood, most fairy tales sever the link between child-birth and sex. An infant's impending appearance is frequently heralded in tales by magical creatures, such as frogs or crustaceans. Early versions of the Grimm tale "Sleeping Beauty," for instance, featured a crab that emerged from the water to inform the queen that she would become a mother. From the 1837 edition onward, a frog assumed the messenger role.[25] Frogs, whose amphibious nature symbolized childbirth, made frequent appearances as harbingers of maternity. Veronika herself receives no such omen, at least not directly: neither her memories of the encounter with Jochen, nor a pair of copulating dragonflies perched on the edge of her boat, clue her in to her condition. Nevertheless, Veronika's instinctive drive toward the water, together with the structural similarities between Hensel's prose and the Grimms' tales, links her experience of childbirth to that of fairy-tale mothers. By indirectly stating that which the Grimms (and Kleist) leave unsaid, however, Hensel draws attention to sexual assault as a motivating factor in tales of virgin birth. Hensel's omission of a redemptive arc for Veronika emphasizes the mother's suffering and inspires an empathetic response on the part of the reader.

Veronika's unexpected—and for her, unexplained—step into mother-hood serves as an ironic echo of the Christian notion of virgin birth, in that she is unable to draw the connection between sex and birth. When asked about the father of her child, Veronika is genuinely bewildered: "Wieso Vater?" (*Gipshut*, 30; Why father?). This darkly humorous dis-connect between cause and effect reminds the reader of the marquise's predicament. Whereas the marquise's lack of awareness connects her to the divine, however, Veronika's naivety, together with an implied cogni-tive disability, renders her an outsider in a society marked by sexism and ableism. As Jill Twark points out, through the combined factors of her

---

25   Jacob and Wilhelm Grimm, "Dornröschen," in *Die Märchen der Brüder Grimm* (Munich: Wilhelm Goldmann, 1980), 180.

intellectual differences and lack of parental supervision, Veronika "never really takes control of her body and grows up amorally."[26] Uneducated and unsupported, she has no recourse against the man who tricked her into sex: not only is she compelled to marry him, but she does so joyfully. On account of her gender, intellectual faculties, and her role as a young apprentice at work, Veronika is constantly marginalized. Her vulnerability to Jochen in particular and society at large highlights the power structures underlying their professional and personal relationships. Without even realizing that the "lustige Gabelstaplerfahrt" (*Gipshut*, 42; fun forklift ride) with Jochen was no simple game—played out on a piece of equipment that itself connotes violent penetration—Veronika finds herself contending with the consequences alone.

As Veronika's son Hans grows up, the differences between them become more pronounced, most strikingly in name. Following Hans's birth, a journalist interested in Veronika's astonishing story gives the child a nickname, Kielkropf. In Germanic mythology, the term "Kielkropf" possesses supernatural associations and often refers to changelings.[27] Although Veronika is obliged to write her own last name in the birth announcement, the moniker sticks. Not only indicative of Hans's extraordinary birth, the name also suggests Veronika's own uncertainty regarding his origins and his future: "[Sie konnte] sich manchmal eines Gefühles nicht erwehren[,] als würde ihr das Kind durch diesen fremden Namen nicht zugehören, als würde es nicht bei ihr aufwachsen, sondern sich entfernen von dem Leben, das sie führte" (*Gipshut*, 41; Sometimes she could not ignore a feeling as though her child, through this foreign name, did not belong to her, as though he did not grow up with her, but rather would distance himself from the life that she led). These unspoken fears cast Hans not as her own flesh but rather as a child of the Siethener Lake, which in the text possesses its own mystical agency. Through intellectual abilities that quickly outpace her own, his political conformity and belief in the socialist system, and even his last name, Hans simply seems not to belong to her. This sense of distance foreshadows their strained relationship later in life, which, following Hans's departure for a long-term work assignment, ends in Veronika's suicide.

Hensel's dark parody of a young woman's introduction to sex and motherhood echoes and subverts the stations of the Maiden's Tragedy, with particular reflection on social class. As the novel opens, the sixteen-year-old already lives alone, as her parents had both been killed in the war. Although the reader assumes that they are dead, Veronika masks her sense

26 Jill Twark, *Humor, Satire, and Identity: Eastern German Literature in the 1990s* (Berlin: De Gruyter, 2007), 250.
27 Elard Hugo Meyer, *Mythologie der Germanen* (Strasbourg: K. J. Trübner, 1903), 181.

of loss by imagining a fairy-tale fate for her parents: "Die Eltern irgendwo noch im Leben oder schon im Tod, was wußte sie! Ihre Vorstellung war, der Krieg habe sie, als sie sich im Wald versteckt hielten, wie Kartoffeln aus dem Sand gezogen und aufgefressen" (*Gipshut*, 8; Her parents somewhere still alive or already dead, what did she know! Her idea was that, as they had hunkered down in the forest, the war had pulled them up like potatoes from the sand and devoured them). For her, "leaving home" is thus realized by the disappearance of her family, and it is this isolation, together with economic and social precarity, that renders her particularly vulnerable to Jochen's advances and the "catastrophe" of sexual assault. Following Hans's birth, Jochen, like Count F., feels a moral obligation to marry the woman he assaulted. Whereas Kleist grants his patrician couple a fragile happy ending, however, Hensel leads her working-class heroine down a much darker path. Veronika's Maiden's Tragedy ends not in acceptance and salvation, as it does for the marquise and many fairy-tale protagonists, but instead concludes in loss and abandonment: Jochen divorces her, and her son, Hans, also leaves eventually. Following a lifetime of abuse and neglect, Veronika ultimately dies by suicide, a bleak contrast to the marquise's social restoration and happy ending.

Unlike the heroines of fairy tales and Maiden's Tragedies, who through the fulfillment of the requisite narrative stations achieve adulthood, Veronika never seems to grow up. She regards the world around her with childlike wonder, demonstrating a profound innocence tied to ignorance rather than virtue. While her son eventually comes of age and moves away, Veronika largely stays the same. Years after his birth, she returns to Siethener Lake in the hopes of rediscovering the old feeling that had once brought her Hans: "Sie wartete auf den Schmerz. Mit jedem Schwimmzug erhoffte sie sich etwas von ihm. Veronika Dankschön wußte nicht, was das sein könnte, das ihr eine Rettung von diesem einzwängenden Gefühl bringen würde" (*Gipshut*, 178; She waited for the pain. With every swim stroke she hoped for something from him. Veronika Dankschön did not know what could bring her salvation from this restrictive feeling). Whereas Rapunzel and her fairy-tale cohort find redemption through maternity and marriage, Veronika remains trapped, an eternal child wishing for rescue.[28] This immobility, combined with damaging relationships and her eventual suicide, points an accusing finger at the surrounding community. Veronika's sexual assault and ensuing treatment contradict the assumptions of equality under socialism in the GDR, a strong indictment of a society that has utterly failed her.

---

28 Hensel's oeuvre often features protagonists who never quite grow up, or who even revert back to childhood. See, for instance, *Lärchenau* (2008), *Hallimasch* (1989; Honey Colored Agaric), and *Tanz am Kanal* (1994; *Dance by the Canal*, 2017).

Veronika's fairy tale–like unworldliness prevents her not only from recognizing the injustices done to her but also from seeking reparations for them. Hensel's depiction of extreme innocence and social and political structures of violence serve as a reminder that keeping girls and women in the dark renders them not virtuous but, rather, vulnerable.

Knowledge and Innocence in Franck's *Die Mittagsfrau*

The abandonment that characterizes Veronika's experiences of motherhood and upsets the progression of the Maiden's Tragedy plays an equally disruptive role in Franck's *Die Mittagsfrau*,[29] which explores themes of knowledge, perceived innocence, and violence. Franck's novel follows the story of Helene Würsich, a young woman of Jewish descent, as she navigates the increasingly threatening political climate of a girlhood before and during the First World War through the years of the Third Reich. Following a troubled childhood, Helene moves to Berlin to stay with her aunt. Subject to the unwanted attentions of her aunt's lover, Erich, Helene finds no refuge there, but her luck seems to change when she meets and marries the engineer Wilhelm. Wilhelm learns of her Jewish heritage and helps her forge a new Aryan identity as Alice Sehmisch. Like the count, Wilhelm appears at first as a rescuer, but his sympathies with National Socialism and knowledge of her secret render him a patent threat. Their marriage is marked by physical and verbal abuse that begins on their wedding night after Wilhelm discovers that Helene is not a virgin. Throughout their union, he repeatedly rapes her, and the text strongly implies that their son, Peter, is a product of this violence. Near the end of the war, Wilhelm leaves his family for another woman. Helene, fighting depression and a stifling indifference to the role of motherhood, struggles to care for her son. She eventually decides that he would fare better without her and leaves Peter at a train station, with the address of a nearby relative in his suitcase.

Through indirect parallels and motifs, as well as direct intertextual references, Franck forges connections to Kleist's novella, capitalizing on themes of innocence and violence. As a young girl, Helene stumbles across a collection of nineteenth-century literature in her father's library, and figures such as Goethe's Werther and Kleist's marquise become her

---

29 The title of Franck's novel hints at another similarity between the two recent texts. "Die Mittagsfrau," or Lady Midday, is a witchlike figure from Sorbian mythology. Franck's narrative mentions the eponymous "Mittagsfrau" by name only once, but Lady Midday, also known as the Pschespoldnitza, plays a central role in Hensel's *Gipshut*.

confidants.[30] In an unstable household with a violent mother, an abusive older sister, and a recently deceased father, this small archive is Helene's only refuge. She seeks solace in these familiar figures, especially the marquise, "deren Ohnmacht Helene noch für sonderbar und unglaublich hielt" (126; "whose fainting fit Helene still thought extraordinary and incredible," *Blindness,* 120). Helene's skeptical response to the marquise's blackout seems a darkly ironic foreshadowing of the sexual violence she herself endures later; for while the marquise's assault is neatly hidden behind a dash, Helene—as well as the reader—must experience Wilhelm's aggressions with extreme clarity.

Like the third stage of the Maiden's Tragedy, the catastrophe, Helene's pregnancy is initiated by violence, and Franck connects this brutality to the perceived loss of innocence on her wedding night. While the abusive Wilhelm would surely have found some "reason" for his cruelty, it is the disruption of Helene's imagined purity that foments his rage. Beyond the question of virginity, Wilhelm is infuriated by Helene's evident knowledge of the act of sex and of her own body. Puzzled by her initial passion, Wilhelm compares Helene to a wildcat,[31] a dehumanizing accusation that stages her pleasure as transgression, and he turns to violence as a means of taming her wayward sexuality. Fully cognizant of the cause of her pregnancy, Helene's knowledge sets her apart from the marquise and Veronika, even as Wilhelm's punishing fascination with innocence connects her story to biblical discourses of virgin motherhood. Her pregnancy is not "immaculate," but Wilhelm's obsession with immaculateness and the virtue that he demands in his victim are closely related to the innocence of the unconscious marquise and the wholly naive Veronika. Wilhelm's use of force against his wife not only functions as a reassertion of control but also constitutes a means by which to divest his wife of any enjoyment of sex, a brutal denial of her knowledge, agency, and self.

Helene's Aryan identity as Alice, an amalgam of traits that he wishes to see in his wife, virtue included, is a construct of Wilhelm's creation, crafted in his imagination and supported by counterfeit documents. His affection for her is contingent on the fantasy of Aryan purity; by calling her Alice, Wilhelm asserts power and knowledge over his wife. The right to name evokes both biblical and fairy-tale practices,[32] and in Wilhelm's case, it signifies a colonizing act that likens Helene to a piece of unclaimed land. Wilhelm's knowledge extends to a form of ownership derived from

---

30   Franck, *Mittagsfrau,* 126.

31   Franck, *Mittagsfrau,* 347.

32   In the Grimm tales "Cinderella" and "Rumpelstiltskin," for example, both power and weakness are tied to the discovery of a name.

naming Helene, an act inextricably linked to violence.[33] Wilhelm projects himself—his will and his sense of identity—upon Helene, whose own name begins to sound like a foreign word to her ears.[34] With every utterance of the name "Alice," the original Helene Würsich seems to disappear, an annihilation of her identity that occurs both metaphorically and legally. Indeed, the first and only time Wilhelm calls her "Helene" is when he comes to realize that he is not her first lover,[35] a subtle acknowledgment that the woman he has created for himself does not exist.

The violence characterizing Helene's marriage also plays a role in the novel's depiction of childbirth. Of the three texts discussed here, *Mittagsfrau* focuses most heavily on the suffering of the mother during labor. Whereas the marquise handily births the babe in less than a sentence, a narrative complement to the mere dash that signaled his conception, Franck's visceral account of labor and birth emphasizes physical and emotional pain.[36] After struggling alone by foot through the icy streets to the hospital, Helene finds herself at the mercy of a midwife whose militaristic manner and intrusive hands seem to be at odds with her own instincts.[37] Like Veronika's experience in the lake, which narratively links the stages of labor with the earlier scene of abuse, Helene's delivery is plagued by memories of violence at the hands of Wilhelm: "Er hatte sie einmal am Ohr gezogen, als er wütend gewesen war, dass sie eine Falte in seinem Hemd übersehen hatte. Er hatte ihr Ohr zwischen seine Finger genommen und sie am Ohr aus der Küche ins Schlafzimmer geschleift. Wieder eine Wehe, das Ziehen war jetzt so schmerzhaft, dass Helene sich unmerklich über dem angespannten Bauch krümmte" (370–71; "He had once pulled her ear really hard when he was in a fury because she had overlooked a crease in his shirt, had taken her earlobe between his fingers and dragged her out of the kitchen and into the bedroom. Another contraction; they were so painful now that Helene bent over her tense belly," *Blindness*, 364–65). Much like the narrator in *Gipshut*, Franck's narrator smoothly transitions from memories of Wilhelm's past cruelty to Helene's immediate suffering during childbirth. Whereas Veronika's memories ironically fail to clue her in to the cause of her pain, Helene is

---

33 Sabina Sestigiani, *Writing Colonisation: Violence, Landscape, and the Act of Naming in Modern Italian and Australian Literature* (New York: Peter Lang, 2014), 3.
34 Franck, *Mittagsfrau*, 346.
35 Franck, *Mittagsfrau*, 346.
36 While much of Helene's story can be read as a subversive retelling of the Grimms' fairy tales, this focus on pregnancy, labor, and suffering constitutes a sharp break from the conventional fairy-tale practice of omitting nearly all references to or experiences of pregnancy, despite the common employment of long-awaited pregnancy as a plot point.
37 Franck, *Mittagsfrau*, 373.

acutely aware of Wilhelm's past and future brutality. The textual parallels linking Helene's labor with the patterns of abuse in her marriage remind the reader that Helene is vulnerable to violence both within and outside of the home, independent of time or space.

As an experienced nurse, Helene is familiar with the processes of labor and birth, and yet her astonishment nearly equals that of Veronika when she discovers that she has borne a son, rather than the long-expected daughter: "Damit hatte Helene nicht gerechnet. Sie hatte nie an einen Jungen gedacht, immer an ein Mädchen" (375; "Helene hadn't expected this. She had never thought of a boy, it was always going to be a girl," *Blindness*, 369). The initial warmth she had felt begins to dissolve as she considers the boy, and the cold relationship she later develops with Peter echoes the distance between herself and her own mother, who had resented her living children for being daughters. Like Veronika, who fears that her child's otherworldly moniker has created a barrier between them, Helene feels wholly disconnected from her son, hesitating even to give him a name.[38] Unlike Wilhelm, who simply decides that Helene should be called Alice, Helene cannot so blithely avail herself of that right. For her, the mother-child bond is not enough to imply closeness or even belonging: "Peter gehörte ihr nicht, sie hatte ihn geboren, aber er war nicht ihr Eigentum und nicht ihre Errungenschaft" (385; "Peter didn't belong to her, she had given birth to him but he was not her property, not her own great achievement," *Blindness*, 379). By dissociating her from the "achievements" of conception and birth, these thoughts further implicate Wilhelm as sole architect of Peter's being, with Helene as unwilling participant.

Unlike Veronika and the marquise and in stark contrast to fairy-tale heroines, Helene feels no joy at the prospect of motherhood, and indeed the role of "mother" seems to be thrust upon her.[39] Rather than liberating her from a period of suffering, as is often the case in Maiden's Tragedies, Helene's initial acceptance of domestic life transforms into a sense of imprisonment within the repressive realm of the family. Her performance of domesticity hinges on the real threat of violence—Wilhelm possesses knowledge of a secret that could kill her—and it ends only when Helene abandons Peter at the train station. After Wilhelm leaves, Helene realizes that she cannot provide what Peter needs and decides to send him to a relative. Despite her good intentions, her actions render her a

---

38   Franck, *Mittagsfrau*, 376.
39   See Alexandra Merley Hill's discussion of "maternal drag" in "Motherhood as Performance: (Re)Negotiations of Motherhood in Contemporary German Literature," *Studies in 20th and 21st Century Literature* 35 (2011): 74–94, and in *Playing House: Motherhood, Intimacy, and Domestic Spaces in Julia Franck's Fiction* (Oxford: Peter Lang, 2012), chapter 4.

stepmother figure, like those in fairy tales, shifting from an obligatory nurturing role to an antagonistic one. Much like the stepmothers in fairy tales who do not satisfactorily embody the maternal and thus become "wicked," Helene fails to perform the mothering role expected of her and is relegated to the role of villain, at least in the eyes of her son.[40] In turning her protagonist into the wicked stepmother, Franck transforms Romantic narrative expectations to reveal a harsher version of the fairy tale, openly exposing and condemning the patterns of violence against women that coerce them into performing domestic roles and ultimately render them perpetrators themselves.[41]

Beyond her vulnerability to her husband within the family circle, Helene also experiences violence within the context of warfare. In the frame narrative at the story's opening, the reader sees the horrors of war through Peter's eyes, including his mother's rape at the hands of Russian soldiers. He witnesses the brutal attack through a crack in the doorway. After the men leave, they find Peter waiting outside on the landing: "Der letzte hatte sich umgedreht und Peter auf deutsch etwas hinaufgerufen: Einen wie dich habe ich auch zu Hause. Pass bloß auf deine Mutter auf, dabei hatte der Soldat lachend den Zeigefinger gehoben" (19; "The last of them had turned and called something up to Peter in German: I have a lad like you at home, keep an eye on your mother. And the soldier, smiling, had wagged one forefinger," *Blindness*, 13). The man's cruelly flippant remark establishes a perverse reorientation of the family structure within the narrative, one in which the invading soldiers take the place of the absent father and husband, exercising the same kind of violence against Helene that she had experienced at the hands of Wilhelm. This reveals a grotesque parallel between the horrors of the battlefield and the domestic circle, illustrating the role that women's bodies play as part of a landscape of spoils, a larger constellation of violence that hinges on

---

40   To distance Helene even further from idealized maternal figures in fairy tales, Franck capitalizes on fairy-tale imagery; for example, in a mushroom-foraging scene in the forest. In an echo of the Grimms' "Hänsel and Gretel," Helene briefly leaves Peter behind as she greedily devours a patch of mushrooms. After an increasingly desperate search, Peter gives up on finding his mother and, like Hänsel, turns toward home. Helene, in contrast, savors the mushrooms and her new-found solitude. By focalizing this scene through both figures' perspectives, Franck creates a fairy tale–like interlude that casts Helene as both negligent mother and empathetic protagonist simultaneously, challenging the conventional fairy-tale binary of "good" and "wicked" women.

41   See Elisabeth Krimmer's "The Representation of Wartime Rape in Julia Franck's *Die Mittagsfrau* and Jenny Erpenbeck's *Heimsuchung*," *Gegenwartsliteratur* 14 (2015): 35–60.

both patriarchal and nationalist sensibilities.[42] Like the marquise, who is threatened by enemy soldiers and her "savior" alike, and like Veronika, who is doubly marginalized via her gender and her intellectual differences, Helene is not safe anywhere.

The "Romance of Rape" in the "Female" Fairy Tale

The traditional paradigm of the Maiden's Tragedy, this familiar fairy tale that guides its female protagonist from girlhood to motherhood, is predicated on sexual violence. For the beleaguered protagonists, the road to salvation hinges on the satisfactory completion of domestic obligations. Typically, the women at the center of these stories have little to no recourse against their aggressors. In evoking these discourses of violence, innocence, and "immaculate" conception, Kerstin Hensel and Julia Franck draw on nineteenth-century traditions, not only through direct allusion to Kleist but also through the employment of fairy-tale imagery and narrative paradigms. This application of the Maiden's Tragedy pattern highlights not only the connections but also the disruptions between nineteenth-century and contemporary literature, especially regarding conceptions of gender. Kleist imagines a heroine who is redeemed through the fulfillment of domestic roles, but the perpetrator of her assault claims his share of her happy ending. The implication in this male-authored text that the marquise *needs* redemption underscores the intensely troubling "romance of rape" thematized in this narrative and so many others that follow the "female" fairy-tale paradigm. In contrast, Hensel and Franck dismantle this romance by emphasizing the consequences of sexual assault for the victim, a gritty deconstruction of the Maiden's Tragedy that subverts the familiar sequence and censures its enduring literary prevalence. Like activist Tarana Burke's engagement with "collective trauma" on a global scale,[43] these authors highlight the structural patterns of violence, inextricably linked to sexism, racism, and ableism, and the enduring pain of assault. In the twenty-first century, Kleist's obfuscating dash is replaced by new narrative devices and symbols, but for the protagonists, who are unable to say #MeToo, the underlying patterns of violence and enforced ignorance, and the oppressing paradigms of female domesticity, remain the same.

---

42 See Anna Froula's preface to *Heroism and Gender in War Films*, ed. Karen A. Ritzenhoff and Jakub Kazecki (New York: Palgrave Macmillan, 2014), xi–xv.

43 Burke, "MeToo."

4: Female Sacrifice, Sexual Assault, and Dehumanization: Bourgeois Tragedy, Horror, and the Making of *Jud Süß*

Deborah Janson

S EXUAL ABUSE AND FEMALE SACRIFICE are constitutive elements of Veit Harlan's notorious Nazi propaganda film, *Jud Süß* (Jew Süss). Promoted by Joseph Goebbels and released in 1940 to foment hatred toward the Jews, this film features the villainous Joseph Süß Oppenheimer, a cunning and greedy financier from Frankfurt's Jewish ghetto who gains favor with Karl Alexander, the new duke of Württemberg. Though loosely based on real events that took place in Stuttgart in the 1730s, the film distorts historical facts—for example, by depicting Oppenheimer as a Jew bent on having his way with bourgeois Christian women. From young maidens forced to perform sexual favors for the duke at Oppenheimer's behest to Oppenheimer's rape of the young, innocent, and already-spoken-for Dorothea Sturm, sexual violence against women propels the film's action. The work thus builds on several established genres that revolve around the abuse and death of beautiful women. These genres span gendered and anti-Semitic expressions of abjection in portraying victimization, violence, and exclusion.

The two cultural antecedents I wish to consider in this context form a surprising pair: eighteenth-century bourgeois tragedy and twentieth-century horror film. The former is well represented by Gotthold Ephraim Lessing's *Miß Sara Sampson* (1755) and *Emilia Galotti* (1772), two works that closely adhere to the tropes of the genre, featuring a close father-daughter relationship, a weak or absent mother, a tyrannical and depraved aristocracy, and the seduction of a virtuous yet corruptible maiden. The horror film, too, prominently features women as victims of sexual abuse, as exemplified by Friedrich Murnau's *Nosferatu, eine Symphonie des Grauens* (1922; *Nosferatu: A Symphony of Horror*), in which a monstrous male character becomes obsessed with hunting down and killing an innocent but alluring female. By discussing features common to these works, this essay illuminates the influence of the German cultural heritage on the making of *Jud Süß*. In turn, these commonalities shed light on representations of victimization central to the #MeToo movement, thereby revealing different manifestations of the rape culture character-istic of male-dominated societies. For example, like the prince in *Emilia Galotti*, perpetrators of sexual assault who belong to the ruling class—to the rich and powerful—may feel they have the right to any woman they fancy without fear of punishment. Conversely—like *Nosferatu*'s Count Orlok or Süß Oppenheimer—rapists may be depicted as "monsters and outliers" who deserve to be punished because they do not behave like normal, upstanding men. In addition to typecasting male predators, these works also call into question the motivations of female victims, reveal-ing the notion common in patriarchal societies that women are "asking" to be assaulted. Demonstrating the heroines' conflicted sexuality, these stories suggest that women strive to maintain their reputation of sexual innocence while secretly longing to be seduced. This depiction reflects the necessity of condemning female desire while sacrificing even the most honorable of women in order to uphold the patriarchal social order.

Although the works I examine in this chapter differ in aesthetics and ideology, they share not only the underlying goal of preserving paternal wholeness but also the corresponding abjection of the female victim—whose vulnerability is always constructed as sexual—and the failure of upstanding male citizens to protect the women they claim to cherish. These male representatives of the social norm—the victims' fathers, fian-cés, and husbands—fit the centuries-old definition of "Man"; that is, they are white, Western, heterosexual, Christian, bourgeois men who have for centuries viewed themselves as the "truly" human and excluded all "oth-ers" from this designation.[1] In *Nosferatu* and *Jud Süß*, the rejection of Man's human others includes not only women but also the monster/Jew, demonstrating the hegemonic and intersectional nature of social exclusion common among patriarchal, sexist, racist, and xenophobic communities.

Corruptible Virtue: Flawed Maidens in Lessing's Bourgeois Tragedies

Building on the genre's British origins, the bourgeois tragedy came of age in Germany in the mid-1750s with the publication of Lessing's *Miß Sara Sampson*. Followed by other notable examples, including Lessing's *Emilia Galotti* in 1772 and Friedrich Schiller's *Kabale und Liebe* (*Intrigue and Love*) in 1784, bourgeois tragedies sought to further the emancipation of the developing middle class by establishing its moral authority over the aristocracy. Lessing in particular focused on the importance of cultivating

---

1   For an in-depth discussion of this exclusionary concept of "Man," see Sylvia Wynter, "Unsettling the Coloniality of Being/Power/Truth/Freedom: Towards the Human, after Man, Its Overrepresentation—An Argument," *New Centennial Review* 3, no. 3 (2003): 257–337.

Mitleid (compassion) among the viewing public, since for him, it was the most desirable of all moral qualities. To this end, he introduced the father-daughter dyad that has become a standard feature of the genre. In both of Lessing's bourgeois tragedies, the father plays a central role as a respected, upstanding citizen who adores and is adored by his loving, pure, and dutiful daughter. Yet despite her virtue, the bourgeois daughter falls victim to a nobleman's seduction and ultimately dies. With this tragic scenario, Lessing sought to arouse compassion in his viewers. Even greater than the sorrow they ought to experience over the death of such an honorable and beautiful young woman, however, was the anguish they should feel for her father. Because his daughter is his most prized possession and an important part of his own identity, her death and the preceding damage to her reputation cause him unbearable suffering. Knowing this, the eighteenth-century viewer shed tears for the father's loss and left the theater a better person.

Although historians have generally lauded the bourgeoisie's efforts to distinguish itself morally, casting bourgeois women as paragons of virtue can hardly be viewed as emancipatory. Indeed, as Susan Gustafson established in her book *Absent Mothers and Orphaned Fathers*, Lessing did not seek to promote a society that treated men and women equally. Instead, his sincere desire to create art that improves an individual's moral character by increasing his capacity for feeling sympathy was bound to a model of subject formation steeped in paternal narcissism. In his works, mothers are either dead, marginalized, or dangerous because their existence poses a threat to the father's authority and to the patriarchal social order that he represents. In fact, Gustafson maintains, even if the mother is not physically present in these works, she is not absent either, serving instead as "an integral component of Lessing's patriarchal aesthetics."[2] Gustafson writes:

> There would be no need for an exclusively patriarchal-aesthetic order, if it were not for the (perceived) threat to that order constituted by the mother. Lessing's tragedies become the stage for the dramatic struggle between fathers and mothers for control over the development of their progeny. The father-daughter dyad masks the mother's presence in the plays. There is a myth of familial unity that reflects a paternal concern for the affirmation of a whole, unified, masculine imago.[3]

---

2   Susan E. Gustafson, *Absent Mothers and Orphaned Fathers: Narcissism and Abjection in Lessing's Aesthetic and Dramatic Production* (Detroit: Wayne State University Press 1995), 14.

3   Gustafson, *Absent Mothers*, 14.

What is narcissistic about the father's relationship with his daughter is, of course, that he sees himself in her. Her behavior must reflect his values, and nothing should encroach upon their unity. His greatest fear, Gustafson writes, "is to become a father . . . without a daughter to mirror and adore him. The mother in the daughter, her maternal body and imagination threaten the father's image of himself . . . as unified with his daughter and sheltered from the mother."[4] Besides the perceived maternal threat, a daughter's developing interest in a man not chosen by her father undermines his authority and further endangers the exclusivity of the father-daughter relationship. In *Miß Sara Sampson*, for example, Sara has run off with her aristocratic suitor, Mellefont, to an inn of ill repute. Though Sara's father, Sir William, is prepared to forgive her transgression provided she still loves him, he waits too long to express how he feels, and as a result is unable to protect her from the tragic events that unfold during the final act, when Sara is poisoned by Marwood (Mellefont's former lover), Marwood escapes, and Mellefont commits suicide. Sara's transgression must have such dire consequences because saving her would not result in the sacrifice needed to reestablish the stability of the patriarchal social order that female desire has threatened. In the end, Sir William decides to raise Arabella—Marwood and Mellefont's illegitimate child—as his own daughter, regarding her as Sara's legacy. In this way, Sir William once again has a daughter to adore him. The narcissistic father-daughter dyad and paternal ideal of wholeness are restored, and the maternal threat is eliminated, at least until Arabella grows up and becomes a sensual young woman and potential mother herself.

Gustafson calls on Julia Kristeva's concept of abjection to explain the necessity of the bourgeois maiden's sacrifice within Lessing's system of paternal narcissism. According to Kristeva, all cultures depend on processes of abjection to expel individuals who disturb "identity, system, order" and do not respect "borders, positions, rules."[5] People who do not uphold values, institutions, and relationships that provide stability to the social contract and to culture and subject formation are criminals within that system—they are "the other" that elicits feelings of disgust and must be excluded. A culture steeped in paternal narcissism requires the abjection of the maternal to preserve the patriarchal rule of law. Lessing's plays exemplify this belief system in several different ways. Either the mother is already dead at the play's outset, as is the case in *Miß Sara Sampson*, or, if still alive, she is depicted as frivolous and may even be held responsible for her daughter's demise. In *Emilia Galotti*, for example, the father's criticism of his wife, Claudia's, priorities and competence as a mother suggests

---

4   Gustafson, *Absent Mothers*, 123.
5   Julia Kristeva, *The Powers of Horror: An Essay on Abjection* (New York: Columbia University Press 1982), 4.

a power struggle over the best way to raise their daughter. In response to Claudia's lament that Emilia will no longer live in the city of Guastalla once she is married to Count Appiani, Odoardo accuses her of wanting to reside in town for the wrong reasons—not for their daughter's education but for access to court functions and other frivolous distractions. Odoardo is horrified to learn that Claudia and Emilia attended a social event at which Hettore Gonzaga, the prince of Guastalla, was present and, even worse, that Claudia is flattered by the prince's obvious interest in Emilia's beauty, vivaciousness, and intellect. Focusing on the salacious possibilities posed by such an encounter, Odoardo scolds his wife for being a vain, foolish mother and tells her that he could not bear to have his daughter's reputation sullied through contact with such a voluptuary.[6] He feels that Claudia has put their daughter's moral development at risk and makes it clear that he could not tolerate his daughter straying from the bourgeois moral code he lives by. This view of female sexuality and maternal ambition as threats to the patriarchal social contract foreshadows the necessity of Emilia's abjection in the play's final scene.

Odoardo is of course correct in his assessment of Hettore Gonzaga's personality and intentions. The prince is a womanizer who enjoys all the wealth, power, and privilege that his position as the local ruler affords him. From the moment he sets eyes on Emilia he is taken by her exquisite beauty and pursues an intimate relationship with her despite the calamitous effect his pursuit will have on Emilia's life. While the prince is less callous than his evil adviser, Marinelli, he represents the depravity and sense of entitlement that typifies the noble class in Lessing's bourgeois tragedies. Count Appiani, in contrast, is as honorable a man as any bourgeois father could hope to have as a son-in-law, despite his noble heritage. As a result, Odoardo is eager to welcome him into the family, and Appiani is similarly enthusiastic about becoming Odoardo's son-in-law, inspired as he is by Odoardo's "manly virtue."[7] The qualities the men admire in each other enhance their self-image and impress on the viewers which standards and personality traits are to be accorded high social value. The play's contrast between paternal virtue and maternal failings is central to Lessing's emphasis on upholding the patriarchal order of the rising bourgeoisie regardless of the cost to women. This explains why the maidens' fiancés, husbands, and fathers fail to protect them and sometimes—as is the case in this play—are even the direct cause of the heroine's death.

The audience learns about the virtues and vices of the different characters and about what took place in any given scene through dialogues

6   Gotthold Ephraim Lessing, *Emilia Galotti*, vol. 2 of *Gotthold Ephraim Lessings sämtliche Schriften*, ed. Karl Lachmann and Franz Muncker, 3rd ed. (Stuttgart: Göschen, 1886), 398.
7   Lessing, *Emilia Galotti*, 403.

that provide conflicting perspectives. Thus, the play makes use of what Andrea Speltz refers to as polyperspectivity, an aesthetic approach that relies on "two or more figure perspectives to describe a particular scene or event."[8] According to Speltz, polyperspectivity was used to discuss problems of female desire in several eighteenth-century works, including *Emilia Galotti*. Lessing's play, Speltz maintains, features "a seemingly asexual, Daphne-like female who flees a male admirer in order to thwart an attack on her innocence."[9] Yet the play casts doubt on the sincerity of its heroine's desire to escape her seducer, leaving open the question about what motivates her actions and raising suspicions about her corruptibility: "Did the heroine flee in order to elude capture, or did she flee in order to conceal her desire to stay, to succumb to her seducer?"[10] A prime example of polyperspectivity in *Emilia Galotti* is provided by the conflicting and ambiguous descriptions of what took place when Emilia went to church alone on her wedding day. Emilia, the prince, and Orsina, the prince's previous mistress who is still in love with him and who sent men to spy on him in church, all offer different versions of this event. When telling her mother about the encounter, Emilia halfway admits that she wanted to sin, but she retracts her confession when her mother expresses disbelief. Nonetheless, she professes "daß fremdes Laster uns, wider unsern Willen, zu Mitschuldigen machen kann!"[11] (that the vice of others can make us accomplices against our will), thus revealing that she has feelings for the prince and therefore believes that she is partly to blame for his advances. Here, the play implies that young, beautiful women become victims of sexual abuse not only because dangerous men pursue them but because of their own moral weakness. They are incapable of living up to standards of female virtue and innocence that have been imposed on them. While Lessing depicts the inner turmoil that arises when moral expectations collide with sensual desires, and by doing so elicits feelings of compassion and fear in his viewers, he does not call into question the necessity of sacrificing women to maintain the patriarchal social order. Similarly, he does not challenge the notion that female desire is as responsible as male aggression in the victimization of women.

More than other characters in the play, Emilia reflects a mix of contradictory traits. She is weak and strong, fearful and decisive, sensual and moral, corruptible and innocent. This combination makes it impossible for her to avoid feeling sexually aroused when she falls victim to

---

8   Andrea Speltz, "Daphne's Desires: Polyperspectivity and Female Happiness in La Roche's *Fräulein von Sternheim*, Wieland's *Agathon*, and Lessing's *Emilia Galotti*," *Seminar* 47, no. 2 (2011): 157–72, here 157–58.

9   Speltz, "Daphne's Desires," 157.

10   Speltz, "Daphne's Desires," 157.

11   Lessing, *Emilia Galotti*, 399.

the prince's seductive powers but resolute enough to choose death over a depraved and immoral existence as his mistress. In the final scene, she admits to her father that she was aroused sensually by the pleasure she experienced at the Grimaldis when she first met the prince and that it took her weeks to control those feelings. With Appiani dead, Emilia recognizes that she is in danger of succumbing to sexual temptation. Having internalized the bourgeois moral code that she learned from her father, she is unable "to reconcile the demands of her morality with the demands of her body."[12] She goads her father into killing her by referencing the fifth-century Roman legend of Virginia, in which a father murders his daughter to prevent her from being taken into slavery, implying that such brave and honorable fathers no longer exist. Thus taunted, Odoardo cannot bear the idea that his daughter could become the prince's whore, and he stabs her to death. Curiously, some literary scholars have blamed Emilia for her father's deed, even though the text provides evidence that Odoardo contemplated killing her before she spoke with him, and even though fathers should protect their children rather than give in to demands that will harm them. Since Lessing based his play on the Roman legend, Odoardo's act of filicide as a means of defending his daughter's honor is not surprising. Yet Lessing's play differs from the original in that it contains no political critique; unlike Virginia's murder, Emilia's death does not result in a popular uprising with progressive political consequences. According to Linda Schulte-Sasse, the goal of eighteenth-century bourgeois tragedies such as Lessing's is to "moralize all citizens, especially the aristocracy, by demonstrating the tragic consequences of the abuse of power."[13] Yet this play's tragic outcome stems as much from Emilia's and Odoardo's internalization of bourgeois moral concepts as it does from the aristocracy's tyranny. Lessing's desire to improve the bourgeoisie's social standing by focusing on moral behavior does little to address class and gender inequities in a manner that would result in real social change. Indeed, at the play's conclusion, Odoardo turns himself over to the authorities; the prince tells Marinelli to go into hiding; and the prince takes no responsibility for what happened to Emilia, justifying his pursuit of her as simply being human. Emilia's death is necessary because the prince's misconduct and Emilia's sensual response to it have disturbed the paternal social order. As will become clear in this essay's discussions of Murnau's *Nosferatu* and Harlan's *Jud Süß*, Lessing's plays articulate an understanding of women's role in society that has persisted over the centuries. As representatives of the #MeToo movement have demonstrated, sexual violence continues to provide the ongoing rationale

---

12 Speltz, "Daphne's Desires," 170.

13 Linda Schulte-Sasse, "The Jew as Other under National Socialism: Veit Harlan's *Jud Süß*," *German Quarterly* 61, no. 1 (1988): 22–49, here 23.

for viewing the sacrifice of female desire and women's lives as appropriate means for restoring order in male-dominated societies.

The Victim as Monster in *Nosferatu*

At first glance, it may seem that the eighteenth-century bourgeois tragedy and the twentieth-century horror film make odd bedfellows. Unlike Lessing's plays, the horror film does not strive to improve its viewers' morals by increasing their capacity to empathize with others. Correspondingly, it features neither a close father-daughter relationship nor the father's devastation over the loss of his daughter. Instead, the horror film seeks to titillate and frighten the audience by mixing sex and violence, often depicting erotically charged situations in which a monstrous male hunts down and kills a young woman. Yet despite some differences regarding intent and the presence or absence of a father (or mother) figure, the genres share an otherwise common constellation of character types and significant themes. Both feature a male antagonist who pursues a beautiful woman; a female protagonist who is pursued; and a traditional, upstanding representative of the Western patriarchal order, who, though he is the heroine's fiancé, husband, or father, proves incapable of protecting her. Both genres also rely on violence toward women to convey their message and propagate the chauvinist notion that women who are associated sexually with anyone other than their socially sanctioned partner deserve punishment. These similarities stem in part from a hegemonic understanding of sex as a form of power that belongs only to (certain) men. Female sexuality is portrayed as different from male sexuality, and women's desire for sexual autonomy is seen as a threat to male dominance. Although neither genre sanctions the predator's pursuit of the heroine, the degree to which he is punished depends on his social standing in the fictional work.

In *Emilia Galotti*, Emilia's upstanding fiancé, Count Appiani, plays a minor role in terms of the number of minutes he appears onstage and the number of lines he speaks. Most of what we learn about his honorable character, we learn from others. Despite his virtues, he is unable to survive the attack on his life, leaving Emilia in the midst of dangerous men, including her father. In *Nosferatu*, by contrast, Ellen's husband, Thomas Hutter, is central to the plot development and appears on-screen for more minutes than any other character. Yet he, too, is incapable of protecting his wife. Hutter's moral probity is less clear-cut than that of Appiani. The film initially presents Hutter as an optimistic, happy-go-lucky fellow who values the bourgeois pleasures that his budding affluence in Wisborg—a small town in northern Germany—affords him. He seems to care about Ellen's happiness yet does not know her well enough to understand her or keep her safe. For example, he thinks the chivalrous act of bringing Ellen flowers will please her, but it saddens her that he has killed the flowers to make her a bouquet. Hutter's employer, a real estate agent named Knock, easily convinces him to accept the lucrative assignment of traveling to a castle in the Carpathian Mountains to sell property in Wisborg to a wealthy client named Count Orlok, who, as we later learn, is Knock's vampiric master, Nosferatu. In accepting the job, Hutter not only dismisses Knock's sinister remark that it will cost him in "sweat and blood" but also scoffs at his wife's sense of foreboding, at warnings contained in a book about Nosferatu that he finds in an inn near the Transylvanian castle, and at the locals' alarm when they learn of his destination. In pursuit of money and adventure, Hutter is blind to danger, blithely ignoring warnings that if heeded could have saved Ellen's life. The threat posed by Count Orlok does not become clear to Hutter until he is directly confronted with it, at which point he has already allowed the count to see a picture of Ellen's "lovely neck" and sold him a house located directly across from his own. When Nosferatu assaults him in his castle at night, Hutter behaves like a damsel in distress, at first freezing and averting his eyes, then hiding under the bedsheets. In his blind pursuit of riches and his weakness when confronted with the power of the "other," Hutter fails to take appropriate action at crucial moments, clearing the way for a monstrous stranger to infiltrate Wisborg and placing not only his wife but all the town's residents in harm's way.

Although Hutter shows concern for his wife's safety both by the speed with which he returns home and his behavior after he has arrived, he is again ineffectual in his attempts to protect her. He makes her promise not to touch the book that he found at the inn, but he leaves it lying around the house for her to find. Unable to resist its pull, Ellen reads the book and learns how she can bring about an end to the "demonic nightmare" that has engulfed her town since Nosferatu's arrival.[14] As an "innocent maiden," she has the power to thwart the vampire's deadly attacks by enticing him to suckle her blood until dawn, when exposure to the sun's rays will kill him. In addition to her altruistic desire to save lives, the film hints at another reason why Ellen is willing to give herself up to the vampire. Through the somnambulistic trances that connected her with Hutter while he was in danger at Orlok's castle, she developed a psychic bond with the count. The film suggests this through several ambiguous scenes. For example, as the two competitors journeyed to Wisborg, Hutter by land and Orlok by sea, it was unclear whose arrival Ellen most anticipated. As we see on the screen and learn from an intertitle, the psychically gifted Ellen frequently sat at the ocean's edge, "scanning

---

14 One of the film's intertitles lets the viewers know what Ellen reads: "Deliverance is possible by no other means but that an innocent maiden maketh the vampire heed not the first crowing of the cock, this done by the sacrifice of her own bloode."

the waves and the horizon as she pined for her beloved." Similarly, when Ellen emerges from another trance exclaiming, "I must go to him. He's coming," the film shows both men approaching Wisborg simultaneously. As was the case in *Emilia Galotti*, the film's heroine appears conflicted and, also like Emilia, is depicted as both intuitive and rational, fearful and decisive, innocent and corruptible. Although Ellen becomes convinced that she must die, not—as in Emilia's case—to save her reputation but to save the townspeople, both women feel attracted to the monsters who pursue them, and in both instances, their deaths restore the mundane, bourgeois, patriarchal social order.

The monster in horror movies, like the antagonist in bourgeois tragedies, is alluring, powerful, and dangerous. Yet much more so than his literary counterpart, the horror-film monster is also frightening in his appearance and insatiable in his predatory appetite. Count Orlok offers the perfect prototype. His tall, shadowy figure enshrouded in a dark cloak, with pale skin, bald head, claw-like fingernails, and ratlike fangs, is terrifying to behold, and his need for human blood is limitless. Yet, Count Orlok is feared not only because of his horrifying appearance but also because of the threat he poses to established social norms, including the dominance of "Man" and the bourgeois institution of marriage. Like other horror-film monsters, and unlike the upstanding but emasculated representatives of patriarchal society such as Thomas Hutter, he is endowed with a sexual potency that captures the viewers' interest. As a hypersexualized male "Other" with fangs rather than a (functioning) penis, Count Orlok resides outside of patriarchy's heteronormativity, requiring his abjection from it. As Linda Williams points out, a horror monster such as Nosferatu is "remarkably like the woman in the eyes of the traumatized male: a biological freak with impossible and threatening appetites that suggest a frightening potency precisely where the normal male would perceive a lack."[15] This difference, Williams continues, "should not be interpreted as an eruption of the normally repressed animal sexuality of the civilized male (the monster as a double for the male viewer and characters in the film), but as the feared power and potency of a different kind of sexuality (the monster as double for the woman)."[16] The vampire's sexual difference aligns him with his female prey. In both instances, power lies in a nonphallic sexuality. Despite their "lack," both the monster and the woman threaten traditional male dominance. Thus,

---

15 Linda Williams, "When the Woman Looks," in *Re-Vision: Essays in Feminist Film Criticism*, ed. Mary Ann Doane, Patricia Mellencamp, and Linda Williams, vol. 3, The American Film Institute Monograph Series 3, no. 3 (Frederick, MD: University Publications of America, 1984), 83–99, here 87.

16 Williams, "When the Woman Looks," 87.

as Heide Schlüpmann suggests, the affinity between Ellen and Count Orlok dooms the heroine from the start:

Die spezifische Relation zwischen beiden, der Frau und dem Monster, der die Aufmerksamkeit des Films gilt, verrät noch eine ursprüngliche Einheit, die sich am Ende auch wiederherstellt. In der Wiedervereinigung gewinnt jedoch nicht der weibliche Blick seine Kraft zurück, sondern der Mann wird von der gespensti-schen Wiederkehr des Bedrohlichen erlöst, wenn auch seiner Gattin beraubt. Oder besser gesagt: in der Erlösung von der Frau besteht die Befreiung.[17]

[The specific relation between the two—the woman and the mon-ster—that is the film's focus betrays an original unity that is restored at the end. Yet the female gaze does not regain its power in the reunion; rather, the man is released from the ghostly return of that which threatens him, though he loses his wife in the process. Or to be more precise: liberation exists in deliverance from woman.]

When hegemonic heterosexual masculinity is threatened in the film, Ellen must be excluded from the sociosymbolic contract, calling to mind the abjection of women in bourgeois tragedies who pose a threat to paternal authority.

The film culminates in the long-awaited and titillating scene in which Count Orlok suckles blood from Ellen's neck. On numerous occasions prior to this, the viewer has seen the count gaze longingly at Ellen from his home across the canal. Once, when she and Hutter are together in her room, she points to the count's framed silhouette, declaring to her husband reproachfully, "That is what I look at—every night!" As the end nears, Nosferatu is again seen standing at his window, causing Ellen to awaken with a fright and to move toward the window with her arms out-stretched, as if under the vampire's spell. While Hutter is asleep in a chair, she throws open the window, a gesture that Nosferatu correctly inter-prets as an invitation. After feigning a faint, Ellen asks Hutter to fetch a doctor, thus clearing the way for her encounter with the vampire. By returning the count's gaze and sending her husband away, the plot makes Ellen responsible for her own victimization. As Orlok climbs the stairs and enters her room, we see his menacing shadow and the fear in Ellen's eyes as she staggers backward in sexualized terror, falls on the bed, and displays her neck for his pleasure. This scene bears witness not only to the horror Ellen is experiencing but also, as Williams points out, to an "affinity between monster and woman" that demonstrates "their similar

17 Heide Schlüpmann, "Der Spiegel des Grauens: Murnaus *Nosferatu*," *Frauen und Film* 49 (1990): 38–51, here 44.

status within patriarchal structures of seeing."[18] Hutter, who represents the status quo, is excluded as his wife and his rival unite. Ellen has allowed herself to be corrupted and, with her blood contaminated, must join her assailant in death. Both she and Count Orlok have threatened the stability of the social contract by transgressing its rules and thus deserve society's abjection. Although Hutter loses his wife, Ellen's sacrifice restores his position in what again becomes a male-dominated, monster-free (and plague-free) society. As the following analysis reveals, a similar scenario occurs in Veit Harlan's *Jud Süß*, which combines elements from bourgeois tragedies and horror films to promote a sexist and anti-Semitic worldview through the denigration of both women and Jews.

Corrupting and Corruptible Monsters: Dehumanizing Man's Human Others in Veit Harlan's *Jud Süß*

In its basic plot structure, *Jud Süß* draws on the contrast between a morally superior middle class and a corrupt and depraved aristocracy characteristic of eighteenth-century bourgeois tragedies. This juxtaposition relies on the usual character types: a loving father; his virtuous daughter; an honorable young man who is the pure maiden's intended; an older, less principled, and more experienced member of the court who pursues her; and the "absent" mother, whom the viewer assumes is dead. Yet as an anti-Semitic film intended to generate hatred toward the Jews, *Jud Süß* blames the harmful events and tragic outcome on Süß's evil scheming and corrupt influence, rather than on the aristocracy as a whole. Without the Jew's infiltration of Stuttgart, its upstanding citizens could have continued to provide moral education on both the private and public levels while maintaining the patriarchal status quo. In replacing the aristocratic villain with a monstrous Jew, the anti-Semitic discourse alters the bourgeois tragedy's goal of reducing tyranny and immorality within German society, blaming social strife instead on the alien and parasitic Jew. In this regard, the film calls to mind horror movies such as *Nosferatu,* in which the villain—like Süß—is an outsider who brings harm to an entire community, possesses a sexual potency that is frightening to the films' respectable men, and lusts after pure bourgeois women, violating them sexually and contaminating their blood.

Already in the film's opening, traditional elements of the bourgeois tragedy are discernable. Dorothea's father, Estate Counselor Sturm, presides over the swearing-in ceremony of the new duke in a room full of solemn men—the estate representatives who share Württemberg's

---

18 Williams, "When the Woman Looks," 85.

governance with the ruling aristocrat. Here and throughout the film, Sturm is presented as the most highly respected member of this most highly respected council. Even more clearly than the fathers in Lessing's plays, Sturm fulfills the dual function of representing the patriarchal social order and serving as head of his family, which consists of himself, his daughter, and her fiancé Karl Faber. Following the swearing-in ceremony, the first scene from within Sturm's home provides viewers with a picture of familial bliss: Dorothea sings a German folk song about love and fidelity while Faber accompanies her on the harpsichord.[19] Like eighteenth-century paintings of women grouped around this instrument, the setting expresses a "sense of peace, harmony and order" within both the family and the culture at large and provides a reassuring impression of the tranquility needed to make reproduction possible.[20] As Schulte-Sasse points out, numerous Nazi films used such images for similar purposes, with women at harpsichords representing domesticity and the associated continuation of the superior "Aryan" culture through reproduction.[21] In the aforementioned scene in *Jud Süß*, the betrothed couple is so blissfully in love that the promise of a joyous future with numerous Christian offspring hangs in the air. Though their love seems destined to last forever, the fleeting kiss that follows the song's conclusion, interrupted by Sturm's return home from court, foreshadows their short-lived marriage. The greeting between father and daughter illustrates the close bond between them as well as Dorothea's deference to her father's authority as she rushes off to carry out his directive to serve the food she has already prepared. During their Sunday dinner of roasted goose, Father Sturm toasts the duke, who has sworn to protect Württemberg and its citizens and to uphold its constitution. This slice of family life thus unites the public and private spheres, suggesting two possible outcomes. Either bourgeois moral ideals will have a positive influence on the entire society, including the aristocracy, or the corrupt and abusive practices of the aristocracy—exacerbated by the Jews who will soon infiltrate it—will have tragic consequences for the bourgeoisie by compromising its maidens' moral integrity and violating their sexuality.

Karl Faber, Dorothea's upstanding fiancé, also demonstrates the bourgeois tragedy's influence on the making of *Jud Süß*. Several traits of Faber's personality reflect cultural discourses that developed in the eighteenth century. On the one hand, he expresses the tender, heartfelt

---

19 The folk song that Dorothea sings, "All mein Gedanken, die ich hab', sind bei dir" (All my thoughts that I have are with you), has been traced back to the Middle Ages. It was popular during the Third Reich and included in many song-books of the period.

20 Schulte-Sasse, "The Jew as Other," 29.

21 Schulte-Sasse, "The Jew as Other," 28.

emotions of the private individual so important to sentimentalism, a midcentury movement of which Lessing was a main representative. This aspect of his personality is apparent, for example, in the above-described scene in which he and Dorothea perform the love song together.[22] In addition, the respect and veneration Faber shows Dorothea's father call to mind the mutual admiration felt by Appiani and Odoardo. On the other hand, when Faber's attention turns to politics, he becomes passionate and heated, taking on a revolutionary persona reminiscent of the fiery protagonists of Sturm und Drang dramas. Yet Faber is not simply cast in the mold of eighteenth-century discourses and works; rather, the character is tainted by National Socialist ideology. For example, what appears to be a desire to eliminate corruption within the aristocracy—in keeping with Sturm und Drang ideals—is actually an ideologically motivated insistence on removing Jews from Stuttgart, a viewpoint that reflects the Nazis' racist exclusion of Jews from German society. Thus, Faber upholds the community leaders' directives rather than rebelling against the bigotry they promote. As a sentimentalist he appears to look forward to a life of marital bliss. At the same time, he exhibits a lack of interest in sexual relations with Dorothea that may have less to do with the blandness modeled by the upstanding husbands or fiancés of bourgeois tragedies or horror movies and more to do with a fascist fear of "contagious lust," as Schulte-Sasse argues. Drawing on Klaus Theweleit, Schulte-Sasse describes this fear as one that "soldierly" men have of losing self-control if they allow themselves to give in to sexual desires.[23] She explains further: "In Theweleit's terms, this signifies the preservation of Faber's body armor; he successfully wards off penetration by the female Other. For a fascist man like Faber, 'blood' is the only thing allowed to flow."[24] Certainly, Dorothea is more bothered than Faber when their embraces are interrupted, and

---

22   Having Faber play the harpsichord in this scene emphasizes the sentimental or even effeminate aspect of his nature, since the harpsichord and its relatives (the virginal, cembalo, spinet, and even the piano—"the most home-bound of instruments") were considered "women's instruments"—appropriate for middle-class girls to learn in preparation for marriage and a life of domesticity. See Rita Steblin, "The Gender Stereotyping of Musical Instruments in the Western Tradition," in "Voices of Women: Essays in Honor of Violet Archer," special issue, *Canadian University Music Review* 16, no. 1 (1995): 128–44, here 137. Like Schulte-Sasse, Steblin cites Richard Leppert, whose study of the significance of harpsichords in eighteenth-century British culture shows "how musical practices helped to assure and preserve male domination of women by limiting female activity to the home" (qtd. in Steblin, 136). See Richard D. Leppert, "Men, Women, and Music at Home: The Influence of Cultural Values on Musical Life in Eighteenth-Century England," *Imago Musicae* 2 (1985): 51–133, here 53.
23   Schulte-Sasse, "The Jew as Other," 42.
24   Schulte-Sasse, "The Jew as Other," 43.

114 ♦ Deborah Janson

more eager than he is to have sex the night they are married. When he objects to sleeping in her bed without her father's approval and claims that her father needs time to get used to the idea, she responds that she has been looking forward to it for a long time. Dorothea is clearly ready for sexual relations, while Faber is not. To remain uncontaminated by lustful contagion, he avoids the temptations posed by women and denies himself the sexual freedoms associated with Jews.

Once the duke hires Süß Oppenheimer as his financial adviser, the depravity that already characterized Stuttgart's nobility worsens. Though the duke pledged allegiance to the people of Württemberg when he was sworn in, his personal desires and interests make it difficult for him to uphold his oath of office. As an egotist who is attracted to lavish excesses but lacks the resources to fund them, he becomes frustrated when the frugal and self-restrained estates representatives deny him money for things they consider luxuries. With Süß's help, the duke's demands are met, and his womanizing becomes obvious. During a ballet rehearsal, for example, he has a "little dark-haired dancer" he fancies brought to him, hoping to secure the artiste's acquiescence to his erotic wishes by offering her a ring that Oppenheimer provides him. Because she submits willingly, the film suggests that women can be bought for a trinket.[25] The interlude with the artiste is followed by a heartbreaking situation when the duke holds a ball that Oppenheimer organizes and to which the townspeople's daughters are invited. Now focusing on a middle-class family named Fibelkorn, the film sets up a subplot that once again reflects the contours of a bourgeois tragedy. While the less-principled mother considers the invitation to this courtly event an honor—a scenario that evokes the mothers in *Emilia Galotti* and *Kabale und Liebe*—her enraged husband regards it as a meat market that will damage the young women in attendance. Yet Mr. Fibelkorn does not prevent his daughters from attending the ball despite his criticism of it. His worst fears are realized when one of his daughters is forced to "entertain" the duke. Süß orders her to show the ruler her legs while a courtly woman lifts her dress to reveal them. Though the girl trembles and sheds tears, it is clear that the duke will not restrain himself. He is concerned only with the satisfaction of his immediate desires, not at all with the tragic effect that the sexual assault will have on the life of this bourgeois maiden.

Just as the duke's behavior is characteristic of the aristocracy in eighteenth-century society, so, too, is Süß Oppenheimer's. Like other members of the court, Süß is ambitious, egotistical, and cruel. He treats the

---

25 Régine Mihal Friedman, "Male Gaze and Female Reaction: Veit Harlan's *Jew Süss* (1940)," in *Gender and German Cinema: Feminist Interventions,* vol. 2, ed. Sandra Frieden, Richard McCormick, Vibeke Petersen, and Melissa Vogelsang (Providence, RI: Berg, 1993), 117–33, here 126.

townspeople like commodities that exist for his pleasure or for the implementation of his devious plans. His role evokes that of the court Jew in the early modern period in that he provides the duke with financial advice and monetary loans in exchange for social privileges and noble status. He also resembles the evil courtly aides in bourgeois tragedies—schemers such as Marinelli in *Emilia Galotti* or Wurm in *Kabale und Liebe*—who use intrigue to elevate their lordship's eminence but ultimately seek to advance their own agenda. Yet Süß is even worse than these evil schemers because of the threat of contamination he poses to the entire community. He first gains access to Stuttgart, whose constitution bans Jews from the city, by offering the duke a low price on jewels for the duchess in exchange for the needed passport. Once he wins the duke's favor, he is granted management of Stuttgart's streets. By collecting taxes and tolls from merchants, he increases his wealth and power but also fuels the townspeople's ire. After Süß convinces the duke to lift the ban against Jews entirely, the conflict between the court and the citizenry can no longer be contained. When the angry estates representatives move to reinstate the prohibition against Jews, Süß encourages the duke to dissolve the council and take full control over Württemberg. He also advises him to borrow foreign soldiers should a popular revolt occur, and arranges the financing. As the escalation of tensions demonstrates, Süß's unbridled greed and ambition pose a threat to the citizens of Württemberg. The film's portrayal of Süß as a conniving Jew who robs Swabians of their livelihood thus reflects the anti-Semitic stereotype that negatively links Jews and money. The film further illustrates the view of Jews as harmful parasites by equating those who enter Stuttgart with a swarm of locusts; that is, with destructive pests that, like rats, are indistinguishable from one another and endanger the German population.[26] By associating Jews with vermin, the film removes

---

26   The association of Jews with locusts calls to mind the association of Jews with rats in Fritz Hippler's 1940 propaganda film *Der ewige Jude* (The Eternal Jew), which appears to have been influenced by *Nosferatu*. In Murnau's film, rats travel westward in Orlok's earth-filled coffins to Wisborg, where they spread the plague in consort with Count Orlok; in Hippler's film, parasitic vermin are associated with Jews who come from Eastern Europe and spread death, disease, and degeneracy throughout the German homeland. *Nosferatu's* relevance for *Der ewige Jude* is also obvious in Hippler's description of his film as "eine Symphonie des Ekels und des Grauens" (a symphony of disgust and horror), a direct reference to the subtitle of Murnau's film, *Eine Symphonie des Grauens*. See Régine Mihal Friedman and Gertrud Koch, "Juden-Ratten—Von der rassistischen Metonymie zur tierischen Metapher in Fritz Hipplers Film *Der ewige Jude*," *Frauen und Film* 47 (1989): 24–35. In addition, a ballad written for *Jud Süß* by Eberhard Wolfgang Möller, one of the film's scriptwriters, makes direct association between vampires, wolves, rats, vipers, and Jews, with Jews described as the most evil of all predators. For the lyrics to this *Bänkellied*, which was not included in the film's

them from the realm of the human, providing an example of "Man's human others"—of human beings who are equated with low forms of life in order to justify their abuse and exclusion.

An examination of the various female characters in *Jud Süß* provides another example of the intersectional nature of social exclusion, showing that in addition to Jews, National Socialists also did not consider women truly human. The film features many more female characters than Lessing's bourgeois tragedies or Murnau's *Nosferatu*, and all of them are portrayed in a negative light. One sees the seductive, scantily dressed Jewess whose father admonishes her for her provocative clothing; the young woman who attends the duke's processional and suffers humiliation when a man pulls at her bodice, revealing her breasts and causing the men around her, including the duke, to laugh; the ballet dancers and bourgeois maidens at the ball who are forced to provide the duke with entertainment when his wife is out of town; and Süß's aristocratic mistress, who lacks compassion and brains. In all these scenes, men regard women as sex objects who exist only for their pleasure and, for this reason, are not worthy of their respect. Only the blacksmith's wife is not depicted in sexual terms; but when she stands beside her husband holding her baby during a confrontational meeting with Süß, Secretary Levy dismisses her with a wave of the hand, telling the blacksmith to "get the wife and kid away from here." This resembles the duke's dismissal of his wife during a moment of intense political turmoil, when he pushes her away, exclaiming, "This isn't a matter for women!" Though the duke holds his wife in higher regard than other women, he still distrusts her, suspecting that she and Süß are having an affair. While it is primarily aristocrats and Jews who denigrate the female characters, the film does little to provide the audience with a needed corrective to its uniformly negative portrayal of women. Other than the blacksmith's wife, mothers in *Jud Süß*—like in other Nazi films—are entirely absent.[27] According to Régine Friedman, this points to a contradiction within National Socialist culture, whereby women were celebrated for their reproductive role, even encouraged "for eugenic reasons to submit to the advances of those SS men who were considered especially pure in race,"[28] but were denied a role in shaping morality. That mothers were not invited to make intellectual contributions to the moral development of German society during the Third Reich is reminiscent of the perceived threat they posed to paternal authority in

---

final version, see Susan Tegel, "Veit Harlan and the Origins of *Jud Süss*, 1938–39," *Historical Journal of Film, Radio & Television* 16, no. 4 (1996): 515–31, here 523.

27 Friedman, "Male Gaze," 132.

28 Friedman, "Male Gaze," 133.

eighteenth-century German society, as reflected in their absence or negative portrayal in Lessing's bourgeois tragedies.

Even Dorothea, who is supposed to be a paragon of bourgeois virtue,
is shown to be morally vulnerable. When Süß's carriage breaks down on
his way to Stuttgart, Dorothea, who offers him a ride, is taken in by his
charm and handsome, manly appearance. Because he is a "Jew in disguise" who wears the clothing and hairstyle of a gentile, she does not
realize how dangerous he is.[29] She admires how well traveled he is and
asks where, among all the places he has been, he feels most at home.
Perpetuating the stereotype of the wandering Jew, Süß declares that the
world is his home, adding coyly that he has never felt more at ease than in
that moment, sitting next to her. Since Dorothea is portrayed as a young
woman who has never been satisfied sexually, it seems possible that Süß's
sweet talk plants a seductive seed in her subconscious. Though Dorothea
tries to avoid him after learning he is a Jew, Süß pursues her at the ball and
later seeks her hand in marriage—a proposal that her father rejects outright, explaining to Süß not only that she is already promised but also that
he would never allow his daughter to bring *Judenkinder* ("Jew-children")
into the world. This scenario illustrates the threat Jews posed to the Nazi
ideal of an Aryan social order and the Nazi emphasis on endogamous
marital relations and paternal authority. After all, it is Sturm who decides
that his daughter will not marry Süß and that Dorothea and Faber will
wed that very night. Not long after this development, Süß has both men
imprisoned for their roles in the revolt against the duke, thereby setting
the stage for the film's tragic conclusion.

Throughout most of the film, Dorothea embodies the National Socialist ideal of "beauty, youth, and health,"[30] as well as virtue and domesticity. Viewers see her serving food, doing housework, playing music, and

---

29 See Weinstein for a discussion of the continuities in the portrayal of Jews
in Weimar and Third Reich Cinema. She argues that in each period, films exhibit
positive and negative views of Jews to varying degrees. While the portrayal of
Süß is primarily negative, he also exhibits political prowess, intelligence, and sex
appeal. This is done both for financial reasons—to make the film a box-office hit
by having the main character appeal to the audience—and to highlight the danger
the Jew in disguise poses. Common to both Weimar and Nazi film is the view of
Jews as Other—as outsiders who thwart order and dissolve structural boundaries through assimilation, making it necessary within each film's plot to contain
the Jew one way or the other to reestablish order. Valerie Weinstein, "Dissolv-
ing Boundaries: Assimilation and Allosemitism in E. A. Dupont's *Das alte Gesetz*
(1923) and Veit Harlan's *Jud Süss* (1940)," *German Quarterly* 78, no. 4 (2005):
496–516, here 497–98.

30 Christiane Schönefeld, "Feuchtwanger and the Propaganda Ministry: The
Transposition of *Jud Süß* from Novel to Nazi Film," in *Feuchtwanger and Film*,
ed. Ian Wallace (Bern: Lang, 2009), 125–51, here 146.

(most frequently) waiting for her men to return. Early on, she awaits them with joy in her heart, but as the political conflict intensifies, her joy turns to anguish. She becomes the suffering woman, stuck at home and sick with worry over the fate of both her father and her husband. The only scenes in which Dorothea is depicted outside the home, other than when she and Faber exchange wedding vows, show her with Süß—in the carriage, at the ball, and finally, in his private chambers, where he rapes her. Her conscious motivation for going to his residence is to beg for her father's release from captivity. Apparently, she has absorbed the idea that Jews (like women) can be enticed by objects of material value, for in her attempt to negotiate with Süß, she offers him her wedding ring. Amused by the very small size of the ring, Süß lures her into his bedroom by saying that he has a much bigger one to show her. Once in the bedroom, the sexual innuendo takes its final sinister turn. It is possible that Dorothea feels partly responsible for what is about to occur, for just before he rapes her, she utters a nearly inaudible prayer that could be interpreted as a plea for forgiveness rather than for help. To ensure her acquiescence, Süß makes Dorothea aware that Faber—in a chamber across the courtyard—is being tortured whenever Süß hangs a white handkerchief out the window. The viewers hear and see him scream during these scenes of torment—further proof, according to Schulte-Sasse, of his "impotence, his inability to prevent the violation of nature and his 'territory.'"[31] As Süß's prisoner, Faber is powerless to protect Dorothea. Instead, she sacrifices her life to save his.

After the rape, Süß orders Faber's release, Dorothea having bought his freedom with her loss of virtue. Viewers then see her staggering to the river, her hair in disarray and a look of revulsion on her face. Like the victim of horror movies, she has become "responsible for the horror that her look reveals."[32] Because she has transgressed her society's values, her abjection from it is unavoidable. She cannot overcome the disgust and self-loathing she feels, caused both by the Jew who has violated her and by her awareness that she has broken the social contract. Mindful that if she were to continue living, she might commit the unthinkable crime of bringing "Jew-children" into the world, she elects to sacrifice herself for the greater good. Like Emilia, she is resolute enough to choose death over a depraved and immoral existence.

Dorothea's suicide unites the townspeople even more strongly against Süß, as can be seen in the angry faces of citizens who gather around Faber as he carries her corpse—a symbol of abjection—to the castle to demand justice. When the duke suddenly dies that night of a heart attack, Süß is captured and imprisoned. His subsequent conviction is not based on

---

31 Schulte-Sasse, "The Jew as Other," 43.
32 Williams, "When the Woman Looks," 86.

charges of treason or various forms of financial misconduct—though he is considered guilty of those crimes—but on an ancient law that prohibits Jews from having sexual relations with Christians. The estate representatives appoint Sturm, regarded as the man most aggrieved by Dorothea's death, to decide Süß's punishment. Following Süß's execution by hanging, Sturm further proclaims that all Jews must leave Württemberg within three days, thereby reinstating the ban against them. This final scene reinforces the idea that Sturm represents paternal authority on both the familial and societal level. As head of his family and leader of the community, he has the power to expel the Jews and restore social harmony.

Although *Jud Süß* is clearly influenced by classical bourgeois tragedies, Lessing, who promoted religious tolerance and the acceptance of Jews in German society, would have decried the film's anti-Semitic focus. The tragedy befalling the Sturm family was not designed to improve the morals of its viewers but to warn Germans about the dire consequences that result from allowing Jews to dwell in their midst. As Süß's example shows, Jews pursue Aryan women, contaminate their blood, and render their offspring valueless to the survival of the Aryan race. As the legal proceedings at the end of the film make clear, the townspeople do not concern themselves with Dorothea as victim of a violent sexual assault, for Süß is not found guilty of rape—of the harm he caused *her*—but of miscegenation, of the threat he posed the white Christian community. As Christiane Schönefeld writes, for National Socialists, "Blood is the measure of difference, and its purity imperative to the definition, containment and protection of the *Volksgemeinschaft*."[33] In light of such concerns, it is clear that not only Süß but also Dorothea must die—since by the end of the film she too has become a carrier of impure blood. Once a model of virtue and purity, she develops into nothing more than an abject sacrifice, expelled from the culture for violating its principles. Having internalized her society's values, Dorothea succumbs to its demands by taking her own life, thereby paving the way for the patriarchal order's return to stability and the continuation of its racist and sexist agenda.

Conclusion

This essay's comparison of important German works from the mid-eighteenth through the mid-twentieth centuries raises several overarching and interrelated questions; namely, who stands to gain from the female sacrifice that takes place in each work, and why is the heroine's sacrifice always envisioned as an attack on her sexuality? The correlation between these two issues is already apparent in Lessing's bourgeois tragedies. As an adherent of the Enlightenment, Lessing sought to elevate the

---

33 Schönefeld, "Feuchtwanger and the Propaganda Ministry," 147.

bourgeoisie's standing above the aristocracy's in moral terms, emphasizing the importance that the bourgeois moral code placed on compassion, fidelity, and—especially for young women—sexual purity. Young maidens were to honor their fathers by embodying the ideal of bourgeois virtue, with any sexual transgression or impure thoughts on their part comprising a threat to the stability of the paternal order. Given the political realities of the eighteenth century, society did not punish the aristocratic seducer who caused the maiden's downfall, but the maiden herself. For example, the prince's attack on Emilia's virtue and the sexual arousal she felt in response to his advances required her abjection from society. In turn, Odoardo's intent to protect his daughter's sexual purity by killing her, followed by his voluntary surrender to his society's justice system, represents his quest to reestablish the stability of the paternal order, as Gustafson's analysis suggests. With the mother's influence criticized or lacking, and the maiden's maternal possibilities eliminated through death, Christian bourgeois men in Lessing's tragedies retain their position of moral authority, thereby setting the stage for future instances of intersectional exclusion.

An important difference between eighteenth-century bourgeois tragedies and Harlan's anti-Semitic rendering of the genre is the status of the film's antagonist. During Lessing's day, criticism of the aristocratic seducers was meant to improve society from within, whereas *Jud Süß* locates "the source of social antagonism in the 'Jew' rather than in feudal powers."[34] Even though Jews resided in Germany, Nazis viewed them as alien invaders. As discussed above, their outsider status links them to villains of horror movies, including *Nosferatu*. Both Count Orlok and Süß Oppenheimer are lecherous and predatory foreigners who must be exterminated so that health and harmony can be restored to the communities they have infiltrated. This is accomplished in both films by having the monsters contaminate the blood of beautiful young women through sexual assault. As Linda Williams asserts, the maiden's body exhibits an "excess of aesthetic perfection" that complements the monster's excessive sexual energy, resulting in a "similar status as potent threats to a vulnerable male power."[35] The traumatized man (the maiden's fiancé, husband, or father) fears that the "power-in-difference" the monster shares with the woman—and with the potential mother residing within her—can

34 Schulte-Sasse, *Entertaining the Third Reich: Illusions of Wholeness in Nazi Cinema* (Durham, NC: Duke University Press 1996), 48.

35 Williams, "When the Woman Looks," 88–90. In her analysis, Williams calls on both Laura Mulvey, "Visual Pleasure and Narrative Cinema," *Screen* 16, no. 3 (1975): 6–18, and Susan Lurie, "Pornography and the Dread of Woman," in *Take Back the Night*, ed. Laura Lederer (New York: William Morrow, 1980), 159–73.

"mutilate and transform" him.[36] A visual illustration of this threat is provided in *Jud Süß* when Faber's hands are being mutilated at the same time that Süß is raping Faber's wife. For men like Faber and Sturm to be free, not only the overly sexualized and corrupting monsters but also their female victims must die. Their sacrifice ensures the continuation of the vulnerable male's sexist and racist rule. Especially under National Socialism, the ideal of racial purity required the criminalization of sexual relations between Aryans and Jews. Although the Nazis clearly did not share Lessing's goal of improving Germans' capacity to feel compassion, their works displayed some similar features of cultural narcissism, such as the necessity of abjecting those who threatened their power and superior status. For Nazis, this was no longer just women, as it was in Lessing's dramas, but also Jews and many others whom they viewed as inferior and onto whom they projected their own shortcomings.

Through its analysis of works by Lessing, Murnau, and Harlan, this essay demonstrates that those who benefit from the sacrifice of women are the self-proclaimed representatives of "Man"—those wounded vulnerable white men who seek to maintain a position of power by projecting an image of themselves as strong fathers and superior leaders. Female sacrifice is connected to the violation of female sexuality in these works because control of female desire and sexual autonomy—women's reproductive capabilities and choices—provides a primary means of regulating who is "on top" in the social hierarchy. Men who view women as possessions regard female sexual freedom as a threat to their authority, and sexual assault committed by others as damage to their property. In general, such men are vulnerable not because they are under actual physical attack but because they are afraid of losing their power, privilege, and hegemonic status. Concerns about women's sexual autonomy and reproductive rights—evident today in the legal challenges to *Roe v. Wade* and the attacks on abortion clinics—thus intersect with concerns about racial purity as well as the need to control nonnormative men. Laws against miscegenation become important when a society wants to control what kinds of babies will be born—what their "race" will be. In situations such as these, a white man in a position of power—for example, the prince in *Emilia Galotti* (or former presidents of the United States)—is likely to receive little or no punishment for violating or harassing a woman, whereas a Jew in German society through the end of World War II (or a Black man living under slavery or during the Jim Crow era in the United States) is likely to be lynched for having contaminated the property of white men. In many twentieth-century horror films, including *Nosferatu* and *Jud Süß*, male bourgeois demands for sexual and racial purity overlap in a way that requires the abjection of both the monsters

---

36 Williams, "When the Woman Looks," 88–90.

and their victims and restores power to the vulnerable leaders of the paternal order. Unfortunately, such intersectional exclusion—typical of cultural narcissism—remains strong in the early twenty-first century as evidenced by the many victims of sexual assault comprising the #MeToo movement. Alternative cultural models are needed that will challenge racial and gender hierarchies and broaden our understanding of the truly human, thereby acknowledging the equal value of individuals across social groups.

5: "Na, wenn du mich erst fragst?": Reconsidering Affirmative Consent with Schnitzler, Schnitt, Habermas, and Rancière

Sonja Boos

Consent

IN HIS 2015 ESSAY "The Sexual is (Not) Political," Slavoj Žižek makes a case against *affirmative consent*, the "yes means yes" sexual rule by which all parties involved in a sexual encounter agree to specific forms of conduct, either through clear, verbal communication or nonverbal cues or actions.[1] Not surprisingly, Žižek considers recent calls to codify "yes means yes" a prime example of the "narcissistic notion of subjectivity" that feeds our "politically correct obsession with protecting individuals from any experience that may hurt them in any way."[2] According to Žižek's polemic, affirmative consent is based on the naive idea that a sex act could be freed of any suspicion of coercion if both participants announce their free and conscious intention to participate. Žižek argues that this false assumption ignores the conflicts resulting from the competing pressures within the Freudian triad between id impulses and a punitive superego.[3] "Under the pressure from the Superego, my Ego says 'no,' but my Id

---

1   Slavoj Žižek, "The Sexual Is (Not) Political," in *The Courage of Hope-lessness: A Year of Acting Dangerously* (Brooklyn, NY: Melville House, 2017), 185–203.

2   Žižek, "Sexual Is (Not) Political," 190.

3   Another point of reference is Freud's essay of 1925 "Negation," in which he argues that repressed material is admitted to consciousness only through deny-ing it: "Negation is a way of taking cognizance of what is repressed; indeed it is already a lifting of the repression, though not, of course, an acceptance of what is repressed." Sigmund Freud, "Negation" (1925), in *The Standard Edition of the Complete Psychological Works of Sigmund Freud*, vol. 19, trans. and ed. James Strachey (London: Hogarth Press, 1961), 235–39, here 235–36. Applied to scenes of sexual coercion, this would suggest that the victim's repressed desire to be raped is expressed through the negative: in her claim that she is being coerced to have sex.

resists and clings to the denied desire? Or (a much more interesting case) the opposite: I say 'yes' to the sexual invitation, surrendering to my Id passion, but in the midst of performing the act, my Superego triggers an unbearable guilt feeling? So, to bring things to the absurd, should the contract be signed by the Ego, Superego, and Id of each party, so that it is valid only if all three say 'yes'?"[4]

Žižek's point in this essay is consistent with his Lacanian interpretation of the superego as an antiethical agency that stigmatizes what it formally commands; namely, the ego's failure to suppress the instinctual demands of the id. As Žižek explains, the superego is "the agency in the eyes of which I am all the more guilty, the more I try to suppress my 'sinful' strivings and meet its demands."[5] In this understanding, it is impossible to withdraw from or reject the fundamental nature of desire that structures the very core of erotic interplay. There is no "neutral position of meta-language [from which to] declare one's readiness to engage in [erotic interplay]," Žižek reasons, since "any such declaration is part of the interplay and either *de-eroticizes* the situation or *gets eroticized* itself" [my emphasis].[6] Žižek is particularly concerned by the first scenario because, he argues, the demand for explicit consent could result in a "long bureaucratic negotiation killing all desire for the act." Note how Žižek uses hyperbole to seduce us into thinking of affirmative consent as a laborious and wary process, rather than a brief but critical part of building a positive sexual culture, as proponents of affirmative consent would maintain. The second scenario, by which the consent negotiation gets "libidinally invested in itself," sparks Žižek's interest because of its aporetic structure, which in his logic culminates in the idea of eroticized rape. Žižek draws his example of a libidinally invested consent negotiation from David Lynch's road-movie *Wild at Heart* (1990). In a scene that is both absurd and over the top, Willem Dafoe's character Bobby Peru propositions Lula (Laura Dern), who initially resists his advances. But soon the scene devolves into a kinky spectacle of sexual manipulation. Dafoe's character gradually overturns Dern's visceral abhorrence into a form of abject desire: with his hands around her throat, Lula reconsiders and "consents," only to have Bobby reject her and leave. Here, as elsewhere in Lynch's films, clichés are mobilized to expose the presence of a rape fantasy as the foundation of romantic fiction. What Žižek's example fails to address, however, are instances where mutual consent and sexual choice lead to hot and desired sex precisely because they are eroticized, as well as those where the absence of consent signals violence.

4   Žižek, "Sexual Is (Not) Political," 187.
5   Žižek, *In Defense of Lost Causes* (London: Verso, 2008), 342.
6   Žižek, "Sexual Is (Not) Political," 188.

The present chapter offers two vastly different case studies, Arthur Schnitzler's play *Reigen* (1903; *La Ronde*) and Corinna Schnitt's short video *Von einer Welt* (2007; *About a World*).[7] Separated by more than a century and conceived by a male author and a female filmmaker, respectively, both the play and the film serve as useful and instructive case studies of the significance of language in the interplay of sexual coercion and consent. The case studies serve to refute Žižek's polemical assertion that language is antierotic, as well as his inherent assumption that sex is not a political act. Taking issue with this essentially patriarchal model, the present chapter suggests instead that language (and its absence) is a powerful tool that can shift (or can fail to shift) agency in sexual acts. This becomes obvious in Schnitzler's and Schnitt's representations of sexual encounters, which are consistent with Jürgen Habermas's and Jacques Rancière's theoretical positions insofar as they put into relief a view of language as a communicative act that pivots on questions of conflict resolution and power relations. In that way, the #MeToo movement finds a historical precedent in these provocative literary and cinematic interventions. Seen through the lens of Habermas's and Rancière's propositions, Schnitzler's play and Schnitt's film challenge patriarchal notions about sex by illustrating how individuals come to inhabit the peculiar gray zone of sexual encounters between explicitly saying "no" to sex and actually desiring to have sex with someone.

The concept of consent appears in both works at the figurative and structural levels, but it is also directly thematized. Dubious versions of "consent" (and in particular, its absence) figure as speech acts that are not only understood as scenes of an ideological interpellation in Žižek's sense but, rather, function precisely as acts, as political gesture in themselves. Hence, this chapter uses a pragmatic model of analysis to explore if and how sexual consent reconfigures the situation in which it is enunciated. Drawing on Habermas's *Theory of Communicative Action* (1984), it explores the theoretical underpinnings of affirmative consent conceived as a form of mutual conflict resolution through compromise in the sense of Habermas.[8] Affirmative consent and *communicative action* both demand of their actors that they harmonize their individual plans of actions with all participants, rather than aim solely at accomplishing their own goals. Conceived in these terms, a successful, equitable sexual encounter would

7   Arthur Schnitzler, *Reigen: Zehn Dialoge* (Vienna: Wiener Verlag, 1903). Arthur Schnitzler, *Plays and Stories*, ed. Egon Schwarz (New York: Continuum, 1982); unless otherwise noted, all English translations are from this edition and are cited as *Plays* and page number. Corinna Schnitt, *Von einer Welt* (*About a World*), 2007, SD video, 9 minutes.

8   Jürgen Habermas, *The Theory of Communicative Action*, trans. Thomas McCarthy, 2 vols. (Boston: Beacon Press, 1984).

be one in which all partners, especially—but not only—the "suitor/ suitress," make concessions as to its form and scope. What, then, are the (felicitous) conditions for sexual consent as communicative action? How would Habermas's conception of a consensus-oriented language play out in a sexual encounter where only one party is sexually interested, and where "compromise" leads to one person engaging in unwanted sex? Drawing on Rancière's work, this chapter inquires into the factors that determine under what conditions the absence of consent turns into what Rancière termed political *disagreement*. It argues that the fictional scenarios outlined in Schnitzler's and Schnitt's works highlight how inequality forecloses consent and causes participants' disqualification as partners in dialogue.[9] Through a close reading of Schnitzler's play and Schnitt's video, Habermas's affirmative view of language and Rancière's affirmation of political speech as an agent of emancipatory social change will be put to a test.

Reciprocity

This chapter takes its cue from Corinna Schnitt's short video *About a World* to think through some of the gender-political implications of sexual assault in relation to the thorny issue of consent. The film shows a dozen nude women who lie motionless and (presumably) defenseless as they are each approached by a single man who caresses and makes erotic overtures to one woman after another, at times tenderly, at other times more assertively (see figs. 5.1 and 5.2). These images of unresponsive women are juxtaposed with text inserts quoting from Habermas's *Theory of Communicative Action* (see fig. 5.3). The irony is apparent: Habermas's concept of communicative rationality requires the actors to have clear, unfettered access to their own reasoning, which is clearly contradicted by the condition of the women in the film who are passed out—asleep or intoxicated. Their speechless passivity disavows Habermas's faith in the kinds of symmetrical communicative interactions that constitute the basis of a procedural, deliberative democracy. The film's aporia is present in many critiques of Habermas's theory of communicative action, which argue that the latter views communication and debate in the public sphere as argumentatively meritocratic and "subscribes to an unrealistic ideal of power-free communication," as Ian McNeely has observed.[10] The film seems to suggest that in view of a culture that condones sexual assault and blames women for their own rape, Habermas's notion of communicative

9   Jacques Rancière, *Disagreement: Politics and Philosophy*, trans. Julie Rose (Minneapolis: University of Minnesota Press, 2004).

10   Ian McNeely, *The Emancipation of Writing* (Berkeley: University of California Press, 2003), 3.

Figure 5.1. Corinna Schnitt, *Aus einer Welt*. Film still. ©Corinna Schnitt.

Figure 5.2. Corinna Schnitt, *Aus einer Welt*. Film still. ©Corinna Schnitt.

rationality, upon which communicative action (and by extension affirmative consent) must be based, is illusory.

Schnitzler's *La Ronde* likewise makes a case against discursive rationality and affirmative consent. The play's critical modality, however, is not irony but candor, and the desire to understand a sexual milieu that centers on the marriage plot, even if the latter is routinely contradicted by pervasive promiscuity. Set in Vienna shortly before the turn of the twentieth century, *La Ronde* consists of ten interlocking scenes between pairs of lovers, whereby each of its ten characters appears in two consecutive

Figure 5.3. Corinna Schnitt, *Aus einer Welt*. Film still. ©Corinna Schnitt.

scenes. All ten scenes are structured around an instance of lovemaking or physical coupling; halfway through each scene in Schnitzler's text there is a row of asterisks, denoting that the stage lights are discreetly dimmed or the curtain is closed while the man and the woman have sex. Although the scandal happens only in the imagination of the reader, it is still unambiguously the event of intercourse that drives each scene's momentum. Crucially, there is not one scene in the play where sexual consent is not in some way in dispute or compromised.

The dialogues preceding the sexual encounters are reminiscent of melodramatic forms. They not only function as conduits for the characters' emotional reactions but effectively drive the drama by underscoring how differently the sexual advances are perceived by the respective actors: as foreplay by "der junge Herr" ("Young Gentleman") who seduces "das Stubenmädchen" ("Parlor Maid"), as monetary bargaining by "die Dirne" ("Whore") who lures "der Soldat" ("Soldier"), as flirting by "die Schauspielerin" ("Actress") who is tempting "der Graf" ("Count"). Although all recipients—except for, predictably enough, "die junge Frau" ("Wife")—initially resist the sexual advances, none of the encounters qualify as a seduction, defined as an "act by which a man entices a woman to have unlawful sexual relations with him by means of persuasions, solicitations, promises, or bribes without the use of physical force or violence."[11] In the legal codes of Schnitzler's time, even the sex

---

11 Jeffrey Lehman and Shirelle Phelps, *West's Encyclopedia of American Law*, vol. 9 (Detroit: Thomson Gale, 2005), https://legal-dictionary.thefreedictionary.com/Sexual+seduction. The Austrian legal code emphasizes the importance of "Eheversprechen" (promise of marriage) as a persuasive means. Moritz von

in scene 6 between "das süße Mädel" ("Little Miss") and "der Gatte" ("Husband") would not have been considered coercive, despite the intoxicated state of the female participant. Audiences with modern sensibilities may hear more than a suggestion of nonconsensual sex and incapacitated rape in her announcing that "mir dreht sich alles" (131; "everything's turning around," 87) and her request that he stop his advances: "Was machst denn? . . . Du in dem Wein muss 'was drin gewesen sein—so schläfrig . . . du, was g'schieht denn, wenn ich nimmer aufsteh'n kann? Aber, aber, schau, aber Karl . . . und wenn wer hereinkommt" (131; "What are you doing? . . . See, there must have been something in the wine . . . so sleepy . . . Hey, what happens if I can't get up? But . . . but look, Karl! . . . If somebody comes in . . . Please . . . the waiter!," 87). But the play takes a more ambiguous view of the encounter, indicating that "das süße Mädel" has voluntarily and intentionally followed "der Gatte" to a *chambre separée* and that she has been there before with other men. When she refers to herself as "Eine, die sich auf der Gassen anreden läßt und gleich mitgeht ins chambre separée!" (117; "a girl who lets you talk to her in the street and goes straight to a private dining room!," 83), she all but admits that she is a "fallen woman" and thus not protected by seduction laws, which did not apply to women of poor reputations. The play's overt theme is not rape but infidelity, and the double standards about sexual morality in late imperial Austrian society.[12] A case in point are the legal stipulations that "seduction" depended on the "previous chaste character" of the victim and a "promise of marriage," which, as Jessica R. Pliley argues, "carved out an implicit type of extramarital sex that could be condoned."[13] It is hardly a secret that Schnitzler ventured among the "fallen women" from the petty bourgeoisie, as do his male bourgeois protagonists who, as W. G. Sebald notes, take economic advantage of prostitutes whom they temporarily "keep" rather than pay. In Sebald's view, Schnitzler's portrayals of these women is sympathetic but ultimately inconsiderate, given that the poet employs melancholy to compensate for his lack of sincere concern or remorse.[14]

Stubenrauch, *Commentar zum österreichischen allgemeinen bürgerlichen Gesetzbuche*, vol. 2 (Vienna: Manz, 1888), 682.

12   See on this Claudia Benthien's astute analysis of how the play undermines and ridicules the "Husband's" ridiculous classification of women into respectable wives and deplorable creatures. Claudia Benthien, "Masken der Verführung: Intimität und Anonymität in Schnitzlers *Reigen*," *Germanic Review* 72, no. 2 (Spring 1997): 130–41, here 137.

13   Jessica R. Pliley, *Policing Sexuality: The Mann Act and the Making of the FBI* (Cambridge, MA: Harvard University Press, 2014), 45.

14   W. G. Sebald, "Die Mädchen aus der Feenwelt—Bemerkungen zu Liebe und Prostitution mit Bezügen zu Raimund, Schnitzler und Horvath," *Neophilologus* 67 (1983): 109–17, here 110–11.

Although *La Ronde* is prescient in its staging of sexual coercion as a systemic social ill, it is not a #MeToo play in the sense that it would consciously and critically deal with issues of sexual assault and violence, let alone put forward a systemic solution. Neither "das süße Mädel" nor the other female characters are unequivocally recognized as victims of male sexual dominance. Schnitzler's agenda does not involve listening to the victims—or "believing survivors," in #MeToo parlance. (Note that the playwright was himself a notorious womanizer who ventured among women from the petty bourgeoisie of the outer districts.) In *La Ronde*, women are just as interested in sex and just as manipulative about getting it as their male counterparts. "Der Dichter" ("Poet") thus seduces "die Schauspielerin" because he wants her to star in his play, while she in turn seduces "der Graf" although (or because) he strikes her as "ein Ehrenmann" (217; "a man of honor," 107). Here as elsewhere throughout the play, sex emerges as a tool to secure financial or societal benefits. But it is also identified as a causal factor in the maintenance of the status quo. Hence the "Husband's" rationalization to his "Wife" in the play's central marital scene where he laments "die vielfachen Erlebnisse, die wir notgedrungen vor der Ehe durchzumachen haben" (90–91; "the many varied experiences we have to go through before marriage," 77), regretting "die Geschöpfe, auf die wir [sexuell] angewiesen sind" (91; "the poor creatures we have to [sexually] resort to," 77). Notably, the spousal relationship is the only one in the play that does not cross lines of class and station. Taken as a whole, the ten scenes provide an instructive glimpse of a wider social reality as the sexual encounters cut across social classes, milieus, and professions.[15] Clearly, the timeliness of the play's subject matter is amplified by its focus on the intersectional dimension of sexual relationships.[16]

---

15 Elizabeth G. Ametsbichler rightly points out that "sexuality acts as an equalizing factor of the social spectrum," as the erotic encounters are depicted "within believable boundaries or crossings of societal lines of the time." At the same time, "the male characters are always of equal or higher class than the women they are with—and are usually in the dominant role." Elizabeth G. Ametsbichler, "'Der Reiz des Reigens': Reigen Works by Arthur Schnitzler and Werner Schwab," *Modern Austrian Literature* 31, no. 3–4 (1998): 288–300, here 292.

16 By broaching the threat of venereal diseases in fin-de-siècle Vienna, as many commentators have pointed out, the play also gives us a wise and timely commentary on the spread of COVID-19 in our time. Schnitzler's depiction is accurate in its suggestion that the spread of a sexually transmitted disease affects all levels of society. As COVID-19 has shown, however, humanly transmitted diseases also follow patterns of social-class differentials in health and mortality. See Laura Otis, "The Language of Infection: Disease and Identity in Schnitzler's *Reigen*," *Germanic Review* 70 (Spring 1995): 65–75, here 67.

La Ronde is a rich and eloquent depiction of the shared understandings and presuppositions that make up the lifeworld in which all, including sexual, encounters transpire. *Lifeworld* is Habermas's term for the informal, unregulated spheres of social life that provide a cultural repository of shared concepts and the deep-seated background knowledge that the members of a linguistic community accept as noncontroversial. For instance, when "das Stubenmädchen" leaves the door of her bedroom open while she undresses, knowing that her employer's son ("der junge Herr") can catch a peek at her, he can rightly assume that she is open to his advances. Another signal (as indicated for the reader in the stage directions) of her willingness is that she coyly "richtet vor dem Spiegel ihre Schneckerln" (36; "arranges her curls in the mirror," 62) before attending to him in his room. It is thus that Schnitzler's provocative play bolsters the rationale of *implied consent* in a male-dominated patriarchal culture.

But *La Ronde* also allows for a critical reading that underscores the regressive nature of the lifeworld it so keenly depicts. Multiple scenes are organized around dialogues in which the conditions for communicative action are manifestly not met. Habermas writes that one condition for communicative action is a shared lifeworld, an "intuitively present, in this sense familiar and transparent, and at the same time vast and incalculable web of presuppositions that have to be satisfied if an utterance is to be at all meaningful i.e. valid or invalid."[17] In addition to such a shared horizon, however, the practice of communication oriented toward mutual understanding also demands that the interlocutors regard each other as equals with respect to their capacity for rational speech and rational evaluation of speech, which will allow them to take up a (defeasible) stance of mutual recognition toward one another.[18] This is the basis of Habermas's claim that the practice of communicative action "always already presuppose[s] those very relationships of reciprocity and mutual recognition around which all moral ideas revolve in everyday life no less than in philosophical ethics."[19] As critics have pointed out, however, Habermas's formal prerequisite stipulating that participants of communicative action are equal may mask the reality of unequal social capital. As Peter Miller argues, "there is no guarantee that a formally symmetrical distribution of opportunities to select and employ speech acts will result in anything more than an expression of the status quo."[20] Nowhere is this claim more obvious

---

17 Habermas, *Communicative Action*, 131.

18 See on this M. S. Russell and A. Montin, "The Rationality of Political Disagreement: Rancière's Critique of Habermas," *Constellations: An International Journal of Critical and Democratic Theory* 22, no. 4 (2015): 543–54, here 543.

19 Jürgen Habermas, *Moral Consciousness and Communicative Action*, trans. Christian Lenhardt and Shierry Weber Nicholsen (Cambridge, MA: MIT Press, 1990), 130.

20 Peter Miller, *Domination and Power* (London: Routledge, 2019), 90.

than in the "Whore's" successive interactions with "der Graf" and "der Soldat." The play's evenly balanced dialogues never eclipse the underlying conflict and division, as in this case a prostitute's dependence on her clients and their control over her. "Die Dirne" even offers her services for free to "der Soldat," who stands higher in the social hierarchy. Implied in Schnitzler's detailed and vivid depiction is the insight that Habermas's *lifeworld* minimizes the risk of dissent, because it is inherently conservative in its social meaning.[21]

Significantly, then, the dialogues identify and make explicit why the preconditions for affirmative consent are not met in the context of these sexual encounters. To put it in the terms of Habermas's theory of communicative action, affirmative consent consists of both an illocutionary act by a speaker and a rationally evaluative "yes/no" position taken by a hearer on the acceptability of the validity claims implicit in what is said. The success of an illocutionary act in establishing an uncoerced agreement depends on the hearer's rationally motivated approval of what is said. In a sexual encounter, then, the utterance "yes" has the illocutionary force of consenting to sex. Her saying so makes it so. Yes means yes. But when "der Gatte" asks "das süße Mädel" if she will see him again (presumably to have sex for a second time), he does not accept "no" or "I'm not sure" as valid answers:

Der Gatte:	Na, willst du . . . bald wieder mit mir hierher . . . oder auch wo anders—
Das süße Mädel:	Weiß nicht.
Der Gatte:	Was heißt das wieder: Du weißt nicht. (138–39)

[Husband:	Well would you like to . . . come here again . . . soon? Or some other place . . .?
Little Miss:	I don't know.
Husband:	Now what's that supposed to mean: you don't know?, 20]

In this interchange, the "little Miss" is obliged to accept the validity claim raised by "der Gatte," who will not take "no" for an answer.

Schnitzler's agenda as a playwright is of a piece with Habermas's investment in unequal power relationships. Schnitzler knows that the freedom to choose sexual partners is not a given, just as Habermas is aware that the freedom to pursue communicative action in an uncoerced manner is not universally enjoyed. Not everyone is given an equal right to speak, and the threat of sanctions may limit what is acceptable to say and what can be challenged. *La Ronde* casts the issue of consent as a problem, the same problem that also haunts Habermas's theory: the fact

---

21 Habermas, *Communicative Action*, 70.

that it ties the meaning of speech acts to the practice of reason-giving. According to Habermas, speech is in need of reasons, and reasons are open to criticism and demand justification. By contrast, affirmative models of sexual consent are based on the notion that "No" is a complete sentence. Participants do not have to commit themselves to explaining and justifying their no. And this is the significance of Schnitzer's intervention. It casts doubt on the notion of autonomous, rational subjects who overcome their merely subjective views by way of rationally motivated, communicative acts. After all, this view of rationality as an emancipative force somewhat paternalistically forecloses the possibility of heterogeneity and difference, or the possibility that an actor might just not want to participate, or might not be invested in mutual understanding, or may not "be" rational. To harken back to the example of Schnitzler's "süße Mädel," Habermas's theory of communicative action knows but fails to acknowledge that when there is a power differential, as when a participant is intoxicated or underage or economically dependent, consent cannot truly exist. Hence the "Little Miss's" answer to the "Husband's" proposition is not only irrelevant but redundant. As the "süße Mädel" cleverly puts it, "Na, wenn du mich erst fragst?" (139; "Why do you have to ask?," 89).

Disagreement

Habermas's discourse theory is premised on the notion of the lifeworld as a platform of agreement: "Subjects acting communicatively always come to an understanding in the horizon of a lifeworld."[22] While Habermas recognizes that this platform is also the condition of the possibility of political disagreement, his approach fails to fully explore the ramifications of power differences in political dialogues. This is because Habermas's theory of communicative action builds on rationality and insists on consensus as the basis of democratic politics. Thus, it does not account for situations when speakers will not or cannot address each other as partners in dialogue. While both Habermas and Rancière theorize a democratic politics that relies on a procedure of argumentation and demonstration, Rancière differs from Habermas on the matter of consensus. Rancière argues that Habermas reduces politics to a rational balancing of interests that takes the parties in dispute as a given; that is, the parties are assumed to at least approximately satisfy certain "idealizing suppositions" that guide the process of argumentation. His performative view of dialogue explicitly rejects Habermas's insistence on a preconstituted subject of locution. Rancière holds that any proper dialogue is not only a rational dispute between multiple interests but also a struggle for one's

---

22 Habermas, *Communicative Action*, 70.

voice to be heard and recognized as the voice of a legitimate partner.[23] In other words, for a dialogue to be called political in Rancière's sense, the object of dispute and the parties in dispute must themselves be in question. While Habermas's notion of understanding (*Verstehen*) presupposes an orientation toward agreement that is driven by communicative rationality, Rancière argues that understanding is rooted in a supposition of equality: agreement and disagreement rest on the presumption that my partner understands what I am saying. For Rancière, the problem with Habermas's notion of a shared preunderstanding is that "it enables certain speakers (those in positions of authority) to exclude subordinates from participating as equal communication partners if they wish, by construing disagreement as a failure of understanding," as Russell notes.[24] According to Rancière, the double meaning of the verb "to understand" reveals how inegalitarian orders implicitly (and falsely) presuppose the fundamental equality of anyone with everyone. As Rancière explains, "'Do you understand?' is a false interrogative whose positive content is as follows: 'There is nothing for you to understand, you don't need to understand' and even, possibly, 'It's not up to you to understand, all you have to do is obey.'"[25]

Schnitzler's play lucidly illustrates the divide between "people who understand problems and people who have only to understand the orders such people give them."[26] When "der Gatte" proposes to take "das süße Mädel" to another place—"Ich werd' dir 'was sagen, mein Schatz, wir könnten jetzt wirklich geh'n" (131; "I'll tell you something, my treasure, now we might really go," 87)—he is not actually suggesting that she has a choice, despite the fact that "we might" is a suggestion that implies a moderate degree of possibility. Rather, when she asks for clarification and declines his idea: "Was meinst denn? . . . Oh nein, oh nein . . . ich geh' nirgends hin, was fällt dir denn ein" (131; "What do you mean . . . Oh oh, no! . . . I wouldn't . . . What an idea!," 87), he retorts more commandingly, "Also hör' mich nur an, mein Kind, das nächste Mal, wenn wir uns treffen, weißt du, da richten wir uns das so ein, dass . . ." ("Now, listen to me, my child, next time we meet, you know, we'll arrange it so . . ."). This exchange demonstrates how individuals with authority exclude partners from equal communication. His comment makes clear who creates the rules and who is required to accept them. As the regulator of the threat of disagreement, "der Gatte" gives "das süße Mädel" an instruction (go somewhere with me) and responds to her question

---

23 Rancière considers Habermas's concept of political rationality "a bit too quick to take as read what is in fact in question." Rancière, *Disagreement*, 44.

24 Russell, "Rationality of Political Disagreement," 545.

25 Rancière, *Disagreement*, 44–45.

26 Rancière, *Disagreement*, 45.

(what do you mean) and disagreement (oh no) with another command (now listen to me). He immediately follows up with a false interrogative (you know) that does not invite her to adopt a critical attitude toward his speech act but instead serves to regulate the threat of her disagreement in this situation. His suggestion that she "know[s]" clarifies that there is no dissenting view that does not, in some sense, constitute a misunderstanding. He assumes that she knows what she is supposed to know (about this type of arrangement), or else if she does not, she only reveals her ignorance. He need not ask for consent and neither must he provide reasons why his utterance is in fact rationally acceptable. Instead, this metadialogue about (the lack of) reciprocity simply underscores a shared preunderstanding according to which he is her superior.

But *La Ronde* also contains an instance of *disagreement* by which a speaker contests her disqualification as an equal partner in dialogue. Rancière argues that for a disagreement to be successful, the speaker must problematize the speech situation itself and indeed break its inegalitarian ordering, the "as if" of the communicative attitude that disavows that her speech is in fact constrained. According to Rancière, such a dispute over the *distribution of the sensible* takes place through aesthetic rupture. The "emancipated spectator," to use Rancière's well-known term, who has begun to engage in a refashioning of reality uses poetic language to reimagine the relationship between the participants of the speech situation.[27] She demonstrates her capacity to produce arguments and metaphors and actively participates in the order of questioning (rather than just understanding). In a double reversal that draws attention to the role of gender in the distribution of the sensible, Schnitzler's play stages an instance of disagreement that *initiates* (rather than deflects) a sexual encounter, and it is the *female* character who is the instigator. In scene 9, "die Schauspielerin" dismisses the "Graf's" objection to having sex with her at midday with the following remark: "Mach' die Augen zu, wenn's dir zu licht ist" (225; "Shut your eyes if it's too light for you," 109). The "Actress's" statement works on two levels, a factual and an ideological one. Argumentatively, her statement suggests that if the "Count" were to shut his eyes, the light would no longer dampen his mood. Metaphorically, however, her statement uses light as a metaphor for propriety and morality, implying that he needs to shut down (let go of) his inhibitions and rationality. The "Actress's" statement both produces the argument (to have sex) and the situation (to adopt her irrational point of view/immoral lifestyle) in which it is understood. In this sense, understanding as it is implied here is not merely successful communication but rather communication that deconstructs the power relationships and standards of propriety in a given community. The "Actress's" performative

---

27   Jacques Rancière, *The Emancipated Spectator* (London: Verso, 2008).

utterance illustrates and challenges the inegalitarian assumptions of the patriarchal order.

Blackout

Not surprisingly, the line between drunk sex and sexual assault is not a concern in a nineteenth-century play. In the final scene of *La Ronde*, "der Graf" wakes up in a "Dirne's" room trying to piece the night together. He registers with surprise that he did indeed go home "mit dem Frauenzimmer" (233; "with that female," 111). Unable to remember if he had sex with the destitute girl, he sheepishly concedes, "Ich war halt b'soffen" (233; "The thing is, I was drunk," 111). "Der Graf" has no memory of what he did when they arrived at her "ärmliches Zimmer" ("mean little room"). He is not sure "Und was ist denn passiert? . . . Also nichts . . . Oder ist was . . .?) (233; "What happened? Nothing . . . or did I?," 111). The "Count" experienced a mental blackout in which he remained functional and conversational but was later unable to remember what he did because alcohol impaired his ability to form new memories.[28] In German, this form of drug-related temporary amnesia is colloquially referred to as *Filmriss*, an apt metaphor comparing the human cognitive apparatus to an analog camera that stops recording when the filmstrip breaks. Less precise and indeed misleading, the English term "blackout" may refer to a period of darkness (as in a city) caused by a failure of electrical power, or it may suggest that a light is suddenly turned off; for example, a stage light between scenes in a play, similar to the *cut to black* in a movie. Although Schnitzler did not intend for the sexual encounters to be shown on stage, the asterisks in the first nine scenes indicate that sexual acts occur, only that they are performed in the dark and hence are not viewed by the audience—a classic blackout scenario where the action continues but is not seen or witnessed. By contrast, the metaphorical expression of the *Filmriss* refers to actions that the actors themselves will be unable to remember.

When, in the play's final scene, an alcohol-induced *mnemonic* blackout takes the place of the theatrical blackouts of the previous scenes, the implications of this substitution are significant—not least because the mnemonic blackout increases the ambiguity of the scene's sexual situation, raising difficult questions about the linkages between gender, victimhood, and agency. During this postcoital morning-after scene, the male partner quibbles, not without some nervous ambiguity, about the possible romantic and sentimental dimensions of his encounter with the

---

28 See on this Sarah Hepola, "Kavanaugh and the Blackout Theory," *New York Times*, September 29, 2018, https://www.nytimes.com/2018/09/29/opinion/sunday/brett-kavanaugh-drinking-blackouts.html.

young prostitute:[29] "Wenn man nur das Kopferl sieht, wie jetzt . . . beim Aufwachen sieht doch eine jede unschuldig aus . . . meiner Seel, alles mögliche könnt' man sich einbilden, wenn's nicht so nach Petroleum stinken möcht' . . ." (236; "If one only sees the head, as now . . . when they wake up . . . they all look innocent . . . upon my soul, one really could imagine all sorts of things if the place didn't reek so of kerosene . . . ," 112). While "der Graf" does not exactly experience his having sex with an underage prostitute as a moral conundrum, there is a slight suggestion of compassion and guilt in his concern for her. He even hints at a view of his sexual conquest as degrading, victimizing, or exploitative to the young girl: "Sag', ist dir noch nie eing'fallen, daß du was anderes werden könntest? . . . Ich mein' aber einen, weißt einen, der dich aushalt, daß du nicht mit einem jeden zu geh'n brauchst" (239–40; "Tell me, did it ever occur to you to do something different? . . . you know: one lover who keeps you, so you don't have to go with just any man," 113). At the same time, "der Graf" worries that his intoxication may have impeded his sexual performance, when he asks the prostitute, "Ob schon manchmal wer bei dir war,—und nichts von dir wollen hat?" (247; "I mean, has it occasionally happened that a man was with you—and didn't want anything?," 115). The girl confirms that he fell asleep on her sofa but also assures him that he "fell for her" ("hab' ich dir besser g'fallen") and that she "fell with" him ("am Divan hing'fallen) [my translation]. "Der Graf" seems relieved to hear that he remained sexually functional and that the prostitute does not doubt his sexual potency. Clearly, his unease arises from a perceived threat to his honor and virility, rather than the girl's safety or well-being. Like the characters in the preceding scenes, "der Graf" is blatantly unconcerned with consent.

Schnitt's *About a World* likewise alludes to the issue of drug-induced blackout and incapacitated rape. Schnitt, however, infuses the topic with a pointedly feminist perspective. Set in a sweeping idyllic landscape, the film radicalizes and simplifies the power relations of Schnitzler's play. It controversially asserts men's systemic power in all matters of sexuality, although its reverse gang-rape scenario paradoxically hints at the possibility of a male claim to victimhood, as the single actor is outnumbered by his female victims.[30] A truly disorienting effect is achieved through the use of multiple look-alike actresses who are caught asleep in various lascivious poses. Viewed as a chronological series of sexual encounters,

---

29 See on this Benthien, "Masken der Verführung," 136 and 139.

30 On the notion of men as the real victims of the #MeToo movement, see Emma Grey Ellis, "How #HimToo Became the Tagline of the Men's Rights Movement," *Wired*, September 27, 2018, https://www.wired.com/story/brett-kavanaugh-hearings-himtoo-metoo-christine-blasey-ford#~:text=%23HimToobecame part of that,domesticviolenceandsexualabuse.

Schnitt's casting seems to illustrate the rationale of prostitution within an unequal gender order, invoking the replaceability of women in the sexual act and within the socioeconomic context of German society. It visually harkens back to Schnitzler's theatrical depiction of sexual substitution as a way to dispel notions of bourgeois "love" and legitimize a new code of "symbiotic sexual relations."[31] A similar idea is expressed by projecting the film in an endless loop that hints at sexual life reduced to its most mechanical, functional level. An alternative reading, however, might see in the film's repetitive pattern a reference to the intricate circular structure of Schnitzler's *La Ronde*, which according to Katrin Schumacher signifies a continual "recycling of sexual energies."[32] In this reading, the endless loop of the film would be suggestive of ongoing histories of sexual desire and erotic love that transcend topical debates and political narratives.

It is true that the film's setting is symbolic of sensual delight: the lush green landscape suggests a locus of erotic seduction. And yet a small creek cuts a meandering fissure in the Alpine meadow, symbolizing a larger, more significant break in the fabric of human erotic and sexual relations. Schnitt's surreal, wordless imagery ironically disaffirms the existence of an ordinary, rational language through which lovers could reach some kind of objective understanding of their shared lifeworld and the erotic nature of their interaction. With its withering depiction of women who are not just silent but incapacitated (or perhaps complicit), the film suggests that Habermas expects too much of his actors, especially with respect to inter-sexual relations as a last bastion of white male dominance and female subordination.

The film's symbolic setting is complemented by a rhetorically purposeful editing style. Schnitt employs dynamic cutting that functions to keep the film on edge and to startle the viewer. The video alternates at seemingly random moments between extreme long shots, governed by a sense of almost complete stillness, and full shots bluntly exposing the viewer to sexual advances that are as conspicuous as they are uncomfortable to witness. In its refusal to adhere to traditional procedures designed to hide the editing, Schnitt's film disassembles temporal continuity—as if alluding to a traumatic memory that cannot be processed into a coherent linear narrative. At the symbolic level, the jump cuts illustrate the tearing of a filmstrip—a Filmriss—that stands in metaphorically for a lapse of memory. As in *La Ronde*, the viewer does not witness any sexual acts. In

---

31   Benthien, "Masken der Verführung," 134.

32   Katrin Schumacher, "Wieder. Einmal. Wieder: Arthur Schnitzlers Akte der Wiederholung," in *Contested Passions: Sexuality, Eroticism and Gender in Modern Austrian Literature and Culture*, ed. Clemens Ruthner and Raleigh Whitinger (New York: Helmut Lang, 2011), 197–208, here 202.

Schnitt's film, however, there is no dialogue from which we could infer that they actually transpired.

There is an obvious disjunction between Habermas's concept of communicative action, so prominently featured in the film's captions, and the themes of *About a World*. The film provides little in terms of cues as to how to achieve understanding in language or how to relate to one another by way of mutual deliberation and argumentation. Instead, the video's ellipses and ambiguities point to aporias that are themselves figures for the moral doubt and legal perplexities regarding sexual assault. In particular, the omission of medium shots and close-ups impedes our sense of knowledge and access; we have to infer what a more probing, lingering camera could make explicit.[33] Although the viewer suspects the man to be a rapist from the earliest moments of the video, an atmosphere of uncertainty is maintained throughout. Not only does the video never confirm that a sexual assault takes place; it also sheds doubt on our ability to prove such a charge. This is partially an effect of the exclusive reliance on high-angle shots that are conventionally used to convey a power differential between viewer and victim. But in *About a World*, high-angle shots place the viewer in an impossible position suspended in midair, as if floating above ground in an extradiegetic act of levitation. If the viewer identifies with the position of the camera, and is thus set up to own the visual field of the film, she is forced to acknowledge that her position defies reality. This only adds to the effect of the dynamic cuts, which are made abruptly apparent to the viewer. To put it in the terms of suture theory, the dynamic cutting from one shot to the next exposes the constructed nature of the spectator's position as "subject" of the film, severing the imaginary wholeness that enables moments of identification with the plenitude of the image.[34]

What we have instead is a lack of personal connection and spatial intimacy. *About a World* foregrounds perspective and the visual limitation of the onlooker in order to contrast this with the unlimited power of a voyeuristic gaze. Schnitt thereby invokes Marcel Duchamp's last major artwork, *Étant donnés* (*Given*), a diorama-like assemblage that implicates the viewer in an act of voyeurism. In this puzzling diorama, on view at the Philadelphia Museum, the viewer spies, through a peephole in an ancient-looking wooden door and a tiny hole in a wall, a nude mannequin in a pastoral setting. The splayed female figure holds up a gas lamp in one hand; a waterfall can be seen cascading behind her. *Étant donnés* is a haunting installation in which the museum visitor is privy to a private

---

33 Bill Nichols, *Representing Reality: Issues and Concepts in Documentary* (Bloomington: Indiana University Press, 1991), 215.

34 See on this Kaja Silverman, *The Subject of Semiotics* (New York: Oxford University Press, 1983), 205–6.

moment that is usually reserved for intimate partners or paying clients. Hal Foster thus reads *Étant donnés* as a "making-physical of perspective" that is facilitated by an "uneasy mixing" of private and public contexts.[35] This is consistent with Rebecca Schneider's reading, by which the nude "becomes emblematic of the scopic field itself," indicating that the work is centrally concerned with the paradigm of perspective.[36]

The self-referential mise-en-scène of *About a World* takes Duchamp's concept of "private pornography made public" one step further by asserting that the contemporary reality of incapacitated rape is a "public secret" that we have simply learned to unsee.[37] In that way, the video mirrors and comments on the culture of binge drinking on American campuses that has become the setting for an epidemic of involuntary intoxication that drastically increases a student's exposure to incapacitated rape.[38] Beyond college campuses, the drawn-out case against Bill Cosby shows that sexual incidents involving intoxicated women occur regularly and often go unpunished.

With its shifts between static extreme long shots and handheld tracking shots, *About a World* oscillates between the representation of an objective reality and a subjective lifeworld—a structure that corresponds to Habermas's two-level social theory, which is built upon his analysis of, on the one hand, a theory of communicative rationality built into subjective, everyday speech, and, on the other hand, an objective theory of modern society and modernization that would overcome modernity's one-sided version of rationalization. In other words, both Schnitt's film and Habermas's social theory are invested in the deep and ongoing entanglement of subjective and objective processes. Schnitt's film does not, however, engage Habermas's dialectical interpretation of the relation between private and public autonomy simply to talk about the objective conditions of feminist struggles. Rather, the film stages an experience that is akin to the particular *distribution of the sensible* that, according to Rancière's now-famous definition, "reveals who can have a share in what is common to the community based on what they do and on the time and space in which this activity is performed."[39] As Tyson Lewis puts it,

---

35 Hal Foster, *Prosthetic Gods* (Cambridge, MA: MIT Press, 2004).

36 Rebecca Schneider, *The Explicit Body in Performance* (London: Routledge, 1997), 67.

37 Rosemary Geisdorfer Feal, Carlos Feal, and Carlos Feal Deibe, *Painting on the Page: Interartistic Approaches to Modern Hispanic Texts* (New York: SUNY Press, 1995), 265.

38 Maria Testa and Jennifer A. Livingston, "Alcohol Consumption and Women's Vulnerability to Sexual Victimization: Can Reducing Women's Drinking Prevent Rape?," *Substance Use & Misuse* 44, no. 9–10 (2009): 1349–76.

39 Jacques Rancière, *The Politics of Aesthetics: The Distribution of the Sensible*, ed. and trans. Gabriel Rockhill (London: Bloomsbury, 2004), 8.

"There is an aesthetic organization at the heart of social life—an aesthetics that defines the spaces, places, and modalities of visibility, audibility, and so forth. This partitioning of the sensible means that certain voices are heard as expressing viable political disagreements while others are heard as mere noise. . . . In other words, a commonsense hierarchy of the audible and the inaudible, the seen and unseen is constitutive of any given social body."[40]

About a World denounces the false assertion of the universal political axiom "We are all equal" that is applied to subjects without a share in the communal distribution of the sensible: those individuals "whose count is always supernumerary" within the police order.[41] Instead, the video reconfigures the sensible so that their claims may be heard and understood. By showing what is typically (and conveniently) unseen and overlooked as readily apparent but not broadly acknowledged, Schnitt's short literalizes the distribution of the sensible and at the same time creates a small rupture in its texture. The video hints at the idea that the social and political ordering may be nothing more than an ideological ruse. It makes the division between unequals appear aesthetically in the form of a disagreement that is staged within the aesthetic regime of art. In that way, *About a World* implicitly poses the problem of consent as one that concerns our consent to *politics* in Rancière's definition.[42] The women's inferred consent to the sexual advances is analogous to *our* veiled consent to the pseudoegalitarian logic of the police order.

As Graham Bowley rightly points out, the #MeToo movement "has established that women who individually once feared their sexual assault allegations would be discounted or dismissed can find corroboration and power when they come forward as a group."[43] Twitter can bring together otherwise isolated and disparate constituencies in order to create a new public based on informed deliberation. The platform has allowed the #MeToo movement to take a communal approach to its analysis of patriarchy, its gesture proceeding from the ideological conviction that misogyny is structural and that survivors can fight it by coming forward. And indeed, the sheer number of #MeToo testimonies has already done much to force systemic change at a social level. It is not hard to imagine how

---

40   Tyson E. Lewis, "Jacques Rancière's Aesthetic Regime and Democratic Education," *Journal of Aesthetic Education* 47, no. 2 (2013): 49–70, here 51.

41   Rancière, *Disagreement*, 58.

42   In his "Ten Theses on Politics," Rancière differentiates between the "politics of the police" and "real" politics "dissensus." Jacques Rancière, *Dissensus: On Politics and Aesthetics*, ed. and trans. Steven Corcoran (London: Bloomsbury, 2015), 27–44.

43   Graham Bowley, "Will the #MeToo Moment Shape the Cosby Case?," *New York Times*, January 18, 2018, https://www.nytimes.com/2018/01/18/arts/television/will-the-metoo-moment-shape-the-cosby-case.html.

the scenarios depicted in *La Ronde* and *About a World*—sexual encounters structured by silence and in the absence of rational consent—could be converted ex post facto into the kind of dissent and uproar that has come to define the #MeToo movement. Looking forward, the play's and the video's exposure of the communicative void surrounding sexual interplay gestures toward the need for societal transformation. In light of the debate surrounding affirmative consent and recent calls for explicit, verbal communication in sexual encounters, we would do well to recall Rancière's assertion that the one speaking is the one who speaks from "a shared world that others do not see" and that these others therefore "cannot take advantage of . . . the logic implicit in a pragmatics of communication."[44] Schnitzler's play and Schnitt's video know that concrete structures of communicative rationality must be coupled with egalitarian redistribution.[45]

---

44 Rancière, *Disagreement*, 38.
45 The editors would like to express their deepest gratitude to Corinna Schnitt for permission to reproduce images from her work.

Part III

Sexual Violence, Warfare, and Genocide

6:   War of the Vulva: The Women of Otto Dix's *Lustmord* Series

Jessica Davis

IN 1921, A SEX WORKER was murdered near German artist and World War I veteran Otto Dix's Dresden studio.[1] According to his friend Kurt Günther, Dix, when questioned by police, claimed that he probably would have had to commit such a murder himself if he had not been able to paint his own murder scenes.[2] Years later, Dix repeated this profoundly disturbing statement to filmmaker Fritz Lang, confessing that he would have to commit a sex crime in real life if he could not create his *Lustmord* (Sexual Death)[3] series on canvas.[4]

This study seeks to understand what Maria Tatar describes as "the drive to disfigure the female body—a representational practice that becomes evident in the many post–World War I works bearing the name of *Lustmord*."[5] Otto Dix's *Lustmord* series (Figs. 6.1–6.6) consists of six works created between 1920 and 1922, one hundred years before the recent "#MeToo" movement. These works depict graphic, grotesque imagery of viciously murdered women, traditionally understood to be sex workers. They are typically nude or in their underclothes, on the bed or nearby on the floor, and in sexually suggestive poses with their legs splayed and their genitalia mutilated. Notably, in a diary he kept while fighting on the front in the First World War, Dix bitterly declared, "Eigentlich, wird im letzten Grunde bloß aller Krieg um und wegen der Vulva geführt" (Actually, in the final analysis all war is waged over and

---

1   Olaf Peters, "'Painting, a Medium of Cool Execution': Otto Dix and Lust-mord," in *Otto Dix*, ed. Olaf Peters (New York: Prestel, 2010), 92–107, 101.

2   Peters, "'Painting," 97.

3   Though *Lustmord* translates to "Lust Murder," prominent scholars, such as Olaf Peters and Maria Tartar, refer to it as "Sexual Death" when translating to English. For the purpose of this chapter, I will do the same.

4   Diether Schmidt, *Otto Dix im Selbstbildnis* (Berlin: Henschel Verlag Kunst und Gesellschaft, 1981), 58.

5   Maria Tatar, *Lustmord: Sexual Murder in Weimar Germany* (Princeton, NJ: Princeton University Press, 1995), 68.

for the vulva).[6] The fact that Dix connects war with women and sex and then later proceeded to attack the vulva on canvas suggests a relationship of cause and effect—linking sexual violence with power.[7] In depicting the mutilation of sex workers, Dix symbolically judged and executed a group of women who are often perceived as representative of the decaying morals of Weimar society and, according to Dix, of a war that, he believed, was caused by the vulva. The destruction of female genitals and of the female form as such also undermines long-held artistic notions of feminine beauty and the female nude in academic art. According to Dix, "Alle Kunst ist Meisterschaft" (All art is mastery),[8] which suggests that the *Lustmord* series could be read as an attempt to figuratively regain mastery over women; if not in the real world, then at least on canvas. It is also possible that Dix's misogyny could have intensified owing to the war, causing him to use women as a scapegoat for his own deteriorating masculine psyche. Therefore, the *Lustmord* series links Dix's hate for Weimar society, the war, and women. To Dix, the sex worker signified the type of debauchery and moral decay that he identified with the Weimar Republic. Conversely, the much discussed, newly emergent type of the "Neue Frau" or "New Woman" who owned her sexuality and fought for the right to work was seen as a threat to an already fragile masculinity in post–First World War Germany. Dix's work suggests that he perceived modern women as threatening and attempted to reverse course by using art to distort their sexuality, stripping them of their identity and power in society.

The implications of the analysis outlined above are damning. Seen in this light, Dix created morbidly violent works to appease his voracious bloodlust aimed at women. Such an explanation, however, does not speak to the root of this hostility. Otto Dix's prewar works consist of realistic

---

6   Cited in Steve Plumb, *Neue Sachlichkeit 1918–33: Unity and Diversity of an Art Movement* (New York: Rodopi, 2006), 89. Unless otherwise indicated, all translations from the German are mine. This accusatory statement is one on which Dix does not elaborate; therefore, we may never know his exact meaning regarding how the vulva is the cause of all wars. In exploring Dix's works, however, one sees two common themes: war and sex. For Dix, both put a man at risk of death—he may die on the battlefield or perhaps from venereal disease. War and sex are also related in terms of procreativity—woman births man, man kills man.

7   The vulva is emphasized in many of Otto Dix's works. One example is the woodcut *Apotheose* (1919; *Apotheosis*), in which the vulva is enlarged and centered, aggressively implying that sex (or the vulva) is central to the downfall of society and the main object of motivation for men. Another example is *Die sieben Todsünden* (1933; The Seven Deadly Sins), in which the sin of lust is portrayed by a woman whose dress folds in the shape of a vulva.

8   Cited in Maria Tatar, *Lustmord: Sexual Murder in Weimar Germany* (Princeton, NJ: Princeton University Press, 1995), 97.

self-portraits and landscapes that are reminiscent of Vincent van Gogh.[9] The First World War marks a clear shift in Dix's oeuvre: his postwar projects focus on suffering, violence, and corruption. Even more damning, large segments of the contemporary German male population appear to have shared his hostility toward women.

The interwar period witnessed the birth of the New Woman. Following the events of the First World War, in which Germany suffered a humiliating loss, enforcing traditional gender roles offered a path toward restoring masculinity and regaining national stability, thus confirming Dix's connection between war and sex. In spite of such efforts to shore up national and individual male pride, however, the Weimar Republic remained plagued by instability. Dix's *Lustmord* series reflects such contemporary social and political turmoil as well as his own mental strain caused by war trauma and by the era's shaken sense of masculinity embodied in the figure of the disabled veteran. Dix's series constitutes an attack on the sexually confident New Woman and on the shifting gender dynamics of his time.

To be sure, the sociopolitical situation in post–First World War Germany impacted Dix's aesthetics and his mental state. It is possible that the violent imagery of his postwar work, which includes the *Lustmord* series, served as a vehicle for homicidal fantasies brought about by shell shock, or what is now known as post-traumatic stress disorder (PTSD), a neurological disease that can lead to flashbacks and violent actions.[10] Artworks alone should not be used as indicators of mental health, but, coupled with Dix's interviews and diary entries, they arguably point to a troubled mental state. I argue that Dix created the *Lustmord* series as an outlet for his hostility toward women because he believed that they were ultimately responsible for all war[11] and because he resented that, unlike traumatized veterans, the New Women were thriving in the postwar period. The *Lustmord* series can thus be seen as Dix "righting" the wrongs he experienced during and after the war. Curiously, the gory depictions and posing of Dix's *Lustmord* women mimic those of the slain men he represented in his earlier *Der Krieg* (1924; The War) series. The maimed woman stands in for the killed male soldier; it is she who deserves death, and in killing her the balance of gender is restored.

---

9 Examples include *Selbstportrait mit Distel* (1912; Self-Portrait with Carnation) and *Sonnenaufgang* (1913; Sunrise).

10 I do not propose to offer an accurate medical assessment of Otto Dix's postwar condition. We can, however, reconstruct from interviews, eyewitness accounts, his diary entries, and, most importantly, his art, a level of emotional turmoil that has since been associated with trauma.

11 Dix's logic is open to interpretation. In many of his works the woman is represented as a femme fatale, a seductress with evil intent. If the vulva is the cause of all war, then arguably war is motivated by lust and sex.

Figure 6.1. Otto Dix, *Der Lustmörder (Selbstbildnis)*
(The Sex Murderer [Self Portrait]), 1920. Oil on canvas
(66⅞ x 47¼ in.). Location unknown. © 2022 Artists
Rights Society (ARS), New York / VG Bild-Kunst, Bonn.

Figure 6.2. Otto Dix, *Lustmord* (Sexual Murder), 1922. Oil on canvas (65 x 53⅛ in.). Location unknown. © 2022 Artists Rights Society (ARS), New York / VG Bild-Kunst, Bonn.

Figure 6.3. Otto Dix, *Lustmord* (Sexual Murder), 1922. From *Tod und Auferstehung* (Death and Resurrection). Etching on paper (16.57 x 19.69 in.). Museum Kunstpalast, Düsseldorf. © 2022 Artists Rights Society (ARS), New York / VG Bild-Kunst, Bonn.

Figure 6.4. Otto Dix, *Lustmord I, Versuch* (Sexual Murder I, Attempt), 1922. Watercolor, brush and ink over pencil on paper (22½ x 19.7in.). Private collection, Germany. © 2022 Artists Rights Society (ARS), New York / VG Bild-Kunst, Bonn.

Figure 6.5. Otto Dix, *Scene I (Mord)* (Scene I [Murder]),
1922. Watercolor, brush and ink over pencil on paper
(19⅛ x 14⅜ in.). Private collection. © 2022 Artists
Rights Society (ARS), New York / VG Bild-Kunst, Bonn.

Figure 6.6. Otto Dix, *Scene II (Mord)* (Scene II [Murder]), 1922. Watercolor, brush and ink over pencil and paper (25⅝ x 19⅝ in.). Otto Dix Stiftung, Vaduz. © 2022 Artists Rights Society (ARS), New York / VG Bild-Kunst, Bonn.

The Horrors of War

Dix, like many of his countrymen, volunteered for service when the war broke out. His motivation and enthusiasm were shared among the working class, who hoped that this war would hasten the end of bourgeois society.[12] Dix's *Selbstbildnis als Soldat* (1914; Self-Portrait as a Soldier; Fig. 6.7) portrays his determined, confident demeanor upon entering the war. This sense of hope and optimism, however, disappeared quickly once Dix witnessed firsthand the horrors of battle. Dix, who was a machine gunner during the war, described what war meant to him in a diary entry from 1915–16: "Läuse, Ratten, Stacheldraht, Flöhe, Granaten, Bomben, unterirdische Höhlen, Leichen, Blut, Schnaps, Mäuse, Katzen, Gas, Artillerie, Schmutz, Mörser, Feuer, Stahl: das ist Krieg! Es ist das ganze Werk des Teufels!" (Lice, rats, barbed wire, fleas, shells, bombs, underground caves, corpses, blood, liquor, mice, cats, gas, artillery, filth, mortars, fire, steel: that is war! It is all the work of the Devil!).[13] This list outlines the subjects of Dix's wartime art, which, as history can attest, is gruesome but not exaggerated. Produced later that year, *Selbstbildnis mit Artilleriehelm* (1914; Self-Portrait with Artillery Helmet; Fig. 6.8) shows just how much the war had changed Dix. Thick, chaotic brushstrokes depict a demented man with shifty eyes and a mouth set into a hard line, a far cry from his self-portrait earlier that same year.

In his later years, the artist described how his wartime experiences affected the content and style of his works and motivated him to take his art in a different direction. In an interview from 1961, Dix stated,

> Der Krieg ist eben etwas so Viehmäßiges: Hunger, Läuse, Schlamm, diese wahnsinnigen Geräusche. Ist eben alles anders. Sehen Sie, ich habe vor den früheren Bildern das Gefühl gehabt, eine Seite der Wirklichkeit sei noch gar nicht dargestellt: das Häßliche. Der Krieg war eine scheußliche Sache, aber trotzdem etwas Gewaltiges. Das durfte ich auf keinen Fall versäumen![14]

> [War is something so beastly: hunger lice, mud, those crazy noises. Is all completely different. You see, with the early paintings, I had the feeling that there was a dimension of reality that had not yet been dealt with: ugliness. The war was a dreadful thing, but awe-inspiring all the same. I could not under any circumstances miss that!]

Clearly, even forty-three years after the end of the First World War, Dix remembered vividly what combat meant to him. The war changed his art

---

12 Eva Karcher, *Otto Dix* (New York: Crown, 1987), 13.
13 Karcher, *Otto Dix*, 4.
14 Karcher, *Otto Dix*, 16.

Figure 6.7. Otto Dix, *Selbstbildnis als Soldat* (Self-Portrait as a Soldier), 1914. Oil on paper (26¾ x 21 in.). Kunstmuseum Stuttgart. © 2022 Artists Rights Society (ARS), New York / VG Bild-Kunst, Bonn.

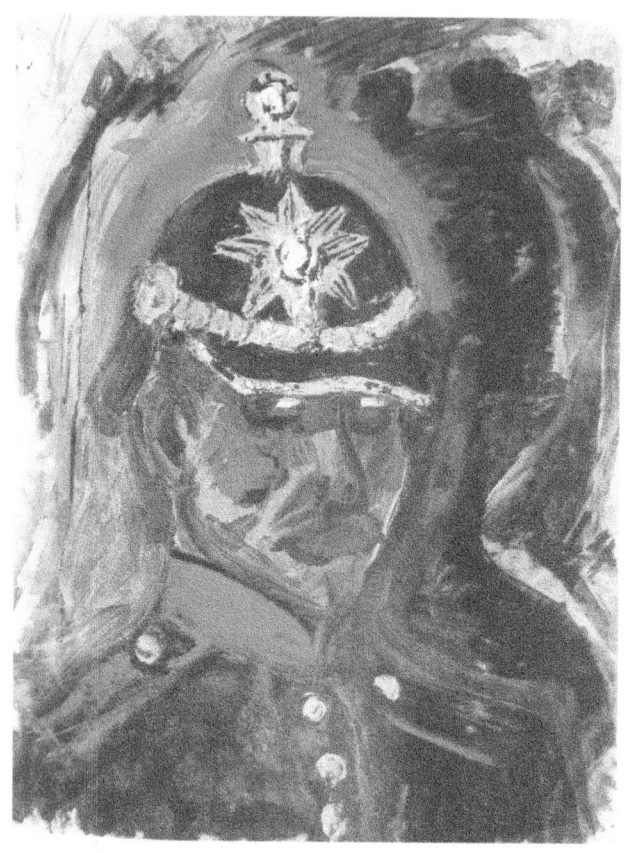

Figure 6.8. Otto Dix, *Selbstbildnis mit Artilleriehelm*
(Self-Portrait with Artillery Helmet), 1914. Oil on canvas
(26.77 x 21.06 in.). Kunstmuseum Stuttgart. © 2022 Artists
Rights Society (ARS), New York / VG Bild-Kunst, Bonn.

and provided him with an opportunity to represent his emotions in a new way. Tellingly, Dix's work during and after the war focused almost exclusively on highlighting the ugliness of humanity.

Shell Shock

German doctors placed responsibility for recovery from shell shock squarely on the shoulders of the patient, not the doctor. Physicians who treated shell shock and hysteria tended to believe that the condition was self-inflicted. Hysteria was also seen as a feminine, even emasculating ailment. After the war, the situation of German veterans who suffered from shell shock deteriorated further; no further research on shell shock was conducted, and by 1926, veterans diagnosed with shell shock no longer received pensions.[15] There was a massive increase in documented cases among German veterans in the 1920s, likely exacerbated by botched treatments.[16] *Zitterers*, or jitterers, as they were called, were a common sight on Berlin's streets, their shaking a typical symptom of extreme emotional distress brought on by trauma. Berlin police went so far as to post warnings about the Zitterer, declaring them to be malingerers, or fakes, conning pedestrians for money.[17]

If Dix indeed suffered from this condition, the negative reception of shell shock patients in public and the painful electroshock therapy methods used to "cure" them might explain why he was reluctant to seek treatment. It is possible that Dix did not begin to feel the symptoms of shell shock until he returned home. And since there were fewer opportunities for treatment in the postwar period, it is also possible that Dix simply did not have access to treatment.

In an interview, Dix described how the war had changed him, indicating that he suffered from sleep disturbances and reoccurring dreams, both symptoms of PTSD:

> Denn ich habe jahrelang, mindestens zehn Jahre lang immer diese Träume gehabt, in denen ich durch zertrümmerte Häuser kriechen mußte, durch Gänge, durch die ich kaum durchkam. Die Trümmer waren fortwährend in meinen Träumen.[18]

---

15 Peter Leese, *Shell Shock: Traumatic Neurosis and the British Soldiers of the First World War* (London: Palgrave Macmillan, 2002), 141.

16 Andreas Killen, *Berlin Electropolis: Shock, Nerves, and German Modernity* (Los Angeles: University of California Press, 2006), 152.

17 Killen, *Berlin Electropolis*, 152.

18 Karcher, *Otto Dix*, 22.

[Because for years, for at least ten years, I always had these dreams, in which I had to crawl through ruined houses, through passageways I could hardly squeeze through. I dreamed continually about rubble and ruins.]

In their book *Treating PTSD in Military Personnel* (2011), Bret A. Moore and Walter E. Penk describe reoccurring dreams of war as an indicator of PTSD among veterans. Tellingly, the dream described above evokes warfare along with feelings of claustrophobia and discomfort, though it is not a direct memory. The fact that Dix lived with this dream for some ten years points to PTSD, since trauma-induced dreams that are not related to PTSD typically stop after a period of about thirty days.[19]

Starting in 1916 while in the trenches, Dix began work on his infamous *Der Krieg* series. Published in 1924, the series comprises fifty engravings in five portfolios. The connection between these artworks and Dix's war experience is obvious. The works, which have inspired countless studies, are a testament to his war trauma and the horrors he endured. According to Eva Karcher, *Der Krieg* indicates that Dix was "psychologically affected by the war."[20] Because Dix worked on this series while still in combat, it can be read as a direct response to his in-the-moment traumatic experiences. At the same time, PTSD is a condition that lingers long after the moment of trauma. In Dix's case, the effects of the war trauma are still evident in his later *Lustmord* series, which acts as a bridge between Dix's wartime experience and his postwar life. Dix was critical of Weimar society, which he saw as the flamboyant and unstable result of Germany's failure in the First World War. Dix perceived his postwar surroundings as ostentatious and corrupt and felt a need to draw his audience's attention to moral and social decay—this time within society, not on the battlefield. This interest continued throughout the 1920s, as evidenced in the *Lustmord* series. In other words, the horrors that Dix saw in the trenches are intimately linked to the horrors he detected in postwar German society.[21]

---

19   Bret A. Moore and Walter E. Penk, *Treating PTSD in Military Personnel: A Clinical Handbook* (New York: Guilford Press, 2011), 273.

20   Karcher, *Otto Dix*, 21.

21   Interestingly, both Dix's *Lustmord* series and his *Der Krieg* series were labeled "entartete Kunst" (degenerate art) by the Nazis, the former for its violence to women and the latter for its unheroic depiction of war. A full set of Dix's *Der Krieg* series was included in the infamous state-sponsored Degenerate Art Exhibition of 1937. Many of Dix's works, including his 1922 *Lustmord* oil painting, are missing, presumed destroyed by the Nazis.

The Weimar Republic and the New Woman

The Weimar era was infamously plagued by hyperinflation for some time. During its peak between 1919 and 1923, Germany witnessed a staggering increase in unemployment; disabled veterans were particularly hard hit by high unemployment rates. Women who were affected by the labor crisis were at times forced to turn to sex work as a means to support themselves and their loved ones. The number of brothels and cabarets increased. Berlin became widely known as the "city of whores," a sexual playground for tourists, with sex workers numbering in the thousands (between 5,000 to 120,000 female sex workers).[22] At the same time, crime rates increased, with sex crimes directed at female sex workers constituting the largest category.

Violent acts against women were a popular subject matter among German artists of the interwar period and are often seen as a response to the perceived ubiquity of the New Woman among the middle class. The term "New Woman" was popularized by American expatriate writer Henry James to describe the rising feminist ideal in a time that witnessed the first wave of feminism in the United States and Europe.[23] First-wave feminists worked to change the social roles of women and advocated for female suffrage. These middle-class women set out to challenge the patriarchal structures in their own households, in the workforce, and in the state. The dichotomy of the private and public spheres was upended by the First World War, which afforded women new employment opportunities and increased freedom. This newfound independence culminated in the success of the suffrage movement in 1919, when German women gained the right to vote. In the 1920s, fashion signaled to onlookers that women were now in charge of their own sexuality: skirts were shorter, hair was trimmed and bobbed; the flapper was born.

The New Woman was seen as a threat by men of all ranks and titles, artists included, who wished to reaffirm the patriarchal system. Indeed, this shift in gender discourses accounts for some of the hostility aimed at women during this time and perhaps explains why Dix and his contemporaries lashed out at women in their art.[24] In her article "*Lustmord*: Inside the Windows of the Metropolis," Beth Lewis argues that social anxiety brought about by the changing role of women was felt deeply by many

---

22 Mel Gordon, *Voluptuous Panic: The Erotic World of Weimar Berlin* (Port Townsend, WA: Feral House, 2006), 27.

23 Hugh Stevens, *Henry James and Sexuality* (Cambridge: Cambridge University Press, 1998), 27.

24 One of Dix's most famous portraits of a New Woman is *Portrait of Sylvia von Harden* (1926), in which he depicts her as masculine, with big hands and a monocle.

artists and intellectuals, who in turn shared their views with their middle-class audiences, who were bent on maintaining the status quo.[25]

The *Lustmord* Series

According to Lewis, post–First World War artists looked to popular urban culture for artistic inspiration and found it in the streets in the form of sex workers and crime, which had become an everyday occurrence in the Weimar Republic.[26] Especially in large cities, such as Berlin and Dresden, crime fed into the sensationalism of the market-driven press, offering attention-grabbing headlines that appealed to the emotions of their readers. Dix's works from this period depict crime and sex work against the backdrop of a glamorous nightclub and/ or among socialites in luxurious clothing, perhaps in an effort to demonstrate to the public that social decadence is accompanied by an aura of ugliness.

Otto Dix was by no means the only artist of the interwar period who addressed the theme of sexual murder. A number of German and Austrian expressionists, including Oskar Kokoschka (1886–1980),[27] and members of Dada Berlin, such as George Grosz (1893–1959), were drawn to the topic.[28] Grosz, who inspired Otto Dix, had a lot in common with the creator of the *Lustmord* series, but it is the differences between the two artists that help us to better understand their aesthetic. In "Painting, a Medium of Cool Execution: Otto Dix and Lustmord," Olaf Peters points to a key difference between Dix and other artists who represented sex murder in their art: Dix did not rely on literary themes.[29] Instead, his *Lustmord* series is deeply personal and autobiographical. In contrast, Grosz's *Lustmord* works were inspired by sensationalist reports in the media and Edgar Allan Poe short stories and are marked by a clear sense of detachment.[30]

Dix's *Lustmord* series consists of six works made after the war, the final five created after his involvement with Dada. The first work of the series, *Der Lustmörder (Selbstbildnis)* (1920; The Sexual Murderer [Self-Portrait], 66⅞ x 47¼ in.; Fig. 6.1 above), is a life-size oil painting that

---

25 Beth Irwin Lewis, "*Lustmord:* Inside the Windows of the Metropolis," in *Berlin: Culture and Metropolis,* ed. Charles W. Haxthausen and Heidrun Suhr (Minneapolis: University of Minnesota Press, 1990), 115.

26 Lewis, "*Lustmord,*" 115.

27 Oskar Kokoschka, *Mörder, Hoffnung der Frauen III* (1909; Murderer, Hope of Women III).

28 Peters, "'Painting,*" 95.

29 Peters, "'Painting,*" 98.

30 George Grosz, *The Mielzynski Affair* (1912/13); George Grosz, *The Double Murder in the Rue Morgue* (1913).

was likely painted after the International Dada Fair of 1920 and is currently missing. George Grosz's *John der Frauenmörder*, 1918; John the Murderer of Women, 34 x 31⅛ in.) possibly inspired this work, since both works are Dadaesque with a collage-like, cartoonish quality. It is therefore significant that Dix's work is larger. A possible reason for this is that Dix was in competition with Grosz and sought to outdo him in size. Moreover, a life-size painting can facilitate engagement with a work.

What unfolds in *Lustmörder (Selbstbildnis)* is sheer chaos. Dix portrays himself as the murderer: flat, fully frontal, and centered. Unlike other artists who depicted sex crimes and chose to focus on the victim, Dix makes himself the subject of this work. The painting shows Dix as a monster with an angular body, potentially a form of personal commentary suggesting that his time on the front morphed him into a bloodthirsty being. His face has a disturbed, crazed expression, with threatening fangs and unfocused eyes. In Dix's left hand is the knife he used to dismember the woman's body while the right holds a leg. Next to Dix's right elbow is a perfume bottle with the inscription "DIX AV." In her article "The Charleston and the Prosthetic Leg: Otto Dix and the Art of the Balancing Act," Karsten Müller argues that the inscription is a play on words, merging Dix's name with that of a well-known brand of cosmetics called "PIXAVON."[31] This, however, does not explain why Dix omitted the letters "O" and "N." More likely, the AV following DIX stands for the Latin *ad vivum*, which means "to that which is alive." This abbreviation is often found on antique prints, usually following the name of the engraver.[32] "Ad vivum" implies that a scene was taken from life; that is, that it depicts actual events. As an academically trained artist who studied engraving, printmaking, and the German Renaissance, Dix would have been familiar with this expression. Thus, in incorporating the words "ad vivum" in his self-portrait, Dix emphasizes that the inaugural work in the series is based on actual events. This, however, is likely not the case. If the image depicts "reality," it is a mental reality taken from Dix's mind.

The painting depicts an action-filled scene; a lamp sways overhead, and all around Dix's angular body are the body parts of his victim, covered in his handprints. There are at least five distinct handprints in all, each smeared on a different part of the dismembered woman's body. The most noticeable print is on the butchered woman's hip next to Dix's left knee. Because the work is life-size, these handprints are likely impressions

---

31 Karsten Müller, "The Charleston and the Prosthetic Leg: Otto Dix and the Art of the Balancing Act," in *Otto Dix,* ed. Olaf Peters (New York: Prestel, 2010), 164–77, 170.

32 "Icones ad vivum Expressae," British Museum, accessed February 25, 2014, http://www.britishmuseum.org/research/collection_online/collection_object_details.aspx?objectId=1425305&partId=1&searchText=ad%20vivum.

of Dix's own hand on the canvas. They are carefully placed, creating the illusion of a hand wrapping around the different body parts. I propose that the handprints act as an index; that is, as a signifier that testifies to the reality of the signified; they show that Dix, the painter, was there and manipulated the body himself: he has been caught "red-handed." Moreover, as handprints, they also stand for the signature of the artist painting the painting. This fusion of art and life evokes the tenets of the Dada Berlin group, who also encouraged the union of life and art.

Dix's *Lustmörder (Selbstbildnis)* can be compared to his earlier self-portrait as a soldier, *Selbstbildnis, grinsend den Kopf aufgestützt* (1917; Self-Portrait, Grinning, Head Resting on Hand; Fig. 6.9). In this work, Dix has given himself a deviant smile, fangs, and shifty eyes. The head resting in the hand suggests contemplation, while the facial expression points to malicious thoughts. The similarity between this earlier self-portrait and the later *Lustmord* work creates a link between the two that ties *Lustmörder (Selbstbildnis)* to the theme of war.

The second painting in the series, *Lustmord* (1922; Fig. 6.2 above) is either missing or hidden in a private collection. An almost life-size oil painting in the manner of *Neue Sachlichkeit* (New Objectivity), it evinces similarities to Dix's earlier Dada-inspired work. Unlike *Der Lustmörder (Selbstbildnis)*, which depicts a murder-in-progress, *Lustmord* portrays the moment right after the murder when the chaos is winding down. The murderer appears to have just gotten away, but blood is still trickling down from the victim's body, forming puddles on the floor. The victim is splayed and falling off the bed, her intestines spilling from a slit in her abdomen—the wound further emphasized through a reflection in a mirror on the wall. The pose is reminiscent of Henry Fuseli's *The Nightmare* (1781), but a disemboweled belly now takes the place of an incubus, suggesting that the mangled female body is itself the dreaded nightmare. *Lustmord* is more disturbing than Dix's earlier work, which conveys a sense of dark humor, because it leaves the viewer wondering what happened and who the perpetrator was. The change in style also highlights the gravity of the situation, since Neue Sachlichkeit paintings, unlike Dada works, are realistically rendered.

A closer look at this painting unveils a window on the back wall with a view of crisp, clean, architectural order. This scene is at odds with the chaos in the interior, thus establishing a stark contrast between the female victim and the surrounding cultural order. According to Dix,

> Alle Kunst ist Exorzismus. Ich male auch Träume und Visionen; die Träume und Visionen meiner Zeit, die Träume und Visionen aller Menschen! . . . Ich habe viele Dinge gemalt, auch Krieg, Albträume,

Figure 6.9. Otto Dix, *Selbstbildnis, grinsend den Kopf aufgestützt* (Self-Portrait, Grinning, Head Resting on Hand), 1917. Black chalk on paper (15⅞ x 15⅜ in.). Private Collection, New York. © 2022 Artists Rights Society (ARS), New York / VG Bild-Kunst, Bonn.

schreckliche Dinge. . . . Malen ist das Bemühen, Ordnung zu schaffen; Ordnung in dir selbst. Es gibt viel Chaos in mir, viel Chaos in unserer Zeit.

[All art is exorcism. I paint dreams and visions too; the dreams and visions of my time, the dreams and visions of all people! . . . I painted many things, war too, nightmares, horrible things. . . . Painting is the effort to produce order; order in yourself. There is so much chaos in me, much chaos in our time.][33]

This statement aligns well with *Lustmord,* suggesting that the woman in the work was slain to produce order. Not order in the physical sense, as the room and body are in disarray, but rather order in the societal sense;

---

33 Reinhold Heller, *Art in Germany 1909–1936: From Expressionism to Resistance* (New York: Prestel, 1990), 171.

by destroying the sexuality of the woman, Dix has taken away her power. In doing so, the hierarchy of gender is restored to its former patriarchal glory. Moreover, the painting could also be read as an attempt to restore order in the artist's own life; by directing his attentions to "murdering" women in a creative medium, he is able to purge himself of his violent fantasies; he cleans up psychic disorder by externalizing it in his art.

A closer inspection reveals that the furnishings in Dix's first and second oil paintings are the same. The swaying lamp and a chair in Dix's earlier work reappear in his 1922 version. Interestingly, this setting resembles the room Dix occupied as a student in Dresden from 1919 to 1922.[34] Also worth noting is a tiny, inconspicuous handprint on the wall in between the victim's legs. It does not appear to be an impression of the artist's own hand; rather, it looks to have been painted and thus less personal. At the same time, however, the handprint was deliberately added, likely to allude to the 1920 painting. The repetition of the furniture and the handprint motif suggests that the earlier work depicts a murder in progress, whereas the later work portrays the aftermath of the same murder. Seen in this light, Dix is the murderer in both works.

An analysis of one of the later five works in Dix's *Lustmord* series suggests that Dix copied the position of his mutilated corpse from a police photography book. Both injuries and placement of the victim in the etching *Lustmord* (1922; Fig. 6.3 above), carried out in the veristic style of Neue Sachlichkeit, resemble those of a corpse in a photograph from Erich Wulffen's *Der Sexualverbrecher* (1910; The Sexual Offender). *Der Sexualverbrecher* offers information about different sexual fetishes, with a whole chapter dedicated to *Lustmord* in general, and contains police photographs of gruesome sexual murders. One such photograph (Fig. 6.10) correlates with Dix's etching (Fig. 6.3). Both the woman in *Lustmord* and the woman in Wulffen's photograph have their stomachs slit from abdomen to genitalia, and one leg is positioned on the bed (or couch in the photograph), with the other sliding off. In the foreground of the etching, two dogs are copulating, further highlighting the charged, sexual atmosphere. The question remains: Why would Dix study an actual crime scene prior to representing it on paper? I propose that, as a practitioner of Neue Sachlichkeit, Dix drew on the language of realism to properly portray his inner violent imagery. Dix once pronounced, "Ich bin so ein Realist, wissen Sie, dass ich alles mit eigenen Augen sehen muss" (You know, I am such a realist that I have to see everything with my own eyes).[35] This indicates that the scene Dix etched had to be accurate so as to become real for the viewer, as well as the artist.

---

34 Tatar, *Lustmord*, 15.
35 Kunstmuseum Stuttgart, ed., *Otto Dix and the New Objectivity* (Ostfildern: Hatje Cantz, 2012), 138.

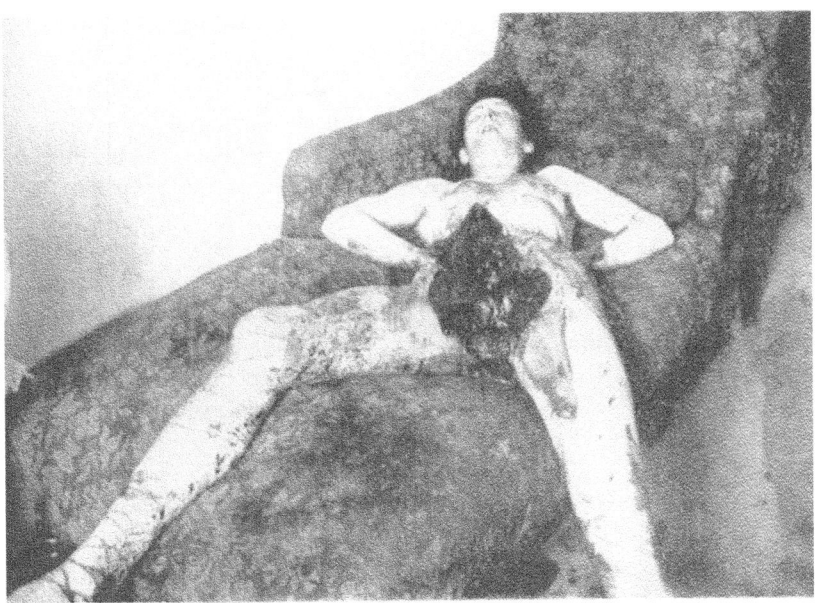

Figure 6.10. Image from Erich Wulffen's *Der Sexualverbrecher* (The Sexual Offender), Berlin: Langenscheidt, 1910, Fig. 9, page 455.

The remaining three works in the series (Figs. 6.4–6.6) are all water-colors in an expressionistic style. Two of these watercolors show the woman alone, hanging limply off the bed, while the third features a grinning man in a bowler hat in the foreground. Not much has been written about these works, and the identity of the man in the latter work is uncertain. There are, however, similarities between Dix's man in the bowler hat and Grosz's man in a bowler hat from *John der Frauenmörder*. While the third painting evokes a work by Grosz, the first two bear similarities to Dix's oil painting *Lustmord* (Fig. 6.2 above). The similar body positions, with the corpse falling off the bed, can be read as a serial killer "calling card," suggesting that both murders were committed by the same person. Thus, the series can be read as Dix's own collection of murders, or the same murder depicted from different points of view, and as a testament to his obsession with the nexus of sex and death. It is possible that the *Lustmord* series provided Dix some mental relief. Dix's diary and testimonies from friends suggest that the artist had violent urges. Thus, one might wonder if the series allowed the artist to express his inner desire for violence in a cathartic manner, substituting a brush for a knife. Interestingly, these works were not intended for Dix's private use, apart from the *Lustmord* oil painting, which hung in his dining room.[36] Rather,

---

36 Müller, "Charleston," 132.

these works, the watercolors and prints especially, were meant for public consumption, which suggests that there was an interest, or at least a sense of morbid curiosity, in such imagery.

Dix's prints and watercolors of sex death were easy to sell in the early 1920s. Hyperinflation peaked in 1922, the same year he finished the series, and middle-class collectors were looking for affordable art as a ready form of investment. Surprisingly, the subject matter was especially attractive to the *Spießer*, or middle-class philistine, who made up much of Dix's clientele.[37] Dix's 1920s correspondence with Johanna Ey, owner of the Galerie Das Ey, reveals that a print version of his oil work *Lustmörder* (Fig. 6.11) was among the prints he wished the gallery to sell.[38] In her memoirs, Ey remarks how beautiful the works were and how easily she managed to exhibit and sell them.[39] Clearly, there was a demand for this type of art, which arguably coincided with the misogynistic beliefs of many German consumers. The public may also have been intrigued by Dix's ability to pierce through the hypocrisy of bourgeois society to reveal the ugliness underneath. This flaunting of sensationalist transgressions enabled Dix to make a name for himself in the art world then as now.

Mädchen am Spiegel

Interestingly, Dix never faced censorship or legal repercussions for his *Lustmord* series (at least before the Third Reich).[40] While they are shocking to the contemporary viewer, at the time his works were understood to be moralizing scenes: a precautionary tale of the "high risk" lifestyle of a sex worker. In 1922, Dix was brought up on charges for obscenity and pornography for his painting *Mädchen am Spiegel* (1921; Girl before the Mirror; Fig. 6.12). This charge was not due to any portrayal of violence against women but, rather, was motivated by the depiction of the woman's pubic hair, vulva, and buttocks.[41] Eventually, the court concluded,

> Die Möglichkeit, dass der erste Gesamteindruck des Bildes ein das Schamgefühl verletzender sein kann, bleibt aber dennoch nicht ausgeschlossen. Dieser Eindruck wird jedoch völlig in den Hintergrund gedrängt durch die bei einiger Versenkung in das Bild unverkennbar moralisierende Tendenz, die der Angeklagte bei Herstellung

37 Heller, *Art in Germany*, 172.
38 Müller, "Charleston," 132.
39 Susanne Meyer-Büser, "Otto Dix—Proletarian Rebel and Big-City Dandy," in *Otto Dix—The Evil Eye*, ed. Susanne Meyer-Büser (New York: Prestel, 2017), 24–68, 34.
40 Heller, *Art in Germany*, 171.
41 Heller, *Art in Germany*, 171.

Figure 6.11. Otto Dix, *Lustmörder* (Sex Murderer), 1920.
Etching on paper (11.6 x 9.8 in.). Private Collection.
© 2022 Artists Rights Society (ARS), New York / VG
Bild-Kunst, Bonn.

des Bildes ernstlich verfolgt hat, wozu übrigens noch die von den
Sachverständigen begutachtete künstlerische Ausführung des Bildes
hinzutritt.

[The possibility that the first full impression of the painting could
offend one's sense of decency cannot be ruled out. After some contemplation, however, this impression recedes into the background
due to the undeniable moralizing tendency recognizable in the
painting, and which the accused seriously sought out in the production of the painting, to which is also to be added the artistic manner of the painter's execution, to which experts in the field have
testified.][42]

---

42 Heller, *Art in Germany*, 171.

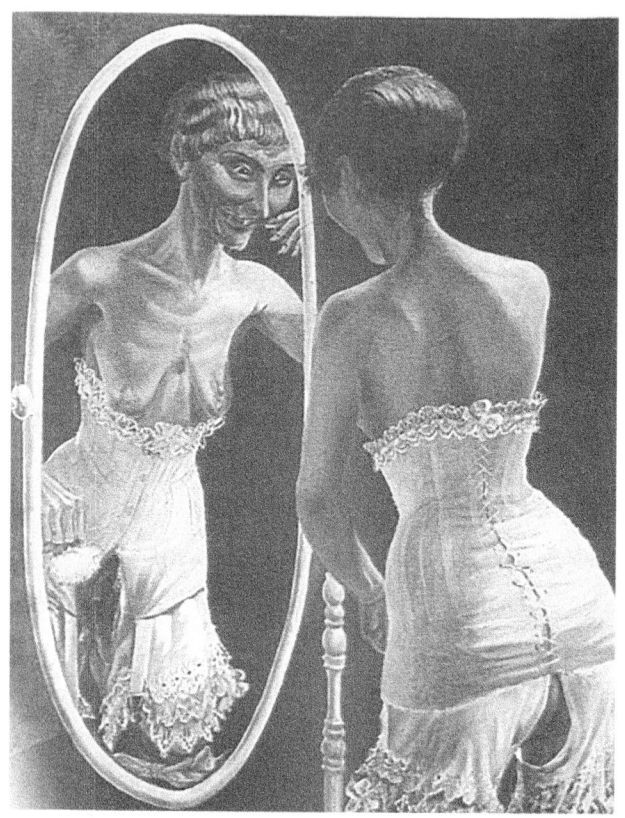

Figure 6.12. Otto Dix, *Mädchen am Spiegel* (Girl before the Mirror), 1922. Oil on canvas, dimensions unknown. Location unknown. © 2022 Artists Rights Society (ARS), New York / VG Bild-Kunst, Bonn.

This statement suggests that the moralizing tale attributed to *Mädchen am Spiegel* outweighs any vulgarity. The lesson seems to be that sex work is an ugly profession that women should not partake in and men should not finance.

Mädchen am Spiegel, an oil-on-canvas painting that is now lost, depicts a sex worker observing herself in the mirror. The use of the word "Mädchen," or "girl," in Dix's title seems cynical, since this woman, whose backside suggests youth, casts an old and haggard reflection in the mirror. The reflection shows a bony woman with sagging breasts and a hard face. Her crazed smile appears to be missing some teeth. The aging sex worker was a common theme in Dix's work. Dix tended to evoke, unsympathetically, the hard life that these women live—a hard life that uses them up and renders them ugly. Because the woman appears young from the back, her elderly reflection exposes her as deceitful. A slit in her undergarments allows easy access to her genitalia, but buyer beware. Dix has done all he can to make this woman sexually undesirable; viewers should not want her—they should be repelled by her and everything she represents. In fact, her face—with its long nose and toothy grin—evokes traditional portrayals of witches. With this work, Dix has stripped the woman of her humanity and attempted to instill in the viewer a sense of horror at her ugliness. We are not meant to feel sympathy but, rather, are justified in our scorn because she let this happen to herself.

Then as now, the public does not care for the life and death of a sex worker; she is the master of her own fate, and her death is her own fault. There is little awareness that prostitution is a last resort for many women. This was particularly so in the Weimar Republic, when hyperinflation made wages and pensions worthless. Dix's *Lustmord* women are not clearly marked as sex workers; rather, sexually promiscuous women and sex workers were often conflated. The *Lustmord* women in a broader sense represent symbolic efforts to silence sexually free, modern women by means of violence and humiliation. Tellingly, the slain woman, not the murderer, is the sinner. The murderer is an instrument of social justice; not the antagonist but rather a vigilante who acts in the best interests of the public.

The 1920s sentiment evident in Dix's painting still reigns true in the 2020s, case-in-point being the representative for Arizona's Fourth Congressional District, Paul Gosar's, 2021 doctored anime Twitter video of him slaying fellow representative Alexandria Ocasio-Cortez, a woman known for her outspokenness and feminist viewpoints. Ocasio-Cortez, like the New Women before her, is a threat to the status-quo and long held notions of gender norms. And like the New Woman, Ocasio-Cortez faced similar persecution in the form of violent visual imagery, no doubt in an effort to humiliate and silence her. In Gosar's eyes, he is the hero of the story; by killing Ocasio-Cortez, he has ridden the world of her "radical" voice.

Dix's and Gosar's points of view need to be left in the past. For too long, the women of Dix's *Lustmord* series have been erased by the focus on the violence of the crime and the reasoning of the murderer. The works treat the victim as a cautionary tale of a loose woman whose sexuality led to her downfall—less a person than a spectacle. In the eyes of the artist, these women embodied a societal problem: they were at the root of all the chaos and uncertainty in his life. Women were the target of his aggression and easy scapegoats for his hardships, the war, and the downfall of Weimar society. By contextualizing Dix's series, we can give the *Lustmord* women a voice. They represent countless real women who were murdered in a similar manner during this time period. Reassessing the visual imagery of Otto Dix's *Lustmord* series with a focus on the mutilated female nude gives us the opportunity to deny power to the abuser and reaffix it to the victim.

7: Death to the Patriarchal Theater! Charlotte Salomon's Graphic Testimony

Maureen Burdock

Life? or Theatre?
An Intersectional Testimony

GERMAN-JEWISH ARTIST Charlotte Salomon (1917–43) recorded her short life in a series of over 1,000 works on paper, all while in exile in France over a period of two years. She overlaid 330 paintings with hand-lettered narratives on tracing paper, while she painted text directly onto some of the later pieces.[1] This collection, titled *Life? or Theatre? A Song-Play* (*Leben? oder Theater? Ein Singespiel*), remained relatively obscure for decades, and it was often categorized as Holocaust art—understandably so, as Salomon was murdered at Auschwitz, and her opus is the "largest single work of art created by a Jew during the Holocaust," according to Toni Bentley.[2] But while she does reveal the effects of social and political violence on herself and her family in a handful of the paintings and texts, the work, despite being exhibited most often in Holocaust museums, is not about the Shoah; it is about the artist's and her family's tragedies and secrets, about her loves, her artistic inspiration and drive, and about her fear of suicidal depression in the midst of war and exile.

Depression among the women in Salomon's family may have been related to domestic abuse. In a thirty-five-page letter to her mentor, Alfred Wolfsohn, which was only made public in 2015, the young artist confesses to fatally poisoning her grandfather. Of course, all autobiographical works are creatively mediated memories of personal experiences, not journalistic reportage. It is possible that this confession is hyperbolic and fictional; nevertheless, even a murderous fantasy informs readers of

---

1   Griselda Pollock, *Charlotte Salomon and the Theatre of Memory* (New Haven, CT: Yale University Press, 2012), 9.

2   Toni Bentley, "The Obsessive Art and Great Confession of Charlotte Salomon," *New Yorker* (July 15, 2017), https://www.newyorker.com/culture/culture-desk/the-obsessive-art-and-great-confession-of-charlotte-salomon.

the extreme nature of the artist's feelings toward the old man. And one could argue that Salomon's letter falls into a different category of life writing than her creative *Song-Play*, one less prone to outlandish fabrications. In her letter, Salomon records her grandfather's insistence that she share a bed with him and her feelings of intense aversion toward him, culminating in the murder. As Bentley observes, Salomon writes that it was Herr Doktor Ludwig Grünwald, not "Herr Hitler," who "symbolized for me the people I had to resist."[3] While it is impossible to substantiate this interpretation, Salomon's *Gesamtkunstwerk* and confessional postscript might well point to a history of sexual abuse. Through a close reading of several of Salomon's images and corresponding texts, I will contend that *Life? or Theatre?* is fundamentally a work of resistance to the intimately and sociopolitically oppressive actors in her life—to the patriarchal theater.

In keeping with the theme of this volume, examining Salomon's work within the context of the contemporary #MeToo movement, I employ critical race theorist Kimberlé Crenshaw's concept of intersectionality, which she theorized in 1989 and further elaborated in 1991.[4] Arising from Black Feminist and Womanist analyses, this framework takes into account the overlapping "isms" of oppression faced by women of color in the United States. Intersectionality can certainly also be applied to European forms of racism, including those faced by Jewish women during the Nazi era. I apply the concept here to elucidate Salomon's work and struggles. It is impossible (or at least inaccurate) to view her suffering as a German Jew without taking into account her oppression as a subject of an overwhelmingly sexist culture with its constant reinforcement of the fallacy that women are inferior intellectually and creatively. Systemic misogyny certainly normalized Salomon's grandfather's abuse, and, in a vacuum of respectful and caring adults who might have helped the young artist to find her way, emboldened her self-appointed mentor, Alfred Wolfsohn, as he capitalized on her needs for affirmation and affection by taking advantage of her sexually. The mental illness in Salomon's family, which affected particularly the women whose intellectual and creative lives were continually stifled and undermined, forms a third vector in this intersectional triad of disadvantages. To examine and to subvert all of these overlapping faces of oppression, Salomon established a multifaceted form of expression.

Importantly, the chimeric form Salomon developed makes room for expressing emotional truths as well as autobiographical facts. Salomon was working decades before the proliferation of US underground

3   Bentley, "Obsessive Art."
4   Anna Carastathis, *Intersectionality: Origins, Contestations, Horizons* (Lincoln: University of Nebraska Press, 2016), muse.jhu.edu/book/48097, 1.

autobiographical and confessional comics that scholars most often identify as foundational to contemporary graphic memoirs, but her genre-
defying work has much in common with that form, which has room for
both emotional and factual veracity. As Elizabeth El Refaie points out,
"some graphic memoirists are much more interested in reflecting their
feelings toward their own past in an authentic manner than in claiming
to portray the 'absolute truth.'"[5] This "emotional truth" is relevant,
especially for women and minorities who have been legitimately afraid to
openly bear witness to violent experiences for fear of reprisal or of being
discredited. As Leigh Gilmore asserts in *Tainted Witness*, historically, race,
gender, sexuality, and doubt stick to women witnesses in various venues,
including in autobiographical literature and comics.[6] Certainly, race and
sexuality "stick" to men as well, but Gilmore's argument here also reflects
Crenshaw's concept of intersectionality, where multiple factors of identity amplify an existing complex of conditions that put women's stories at
greater risk for being discredited.

Salomon was a Jewish artist during the Third Reich. The Nazi conflation of Judaism with mental illness and "degenerate" modern art, as Ariela
Freedman points out, already placed the young Salomon in an extremely
perilous position.[7] Add her gender and her familial history of depression
and suicide to these already implicating vectors, and one begins to understand what the young artist was up against. Further, Freudian ideas such
as his concept of "penis envy," which he published in a paper in 1905,
cast suspicion on every young woman in cases of incest, as girls, according
to him, were forever seeking the missing appendage. This inherent need
to possess a phallus, according to Freud, gives rise to the Oedipus complex, a condition where young girls are compelled to reject their mothers
and to make their fathers into their love objects.[8] Salomon would almost
certainly not have dared to openly accuse her grandfather of sexual abuse
for fear of being disbelieved and discredited (or blamed). By examining
the artist's emotional truths and the ghostly impressions that emerge
from her visual and textual poetics, and by reading her work as a prototypical graphic narrative, I hope to bring to light the extraordinary testimony of a groundbreaking artist whom we might understand better now,
in the age of #MeToo and confessional comics. I will use the frame of

---

5   Elizabeth El Refaie, *Autobiographical Comics: Life Writing in Pictures*
(Jackson: University Press of Mississippi, 2012), 44.

6   Leigh Gilmore, *Tainted Witness: Why We Doubt What Women Say about
Their Lives* (New York: Columbia University Press, 2018), 5.

7   Ariela Freedman, "Charlotte Salomon, Degenerate Art, and Modernism as
Resistance," *Journal of Modern Literature* 41, no. 1 (Fall 2017): 3–18, here 5.

8   Sigmund Freud, *Three Essays on the Theory of Sexuality*, 1905, https://
www.sigmundfreud.net/three-essays-on-the-theory-of-sexuality-pdf-ebook.
jsp, 45.

intersectionality to first examine Salomon's creation of a groundbreaking multifaceted literary-artistic form; then I will elaborate on her role as a young modernist artist within the context of the Third Reich. Next, I will examine Salomon's choice of the title *Life? or Theatre?* and her rejection of her grandfather's oppressive patriarchal charade in favor of her own intimate creative production. This leads me into a discussion of the very specific and personal ways in which the young artist embraces her inherent genius by choosing fine art as her life path, in defiance of the other, very limited roles available to women of that time and place. Next, I show how Salomon's much older mentor and lover, Alfred Wolfsohn, exploited her need for affirmation and guidance, and how this relationship may well have triggered Salomon's existing issues related to childhood sexual abuse. Following Griselda Pollock and using close visual and literary analysis, I trace the clues Salomon left for us to detect this theme of abuse. The graphic testimony she left before her tragic murder at Auschwitz might well serve as inspiration for today's #MeToo activists.

Salomon's Chimeric Code

Charlotte Salomon's "strange work," as she called it, has become better known over the past few decades, but it continues to elude being *knowable*, as Freedman puts it.[9] Salomon's work can be parsed using literary or art historical analysis. Art historian Griselda Pollock's approach in her definitive work, *Charlotte Salomon and the Theatre of Memory*, is to focus on individual paintings rather than to analyze the work as a single narrative, as the author explains in a short film made by her publisher.[10] This recognition of Salomon as a serious modernist artist is vital. Too often, women artists have been reduced to intimate spheres, to tidy trick-pony stories that minimize their art-historical significance: "How quaint, and she painted, too!" Tellingly, after the first publication of her work in 1963, as Bentley expounds, Salomon was referred to for decades as "Charlotte," in a "misguided attempt to market her as a sister diarist to

---

9   Freedman, "Charlotte Salomon," 5.

10   Pollock states, "My approach to Charlotte Salomon's *Life? or Theatre?* is to focus on individual paintings. That's to say, I break the idea of a single narrative. I bring my art historical approach to say, 'What am I seeing? How is this being made? How is the material process of literally putting the paint on?' I try to understand the relationship between the act of painting and the images that came into being as she did so because this is not illustration, this is not an existing story. She wanted to confront what the events she painted looked like but also what they felt like. And for this she invented an extraordinary range of painting." "Griselda Pollock Discusses the Life and Work of Charlotte Salomon," *Yale Books Blog*, February 21, 2018, yalebooks.co.uk/display.asp?k=9780300100723, 04:15–05:00.

Anne Frank, which has served both to render her all but anonymous and to defang her ferocious work."[11] Departing from this reductive approach, postmodern feminist scholarship has made room for the biographical without diminishing the historic significance of the artist. I propose that, ideally, Salomon should not be regarded as only an artist or read as solely a writer. She invented a complex system—a chimeric composite comprised of thousands of pieces—that entreats chimeric methods of evaluation: careful reading, visual analysis, and affective and transdisciplinary engagement to decode it.

The term *chimeric* is more fitting here than *hybrid*. Whereas hybrid creatures are merged seamlessly into a new and legible whole (think pluot or Bernedoodle), the Chimera is a creature composed of disparate parts that all keep the integrity of their own forms despite their uneasy coexistence. The word *Chimera* comes from Greek mythology: a monster with a lion's head, a goat's body, and a serpent's tail. This image is useful in thinking about Salomon's intersectional life and work because the Chimera insists that we look at all of her parts, but also that we simultaneously look at her as a whole entity. All of the parts are juxtaposed for good reasons, like pieces of a puzzle; in their union, a multiplicity of meanings is created that exceed the individual components. The chimera metaphor echoes the concept of intersectionality. While less in-demand aspects of identity are often subsumed into a seamless hybridic and saleable entity under capitalism, the disparate elements of a chimeric identity are not as easy to streamline and brand.

In the interest of viewing Salomon's work as chimeric and genre-defying, it makes sense to employ contemporary methods used by scholars who analyze autobiographical comics. As Freedman has suggested, "Perhaps Salomon's strange invention comes closest to the contemporary form of the confessional graphic memoir . . . in its seriality, its representation of time as space, its 'autobiofictionalographical' qualities, and its complex mobilization of word and image."[12] A growing number of graphic memoirists since Salomon have interwoven autobiographical and psychological insights with cultural and political observations. The most celebrated work along these lines is Art Spiegelman's *Maus* (1980–91), which he began to create serially in the 1970s. Through drawings and writing, Spiegelman works through his parents' (especially his father's) ordeal of surviving the Holocaust while simultaneously exploring his

---

11   Bentley, "Obsessive Art."

12   Freedman uses Lynda Barry's neologism, "autobiofictionalography," which Barry coined in *One! Hundred! Demons!* (Seattle: Sasquatch Books, 2002). Ariela Freedman, "Charlotte Salomon's Life? or Theater? A Melodrama?" in "A Dossier of Essays on Melodrama," special issue, *Criticism* 55, no. 4 (Fall 2013): 617–36, here 618.

own fraught relationship with his father. As in Salomon's work, personal memories and motivations, familial interactions, and historical events are interlaced to create a complex new whole. It is precisely in their intertwining that these components bear witness to a more complete truth than they would on their own. Andrew Kunka looks at autobiographical comics and their creators' goals of bearing witness to facts while also revealing emotional veracity. He points out that authors of autobiographical prose can use figurative language without altering truths: "'I felt like a mouse in a trap' or 'I was a mouse, caught in a trap'" will not confuse readers as they are accustomed to metaphor and simile as literary conventions. Creators of comics, however, can actually render the figurative as literal. In Spiegelman's work, the Jews aren't *like* mice; they *are* mice. "The mental process that the visual allegory requires for readers to decode the narrative is different from and more complex than the tools available to the prose autobiographer," Kunka asserts.[13] In this vein, Salomon created allegories, drawing from various art-historical periods from the Renaissance to the modern, and established her own visual vocabulary generated from mythology, dynamic psychology, and musical lyrics, and from her own lived experiences and feelings. She chose to use the twenty-six standard letters (plus three umlauts and one ligature) of the German alphabet and three primary colors to create her opus. She included references to tunes, some well-known, others either obscure or invented to fit her own moods. Salomon tactically combined these textual, visual, and lyrical elements to create a unique codification of her life—a codification she literally (as I will later show) urges us to decrypt.

Salomon's work exceeds simple categorizations and insists on a complex and comprehensive analysis. When one part is left out, the whole puzzle loses its integrity and meaning. The first publication of *Life? or Theatre?*, by Paul Tillich and Emil Straus in 1963,[14] for example, framed the work as a diary, despite the fact that Salomon created the work after the described events had taken place and that she wrote it in the third person. This 1963 publication also omitted all references to Salomon's family history of suicide, which is one of the most important themes in the work. This is an example of hybridization that serves a particular consumer demand, making invisible and inaudible those aspects of Salomon's intersectional identity that might distract from selling a specific type of cultural product to a particular audience.

---

13 Andrew Kunka, *Autobiographical Comics* (London: Bloomsbury Academic, 2018), 7.

14 *Charlotte: A Diary in Pictures by Charlotte Salomon; Comment by Paul Tillich; Biographical Note by Emil Straus* (London: Collins, 1963).

Modernist Un-conventions

Throughout her short life, Charlotte Salomon was confronted with impossible challenges. She was born in 1917 into an assimilated Jewish German family in Berlin. In addition to facing anti-Semitism and the horrors of Nazi Germany, she also had familial tragedies to contend with. Six of her close relatives, including her mother, aunt, and grandmother, all committed suicide. Charlotte's survival depended on her ability to translate herself into a work of art, to create something meaningful in the midst of so much death, and that work—that meaningful soul-baring life-affirming creation—was too complex, too large, too difficult, too painful, too beautiful, hopeful, and irrepressible, to fit within one tidy genre. Freedman and Pollock have shown how Salomon's art was decidedly modernist. Salomon was formally trained and certainly exposed to modern artists and art movements. She would have been familiar with the work of Vincent van Gogh, Marc Chagall, Ernst Ludwig Kirchner, Käthe Kollwitz, Otto Dix, George Grosz, Edvard Munch, and Pablo Picasso. She also would have been exposed to Dadaist and surrealist work. Dada artists had been busy disrupting conventions, creating text-based art and art-based texts, using every means at their disposal to respond to the horrors of the First World War and the societal fragmentation and political strife that marked the early part of the century. Artists like Hannah Höch, André Breton, and Marcel Duchamp had devoted themselves to disrupting the staid and stolid superstructure of German society at that time, from the Wilhelmine education system to the established patriarchal and nationalistically inclined art world. Höch's photomontages and paintings are an apt example of how modernist artists were recombining disparate elements chimerically, purposely confusing audiences and art markets. In her montages, male and female body parts collide with animal, vegetable, and mechanical elements, resulting in grotesque composites, monster images that serve to dismantle illusions of seamlessness. Modernist work served as foil to the patriarchal status quo and its penchant for simple binaries and for the easily assimilable—the definable, predictable, and saleable products preferred by the mainstream.

In order to survive with her sanity intact, Salomon, like her contemporaries, fought against the despotic political and the very personally tyrannical family patriarchs hounding her. She saw the latter, the intimately oppressive foe, embodied in her grandfather, Herr Doktor Ludwig Grünwald, whom she names "Herr Dr. Knarre" in her work. The thirty-five-page letter mentioned above, written by Salomon after she completed *Life? or Theatre?* and kept private by the artist's parents for decades, came to light in 2015. In "Charlotte Salomon's letter to Amadeus Daberlohn" (her fictional name for Alfred Wolfsohn), now held at the Jewish Historical Museum in Amsterdam, she describes the impact her grandfather had on her state of mind while she was in exile with him in France. She reports getting threatening and mean-spirited letters from him while they were briefly living apart; but her residency permit in France was dependent on her role as his caretaker. It is clear that she dreaded his return to her care: "My happiness was at an end," she writes. "Absolutely at an end from brilliant sunlight into grey darkness back to my grandfather playing his '*theater of civilized, cultured men*'" (emphasis mine).[15] I believe that this sentence, more than anything else, points to the artist's intentions behind the title of her work.

Salomon's Private versus the Patriarchal Theater

Various theories have emerged to explain the title of Salomon's opus, *Life? or Theatre?* Some scholars have suggested that "theater" in this case alludes to various categories in the performing arts—Brechtian theater, *Singspiele*, the subversion of *Singspiel* into Salomon's "*Singespiel*"; by adding the additional syllable, Freedman suggests, perhaps Salomon meant to disrupt the conventional notion of this musical theater genre.[16] But it is also plausible that the artist used the term "theater" to represent her grandfather's charade, the posturing of the so-called civilized and cultured man. I suggest that her title alludes to that patriarchal drama, the self-congratulatory theater of powerful men who create their world at the expense of those it excludes: those who are not allowed in the theater, let alone on the stage or in the spotlight. There is an expression in German, *Mach kein Theater!* (Don't create drama!), that is associated with women's tendencies toward "hysterical" behavior. The exclusion of women from the realm of high drama expressed in this phrase goes back to Greek antiquity. Aristotle believed that women were deformed humans, and thus only men were allowed to play women's roles in the Athenian theater. The patriarchal theater as established by Aristotle was a space for working out overpowering emotional issues and stimulating valuable catharsis in its audiences, thus ridding society of emotional excesses and allowing it to function smoothly. In contrast, the idea of females "making theater" evokes the antithesis of order, as women were believed to be constitutionally incapable of controlling emotional excess. In ancient Greek texts, the womb (Greek *hystera* being the word for uterus) was an impish free agent, a tiny mischievous creature roaming a woman's body, lodging itself rudely in various places including her brain, and thus causing its host to

---

15 Charlotte Salomon, *Life? or Theatre?* (New York: Duckworth, 2017), 805. I will be citing this edition throughout the rest of this chapter.

16 Freedman, "Charlotte Salomon's *Life? or Theater?*," 626.

act hysterically and to blow events and feelings well out of proportion.[17] Though this notion was discarded in the seventeenth century, the essence of this belief in a disorder that overwhelmingly affects women clung on, even into the modern era.

In the 1880s, Austrian physician and physiologist Josef Breuer's "hysterical" patient, Bertha Pappenheim (known under the pseudonym Anna O.), would fall into a self-hypnotic trance and tell Breuer "fairy tales" from what she called her "private theater." The Viennese-Jewish Pappenheim, who would later become a groundbreaking feminist activist, reportedly replied to a complaint about Jews not being granted enough space, "We don't need space; we have spiritual space that knows no limits."[18] Like Pappenheim, who unapologetically claimed the theatrical space of her own brilliant imagination, Salomon drew from her own "theater"—from her private spiritual and creative life—in defiance of that other, uncompromisingly antifeminist, killjoy theater of the oppressive patriarch.

Salomon's grandfather and his theater of civilized and cultured men stood for everything Salomon hated—hated with a murderous rage and needed to purge in order to live. While the artist portrays all other people in her life with uncommon maturity and profound compassion, her grandfather stands outside of that circle of sympathy as the clear antagonist of *Life? or Theatre?* In the letter mentioned earlier, the artist confesses to watching her grandfather die after cooking him an omelet laced with morphine opium veronal. Her grandparents had brought the poison with them when they went into exile in France so they could commit suicide together if their money ran out. What would have made Salomon hate a close relative enough to commit murder? While I will examine the possibility of a correlation between the artist's repugnance, the suicides in her family, and a sexually predatory grandpa, I have found several other reasons, spelled out by Salomon, for her lethal hatred that suggest that predatory sexual behavior was one facet of a larger complex of overlapping oppressive behaviors and events. Moreover, as I suggested earlier, it is an entire system (social, psychological, medical, and economic) that enables and exculpates abusers by discrediting and further disempowering women and girls, especially, in this case, non-Aryan women, and especially women with a history of mental illness. Of course, this is not to say that Salomon's grandfather was prejudiced against his grandchild because

---

17 H. Boeker, "Hysteria," in *Encyclopedia of Neuroscience*, ed. Marc D. Binder, Nobutaka Hirokawa,and Uwe Windhorst (Berlin: Springer, 2009), https://doi.org/10.1007/978-3-540-29678-2_2331,1905.

18 Melinda G. Guttman, "'One Must Be Ready for Time and Eternity': The Legacy of Bertha Pappenheim," *On the Issues* 5, no. 4 (1996): 42, ProQuest, https://search.proquest.com/scholarly-journals/one-must-be-ready-time-eternity-legacy-bertha/docview/221139440/se-2?accountid=14505, 1.

she was Jewish, but her Jewishness in that time and place certainly diminished the circle of potential witnesses—of people she could have turned to for help.

The overarching motivation for Charlotte's desire to stand firm against the old man is that he seeks to destroy Charlotte's vitality and sanity. He ridicules and undermines his grandchild at every turn. On a sunny day in the garden of the American benefactress's villa in France, where Charlotte and her grandparents have taken refuge, Charlotte's grandmother asks her, "Are you here in the world only to paint?" And Grandfather chimes in, "You are much too lenient with her. Why shouldn't she work as a housemaid, like all the others?" (Salomon, *Life? or Theatre?*, 696). Grandmother Knarre then backpedals, coming to Charlotte's rescue: "Because, whatever happens, if it's at all possible I wish to prevent that [that is, that Charlotte should have to give up painting and work as a housemaid]" (Salomon, *Life? or Theatre?*, 697). Salomon in this way presents her grandmother as somewhat befuddled by young Charlotte's commitment to painting, but her grandfather as utterly dismissive of her very essence. "Knarre" in German means to creak or rattle, which could refer to his antique patriarchal condescension. It is also a colloquialism for a gun. The young artist must disarm the old Knarre; it is a matter of survival. Further, she must resist his attempts, and by extension those of the theater of cultured men, to undermine her if her besieged spirit is to survive. Salomon fears the demise of her sanity and creativity more than she fears actual death. As she explains in her letter, her physical survival was tied to her role as her grandfather's caretaker, since her residency permit was dependent on her continuing in that role. *Life? or Theatre?* is not only about Salomon's struggle to stay alive; it is overwhelmingly about her quest for a *meaningful* life as a cultural creator at a time when the combination of her gender and her Jewishness made this practically impossible.

The Juno in Her

Salomon directly links her drive to become an artist with the increasingly terrifying political situation. The first page of "Act Two" (Salomon used the conventions of a playwright to section her work) chronicles the Nazi takeover of power on January 30, 1933. A mob of figures holds aloft a big red flag emblazoned with a backward swastika, as though reflecting history in a mirror. This emblem continues to infest the pages that follow; it invades everything, as Freedman and Pollock have pointed out, including wallpaper, textiles, clothing . . . it literally becomes enmeshed with the fabric of Salomon's world. These pages reveal how Jews, including Salomon's father, whom she calls "Doctor Kann" in this work, are driven out of their jobs and government positions. At the same time, the rapid Nazification of school must have made life utterly intolerable for Salomon.

At the end of her wits, Charlotte Kann (Salomon's name for herself in this work) stands demurely yet resolutely, arms crossed, before her father (Salomon *Life? or Theatre?*, 176; Fig. 7.1). Both are garbed in dark blue against a mostly mustard-yellow background that is infected with more inverted red swastikas. Salomon's text overlay for this image reads, "*over and over again,* I won't go back to school. You can do with me what you will . . . ," and her father answers, "Just see your finals through, that's all I ask of you."

The next page shows Charlotte Kann from a posterior aerial view, still clad in deep blue, hunched over a desk, painting utensil in hand as she makes marks upon a paper (Salomon, *Life? or Theatre?*, 177; Fig. 7.2). The desk, a lighter blue rectangle that cuts the page into thirds diagonally, is set sharply against a background, similarly hued yellowish as the previous page. Only now the swastikas are gone. Instead, energetic short strokes and dabs of sunshine yellow have taken their place. A few gold sparks appear to fall onto Charlotte's desk. A notation at the top of the text overlay states "*Mel[ody]: ich hört ein Bächlein rauschen* (Tune: I heard a babbling brook)." This is the first line of a song by Franz Schubert, the early nineteenth-century Romantic composer. The song can be understood as an invitation to follow one's muses or creative impulses, as the first-person narrator of the song is moved to follow a little stream until he is completely lost in its enchanting burbling.

Swastikas thus dispelled by the *Rausch* (*rauschen* means the rushing of water, but *Rausch* also means a pleasant state of stimulation, exhilaration, or intoxication—an artist's high, in this case), Charlotte Kann muses, "Perhaps I could learn to draw, that might be just the thing" (Salomon *Life? or Theatre?*, 177). On the following page, Charlotte consults with her stepmother, the famous singer Paula Lindberg, playfully dubbed Paulinka Bimbam in *Life? or Theatre?* Charlotte adores Paulinka and had formed a fierce bond with her after losing her biological mother. Despite their very loving interactions earlier in the book, Paulinka and the now teenaged Charlotte do not always see eye to eye. In response to Charlotte voicing her desire to study art, Paulinka informs Charlotte that she will "only respect a person who can make money and earn a living. Because that's what's important" (Salomon, *Life? or Theatre?*, 178). Paulinka's message comes across as patronizing, and Salomon's portrayal of her is caricaturized; Paulinka's figure is depicted as large and looming. Her dominant chin juts aggressively toward the diminutive figure of Charlotte. The singer's blouse is covered in hatch-marks reminiscent of the oppressive swastika symbol from earlier in Act Two, and so is the light-blue ground on which the two figures stand. The yellow behind them is muted and pale. On the next page, Paulinka is seen approaching the Strassburger Feige School of Fashion Design. She explains that she has a daughter who is not particularly talented, to which the school director

Figure 7.1. Charlotte Salomon, *Life? or Theatre?*, 176. Collection Jewish Museum, Amsterdam. © Charlotte Salomon Foundation.

responds reassuringly that her daughter will soon be earning money. The plan fails, however; Charlotte hates the school and her teacher, who ultimately pronounces her talentless. "No, I refuse to stay here with this stupid old cow, where through the dirty window even the sun's bright ray can only dimly play," Charlotte defiantly concludes (Salomon, *Life? or Theatre?*, 192). She is looking for the sparks, the full sunshine, the

Figure 7.2. Charlotte Salomon, *Life? or Theatre?*, 177. Collection Jewish Museum, Amsterdam. © Charlotte Salomon Foundation

Rausch. She persists in her choice to become an artist and, with the aid of private drawing lessons, eventually garners acceptance into the Academy of Arts in Berlin.

The immense challenge of finding meaning and purpose and, importantly, *acceptance* as an artist is arguably the most important theme throughout this work, particularly before Salomon is exiled. The artist's portrayal of female characters reveals changing gender roles of the modern era. Paula Lindberg, aka Paulinka Bimbam, in some ways exemplifies the emergence of the New Woman figure in the artistic, literary, and cultural landscape of the Weimar era.[19] Salomon goes into some detail about the famous singer's biography. Before marrying Charlotte's father, Paulinka had turned down a marriage proposal from a certain Professor Singsong, a divorced father, opera conductor, and doctor. Paulinka decided, "A man like that demands that honorable women devote their entire time to him. . . . Gone is the dream of the singer if I join my life to his. So, although deeply touched, she remained firmly resolved not to marry him" (Salomon *Life? or Theatre?* 85). Paulinka, while devoted to her art and very successful, still adheres to bourgeois financial and societal expectations. She is a career woman with a family and also does volunteer work. Her dilettante self-appointed voice teacher, Alfred Wolfsohn aka "Amadeus Daberlohn," tells her she will have a nervous breakdown if she keeps up this pace (Salomon, *Life? or Theatre?* 303). Paulinka rejects Daberlohn's presumptuous suggestion. The singer supports Charlotte's desire to study art only conditionally, with the caveat that her education will result in an economically sustainable career. A conversation between Paulinka and Charlotte following a visit from Daberlohn reveals Paulinka's rather harsh judgement of Charlotte's choice to pursue her study of fine art after the fashion design avenue has dead-ended. Importantly, it is Daberlohn who accepts and encourages Charlotte.

The young artist remarks to Paulinka that "of all your friends, [Daberlohn] is the only sensible person," to which Paulinka responds, "Yes, you suit each other quite well, he's just as crazy as you are. Since he's really tremendously gifted, he can afford to be like that" (Salomon, *Life? or Theatre?* 369–70). Paulinka insinuates, of course, that Charlotte *can't* afford the same freedoms as she is *not* gifted (and not male). Furthermore, Paulinka insinuates that the idea of artistic dedication

---

19 Sociologist Carol Schmid describes the emergence of the New Woman archetype during the Weimar period: "During the interwar period, urban modernism was linked to contending ideals of womanhood. Women's participation in a culture of leisure, consumption and body consciousness created images of the New Women in Berlin . . . during the 1920s and early 1930s. Weimar Berlin . . . [was] a laboratory for change in women's roles." Schmid notes a clear link between consumerism and this New Woman figure. She rejects *Kinder, Kirche, und Küche* (children, church, and kitchen) ideals of traditional gender expectations and values her independence and ability to participate in capitalist society. "The 'New Woman,' Gender Roles and Urban Modernism in Interwar Berlin and Shanghai," *Journal of International Women's Studies* 15, no. 1 (2014): 1–16, here 1; ProQuest, https://search.proquest.com/scholarly-journals/new-woman-gender-roles-urban-modernism-interwar/docview/1504068912/se-2?accountid=14505.

above all else is lazy and selfish. Charlotte, still referring to Daberlohn, tells her, "I find it unjust that such gifted people should have to struggle like that for a living," to which Paulinka responds, "Much of it is his own fault. Like you, he likes to take his ease and only do things that please" (Salomon, *Life? or Theatre?* 373). In response to this conversation, "Charlotte is depressed that . . . those who are incapable of compromise because they are searching for the truth, lack the most basic requirements of daily sustenance" (Salomon, *Life? or Theatre?*, 374). Clearly, she counts herself among those who are unable to compromise. She knows that art is her calling, despite the overall lack of encouragement. She disidentifies with Paulinka, the modern bourgeois woman who tries to do it all. At the same time, the traditional role of housewife and mother is also out of the question.

Unlike the New Woman embodied by Paulinka, Franziska Kann, Charlotte's biological mother, had given up her career after marrying Dr. Kann. "No, she could never be happy with that husband and that child. Because all he ever thought about was his career and she was left at home to be nothing but a housewife," Salomon writes of her (Salomon, *Life? or Theatre?*, 142). Franziska had met Dr. Kann, the surgeon, when she was working as an operating nurse. Their romance began when she had to wipe his nose while he was operating. This could be construed as a rather adorable act of care and sanitation, but the vision of a woman wiping a man's nose can also be interpreted as satire of gendered expectations. Franziska's parents, Mr. and Mrs. Knarre, had haltingly given their consent to the marriage, and Salomon narrates that they—especially Mrs. Knarre—look depressed at the civil wedding ceremony (Salomon, *Life? or Theatre?*, 25). In light of later revelations in the book, it is plausible to deduce from this that Mrs. Kann, Charlotte's grandmother, is thinking of her own unhappy marriage and of her other daughter, Franziska's younger sister, Charlotte (for whom Charlotte Salomon is named), who committed suicide. The wedding-day sadness is a premonition of a marriage that will go terribly wrong. And indeed, a few years later, when Dr. and Mrs. Kann's baby Charlotte is eight years old, depression grips Franziska, and she jumps out of a window to her death.

The window is a metaphor throughout *Life? or Theatre?* for the thin translucent pane between lonely domesticity and a vibrant and worldly life beyond the home, between merely staying alive and truly living, and for the choice, ultimately, between death and life. André Breton, the self-named "Pope of Surrealism," refers to a window as the dividing line between wake and sleep, rationality and the subconscious, the dream world, and madness. In his 1924 *Manifestoes of Surrealism*, Breton reports hearing a strange phrase as he lies, one evening, between sleep and wakefulness: "There is a man cut in two by the window." The phrase is accompanied by a faint image of a man "cut halfway up by a window perpendicular to the axis of his body."[20] Breton's liminal auditory and visual hallucination comes in the midst of his preoccupation with Sigmund Freud's experiments with automatic, stream-of-consciousness narration, which Freud codified after Bertha Pappenheim, as mentioned earlier, had originated the method in her sessions with Breuer and later Freud.[21] The surrealist idea of a creative, authoritarian-resistant, antifascist inner landscape set against the dominant world of so-called rational phenomena lorded over by the theater of civilized and cultured men would have been familiar to Salomon. She, like Pappenheim, chose to draw from her own "private theater" as a method of self-investigation and as a form of resistance to the patriarchal theater.

A third feminine social construct, in line with surrealist and Jungian ideas, haunted the margins of modern society. Less well known than the New Woman or the traditional housewife, the concept of the liberated woman, the madly creative feminine genius, or, more appropriately, Juno, was also increasingly visible in the cultural landscape.[22] This wild and irrepressible anima, this psychologically and sexually liberated woman archetype was gaining visibility in and through the arts. She stood in resistance to traditional and bourgeois expectations. She loved freely; she painted and wrote and was in tune with occult truths. As exemplified by Salomon's contemporary, the British esoteric feminist artist-writer Leonora Carrington (also born in 1917, also in exile in France as the Nazis invaded), her body was the body of the world. The suffering of the world under fascism was in her belly. She held the key to salvation, her own and the world's. Echoing Salomon's statement that "my grandfather was the symbol for me of the people I had to resist" (Salomon, *Life? or Theatre?*, 801), Carrington testifies that she "was as frightened of [her] family as of the Germans."[23] Even more than Salomon's family, Carrington's British industrialist father was wholly unsupportive of her choice to be an artist and tried to keep her institutionalized. When confronted with the possibility of rape by the Germans, Carrington responded that she feared "the thought of robots, of thoughtless, fleshless beings" far more than anything else.[24] When Salomon paints women at windows, herself included, she paints the

---

20 André Breton, *Manifestoes of Surrealism*, trans. Richard Seaver and Helen R. Lane (Ann Arbor: University of Michigan Press, 1969), 21–22.

21 Guttman, "One Must Be Ready," 1.

22 Every Roman man was thought to have his own personal genius as a guardian spirit from birth to death. The word was cognate with Arabic *djinnie* or *genie*. Each woman had a corresponding female guardian spirit called a *juno*. H. J. Rose, *Religion in Greece and Rome* (New York: Harper, 1959), 217.

23 Leonora Carrington, *Down Below* (New York: New York Review Books, 2017), 67.

24 Carrington, *Down Below*, 6.

choice between convention and freedom, between self-annihilation and self-expression, between thoughtless, fleshless beings—the vitality-negating grandfathers—and life.

Salomon depicts her mother standing at the window, longing for a life beyond her caged existence, and in lieu of this, at least a beautiful afterlife filled with liberty and with angels (Salomon, *Life? or Theatre?*, 148–49). Much later in the work, Salomon paints the window from which her grandmother throws herself (Salomon, *Life? or Theatre?*, 759). The panel has no text and sparse visual information, just a rough pinkish-red shape suggesting her grandparents' bed and then urgently intersecting lines, blue-purple and gold, to denote the open window, and a figure with its back to the viewer, arms raised to look almost like a sickle (the Grim Reaper?) on the other side of this window, launching itself into the void. On the next page, Charlotte stands at the open window, head tilted down as though she is gazing at her grandmother's crumpled body below. This time, the paint is thickly layered and multihued and fills most of the page; there is no text (Salomon, *Life? or Theatre?*, 760). Finally, on the following page, Charlotte's figure stands, slightly bent at the hips, witnessing the distorted shape of her grandmother's body. Words painted in thick, dark-red paint cover Charlotte's form from head to toes, obscuring her eyes and hands. The words say, "May you never forget that I believe in you." They are Daberlohn's words. They are the words that had kept Charlotte alive, and the words she had tried to use, albeit unsuccessfully, as medicine to cure her grandmother's depression.

After her grandmother's first suicide attempt, Charlotte cares for her, sleeps next to her, sings to her, and, finally, shows her one of her paintings of Daberlohn. "That man is going to save you," she tells the fragile older woman (Salomon, *Life? or Theatre?*, 734). And then she explains,

> If you think about it, you can look back on a wonderful, full life. Apart from anything else, you've found a great deal of satisfaction and you have succeeded in expressing in poems many things that are denied to others. Some of your most recent poems are positively inspired, and I am convinced that a great literary talent has been lost in you. So I'll make you the following proposition: Instead of taking your own life in such a horrible way . . . why don't you make use of the same powers to describe your life? I am sure there must be some interesting material that weighs on you, and by writing it down you will liberate yourself and perhaps perform a service to the world. (Salomon, *Life? or Theatre?*, 735–36)

Charlotte wants to be for her grandmother what Daberlohn is for her: the voice of support for her Juno, the liberatory voice that will set her free from the grandfather's theater, from her depression, from her suicidal thoughts.

Io and Jupiter

"May you never forget that I believe in you." Daberlohn had first said these words to Charlotte shortly before she left Berlin—the only home she had ever known—to join her grandparents in exile. Salomon paints a complicated relationship between young Charlotte and the much older Daberlohn. While she became very reliant on his mentoring and personal interest, he clearly possesses most of the power in their relationship. He has a fiancé whom he infantilizes and continually sidelines while pursuing other love interests, he pines after Paulinka, and he toys with Charlotte's emotions, basking in her adoration one moment and callously snubbing her the next. Just before leaving Berlin for the Mediterranean, Charlotte had gone to Daberlohn's place, under the pretense of saying goodbye to an aunt, and they had spent time horizontally, as lovers do, wrapped together. From this vantage point, Daberlohn showed Charlotte a spot on his ceiling that he claimed represented Io and Jupiter. In some versions of the Roman myth, Jupiter takes on various disguises when he cheats on his jealous wife, Juno.[25] He changes form, becomes animal or vapor, a swan or a cloud. In Antonio da Correggio's sixteenth-century painting of Jupiter and Io, Io is shown in the throes of sexual euphoria, wrapped in the vaporous hands of a metamorphosed Jupiter. She accepts his misty kiss; he is barely there but unmistakably felt. Daberlohn and Charlotte, reclining, are similarly wrapped in a watery blue cocoon, and the words "It represents Io and Jupiter" are inscribed in red paint above their heads (Salomon, *Life? or Theatre?*, 676). On the facing page, the lovers are upright, now in a *Pietà*-like pose together, with Charlotte kneeling before Daberlohn like a supplicant.[26] His hands are on her shoulders as though blessing her. To their right, red and blue painted text wraps around a dark rectangular form: "And here is a farewell gift—a picture, 'The Darkest Day'—and I ask you not to forget that I love life and affirm it threefold. In order to love life completely, perhaps it is necessary to embrace and comprehend its other side: death" (Salomon, *Life? or Theatre?*, 677). The

---

25 Some mythographers note that Io and Juno were versions of the same goddess and that Juno's jealousy is thus a patriarchal fiction. Jupiter was primarily a rain god, so his transformation into misty cloudlike forms could also allude to that aspect. Barbara Walker, *The Women's Encyclopedia of Myths and Secrets* (Edison, NJ: Castle Books, 1996), 449.

26 I use the word *Pietà* here to describe Salomon's painting of the two figures. Though the *Pietà* is commonly known as the Virgin Mary holding the dead body of Christ, the term has been used for similar triangular-shaped compositions. The word derives from the Latin *pietas*, piety, loyalty, commiseration, devotion, and the concept has been employed by other artists, including Käthe Kollwitz, to show a compassionate figure caressing or holding a second subject in a pitiable state.

last page of this sequence shows a dusky repetition of the *Pietà*, teacher and student, priest and supplicant, or, employing a more vulgar interpretation, the scene suggests fellatio. This time, the words painted to the right of the lovers take up as much space on the page as the figures: "May you never forget that I believe in you" (Salomon, *Life? or Theatre?*, 678).

Daberlohn is Charlotte's Jupiter, the misty presence that is always there, always embracing her when nothing else gives her peace or joy or strength. It seems that Charlotte is in love with the *idea* of Daberlohn, and with Daberlohn's ideas, rather than with the actual person, who lets her down again and again. She is hypnotically drawn to this much older man. When they first met, Charlotte was in her late teens and Daberlohn in his forties. In her painted letter to him, dated February 1943, she writes, "I had—only too naturally—absolutely no attraction for you" (Salomon, *Life? or Theatre?*, 801). Like Leonora Carrington's affair with the much older artist Max Ernst, Charlotte's infatuation with Daberlohn ignites when he opens a window for her to another, much more fulfilling, world. Charlotte's love was likely borne of her basic need for acknowledgment of her essence, purpose, person. Daberlohn is the one person who believes in her or, more importantly, believes in her capacity as an artist whose work wells up from that "private theater," so important in modern art and psychology. She was terrified that she, too, would go mad and become suicidal, like her maternal aunt, her mother, and her grandmother. Daberlohn's methods for inspiring his students to metamorphose their inner demons into creative expression remained vital for Salomon after she fled Berlin.

Alfred Wolfsohn, on whom Daberlohn is modeled, had suffered severe shell shock as a result of his experiences as a medic during the First World War. When psychiatric treatments failed to help him, he began to experiment with applying Carl Jung's psychological processes to nonverbal vocalizations. He first experimented on himself, making a range of primal sounds based on the anguished vocalizations he had heard in the trenches, the voices that haunted him. He began to push the high and low notes as far as possible each day, to see how far he could expand his vocal range. Wolfsohn then wanted to share his methods to help others, and he entered the Salomon-Lindberg residence with that intention: to teach the already famous singer. At the Salomon-Lindberg home, Wolfsohn eventually took on other students as well. After fleeing Nazi Germany for London in 1943, Wolfsohn established the Alfred Wolfsohn Voice Research Centre and continued teaching his methods there. Paul Newham, a British writer inspired by Wolfsohn's work, describes the experiences of one of Wolfsohn's former students, Marita Gunther, who would later become the guardian of his estate.

Newham notes that "Wolfsohn believed that the dream was the prime source of everything that we understand as art, such as music, poetry, and painting . . . and he discovered that singing could be likened to dreaming; while the dream reflected the different aspects of the psyche in pictures, the voice could reflect psychological images in sound." According to Newham, Marita Gunther said that Wolfsohn "studied in detail the theories of Jung and believed that the 'concepts of archetypes, shadow, animus and anima were not only visible but could be made audible.'" Gunther also described Wolfsohn's unique approach to teaching. She witnessed "what was happening between teacher and pupil; it was the give and take on both sides, this incredible concentration and intensity emanating from both."[27] In *Life? or Theatre?* Daberlohn believes that Paulinka must fall in love with him in order for his methods to be truly effective, but she, as a mature woman with life experience and considerable agency as an internationally known singer, rejects his advances. Charlotte had none of these intersecting advantages, which would have made her able to say no to this vulturous person. There was evidently a psychosexual element to Daberlohn's approach. Throughout the main section of *Life? or Theatre?* he is condescending and annoying and not even attractive to Charlotte, but in an endless ocean of negation she clings to him—to a few encouraging words from him—like a drowning man clings to a bit of driftwood. After he had asked her to illustrate an entire book for him as a birthday present, and she, after much unpaid labor, delivers the work to him, he cannot be bothered to take a few moments to look at what she has done. During the two weeks that follow, Charlotte is distressed and even thinks about throwing herself out of the window, but she concludes that Daberlohn is not worth it. She finally begins to wonder if she was nothing but a guinea pig for his experiments (Salomon *Life? or Theatre?*, 570–90).

Something Cold, Resembling Death

Salomon may have fallen prey to Wolfsohn's rather predatory impulses as the result of an existing history of sexual abuse. The secretive nature of their affair suggests as much. Charlotte meets with Daberlohn only surreptitiously. Secrecy, as psychologists who work with survivors of incest will attest, is one of the behavioral patterns that characterize abusive relationships and often persist into adulthood. Pedophiles often tell their victims that the sexual acts should be kept secret and even threaten to retaliate with violence if the child were to speak out. This, together with the child's relative powerlessness and fear of being disbelieved (in a game of "he said versus she said," the child innately knows who is likely to be believed), sparks a pattern of silence and secret-keeping that cannot easily be broken.

---

27 Paul Newham, "Jung and Alfred Wolfsohn," *Journal of Analytical Psychology* 37, no. 3 (1992): 323–36, here 327–28, doi:10.1111/j.1465-5922.1992.00323.x.

Art historian Griselda Pollock has already, quite convincingly, explored the idea that Salomon may well have been subjected to incest by her abusive grandfather. In Pollock's chapter "The Monster," she builds a case for this supposition, using as proof, among other things, the grandfather's insistence that Charlotte share a bed with him after their release from the Gurs concentration camp (interestingly, Salomon chooses not to describe the concentration camp experience at all). "I don't understand you," old Herr Knarre says to his young granddaughter. "What's wrong with sharing a bed with me—when there's nothing else available? I'm in favor of what's natural." Charlotte retorts, "Don't torment me. You know exactly what I have to do" (Salomon, *Life? or Theatre?*, 777). In the painted image, Herr Knarre, clad in a nightshirt, gestures toward a rectangle suggesting a bed. His white shirt, long white beard, and slightly outstretched hands make him look like some sort of prophet, a parody of a holy man receiving divine information about "what's natural." The brushstrokes in this image look energetic, impatient, possibly angry. In the lower left corner of the page, Charlotte kneels, facing away from the bed and the lascivious old man, with one hand inside her suitcase. What is it that she has to do? Is she reaching into the suitcase for the flask of veronal with which she will poison him? Behind the two figures, discordant diagonal strokes of color dance like the kaleidoscopic vision that precedes an ocular migraine, obliterating any horizon. Pollock points out the similarity between the grandfather's pose here—the long, slightly extended arms—and an earlier painting of a massive animated skeleton, arms similarly reaching, looming above eight-year-old Charlotte in a dark hallway right after her mother died.[28] She had been told that her mother had died of influenza when, in reality, her mother had committed suicide. Following this great loss, little Charlotte had been unable to sleep, awakening several times a night. The text overlaying the skeleton image reads, "And whenever she has to walk along the endless, wide, high, dark passage in her grandparents' home, she imagines something terrible, with skeleton's limbs, that has something to do with her mother. Then she is filled with panic and begins to run, run, run. . . ." (Salomon, *Life? or Theatre?*, 50). When I first read this, I felt that the looming skeleton and the little girl's fear and night terrors could very well have been the result of her mother's recent death. The loss of her mother would have been an event traumatic enough to unleash such nighttime anguish! But then another passage, later in the work, also related to death and distinctly pointing to sexual trauma, caught my attention.

Before Charlotte's exile from Berlin, Daberlohn and Charlotte go boating. Salomon writes that, as he looks at Charlotte sitting in the boat, "his passion for experimenting is aroused. . . ." (Salomon, *Life? or*

---

28   Pollock, *Charlotte Salomon*, 219.

Theatre? 552). "Experimenting" seems to be Salomon's code word for sexual capers. The introduction of a sexual dimension to their interactions is in line with the apparent psychosexual component of Daberlohn's experimental "mentoring" process. As they arrive at a sandy bay obscured by reeds, they rest. Salomon paints Daberlohn and Charlotte's figures horizontally reclining, with the text overlay explaining, "He pursues his 'experiments' which impassion him as always. Charlotte remains motionless—something he has never seen during all his long years of experience. He senses something cold, resembling death, and looks surprised and concerned" (Salomon, *Life? or Theatre?*, 555). Despite his surprise and concern, Daberlohn does not stop. Several more iterations of the horizontal couple in missionary position follow, the last of which is painted with a cocoon of sunshine gold, reminiscent of the *Rausch* scene of Charlotte painting that I described earlier. The overlaying text reads, "But suddenly his hypersensitive nerves are touched by a firelike current. . . ." (Salomon, *Life? or Theatre?*, 557). In the next painting, the figures are lying side by side, Daberlohn on one elbow, the other hand touching his forehead as though shielding his eyes from the sunny glow that still envelops them. Charlotte is painted as impassively lying on her back, eyes closed. The text continues, "It was only a second. Charlotte is lying there as if it were not she who had brought about this fiery stream. Perhaps if Daberlohn had known old Mrs. Knarre, he would once again have noted a family resemblance—*just as you can after reading the Epilogue*" (Salomon, *Life? or Theatre?*, 558; emphasis mine). This is one of the very few places in her work where the artist breaks the fourth wall and speaks directly to the reader. She urges us to read her epilogue, to notice old Mrs. Knarre's suicidal desperation and ensuing annihilation, and to *compare* the old woman's incapacitating, dire distress with Charlotte's own paralyzing anguish. Salomon's description of her corpselike posture in response to Daberlohn's sexual passion evokes current understandings of sexual trauma–induced dissociation.

Trauma researchers have, in recent years, recognized several reactions of the brain to trauma and posttrauma, in addition to the notion of the "fight or flight" response, first described by American physiologist Walter Bradford Cannon in 1915. This response is stimulated by the sympathetic nervous system when one is faced with danger, real or anticipated. A third reaction to perceived threat, more recently added to "fight or flight," is to freeze or dissociate. Salomon describes herself as "paralyzed" following her grandmother's first attempted suicide; she portrays herself lying stiff as a board, again on her back, unable to move (Salomon, *Life? or Theatre?*, 709). To freeze is to become quite literally incapable of making a choice or of running away. A fourth response has also been suggested, a fawning reaction that is common in those who experienced childhood physical or sexual abuse. In this response, coined by Pete Walker in 2013, survivors of abuse hurry to appease and please in order to avoid conflict, even if their actions put them in further danger.

Charlotte obviously lacks interest in sex with Daberlohn and is possibly being triggered by the advances of this significantly older man. She lies stiffly on her back, corpselike, dissociating herself from the scene. And yet she continues to cavort with him, unable to say no. A thunderstorm blows in, and she suggests, in defiance of common sense, that they go for a swim. This too is characteristic of behavioral patterns of sexual abuse survivors: the headlong rush into more potentially harmful, self-negating, or even deadly situations. Why not go swimming in a thunderstorm? Salomon now paints and describes Charlotte and Daberlohn immersed in the water during the storm, listening to thunder and watching the lightning, enveloped in thick blue brushstrokes. Charlotte appears to be floating on her back, while he is on top or close to her side. The two figures are entwined, an amorphous red blob in the blue lake. The large red painted letters above the pair insist, "Continue comparing" (Salomon, *Life? or Theatre?*, 561). Again, Salomon provokes us to look and to compare. She urges us to read her epilogue and to crack her code of silence.

Paradoxically, despite the real possibility that Wolfsohn, who was in his early forties, had predatory tendencies, and that Salomon, barely out of her teens, was unhappily triggered by his sexual and sexualizing "experiments," his ideas and supportive words were a vital tonic for the sensitive and deeply intelligent young artist. Following a month-long internment at Gurs concentration camp in the Pyrenees, from which Salomon and her grandfather were released owing to his bad health, she suffered a nervous breakdown. She visited a local psychologist and resistance leader, Dr. Georges Moridis, who had helped Salomon's grandmother after her first suicide attempt. Dr. Moridis suggested that Salomon paint in order to save herself. It would have been easy to follow this advice, as Wolfsohn's encouragement and her modern-art education at the Akademie der Künste had already empowered her to open that window to her own private theater, to explore her psyche and draw from even the darkest aspects as a source of artistic inspiration. She sequestered herself for the duration of 1942 in a hotel room in Saint-Jean-Cap-Ferrat, where she dedicated her time and strength to the monumental project that would become her groundbreaking opus: *Life? or Theatre?*

The Patriarchal Theater Is Dead

Salomon's work is at odds with autobiographical literature that adheres to a redemptive framework. She also cannot be framed solely as an innocent young victim of the Holocaust. Charlotte Salomon's identity and her work are chimeric and thus necessitate intersectional and transdisciplinary methods of comprehension. Thus, she does not fit the plotline that attracts school groups who are being taught about genocide through the experiences of someone relatable, as do carefully edited versions of Anne Frank's diary (with references to her burgeoning sexuality removed).[29] Salomon's work is confessional, though she does not seek absolution, and chimeric. Like modern-day graphic memoirists, she documented her life with serial renderings and story, with metacognitive insights, and with references to the political events of her day. And cleverly, with a spidery silver thread, she interwove her complex story with a distressing subtext that she literally urges us to follow. Her secret affair with Daberlohn alerts us to this thread, as does the painting of the skeleton in the hallway. No matter where one picks up this thread, once it is noticed, it is painfully easy to follow.

Like creators of today's autobiographical comics, Salomon painted and wrote *Life? or Theatre?* in order to draw herself out of the darkness. The process itself was her lifeline, her resistance against the intimate tyranny of her grandfather and the political, racist tyranny of the Nazis. Modern-day artist Miriam Katin crafted two graphic memoirs decades after she and her mother fled the Nazi invasion of Budapest. In beginning *Letting It Go*, the second of her two works, she draws her view out of the window of her New York apartment over four panels with the words, "So, where does a story begin? And if you are inside that story now; in that situation and it hurts and say you can draw; then you must try and draw yourself out of it."[30] The process of re-membering wounded and silenced parts of the chimeric self through drawing and telling opens windows, even those that had long been boarded shut. By drawing from her private theater and by drawing herself out of oppressive, hurtful situations, Salomon courageously became the curator of her own memories and affective truths.

For marginalized creators, those truths have too often been obscured and discredited by the soulless, fleshless beings that populate the patriarchal theater of so-called civilized and cultured men. As Sidonie Smith points out in speaking to the myth of the universal, masculine, normative autobiographical subject, "The tyranny of the arid 'I' . . . obscures through a gray and shapeless mist everything colorful that lies within its vision. And it implicitly issues a challenge to the woman who, in entering the textual space of that 'I,' would appropriate the position of the

---

29 Anne Frank's father removed significant sections of his daughter's work before its original publication in 1946. He took out portions that reflected her burgeoning sexuality and passages where she expressed dislike of co-occupants of the secret annex where she was hiding. Anne Frank, "Foreword/Publishing History," *Anne Frank: The Collected Works*, ed. Mirjam Pressler (London: Bloomsbury Continuum, 2019), 5–6.

30 Miriam Katin, *Letting It Go* (Montreal: Drawn & Quarterly, 2013), n.p.

autobiographical subject."[31] This appropriation has historically caused much trouble for women who dare to tell their fraught stories. Bearing witness to one's own truths still comes with plenty of hazards, as Gilmore asserts: "When the witness is a woman, and especially when the harm includes sexual violence, she will be subjected to practices of shaming and discrediting that preexist any specific case."[32] Race, gender, and sexuality "stick" to Salomon as female witness, as Gilmore puts it, amplifying the potential for discrediting.

Though Charlotte Salomon tragically did not survive the Holocaust, her magnificent graphic testimony did endure in France, and when her parents, who had lived through the war in Amsterdam, were finally able to search for signs of their beloved daughter, they were astonished to uncover her voluminous body of work. In a moving 1963 interview for the *Pariser Journal*, Salomon's father says that Charlotte "surely would have become a talented artist."[33] Though he acknowledges the progress his daughter had made as an artist, his wording also struck a discordant note in me. Would have *become*? She *was* a talented artist, and it struck me that many, even her own parents, still refuse to believe what her phenomenal work has long proven. It is on that ground of legitimacy and veracity, the very ground Salomon was struggling to assert, that a life is built, that a life is lived, that a life is remembered.

What would have happened to Charlotte Salomon, had she lived? What further works would she have contributed, had the Nazis not effectively lobotomized Germany by murdering its most important Junos and geniuses? I cannot help but wonder how Salomon's life and work would have unfolded, had she had the decades that, for example, Leonora Carrington had. Both artists, as I mentioned earlier, were born in 1917, both were deeply inspired by modern art movements, and both allied themselves with older men who took on for them, for better or for worse, mentor roles that included sexual dimensions. In Carrington's case, after her lover, Max Ernst, was interned in a concentration camp as a "degenerate artist," Carrington suffered a psychotic break and was sent to an insane asylum in Spain where she underwent horrific treatments. Shortly after this ordeal, she again met Ernst (who had been released) in Lisbon. She reported that she was free from the spell he had once exercised over her.[34] Carrington would spend the rest of her long life in Mexico City, as

---

31   Sidonie Smith, *Subjectivity, Identity, and the Body: Women's Autobiographical Practices in the Twentieth Century* (Bloomington: Indiana University Press, 1993), 3–4.

32   Gilmore, *Tainted Witness*, 5.

33   Albert Salomon and Paula Lindberg, interview for *Pariser Journal*, 1963. Jewish Cultural Quarter (Amsterdam) Online, accessed December 9, 2020, https://youtu.be/NlytljkojGo, 3:50–3:55.

34   Marina Warner, "Introduction," in Carrington, *Down Below*, xxi.

part of a vibrant community of artists who had found refuge from fascism there. She died in 2011, at the age of ninety-four. Mexico claims her as one of the nation's most treasured artists. What if Salomon had been with us that long?

It is remarkable that Salomon was able to produce her magnificent, genre-defying opus under such duress and at such a young age, and that she was able to break free of the intimate as well as the sociopolitical tyrants and tyrannies that surely would have broken most young artists' spirits. When faced with the choice between life and her grandfather's theater of civilized and cultured men, the artist chose life. Despite a short lifetime of tragedy, during which Salomon was likely haunted by a history of sexual abuse and by her familial tragedy of suicides, she chose life, again and again. On their way back to the refuge in Villefranche from the Gurs concentration camp, after having refused to sleep next to him, Charlotte muses, "You know, Grandpa, I have the feeling the whole world has to be put together again. He replies, "Oh, go ahead and kill yourself and put an end to all this babble" (Salomon, *Life? or Theatre?*, 786–87). But at the end of her letter to Wolfsohn, as she watches her grandfather slipping away from the poisonous omelet that she had just served him, it is Salomon who has the last word:

> As grandfather already fell asleep gently by intoxication with the Veronal omellette and as I made a drawing of him—it felt to me as though a voice called out: Theatre is dead! Perhaps dearest it is actually true that with this war even the theater that's played out by humanity comes to an end so that all of humankind tested by hard pain and experience moves toward a truer life-affirming life. I thank you. I almost want to say: Amen. (Salomon *Life? or Theatre?*, 805).

8: #MeToo and Wartime Rape: Looking Back and Moving Forward

Katherine Stone

A FUNDAMENTAL ASSUMPTION of memory studies is the idea that collective remembrance is a highly mediated version of "history-in-motion," which "remak[es] the residue of past decades into material with contemporary resonance."[1] The recent graffitiing of Seward Johnson's sculpture *Unconditional Surrender* offers a pertinent example of this process of recasting. Modeled on the iconic photograph by German-Jewish émigré Alfred Eisenstaedt, the statue depicts US Navy sailor George Mendonsa passionately embracing a pliant nurse on September 2, 1945. This image was initially celebrated as a visual encapsulation of the joy of VJ Day; in 2005, however, an Austrian-Jewish refugee named Greta Zimmer Friedman identified herself as the photographed woman and revealed that the kiss had not been consensual.[2] This disclosure cast the title of Johnson's work in a new light, exposing the extent to which women's sexual passivity and the fine line between consent and coercion are naturalized—if not romanticized and eroticized in Western cultures.[3] It took #MeToo to disturb the narrative. When Mendonsa's death in February 2019 was widely reported in obituaries, a protestor sprayed the Sarasota statue with the words "#MeToo." This graffito embodied the work's altered status as feminist cipher for "the normalization of assault."[4] Conversely, the fact that local authorities categorized the #MeToo tag as vandalism and

---

1   Barbie Zelizer, "Reading the Past against the Grain: The Shape of Memory Studies," *Critical Studies in Mass Communication* 12, no. 2 (1995): 214–39, here 216–17.

2   The graffitiing and subsequent debate in the US press were not picked up in Germany or Austria, although some outlets referred to the furor in their obituaries of Mendonsa.

3   See Audrey Reeves, "Kisses at the Memorial: Affective Objects, US Militarism, and Feminist Resistance at Sites of Wartime Memory," *Critical Military Studies* (2020), advanced online publication: 1–17, here 2, https://www.tandfonline.com/doi/abs/10.1080/23337486.2019.1686900.

4   Stuti Pachisia, "Graffiting #MeToo," *SOAS* Blog, February 25, 2019, para 2, https://www.soas.ac.uk/blogs/study/graffiting-metoo/.

removed it suggests the difficult entanglement of sexual politics and history with national identity.

Several scholars have considered the memorial dynamics at the heart of #MeToo. For instance, Laura Moisi analyzes the "temporal engagement" integral to the public sharing of stories, which she calls a form of "navigating the past with the tools (words, concepts, ideas) of the present."[5] This chapter contributes to such discussions by specifically examining how #MeToo has the potential to shift our understanding of history. First, I elucidate the relevance of the past to debates and scholarship under the sign of #MeToo and discuss the extent to which historicization has been used to downplay the systemic dimensions of rape culture in the present. Part 2 of this chapter explains the implications of such historical thinking for how Germany remembers its history of sexual violence, especially in the context of World War II. It links the exploitation of sexual violence within memory politics to broader trends in rape culture and unpacks how conceptual shifts attributed to #MeToo are being taken up in scholarship and political discourse surrounding conflict-related sexual violence (CRSV). The chapter closes by modeling how #MeToo can advance memory studies through a close reading of Ralf Rothmann's best-selling novel *Der Gott jenes Sommers* (2018; *The God of That Summer*, 2022). Ultimately, I argue that #MeToo has not merely provided new frames for discussing history. Looking back at the past also illuminates patterns of misunderstanding, silencing, and trivialization that go some way toward explaining the explosion of storytelling under the hashtag #MeToo. My reflections thus also signal changes that are necessary to ensure that this movement does not suffer the same fate as previous consciousness-raising campaigns.

#MeToo and the Specter of the Past

Three years after the hashtag #MeToo was first used to interpellate women's accounts of harassment and assault, it is clear that the locution has not merely provided a collective frame for recognition and a rallying cry for change. Rather, #MeToo has a disclosive quality that refigures the unremarkable as conspicuous, rendering "unlistened-to stories" and previously unreadable experiences both visible and intelligible.[6] There is

5   Laura Moisi, "Collective Reckonings: Re-Writing Trauma, Memory and Violence on Social Media," unpublished manuscript, n.d., 9, accessed October 15, 2020, https://www.academia.edu/39742504/Collective_Reckonings_Re_Writing_Trauma_Memory_and_Violence_on_Social_Media.

6   Sarah Colvin, "Unerhört? Prisoner Narratives as Unlistened-to Stories (and Some Reflections on the Picaresque)," *Modern Language Review* 112, no. 2 (2017): 440–58.

a historical dimension to this process. As Sara Ahmed writes, "Having names for problems can make a difference. Maybe before, you could not quite put your finger on it. With these words as tools, we revisit our own histories, we hammer away at the past."[7] Such work of remembering and revision is at the heart of debates about #MeToo, which possess a peculiar temporality. The shock that followed the outpouring of tweets belies the fact that previous viral hashtags such as #everydaysexism and #aufschrei were also heralded for breaking taboos about the ubiquity of sexual harassment and abuse. Furthermore, the words "me too" circulated in grassroots movements long before Twitter, most notably in Tarana Burke's activism. Given Burke's relative anonymity within mainstream #MeToo conversations, Karen Boyle advises retaining the analogue expression "Me Too" to denote the temporal dimensions of the "long, if unevenly intersectional, history" of consciousness-raising and speaking out.[8] After all, the systemic character of sexual assault was a driving concern of *die neue Frauenbewegung* (the new women's movement), which succeeded in introducing legislation against sexual harassment in the workplace in 1994 and marital rape in 1997, albeit while failing to address its own universalism and bias until well into the new millennium.[9]

Such examples of short and selective memory are not the sole reasons why a historical perspective on #MeToo is fruitful. Historicization has been a common mode of defense for the accused, who justify their actions with reference to the world of their formative socialization, as though abuse were a generational issue.[10] According to Clare Hemmings, such false historicization insinuates that feminist advocacy was either previously absent or wholly ineffective, eliding the pervasiveness of similar crimes and barriers to justice in the present:

> Feminist campaigns against sexual violence are thus caught in the curious temporal plays underpinning fantasies of gender and sexual equality as almost if not quite yet achieved. Thus sexual violence feminism can ironically enough be framed as the one kind

---

7   Sara Ahmed, *Living a Feminist Life* (Durham, NC: Duke University Press, 2016), 33.

8   Karen Boyle, *#MeToo, Weinstein, and Feminism* (Basingstoke, UK: Palgrave Macmillan, 2019), 5.

9   Encarnación Gutiérrez Rodríguez, "Frau ist nicht gleich Frau, nicht gleich Frau, nicht gleich Frau . . . : Über die Notwendigkeit einer kritischen Dekonstruktion in der feministischen Forschung," in *Kategorie: Geschlecht? Empirische Analysen und feministische Theorien*, ed. Ute Luise Fischer, Marita Kampshoff, and Mathilde Schmitt (Opladen: Leske + Budrich, 1996), 163–90.

10   Karen Boyle, "The Sex of Sexual Violence," in *Handbook of Gender and Violence*, ed. Laura Shepherd (Cheltenham, UK: Edward Elgar, 2019), 101–14, here 111.

of feminism that everyone can agree on: one that identifies sexual and gender-based violence as the basis of gender oppression, while simultaneously positioning widespread sexual violence as part of the actual or (soon to be) past. Part of the shared cultural horror of the #MeToo campaign is indeed that sexual abuse is both anachronistic and ever-present.[11]

In the next section of this chapter, I use a German example to show that similar dynamics are at play in Western political campaigns against CRSV, which decry the continued prevalence of gender-based violence elsewhere yet present these iniquities as distinct from and unrelated to one's own histories of sexual violence in war and peace.

#MeToo and Mobilizing Memory

Marianne Hirsch has argued that "to mobilize memory means to find in it a dynamic potential for transformation that counters backward-looking movements that attempt to restore a legendary or mythic past, or, worse, that serve nationalist and divisive ends."[12] These issues are particularly pertinent for the memory of CRSV, which has long featured in national commemoration only insofar as it can be instrumentalized for political purposes. As recently as June 2010, the deputy chairman of the Christian Democratic Union in Berlin, Michael Braun, caused controversy by petitioning the House of Representatives to erect a memorial "für die ab Frühjahr 1945 in Berlin geschändeten Frauen" (to the women who were defiled in Berlin in spring 1945).[13] The rationale presented to the Senate repeats this language of shame. The stigmatizing—and potentially retraumatizing—construction of survivors caused alarm among parliamentarians and commentators.[14] Historian Regina Mühlhäuser

11 Clare Hemmings, "Resisting Popular Feminisms: Gender, Sexuality and the Lure of the Modern," *Gender, Place & Culture* 25, no. 7 (2018): 963–77, here 971.

12 Marianne Hirsch, "Introduction: Practicing Feminism, Practicing Memory," in *Women Mobilizing Memory*, ed. Ayşe Gül Altınay, María José Contreras, Marianne Hirsch, Jean Howard, Banu Karaca, and Alisa Solomon (New York: Columbia University Press, 2019), 1–23, here 2.

13 "Braun fordert Denkmal für geschändete Frauen," *Berliner Rundschau: Das Magazin der CDU Berlin*, June 2010, https://www.cduberlin.de/image/inhalte/22_br_jun10.pdf.

14 See Stefan Jacobs and Sigrid Kneist, "Sollte es ein Denkmal für missbrauchte Frauen geben?" *Tagesspiegel*, June 17, 2010, para 6, https://www.tagesspiegel.de/berlin/pro-und-contra-sollte-es-ein-denkmal-fuer-missbrauchte-frauen-geben-vor-fuenf-jahren/1869338.html.

questioned whether the CDU had any interest in women's experiences or whether it simply sought to exploit these experiences to further its own memory political agenda.[15] Others questioned the geographic and historical restriction of the monument, a decision that smacked of revisionism. This brief example illuminates the entanglement of memory and gender politics.[16] In this case, prevailing interpretations of sexual violence as shameful taint the interpretation of historical violence. Cultural memory has the potential to enshrine such damaging interpretations of sexual violence, objectifying the survivors and isolating their "defilement" from the actions of perpetrators and the symbolic and structural nexus in which these crimes occur. It freezes these women in hyperconstructed moments of shame, denying their agency and autonomy. At their worst, cultural memories that pivot around the violation and degradation of "our women" fortify myths that associate women's actual bodies with the nation and provide symbolic justification for future violence.[17] Such rhetoric has ultimately "participated in the making of a world that tends to care little about violated bodies."[18]

Providing a full review of the complicated memory politics surrounding wartime rape in divided and unified Germany would be a chapter, if not a book, in itself. Previous scholars have done excellent work reconstructing the cultural memory of wartime rape, unearthing a wealth of testimonies and narratives that have circulated in postwar society and demonstrating the politicization of memory in different contexts. Elisabeth Krimmer shows that legacies of stigma and traumatization, combined with the political and ethical hazards of remembering and representing violence in a perpetrator nation, mean that sexual violence has tended to become "invisible even in texts that explicitly address the topic of wartime rape."[19] The above example is merely one illustration of the way that women's experiences and subjectivity have been erased within

---

15   Cited in Zoé Sona, "Debatte über Denkmal für Vergewaltigte: Das Mahnmal," *TAZ*, July 30, 2010, para 3, https://taz.de/Debatte-ueber-Denkmal-fuer-Vergewaltigte/!5138175/.

16   I develop this argument in "The Mass Rapes of 1945 in Contemporary Memory Culture: The (Gender) Politics of Metaphor and Metonymy," *European Journal of Cultural Studies* 21, no. 6 (2018): 707–23.

17   Julie Mostov, "Sexing the Nation/Desexing the Body: Politics of National Identity in the Former Yugoslavia," in *Gender Ironies of Nationalism: Sexing the Nation*, ed. Tamar Mayer (London: Routledge, 2010), 89–112, here 90.

18   Sabine Sielke, *Reading Rape: The Rhetoric of Sexual Violence in American Literature and Culture, 1790–1990* (Princeton, NJ: Princeton University Press, 2009), 3.

19   Elisabeth Krimmer, *German Women's Life Writing and the Holocaust: Complicity and Gender in the Second World War* (Cambridge: Cambridge University Press, 2018), 115.

German memory culture. This phenomenon provides some insight into the reasons why #MeToo erupted with such force in 2017. It also elucidates why any assessment of the impact of #MeToo on German memory culture must do more than simply diagnose an uptick in narratives about women's experiences of abuse at the close of World War II. Writing about CRSV more broadly, Doris Buss has commented on the double-edged quality of visibility, noting that the presence of a topic on the public agenda—or, for our purposes, in cultural memory—is not the same as the "analytical sense of sight as a metaphor for refocusing what is known and can be known about conflict and gender. The hyper-visibility produced through the first register of 'making visible' has eclipsed some of the richness promised by the second."[20] The debate about Braun's proposal for a memorial offers an unsavory example of the tension between these two forms of visibility.

Researchers in a wide range of disciplines have begun to explore how #MeToo might transform political discourse, scholarship, and cultural representations of CRSV. The year 2018 saw the Nobel Peace Prize awarded to rape survivor and campaigner Nadia Murad and doctor and activist Denis Mukwege. The chairwoman of the Nobel committee, Berit Reiss-Andersen, remarked that "Metoo and war crimes are not quite the same. But they have in common that they see the suffering of women, the abuse of women, and that it is important that women leave the concept of shame behind and speak up."[21] More broadly, #MeToo has discernibly impacted on discourse surrounding CRSV in three main areas. First, historians and advocates have leveraged #MeToo to reconsider and publicize historical cases of sexual abuse and assault.[22] Historian Anna Hájková has written about the Holocaust's "#MeToo moment," referring to a surge in research on gendered violence endured by those in the ghettos, in camps, and in hiding, not to mention after liberation. Hájková insists on the necessity of discussing this aspect of the Holocaust openly:

20 Doris Buss, "Seeing Sexual Violence in Conflict and Post-Conflict Societies: The Limits of Visibility," in *Sexual Violence in Conflict and Post-Conflict Societies: International Agendas and African Contexts*, ed. Doris Buss, Joanne Lebert, Blair Rutherford, Donna Sharkey, and Obijiofor Aginam (New York: Routledge, 2014), 3–27, here 15.

21 Crispin Kyalangalilwa, Ted Siefer, and Nerijus Adomaitis, "Congolese Doctor, Yazidi Activist, Champions in Fight against Rape in War, Win Nobel Peace Prize," *Reuters*, October 5, 2018, https:// www.reuters.com/article/us-nobel-prize-peace/congolese-doctor-yazidi-activist-champions-in-fight-against-rape-in-war-win-nobel-peace-prize-idUSKCN1MF0YB.

22 See, for example, Gary Nunn, "Bangka Island: The WW2 Massacre and a 'Truth Too Awful to Speak,'" *BBC News*, April 18, 2019; Nicole Percy, "In the #MeToo Era, Women Used as Sex Slaves by Japanese in WWII Are Still Seen as Prostitutes, Not Victims," *CBC News*, July 7, 2018.

The society of Holocaust victims was a human society. As in ours, some people chose to engage in sexual violence. For some of them, this was a pattern carried over from earlier life; for others, it was conduct that emerged from their experience of persecution. The victims, men and boys, women and girls, were almost always shamed into silence.[23]

Hájková's reflections on the social norms that shape cultural memory feed into the second consequence of #MeToo for the interdisciplinary field of research into CRSV. Historians have examined how the (gendered and racial) dynamics of what Leigh Gilmore calls "tainted witness" seep into historical praxis.[24] For example, Ruth Lawlor pushes historians to interrogate the victims deemed credible—averring that "records demand cultural translation."[25] Finally, researchers have taken #MeToo as an opportunity to assess the increased visibility of CRSV on the global stage and audit the foci and blind spots of previous discourse. After all, in many respects, advocacy on CRSV has developed along chronologically parallel tracks to the #MeToo movement, from the significance of "silence breakers" to the role that celebrities have played in enhancing the visibility of preexisting struggles.[26] There are likewise instructive parallels between critiques of the "carceral turn" in feminism and international relations, which has been influential both in #MeToo and in the fight against CRSV.[27]

23 Anna Hájková, "The Holocaust Is Having a #MeToo Moment," *Tablet*, October 8, 2019, https://www.tabletmag.com/sections/news/articles/holocaust-metoo-moment. See also Marisa Fox-Bevilacqua, "It's Time for a Holocaust #MeToo Reckoning," *Forward*, February 5, 2018, https://forward.com/opinion/393518/its-time-for-a-holocaust-metoo-reckoning/.

24 Leigh Gilmore, *Tainted Witness: Why We Doubt What Women Say about Their Lives* (New York: Columbia University Press, 2017).

25 Ruth Lawlor, "Contested Crimes: Race, Gender, and Nation in Histories of GI Sexual Violence, World War II," *Journal of Military History* 84, no. 2 (2020): 541–69, here 542; Amy Stanley, "Writing the History of Sexual Assault in the Age of #MeToo," *Perspectives on History*, September 24, 2018, https://www.historians.org/publications-and-directories/perspectives-on-history/november-2018/writing-the-history-of-sexual-assault-in-the-age-of-metoo.

26 See Inger Skjelsbæk, "Silence Breakers in War and Peace: Research on Gender and Violence with an Ethics of Engagement," *Social Politics: International Studies in Gender, State & Society* 25, no. 4 (2018): 496–520, here 497. On celebrity activism, see Jelke Boesten, "On Ending Sexual Violence, or Civilizing War," King's International Development Institute Working Paper, February 2015, 3, file:///C:/Users/kstone/AppData/Local/Temp/Boesten-IDI-Working-Paper-2015-02.pdf.

27 See Sahla Aroussi, "'Women, Peace and Security': Addressing Accountability for Wartime Sexual Violence," *International Feminist Journal of Politics* 13, no. 4 (2011): 576–93; Karen Engle, "A Genealogy of the Centrality of Sexual

For Inger Skjelsbæk, #MeToo offers opportunities to take stock and foreground new issues, such as hegemonic masculinity and the structural inequalities that facilitate male privilege and abuses of power.[28] The response to CRSV, by contrast, "has been predominantly and historically focused on protection and mitigation of the impact on victims. The predator, or perpetrator, and the sociopolitical context which encourages, or silently accepts, and permits, this behavior have far too often been sidelined."[29] One reason for these priorities is the cogency of concepts such as "rape as weapon of war" and "genocidal rape," which emphasized the centrality of sexual violence to processes of conflict and secured political interest in the topic. Used too narrowly, however, these terms mask the complexity of CRSV. The strategic frame has arguably "rubbed out" the sexual from CRSV; it has, moreover, obscured and normalized other examples of gender-based violence before, during, and after conflict.[30] Against this background, Nicola Popovic and Anna Antonakis argue that #MeToo has helped to "unveil the power structures and gendered hierarchies that are mobilized so easily in times of war and conflict."[31]

In general, #MeToo has been credited for transporting what Boyle calls "continuum thinking" into mainstream discussions of sexual violence. Liz Kelly developed this concept in *Surviving Sexual Violence* (1988) to elucidate "how 'typical' and 'aberrant' male behavior shade into one another."[32] Against accusations that #MeToo has attempted to criminalize "trivial" forms of harassment by conflating them with violent misdemeanors, Boyle draws on Kelly to insist that the continuum is not a

Violence to Gender and Conflict," in *The Oxford Handbook of Gender and Conflict*, ed. Fionnuala Ní Aoláin, Naomi Cahn, Dina Francesca Haynes, and Nahla Valji (New York: Oxford University Press, 2017), 132–44.

28   Skjelsbæk, "Silence Breakers," 497.

29   Doris Buss, "Making Sense of Genocide, Making Sense of Law: International Criminal Prosecutions of Large-Scale Sexual Violence," in *Genocide and Gender in the Twentieth Century: A Comparative Survey*, ed. Amy E. Randall (London: Bloomsbury, 2015), 277–97, here 284; Maria Eriksson Baaz and Maria Stern, "Curious Erasures: The Sexual in Wartime Sexual Violence," *International Feminist Journal of Politics* 20, no. 3 (2018): 295–314.

30   Buss, "Making Sense of Genocide," 284; Eriksson Baaz and Stern, "Curious Erasures," 302.

31   Nicola Popovic and Anna Antonakis, "Centering War's 'Side Effects': The Institutionalisation of Conflict-Related Sexual and Gender-Based Violence in International Law and Its Translation into National Action Plans," in *Gender Roles in Peace and Security*, ed. Manuela Scheuermann and Anja Zürn (Cham, Switzerland: Springer, 2020), 103–26, here 104.

32   Liz Kelly, *Surviving Sexual Violence* (Cambridge: Polity, 1988), 75.

monolith.[33] Rather, it "exists within any individual woman's lifetime and connects different women's experiences under patriarchy, even as these experiences are differentiated in relation to overarching socio-political structures (for example, in conditions of war or systems of slavery) as well as through the intersections of gender with other structural forms of oppression such as race, dis/ability, age, or sexuality."[34] While contextual differentiation is vital, certain dynamics of gender and sexuality transcend the dividing line between peace and conflict: the vulnerability that comes with economic and social precarity; cultural norms that promote male sexual aggression and privilege; rape myths that deign only certain victims worthy of empathy; the relationship between stigma and silence; the perils of speaking out; and atmospheres of impunity. Jelke Boesten therefore argues that "it might not be wise to separate war and peace as political contexts if the aim is eradicating sexual violence."[35] During its presidency of the United Nations Security Council, Germany has championed such approaches as part of its "Frauen, Frieden und Sicherheit" (Women, Peace, and Security) agenda, which oversaw the passing of Resolution 2467, the first to recognize that "sexual violence in conflict occurs on a continuum of interrelated and recurring forms of violence against women and girls, and . . . exacerbates the frequency and brutality of other forms of gender-based violence."[36] In the remainder of this chapter, I show how Ralf Rothmann's bestselling novel *Der Gott jenes Sommers* imports these conversations into its exploration of sexual violence in 1945.

#MeToo and Continuum Thinking
in *Der Gott jenes Sommers*

Ralf Rothmann (1953–) has become one of Germany's foremost writers, with ten novels to his name as well as two plays and several collections of short stories and poetry. The recurring backdrop of his writing is the Ruhrgebiet of his formative years and period as a blue-collar worker. Since the 1990s, the so-called Ruhrgebiets-Romancier (Ruhr-area novelist) has achieved acclaim as one of Germany's best storytellers, garnering

33 Boyle, *#MeToo*, 52.

34 Boyle, "Sex of Sexual Violence," 101.

35 Boesten, "On Ending Sexual Violence," 4.

36 Office of the Special Representative of the Security General on Sexual Violence in Conflict, "Landmark UN Security Council Resolution 2467 (2019)," April 29, 2019, https://www.un.org/sexualviolenceinconflict/press-release/landmark-un-security-council-resolution-2467-2019-strengthens-justice-and-accountability-and-calls-for-a-survivor-centered-approach-in-the-prevention-and-response-to-conflict-related-sexual-violence/.

widespread coverage in the feuilletons and top literary prizes.[37] *Im Frühling sterben* (2015; *To Die in Spring*, 2017) was a runaway success and translated into twenty-five languages. It follows seventeen-year-old dairy hand Walter Urban, loosely modeled on the author's father, after he is recruited by the Tenth SS Panzer Division "Frundsberg" to fight on the eastern front in February 1945. *Der Gott jenes Sommers* forms a diptych with this work; Walter features as the object of twelve-year-old Luisa's affections. Her father is an admiral's steward who runs the military canteen in Kiel; when the bombing campaigns intensify, his family relocates to the rural estate managed by his stepdaughter, Gudrun, a leader in the "Kreisfrauenschaft" (district women's group), and her husband, Vinzent, an SS officer high up in the regional administration. The novel charts the family members' divergent responses to the war's growing presence in their daily lives, especially Luisa's increasing awareness of the prejudice and persecution within her local environment. Luisa's mother is equally intolerant and bigoted toward the Jewish community as toward the burgeoning numbers of refugees from the east who are allocated quarters on the estate. Their arrival sparks a distorted sexual awakening for Luisa, whose eyes are opened to the brutal realities of sexuality via rumors about rape. Moreover, she picks up the community's gossiping about her elder sister, Sibylle, who flouts the sexual mores of the time and engages in an affair with Vinzent.

The novel closes soon after the British Army occupies the area. By this point, Luisa's father has committed suicide, and Sibylle is missing, having been arrested by the Gestapo. It is unclear whether her detention is linked to her "asocial behavior" or some other offense fabricated by a jealous Gudrun. Luisa is contemplating entering the novitiate, seeking proximity to the nuns who represented the only beacon of humanity in her community during the Third Reich. Although religion otherwise plays a minor role in bookish Luisa's existence, the themes of hope and faith resound in the embedded narrative written by a fictional witness of the Thirty Years' War, Bredelin Merxheim. The framed narrative—"Der Chronik vom Ochsenweg" (The Ochsenweg Chronicle)—is told in alternating chapters and marked by an alienating register shift that approximates baroque diction to describe the indiscriminate brutality of war. Amid this chaos, Merxheim and his associate seek to create a spiritual refuge in the center of a lake. Although a storm sinks the floating chapel, Merxheim considers the endeavor a success, a permanent icon of his faith. As the novel draws to a close, it is unclear whether Luisa's desire to join a convent represents a similar confirmation of faith, or whether it is a form of escapism.

---

37 Doja Hacker, "Diskretion des Kindes," *Der Spiegel*, September 28, 2004, https://www.spiegel.de/spiegelspecial/a-320397.html.

Critics have questioned the quasi-transcendental framing of *Der Gott jenes Sommers*, the novel's tendency to idealize Luisa as largely unstained by her bigoted environment, and its limited attention to the political and military actions of figures like Vinzent and Gudrun.[38] These accusations risk painting Rothmann's depiction of the bombing war, refugees, and wartime rape in a revisionist light. I would argue, however, that *Der Gott jenes Sommers* intertwines histories of individual responsibility and state violence with personal stories of suffering, creating a differentiated picture of genocide and war that moves beyond moral binaries conflating victimhood with innocence that circulated in earlier representations of *Heimat* (homeland) and German wartime suffering. The novel's depiction of the final dreadful stages of World War II in no way obscures the bigotry and self-interest of a local community that supports the regime and turns a blind eye to its brutality.

We are introduced to Luisa as she reaches the cusp of adolescence, wavering between childlike ignorance and an awareness of her previous naivety. Frequently, this perception is expressed intuitively through feelings of embarrassment or, in the case of uncomfortable knowledge, a preference for looking away; for instance, when she encounters a large group of slave workers digging trenches along the riverbank. This reaction is mirrored in the final chapter, when Luisa catches sight of British soldiers disinfecting and tearing down the barracks that served as a labor camp and digging up corpses. Again, "Luisa wendete sich ab" (Luisa turned away).[39] This gesture is ambivalent. Contrary to her previous diffidence, Luisa now openly casts aspersions on Vinzent, who has been executed for crimes against the Geneva Convention. She also mentions that Gudrun now works as a secretary for the former gauleiter. Her distaste is apparent in her matter-of-fact summary of her relatives' whereabouts, although she withholds explicit judgment. Rather than resorting to ostentatious didacticism, the novel immerses the reader in the immediacy of Luisa's perspective, in her slow and difficult processes of awakening to the cruel world around her. This cruelty is manifest in the petty, judgmental, and selfish behavior of the adults, but also in the novel's depiction of sexual politics. Rothmann's depiction of sexual relations bolsters the work's message about the iniquity of the home front.

Judging by the opening chapters, readers might be forgiven for expecting the novel to rehash hackneyed memory scripts that use the threat of CRSV to conjure up the specter of the barbarous occupier. Such images

---

38 See Hans-Jürgen Benedict, *"Wär ich allmächtig, ich würde retten, retten": Aufsätze zur Gottesfrage in der deutschen Literatur* (Stuttgart: Kohlhammer, 2019), 205.

39 Ralf Rothmann, *Der Gott jenes Sommers* (Berlin: Suhrkamp, 2019), 249. Subsequent references are cited in text. All translations are mine.

saturate the mise-en-abyme "Die Chronik vom Ochsenweg," which describes the presence of "ledige Männer, die machten sich unkeusch mit einer Handvoll Weibshaar" (13; unwed men who unchastened themselves with the locks of wenches by the fistful) and who "trieben . . . ihre viehische Lust mit den zartesten Jungfrauen sowohl als mit Greisinnen, stachen ihnen die Augen aus" (90; discharged . . . their bestial lust with the most tender virgins and crones, stabbed out their eyes). This cruelty is mirrored in the graphic copperplate engravings that adorn the walls of Vinzent's villa, a glorification of war that portends his desensitization to human suffering. Such presentations of CRSV as exceptional brutality and bestiality normalize "rape, loot, and pillage" as inevitable by-products of war and risk turning violence into a spectacle that objectifies victims. In this respect, the chronicle mirrors the atrocity propaganda circulated by the Nazis in the closing stages of the war. Rothmann implies the influence of such "Greuelgeschichten" (atrocity stories) early in the novel when Luisa hears that refugees had endured rape by "die asiatischen Horden" (33; the Asiatic hordes). Such racist locutions suggest the difficulty of disentangling testimony from propaganda and ideology.[40] Into the Cold War, the memory of wartime rape bolstered West Germany's efforts to present the Christian West as more civilized—echoing Nazi arguments—and therefore as morally and politically superior to the Communist East.[41] Such propaganda became ossified as a cultural memory that only superficially educed women's experiences to channel fear, outrage, and disgust toward the perpetrators and the political systems they represented. The contemporary salience of such memory narratives resides in their imbrication with rape myths that demonize perpetrators as other to the moral and national community, as we see today in right-wing anti-immigrant rhetoric. Such rhetoric elides the systemic nature of sexual violence in the in-group. When current and past sexual violence is politicized as part of nationalist narratives, the actual crime of sexual violence, the experience of victims and survivors, and the responsibility of the community are elided. As Sabine Sielke has argued in her study of what she calls the "rhetoric of rape," such highly mediated rape narratives are "first and foremost interpretations, readings of rape that, as they seem to make sense of socially deviant behavior, oftentimes limit our understanding of sexual violence."[42]

While Rothmann's discussion of wartime rape initially seems to recycle stereotypical narratives painting sexual violence as an animalistic outgrowth of war, closer inspection reveals that he in fact writes against

---

40 Krimmer, *German Women's Life Writing*, 113.

41 Júlia Garraio, "Hordes of Rapists: The Instrumentalization of Sexual Violence in German Cold War Anti-Communist Discourses," *RCCS Annual Review* 5, no. 5 (2013): 46–63.

42 Sielke, *Reading Rape*, 2–3.

the grain of propagandistic narratives that naturalize sexual violence as an inevitable part of conquest. He complicates this rhetoric of rape by foregrounding women's perspectives. Finding herself alone with one of the younger refugee women, Luisa allows her curiosity to get the better of her, and she asks whether Elisabeth was raped. Elisabeth is surprised by Luisa's guileless candor but responds honestly. Rothmann's use of direct speech provides a first-person perspective, however brief, that is rare in German representations of wartime rape. Hans-Ulrich Treichel's *Tagesanbruch* (2015; Daybreak) is a notable exception. It remains to be seen whether #MeToo will prompt a broader cultural shift that begins to imagine survivors of wartime rape as agents of their own story and subjects whose lives are not solely defined by their experiences of violence. *Der Gott jenes Sommers* offers some cause for optimism. Rather than recapitulate the mechanics of assault, Elisabeth describes her sense of entrapment and the lasting physical effects of her abuse, such as the nauseating effect of the smell of schnapps. Despite the melancholy that settles over her features when she remembers her rape, Elisabeth does not let the attack define her; instead, she is focused on bringing her family through the war.

The fact that Elisabeth is in a relationship with Walter, the object of Luisa's infatuation, reinforces the extent to which rumors of rape form the backdrop to Luisa's coming of age. Moreover, a scene in which Luisa interrogates Sibylle about rape warps the typical scenarios through which older sisters initiate their siblings into the mysteries of sex. Luisa asks Sibylle whether it is true that soldiers leave women alone if they suspect they have syphilis. This question earns bitter laughter: "Na, da würde ich mir mal keine Illusionen machen. Die Kerle sind so spitz auf Weiberfleisch—ob man nun Krankheiten hat oder nicht, interessiert die einen Dreck" (43; Well, I wouldn't be under any illusions there. The fellers are so hot for a bit of skirt—they won't give a toss whether you've got some disease or not). With her reference to "die Kerlen" rather than "die Russen," she evokes a continuum of heterosexual behavior that transcends both the boundaries between war and peace and between nationalities. After her characteristically cocksure reply, Sibylle concedes, "Ja, wahrscheinlich tut es weh . . . sehr weh. Aber schrei nicht, zapple nicht und mach dich nicht steif, sonst wird dir alles gebrochen. So hab ich's jedenfalls gehört" (43; Yes, it probably does hurt . . . a lot. But don't cry out, don't struggle, and don't freeze up, otherwise they'll break every bone. At least that's what I've heard). This afterthought is the only indication that the affair between Sibylle and Vinzent was not always consensual.

Luisa's sexual awakening is accompanied by a series of harsh lessons about heterosexual relations and male sexual aggression that shatter the romantic myths that she has picked up through her voracious reading. The longest chapter depicts a decadent party at Vinzent's villa. Sibylle cuts a libertine figure among the Nazi wives and girlfriends who embody historical clichés about puritanical Nazi femininity. Luisa watches disapprovingly as her increasingly inebriated sister is courted by a circle of grotesque admirers, and she overhears one of the would-be gallants crudely announce: "Das Ziel ist ausgemacht, die Kräfte sind gesammelt. Der Zeitpunkt könnte besser nicht sein. Wer hackt sie zuerst?" (173; We've got our target, the forces have been rallied. The timing couldn't be better. Who's going to whack her first?). The violent military language suggests the extent to which aggressive male sexuality and derogatory attitudes toward women are normalized in this group. As Mühlhäuser writes, sexual banter fomented comradeship and served as a pathway to initiation for would-be soldiers in the Third Reich.[43] An odious illustration of this thesis comes toward the end of the novel, when Luisa is accosted by Hitler Youths making obscene gestures, no doubt already well aware of military rhetoric presenting sex as a privilege and reward for soldiers' sacrifices.[44] Hitler is even quoted as having said that "wenn der deutsche Mann als Soldat bereit sein solle, bedingungslos zu sterben, dann müsse er auch die Freiheit haben, bedingungslos zu lieben" (if we expect German men to be ready as soldiers to die unconditionally, then they also ought to have the freedom to love unconditionally).[45] This certainly seems to be a given at Vinzent's party. Luisa's father wryly comments on the debauchery, noting that "Soldaten auf Fronturlaub nutzen jede Sprungfeder, um das Heer aufzufrischen" (193; soldiers on furlough take advantage of every mattress to replenish the army). It is little wonder that this ideal of masculine virility and female availability impacted on soldiers' treatment of women in the occupied territories, ghettos, and camps.[46]

The novel's focus on Vinzent emphasizes the fact that these ideas about sexual access and power originate in civilian society. During the party, he tries to get Luisa alone, eventually coercing her to follow him into the state-of-the-art bunker. The pressure of his cufflinks through her cardigan symbolizes his forcefulness. Implicitly she senses a hierarchy of emotional and behavioral norms that compel her to subordinate her own feelings: "Luisa war ratlos, schluckte leer. Sich stärker als innerlich zu sträuben, wäre ihr unhöflich vorgekommen. Er war der Gastgeber, ihr Schwager zudem, und dass ihre Reserve ihn beleidigen könnte, machte

43   Regina Mühlhäuser, "Reframing Sexual Violence as a Weapon and Strategy of War: The Case of the German Wehrmacht during the War and Genocide in the Soviet Union, 1941–1944," *Journal of the History of Sexuality* 26, no. 3 (2017): 366–401, here 399.

44   Mühlhäuser, "Reframing Sexual Violence," 386. See also Thomas Kühne, *Kameradschaft: Die Soldaten des nationalsozialistischen Krieges und das 20. Jahrhundert* (Göttingen: Vandenhoeck und Ruprecht, 2006).

45   Cited in Kühne, *Kameradschaft*, 385.

46   Kühne, *Kameradschaft*, 386.

ihr mehr Angst als der Keller" (178; Luisa was at a loss and gulped. To resist more than internally seemed impolite. He was the host, and her brother-in-law at that, and the idea that her reservation might offend him scared her more than the cellar). In its depiction of the power dynamics that underpin sexual abuse, *Der Gott jenes Sommers* thus reflects the themes that have come to dominate post-#MeToo discourse. Vinzent is fully aware of the status differential, calling Luisa "mein Milchmädchen" (my little dairymaid). Class divisions and snobbery are among the novel's central motifs, also evident in the family's sense of superiority over the "refugees," that is, the bedraggled peasants from the East who are crammed into the outbuildings.

Beyond its focus on the dynamics of power and coercion, the novel's ethics of representation are wholly compatible with the post-#MeToo world. An extensive body of feminist scholarship has engaged with the perils of representing sexual violence in word and image, warning of the risks of reproducing the objectifying perspective of the perpetrator and eliminating the victim's subjectivity. Rothmann circumvents these risks with his focus on Luisa's emotional reaction to Vinzent's actions. The effect of these narrative choices is clear in the following excerpt:

> Er [stieß] einen seltsamen Laut aus . . . ein spaßhaftes Knurren. Sein Schatten schob sich über sie, die Fliege streifte ihre Wange, und sie wusste vor Entsetzen nicht, ob sie lachen oder schreien sollte. "Nein, lass das!" zischte sie, "Wir werden ganz schmutzig." Mit beiden Händen schlug sie nach ihm, vor Unglauben schwach. Aber er grinste nur. (178–79).

> [He emitted a strange sound . . . a facetious growl. His shadow thrust itself over her, his bow tie caressed her cheek and, in her horror, she did not know whether she should laugh or cry. "No, stop that," she hissed. "We're going to get all dirty." She used both hands to thrash at him, weak with disbelief. But he simply grinned.]

The adjectives describing Vinzent's actions evoke a jocular atmosphere that contrasts starkly with Luisa's fear and outrage, showing his failure to acknowledge or take seriously her resistance, perhaps unsurprising given Western culture's idealization of female sexual passivity and coyness. One of the songs playing in the background is "Mein Herz hat heut' Premiere" (My Heart Premieres Today) from the musical comedy *Wir machen Musik* (1942; We're Making Music), which contains the lyrics "und wenn ich mich auch wehre, / mein Herz schlägt nur für dich" (189; even if I resist, / my heart beats only for you). Yet Rothmann's description does not eroticize resistance; indeed, it appeals to the abject. Vinzent's kisses remind Luisa of her mother's fetid handkerchiefs; in her shock, she wets herself and struggles to breathe under his weight. When

Luisa makes a final attempt to get him to stop, he fully covers her. This blatant violation of her will evokes Mieke Bal's argument that "rape itself cannot be visualized . . . because rape makes the victim invisible. It does that literally—first the perpetrator covers her—and figuratively—then the rape destroys her self-image, her subjectivity."[47] Vinzent completely disregards Luisa's autonomy, only stopping his assault when Luisa vomits, an involuntary somatic reaction that directly impacts on him.

Der Gott jenes Sommers offers a neat example of Kelly's and Boyle's employment of the concept of the continuum to signify how women's histories inform their interpretations of the present. By this point of the novel, Luisa's understanding of sensuality has been shot through with violence. After recovering from her nausea, Luisa asks, "War das jetzt ein Zungenkuss? . . . Willst du mich vergewaltigen?" (180; Was that a French kiss? . . . Do you want to rape me?). This slippage between the sensual and violent is reminiscent of Boyle's explanation that women's understanding of what is "typical" behavior stems from both cultural narratives and personal encounters.[48] Luisa's few lessons about sex suggest that sensuality and violence are intimately connected. To give just one example: earlier Luisa had witnessed a man chasing a shrieking paramour into the garden, prompting Gudrun to remark, "'Männer sind Kinder, stimmt's? Immer wollen sie Fangen spielen. . . . Männer mögen nämlich keine Bohnenstangen, weißt du. Wenn die auf ihre Art hinfassen, ist es immer besser, ein bisschen gepolstert zu sein.' Sie lächelte" (158–59; "Men are children, you see? They always want to play catch. . . . See, men don't like beanstalks, you know? When they grab you like they do, it's always better to have a bit of padding." She smiled). Her smile draws attention to the glaring contrast between the comment about male roughness and Gudrun's accepting and ultimately trivializing response. It is therefore unsurprising that Vinzent laughs at Luisa's perception of their encounter: "Vergewaltigt wird hier niemand. . . . Wir sind keine Barbaren, wir sind Verwandte, oder? Wir machen das in familiärem Einvernehmen, Kind. Ich tue etwas für dich, du tust was für mich?" (180; Nobody's being raped here. . . . We aren't barbarians, we're relatives, aren't we? We're doing this in familial concord, little one. I'll scratch your back and you scratch mine?). Here he demonstrates his power of definition, marshaling prevailing conceptions of rape as defined by extreme violence and the actions of deviant strangers (or, in the context of war, foreigners).

There is no doubt that the novel's interest in structures of coercion and inequality resonates in the light of #MeToo and makes *Der Gott jenes Sommers* one of the more nuanced memory narratives to deal with CRSV.

47 Mieke Bal, *A Mieke Bal Reader* (Chicago: University of Chicago Press, 2006), 44.
48 Boyle, "Sex of Sexual Violence," 108.

Yet its depiction of sexual perpetrators is somewhat lacking in complexity. After lecturing Luisa on the meaning of rape, Vinzent proceeds to masturbate in front of her. All that she sees through the opening of his trousers is the silver skull on his ring, a clunky metaphor linking Vinzent's misconduct with his Nazi beliefs. The novel ultimately eliminates Vinzent (he is executed). After her convalescence, Walter is the only male figure with whom Luisa engages. He nobly rejects her advances, however, when he realizes how young she is. This raises the question: What happened to the sexual perpetrators—those who exploited the war to attack members of their own nation and enemy populations—after 1945?

Much like the media's obsession with larger-than-life perpetrators like the movie producer Harvey Weinstein, Rothmann's focus on Vinzent as a bogeyman and product of an inhuman, but soon to be vanquished, regime, arguably risks overshadowing broader structural issues. Burke has vociferously opposed this distortion of #MeToo within the media.[49] Rosalind Gill and Shani Orgad likewise call for more detailed engagement with what they call the "monstrous capitalist, patriarchal and sexist system that has produced, sustained and rewarded these 'bad apples' over decades."[50]

Contextualizing CRSV during World War II as part of longer histories of structural violence would provide one way of integrating wartime rape into public memory of the war, without reproducing bathetic and politically suspect narratives of German victimhood.[51] A complex understanding of victims and survivors as agents would be integral to this project. In *Der Gott jenes Sommers*, each character experiences different forms of sexual abuse and coercion; each interprets and responds to the experience in her own way. After her initial shock, Luisa resolves to make the experience uncomfortable for Vinzent rather than passively participate in an erotic scenario choreographed by her aggressor. Defiantly, she asks whether he had executed a British pilot who had crashed near the estate and fulminates that the Allies are already holding Germans to account for breaches of the Geneva Convention. In response, Vinzent ponders where she has gained this information. His firm grip on her thigh offers Luisa a wordless invitation to buy his silence regarding the source

---

49 Elizabeth Adetiba and Tarana Burke, "Tarana Burke Says #MeToo Should Centre Marginalized Communities," in *Where Freedom Starts: Sex, Power, Violence, #MeToo* (London: Verso, 2018), 8–37, here 15.

50 Rosalind Gill and Shani Orgad, "The Shifting Terrain of Sex and Power: From the 'Sexualization of Culture' to #MeToo," *Sexualities* 21, no. 8 (2018): 1313–24, here 1320.

51 Scholars have begun to address the marginalization of CRSV in official fora of commemoration. See Janet Jacobs, "The Memorial at Srebrenica: Gender and the Social Meanings of Collective Memory in Bosnia-Herzegovina," *Memory Studies* 10, no. 4 (2017): 423–39.

of her knowledge. She stands up and allows him to guide her hand to pleasure him manually. The narrative carefully decodes her actions and emotions, discouraging the reader from equating agency with consent. "Zum Weinen war ihr," we read, "aber für die Traurigkeit, die sie fühlte, gab es wohl keine Tränen, und so versuchte sie ein Lächeln" (185; She wanted to cry, but there were no tears to express the sadness she felt, so she ventured a smile). When she wipes her face and hands on his handkerchief, she notices her eyelashes look like "ausgerissene Fliegenbeine" (plucked-off fly legs), a zoomorphic simile that reflects philosopher Louise du Toit's conception of sexual assault as a "spirit injury" that disturbs the individual's previous relationship to the world: "she now sees, inhabits and lives an alien Körper, a dead weight of flesh, a mortal, vulnerable, breakable thing that obstructs, exposes, and threatens rather than shelters."[52] Luisa is not, however, plunged into a state of permanent self-abjection, impotence, and dereliction. According to Kelly, continuum thinking involves recognizing that "women's reactions to incidents of sexual violence at the time, and the impact on them over time, are complex matters."[53] In *Der Gott jenes Sommers*, sexual assault is merely one of the hardships that these women endure given the historical setting. Soon after Vinzent's abuse, Luisa contracts typhoid fever, learns that Sibylle is missing, and finds the dead body of her father. Like Elisabeth, moreover, Luisa does not let Vincent's actions define her or her relationship to sensuality. When Walter returns from a prisoner-of-war camp, Luisa does not shrink from a possible amorous encounter but, rather, dons her high heels and tries to kiss him.

Rothmann's ambivalent representation of the relationship between Sibylle and Vinzent also challenges rape myths that specify how survivors should respond to their experiences of violence and that freeze them in the identity of victims. Sibylle refuses to be cowed by the circumstances of the crumbling wartime society and grasps the hedonistic pleasures of life. Vinzent offers one route to such gratification. She brashly tells her mother, "Dem ist klar, dass er liefern muss. . . . Und falls er wirklich keine [Vorräte] haben sollte, gibt es bei mir auch nichts mehr, verstehst du. Dann ist der Laden für den Herrn Sturmführer eben dicht" (32; He knows full well that he has to deliver. . . . And if he really doesn't have any provisions, then I won't be laying out anymore either, understood. It'll simply be shop shut for Mister Sturmführer). While Sibylle's affair with Vinzent blurs the lines between consent and pressurized sex, she is an active participant in the relationship and, arguably, infatuated with him. Rothmann's narrative thus resists facile judgments. Feminist scholars and

52 Louise du Toit, *A Philosophical Investigation of Rape: The Making and Unmaking of the Feminine Self* (New York: Routledge, 2009), 84.
53 Kelly, *Surviving Sexual Violence*, 76.

activists criticize the extent to which the "reality" of rape is frequently judged according to the recognizability, and therefore credibility, of a victim's trauma. Yet as Boyle points out, the idea that sexual assault is "always and only devastating (and, so, rare) clashes with the assertion that rape and sexual assault take many forms and are depressingly routine."[54] Within the context of #MeToo, skeptics questioned why figures such as actors Rose McGowan and Ashley Judd continued to pose for pictures with Weinstein after their alleged assaults, suggesting that "real" victims would not have been capable of doing so. With its portrayal of the agency of Sibylle, Luisa, and Elisabeth, who take ownership of their experiences, their memories, and the impact of the assault on their subsequent lives, *Der Gott jenes Sommers* contributes to a broader dismantling of such rape myths and lays the groundwork for a reconsideration of women's vulnerability and possibilities for agency in times of war.

Looking Back and Moving Forward

The starting point for my analysis of Rothmann's novel was Sara Ahmed's conviction that feminist practice is often a mode of "memory work" that expands on the present and thus enables us to "make sense of how different experiences connect."[55] Looking back at World War II via narratives such as *Der Gott jenes Sommers* allows readers to draw connections between past and present but also between different contexts; namely, between times of war and ostensible peace. This chapter has argued that it is necessary to consider CRSV in the context of discussions about #MeToo precisely because "war dramatically complicates the boundary between truly consensual and violent, forced, coerced, or in some way publicly shameful sexual relationships."[56] It epitomizes a new phase in the cultural memory of CRSV by representing the complex relationship between precarity and consent and by giving survivors a voice and subjectivity that expands on one-dimensional notions of victimhood. With its literary reflections on continuums of sexual violence, toxic cultures of masculinity, and gender inequalities, it is thus a memory narrative for the #MeToo age.

In this respect, the novel mirrors *Die Mutter meiner Mutter* (2015; My Mother's Mother) by Sabine Rennefanz, which tells the story of the narrator's grandmother, a refugee who suffers sexual assault not by Russian occupation forces but at the hands of a returning German

---

54 Boyle, "Sex of Sexual Violence," 104.

55 Ahmed, *Living a Feminist Life*, 22.

56 Annette Timm, "The Challenges of Including Sexual Violence and Transgressive Love in Historical Writing on World War II and the Holocaust," *Journal of the History of Sexuality* 26, no. 3 (2017): 351–65, here 365.

soldier, who is eventually pressured into marrying her to avoid the scandal of pregnancy. By expanding on the normative script of sexual violence circa 1945 and revealing the normalization of sexual aggression on the home front, Rothmann and Rennefanz deepen our understanding of the cultural attitudes and structural disadvantages that fed into the abuse of enemy women by German soldiers, led to assaults on German women by Allied soldiers, and contributed to a cultural memory that has objectified and disempowered women. These recent novels offer some hope that #MeToo might provide new templates for telling stories about historical sexual violence, as well as for understanding contemporary examples of CRSV and the continuums of violence that transcend war and peace.

As Jessie Kindig notes, moreover, adopting a historical perspective on current movements can provide "an antidote to . . . false narratives of shock" and "offer the potential for different futures."[57] Feminist memory work must share #MeToo's desire to deconstruct rape myths that influence when and how sexual violence is addressed, recognized, and understood. After all, like rape culture, cultural memory and national identity are constituted through the relations of power that structure a given society. And so, unless we can heed the lessons of the past about the reality of sexual violence, future cries of #MeToo are likely to fall on deaf ears.

---

57   Jessie Kindig, "Introduction," in *Where Freedom Starts: Sex, Power, Violence in #MeToo* (London: Verso, 2018), 17–27, here 10.

Part IV

The Institutions of #MeToo

9: Boarding-School Novels around 1900: The Relation of Male Fear of Women to Male-Male Seduction and Sexual Abuse in Hesse, Musil, and Walser

Niklas Straetker

I N THE EARLY TWENTIETH CENTURY, the German-language literary scene witnessed the sudden proliferation of boarding-school novels, many of which feature scenarios of (predominantly) male-on-male sexual abuse and/or seduction at crucial points in the plots. Hermann Hesse's *Unterm Rad* (1906; *Beneath the Wheel*, 1968), Robert Musil's *Verwirrungen des Zöglings Törleß* (1906; The *Confusions of Young Törless*, 1955), and Robert Walser's *Jakob von Gunten* (1909; *Jakob von Gunten*, 1969),[1] three highly prominent works in the German-language literary canon, share a common setting: all-male boarding schools. As these institutions sequester students from their surroundings, contact with girls and women is limited. In each of the novels, there is only one female figure who plays a larger role and who thus serves as a semantically overcharged representation of womanhood as such. Especially in *Unterm Rad* and *Törless*, the lone female character embodies the dangerous world outside the institutions. She is portrayed as a voracious, lascivious, overpowering, and swamp-like entity that threatens to destroy the orderly recursive formalism of the teenage boys' lives.

---

1 See Hermann Hesse, *Unterm Rad* (Frankfurt am Main: Suhrkamp, 1985), trans. Michael Roloff as *Beneath the Wheel* (New York: Picador, 2003 [1968]); Robert Musil, *Die Verwirrungen des Zöglings Törleß* (Hamburg: Rowohlt, 2013), trans. Eithne Wilkins and Ernst Kaiser as *Young Törleß* (New York: Pantheon, 1955); Robert Walser, *Jakob von Gunten* (Zurich: Suhrkamp, 1985), trans. Christopher Middleton as *Jakob von Gunten* (New York: NYRB, 1999 [1969]). In this paper, I do not quote from the first English translation of *Törleß* but, instead, from *The Confusions of Young Törleß*, trans. Shaun Whiteside (New York: Penguin, 2001), whose syntax and vocabulary capture the peculiarities of the German original more closely.

It may seem counterintuitive that some men perceived women as menacing, violent forces, not only in novels but in the broader masculine imagination as such at a time when, by any objective standards, woman's emancipation and empowerment faced much greater resistance than they do today.[2] This is even more puzzling if one considers the contemporary trope of the "hysterical" woman.[3] It would appear, however, that a hundred years ago, the male protagonists of many a novel and autobiography traded accounts of how they had suffered and feared unsolicited sexual advances by women: #they too, that is. Such (oftentimes fictional) anecdotes cannot belie the larger historical reality of oppression and sexual abuse inflicted on women at the hands of men.[4] Unlike today's #metoo accounts, those anecdotes often targeted a unitary bogeywoman and, in doing so, were more invested in constructing a distorting cultural trope[5] than relating actual experiences.

Nonetheless, at the level of rhetoric, such male fear of women is oddly similar to the "female fear of male aggression" that is strongly emphasized in parts of the #metoo movement. While such female fear is well founded and empirically justified, some feminists have nonetheless claimed that highlighting it one-sidedly may itself encroach on women's agency, perpetuating a belief in women's powerlessness.[6] Throughout this chapter, I explore and historicize possible connections and parallels

---

2   This is well documented in Klaus Theweleit, *Männerphantasien*, 2 vols. (Frankfurt am Main: Roter Stern, 1977–78); in English as *Male Fantasies*, 2 vols., vol. 1 trans. Stephen Conway (Cambridge: Polity, 1987); vol. 2 trans. Chris Turner and Erica Carter (Cambridge: Polity, 1989).

3   The Freudian trope of the overly sexual, yet weak, hysterical woman is, of course, markedly different from that of the "overpowering woman." See George L. Mosse, *The Image of Man: The Creation of Modern Masculinity* (Oxford: Oxford University Press, 1996), 85, for a contextualization of the hysteria discourse. It is unfortunate (even careless), however, that Mosse does not even mention Theweleit's hugely influential study. Mosse refers to several "dangerous woman" tropes from around 1900 but not to the trope of the overpowering, voracious woman. He comes closest to describing the latter in his discussion of seemingly "virile women" (104) in the late-nineteenth-century feminist movement, but this type is "sexless" and more akin to the flapper "with her short hair, mannish clothes, and the cigarette dangling from her lips," whereby "she seemed to efface gender" (147).

4   Mosse rightly highlights this, asserting that despite the growing feminist movement in the early twentieth century, "men's superiority was not yet seriously at risk." *Image of Man*, 144.

5   My use of the term "trope" here presupposes its ordinary, broad meaning (close to "prototype" or "stereotype"), not the particular ones it receives in Hayden White's or Jacques Derrida's "tropologies."

6   See, for instance, Svenja Faßpöhler, *Die potente Frau: Für eine neue Weiblichkeit* (Berlin: Ullstein, 2018).

between the contemporaneous and present discourses and realities of gender relations. Since the study of modern sexuality has given rise to significant scholarly disagreements over the last decades—most notably after Foucault published the first volume of his *History of Sexuality* in 1976—I engage in a discussion of methodology and theory before dealing with the three novels.

In my analysis of the novels, I then elucidate the causal and contiguous relations between institutional formalization, male-on-male sexual abuse/seduction, and the constructions of dangerous oversexualized femininity, taking both form and content into consideration. Drawing on Rüdiger Campe's concept of the *novel of the institution*,[7] I demonstrate that the intense overdetermination of sexuality fulfills an important function: the violent repression of corporeality grounds the lifeless formalization that characterizes not only the diegetic boarding schools but also the recursive and quasi-institutional structural organization of the novels. In a final section, I assess how far this historical dynamic involving explicit and implicit homoeroticism, violence, and fear of women may still have a bearing on our present time.

Historicizing "Homosexuality," "Sexual Abuse," and "Seduction"

The search for continuities and parallels between present and past cultural constellations runs the risk of becoming entangled in conceptual confusions. This is illustrated not least by such terms/concepts as "homosexuality," which was not coined before the late nineteenth century, or "sexual abuse" and "seduction," whose ordinary and legal meanings have changed significantly over time. All these terms need to be elucidated and historicized in their contemporary discursive environments.

It is worth emphasizing that forms of sexuality that we would now characterize as "statutory rape" or "sexual misconduct" would have appeared to be instances of "benign" seduction to the contemporaneous public and/or the law. For example, in the twenty-first century, a teacher who seduces or woos an adolescent student raises legal and moral concerns about gender, legal age, class, propriety, and power differences

---

7   See Rüdiger Campe, "Kafkas Institutionenroman: *Der Proceß, Das Schloß*," in *Gesetz: Ironie*, ed. Rüdiger Campe and Michael Niehaus (Heidelberg: Synchron, 2004), 197–208; Rüdiger Campe, "Das Bild und die Folter: Robert Musils *Törleß* und die Form des Romans," in *Weiterlesen: Literatur und Wissen*, ed. Ulrike Bergermann and Elisabeth Strowick (Bielefeld: transcript, 2007), 121–47; Rüdiger Campe, "Robert Walsers Institutionenroman: *Jakob von Gunten*," in *Die Macht und das Imaginäre*, ed. Rudolf Behrens and Jörn Steigerwald (Würzburg: Königshausen & Neumann, 2005), 235–50.

that would have appeared in a radically different light in, say, the German or Austro-Hungarian Empires.[8] Relatedly, Sigmund Freud's early *seduction theory*, which he abandoned when developing his concept of infantile sexuality, has recently gained renewed prominence in literary and cultural studies.[9] In his early work, Freud believed that certain neuroses develop when a pubescent person begins to understand unconsciously that certain childhood interactions with adults that seemed rather harmless or perhaps awkward to him/her at the time were forms of sexual abuse all along. If Freud's observation is valid, we need to take into account yet another level of temporal and conceptual incommensurateness; namely, how one and the same person's interpretations of sexually charged interactions change over time.

The contemporary #MeToo movement has likewise drawn attention to cases in which a person realized retroactively, belatedly—Freud's German term is *Nachträglichkeit*—that past sexual interaction(s) that were not perceived as malicious at the time constituted sexual abuse and could be the reason for persistent mental-health problems. In retrospect, a coworker's seemingly innocent touches or a superior's failed or successful attempts to seduce (or: abuse) may appear in a much darker light. However, if Freud's analysis of a prepubescent child's interaction with an adult is thus applied to "acts of seduction" as such, the concept of *Nachträglichkeit* may become extended to such a degree that it loses its explanatory value and turns into an overdiagnosed passe-partout.[10]

---

8   In Wilhelminian Germany, the seduction of a fourteen-year-old girl by a male adult authority figure could be tolerated if it was understood as a "promise of marriage" (*Heiratsversprechen*). See Volker Berghahn, *Das Kaiserreich 1871– 1914: Industriegesellschaft, bürgerliche Kultur und autoritärer Staat*, Handbuch der deutschen Geschichte (Stuttgart: Klett-Kotta, 2013), 130. Conversely, the empire demanded that "female teachers" be celibate (*Lehrerinnenzölibat*) and made it impossible for them to marry. See Ute Planert, *Antifeminismus im Kaiserreich: Diskurs, soziale Formation und Mentalität* (Göttingen: Vandenhoeck & Ruprecht, 1998), 55.

9   Jean Laplanche, *New Foundations for Psychoanalysis*, trans. David Macey (Oxford: Blackwell, 1989 [Fr. 1987]), attempted to rehabilitate Freud, devoting the entire second part of the book to a "generalized theory of seduction."

10   One may think, for instance, of the case of actress Asia Argento, who helped initiate the movement by credibly accusing producer Harvey Weinstein of sexual assault, only to then have her sincerity retroactively questioned when the actor Jimmy Bennett accused her of "statutory rape." Bennett alleged that he and the then-adult Argento engaged in sexual interactions when he was seventeen. At the time he perceived the relationship as consensual; later, however, he realized that the "fallout . . . was so traumatic that it hindered Mr. Bennett's work and income and threatened his mental health." See Kim Servento, "Asia Argento, a #MeToo Leader, Made a Deal with Her Own Accuser," *New York*

How far, then, is it reasonable, in the present, to imbue an event with meanings—concerning both individual psychological development and socially conventionalized linguistic denotation—that did not exist (or did so only latently) at the time of its original occurrence? This question poses itself not only when specific interactions with or acts of aggression by others are evaluated but also in the case of someone's apparent "homosexuality," a term whose current definition is radically different from its meaning when it was coined in the latter third of the nineteenth century.[11] The establishment of the homosexual/heterosexual binary is often considered to have been functionally coextensive with or an offshoot of the creation of modern heteronormative "sexuality" as such. According to Foucault and later Judith Butler, an "essentialist fiction" of binarily opposed sexes arose via a synthesis of what were in fact disparate pieces of medical, biological, and psychological knowledge, thereby concealing its own constructedness under the guise of scientific objectivity.

Well before the establishment of modern "heteronormativity," homoerotic interactions had been criminalized, of course. In Prussia, "sodomy" continued to be a crime even in the "enlightened" legal code (*ALR*) of 1794, though it was no longer punishable by death. In fact, Bavaria's post-Enlightenment legal code was the only major German-language codex that followed the example of France, where "sodomy" had been decriminalized in 1791. With the establishment of the German Empire in 1871, the German criminal code decreed, in the infamous §175, that sex

---

Times, August 8, 2019, https://www.nytimes.com/2018/08/19/us/asia-argento-assault-jimmy-bennett.html.

11 The Austro-Hungarian journalist Karoly Maria Benkert is considered to have been the first to use the term, in an 1868 letter. While Michel Foucault credits the neurologist Carl Westphal with introducing it in 1869–70, Westphal used the term *konträre Sexualempfindung*. Richard von Krafft-Ebing employed "homosexual" in his highly influential *Psychopathia Sexualis* from 1886, cementing its usage in the psychiatric and medical discourse. While originally understood as a pathological deviation from "normal" sexuality, "homosexuality" has since accrued innumerable influential definitions. Freud famously understood it as an *inversion*, emphasizing early-childhood cathexes rather than innate dispositions, and the Abrahamic religions have considered homosexuality to be a matter of free and thus condemnable choice. Cf. Vern L. Bullough, *Homosexuality: A History* (New York: Routledge, 1979), 1–16. At the present time, the dominant, liberal understanding, at least in the so-called West, is that one's sexual preferences are largely based in one's biology, which is a rebuttal to religious views. How far this causes problems for decidedly constructionist approaches will be analyzed in the next section.

between men was punishable with a prison sentence.[12] It is true that the German Empire's new penal code punished only homoerotic *acts*. Yet the fact that they were, in some regions, *re*criminalized in the first place indicates that the code was already affected by a notion of "homosexuality" as an apparently deep-seated, pathologically deviant disposition which single acts merely express or instantiate.[13] Similarly, regarding violent crime, promiscuity, arson, or even financial fraud, the late nineteenth century replaced act-based conceptions with characterological ones, as biopolitics established itself as a dominant paradigm.[14]

In fact, the question of what the introduction of "homosexuality" signified on a larger sociocultural scale has elicited very different responses along (or rather: at the extreme points of) a continuum between constructionism and essentialism. Most scholars of sexuality firmly oppose those researchers, sometimes dubbed (rightly or wrongly) "essentialists" or "biologists," who have claimed that "homosexuality" was simply a new term for or merely a modification of a concept, action, or quality that had already been engaged with for thousands of years in philosophical, religious, and legal writing.

In this chapter, however, following neither constructionist nor essentialist approaches, I instead attempt to provide a "thick description"[15] of three novels against their historical backdrop, especially the early discourse on "homosexuality" around 1900. I thus explore the dialectic, underlying all three novels analyzed here, between the autonomous choices of individuals and the material, natural, social, and historical factors that to a smaller or larger (deterministic) degree influence those choices.[16]

---

12 See Hans-Georg Stümke, *Homosexuelle in Deutschland: Eine politische Geschichte* (Munich: C. H. Beck, 1989), 21–26.

13 See Thomas Vormbaum, *A Modern History of German Criminal Law*, trans. Margaret Hiley (Berlin: Springer, 2014), 112–13. Vormbaum quite convincingly places himself between Foucauldian discourse analysis and the classic history-of-ideas approach.

14 This, of course, is one of Foucault's main points in the first of the three volumes of his *Histoire de la sexualité* (1976–2021; *History of Sexuality*, 1979–2021). For a more concrete history of the change to a characterological conception of criminality in German-language countries, see Peter Becker, *Verderbnis und Entartung: Eine Geschichte der Kriminologie des 19. Jahrhunderts als Diskurs und Praxis* (Göttingen: Vandenhoeck & Ruprecht, 2002), especially 281–82.

15 Cf. Clifford Geertz, "Thick Description: Toward an Interpretative Theory of Culture," in *The Interpretation of Cultures* (New York: Basic Books, 1973), 3–30. My interpretations of the novel are thus informed by hermeneutic close readings that focus on form aesthetics and semiotic overdetermination.

16 A convincing example of a study that dialectically engages structural, symbolically interactionalist, and individual-centered hermeneutic analyses is Susan Faludi, *Stiffed: The Roots of Modern Male Rage* (New York: William Morrow

Unterm Rad—First Signs
of the *Institutionenroman*

Unterm Rad is the most straightforward of the three boarding-school novels. It tells the story of Hans Giebenbarth, a smart boy from a humble southwest German background, whose stellar academic achievements qualify him to take (and pass) the entrance exam to a state-run elite boarding school for future civil servants. When the students enter the boarding school, their lives undergo two significant changes. First, at their former schools the students all distinguished themselves by their academic performance. At the new school, however, a "re-entry," that is, a recategorization of students based on their current scholarly accomplishments, creates new hierarchies and thus threatens to relegate a student who previously occupied the top end of the scale to its bottom.[17] Second, at his former school, Hans had enough leisure to integrate the cultural content he was presented with in the classroom into his lifeworld. In the new boarding-school environment, however, excessive examinations all but eliminate any chance to apply humanistic and scientific knowledge in real life.

Hesse's novel, which depicts boarding-school life as highly repetitive and deprived of meaning and pleasure, already exhibits, contentwise, classic traits of what Rüdiger Campe calls the "novel of the institution." Whereas the nineteenth-century bildungsroman narrates the "Gang des Subjekts durch die Institutionen" (subject's moving through the institutions), the novel of the institution is concerned with authorities that institute a life ("Instanz, die ein Leben instituiert"),[18] insofar as the institution both produces and hinders, or even destroys, one's autobiography, one's individuality, and one's life.

None of the novels discussed here instantiates the most extreme version or ideal type of the *Institutionenroman*, that is, the *complete* collapse of the difference between form and content, life and formalization, progress and recursion. This means that while or perhaps because the institutionalization of life and narrativity threatens to dissolve the sense of individual human personhood in these novels, more traditionally humanistic concerns, such as "hermeneutic meaning," "development," "mind and body equilibrium," "affectivity," or even "love," still hold claims on

---

Paperbacks, 2019 [1st ed., 1999]). Faludi does not presuppose systemic determinism. The book's original subtitle was *The Betrayal of the American Man.*

17 "Re-entries" of already-made distinctions, such as fiction/reality at a lower level, e.g., as a (fictional) play within the (already fictional) play, are prominently discussed in theories of systemic and institutional organization, not least in Niklas Luhmann's.

18 Campe, "Kafkas Institutionenroman," 199. All translations from Campe's texts are mine.

both artistic production and on the individual human being. Each time, those concerns adapt themselves to and counteract the peculiarities of the institutional settings in idiosyncratic ways.

In the case of *Unterm Rad*, the institutionalization of life is broken open by means of a kiss Hans shares with a fellow student, the *Schöngeist* (aesthete) Herrmann:

> Beide sahen nun einander ins Gesicht, und wahrscheinlich sah jeder in diesem Augenblick des andern Gesicht zum ersten Male ernstlich an und versuchte, sich vorzustellen, daß hinter diesen jünglinghaft glatten Zügen ein besonderes Menschenleben mit seinen Eigenarten und eine besondere, in ihrer Weise gezeichnete Seele wohne. Langsam streckte Hermann Heilner seinen Arm aus, faßte Hans an der Schulter und zog ihn zu sich her, bis ihre Gesichter einander ganz nahe waren. Dann fühlte Hans plötzlich mit wunderlichem Schreck des andern Lippen seinen Mund berühren.

> [Now they faced each other and at this moment each took his first serious look at the other and tried to imagine that these boyishly smooth features concealed a particular personality and a soul of its very own. Hermann Heilner slowly extended his arm, took Hans by the shoulder and drew him to him until their faces almost touched. Then Hans was startled to feel the other's lips touch his.][19]

Here, the adolescents' interaction is described in the linguistic register of "romantic love," despite its homoerotic—that is, at the time, transgressive—nature. In this aspect, *Unterm Rad* is markedly different from *Jakob von Gunten* and especially *Törleß*, both of which intertwine homoeroticism with torture, abuse, and/or dangerous seduction, and throughout Hesse's novel, the effects of institutionalization are not as extreme as in Musil and Walser. In *Unterm Rad*, the teachers are strict and impose arbitrary punishments, such as detention or writing lines on the chalkboard, but the students do not perceive them as all-pervading draconian authorities. Similarly, the everyday relationships between the students are not marked by the brutal power divides that characterize *Törleß*.

This may be because significant parts of *Unterm Rad* are not set in the boarding school, meaning that the students' experiences at school are framed by a before and after. We are provided with a biography of the protagonist and the possibility of a romantic, free, fulfilling, and perfectible life. That is, life as it (seemingly[20]) unfolds in the bildungsroman

---

19   Hesse, *Unterm Rad*, 230; *Beneath the Wheel*, 78.

20   Friedrich Kittler, "Über die Sozialisation Wilhelm Meisters," in *Dichtung als Sozialisationsspiel: Studien zu Goethe und Gottfried Keller*, ed. Friedrich Kittler and Gerhard Kaiser (Göttingen: Vandenhoeck & Ruprecht, 1978), 13–124,

still serves as an ideal that the protagonists value and seek to recuperate in opposition to the institution. Hesse's novel still portrays a temporally and spatially progressive and extensive journey of development of its protagonist, whether it is considered a chimera or not. Therefore, in *Unterm Rad*, the bildungsroman, rather than merely being invoked *ex negativo*, still determines parts of both the plot schema and the operation of narration itself.

In the more fully realized novels of the institution, the recursive, formalized, and atemporal processes of institutionality determine not only the protagonists' concrete experiences (or lack thereof) in the institution of the boarding school but also the novels' formal/structural components; that is, their narrators' techniques/positions and the "ontologies"/structures of the narrated worlds as such.[21] For the repetition of the protagonists' everyday lives in their respective closed-off and strictly regulated institutions is not counteracted, as is still the case in *Unterm Rad*, by, say, an omniscient narrator's comments or broken up by analepses, prolepses, changes in focalization and tempo, or alternations between temporal compression and overextension. Rather, the narration is often itself redundant, deliberately restricting itself to or progressively increasing somewhat machinelike patterns of recursion. The typically modernist

---

claims that the subject's formation in the bildungsroman has never been autonomous but rather is underpinned by a hidden institutional disciplinary power (the Tower Society) in the Foucauldian sense. Campe concurs yet highlights that in the Institutionenroman proper institutionality is by no means hidden. Rather, it fully determines both form and content of the narrative.

21 In almost all narratological models the *form* of the narrative has to do with the position (inside or outside the narrated world, for instance) inhabited and techniques (analepsis, prolepsis, temporal compression, etc.) used by the narrating entity. The *content*, on the other hand, concerns what happens to whom ("Joe is run over by a car"). In between, however, we find the "structure of the narrated world," its motifs, its schemas, its configuration of semantic oppositions (inside/outside, cause/effect) and topology (transition from unmarked to marked territories). There are narrative worlds, for example, where dying is not possible or where the natural laws of our world do not obtain. Such narrative structures are similar to the abstract functions of folktales identified by Vladimir Propp or the semiotic topographies described by Yuri Lotman. Gérard Genette proffered a somewhat similar triadic model, consisting of *narration* (narrating), *récit* (narrative), and *histoire* (story), with *récit* occupying a threshold or synthesizing position between the narrator's techniques/position and the meaning of the concrete, graspable events that are narrated. See Gérard Genette, *Narrative Discourse: An Essay in Method*, trans. Jane E. Lewin (Ithaca, NY: Cornell University Press, 1983 [1st. ed., 1972], 25–29.

tendency of substituting the paradigmatic for the syntagmatic may thus be said to reach one of its purest forms in the novels of the institution.[22]

Homoeroticism and Homosexuality in *Unterm Rad*

The comparatively mild institutionalization of life and narration in *Unterm Rad* may then be one of the reasons why, here, homoeroticism is by no means linked as strongly to abuse and dangerous seduction as it is in the two other novels. While the kiss shared between Hans and Hermann will, however, strike most present-day readers as innocent and benign, perhaps as Hermann's rather courageous seduction of Hans, the novel's narrator considers it necessary to comment explicitly on this event as if to anticipate prejudiced interpretations:

> Ein Erwachsener, welcher die kleine Szene gesehen hätte, hätte viel-leicht seine stille Freude an ihr gehabt, an der unbeholfen scheuen Zärtlichkeit einer schamhaften Freundschaftserklärung und an den beiden ernsthaften, schmalen Knabengesichtern, welche beide hübsch und verheißungsvoll waren, halb noch der Kindesanmut teil-haftig und halb schon vom scheuen, schönen Trotz der Jünglingszeit überflogen.

> [An adult witnessing this little scene might have derived a quiet joy from it, from the tenderly inept shyness [of their bashful declaration of friendship, N.S.] and the earnestness of these two narrow faces, both of them handsome, promising, boyish yet marked half with childish grace and half with shy yet attractive adolescent defiance.][23]

---

22   I use the Saussurean terms "paradigma" and "syntagma" in the sense of "selection" and "combination" as developed by Roman Jakobson, "Linguistics and Poetics," in *Style and Language*, ed. Thomas A. Sebeok (Cambridge, MA: MIT Press, 1960), 350–77. The Kafka scholar Manfred Engel rightly considers "paradigmatic narration" to be characteristic of modernist prose texts. In this kind of narration, the plot becomes more of a loose frame assembling episodes structurally similar to such a degree that their temporal sequence may at times be upended: "Die Handlung bildet nur einen Rahmen . . . , der mit Episoden ausge-füllt ist, die einander strukturähnlich sind und sich in ihrer Reihenfolge oft vertau-schen ließen. Eine ähnliche 'Paradigmatisierung' des Erzählsyntagmas ergibt sich häufig auch dadurch, dass der Iterativ (also die Schilderung immer wiederkeh-render, gewohnheitsmäßiger Handlungen) über den Singulativ dominiert." Man-fred Engel, "Kafka lesen—Verstehensprobleme und Forschungsparadigmen," in *Kafka Handbuch: Leben, Werk, Wirkung*, ed. Manfred Engel and Bernd Auerochs (Stuttgart: Metzler, 2010), 411–27, here 413.

23   Hesse, *Unterm Rad*, 230; *Beneath the Wheel*, 79. A genitive attribute in the original German is left out in the English translation. I have added my transla-tion of it in square brackets.

For the narrator, these homoerotic elements seem to constitute rather benign expressions of affection as well as attempts to wrestle a sense of meaning and purpose from the evermore formalizing life cycle in the institution. This narratorial evaluation and the apparent need to make it explicit may indicate the stigma placed on homoeroticism, especially since homoerotic acts had been increasingly pathologized since the late nineteenth century, under the name of "homosexuality," as expressions of innate deviance. In that view, Hermann's seducing Hans would appear as abuse and a sign of moral and sexual degeneration.[24]

The question of whether and to what extent the kissing scene and the narrator's comments amounted to a breach of social taboo will yield different answers, however, depending on whether and to which extent one believes that the construction and pathologization of "homosexuality" reconfigured late-nineteenth-century discourses and attitudes on homoeroticism. As mentioned above, according to Butler- or Foucault-inspired approaches, such discursive breaks radically transform the *historical a priori*, including the foundational categories through which one conceives, reasons in, or can speak about the world. Viewed from a dialectical-hermeneutical perspective, to which this paper adheres, the introduction of "homosexuality" certainly reshaped the medicopsychological and juridical discourses significantly and influenced other specialized discourses and the zeitgeist as such. Yet it did not, and, of necessity, could not,[25] completely override or reconfigure rivaling conceptions of sexuality or prevent individuals from taking a reflective stance on them, as is to be shown below.

In the German-language literary scene of the early twentieth century, unmistakably homoerotic writings flourished, published by proponents of philhellenism and pioneering members of the German Youth Movement, such as, perhaps most notoriously, Hans Blüher. Blüher's 1910s and '20s books on the foundational homoeroticism of the *Wandervogelbewegung* (Wandering Bird Movement) and "male society" as such were widely read, among others by Franz Kafka, whose novel *The Castle* (1926), another Institutionenroman brimming with homoeroticism, was strongly influenced by them.[26] Blüher intended to refute the widespread assumption that the institution of marriage between man and woman was necessary to control and channel the otherwise destructive sexual drive. Instead, he

---

24 This connects to our earlier discussion of what was considered acceptable seduction in the German Empire.

25 Since a dialectic approach precludes the assumption of material, social, cultural, or linguistic quasi-determinisms.

26 See Benno Wagner, "Allogenität und Assemblage: Kafkas 'Schloss' mit Blüher und Latour," *Internationales Archiv für Sozialgeschichte der deutschen Literatur* 38, no. 1 (2013): 64–99.

imagined a quasi-metaphysical Eros that both transcended and fused with mere corporeal sexuality:

> Man hat mit der "Sexualität" gerechnet, wie als komme sie beim Menschen in reiner Form—als gleichmäßiger undurchbrochener Trieb—vor, und man hat vergessen, daß in ihr der Eros eingefügt ist, und daß Eros das Gesetz der Besonderung enthält.[27]

> ["Sexuality" has been treated as though it existed in its pure form within the human—as a stable, unbroken drive—and it has been forgotten that the Eros is integrated in sexuality, and that Eros contains the law of particularization.]

Blüher also discussed widespread homoerotic interactions in the military and all kinds of male societies, not to denounce homosexuality but to buttress his claims of its civilizing effects and superiority to male-female relations.[28]

The fact that Blüher was not criminally charged for spreading such ideas in his widely read writings (which were not indexed, either) testifies to a double standard in Wilhelminian society: on the one hand, and from a biopolitical perspective, "homosexuality" was understood as a pathological deviation from the norm, endangering the health and vitality of the *Volkskörper* (body of the nation) and its reproduction. Such an assessment was prevalent in much of medicine, biology, psychiatry, and even jurisprudence (despite its determination to preserve the notions of individual free will and responsibility against biopolitical conceptions of crime).[29] On the other hand, it was not at all the case that homoerotic acts were only practiced in the most private of settings. Its widespread occurrence in the military, in youth movements, boarding schools, or in nightclubs was apparent to those not willfully blind.[30] When "homosexuals" were

---

27 Hans Blüher, *Die Rolle der Erotik in der männlichen Gesellschaft*, vol. 2: *Familie und Männerbund* (Jena: Eugen Diederichs, 1920), 7. See also Mosse, *Image of Man*, 144.

28 Cf. Sebastian Zilles, *Die Schulen der Männlichkeit: Männerbünde in Wissenschaft und Literatur um 1900* (Cologne: Böhlau, 2017), 119. Blüher, however, not only endorsed homoerotic acts between adults, which in today's Germany are perfectly legal and for the most part uncontroversial. He also spoke out emphatically for pederasty, citing the cultural accomplishments of the ancient Greeks, whom he admired, as evidence for its benefits. Sexual relationships between adult "scoutmasters" and adolescents, which nowadays constitute statutory rape, were not uncommon within the German youth movement. See Blüher, *Erotik*, 38–39.

29 Cf. Vormbaum, *German Criminal Law*, 122–23.

30 Cf. Stümke, *Homosexuelle in Deutschland*, 29, speaks of no less than forty "speakeasies" for homosexuals in Wilhelminian Berlin alone.

denounced to the authorities, which was rather rare,[31] this did not necessarily happen out of moral or biopolitical concerns or because the concerned parties were discovered in flagrante delicto. Many denouncers had
long been aware and tolerant of the respective person's homosexuality or
had even themselves engaged in homoerotic acts at some point. Thus, the
denunciations were often motivated by personal vendettas or the hope of
gaining political and institutional power through the removal of a rival.
This was exemplified by the high-profile cases of the 1907 Eulenburg
affair involving the kaiser's inner circle and, later, Hitler's 1934 neutral-
ization of Ernst Röhm and the SA elite.[32]

It therefore remains unclear to what degree the narrator's justifica-
tory comments about the kiss shared between the boys struck the contemporaneous readership of *Unterm Rad* as transgressive, offensive, or
even unexpected. In the fictional world of the novel, there are, in any
event, no indications that their erotically and romantically charged relationship is uncommon or in need of being kept secret at all costs. Rather,
given the students' otherwise boring and uneventful days, it is the logic of
the boarding school itself that creates, as its own corrective, the allure of a
Männerbund (men's association). After all, in *Unterm Rad*, feeling, consciously or unconsciously, that one is part of an overarching Männerbund
not only fosters a sense of belonging and mysterious erotic tension, but
also promises access to a deeper meaning that the mechanized boarding-
school routine does not provide or even erodes.

The Appearance of the "Dangerous Woman" Trope

In *Unterm Rad*, improper seduction, lasciviousness, and danger are not
associated with homoeroticism but with the girls Hans meets once he has
left the boarding school. They exude a disquieting air, as illustrated in this
interaction with a girl named Emma:

> Und es schien ihm aus einer großen Nachtferne her zu tönen, als
> das Mädchen ganz leise fragte: "Willst du mir einen Kuß geben?"
> . . . Ein heftiger Schauder lief ihm über den Leib, als er mit scheuen
> Lippen den Mund des Mädchens berührte. Er zitterte augenblick-
> lich wieder zurück, aber sie hatte seinen Kopf mit den Händen
> umfaßt, drückte ihr Gesicht in seines und ließ seine Lippen nicht

---

31   Oftentimes, witnesses of respected citizens' homoerotic interactions preferred blackmailing them, even baiting them into having sex for that purpose. See
Stümke, *Homosexuelle in Deutschland*, 25–27.

32   Cf. Stümke, *Homosexuelle in Deutschland*, 42–44 and 100–106.

los. Er fühlte ihren Mund brennen, er fühlte ihn sich anpressen und gierig festsaugen, als wolle er ihm das Leben austrinken.

[Her voice seemed to reach him from far-off in the night when she said very softly: "Do you want to kiss me?" . . . A strong shudder ran through his body as he shyly placed his lips on the girl's mouth. He shied back trembling at once but the girl had seized his head, pressed her face to[33] his and would not let go of his lips. He felt her mouth burn, he felt it press against his and cling to him as if she wanted to drain[34] all life from him.][35]

Even contemporary readers will likely perceive Emma's behavior as overly aggressive, and Hesse clearly relies on the trope of the succubus to characterize it. Structurally, however, Hans's interaction with Emma does not appear strongly motivated by prior or subsequent plot developments—rather, it draws attention away from the male-male romance. For when Hans encounters her, he is already depressed and almost suicidal. Earlier, his world fell apart when Herrmann, an artistically inclined Schöngeist and general rebel-without-a-cause, was expelled from the school. Hermann was tracked down in a neighboring village days after leaving the institutional premises without permission and was made to leave the school as a consequence. In other words, the expulsion had nothing to do with any suspicion of homosexuality. Sometime later, Hans, now failing exam after exam, was expelled as well, on account of insufficient grades. He turned into a nihilist after losing his friend and undergoing the boarding school's sense-draining formalization and mechanization of life for too long. Stranded back home, he plans to commit suicide.

This resolution is stalled temporarily when he becomes a locksmith apprentice, which reestablishes within him a certain sense of purpose and connection with the world. After a night of binge drinking with his coworkers, however, he is found dead in a river. The text leaves open whether his death was an accident or suicide. He encounters Emma sometime between his expulsion from the school and his death. The interaction with her presents as a "moment of delayed suspense" (*retardierendes Moment*) that potentially slows (or accelerates) Hans's downward spiral, but the text does not offer support for either conclusion. One might surmise that, for Hans, everything would have changed for the better had Emma been depicted as deeply caring and imbued with a chaste eroticism, which would have made her a viable replacement for Hermann. Yet Emma appears as if out of thin air, not having played any

33 Or "into," N.S.
34 Or "drink," N.S.
35 Hesse, *Unterm Rad*, 300–301; *Beneath the Wheel*, 156.

role in the narrative before; consequently, she is a rather poorly conceived deus ex machina.

Since the narrative logic of Emma's occurrence and the evocation of
the succubus trope are somewhat gratuitous, it makes sense to consider
them manifestations, within the literary text, of a broader cultural sub-
strate. The use of such tropes was widespread in early-twentieth-century
German-language novels, as elaborated by Klaus Theweleit in his highly
influential *Männerphantasien* (1977–78; *Male Phantasies*, 1987–89).
Theweleit argued that narratives featuring closed-off, potentially militaristic *male societies* of any kind tend to present women not as weak or
irrelevant objects of patriarchal domination but rather as dangerous, voracious, infectious, salacious floods and masses that threaten to contaminate
the imagined purity and nobility of male organizations. Indeed, *all* the
novels discussed here exhibit these tropes to a certain degree.[36]

This type of male fear of women, however, is different from the male
fear of being humiliated by or in the eyes of women that Michael Kimmel
has identified as crucially undergirding American "hegemonic masculinity"—and, one may extrapolate, Western masculinity as such—since the
nineteenth century. Kimmel argues that this fear reveals itself, if analyzed
more closely, as more of a surface effect of the deeper-lying male fear of
other *men*, even calling this "the great secret of American manhood."[37]
According to such a triangle of desire,[38] the fear of becoming the object
of women's negative judgments and evaluations, which appear to determine male self-worth, has in fact always been the fear of being looked
down upon and considered impotent by other men, thereby lowering
one's position within intramale hierarchies. In this view, men are cease-
lessly and exclusively engaged in a game of comparison with each other,

---

36 See especially the entire chapter 2 of the first volume, which is fittingly
entitled "Floods, Bodies, History."

37 Kimmel characterizes this fear as follows: "That nightmare from which we
never seem to awaken is that those other men will see that sense of inadequacy;
they will see that in our own eyes we are not who we are pretending to be. What
we call masculinity is often a hedge against being revealed as a fraud, an exaggerated set of activities that keep others from seeing through us, and a frenzied effort
to keep at bay those fears within ourselves." Michael S. Kimmel, *The Gender of
Desire: Essays on Male Sexuality* (Albany: SUNY Press, 2005), 35.

38 Interestingly, Kimmel neither mentions nor references René Girard's influential concept of *mimetic desire* when stating that men in fact desire and fear to
be evaluated by other men, and only seemingly by women. This is unfortunate,
considering how well-thought-out Girard's analyses of unconscious triangles of
desire and their relation to the latent threat of violence are. See, for instance, René
Girard, *Violence and the Sacred*, trans. Patrick Gregory (Baltimore: Johns Hopkins
University Press: 1979 [1st ed., 1972]), 143–68.

234 • Niklas Straetker

meaning that "women themselves often serve as a kind of currency that men use to improve their ranking with other men."[39]

Conversely, the male fear of women that characterizes male societies in the early twentieth century does not even pretend to be linked to women's judgments. If anything, the fear of swamplike women can be likened to the fear of dark, overwhelming forces—"savage" peoples, wild animals, bacterial diseases, the dirty proletariat, or uncontrollable natural disasters—that so-called civilized societies saw themselves threatened by and defined themselves against around 1900.[40] Fearing swamp-women's judgments regarding male status would then be as nonsensical as fearing those made by tigers, wolves, or crocodiles. There is fear, but it is the fear of the dangerous power that is the other.

Törleß—Torture as the Recuperation of Meaning

Robert Musil's *Törleß*, which is set in a military-style academy for teenage boys, relies on the trope of the dangerous female too. When the students steal away to a little village close to their isolated boarding school, young Törleß visits the prostitute Božena (as had many of his fellow students before him). Depicted as coarse and dirty, Božena figures as the beast to the (imagined) beauty and nobility of the teenage cadets.[41] In Božena's world, the teenagers seem like naive little boys. Once they are among themselves within the confines of their boarding school, however, they constitute a rigid, hierarchically structured male society that is much more threatening than the one we encounter in *Unterm Rad*.

In both content and form, *Törleß* is significantly more complex than *Unterm Rad*. Musil evokes the bildungsroman, but it is no longer, as it

---

39 See Michael S. Kimmel, *Manhood in America: A Cultural History* (New York: Oxford University Press, 2006 [1st ed., 1996]), 4.

40 This is one of the main claims in Mosse, *Image of Man*, especially 56–76, where he presents the many "countertypes" Western men and societies defined themselves against. As already mentioned, however, Mosse fails to address the trope of "woman as overwhelming flood."

41 Whenever Törleß is in the presence of or (involuntarily) remembers Božena, he is both repulsed and drawn in by her "ätzenden Hässlichkeit" ("corrosive ugliness") and "fauler, süßer Geruch" ("rotten, sweet smell"); his interactions with her are characterized as a "grausamer Kultus der Selbstaufopferung" ("a cruel cult of self-sacrifice"). Musil, *Verwirrungen*, 156, 64, 41; *Confusions*, 124, 49, 31. That he feels overwhelmed by her is very apparent: "Er starrte mit einem versteinerten Lächeln in das wüste Gesicht über dem seinen, in diese unbestimmten Augen, dann begann die Außenwelt klein zu werden" (49; "With a petrified smile he stared into the ravaged face above his own, into those vacant eyes, then the outside world began to grow smaller," 38).

still was in Hesse's novel, nostalgically affirmed as the preferable alternative to the Institutionenroman, which is more suitable for representing modern institutionalized life. *Törleß* still evokes classic bildungsroman scenarios on its very first and very last pages: the protagonist takes leave of his family, embarks on his journey, and, at the end, returns home. Törleß's experiences at the institution, however, do not complement and are not integrated into his former life but rather break with it radically. This break is not set up as a contrast of the supposed warmth of the family, as an object of longing, with the coldness of the institution. Rather, once he finds himself in his institutional environment, it is as though his family and his private biography did not exist anymore or, in fact, never existed in the first place. This is most clearly shown when Törleß, shortly after arriving at the institution, suffers from "fürchterlichem, leidenschaftlichem Heimweh" ("terrible, passionate homesickness")[42] but soon thereafter becomes incapable of evoking the image of his mother. According to Campe, this scene captures "die Leere eines Platzes, an dem kein Bild ist, aber sein Fehlen—sein Fehlen, das die Kraft, von der man im Nachhinein meint, sie habe das Bild hervorgebracht, an seinem leeren Platz zurückgelassen hat" (the emptiness of a location where there is no image but its absence—its absence left at its empty location by the force that in hindsight one believes to have generated the image).[43]

As this episode shows, whereas *Unterm Rad* largely employs a conventionally realistic narrative, *Törleß* only appears to do so. *Törleß* does not contain the grotesque, exceedingly improbable elements we find in Kafka's or Walser's texts; rather, it relies on a hyperrealistic narration that compresses, increases, distills, and exacerbates common psychological reactions. The lack of *Anschaulichkeit* (clarity) of images, of meaning and representation (which anyone who has encountered institutional mechanisms might have felt at some point) is pushed to the brink of a general bleak *Bildlosigkeit* (absence of images), further underlined by Törleß's obsession with the referentiality of imaginary numbers (expressed in aesthetic terms as the problem of the sublime).

Whereas *Unterm Rad* operates against the backdrop of the protagonist's family and former life, which he remembers and which serve as a corrective, *Törleß* cuts off the past. And yet, while the protagonist is cut off from his previous life, he does not lose his desire, conscious or not, for presence and meaning. In *Unterm Rad*, these claims are actualized and channeled into the homoerotic romance between Hans and Herrmann. In *Törleß*, no romance fulfills the protagonist's longing. The students' lives are made to fit the institution, as they are increasingly formalized and deprived of meaning. In this context, only a violent antidote proves

---

42 Musil, *Verwirrungen*, 9; *Confusions*, 4.
43 Campe, "Das Bild und die Folter," 127.

236 ♦ Niklas Straetker

capable of counteracting and, at the same time, confirming the process of
self-emptying. In Hesse's novel, Hans and Hermann's romance helps them
to find meaning and affection from within an institution in which meaning dwindles away. In *Törleß*, where romantic experiences persist only as
empty dispositions, only the violence of sexual torture, which Törleß and
two fellow students begin to inflict on a student named Basini, appears to
offer access to meaning:

> Da war nun etwas zum ersten Male wie ein Stein in die unbestimmte
> Einsamkeit seiner Träumereien gefallen; es war da; da ließ sich nichts
> machen; es war Wirklichkeit. Gestern war Basini noch genau so
> wie er selbst gewesen; eine Falltüre hatte sich geöffnet, und Basini
> war gestürzt. Genau so, wie es Reiting schilderte: eine plötzliche
> Veränderung, und der Mensch hat gewechselt.

> [Something had dropped for the first time like a stone into the vague
> loneliness of his daydreams; it was there; there was nothing to be
> done about it; it was reality. Yesterday Basini had been exactly as he
> was; a trapdoor had opened, and Basini had fallen. Exactly as Reiting
> described: a sudden alteration, and the person was someone else.][44]

Although such a new "reality" of torture seems eruptively to awaken and
actualize Törleß's longing for meaning, purpose, and affection, its anar-
chic potential has always already been absorbed by institutionality. For
one thing, the torture only begins after Basini is found to have stolen
from other students, a rule violation that his future tormentors believe
legitimizes or even demands punishment. This punishment then is institutionalized; that is, it becomes a ritual of paralegal torture and sexual
degradation, held in a hidden chamber of the boarding school. In other
words, torture itself functions as an institution within the institution, and
its regulated process mirrors and repeats, in a manner evocative of de
Sade, the cadets' formalized and rule-based everyday life at the boarding school. Rather than being subverted, institutionality has absorbed the
presence of meaning and corporeality even more exhaustively.

   This peculiar double bind of rebellion and co-optation guarantees
institutionality in the first place insofar as attempts to undermine the
institution ultimately serve to perpetuate and legitimize it. Here, as one
starts to probe more deeply, the origin of institutionality and the authority it creates become, as JacquesDerrida or Walter Benjamin would put
it, elusive and mystical.[45] Musil's epigraph, the famous quotation from

---

44   Musil, *Verwirrungen*, 64; *Confusions*, 49.
45   Cf. Jacques Derrida, "Force of Law: The Mystical Foundation of Authority," trans. Mary Quaintance, *Cardozo Law Review* 11 (1989–90): 920–1045;
Walter Benjamin, "Zur Kritik der Gewalt [1920/21]," in *Gesammelte Schriften*,

Maurice Maeterlinck, anticipates the mysticism behind the structured clarity of cruelty in Törleß:

> Sobald wir etwas aussprechen, entwerten wir es seltsam. Wir glauben in die Tiefe der Abgründe hinabgetaucht zu sein, und wenn wir wieder an die Oberfläche kommen, gleicht der Wassertropfen an unseren bleichen Fingerspitzen nicht mehr dem Meere, dem er entstammt. Wir wähnen eine Schatzgrube wunderbarer Schätze entdeckt zu haben, und wenn wir wieder ans Tageslicht kommen, haben wir nur falsche Steine und Glasscherben mitgebracht; und trotzdem schimmert der Schatz im Finstern unverändert.

> [As soon as we put something into words, we devalue it in a strange way. We think we have plunged into the depths of the abyss, and when we return to the surface the drop of water on our pale fingertips no longer resembles the sea from which it comes. We delude ourselves that we have discovered a wonderful treasure trove, and when we return to the light of day we find that we have brought back only false stones and shards of glass; and yet the treasure goes on glimmering in the dark, unaltered.][46]

If it is true that the origin of authority and institutional order must remain mystical, then its complex formalizations and regulations lack actual necessity or ultimate justifiability and thus appear to be driven by a pure aestheticism that re-creates formalized orders for the sake of mere self-continuation. The hierarchical Männerbund, though incapable of signifying anything outside of itself, becomes its own purpose:[47] its raison d'être consists in lending a Schillerian *Anmut und Würde* (grace and dignity), if only in a formal sense, to its members, who will do anything to

---

vol. 2, pt. 1, ed. Rolf Tiedemann and Hermann Schweppenhäuser (Frankfurt am Main: Suhrkamp 1977), 179–203.

46 Musil, *Verwirrungen*, 8; *Confusions*, 1.

47 Before turning to Walser's *Jakob von Gunten*, it seems worth mentioning that formalized rituals of torture also figure prominently in Ernst von Salomon's autobiographically inspired novel *Die Kadetten* from 1933, which is based on his time at a Prussian military academy in the 1910s. See Ernst von Salomon, *Die Kadetten* (Hamburg: Rowohlt, 1957 [1933]). Von Salomon's novel lacks the psychological complexity and aesthetic intensity of Musil's hyperrealism, but it too represents, almost in the documentary manner of historical positivism, the practices and mechanisms of institutionality as well as the gender tropes we encounter in *Törleß* and *Unterm Rad*. After his time in the cadet academy, von Salomon, to whom Theweleit devotes much attention in *Männerphantasien*, unsurprisingly became ultraconservative and joined a Freikorps. His relationship with the Nazis was fraught with ambivalence, though.

prevent its undoing by the then-contemporary tropes of chaotic flood, wet mud, swamp, or the bottomless sea that, to them, is womanhood.[48]

Jakob von Gunten—Teacher-Student Relationships between Seduction and Abuse

In Robert Walser's *Jakob von Gunten*, mysticism and aestheticism also figure prominently. Indeed, while they operate respectively as the latent base and superstructure of the narrated world in *Törleß*, they are woven directly into the diegesis of Walser's novel, thus openly blurring the distinction between conventionally realistic storytelling and avant-garde fantasy. *Jakob von Gunten* sheds any pretense of conventional realism when it is revealed that the entire curriculum taught at the Benjamenta servant school, the boarding school where Jakob is enrolled, consists of one single, infinitely repeated lesson entitled "Wie hat sich der Knabe zu benehmen?" (How is the boy supposed to behave?). This lesson is based on a single textbook with the fitting title "Was bezweckt Benjamenta's Knabenschule?" (What does the Institute Benjamenta aim at?).[49] In other words, the only purpose of this school is to teach its own purpose and thus its own deprivation of meaning.

Although this and other grotesque elements illustrate the absurdity of institutionality for institutionality's sake in its purest form, the erosion of sense and meaning in *Jakob von Gunten* does not generate the same kind of oppressive inexorability and then compensatory operations that we see in *Törleß* or *Unterm Rad*. This may be in part because the Institute Benjamenta, unlike the other two boarding schools, is located in the heart of a metropolis; the students are free to frequent its attractions at will. By virtue of this open structure, the grotesque monotony of the lessons at Benjamenta is counteracted by the "wild anmutenden Märchen" (wild-seeming fairy tale), the "Geschiebe und Gedränge" (shoving and squeezing), "Rasseln und Prasseln" (rattling and pattering), "Geschrei, Gestampf, Gesurr und Gesumme" (screaming, stomping, whirring, and humming) of the metropolis.[50] As the alliterations, onomatopoeia, and rhymes in the syntagmas just quoted indicate, however, city life may provide a welcome diversion from the institute's monotony,

---

48 Cf. Theweleit, *Männerphantasien*, 1:456; *Male Fantasies*, 1:359.

49 Walser, *Jakob* (German ed.), 8–9.

50 Walser, *Jakob* (German ed.), 37. I added my own translations in parentheses to capture the original German more literally. Middleton translates the sentences containing the expressions in question as follows: "Often I go out onto the street, and there I seem to be living in an altogether wild fairy tale. What a crush and a crowd, what rattlings and patterings! What shoutings, whizzings, and hummings!" (36).

but it does not rise beyond eclectic and impressionistic aestheticism. The institute effects deprivation of meaning via recursive monotony, the city by means of eclectic diversity.

Unsurprisingly, then, city life does not satisfy Jakob, and mystification serves to counteract the arbitrariness and senselessness of both the boarding school and urbanity. Unlike *Törleß*, however, Walser's novel does not rely on formalized rituals of torture, since the senselessness it depicts does not manifest as an oppressive, all-pervasive formalization of every individual action but rather as the complete interchangeability of any purpose. Jakob only gains a sense of the latter *ex negativo* when he becomes aware of the secret chambers in the institute, where he expects to find a grounding reason for the arbitrariness of institutional life. These secret halls, institutions within the institution, are the private chambers of Mr. and Mrs. Benjamenta. The latter, herself a teacher, is, however, not the wife but the sister of the institute's principal. Through this couple, Walser establishes a half-oedipal, half-incestuous *Familienroman* (family saga) setting, in which the educators figure as stand-ins for the biological family (much like the ducal boarding school Friedrich Schiller attended and re-created in his play *Don Carlos* [1787]).[51]

This peculiar oedipal configuration all but guarantees strong libidinal investment on the part of Jakob: it leaves one parental slot empty while at the same time installing a sibling as both an ersatz parent and romantic rival for parental affection. Unsurprisingly, then, Jakob cathects both Benjamentas in the course of the novel. Walser, unlike Hesse and Musil, does not employ the trope of women as dangerous floods of salaciousness. Instead, he depicts the *Fräulein* as an angelic, ethereal being, yet also one who actively seduces her students and seems capable of ruining them if crossed, which imbues her with a siren-like quality.

The principal prevails in the end, however, likely because of his position as secretive, ultimate authority that mainly operates, *schaltet und waltet* (reigns and rules), from within the closed-off chambers of the institute and thus provides ample space for projection. In their private conversations, the principal displays his absolute power over Jakob and all students by repeatedly emphasizing that he could, should, and would like to "durchprügeln" (whack) Jakob. But this threat of physical violence remains just that, a mere threat, another aestheticism, a shrewd citation of the allure of sadomasochism rather than its actual implementation. Moreover, the principal's behavior turns out to have been part of a deliberate strategy of seduction all along, motivated by his love and desire for

---

51 See Friedrich Kittler, "Carlos als Carlsschüler: Ein Familiengemälde in einem fürstlichen Hause," in *Unser Commercium: Goethes und Schillers Literaturpolitik*, ed. Wilfried Barner, Eberhard Lämmert, and Norbert Oellers (Stuttgart: Cotta, 1984), 241–73.

Jakob, though it is not quite clear whether as a son, a friend, or a lover. At the end of the novel, Jakob dreams that he and the principal are traveling on camels through an Orientalist setting of Arabian deserts, smells, sounds, and licentiousness. When Jakob wakes up, he and the principal really leave the institute and travel to the Orient, whereby the principal's game of seduction has finally become Quixotic reality.

The sexual abuse of power presented in *Jakob von Gunten* is different from that depicted in Musil or von Salomon. In all cases, the abuse is conditioned on the deprivation of meaning and recursion of extreme forms of institutionality. But the scenarios of physical humiliation and torture that define *Törleß* and autobiographical novels like *Die Kadetten* derive from an emphasis on brutality, drill, and hierarchy that is significantly reduced in most, if not all, military and paramilitary institutions in the German-speaking world of today. In addition, realistic scenes of sexual abuse involving extreme physical humiliation and torture also occur in contemporary boarding-school novels, such as Norbert Gstrein's *Einer* from 1988 or Michel Houellebecq's *Elementary Particles* from 1998, and neither features any military setting. It would appear that the ideal hotbed for such scenarios is constituted by the closed-system, pressure-cooker dynamic that arises if an institution does not provide any outside lines of flight.

Conclusion

Although Ms. Benjamenta, the female character in *Jakob von Gunten*, does not actualize the trope of the swampy, voracious, and overpowering woman who induces a certain disgust in the refined male adolescents, her more ethereal qualities do not prevent her from being perceived as equally dangerous and powerful by Jakob. Angelic though she may be, her power over Jakob does not arise from any kind of "exquisite fragility" that is worthy of protection and casts its spell over the male gazer. Rather, she is a very concrete authority figure owing to both her official position in the institution and her gracious yet resolute behavior. In other words, just as the female characters in *Unterm Rad* and *Törless*, she does not show any signs of brittleness or fear of men. On the contrary, in all three novels it is the male characters who are in one way or another scared of women.

Clearly, an attempt to draw parallels between tropes of dangerous women and male fear in fictional texts from a hundred years ago, on the one hand, and current social realities, on the other, only goes so far. At the same time, the tropes discussed above not only populate diaries, letters, and autobiographical writings from the early twentieth century but are also widespread among men and boys today. In particular, the age-old but nowadays almost grotesquely ubiquitous male sexual paranoia of not being well-endowed enough[52] or performing inadequately is omnipresent in contemporary culture. Similarly, and more closely corresponding to the "overpowering woman" trope, the recent publicizing of men's fear of having their members broken and squashed while at the mercy of the woman's pace in certain positions during sexual intercourse has inverted even the oldest of masculine gender tropes: the penetrating, active, possibly violent male versus the receiving, passive, suffering female.[53]

The penis-breaking woman's actions of squashing, smashing, or breaking abound with masculinist connotations. Such conceptual travel also illustrates that even the two leading categories of aesthetic discourse since Edmund Burke and Immanuel Kant's conceptions in the eighteenth century[54]—namely, the beautiful and the sublime—are subject to those oscillations: it is not at all clear that the "beautiful" connotes femininity and the "sublime" masculinity. The organic formality of male societies, for example, is much closer to Kant's conception of the beautiful and its "pure formal purposiveness,"[55] whereas imagining women as devouring oceans or penis-breaking agents exemplifies the overwhelming, fear-inducing power normally associated with the sublime. In any event, the social roles seem, in this view, far from deep-structurally enshrined, both today and around 1900.

While the "overwhelming swamp-woman" trope serves as the foil against which the male psyche constitutes itself in boarding-school novels, its present pervasiveness among men can no longer be explained in reference to closed-off male societies. They have become largely anachronistic, after all. Notwithstanding, today's male fear of women still is predicated

---

52 Cf. Susan Bordo, "Does Size Matter?" in *Revealing Male Bodies*, ed. Nancy Tuana, William Cowling, Maurice Hamington, Greg Johnson, and Terrance Mac-Mullan (Bloomington: Indiana University Press 2002), 19–37. The intensity of that paranoia has increased significantly since porn tubes entered the scene in 2006. The recent Twitter-spawned concept of "big-dick energy" seems to want to deconstruct the obsession by implying that it is not a man's physique but his character that determines penis energy. It is not clear if this ubiquitous meme will subvert or reinforce this paranoia.

53 A simple Google search reveals an uncanny number of recent magazine articles in *Vice, Cosmopolitan, Ladbible*, etc. that deal with this phenomenon. They are authored by men and women alike.

54 See Immanuel Kant, *Kritik der Urteilskraft* [1790], ed. Heiner F. Klemme (Hamburg: Meiner, 2009), §23, pp. 206–209.

55 It is tempting to describe the systemic recursivity of institutions and the hierarchical composition of male societies as "mechanistic." This, however, misses the point that their individual parts do not stand in a purely linearly causal relation to another but, rather, are holistically interdependent and serve a common purpose. They function similarly to what Émile Durkheim called the "organic division of labor" in modern societies.

on *institutionality*. For the recursive formalization of life and meaning has increasingly left the confines of concrete institutions and "colonized" today's lifeworld as such, the algorithmization of tastes and interests since the onset of the Web 2.0 being only the latest piece of evidence for this.[56] Nowadays, Hollywood and academia, among others, can be considered examples of closed-off institutions characterized by an interdependence of recursively formalized life, humiliation, and sexual abuse. There, the abuse is predominantly inflicted on women, its widespread occurrence having become strikingly clear in the course of #MeToo. Given not only the sheer number of incidents of men's predatory behavior reported in recent years but also the virtual, conjured-up nature of the male fear of "overwhelming swamp-women," it is very understandable that the trope of the "scared man" has been somewhat neglected within the #MeToo movement. This emphasis, however, has the unintended consequence of reifying and perpetuating the trope of the "scared woman"; thus, it may be helpful to think of these tropes as a complementary unit.

To be sure, highlighting male fear can serve to trivialize and cancel out female fear and dismiss a woman's lived experience, thereby reproducing the societal status quo. It can, however, also be harnessed for change insofar as it asks us to analyze how, in everyday interactions at the workplace and at social gatherings of any kind, *women* are feared even (or precisely) by those men who attempt to assume an air of machismo. Being aware of male fear shows that women are not perceived as helpless prey but rather as powerful agents. To be very clear, attesting the existence of such male fear of women (and their judgments) must not translate into a plea for sympathy with men who act on it. Indeed, it is precisely the attribution of agency to women that often motivates a violent response designed to purge the male body of its fear.[57] Yet inquiring—as a family member, friend, therapist, scholar, or participant in public discourse—into whether that fear plays a role in the development of society's or specific men's misogynistic attitudes can be useful when seeking to nip them in the bud or transform them.

Though the trope of the "overpowering woman" is itself often a misogynistic one, its tenacity could perhaps be harnessed to help explode or transform the trope of women as overwhelmed and scared victims. In the German #MeToo discourse, influential *Spiegel* columnist Margarete

---

56 Cf. Jürgen Habermas, *The Theory of Communicative Action*, vol. 2: *Life-world and System: A Critique of Functionalist Reason*, trans. Thomas McCarthy (Boston: Beacon Press, 1987 [1st ed., 1981]), 356.

57 It is well known, for instance, that some notorious serial or mass murderers targeting women were beset by a thoroughly paranoid fear of everything female. Prominent examples include Edmund Kemper and Elliot Rodger, the perpetrator of the 2014 Isla Vista killings, whom some media labeled "The Virgin Killer."

Stokowski and philosopher Svenja Faßpöhler engaged in a high-profile discussion of the concept of "victimhood."[58] Faßpöhler does not deny the existence of sexual harassment and degradation of women in many social settings but warns against leveling distinctions between disrespectful and machoistic male transgressions, such as sexist comments and touching women's hair or shoulders, on the one hand, and clear acts of assault, violence, and rape, on the other. Concurring with Faßpöhler, I argue that, in referencing pervasive social structures that cannot but infest gender performance and experience, certain #MeToo discourses run the risk of chipping away at women's (and, for that matter, men's) ability to discern, on a case-by-case basis and with the help of a hermeneutic reasoning, violent sociopaths from those men who degrade and belittle women while barely disguising how scared they are of sex, women, and modern life as such. Men need to take responsibility and evolve, but some may not be able to do so on their own, even if it is their duty. Women do not have the moral duty to pull men out of holes that the latter have dug for themselves and from where misogyny is being spewed; not at all. Still, recognizing and reflecting on the dialectic of male fear of women and men's aggressive and sexist behavior may help us reduce and remedy gender trouble in our personal lives, society, and the media.

---

58   As part of the Ullstein *resonanzraum* lectures in May 2018: https://www. youtube.com/watch?v=CgFGTXKRuhQ.

10: Breaking the Silence about Sexualized Violence in Lilly Axtser's and Beate Teresa Hanika's Young Adult Fiction (YAF)

Anna Sator

Adolescence is generally regarded as a developmental phase in which most young adults begin to explore their sexuality. One might argue that Western culture is marked by pervasive sexualization—especially in popular culture—and that this heightened awareness of sexuality also plays an increasingly explicit role in Young Adult Fiction (YAF), although there are successful examples of YAF, such as the Harry Potter series (1997–2007) or Cornelia Funke's *Tintenherz* (2003; *Inkheart*, 2005), that mostly eschew explicit mentions of adolescent sexuality. YAF often depicts adolescent sexuality as uncontrollable, awkward, and sometimes dangerous. Abuse of power and sexual assaults are often not labeled as such, nor are they problematized within the narrative. Many story lines draw on old myths of the complicity of victims; or they portray sexualized violence as a "natural" form of interaction between the sexes.

Feminist research uses the term "sexualized violence" to refer to all forms of violence that weaponize sex and sexuality in order to exert power. Mithu Sanyal, for example, offers a powerful definition of rape: "Das ist der Grund warum Feministinnen heute von sexualisierter Gewalt—und nicht von sexueller—Gewalt sprechen, um deutlich zu machen, dass Sex zwar die Waffe, nicht aber die Motivation einer Vergewaltigung ist" (That is why feminists today speak of sexualized violence—and not sexual violence—to make it clear that sex is the weapon but not the motivation for rape.)[1]

This chapter aims to illustrate how key moments connected to the #MeToo movement, including introducing the topic of sexualized violence into public discourse and labeling it as such, also had an impact on YAF. Indeed, YAF can empower young adults to explore sexual desires

---

1   Mithu M. Sanyal, *Vergewaltigung: Aspekte eines Verbrechens*, Nautilus Flugschrift (Hamburg: Edition Nautilus, 2016), 41.

while setting limits, and it can provide guidance to those affected by sexualized violence. In the following, I analyze two novels that offer unique takes on the topic: Beate Teresa Hanika's *Rotkäppchen muss weinen* (Little Red Riding Hood Has to Cry)[2] and Lilly Axster's *Die Stadt war nie wach* (The City Was Never Awake).[3] Both prizewinning novels portray the psychological and social effects of abuse on adolescents. In the end, the characters manage to break free of the taboo surrounding sexualized violence; they speak out, advocate for one another, and thus regain their agency. Because both texts contextualize sexual abuse, it does not dominate the narrative: Hanika's novel contrasts abuse with friendship and a first crush, while Axster's story depicts not only abuse but also self-determined forms of consensual sexuality between young adults.

Adolescence and Sexuality

The representation of young adults in fiction changes along with changing sociocultural images of adolescence. Since the mid-twentieth century, the lines between adolescence and adulthood have become increasingly blurry, especially since the end of adolescence is no longer clearly marked by easily identifiable life events, such as moving out of the parental home or getting a job. In general, as Vera King and Susanne Benzel point out, adolescence is defined as the stage between childhood and adulthood and is closely connected to the development of psychological, cognitive, and social skills; it is associated with puberty and thus with sexual maturation.[4] King and Benzel explain that, more often than not, adolescence is perceived as a time of crisis and conflict,[5] particularly with respect to gender and sexuality:

> In der Phase der Adoleszenz werden Geschlechterentwürfe und -unterscheidungen sowohl hervorgebracht als auch reproduziert, insofern in dieser Lebensphase eine Vergeschlechtlichung der sozialen Rollen stattfindet und Heranwachsende in die unterschiedlichen Praxen der Geschlechterordnung einsozialisiert werden. Jugendliche sind in verstärktem Maße konfrontiert mit den Veränderungen des

---

2   Beate Teresa Hanika, *Rotkäppchen muss weinen: Roman* (Frankfurt am Main: Fischer, 2009).

3   Lilly Axster, *Die Stadt war nie wach: Roman* (Vienna: Zaglossus, 2017).

4   Vera King and Susanne Benzel, "Adoleszenz: Lebensphase zwischen Kindheit und Erwachsensein," in *Handbuch Interdisziplinäre Geschlechterforschung*, ed. Beate Kortendiek, Birgit Riegraf, and Katja Sabisch, Geschlecht und Gesellschaft (Wiesbaden: Springer Fachmedien Wiesbaden, 2019), 1075–82, here 1076.

5   Vito Paoletić, "Der Adoleszenzroman Heute: Eine Herausforderung für Jung und Alt," *Libri et Liberi* 7, no. 1 (2018): 93–108, here 95

Körpers und den damit verbundenen biographischen, familialen und generationalen sowie kulturellen geschlechtstypischen Bedeutungen.

[In the stage of adolescence gender concepts and differences are both produced and reproduced, since during this phase of life the gendering of social roles takes place and young adults are socialized into the different habits in the gender order. To a significant degree, young adults are confronted with their changing bodies and the attendant biographical, familial, and generational as well as cultural gender meanings.][6]

Such moments of crisis may present challenges, but they can also help to redefine gender norms and expectations of what a male or female body should be. At the onset of adolescence, the not-yet-mature young adult must cope with a changing and sexually maturing body. This changing body then has to be reclaimed within the framework of the current gender order.[7]

Marion Rana argues that Young Adult Fiction is closely linked to its cultural and historical context and thus affected by the increasing sexualization of Western society and especially by popular culture. And yet, while we are surrounded by representations of sex in the media, talking about personal sexual relations is still taboo. This bifurcation is also evident in YAF, which often emphasizes the danger inherent in sexual acts and promotes a purification of sexuality.[8] (It has been much discussed in relation to Stephenie Meyer's Twilight Saga, for example, where abstinence is constructed as essential for Bella's survival.) The resulting images of adolescent sexuality often convey traditional gender roles and problematic takes on sexualized violence. Conversely, scholars such as Silja Matthiesen have argued that it is not helpful to frame today's adolescents as "Generation Porno." Such a label is apt to stir fears of a supposedly declining sexual morale of adolescents while framing adolescent sexuality as problematic, even though research shows that today's teenagers do not have sex earlier, nor are there more unplanned pregnancies. Some scholars claim that countries with more restrictive attitudes toward teenage sexuality have more problems related to sexual matters.[9] Frequently, the great-

6   King and Benzel, "Adoleszenz," 1077.

7   King and Benzel, "Adoleszenz," 1077–78.

8   Marion Rana, "Sexualität und Macht: Sexuelle Handlungsgewalt in der aktuellen Jugendliteratur," *kids + media*, no. 2 (2013): 44–57, here 44, https://www.kids-media.uzh.ch/dam/jcr:00000000-7c15-f537-0000-00000ea50526/rana.pdf.

9   Silja Matthiesen, Jasmin Mainka, and Ursula Martyniuk, "Beziehungen und Sexualität im Jugendalter," in *Sexuelle Vielfalt und die UnOrdnung der Geschlechter: Beiträge zur Soziologie der Sexualität*, ed. Sven Lewandowski and

est problem in this respect is not saturation in sexual images but a lack of sex education in schools and a taboo regarding sexuality at home.[10] Christina Lötscher argues that the internet and easily accessible porn led to a youth culture in which young adults are constantly comparing themselves to others and are sexualized quite early. In addition, many teenagers struggle with social pressure and a sense that they have to have sexual experiences and that these experiences should include certain practices.

Lötscher sees YAF as a medium capable of conveying reassurance that young people should feel free to find their own sexuality and preferences in their own time and that they should not let themselves be influenced by societal expectations and cultural images.[11] Sexuality and love were a topic of traditional girls' literature until the 1970s—though those novels were typically more concerned with finding a good husband rather than exploring one's sexuality: "[Sexualität] tritt wenn überhaupt nur in Form heftiger Küsse auf und dient natürlich nur der Fortpflanzung" ([Sexuality] occurs, if at all, only in the form of ardent kisses and of course serves only reproductive purposes).[12] Recent German and Scandinavian YAF novels are approaching sexuality with greater openness, exploring how desire and love are connected, or if they have to be connected at all. But most novels still cleave to heteronormative concepts.[13] Coming-of-age stories that are outside this paradigm are mostly problem-oriented. Consequently, there are very few positive models for young adults that explore nonheteronormative constructions of gender and sexuality.[14] "The majority of YAF still reinforces traditional notions of gender and sexuality."[15]

Cornelia Koppetsch, KörperKulturen (Bielefeld: transcript, 2015), 219–48, here 219–20.

10   Journalist Teresa Bücker draws attention to the ambivalent role of the internet: it offers easy access to information, especially for LGBTIQ adolescents, but at the same time these same groups are likely targets of social-media campaigns. Teresa Bücker, "Ist es radikal, Jungen beizubringen, nicht zu vergewaltigen?," *Süddeutsche Zeitung Magazin*, January 29, 2020, https://sz-magazin.sueddeutsche. de/freie-radikale-die-ideenkolumne/vergewaltigung-aufklaerung-jungen-88318.

11   Christine Lötscher, "Wenn Sex nur nicht so furchtbar gefährlich wäre: Sexualität in der aktuellen Jugendliteratur," *Buch & Maus*, no. 1 (2010): 2–4, here 3.

12   Petra Josting, "Verliebte Jungs, verliebte Mädchen: Liebe und Sexualität in aktuellen Texten der Kinder- und Jugendliteratur," in *Sexuelle Vielfalt im Handlungsfeld Schule: Konzepte aus Erziehungswissenschaft und Fachdidaktik*, ed. Sarah Huch and Martin Lücke, Pädagogik (Bielefeld: transcript, 2015), 151–68, here 153.

13   Lötscher, "Wenn Sex nur nicht so furchtbar," 4.

14   Josting, "Verliebte Jungs, verliebte Mädchen," 155.

15   Carrie A. Platt, "Cullen Family Values: Gender and Sexual Politics in the Twilight Series," in *Bitten by Twilight: Youth Culture, Media, and the Vampire Franchise*, ed. Melissa Click, Jennifer Stevens Aubrey, and Elizabeth Behm-Morawitz (New York: Peter Lang, 2010), 71–86, here 75.

It is noticeable that novels like Charlotte Roche's *Feuchtgebiete*[16] (2008; *Wetlands*, 2009) or Jaromir Konecny's *Doktorspiele* (Doctor's Games)[17] are generally denounced in the media for depicting sexuality too explicitly for an audience that is not yet mature enough. This suggests that societal images and ideals of (the imagined absence of) child and teenage sexuality collide with the lived reality of young adults.[18] Not only is adolescent sexuality taboo, but teenagers are denied sexual agency. Sex education and open dialogues as well as appropriate depictions of adolescent sexuality are necessary in order to address and combat sexualized violence. Young adults who are exploring their sexuality need to understand the concept of consent in order to be able to respect their own boundaries and those of the people they interact with.

Sexuality and Violence

Writing about sexualized violence is a sensitive topic, and one's choice of words must be scrupulous. In this chapter I use the German term *Betroffene*, which translates as "individuals affected by sexualized violence." I do this because the most frequently used terms—"victim" and "survivor"—are both burdened with problematic implications that continue to shape public perceptions of sexualized violence: unlike the term "victim," the word *Betroffene* does not connote passivity; and unlike "survivor," it does not conflate the experience of sexualized violence with death.[19]

Sexualized violence is a gendered problem: statistically, most Betroffene are female, and the majority of perpetrators are men: "Es ist auffällig, dass über sexuelle Gewalt häufig nicht als spezifisches Verbrechen gesprochen wird, sondern als eine Art Risiko der *conditio humana*—solange diese Menschen Frauen sind" (It is striking that sexual violence is often not discussed as a specific crime, but as a sort of risk of the human condition—as long as these humans are women).[20] In both cultural and literary narratives as well as in legal procedures, sexualized violence is often represented as "normal" heterosexual foreplay. This portrayal runs

---

16 Charlotte Roche, *Feuchtgebiete: Roman* (Cologne: DuMont, 2012).

17 Jaromir Konecny, *Doktorspiele: Roman* (Stuttgart: dp DIGITAL PUBLISHERS GmbH, 2018).

18 Kristina Lareau, "Nostalgia for a Childhood Without: Implications of the Adult Gaze on Childhood and Young Adult Sexuality," *Libri et Liberi* 1, no. 2 (2012): 235–44, 236, https://doi.org/10.21066/carcl.libri.2012-01(02).0042.

19 This is not meant to belittle the experience of sexualized violence in any way, but to critique public expectations and discourses about Betroffene. Sanyal, *Vergewaltigung*, 93.

20 Sanyal, *Vergewaltigung*, 11.

the risk of making sexualized violence invisible and impedes efforts to promote sexual self-determination. Because of such cultural images, legal procedures, and societal norms, sexualized violence remains a taboo, and rape myths are omnipresent: one such frequently invoked myth casts victims of sexual violence, especially girls and women, as seductive accomplices.[21] Consequently, girls and young women grow up in the belief that they have to be permanently on guard:

> Nach wie vor gehört die Warnung vor Vergewaltigung zu den Initiationen in die Geschlechterverhältnisse. Zuweilen noch vor jeglicher Form sexueller Aufklärung erfahren Mädchen, dass sie aufpassen müssen—in der Regel ohne nähere Informationen, wie sich das gestalten soll.

> [The warning against rape is still one of the initiations into gender relations. Sometimes even before any form of sexual education, girls learn that they have to be careful—usually without further information about how this should be done.][22]

This misconception of sexualized violence suggests that there is some kind of secret code that could protect girls and women from being assaulted—at the same time as it is implied that experiencing sexualized violence is a result of not sticking to this code and therefore one's own fault—which is widely known as victim-blaming. Another rape myth concerns the widespread notion that rapes are committed by unknown assailants even though research shows that most perpetrators are relatives or friends of the Betroffene. Moreover, perpetrators are often pathologized and depicted as inherently evil.[23] This "othering" of offenders is often combined with the assumption that the offender is a single man who is driven to sexual violence because he does not have a wife—an assumption that also points to the heteronormative logic of our cultural thinking about sexualized violence.

It is one of the signal achievements of the women's movements in the 1970s that forms of sexualized violence, such as rape, are now defined as acts of power and violence rather than erotic desire.[24] Unfortunately, however, research on sexualized violence is still marginalized in German criminology, and some recent papers by criminologists still reference rape

---

21   Dirk Bange, "Geschichte der Erforschung von sexualisierter Gewalt im deutschsprachigen Raum unter methodischer Perspektive," in *Forschungsmanual Gewalt*, ed. Cornelia Helfferich, Barbara Kavemann, and Heinz Kindler (Wiesbaden: Springer Fachmedien Wiesbaden, 2016), 33–49, here 33–36.

22   Sanyal, *Vergewaltigung*, 12.

23   Bange, "Geschichte der Erforschung," 38.

24   Bange, "Geschichte der Erforschung," 39.

myths.[25] Such rape myths perpetuate gendered power structures, reinforce heteronormativity, and construct the female body as an object of pleasure and reassurance of male potency.[26] As Karin Theurer emphasizes, all too often sexualized violence is relegated to the private realm and thus rendered invisible. Mithu Sanyal points out that the motif of shame in the context of rape is closely linked to the image of rape as a form of robbery—and to the belief that a woman's value lies in her sexual purity.[27] Research on sexualized violence shows that Betroffene are often unwilling to go to the police because they fear social stigmatization and other forms of intersectional discriminations that might affect their social status.[28] Furthermore, even if Betroffene speak out, they are confronted with rigid expectations regarding the emotional status and behavior of persons who have experienced sexualized violence. For example, an individual's credibility is often tied to whether she is publicly perceived to "suffer enough."[29]

A number of surveys and studies show that experiences of sexualized violence are a daily feature of (especially female) adolescence.[30] Estimates of the number of unreported crimes in 2018 suggest that every seventh to eighth individual in Germany has experienced sexual violence in their childhood and adolescence. Further, it is estimated that at least one or two students in every class are affected by sexual violence.[31] Katrin Bickler states in her 2011 study that over 8 percent of girls and 3 percent of boys are sexually abused before reaching the age of majority.[32] Bickler states further that children in our society often do not learn that sexualized violence exists, nor are they informed that individuals from their social network might abuse them sexually or that they have the right to defend themselves. Consequently, very few girls and boys are able to

---

25 Bange, "Geschichte der Erforschung," 34–36.

26 Karina Theurer, "Recht und Literatur: Narrative der (Un-)Sichtbarmachung sexualisierter Gewalt," *Kritische Justiz* 48, no. 4 (2015): 434–45, here 434–36, https://doi.org/10.5771/0023-4834-2015-4-434.

27 Sanyal, *Vergewaltigung*, 82.

28 Theurer, "Recht und Literatur," 436.

29 For more detail, see Sanyal, *Vergewaltigung*, 76–101.

30 Marion Rana, "Sexualität und Macht," 51; Katrin Bickler, *Sexueller Missbrauch als Thema der neueren Kinder- und Jugendliteratur* (Freiburg im Breisgau: Fillibach, 2011), 7.

31 Unabhängiger Beauftragter für Fragen des sexuellen Kindesmissbrauchs, "Fakten und Zahlen zu sexueller Gewalt an Kindern und Jugendlichen" (June 2019): 1–2, accessed August 23, 2020, https://www.dji.de/fileadmin/user_upload/bibs2019/Zahlen_Fakten_sexuelle%20Gewalt%20an%20Minderj%C3%A4hrigen.pdf.

32 Bickler, *Sexueller Missbrauch*, 11.

stop the abuse.[33] As a result, there is an urgent need for age-appropriate and diverse representations of sexuality and sexualized violence. Such information should be an integral part of school curricula, social discourse, and literature.

In reproducing, recoding, or neutralizing acts of sexualized violence, literary narratives draw on cultural knowledge. Such narratives can preference or omit the perspectives of victims and thus highlight or obscure inherent contradictions. They can even situate acts of sexualized violence in a framework of (unilateral) love that offers only the perpetrator's point of view.[34] Another problematic narrative concerns the representation of sexualized violence as a punishment for women who laid claim to sexual self-determination.[35] Platt argues that even today female sexuality is still portrayed as a "threatening force" in some YAF novels, but such narratives about the need to repress sexual desire or the dire consequences of unwanted pregnancy are now less common.[36] Still, popular narratives such as the Twilight series portray sexuality as a dangerous force and possibly discourage young adults from exploring their sexuality and boundaries. I will elaborate on this issue in the next section.

Since the 1970s, social movements and feminist interventions have challenged rape myths. But even today the experiences collected under the hashtags *MeToo* or *aufschrei*[37] are devalued, ridiculed, or belittled as petty scheming against powerful men, in spite of much research that disproves such claims.[38] This backlash shows how difficult and laborious it is for societies to challenge traditional beliefs about gender, sexuality, and, especially, sexual self-determination. The societal changes that inspired these hashtags show how important it is to share experiences of sexualized violence and to name them as such. It is also crucial to have access to a diversity of narratives. Such multiplicity encourages a variety of socially accepted responses to sexualized violence because it recognizes that healing occurs in different, highly individualized ways. For example, Mithu Sanyal argues that the imperative to break the silence can be

---

33   Bickler, *Sexueller Missbrauch*, 13.

34   Theurer, "Recht und Literatur," 437.

35   Hadassah Stichnothe, *Der Initiationsroman in der deutsch- und eng-lischsprachigen Kinderliteratur* (Heidelberg: Carl-Winter-Universitätsverlag, 2016), 43.

36   Platt, "Cullen Family Values," 75.

37   This hashtag, introduced in 2013, is used in German-speaking countries to share experiences with sexism and sexualized violence.

38   The slogan "Missbrauch mit dem Missbrauch" (abuse with the abuse) was used in the 1990s to critique public discourses on sexualized violence, such as the claim that women exaggerate or lie about being assaulted to get financial or other advantages. Bange, "Geschichte der Erforschung," 40.

counterproductive if it pressures Betroffene into sharing their experience in detail (and in public) without consideration for their need for privacy.[39]

It typically does not take long for societal upheavals and changes to be incorporated into YAF: literary critic Manuela Kalbermatten cites the pussy-hat movement and the MeToo debate, which have been adopted internationally at breathtaking speed in YAF, as the most recent example of this process. While there is a growing number of explicitly feminist and antisexist YAF, there are also many narratives that promote a return to traditional gender roles. Similarly, gender marketing has become common again.[40]

Young Adult Fiction and Sexualized Violence

YAF models how to deal with one's changed body and sexuality, which relationships and lifestyles are desirable, how to deal with difference, and, ultimately, how one can make gender relations work. Thus, YAF can make certain individuals and ways of life invisible: it can reassure or devalue; and it shows who is allowed to speak and to participate.[41] YAF is entertainment, but it is also performative. According to Martina Aigner, YAF can be preventative, sensitizing, and educating. As a coping mechanism, YAF can show options for taking action and breaking taboos; it can also serve as an important tool for prevention work.[42]

YAF focuses on three main topics: love/sexuality, the search for one's identity, and the relationship between parents and young adults. Since the advent of LGBTIQ movements and the discursive changes that followed in their wake, sexuality is discussed more openly and no longer reduced to heterosexual desire. In addition, more novels now address sexual abuse and sexualized violence explicitly.[43] But as Marlene Kruck points out,

---

39 Sanyal analyzes the case of Natascha Kampusch, who was accused of lying in her autobiography because she did not address every detail of her abuse: *Vergewaltigung*, 83–84.

40 Manuela Kalbermatten, "Aufmarsch der Jungfeministinnen: Jugendbücher kritisieren Sexismus," *JuLit/Arbeitskreis für Jugendliteratur*, no. 2 (2019): 19–21, here 20–21.

41 Kalbermatten, "Aufmarsch der Jungfeministinnen," 19–20.

42 Martina Aigner, "Sexualisierte Gewalt in Jugendbüchern: Eine exemplarische Inhaltsanalyse der deutschsprachigen Literatur für 12 bis 16-jährige, erschienen im Zeitraum von 1995 bis 2006" (Diplomarbeit, University of Vienna, 2007), 52.

43 Nadine Bieker, "Weiblichkeitsbilder im aktuellen Adoleszenzroman am Beispiel von Tamara Bachs Roman Marienbilder," in *"Die Zeitalter werden besichtigt": Aktuelle Tendenzen der Kinder- und Jugendliteraturforschung—Festschrift für Otto Brunken*, ed. Gabriele von Glasenapp, Andre Kagelmann, and Felix Giesa (Bern: Peter Lang), 271–291, here 274.

there is still a dearth of novels that offer proper sex education, address corporeality and sexuality, and clearly name areas of danger and transgressions of boundaries.[44]

YAF increasingly functions as a medium of social critique, not only of identification.[45] Nevertheless, such critique is generally funneled through the perspective of an adolescent (predominantly white male) hero who embarks on a "social-sexual" search for identity[46] and whose perceptions are therefore limited. Even so, the focus on the search for identity opens up space to illustrate the impact of sexual violence on Betroffene and to portray coping mechanisms. Concepts of the family are changing as well: the notion of the family as a safe haven is being deconstructed, and the relationship between parents and young adults is often presented as a friendship rather than a power structure, which, in turn, makes it possible to address sexuality and sexualized violence.[47]

The unease surrounding adolescent sexuality is evident not only in the narrative style of a work but also in the types of conflicts that the protagonists deal with. Sexual desire is often depicted as a disruptive, disturbing, and even terrifying force that the teenage protagonists cannot integrate into their identities. This sense of alienation can be traced to the temporal disconnect between the maturation processes of body and psyche. Marion Rana argues that this sense of alienation is one reason why teenage vampire stories are so popular: erotic desire is removed from everyday contexts and transferred to the fantasy realm of vampires, which is unreal and hence less threatening.

Sexualized violence is not a new topic in YAF, although the portrayal and implications have changed fundamentally. The 1930s racist image of the black or Jewish man who chases (German) girls and women lives on in the 1990s fear of an unknown predator who lurks in the dark.[48] Moreover, Bickler argues that novels that depict sexualized violence without discussing sexuality and violence do not alleviate fear but rather fuel it. Although narratives that are told from the perspective of the

---

44 Marlene Kruck, *Das Schweigen durchbrechen*, vol. 1: *Sexueller Missbrauch in der deutschsprachigen Kinder- und Jugendliteratur*, Geschlecht, Gewalt, Gesellschaft 2 (Berlin: Lit-Verlag, 2006), 2–3.

45 Hans-Heino Ewers, ed., *Jugendkultur im Adoleszenzroman: Jugendliteratur der 80er und 90er Jahre zwischen Moderne und Postmoderne*, Jugendliteratur—Theorie und Praxis (Weinheim: Juventa-Verlag, 1997), 7–12, here 7.

46 Paoletić, "Der Adoleszenzroman heute," 97.

47 Jana Baroková, "Ein Thema der problemorientierten Jugendliteratur als Bruch der Tabuzone," *Brünner Hefte zu Deutsch als Fremdsprache* 7, no. 1–2 (2014): 2–25, here 5–6.

48 In the last decade, this imaginative repertoire of potential offenders has included "the Arabic man," owing to a fear of refugees stirred by right-wing populism.

Betroffenen have increased in number since the 2000s, not all of them
are helpful for Betroffene.[49] Marlene Kruck notes that recent YAF publications approach sexualized violence differently. Even so, her thorough
study on sexual abuse in German children's and YA fiction concludes that
most novels that present sexualized violence rely on clichés and are not
very informative.[50]

To provide greater international context, I want to address the depiction of sexuality and sexualized violence in one of the most popular US
imports to Germany, the Twilight series, before I proceed to an analysis of two German novels.[51] Stephenie Meyer's Twilight series has been
discussed controversially not only in public forums but also in academia.
Bella Swan is variously seen as a postfeminist Red Riding Hood[52] or as the
eternal damsel in distress. Thus, Öteyaka and Ayan's article "Postmodern
Red Riding Hood" argues that "sexuality and power relations are the
common grounds of both the fairy tale and the Twilight series."[53]
Lötscher claims that the characters of Bella and Edward are paradigmatic
for the way popular media depict gender roles. She notes further that
Meyer's narrative is informed by an anthropology that relies on biblically
conservative and biologistic thought, even if her narrative style opens up
a fantastic space for adolescent dreams and desires and for the exploration
of adolescent sexuality.[54]

Lötscher's critique focuses on the depiction of Edward as a seductive vampire. She argues that the text presents men as sexually aggressive
by nature and that being intimate with Edward is identified with mortal danger.[55] Platt states more generally that "Meyer likens the desire for
somebody's body to the desire for their death."[56] Even when Edward
and Bella are married, their sexual intercourse is depicted as dangerous and hurtful for Bella who is left with bruises and broken ribs (and

---

49 Bickler, *Sexueller Missbrauch*, 35–36.
50 Kruck, *Das Schweigen durchbrechen*, 6.
51 Renate Reichstein links the popularity of translated bestsellers from the
UK and the US with the fact that novels and film versions are released almost
simultaneously but also with the larger size of the combined book markets in the
UK and US. Renate Reichstein, "Alles Gute kommt von Westen?," *JuLit/Arbeits-
kreis für Jugendliteratur*, no. 1 (2017): 27–31.
52 Işıl Öteyaka and Meryem Ayan, "Postmodern Red Riding: Bella Swan in
the Twilight Series," *Pamukkale University Journal of Social Sciences Institute*, no.
34 (2019): 123–32, https://doi.org/10.30794/pausbed.406632. The authors'
postfeminist argument that Bella (Red Riding Hood) seduces the wolf (Jacob) is
not entirely convincing.
53 Öteyaka and Ayan, "Postmodern Red Riding," 124.
54 Lötscher, "Wenn Sex nur nicht so furchtbar," 2.
55 Lötscher, "Wenn Sex nur nicht so furchtbar," 2.
56 Platt, "Cullen Family Values," 83.

pregnancy, of course). Some critics have compared Bella's comments on the consequences of marital intercourse to those of rape victims who blame themselves for being assaulted.[57] Another point of criticism concerns the idealization of Edwards's overprotectiveness and Bella's corresponding status as damsel in distress. This perpetuates "the idea that young women are objects to be possessed, cherished, and defended from every danger by the men in their lives,"[58] which, in Bella's case, includes Edward himself.

Another important aspect of the novels under consideration concerns female sexuality. According to Melissa Ames, most vampire fiction, including Twilight and L. J. Smith's Vampire Diaries series, relies on stereotypical notions of female sexuality: a young woman is initially torn between two men, but in the end the story reasserts traditional family values.[59] Although female sexuality is depicted as active, and, overall, Bella is more sexually aggressive than Edward, the sexual politics of their partnership are conservative.[60] Bella's sexuality is policed by Edward; it is reduced to its procreational function and promotes the sanctity of life.[61] Platt concludes that "this image of female sexuality is far from empowered and . . . even more troublesome given the large number of female fans that make up the readership. As other scholars have noted, leisure reading serves as an important form of socialization, teaching young girls what it means to be feminine, and how they should relate to themselves, to other women, and to the men in their lives."[62]

As I will show, the conservative sexual politics of Twilight do not extend to all YAF. In the following, I discuss the representation of sexualized violence and its consequences in two YAF novels: *Die Stadt war nie wach* und *Rotkäppchen muss weinen*. After short plot summaries, I will analyze the depictions of the protagonists and perpetrators and of their social environments. In addition, I discuss the representations of sexualized violence along with discourses on how to prevent it.

Beate Teresa Hanika's *Rotkäppchen*, published in 2009, offers a powerful narrative about trauma, friendship, and first love. It depicts two weeks in the life of the heroine, Malvina, whose grandfather sexually assaults her. This abuse reactivates suppressed childhood memories.

---

57 Melissa R. Ames, "Twilight Follows Tradition: Analyzing 'Biting' Critiques of Vampire Narratives for Their Portrayals of Gender & Sexuality," in *Bitten by Twilight: Youth Culture, Media, and the Vampire Franchise*, ed. Melissa Click, Jennifer Stevens Aubrey, and Elizabeth Behm-Morawitz (New York: Peter Lang, 2010), 37–53, here 40–41.

58 Platt, "Cullen Family Values," 72.

59 Ames, "Twilight Follows Tradition," 49.

60 Platt, "Cullen Family Values," 80; Ames, "Twilight Follows Tradition," 49.

61 Platt, "Cullen Family Values," 73.

62 Platt, "Cullen Family Values," 84.

Rotkäppchen also draws attention to the grave consequences for a victim of abuse whose parents do not believe her story. At the same time, the novel portrays strong female characters, who offer a contrast to the story of abuse and victimization, and it clearly labels the grandfather's actions as sexual assault through the first-person perspective of Malvina. The title and paratext on the dust jacket reference the story of Little Red Riding Hood. Like Little Red Riding Hood visiting her grandmother, Malvina visits her grandfather with a basket full of supplies: she is like "Rotkäppchen—weil der Wolf sie längst in seiner Gewalt hat" (Red Riding Hood—because the wolf has long had her in his grip). Neither the motif of Red Riding Hood nor the image of the wolf as a sexual perpetrator are unique to this novel. Bettina Scheichelbauer's thesis on sexual abuse in YAF finds numerous intertextual references to the wolf and/or Red Riding Hood in YAF that addresses sexual abuse.[63] Catherine Orenstein's study on changing versions and interpretations of Little Red Riding Hood shows that this tale "speaks to enduring themes about men and women, of gender roles and how they change."[64]

The child psychologist Bruno Bettelheim interpreted Red Riding Hood as an allegory for the seductiveness of budding sexuality. In his argument, the sexual assault is the fault of the Betroffene and a just punishment for being sexually active "too early." Bettelheim also notes that any sexual contact would be traumatic for Red Riding Hood, because she is not mature enough for it. This recalls notions of teenage purity and denies that adolescents are capable of consensual sexual interactions.[65] Moreover, Orenstein demonstrates that older versions of the story feature a different plot; several of these narratives highlight Red Riding Hood's resilience and let her escape. Bettelheim's psychoanalytical approach is ill equipped to make sense of these versions.[66]

Lilly Axster's *Die Stadt*, published in 2017, takes a different approach. Much like *Rotkäppchen*, *Die Stadt* contrasts abusive behavior with first experiences of sexuality between consenting young adults. Told from a third-person narrative perspective, the novel alternates between the points of view of five friends: Reza, Hannes, Minh, Tony, and Ayo. While all five are affected in different ways, the direct Betroffene of the abuse do not give voice to their experiences. The story begins after Reza has become an involuntary witness to a sexual assault committed by a

63 Bettina Scheichelbauer, "'Damit ich dich besser fressen kann!': Intertextualität in jugendliterarischen Erzähltexten über sexuellen Missbrauch" (Diplomarbeit, Universität Wien, 2015), 1.
64 Catherine Orenstein, *Little Red Riding Hood Uncloaked: Sex, Morality, and the Evolution of a Fairy Tale* (New York: Basic Books, 2002), 13.
65 Bruno Bettelheim, *Kinder brauchen Märchen* (Munich: dtv, 1999), 199.
66 Orenstein, *Little Red Riding Hood Uncloaked*, 71.

teacher. On the dust jacket, readers are told, "Machtmissbrauch durch einen Lehrer verunsichert die Freundschaften und das Begehren der Jugendlichen" (Abuse of power by a teacher troubles friendships and desires of young adults).

The narrative perspective in *Rotkäppchen* is solely that of Malvina, a first-person narrator, and is presented in present tense. Thus, the reader is drawn into Malvina's story, which gradually unfolds the truth about her abuse. The text offers a credible portrayal of a coming-of-age story that focuses on the abuse but also on Malvina's problems with her family, her wish to be taken seriously by adults, a close friendship, and the impact of first love on a friendship. Malvina is an average teenager in an average German suburb with an average dysfunctional family. Thus, the story lends support to studies that suggest that sexual abuse is not a matter of social background or place of residence. In *Die Stadt* the narrative is multiperspectival, but the voices of abused pupils remain unheard. The responses and behavior of Hannes's little brother, Jonathan, are accessible to the reader only through the perspectives of Hannes and Reza.

Axster uses the gender gap—*Schüler_innen* for pupils (*Die Stadt*, 9)—not only when referring to groups but also when the five protagonists are mentioned. Thus, readers come to understand that at least one of the characters does not self-identify within binary categories. Hannes, for example, is not only called "Fee" (*Die Stadt*, 14; fairy) on several occasions but also wears their hair and style in a nonconforming way. In addition, the five friends come from different social backgrounds: Minh and Tony have single mothers; Hannes was adopted before his parents had a biological child; Reza's parents immigrated to Germany; and Ayo struggles with her Black German identity. One narrative thread focuses on Reza's attempts to cope with the abuse he witnessed; other threads deal with the classic topics of YAF: Minh is in love with Tony, who is in a relationship with Reza, but is not quite sure about her sexual identity. Hannes and Ayo secretly rent a flat because they are eager to be seen as adults. Ultimately, all of them struggle with their parents in one way or another.

The perpetrators in both novels are extremely manipulative. They use their positions of power to groom and isolate the Betroffene and to frame them as unreliable if they speak out. When the grandfather begins to abuse Malvina, he tells her that she should seek to please him for the sake of her cancer-stricken grandmother, who would not get better unless her husband was happy (*Rotkäppchen*, 143). Later, when Malvina disobeys him, he accuses her of having killed her grandmother (173). He also tells her that she has to keep "their" secret (127) because nobody would believe her anyway. When she tells her father and brother that her grandfather kissed her, they do nothing except inform the grandfather that she told on him:

Weißt du, was du deinem Papa und Paul da über uns erzählt hast,
das war nicht schön von dir. Aber der Papa hat dir sowieso nicht
geglaubt. Und weißt du auch warum? . . . Weil er immer mir glaubt.
Weil ich sein Vater bin. Was du ihm auch erzählst, er glaubt dir
nicht. (66)

[You know, what you told your father and Paul about us, that was
not nice of you. But your dad didn't believe you anyway. And do
you know why? . . . Because he will always believe me. Because I am
his father. Whatever you tell him, he won't believe you.]

He isolates her from her best friend, Lizzie; her boyfriend, Klatsche; and
his attentive neighbor, Bitschek, who tries to talk to Malvina when she
has to visit her grandfather (12, 93–94, 98). The text offers a detailed
portrayal of the grandfather's strategies. It shows how he grooms Malvina
and keeps her from talking to others while never leaving any doubt that
he is a perpetrator.

While readers learn much about the grandfather's strategies, they do
not gain much insight into the psyche of the perpetrator in *Die Stadt*,
Stoibler, who is introduced as the guidance counselor at the school and
as the best friend of Minh's mother. When Reza becomes an involuntary witness of Stoibler's assaults in the school's storage room, Stoibler
pretends that Reza observed one of Stoibler's "therapy" sessions. In
these sessions, Stoibler, who is mostly referred to only by his last name,
explains that masturbating in front of him (and others) can help students
heal from sexual assault—even those students who do not remember any
past trauma (*Die Stadt*, 32–33). Stoibler targets vulnerable students, convinces them that they have been abused, and therefore that they must partake in his "healing" program. He also lures students with gifts, including
an expensive phone that, as Reza discovers, he gave to Hannes's brother
(32–33, 47, 88). When Reza tells Minh about the sexual abuse he witnessed, Minh is confused at first but then wants to take action. At this
point, Stoibler tries to discredit her by telling Minh's mother that Minh
has a crush on him. Minh's mother believes Stoibler because he is her
best friend, even though she knows that her daughter is not interested in
men (125). When Reza speaks out during a presentation at a conference,
Stoibler is revealed as a master manipulator:

Ich bin sicher, es gibt einen wahren Kern in diesem schrecklichen
Beispiel, das Reza vorgetragen hat, und wie wir alle wissen, werden,
gerade im Fall von sexualisierter Gewalt, von Betroffenen häufig
Vertrauenspersonen an Täterstelle gesetzt, aus der Hoffnung heraus, diese mögen Verständnis haben und die Beschuldigung, die
eigentlich ein Hilfeschrei ist, aushalten. Ich gebe zu, dass es mich
persönlich schockt und kränkt, für diese Rolle offenbar auserkoren

zu sein. . . . Und ja, Reza, ich halte es aus an die Stelle von jemand anders gesetzt worden zu sein und ich werde alles in meiner Macht Stehende tun, um Licht in die Sache zu bringen und einem möglichen Missbraucher das abscheuliche Handwerk zu legen. (*Die Stadt*, 141)

[I am sure that there is a kernel of truth in this horrible example that Reza just gave to us. And we all know that those affected often put people they trust in the position of the perpetrator, especially in cases of sexualized violence, because they hope that they will understand and are able to endure the accusation that is really a cry for help. I admit that I am personally shocked and aggrieved that I have obviously been chosen for this role. . . . And yes, Reza, I am willing to endure that you put me in the position of someone else and I will do everything in my power to shed some light on this issue and to put an end to the terrible actions of a possible abuser.]

Both Malvina's grandfather and Stoibler fit the paradigms established by studies of sexual abuse: They present their abuse as forms of help or love. At the same time, they isolate and silence the Betroffenen, convincing them that no one would believe them, while undermining the credibility of the Betroffenen in their social circle.[67] It is very important, however, that the text clearly label the perpetrator as such: Aigner notes that only half of all YAF novels on sexualized violence do so.[68]

In both texts, the protagonists experience an overwhelming feeling of helplessness during the first experience of abuse. Later, this sense of helplessness is accompanied by other feelings, including shame, guilt, or confusion. Studies of the symptoms of sexual abuse in children and young adults list not only a decline in physical health but also withdrawal into the self and feelings of shame and guilt.[69] The fact that the texts depict a variety of feelings and a whole series of symptoms of abuse is potentially conducive to processes of healing as well as prevention.[70]

Both Reza and Malvina are experiencing speechlessness and paralysis during or shortly after the assault. For Reza, the act of witnessing abuse is portrayed as confusing and unsettling. He does not trust his feeling that something is amiss but, rather, doubts himself, wondering if what he saw

---

67 Bickler, *Sexueller Missbrauch als Thema*, 9–26; Kruck, *Das Schweigen durchbrechen*, 21–49.

68 Aigner, "Sexualisierte Gewalt in Jugendbüchern," 85.

69 Unabhängiger Beauftragter für Fragen des sexuellen Kindesmissbrauchs, "Missbrauch—Symptome können Signale sein," accessed August 26, 2020, https://beauftragter-missbrauch.de/praevention/was-ist-sexueller-missbrauch/ missbrauch-symptome-koennen-signale-sein.

70 Kruck, *Das Schweigen durchbrechen*, 179.

was therapy or abuse (*Die Stadt*, 9, 15). He feels ashamed because he did not leave the room immediately and because Hannes's brother was there (32–33). Reza is afraid that no one will believe him, especially since he is accusing a popular teacher: "Niemand wird ihm, Reza Rahmay, einem miserablen Schüler glauben" (57; Nobody will believe him, Reza Rahmay, a lousy student). Similarly, Malvina is not able to move the first time her grandfather kisses her (*Rotkäppchen*, 14). She feels ashamed and is afraid that she might lose her best friend, Lizzie, and her crush, Klatsche, if she told them (219). When she is finally able to speak about the abuse, she reflects,

> Andere wären vielleicht nicht so feige gewesen, denke ich, vielleicht wäre es aber auch vielen gegangen wie mir, viele hätten sich auch gedacht, das halte ich doch aus, noch einen Tag und noch einen, morgen rede ich oder übermorgen oder vielleicht irgendwann. Man denkt nicht daran, dass das Geheimnis jeden Tag wächst, jede Stunde macht es größer und unaussprechlicher. (*Rotkäppchen*, 219)

> [Others might not have been so cowardly, I think, but many people might have responded as I did, many would have thought, I can stand it, one more day and one more, tomorrow I'll talk or the day after tomorrow or maybe sometime. One doesn't think about the fact that the secret grows every day, every hour makes it bigger and more inexpressible.]

The representation of the physical and psychological effects of sexual abuse can also raise awareness and help bystanders to recognize possible signs of abuse. Both Malvina and Reza start to seclude themselves. Reza develops a stress-induced cough (*Die Stadt*, 37), and Hannes observes that their brother's underwear shows traces of feces and that he struggles with hygiene (70–71). Malvina suffers from episodes of vertigo and fainting in addition to symptoms of dissociation (*Rotkäppchen*, 141–42, 144, 158, 93–96, 100, 136). She also experiences a tingling sensation that she does not understand:

> Mein Herz klopft ganz schnell, ich kann es schon wieder hören, im Kopf und hinter meiner Stirn macht sich dieses komische Kribbeln breit, ich weiß jetzt, was dieses Kribbeln ist, das wusste ich die ganzen Jahre lang nicht. Dieses Kribbeln ist Angst, ganz scheußliche Angst. (*Rotkäppchen*, 93)

> [My heart beats very fast, I can already hear it again, in my head and behind my forehead this weird tingling feeling spreads, now I know what this tingling is, I did not know all those years. This tingling is fear, terrible fear.]

While *Die Stadt* features no additional references to sexualized violence besides the abuse by the teacher, *Rotkäppchen* contains two. Tellingly, Malvina's mother warns her not to ride a bike alone (16). The remark alludes to the notion of the unknown perpetrator who lies in wait for girls. It is remarkable that Malvina's mother is concerned about a bike ride but ignores Malvina's accusations against her grandfather. Similarly, we learn through flashbacks that Klatsche and his gang stole Malvina's and Lizzy's clothes when they were taking a bath in a rain barrel, and they had to escape almost naked. Malvina confesses that she could have died of shame in that moment and that she felt the boys' gazes on her back and bottom (161–62). Here the childish play of stealing clothes turns into a humiliating ritual with clear sexual connotation. The incident, however, is not clearly framed as sexualized violence but, rather, presented as a game, though later Klatsche does apologize to Malvina and understands that his behavior was offensive (183). YAF should address not only sexual abuse and rape but also other forms of sexualized violence. In this sense, *Die Stadt* and *Rotkäppchen* are exemplary. We need novels that move beyond the constellation of male perpetrator and female Betroffene, even if this is statistically the most common type of sexual violence. Making all forms of sexual violence visible is a crucial aspect of prevention.

Unfortunately, the representation of sexualized violence in *Die Stadt* and *Rotkäppchen* is exceptional. YAF frequently features scenes of sexualized violence, but they are typically not labeled as such; nor are they problematized. Two of the most popular works of YAF, Twilight and The Vampire Diaries, trivialize the harmful effects of sexualized violence: both depict control and even abuse as "normal" aspects of heterosexual relations.[71] In these texts, young women and girls are taught to perceive unwanted comments on their bodies as compliments. Narratives of being "crazy in love" and therefore incapable of respecting boundaries normalize transgressive behavior.[72] Sexuality is often shown to endanger the purity of female characters; if the text depicts sexual activities, they tend to be clinically clean. There is rarely room for a realistic representation of the first sexual encounter. *Die Stadt* is truly exceptional in this regard. It contrasts abuse with consensual adolescent sexuality, including all its awkwardness and bodily fluids (18). In addition, the text goes beyond the heteronormative frame and features a diverse cast of characters.

Fiction impacts our view of sexuality and gender and of sexualized violence. If YAF stopped normalizing and/or omitting sexualized violence, young adults might be encouraged to assert their boundaries and to speak out about abuse. Social interventions like the #MeToo movement offer a public stage for Betroffene and make it easier to address

---

71   Rana, "Sexualität und Macht," 46–48.
72   Rana, "Sexualität und Macht," 52.

sexualized violence in YAF. YAF can reach many adolescents and communicate to them the concerns of #MeToo while providing those who are affected with identification and coping options. Furthermore, YAF can raise young adults' awareness of the problems of sexualized violence and demand changes in contexts that are relevant to them; it can model how to defend oneself and how to seek help. Visibility, however, remains probably the most important challenge, a challenge that is also at the heart of the various movements around #MeToo: After all, if we want to solve problems, these problems must first become visible.

In YAF, as in the #MeToo movements, some topics remain marginalized or unexplored. For example, at present, precious few narratives deal with the concept of toxic masculinity. While it is important to make sure that the victims of sexualized violence have a voice and that we listen to them, it is also imperative that YAF portray young men whose sexuality is not defined by dominating and degrading women. We need novels about characters who struggle against becoming a perpetrator. The continued suffering from sexualized violence demands a social and political rethinking of gender relations, a culture of consent and open dialogue. We need visibility, a diversity of narratives, and fundamental change in our societal approach to sexual violence. As Bücker puts it, defending against unwanted behavior is the second step; the first step is to avoid this behavior altogether.[73]

---

73 Bücker, "Ist es radikal?"

11: "Eine gigantische Vergewaltigung": Rape as Subject in Roger Fritz's *Mädchen mit Gewalt* (1970)

Lisa Haegele

THE BEST-KNOWN DIRECTORS of the Young German Cinema—the burgeoning art cinema movement in West Germany in the 1960s—later became the internationally celebrated auteurs of the New German Cinema in the 1970s and early 1980s. Funded largely by the newly established Kuratorium junger deutscher Film (Young German Film Subsidy Committee), the early feature films of Volker Schlöndorff, Alexander Kluge, Rainer Werner Fassbinder, Werner Herzog, and Edgar Reitz broke from the traditions of commercial genre cinema—mockingly dubbed "Papas Kino" (Daddy's Cinema) by the young directors—that had dominated the West German film industry since the 1950s. While scholars have tended to focus their attention on these directors, the films of many others in the Young German Cinema movement have been ignored, including the so-called Neue Münchner Gruppe (New Munich Group), a small group of filmmakers based in Munich's hip Schwabing district. First identified as a group by film critic Enno Patalas in 1966, these directors—among them Rudolf Thome, Klaus Lemke, Eckhardt Schmidt, May Spils, and Roger Fritz—rebelled against the abstract intellectualism and serious sociohistorical criticism endorsed by their better-known peers. Inspired largely by the French New Wave and Hollywood B-films of the 1930s and 1940s, the New Munich Group directors opted instead for simple stories, fashionable young protagonists, visually appealing settings, and rock 'n' roll soundtracks.

This essay examines the New Munich Group film *Mädchen mit Gewalt* (1970; Girl with Violence), which was released in English as *The Brutes* and *Love by Rape* in 1970 and as *Cry Rape* for its 1975 rerelease in the United States.[1] Shot in English and later dubbed in German,[2] the film

---

1   "The Brutes (1970)," IMDb, accessed December 9, 2020, https://www. imdb.com/title/tt0066116/?ref_=tt_mv_close.

2   Klaus Löwitsch and Helga Anders dubbed their voices in the German version, but Arthur Brauss did not. The original English-language version of the film

was directed by Roger Fritz, known also for his work as producer, actor, photographer, journalist, and cofounder of the popular West German youth magazine *twen*.[3] The last film in Fritz's so-called Mädchen-Trilogie (girl trilogy),[4] *Mädchen mit Gewalt* centers on the abduction and rape of a young woman named Alice, played by Fritz's then wife, Helga Anders, by two men over the course of an evening in a gravel quarry on the outskirts of Munich.[5] On its surface, the film seems to offer us little more than a misogynistic rape fantasy and sexploitation, a popular style in European low-budget cinema that became especially popular in West Germany with the *Schulmädchen-Report* (schoolgirl report) film cycle.[6] Marketed internationally and domestically as a B-film, *Mädchen mit Gewalt* premiered in February 1970 at the Europa-Filmpalast in Munich, a so-called Bahnhofskino (train station theater) that screened cheaply produced genre films and exploitation fare from around the globe in the 1960s and 1970s.[7]

By viewing *Mädchen mit Gewalt* more closely, however, this essay shows how the film departs from more popular representations of rape

---

is considered missing. "The Brutes (1970)," IMDb.

3   Fritz passed away at the age of eighty-five on November 26, 2021. Christian Mayer, "Ein herrlich unbescheidener Lebenskünstler," *Süddeutsche Zeitung*, November 29, 2021, https://www.sueddeutsche.de/muenchen/ muenchen-roger-fritz-fotograf-nachruf-1.5476304.

4   The first two films in the series were Fritz's feature film debut, *Mädchen, Mädchen* (1967; Girls, Girls) and *Häschen in der Grube* (1968; Rabbit in the Pit), both of which also featured Anders as the star.

5   Helga Anders had her own kind of #MeToo moment when she appeared as one of many women on the front cover of *Stern* magazine on June 6, 1971, with the headline "Wir haben abgetrieben!" (We've had abortions!). Not unlike the contemporary #MeToo movements, this public campaign initiated by well-known feminist Alice Schwarzer is often regarded as the event the launched the feminist movement in West Germany. Alice Schwarzer, "Die *Stern*-Aktion und ihre Folgen," *Emma*, April 1, 2011, https://www.emma.de/ artikel/wir-haben-abgetrieben-265457.

6   See Tim Bergfelder, *International Adventures: German Popular Cinema and European Co-Productions in the 1960s* (New York: Berghahn, 2004), and Jennifer Fay, "The Schoolgirl Reports and the Guilty Pleasure of History," in *Alternative Europe: Eurotrash and Exploitation Cinema since 1945*, ed. Ernest Mathijs and Xavier Mendik, 39–52 (London: Wallflower Press, 2004).

7   Christian Horn, "Die wilde bunte Welt des Bahnhofskinos," *Goethe-Institut*, August 2016, https://www.goethe.de/de/kul/flm/20819186.html. In the United States, the film was distributed by Joseph Brenner Associates, a company that distributed grindhouse and exploitation films from around the globe. The company advertised *Mädchen mit Gewalt* with sensationalist and misogynistic headlines such as "Force Adds to the Sport!," "Does She Really Hate It?," and "Is She Prey . . . or Playmate?" "The Brutes (1970)," IMDb.

in the cinema by emphasizing the victim's "secondary victimization" by the legal system and patriarchal society long after the on-screen physical attack. In this way, the film taps into the discipline of victimology that, spurred by the growing feminist movement, emerged in the early 1970s to compensate for the predominating focus on male perpetrators in studies of sexual violence.[8] Speaking out against their sexual assaulters and years of silencing, intimidation, and discrimination they have had to endure, the voices contributing to today's #MeToo movements reveal how "secondary victimization" remains an ongoing problem that sexual assault victims are seeking to redress.

Rejected from the Young German Cinema canon, *Mädchen mit Gewalt* disappointed critics for failing to address larger, putatively more important questions of national politics, history, and representation. In this chapter, I argue that the film's failure to link its subject of rape to more abstract, masculinist notions of nation and national identity—its failure to meet the standards of a "good" art film, in other words—is precisely where the film succeeds from a feminist perspective. To be sure, Fritz's film could hardly be called a "feminist" film in the vein of 1970s feminism. Rather, this essay draws out the film's feminist sensibilities by taking Vicki Callahan's understanding of feminism as a "deep-time project" with "multiple points of entry"[9] as its point of departure. Acknowledging that, to quote Callahan, "the history that we present as feminists always implies a kind of reclaiming, rewriting, and recontextualization of materials," the essay teases out strands of the film in the mode of a "Feminism 3.0," that is, a transgenerational, decentered, "new networked . . . and deep-time inflected phase of feminism"[10] that is not anchored within a single text or particular moment in history. Reclaiming *Mädchen mit Gewalt* within and for the present era of #MeToo, the essay recovers the story of a victim of sexual assault in a film that had been long written off as unworthy of attention.

Undoing Rape as Metaphor

Mädchen mit Gewalt opens with Mike (Arthur Brauss) and Werner (Klaus Löwitsch, who won the German Film Award in 1970 for his performance), two office colleagues who spend their weekends seeking out, abducting, and sexually violating young women. Early in the film, Mike and Werner meet Alice at a go-cart track before joining her and her friends for a drink

---

8   Duncan Chappell, Gilbert Geis, and Faith Fogarty, "Forcible Rape: Bibliography," *Journal of Criminal Law and Criminology* 65, no. 2 (1974): 248.

9   Vicki Callahan, ed., *Reclaiming the Archive: Feminism and Film History* (Detroit: Wayne State University Press, 2010), 4.

10   Callahan, *Reclaiming the Archive*, 5, 7.

at the bar. When one of Alice's friends suggests moving the party to the Autobahnsee, a lake along the highway in Augsburg, for a late-night bonfire and swim, Mike and Werner jump at the opportunity to offer Alice a ride. Rather than bring her to her friends, however, the men take Alice to a dark and remote gravel quarry off the highway. While waiting for her friends, Alice takes off her dress and goes for a quick dip in a pond as the men watch her from afar, disappointed that she keeps her underwear on and does not turn to face them. Once Alice realizes that she has been duped and that her friends will not be joining them, she demands a ride home. The men then begin to torment her psychologically, promising to take her home if she wins at a game of hide-and-seek. When it is her turn to hide, she tries to escape the quarry, but Werner quickly catches up to her, throws her to the ground and rapes her as Mike watches. The second half of the film begins in the early morning the next day in a setting that strongly evokes the bright, barren desert landscapes in Westerns. Now Mike tries to gain control over Alice, leading to a violent altercation between him and Werner. Alice begins to show signs of "Stockholm syndrome"—a term first used by the media in 1973 in connection with the Norrmalmstorg bank robbery and hostage crisis in Stockholm[11]—and implores the men to stop fighting. At the end of the film, the police arrive by helicopter and take Alice aside to ask whether the men threatened her. When she replies that they did not, the officer asks again, "Es ist Ihnen also nichts passiert, was Sie nicht wollten?" (Nothing happened to you that you didn't want?). She insists that that is the case, and so the officers leave Mike and Werner with just a small trespassing fine. The main score, "Soul Desert" by the Krautrock band Can, enters the soundtrack as Mike and Werner drive off with Alice pressed tightly between them. In the last shot of the film the police fly out of the quarry in their helicopter.

Mädchen mit Gewalt belongs to a long list of films produced in the early 1970s that depict rape: Sam Peckinpah's rape-revenge film *Straw Dogs* (1971),[12] Alfred Hitchcock's *Frenzy* (1972), John Boorman's *Deliverance* (1972), Wes Craven's B-horror film *Last House on the Left* (1972)—based on Ingmar Bergman's Swedish art film *Jungfrukällan* (*The Virgin Spring*, 1960)—Meir Zarchi's *I Spit On Your Grave* (1978), and a plethora of sexploitation B-films produced in and distributed

11 Andrew M. Colman, "Stockholm Syndrome," in *Oxford Dictionary of Psychology*, 4th ed. (Oxford: Oxford University Press, 2015), https://www-oxford reference-com.libproxy.txstate.edu/view/10.1093/acref/9780199657681.001.0001/acref-9780199657681-e-8014.

12 Sam Peckinpah allegedly ordered a copy of *Mädchen mit Gewalt* before filming *Straw Dogs*. Jack J., "Mädchen mit Gewalt (Roger Fritz, West Germany, 1970)," *En lejemorder ser tilbage* (blog), February 21, 2018, http://enlejemor dersertilbage.blogspot.com/2018/02/madchen-mit-gewalt-roger-fritz-west.html.

widely across Europe. In West Germany, Michael Verhoeven's anti-war film *o.k.* (1970) and Rainer Werner Fassbinder's television drama *Wildwechsel* (1972; Wild Game Crossing, released in English as *Jail Bait*) portray the rape of a young girl, played in both films by the rising New German Cinema star Eva Mattes. In *o.k.*, Mattes plays Phan Thi Mao, a young Vietnamese girl who is raped and murdered by a group of American soldiers;[13] in *Wildwechsel*, the thirteen-year-old Hanni is raped by her father. Both films elicited scandals: while *o.k.* led to the cancellation of the entire 1970 Berlin International Film Festival, where it premiered, *Wildwechsel* sparked a heated debate between Fassbinder and the original author of the play on which it was based, Franz-Xaver Kroetz, who publicly condemned Fassbinder's adaptation and tried to prevent its release in theaters.

Significantly, the controversies surrounding *Wildwechsel* and *o.k.* were based not on the films' depictions of rape per se but, rather, on broader issues related to artistic license and (male) authors' rights. In *Lustmord: Sexual Murder in Weimar Germany*, Maria Tatar discusses a similar phenomenon in the context of Weimar expressionism.[14] She argues that the female victim of sexual murder depicted on the canvas "disappears" as the "transgressive genius" of the male artist and his technique—and that of the killer, with whom the artist often identifies—become the primary focus of the artwork.[15] Analyzing Otto Dix's *Lustmord* paintings, Tatar writes,

The artist . . . becomes less criminal perpetrator than cultural hero. It is his biographical connection with what is represented and his artistic brilliance in representing it that eclipses the subject matter on the canvas and, as we have seen, turns him and his transcendent artistic authority into the subject of critical analysis. The corpse vanishes as the work of art and its creator enter the foreground to serve as the center of attention.[16]

---

13 By playing a Vietnamese girl, Eva Mattes, a white German woman (in 1970 a sixteen-year-old girl), performs "ethnic drag," a phenomenon imbued with various and sometimes conflicted meanings in West German culture after Nazism. Mattes's performance deserves a more detailed exploration than can be provided here. See Katrin Sieg's essential book on the topic, *Ethnic Drag: Performing Race, Nation, Sexuality in West Germany* (Ann Arbor: University of Michigan Press, 2004).

14 Maria Tatar, *Lustmord: Sexual Murder in Weimar Germany* (Princeton, NJ: Princeton University Press, 1995).

15 Tatar, *Lustmord*, 18.

16 Tatar, *Lustmord*, 17.

She concludes that "artistic identity and masculine identity come to be founded on and constituted through acts of disfiguring, murderous violence."[17]

Similarly, the discussions surrounding sexual violence in *o.k.* and *Wildwechsel* focused entirely on the male artist and his rights to artistic expression rather than on the violated female subject. Verhoeven's *o.k.* relates the kidnapping, rape, and murder of Phan Thi Mao, a twenty-one-year-old Vietnamese woman, by four American soldiers in Vietnam in 1966. It was rejected by the jury at the Berlin International Film Festival—presided over that year by American film director and producer George Stevens—for stoking antagonistic sentiment between West Germany and its new political ally, the United States.[18] As Kris Vander Lugt notes, the scandal was based not on the film's explicit depiction of rape but on "Verhoeven's implicit critique of American foreign policy" and the film's subsequent "censorship" by the festival jury,[19] which prompted other filmmakers to retract their films in protest.[20] Much like *o.k.*, Fassbinder's *Wildwechsel* stirred up public controversy. Franz-Xaver Kroetz denounced the film, and its incestuous rape scene in particular, as an "obscenity," sparking a public debate between the two artists about artistic license and adaptation rights.[21] In these discussions, the rape victim vanishes as the male *Autor* defends his right to creative or political self-expression, through which he is perversely positioned, to quote Tatar, as a "casualty of [his] sacrificial victim" and a "cultural hero."[22]

Deemed detrimental to the festival's mission of fostering understanding among nations, the rape of Phan Thi Mao in Verhoeven's film became linked to questions of national reputation and international relations that further obscured the subject of sexual violence as such. Even in more recent film scholarship and criticism there remains a tendency to contextualize rape within masculinist notions of politics and nation that usurp and overwrite the experience of the victim. For example, Adam Lowenstein writes that the brutal rape of seventeen-year-old Mari (Sandra Peabody) in Wes Craven's *Last House on the Left* "serves as the locus for anxieties concerning the nation as feminized and susceptible to violation

17 Tatar, *Lustmord*, 18.

18 Kris Vander Lugt, "30 June 1970: A Faltering Berlinale Founders on *o.k.* Controversy," in *A New History of German Cinema*, ed. Jennifer M. Kapczynski and Michael D. Richardson (Rochester, NY: Camden House, 2012), 433.

19 Vander Lugt, "30 June 1970," 433.

20 "Berlinale im Juli," *Filmreport* 12/13 (1970): 3.

21 Thomas Thieringer, "Ist der Autor Freiwild für die Produzenten?," *Kölner Stadt-Anzeiger*, March 15, 1973.

22 Tatar, *Lustmord*, 18.

in the Vietnam era."[23] In West Germany, Helma Sanders-Brahms's semi-autobiographical film *Deutschland bleiche Mutter* (*Germany Pale Mother*, 1980) invited metaphorical readings that linked the rape of Lene (Eva Mattes), its female protagonist, to the "'rape' of Germany by the Allies"[24] and to "Germany's 'rape' by Hitler."[25] For Susan E. Linville, these reductive and "totalizing analogies between Lene and Germany" show how critics, despite their efforts to "weed out retrograde, masculinist discourse in films," ironically "end up articulating a smaller and smaller range of possibilities for feminism."[26] These readings of rape become even more problematic when viewed in the context of working through historical trauma: read as an allegory for national victimization, rape serves to help process wartime violence, through which it becomes—in a perverse paradox—implicated in narratives of recovery and healing. These readings indirectly condone violence against women by sublimating sexual assault into an allegory whose purpose is to reaffirm and rebuild national integrity. Such metaphorical interpretations of rape are perhaps not so surprising given that the United Nations did not consider sexual violence in areas of conflict a war crime until 2008.[27]

Unlike other films in the 1970s that deal with rape, Roger Fritz's *Mädchen mit Gewalt* frustrated readings that tried to link the sexual violence in the film to ostensibly more "meaningful" aesthetic debates and issues regarding national politics and identity. One critic, for example, bemoaned the film's failure to realize its political potential:

> Kein progressiver Jungfilmer, der nicht von einem deutschen Western mit politischem Hintergrund träumt. *Mädchen mit Gewalt* ist ein deutscher Western und politisch gemeint. Aber die Konzeption ist falsch. Sie bewirkt nichts als Amüsement über Schweinerei und Gewalt. In der Isolation der Kiesgrube kann kein gesellschaftliches Verhalten nachgewiesen werden. Es fehlt eigentlich nur noch, dass auf Vietnam angespielt wird.

23 Adam Lowenstein, *Shocking Representation: Historical Trauma, National Cinema, and the Modern Horror Film* (New York: Columbia University Press, 2005), 115.

24 Ellen E. Seiter, "Women's History, Women's Melodrama: *Deutschland, bleiche Mutter*," *German Quarterly* 59, no. 4 (Autumn 1986): 580.

25 Barbara Hyams, "Is the Apolitical Woman at Peace? A Reading of the Fairy Tale in *Germany, Pale Mother*," in *Perspectives on German Cinema*, ed. Terri Ginsberg and Kirsten Moana Thompson (New York: G. K. Hall, 1996), 346.

26 Susan E. Linville, *Feminism, Film, Fascism: Women's Auto/biographical Film in Postwar Germany* (Austin, TX: University of Austin Press, 1998), 65.

27 T Vishnu Jayaraman, "Rape as a War Crime," *UN Chronicle*, accessed December 9, 2020, https://www.un.org/en/chronicle/article/rape-war-crime.

[There is no progressive Young German filmmaker who does not dream of a German Western with a political backdrop. *Mädchen mit Gewalt* is a German Western and is meant to be political. But the approach is wrong. The only effect is amusement at brutishness and violence. In the isolation of the gravel quarry behaviors of society cannot be exemplified. The only other thing missing is its allusion to Vietnam.][28]

Echoing these complaints, other critics attacked the film for failing to provide any psychological or sociological motives that could explain the perpetrators' behaviors: "Der Film bedeutet gar nichts, als die Aufzeichnung eines Falles, der isoliert da steht und nichts über Verhaltensweisen einer Gruppe oder Schicht aussagen kann" (The film means nothing but the description of a case that stands alone and can say nothing about the behaviors of a group or class).[29] For another reviewer, the film "liefert keinen soziologischen Hintergrund [und] bringt seine Story ohne psychologische Vorgeschichte. Dauer und Massivität der Prügelszenen regen keineswegs dazu an, über eventuelle hintergründige Motivationen nachzudenken" (provides no sociological background [and] delivers its story without a psychological backstory. Duration and severity of the fight scenes hardly compel one to think about possible underlying motives).[30] A more recent review, published upon the film's DVD release in 2015, linked the film's critical failure to Fritz's affinity for popular cinema, a style that Fritz's better-known peers in the Young German Cinema resolutely rejected: "Dass so mancher dem Film nicht zugetraut hat, ein ätzendes Sittenbild der damaligen BRD [Bundesrepublik Deutschland] zu zeichnen, mag an Fritz' Begeisterung für das populäre Kino liegen" (That so many people did not give the film credit for painting a searing moral picture of the FRG [Federal Republic of Germany] at the time is probably due to Fritz's enthusiasm for popular cinema).[31]

Contradicting such negative assessments of the film's seemingly noncritical stance, this essay suggests that the film's failure to convey a critique of the moral state of the nation—"ein ätzendes Sittenbild der damaligen BRD"—is precisely where the film opens up space for feminist interpretation. Borrowing Vivian Sobchack's differentiation between rape as *subject* versus *object* in the cinema,[32] I show how *Mädchen mit Gewalt*

---

28 Hellmut Haffner, "Mädchen mit Gewalt," *Sonntagsblatt*, April 12, 1970.

29 "Das Leben ist halt so," *Spandauer Volksblatt*, May 27, 1970.

30 "Lust am Brutalen: 'Mädchen mit Gewalt' im Minilux," *Telegraf*, June 5, 1970.

31 Michael Kienzl, "Mädchen: Mit Gewalt—Kritik," Critic.de, June 6, 2015, https://www.critic.de/film/maedchen-mit-gewalt-8323/.

32 Vivian Sobchack, "*No Lies:* Direct Cinema as Rape," *Journal of the University Film Association* 29, no. 4 (Fall 1977): 13–18.

presents rape as subject by emphasizing Alice's "secondary victimization" or "secondary rape"—issues that were only slowly entering into public discourse in West Germany at the time[33]—in the form of slut shaming, victim blaming, and silencing long after the physical assault, particularly by the criminal justice system. By maintaining its focus on the experience of Alice as victim, the film rejects the more abstract, androcentric readings of sexual violence that other Young German films invite. By the same token, the film resists the convenience of a neatly packaged "social message" that would misleadingly explain away the problem of rape by attributing it to a particular social class or psychopathology.

"Eine gigantische Vergewaltigung" (A Gigantic Rape): Alice's "Secondary Victimization"

In "*No Lies*: Direct Cinema as Rape," Vivian Sobchack points out that rape in the cinema has tended to focus on the sexual and physical nature of the act, on rape as "an *activity*."[34] From D. W. Griffith's early American classic *The Birth of a Nation* (1915) to Lamont Johnson's 1976 rape-revenge thriller *Lipstick*, this action- and movement-centered treatment of rape "has much to do with the supposed 'nature' of the film medium."[35] Sobchack elaborates:

---

33 Hans Joachim Schneider, "Das Verbrechensopfer im Sozialprozess: Fortschritte der Viktimologie-Forschung," *JuristenZeitung* 32, no. 19 (October 7, 1977): 632. In 1977, West German criminologist Schneider noted that legal reforms and social programs supporting victims of violence were developing more slowly in West Germany than in other parts of the world, such as the United States, Poland, and Japan (632). In 1976, the West German government finally put a law into effect allowing victims of violence to seek compensation, years after Austria had passed a similar law (621). The problem of revictimization, Schneider stressed, was hardly addressed in West Germany: "Viktimologisch geschulte Psychologen und Psychiater müssten die psychischen und sozialen Schäden mit den Verbrechensopfern und ihren Angehörigen durcharbeiten. In dieser Hinsicht geschieht in der Bundesrepublik Deutschland nicht nur fast nichts. Durch verfehlte Reaktionen im sozialen Nahraum des Opfers und durch die formellen Instanzen der Sozialkontrolle, die Polizei und Gerichte, werden die Schäden vielmehr noch verschärft" (628; Psychologists and psychiatrists trained in victimology would have to work through the psychological and social damage with the victims and those close to them. In this respect nothing is happening in the FRG, and not only that. Rather, the damage is exacerbated by misguided responses in the victim's social circle and by the formal instances of social control: the police and the court).

34 Sobchack, "*No Lies*: Direct Cinema as Rape," 14 (emphasis in original).

35 Sobchack, "*No Lies*," 14.

272 ♦ LISA HAEGELE

The movies have always had an affinity for that which moves; and, all moral and social judgments aside, one has to admit that scenes of sexual and physical assault move. They are a veritable frenzy of activity. Thus, on a visual level alone, it is nearly impossible for even their brief presence in a movie not to inform and often overshadow the entire film, and particularly the relatively more quiescent and inert scenes of emotional and physical turmoil which, though they may occupy more screen time, make much less mark on one's visual memory.[36]

By emphasizing the physical and frenzied nature of sexual assault, cinematic rape scenes, she argues, inevitably "overpower and delimit the film's broader definition of rape."[37] At the same time, they exempt audiences from acting morally because they are safely contained within the structure of narrative cinema, where they take the "shape of a *fait accompli* in which we cannot possibly intervene."[38] Embedded in films with a predestined beginning, middle, and end, the rape has already occurred before it appears on-screen, thus relieving us of our moral responsibility to act. In these instances, rape is passing "object rather than subject."[39]

The rape sequence in *Mädchen mit Gewalt* is no different than the frenzied scenes that Sobchack critiques. When Werner finally catches up to Alice after her failed attempt to escape, he pins her down in a long shot and begins to tear off her clothes. The camera slowly tracks forward, and a series of countershots show Mike in his car, smiling deviously, as he quickly drives toward them from the other side of the quarry. In a dizzying sequence, Alice struggles to push Werner off her in several quick handheld close-up and extreme close-up shots at various high, low, and oblique angles. Accompanied only by the sounds of the car's engine, Werner's laughter, and Alice's hits and cries, Werner flips Alice over on top of him, holds her thighs down with his forearms, and proceeds to rape her in the glaring light of Mike's high beams. After slapping Werner's face to no effect, Alice finally slumps over, exhausted. The sequence ends with a point-of-view shot from Alice's perspective of the high beams in close-up, followed by a match cut to a lamp in the quarry the next morning.

While the rapid editing and hectic, disorienting movements in the rape sequence are typical of the scenes that Sobchack describes, the second half of the film overshadows the on-screen physical attack in its visual and emotional intensity. In a sequence that lasts over ten minutes—Fritz's favorite to film, as he mentions in the DVD audio commentary—Mike proceeds to explain to Alice in excruciating detail the revictimization she will have to endure once she files a police report

---

36 Sobchack, "*No Lies*," 14.
37 Sobchack, "*No Lies*," 15.
38 Sobchack, "*No Lies*," 14.
39 Sobchack, "*No Lies*," 14.

against him and Werner. When Alice threatens to press charges against them, Mike defuses her threat by offering to "help" her, explaining in a condescending, matter-of-fact tone how she should proceed. He asserts his dominance by demeaning her intellectually and forcing her to speak. Unlike Werner, who becomes uneasy when Alice calmly insists that her father will kill them, Mike, unmoved, begins to assault her by shaming her: "Vergiss es. Steck ihm die Geschichte, dann weißt du, was er von dir hält" (Forget it. Tell him, then you'll know what he thinks of you). Once she tells him the name of her home street, he interrupts her to give her the police district number where she will have to file her report. He asks her to imagine herself in front of the police and to state her intention, to which she reluctantly responds, "Ich will . . . eine Anzeige machen" (I want . . . to make a complaint). Again, he interrupts: "*Erstatten*. Man *erstattet* eine Anzeige. Das musst du dir merken. Ohne die Vorschriften zu beachten, kommt man bei der Polizei nicht durch" (*File*. One *files* a complaint. You'll have to remember that. If you don't follow the rules, you won't get anywhere with the police [my emphasis]). Mike uses the "Amtssprache" (official language)—with which she is "of course not yet familiar"—to belittle her and hijack her experience into a discourse that is not her own, explaining, for example, the gross euphemisms and initialisms "GT" for "Geschlechtsteil" (genitals) and "HWG" for "häufig wechselnder Geschlechtsverkehr" (promiscuous behavior). In his most pernicious coercion, Mike forces Alice to say that she was raped, an admission that she is not yet ready to make. The camera zooms in slowly to a close-up of him as he presses her: "Sag es. Man hat mich vergewaltigt. Man hat mich vergewaltigt, sag's!" (Say it. Someone raped me. Someone raped me, say it!). By dictating the terms through which she comes to admit, "Man . . . man hat mich . . . vergewaltigt" (Someone . . . someone . . . raped me), Mike takes over her voice and lays claim to her deeply personal experience, robbing her of her autonomy even further. Stripped of her authority over her experience, Alice is rendered powerless and deprived of the language that could help her come to terms with her experience, to rename it, to control the narrative in order to move past it.

Mike continues to assault Alice by describing in explicit detail the police questioning and medical procedure to which she will be subject when she files her report. While Alice sits hunched over on a scrapped tire, the camera follows Mike around in medium- to medium-close-up tracking shots taken at various angles, emphasizing his dominance and agency. In a menacingly ironic tone, he mentions that the officers in her police district are "schon in Ordnung" (pretty okay). When she arrives at the station, he notes, the officers will stare at her as they wait for her to state her intention. Mike explains that Police Chief Müller will then call her into his room for questioning, adding, "Ich weiß zwar nicht, ob du mit ihm allein sein willst" (But I don't know if you want to be alone with him) and "Ihn interessiert nämlich alles, aus dienstlichen Gründen, natürlich" (He's interested in everything, for official purposes, of course). Posing as the police chief, he questions her: "Wie ist es passiert? Wer hat Ihre Beine gespreizt? Wo war Ihr Schlüpfer? Wurden dabei Ihre Schamlippen verletzt?" (How did it happen? Who spread your legs? Where were your panties? Were your vaginal lips injured?). After Alice bursts out, "Das ist nicht wahr!" (That's not true!), Mike continues, "Es macht ihnen Spaß, ein hübsches Mädchen nach den intimsten Dingen zu fragen. Wie lange hat er Sie vergewaltigt? Ist es zu einem Samenerguss gekommen? Ein-, zwei-, dreimal? Haben Sie sich gewehrt? Ach so, nur anfangs haben Sie sich gewehrt, danach hat's Ihnen gefallen" (They enjoy asking a pretty young girl the most intimate things. How long did he rape you? Did he ejaculate? Once, twice, three times? Did you defend yourself? Oh, just in the beginning you defended yourself. After that you liked it). Mike proceeds to question her about the size of Werner's penis, whether the insertion hurt, and in what position the penetration occurred before elaborating ad nauseam on how the medical staff will handle her:

> Am liebsten würden sie dich auf den Tisch legen, dich ausziehen und untersuchen, einer nach dem anderen. Aber bedauerlicherweise dürfen sie das nicht, denn dafür ist der Polizeiarzt da. Dann bringt man dich hin und du wirst sehr intensiv untersucht, ob du Verletzungen hast, der Zustand der Vagina, sind Samenspuren drin. Du wirst vermessen, auf Geschlechtskrankheiten untersucht. Das Gericht muss sich später ein sehr genaues Bild machen können.

> [They'd rather put you on the table, undress you and examine you, one after the other. But unfortunately, they're not allowed to do that—that's what the medical examiner is for. They'll take you there and you'll be examined very intensively, whether you have injuries, the condition of the vagina, are there traces of sperm. You'll get measured, tested for sexually transmitted disease. The court will have to have a really precise picture later.]

After prompting Alice to imagine the humiliating and invasive procedure, Mike grabs her arm and pulls her up to confront Werner in the "Gegenüberstellung," the suspect lineup. He commands her to look directly into Werner's face and tell him what he did. When she hesitates, Mike threatens her in the guise of reassurance: "Die Polizei ist ja dabei, es kann dir nichts passieren" (The police are there, nothing can happen to you). Playing along, Werner defends himself by insisting that Alice wanted to have sex with him and that she intentionally aroused both of them. As Alice begins to look increasingly defeated, Mike again reassures her in a threatening way, reclaiming his power over her by building her trust: "Wir sind nicht auf der Polizei, da brauchst du keine Angst zu haben. Wir sind unter uns!" (We're not at the police station, no need to be afraid. It's just us!)

Mike continues to intimidate and demean Alice until she breaks down at the end of the sequence. In the last stage of his imaginary scenario, Mike shames Alice for being sexually active, a fact he says will ultimately convince the jury of Werner's innocence. If the jury finds out that she is "eine Person mit HWG" (a person with a history of promiscuous behavior), then she will lose her credibility as witness. After all, he asks, "Was ist denn das für ein Mädchen, das mit wildfremden Männern in ein Auto steigt? Denk mal drüber nach. Da kann dir auch der Staatsanwalt nicht mehr helfen" (What kind of girl gets into a car with complete strangers? Think about it. Even the prosecutor can't help you there). He tells her to imagine Werner as the prosecutor and that she is on the witness stand facing a silent and sexually aroused audience. Speaking for Werner as prosecutor, Mike addresses Alice in an extreme low-angle shot and continues:

> Kann es nicht auch so gewesen sein, dass Sie es waren, die [die Angeklagten] erst dazu animiert hat? Sind die Angeklagten durch Ihr Nacktbaden in dem See zu geschlechtlichen Einlassungen nicht direkt provoziert worden? Wie erklären Sie sich den Umstand, dass Ihre Vagina trotz vorgeblich brutalem Geschlechtsverkehr nicht verletzt worden ist? Geht daraus nicht hervor, dass Sie geholfen haben? Ja, den Verkehr *wollten*?

> [Can it also be the case that you aroused the defendants first? Were the defendants not directly provoked sexually by your bathing nude in the lake? How do you explain the fact that your vagina is uninjured despite the allegedly brutal sexual intercourse? Does that not show that you helped? That you, in fact, *wanted* it? (My emphasis)]

In a zoom-in to a close-up shot, Mike finally becomes emotional, raising his voice and speaking with increasing tempo before concluding angrily: "Das ist nämlich nicht der Staatsanwalt. Das ist Werner, der dich vergewaltigt hat. Schau ihn dir an, dieses Vieh. Aber glaub ja nicht, dass der Staatsanwalt viel besser ist. Er wird dich genauso hetzen wie die Richter, die Zeugen der Verteidigung, der Verteidiger, die Presse, wir, dein Vater, das ist doch eine gigantische Vergewaltigung!" (But that's not the prosecutor, that's Werner, who raped you. Look at him, the pig. But don't think that the prosecutor is much better. He's after you just like the judges, the defense witnesses, the defense lawyer, the press, us, your father. Now that is one gigantic rape!). At that point, Alice, visibly stunned, breaks down and begs them not to take her to the police, promising to do anything they want in return.

Unlike the more conventional cinematic treatments of rape that emphasize the moment of the physical and sexual attack, the definition of rape in *Mädchen mit Gewalt* extends beyond the physical act to include the discrimination, rejection, and abuse that victims of rape experience in the justice system and in personal relationships when they come forward. Taking place in the strikingly bright light of day, the sequence after the physical rape demonstrates that the act of violence is not contained and concealed in the dark of the previous night but, rather, continues into broad daylight; that is, in the full transparency of the law and everyday social life in the patriarchy. The excessive duration of the sequence and its vivid mise-en-scène create a strong affective charge that surpasses that of the previous sequence. While the campfire still blazes behind Alice, shots of Mike against the monochrome blue-gray sky and the horizon of the quarry wall enhance his overbearing and seemingly unescapable presence (fig. 11.1). Rather than create visual depth, the long shots in the film are dominated by horizontal lines and a minimalist color palette of sea greens and browns that lend a flatness to the images. By creating tension between depth and flatness, these images generate an agoraphobic affect. This affect is heightened by the glaring afternoon sun that permeates the setting and by the rusty, burnt scraps of wood and metal littered throughout the quarry. In these vast, seemingly endless spaces, we are forced to endure the violence with Alice for the remainder of the film without relief.

While the "secondary rape" sequence does not feature dramatic, quick cuts like the earlier rape sequence, the camerawork brings to striking visualization the psychological violence inflicted upon Alice. Right before Mike grabs Alice by the arm to bring her to Werner, he walks directly toward the camera, followed by a cut to a close-up of his buttocks as he walks away. By creating the impression that Mike walks straight *through* the camera, the shot sequence emphasizes his penetrative violence that transcends physical boundaries, omnipresent and far-reaching. In one of the most memorable shots of the sequence, the camera zooms in to an extreme close-up of Alice's eye while Mike interrogates her from off-screen about the specifics of the act of penetration and whether it hurt. In contrast to the scene in which Alice looks directly into Mike's headlights after Werner rapes her, which causes her pupils to contract, the gradual zoom in to her eye during Mike's questioning demonstrates the pervasiveness and long-lasting imprint of her revictimization. The shock she experiences during and shortly after the rape as (an albeit temporary) form of psychological protection against Werner's forced penetration—illustrated by the narrowing of her pupils as a protective autonomic reflex against the bright, piercing headlights—cedes to the less obvious but deeply invasive violence of shame, guilt, and disgust that the law and patriarchal society force upon her and that she internalizes after the attack. The violence of Alice's revictimization registers affectively with the viewer through the zoom-in, pulling us uncomfortably close to Alice to meet her eye to eye as Mike continues to humiliate her and embarrass us with his graphically explicit interrogation (fig. 11.2).

Figure 11.1. Dawn breaks over the desolate quarry in *Mädchen mit Gewalt*, dir. Roger Fritz, 1969, 94 min., Roger Fritz Filmproduktion. DVD Screenshot: Media Target Distribution GmbH, 2016.

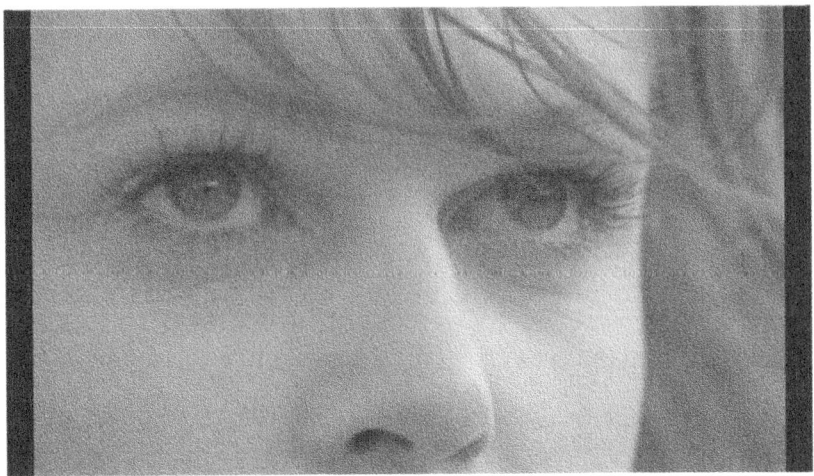

Figure 11.2. The camera zooms in to an extreme close-up of Alice as Mike threatens her in *Mädchen mit Gewalt*, dir. Roger Fritz, 1969, 94 min., Roger Fritz Filmproduktion. DVD Screenshot: Media Target Distribution GmbH, 2016.

Alice's rape continues even at the end of the film when she refuses to admit to the police that Mike and Werner assaulted her. Silenced by shame and fear, she maintains that Mike and Werner did not hurt her and insists on riding back home with them. After one of the officers looks at her from top to bottom and observes, "Man sieht doch, dass Ihnen etwas geschehen ist. Ihr Kleid zum Beispiel" (You can see that something happened to you. Your dress, for example), Alice seems to be reminded of Mike's earlier warning that she might not want to be alone with the police, yet another pair of "complete strangers" offering her a ride. After Mike pays the police a five-mark fine for "unbefugten Feuermachens auf Privatgelände" (unauthorized burning on private property), the camera cuts to a close-up of him smiling before following his gaze downward to the ticket in his hands. Reduced to a grossly incommensurate offense of, in another euphemistic turn of phrase, "trespassing" on "private property," the crime of sexual assault, the ending suggests, can be paid off for a mere five marks, as though it were only a small misdemeanor. Under the aegis of the law, in other words, Alice can be purchased for a negligible fee. Like the legal euphemisms that Mike explained to Alice earlier, the analogy between rape and "trespassing" sublimates sexual violence into a palatable discourse that not only hides that violence but perpetuates it in the process. As Alice rides off pressed between her two assaulters, the film shows that she will remain subject to their psychological violence and abuse even beyond the space of the quarry. Rape in this film is hardly a fait accompli. Rather, it is an ongoing act of violence that continues into the victim's everyday life long after the physical attack.

Because the police fail to incriminate Mike and Werner, some critics drew attention to what they viewed as the film's antipolice stance: "Zugleich ist dies ein Film gegen die Polizei. Denn als die schließlich mehr aus Zufall auftaucht—erscheint sie zwar sehr gutwillig, aber in erster Linie doch als eine Versammlung von 'Dämlacks'" (At the same time, this is a film against the police. For when they finally show up mostly out of coincidence, they appear to be well-meaning, but above all as a gathering of idiots).[40] The assessment that the police officers are simply inadequate and fail to bring Alice's perpetrators to justice ignores the film's larger critique of the very system that the officers represent; namely, as one that punishes, rather than protects, victims of sexual assault. Overlooking the film's emphasis on Alice's "secondary rape" by the law, the focus on the incompetence of individual officers suggests that the law *can* restore justice to the victim when practiced properly by those who represent it. One critic for *Der Spiegel* even questioned whether guilt, shame, and silencing really exist in the legal system: "Das geschändete Mädchen, soll das Publikum glauben, geht nicht zur Polizei, nur weil die 'Bullen' fragen könnten, 'Wie lang war sein GT?'" (The audience is supposed to believe that the defiled girl won't go to the police simply because the "pigs" could ask, "How long was his penis?").[41] Clearly, *Mädchen mit Gewalt*

---

40 Klaus U. Reinke, "Böser Spaß an der Gewalt: 'Mädchen mit Gewalt,' der zweite Spielfilm von Roger Fritz," *Handelsblatt*, March 2, 1970.

41 "Scharfe Linse," *Der Spiegel*, February 23, 1970, 168, https://www.spiegel.de/spiegel/print/d-45202892.html.

baffled critics who could not imagine that the violence exacted upon Alice after the rape—if they acknowledged it at all—could be more traumatic or harmful than the physical act itself. These reviews bring into relief the film's feminist charge at a time when sexual assault victims were only beginning to be heard as subjects.

By the end of the film, Alice finds neither justice nor revenge. Unlike the better-known films in the 1970s that depict rape, *Mädchen mit Gewalt* refuses to offer viewers the satisfaction of a more popular rape-revenge story. Moments before the police arrive, Mike holds a knife to Werner, ties him up to a concrete mixer, and threatens to castrate him. When Werner cries out for Alice to help him, Mike suggests that they let her decide and calls her over. Alice walks toward them and stops in the center of the frame in a medium wide shot, evoking the image of the cowboy in Western shoot-out scenes. Then she calmly states, "Macht, was ihr wollt" (Do what you want). In a long shot, Mike meets Alice halfway and drops the knife in front of her. She picks up the knife and slowly approaches Werner while Mike walks off into the distance. With a look of both exhaustion and resolve, Alice walks toward the camera and stops in close-up range. When Werner reacts, "Los! Schneid mich endlich ab!" (Come on! Cut me free!), she looks straight into Werner's eyes and gives the slightest smirk, her eyes gleaming from behind the shadow on her face as though she is eager for revenge (fig. 11.3). Instead of cutting off Werner's penis, however, Alice proceeds to cut the rope and frees him. Werner, seemingly unsurprised, stumbles off with a wide grin. On one level, by showing empathy with her rapist-kidnapper, Alice appears

Figure 11.3. Alice contemplates revenge in *Mädchen mit Gewalt*, dir. Roger Fritz, 1969, 94 min., Roger Fritz Filmproduktion. DVD Screenshot: Media Target Distribution GmbH, 2016.

to have "Stockholm syndrome"; on another level, however, by releasing instead of castrating Werner, she refuses to participate in and act as a conduit for the men's continued violence. Thwarting viewer expectations and desires for violent retribution, Alice refuses to act as aggressor in a simple role reversal that, by keeping the perpetrator-victim dichotomy intact, would serve more to preserve than fundamentally unsettle male dominance.

More importantly, by denying viewers the pleasure of retaliation against Alice's rapists, the film avoids producing a fantasy in the vein of what Lauren Berlant has coined "cruel optimism."[42] Berlant defines the concept as a relation "that exists when something you desire is actually an obstacle to your flourishing. These kinds of optimistic relation . . . become cruel when the object that draws your attachment actively impedes the aim that brought you to it initially."[43] She continues,

> [The] affective structure of an optimistic attachment involves a sustaining inclination to return to the scene of fantasy that enables you to expect that this time, nearness to this thing will help you or a world to become different in just the right way. But, again, optimism is cruel when the object/scene that ignites a sense of possibility actually makes it impossible to attain the expansive transformation for which a person or a people risks striving; and, doubly, it is cruel insofar as the very pleasures of being inside a relation have become sustaining regardless of the content of the relation, such that a person or a world finds itself bound to a situation of profound threat that is, at the same time, profoundly confirming.[44]

Rape-revenge films are cruelly optimistic because they project violent, liberating fantasies of female victim-turned-avenger that, by producing pleasurable, empowering affects, distract and contain feminist motivations to bring about real change. Rape-revenge stories, in other words, work to ensure that male violence and oppression remain undisturbed by offering feminist fantasies of retribution that create a sense of release, gratification, and temporary fulfilment. By advocating female liberation through violent, often murderous, revenge, the films ensure that that liberation remains an impossibility, relegated to the realm of mere fantasy, whose power rests on its promise and attraction. Through Alice's refusal to exact brutal revenge on Werner, *Mädchen mit Gewalt* resists the cruel optimism of rape-revenge fantasies, opting instead to emphasize the enduring, deeply complex, and not-so-easily solvable struggles that victims of sexual

42 Lauren Berlant, *Cruel Optimism* (Durham, NC: Duke University Press, 2011), 1.
43 Berlant, *Cruel Optimism*, 1.
44 Berlant, *Cruel Optimism*, 2.

assault have to face in the real world. By disappointing viewers who have come to expect and yearn for a violent act of retaliation, the film draws attention to our very attachment to those empowering, vivid fantasies of vigilante justice that suspend action by holding out hope.

Conclusion: Alice, Helga, and #MeToo

Rape in Roger Fritz's *Mädchen mit Gewalt* is not a singular, self-contained event that is quickly forgotten or resolved. By presenting rape as subject rather than object, the film offers a definition of sexual assault that resists easy integration into grand narratives about national politics, aesthetics, and history that were the foundation for Young German film criticism. Viewed in the era of #MeToo, the film becomes especially relevant: not only does it refuse to provide a quick and titillating few "minutes of action"[45] that are quickly forgotten—to recall the horrendous comment made by the father of convicted rapist Brock Turner to downplay the seriousness of his son's crime—but it also encourages us to restitute films that have been excluded from national cinema histories for presenting sexual violence in ways that do not conform to critics' often grossly hypocritical standards. Reduced to and written off as mere sensationalism for failing to meet those standards, *Mädchen mit Gewalt* and similar films are blocked from entering into critical dialogue and become limited in their distribution and accessibility, if they are made accessible at all. *Mädchen mit Gewalt* draws attention to the sexism in film criticism as a kind of "secondary victimization," abducting, overwriting, and effacing on-screen victims of sexual violence so that they remain unseen and unheard.

If we approach feminist film criticism as, to return to Vicki Callahan, a "deep-time project" and "discovery process with . . . multiple points of entry,"[46] then we can bring stories like that of Alice into visibility. Alice's story emerges once we look past the often-unquestioned authority of the male author/director, male critics, and gatekeepers of the canon. The rediscovery of Alice leads us, in turn, to the forgotten story of Helga Anders, the actress who plays her, who had spoken out about her treatment by the sexist film industry before she died of heart failure at the age of thirty-eight.[47] Anders's career has been clouded over by her early

---

45 Michael E. Miller, "'A Steep Price to Pay for 20 Minutes of Action: Dad Defends Stanford Sex Offender," *Washington Post*, June 6, 2016, https://www.washingtonpost.com/news/morning-mix/wp/2016/06/06/a-steep-price-to-pay-for-20-minutes-of-action-dad-defends-stanford-sex-offender/.

46 Callahan, *Reclaiming the Archive*, 4.

47 Anders commented shortly before her death, "Ich bin eine Frau über dreißig, aber für meine Produzenten immer noch ein 18jähriger Brigitte-Bardot-

death, described in her obituary in *Der Spiegel* as the inevitable outcome of her alcohol and drug addiction and purportedly reckless, "hysterical" behavior: "Zuletzt machte sie mehr mit Nervenzusammenbrüchen, Randale [*sic*] und Autokarambolagen als mit Schauspielerei von sich reden. Alkohol und Tabletten und wohl auch ihre Umgebung ruinierten die einstige Lolita des deutschen Films" (Toward the end she drew more conversation around her nervous breakdowns, rampages, and car wrecks than her acting. Alcohol, pills, and probably also her environment ruined the former Lolita of German cinema).[48] The author of the obituary reduced Anders's acting career to a series of roles as the scantily clad sex object: "In rund 150 Fernseh- und Filmrollen spielte sie mal mehr, mal weniger bekleidet die süße Schöne. Sie . . . spielte in Filmen wie 'Mädchen mit Gewalt,' deren emanzipatorischer Anspruch in der Frage gipfelte: 'Wollen Sie von mir gebumst werden?'" (In about 150 television and film roles she played the sometimes more, sometimes less clothed sweet beauty. She played in films, for example, "Mädchen mit Gewalt," whose emancipatory pretense peaked in the question: "Do you want to be screwed by me?")[49]

This project, then, is as much about recovering Alice's story of sexual assault and revictimization in a neglected film as it is about rediscovering, reclaiming, and reattributing critical value to the work of an actress who struggled to gain respect and recognition in a sexist industry. Anders's performance as Alice resonates in the contemporary era of #MeToo, breaking out of and past the sexist dismissals that her work garnered in her lifetime. Leading us from one moment of rediscovery to the next, *Mädchen mit Gewalt* demonstrates how an approach to feminist film history as a "deep-time," decentered, and multiangled process of discovery can expose new voices and possibilities for feminism in places one might least expect.

Verschnitt mit Schmollmund. Das kann nicht gutgehen" (I'm a woman over thirty, but for my producers I'm still an eighteen-year-old Brigitte Bardot imitation with a pout. That can't go well). "Gestorben: Helga Anders," *Der Spiegel*, April 7, 1986, 278, https://www.spiegel.de/spiegel/print/d-13517369.html.

48 "Gestorben: Helga Anders," 278.
49 "Gestorben: Helga Anders," 278.

12: Elfriede Jelinek and Ingeborg Bachmann: Transformations of the Capitalist Patriarchy and Narrating Sexual Violence in the Twentieth Century

Aylin Bademsoy

THE BLOODY HEAD OF A RAPIST lying in the center of a little town in Turkey made headlines in Turkish media in 2013.[1] This was not the first and certainly not the last time a woman sought to restore justice on her own after the institutional apparatus of the patriarchal state had failed her. *Clara S.: Eine musikalische Tragödie* (1981; *Clara S. [A Musical Tragedy]*, 2001), a play written by Elfriede Jelinek, concludes with a similar scenario: the long-neglected artist Clara S., an explicit reference to the pianist Clara Schumann, ends up talking to the head of her freshly strangled husband, Robert Schumann. In Ingeborg Bachmann's *Malina* (1971), the female narrator, instead of fighting back, disappears into the wall that previously marked the border of her entrapment. Bachmann's and Jelinek's respective works establish a relationship to social history that can be read as reflections of the (diverging) modes of oppression of the "feminine," on the one hand, and as testimonies of ideological transformations within the capitalist patriarchal order, on the other. Utopic scenarios—for example, in Bachmann's *Malina*—end up demonstrating the inevitability of immanence as attempts to entirely transcend the trajectories of history necessarily fail.

Whereas the "modern" gender dichotomy and the entrapment of the "female" in the private sphere is central to Bachmann's novel, in Jelinek's work women's inclusion in the sphere of production poses a new challenge to emancipation: labor, which was expected to be a step

1   "Tecavüzcüsünün kafasını kesip köy meydanına atmıştı! Yargıtay'dan flaş karar" (She cut off her rapist's head and threw it in the village square! Flash decision from the Supreme Court). Hürriyet.com.tr, September 21, 2017, https://www.hurriyet.com.tr/gundem/tecavuzcusunun-kafasini-kesip-koy-meydanina-atmisti-yargitaydan-flas-karar-40586057.

toward liberation, is unveiled as yet another mutation of capitalist patriarchy. In this essay, I argue that differences in the literary responses to patriarchal violence can be theorized in line with transformations within capitalist production in the twentieth century, from Fordist production to post-Fordism[2] and from modernity to postmodernity, as scholars in the humanities have argued. Whether the latter transition took place is doubtful; the works examined here reflect an increase of cynicism or cultural pessimism, an accusation frequently leveled at Theodor W. Adorno. In order to show that the works of Bachmann and Jelinek speak to the changing conditions of production and to the attendant ideological shifts, I will examine each in relation to their respective historical moments and changing modes in the oppression of the "feminine" in capitalist economies, turning first to Bachmann, with an emphasis on her novel *Malina*, and thereafter to Jelinek's play *Clara S.*

As a historical framework, an epoch cannot be defined solely on the basis of its "posthumousness," and it stands to reason that the notion of "postmodernity" will either prove to be insufficient owing to the potential eternality implicit in the term itself, or renamed and rethought in the future, perhaps at the dawn of a postfascist, postnational, and postcapitalist era. Despite globalization, the synchronicity of epochs cannot be assumed. And yet, numerous "real" and "fictional" examples from across the globe, including the recent surge of the #MeToo movement in the centers of capitalist patriarchies, show that the fight against sexual harassment and assault is a common struggle, even if women worldwide are separated by large socioeconomic gaps. Although it manifests in different forms over diverging geographies, the problem of sexual violence cannot be separated from the root issue of oppression, exploitation, and devaluation of the "feminine" in capitalist centers and outposts alike. Beginning with what some may label "postmodernity," oppression appears in a new guise in the "centers," now touting the twofold exploitation as "emancipation."

Marxist critic Roswitha Scholz's theory of value dissociation offers an important perspective for understanding the relation between the notions of *value* and the *feminine* within capitalist patriarchies against a background of transforming material and ideological conditions during the twentieth and early twenty-first centuries. Following Carol Hagemann-White, Scholz argues that the "modern system of gender/sex dualism" (*Zweigeschlechtlichkeit*) took shape only in the eighteenth century and that

---

2   According to Roswitha Scholz, post-Fordist "turbo-capitalism" brought about a flexibility in terms of identities and gender, but it did not free women from being primarily responsible for reproductive work. Roswitha Scholz, *Das Geschlecht des Kapitalismus, Feministische Theorien und die postmoderne Metamorphose des Patriarchats* (Bad Honnef: Horlemann, 2000), 46.

the changes it has since undergone have been drastic;[3] with the dawning of "postmodernity," it seemed that traditional gender roles were about to be overcome, but the much-touted equality through inclusion in the job market was not realized. Although (middle-class) women were quasi-liberated from the domestic sphere, the subordination of the feminine persisted in the public sphere. The beleaguered position of women is mirrored in Bachmann's and Jelinek's texts. In Bachmann's novel *Malina*, the struggle against the allegorical "fatherland" ends with the murder of the female author and narrator, while Jelinek's play concludes with the murder of the figure who embodies the patriarchal order before the complicit protagonist, Clara, dies as well. I argue that both works represent literary responses to violence targeting women or the feminine in general insofar as it is dissociated from a positive notion of value. Yet whereas Bachmann's work was often read as one where female victimhood manifests itself, Jelinek clearly opposes the victim myth.

The theory of value dissociation rests on earlier Marxist-feminist theories asserting that reproductive (domestic) work remains unpaid because it is not quantifiable in terms of time/hours. Domestic work follows a different time-logic, even though it is just as constitutive for the functioning of capitalism as "abstract," paid labor.[4] The dialectic relationship between value and its flip side, nonvalue, is central for Scholz's theory. Unlike her predecessors, Scholz embeds the cultural-symbolic and sociopsychological dimensions into the theorization of value, without reverting to personifications of capital that risk reproducing anti-Semitic ressentiments or universalizing the oppression of women as a transhistorical phenomenon.[5] As postmodernity did not bring about the desired end of oppression based on sex or gender, it has become clear that simply providing

---

3   In earlier centuries, "women" were viewed as different versions of "men." Scholz, *Geschlecht des Kapitalismus*, 38. Following Regina Becker-Schmidt's thesis, Scholz argues that the complementary emergence of housework and abstract labor in accordance with instrumental reason is a "modern" phenomenon (51). The term "modern" does not seek to reject the prehistory of patriarchy but to highlight its specific form within capitalist modes of production (39). Thus, both "masculinity" and "femininity" are conceived as dynamic, as the dualism of abstract labor and reproductive work brought about an unprecedented transformation of gender/sex relations (52).

4   Scholz, *Geschlecht des Kapitalismus*, 43. Although Scholz does not agree with Elisabeth Beck-Gernsheim and Ilona Ostner in every respect, the notion of a "sociopsychological" dimension of capitalist divisions of labor owes much to their 1978 study "Frauen verändern—Berufe nicht? Ein theoretischer Ansatz zum Problem von Frau und Beruf," *Soziale Welt* 3 (1978): 257–87. Frigga Haug's and Regina Becker-Schmidt's theories similarly impacted Scholz's work, most of which was published in the Marxist value-critique journal *Exit*.

5   Scholz, *Geschlecht des Kapitalismus*, 51.

remuneration for women's labor—often still not equal to men's pay—is a partial remedy at best. While "reproductive" work remains unpaid, pleading for its remuneration along with inclusion in the job market would only curtail dissent rather than bring about radical change. Instead, we need a radical transformation, if not an abolition, of the separation of the spheres of production and consumption.

In this essay, I examine Ingeborg Bachmann's and Elfriede Jelinek's varying takes on the concept of value and on women's role in a society founded on this concept, as well as their attempts to revolt against it by literary means. While doing so, I trace discrepancies back to historical conditions[6] that gave rise to diverging levels of agency and shifts in the conceptualization of utopic societies. In both Bachmann's and Jelinek's writings, the notion of value is entangled with the violent oppression of women by capitalist patriarchies, although in fundamentally different ways. In Bachmann's *Malina*, value is not only inscribed within the "classical" (or, perhaps, modern) division of space and labor but is particularly important for her concept of utopia, which, albeit only on a superficial level, challenges the legitimacy of private property and the trajectory of technological development under capitalist production.[7] Indeed, Bachmann's narrator disappears into a crack in the wall at the end of the novel. Her second-chapter dream sequence, however, titled "The Third Man" after the eponymous British film noir set in postwar Vienna, begins with a narrator who is helpless against her father's violent attacks but ends with her attempts to rise against him: she throws objects that had previously targeted her back at her father. Jelinek, in turn, ironically unveils the proximity of her (female) figures to the commodity form. Unlike lucrative investments, however, women "lose" value; for example, through aging. In *Clara S.*, sexual exploitation and artistic repression of female figures

---

6   In *The Cemetery of the Murdered Daughters* (Amherst: University of Massachusetts Pressbooks, 2006), Sara Lennox suggests that history conditioned not only Bachmann's work but also the various readings and interpretations of it throughout the 1970s, '80s, and '90s. This also applies to my reading of Bachmann and Jelinek.

7   In her essay "Tagebuch: Beitrag zur Probenummer einer internationalen Zeitschrift," Bachmann critiques the "market" that also subsumes cultural "goods"—*Kulturgüter*. Ingeborg Bachmann, *Die Wahrheit ist dem Menschen zumutbar* (Munich: Piper, 1981), 68. She does not discuss market capitalism in depth, however, and is likely influenced by the Frankfurt School, perhaps by Theodor W. Adorno's essay on the culture industry in *Dialektik der Aufklärung* (1944; *Dialectic of Enlightenment*, 1972) or, as Sigrid Weigel argues, by Walter Benjamin. See Weigel, "Öffentlichkeit und Verborgenheit: Zur literaturpolitischen und persönlichen Konstellation von Ingeborg Bachmanns Frankfurter Poetikvorlesung," in *Ingeborg Bachmann und Paul Celan: Historisch-poetische Korrelationen*, ed. Georg Wimmler (Berlin: De Gruyter, 2014), 12.

go hand in hand, while fascism and delirium culminate in mariticide—the murder of her husband—and subsequently the mysterious death of Clara herself. While the protagonist here is based on a nineteenth-century pianist, it is clear that the threat of exploitation she is confronted with is not a matter of the past but, rather, remains an instrument of oppression even now. It is also no coincidence that (the real) Clara Schumann's lifetime anachronistically intersects with the industrial revolution in Germany. The nineteenth-century industrial revolution and the rise of fascism in the twentieth century are two key factors building the foundation for the contemporary exploitation of the female body—its productivity as well as its reproductivity.

Ingeborg Bachmann's works have often been discussed under the rubric "victimhood" rather than resistance or revenge; even the women in the short story "Among Murderers and Madmen" (1961), who kill their husbands in their dreams, cry in regret after the murder. Bachmann's Undine in "Undine geht" ("Undine Goes," in the collection *Das drei-ßigste Jahr* [1961; *The Thirtieth Year*, 1964]) retreats from society, and the female narrator in *Malina* disappears into the wall; in both texts an allegorical figure of patriarchal violence, Hans or the unknown murderer, disposes of the woman in a rather subtle way. For Bachmann, society is a killing site, consisting of predominantly male murderers.[8]

Utopia, Nightmares and Modernity: Gender Relations in Ingeborg Bachmann's *Malina*

As Sara Lennox demonstrates in *The Cemetery of the Murdered Daughters* (2006), the vast majority of Bachmann research focuses either on questions of écriture féminine or relates issues of gender to Nazism and its postwar trajectories in Austrian literature. One of the most prominent poets of postwar Austria, Ingeborg Bachmann responded early on to Theodor W. Adorno's dictum on lyric poetry after Auschwitz.[9] Despite

---

8   Bettina Bannasch's *Von vorletzten Dingen: Schreiben nach "Malina"; Ingeborg Bachmanns "Simultan"-Erzählungen* (Würzburg: Königshausen & Neumann, 1997) focuses on Bachmann's neglected late work *Simultan* (1972; Simultaneous). Bannasch claims that the persecutors in Bachmann's works are male, such as Jordan in the novel fragment "Der Fall Franza" (1978; The Case of Franza), and do not represent individuals but rather the general public (40, 170). Also, *Malina* complicates and disrupts the gender dichotomy, especially since Bachmann considered Malina an alter ego of the "I." The work has repeatedly been discussed in regard to *Ich-Spaltung* or androgyny. Yet here too, it is the "male" part that murders; see Bannasch, *Von vorletzten Dingen*, 178.

9   Eva Revesz, "Poetry after Auschwitz: Tracing Trauma in Ingeborg Bachmann's Lyric Work," *Monatshefte* 99, no. 2 (2007): 194. In "Cultural Criticism

her success as a poet, *Anrufung des Großen Bären* (1956; Invocation of the Great Bear) was the last book of poems published in her lifetime. As Hans Höller's 2015 monograph, *Ingeborg Bachmann*, shows, recent Bachmann scholarship also centers on the ramifications of fascism in her oeuvre, which includes poems, radio plays, essays, libretti, translations, letters, novel fragments, and one finished novel, *Malina*. And yet there is no consensus about Bachmann's thinking on fascism or about her status as a "feminist writer." In both respects, she has been accused of self-victimization: on the basis of sex/gender and by relating the oppression of women to the persecution of Jews during the Nazi regime.[10] Various readings of Bachmann have defended *Malina* against such accusations. As Lennox points out, the focus on self-victimization can also be read as a critique of the zeitgeist, a critical metacommentary on postfascist women's self-victimization in response to accusations of complicity, or perhaps remorse. In her recent dissertation on performativity in *Malina*,[11] Caroline Jebens attempts to correct those interpretations that suggest that Bachmann's work parallels the victimhood of female figures and of Jews. Instead, Jebens interprets Bachmann's portrayal of victimization as a commentary on the kinship of fascism and patriarchy. Even so, one would do well to remember that women can be complicit in patriarchal structures (and Jews in racist systems of oppression).[12] After all, while the Nazi state was marked by radically patriarchal structures, it was supported and sustained by women as well as men. Furthermore, even though we might want to attribute the most extreme formation of patriarchy (so far) to fascism, it should not be forgotten that the patriarchy exists on a continuum. The "Woman = Mother = Housewife" equation has its origins in bourgeois ideology, which is perfectly mirrored in, for example, Johann Wolfgang von Goethe's works. Several recent studies confirm that Bachmann identified with the (Jewish) victims of the Nazi regime. According to Eva Revesz, Bachmann conflated her own "traumatic"

---

and Society," published in *Prisms* in 1967, Adorno refers to lyric poetry but also to literary and cultural criticism and ultimately to *Erkenntnis* (understanding) itself. In this respect, his famous pronouncement is a critical metacommentary on his own "work," which he nevertheless pursued further, albeit with an awareness of a potential relapse into barbarity, Theodor W. Adorno, *Prisms* (Cambridge, MA: MIT Press, 1997), 34.

10 Lennox, *Cemetery*, 2–3.

11 Caroline Jebens's dissertation on performativity in *Malina*, "Seltsame Worte, seltsamer Wahn? Erzählstimme und Geschlecht in Ingeborg Bachmanns *Malina* (1971)" (Art & Sciences Electronic Theses and Dissertations 1284, 2018) reaffirms Lennox's thesis about the historicity of literary scholarship, which is strongly influenced by Walter Benjamin's *Geschichtsphilosophie* (philosophy of history).

12 Jebens, "Seltsame Worte," 74.

separation from Max Frisch and her subsequent stays in hospitals with the "cruel and torturous experimentation by Nazi doctors," an attitude that Revesz characterizes as a "projective identification with the victims."[13] Sandra Boihmane's 2014 thesis elaborates multiple meanings and functions of the word "Malina" as an *Erinnerungsort* (place of remembrance), including the use of "Malina" as a code word for hiding places during World War II. Boihmane also argues that the rape discourse in the dream sequence reverts to the male perpetrator–female victim binary.[14] Alexandra Kurmann and Sigrid Weigel claim that Bachmann's empathy with Jewish victims of the Holocaust originated in her close relationship to some survivors and that the codeword "Malina" indicates a "shared secret language."[15]

These insights point to a concrete historical locatedness that is diametrically opposed to the text's allusions to the transhistorical oppression of women and everlasting war.[16] It would appear that historicity and universality coexist in Bachmann's text, and perhaps it was Bachmann's aspiration to mediate transcendence and immanence dialectically. Contrary to the claims of cultural pessimism in Bachmann's writings, Elfriede Jelinek interprets the vanishing into the wall as a rather optimistic ending: "At least there is a place where women can retreat to."[17] And as I noted earlier, there is an attempt to resist: at the end of the sequence of nightmares, the "dream-I" throws objects hurled at her back at her father.

---

13 Revesz, "Poetry after Auschwitz," 197–98. Presumably it was easy for a postwar "Austrian" writer to identify with the victims, as the myth of victimhood was supported by the Declaration of Moscow in 1953 and remained predominant in Austria until Kurt Waldheim's presidency in the 1990s. Bachmann is, however, critical in regard to "reconciliation," as is evident, for example, in "Tagebuch: Beitrag zur Probenummer einer internationalen Zeitschrift," in *Die Wahrheit ist dem Menschen zumutbar* (1981).

14 Sandra Boihmane, *Malina—Versteck der Sprache: Die Chiffre "Malina" in Ingeborg Bachmanns Werk und in Zeugnissen von ZeitzeugInnen* (Berlin: Neofelis, 2014), 145–46.

15 Alexandra Kurmann, "What Is Malina? Decoding Ingeborg Bachmann's Poetics of Secrecy." *Women in German Yearbook* 32 (2016): 76–94, here 77.

16 See also Monika Albrecht and Dirk Göttsche: "Just as Horkheimer and Adorno equate the beginning of enlightenment with that of world history, Bachmann seems to locate the origins of today's gender problematic in prehistoric times when myth developed. It seems, therefore, doubtful that Bachmann, as it has been claimed, does bring up for discussion the "incompatibility of the male and female principle . . . as an 'eternal' conflict that equally concerns man and woman." Lennox, *Cemetery*, 75.

17 Cited from the documentary film *Der Fall Ingeborg Bachmann* (1990), directed by Boris Manner.

Malina famously ends with the sentence: "It was murder." Perhaps this does not, as has been suggested, allude to autobiographical[18] experiences and a prophetic prediction of her own death. Rather, it speaks to the violent death of the utopia of a liberated society, which features in the first chapter of the novel in italics:

Ein Tag wird kommen, sie werden frei sein, es werden alle Menschen frei sein, auch von der Freiheit, die sie gemeint haben. Es wird eine größere Freiheit sein, sie wird über die Maßen sein, sie wird für ein ganzes Leben sein . . .

Ein Tag wird kommen, an dem die Menschen die Savannen und die Steppen wiederentdecken, hinausströmen werden sie und ihrer Sklaverei ein Ende machen, die Tiere werden unter der hohen Sonne zu den Menschen treten, die frei sind, und sie werden in Eintracht leben, die Riesenschildkröten, die Elefanten, die Wisente, und die Könige des Dschungels und der Wüste werden sich mit den befreiten Menschen vereinbaren, sie werden aus einem Wasser trinken, sie werden die gereinigte Luft atmen, sie werden sich nicht zerfleischen, es wird der Anfang sein, es wird der Anfang sein für das ganze Leben . . .

Ein Tag wird kommen, an dem die Frauen rotgoldene Augen haben, rotgoldenes Haar, und die Poesie ihres Geschlechts wird wiedererschaffen werden . . .

Ein Tag wird kommen, an dem die Menschen rotgoldene Augen und siderische Stimmen haben, an dem ihre Hände begabt sein werden für die Liebe, und die Poesie ihres Geschlechts wird wiedererschaffen sein . . .[19]

[*A day will come, they will be free, all people will be free, even from the freedom they had intended. There will be a greater freedom, beyond measure, a freedom to last a whole life long.*

A day will come when human beings will rediscover the savannas and the steppes, they will inundate them and put an end to their slavery, at high noon the animals will approach the humans who are free, and they will live in unity, the giant tortoises, the elephants, the bison, and the kings of the jungles and the deserts will be reconciled with the liberated people, they will drink from one water, they will breathe the purified air,

---

18 It is almost bizarre how much attention scholars paid to Bachmann's biography, while Bachmann herself, in her speech for the Anton Wildgans Prize, critiqued the blending of author and works.

19 Ingeborg Bachmann, *"Todesarten"-Projekt: Kritische Ausgabe*, vol. 3.1: *Malina* (Munich: Piper, 1995), 427–28, 449, 451.

they will not mangle one another, it shall be the beginning, it shall be the beginning for a whole life . . .

A day will come when all women have redgolden eyes, redgolden hair, and the poetry of their sex, their lineage, will be recreated . . .

A day will come when all mankind will have redgolden eyes and starry voices, when their hands will be gifted for love, and the poetry of their lineage shall be recreated.][20]

In *Malina*, utopia flares up only briefly, scattered across pages, only to disappear again. The narrator outlives the utopia but ultimately vanishes as well. Although there is no "vengeance" in Bachmann's narratives, the patriarchal mode of production, which gave rise to various forms of fascism in the twentieth century, is the locus of oppression. Therefore, her utopia prioritizes the liberation of "women"; only thereafter can the liberation of all humankind follow and all eyes turn "redgold," an allusion to Paul Celan's poem "Todesfuge" (1948; "Fugue of Death," 1962).[21] Liberation is linked to the abolition of the division of "gold" and "ash," the golden hair of Margarete and the ashen hair of Sulamith.

Ein Tag wird kommen, an dem unsere Häuser fallen, die Autos werden zu Schrott geworden sein, von den Flugzeugen und von den Raketen werden wir befreit sein, den Verzicht leisten auf die Erfindung des Rads und der Kernspaltung, der frische Wind wird niederkommen von den blauen Hügeln und unsere Brust weiten, wir werden tot sein und atmen, es wird das ganze Leben sein.

In den Wüsten wird das Wasser versiegen, wir werden wieder in die Wüste können und die Offenbarungen schauen, die Savannen und die Gewässer in ihrer Reinheit werden uns einladen, die Diamanten werden im Gestein bleiben und uns allen leuchten . . .[22]

---

20 Ingeborg Bachmann, *Malina* (New York: Holmes & Meier, 1990), 76–77 and 87–88.

21 Paul Celan, *Gesammelte Werke in fünf Bänden*, vol. 1: *Gedichte I* (Frankfurt am Main: Suhrkamp, 1983,) 41–42. Some research has been conducted on Celan references in Bachmann's work; for example, in the epilogues to Bachmann's and Celan's correspondence, *Herzzeit: Ingeborg Bachmann–Paul Celan; Der Briefwechsel* (Frankfurt am Main: Suhrkamp, 2008); in Eva Revesz's "Poetry after Auschwitz"; and by several authors in *Ingeborg Bachmann und Paul Celan: Historisch-poetische Korrelationen*, ed. Gernot Wimmer (Berlin: De Gruyter, 2014).

22 Bachmann, *"Todesarten"-Projekt*, 455.

[A day will come, when our houses will fall, all cars will have become scrap metal, we will be freed from all airplanes and rockets, renounce the invention of the wheel and the ability to split the atom, the fresh wind will come down from the blue hills and our breast will expand, we will be dead and still breathe, it shall be our whole life.

All water will run dry in the deserts, once again we will be able to enter the wilderness and witness revelations. Savanna and stream will invite us in their purity, diamonds will remain embedded in stone and illuminate us all . . .][23]

The call to forego the discovery of the wheel and nuclear fission can be read as a fundamentally reactionary position, as it evokes a return to a romanticized *Urzustand* (originary state). Yet it can also be read as a critique of the course of history, which does not represent linear progress but paved the way for *commodity society*[24] and its as-yet most destructive form, fascism. In Bachmann's vision, the diamonds must shine for everyone. This implies that for this oppression to end, private property must be overcome, and the very notion of value must be radically called into question and separated from an exploitative relationship to nature. In a short draft entitled "Jede Jugend ist die Dümmste" (Every Youth is the Dumbest), Bachmann reflects on the failure of existing socialist regimes, such as the Soviet Union. She approaches the problem from a point of view that is atypical for the traditional left but bears some resemblance to Scholz's arguments, since Scholz also problematizes the compulsive structures of the bureaucratization and fetishization of labor in socialist regimes:

Die Arbeit ohne Orgiasmus. An Stelle des Fegefeuers die Bürokratie. Der Kommunismus, der seinen Anfang nicht begreift und sich schon verwalten will. Marx und Lenin werden erst studiert werden, wenn die helleren Köpfe nach ihnen am Ziel gemessen werden und nicht mehr am Anfang. . . . Der Kommunismus muss Luxus sein, oder er wird nicht sein. . . . Die Welt hat keine zugelassenen Feiertage, sie ist ein Feiertag.[25]

[Work sans orgasm. In place of purgatory, bureaucracy. A communism that does not understand its beginnings and already wants to administer itself. Marx and Lenin will be studied only when the

23 Bachmann, *Malina*, 90.
24 Lennox stresses Bachmann's disregard for capitalism based on an interview in which Bachmann characterizes her writing as testimony to her continuing hope for society to change. Lennox, *Cemetery*, 41–42.
25 Bachmann, *Malina*, 133–34.

brighter minds after them will be measured by objectives and not by the beginning. . . . Communism must be luxury, or it shall not be. . . . The world does not have authorized holidays, it is a holiday.]

Bachmann's critique of contemporary socialist regimes focuses on the contrast between their political reality—the purgatory of bureaucratic frenzy and obsession with labor—and the image of a liberated society. Central to her point is the condition of work or labor, which is detached from pleasure in both socialist countries and the Western bloc. Perhaps inspired by Herbert Marcuse's *Eros and Civilization* (1955), Bachmann notes the forgotten goal of liberation and the subordination of the pleasure principle to the performance principle. Bachmann's scenario here links "communism" to the notion of utopia, redefining it in her own terms: hedonism and liberation are fundamental rationales.

Bachmann's texts have often been read as portrayals of the *conditio humana*;[26] but Bachmann herself considered the reconfiguration of time and space one of literature's strong points, as she explains in the first of her Frankfurt Lectures. Such a reconfiguration can be interpreted as an act of "resistance": after all, the strict organization of time and space paved the way to "modernity" and to the so-called postmodern, late capitalist era.[27] To be sure, Bachmann's dream state enhances an idiosyncratic fabric of time and space. Even so, however, the composition of the dream is contingent upon Bachmann's historical locatedness, no matter how much it alternates or opposes the current moment. Bachmann's "aesthetic opposition to the modern deformation of the soul," in Michael Minden's words, is an opposition to the contemporary condition;[28] critique cannot fully

---

26 In "The 'Hearing I': Sounding the 'Conditio Humana' in Ingeborg Bachmann's 'Ein Geschäft mit Träumen,'" *Journal of Austrian Studies* 52, no. 3 (2019): 19–40, Caroline Kita critiques Sigrid Weigel, suggesting that Bachmann's *conditio humana* is not transhistorical but conditioned by the postwar era. According to Roland Barthes, *conditio humana* is the foremost example of a myth that seeks to define history as nature. Roland Barthes, *Mythen des Alltags* (Berlin: Suhrkamp, 2013).

27 More than anything else, the conditions of production determine the organization of time and, consequently, the dynamics of value, as Moishe Postone argues in *Time, Labor and Social Domination* (Cambridge: Cambridge University Press, 1993). Bernhard Siegert's "(Nicht-)am Ort: Zum Raster als Kulturtechnik," *Wissenschaftliche Zeitung der Bauhaus-Universität Weimar*, Heft 3 (2003): 92–104, evaluates processes of arranging and dividing up space and "locating" people as bureaucratic endeavors that paved the way for urban, modern "life," evidenced, for example, in the exclusion of nomadic people on the basis of their nonlocalizability. He also elaborates on the transformation of this social phenomenon in the "postmodern" era.

28 Michael Minden, "Modernism's Struggle for the Soul: Rainer Maria Rilke's *Die Aufzeichnungen des Malte Laurids Brigge* and Ingeborg Bachmann's

detach itself from its moment in time. Immanence is revealed especially when literature attempts to transgress toward the utopic: even though national borders are repealed, the utopian scenario relapses to feudality, to the age of princesses and princes, to the mythical and to fairy tales that sought to revive the feudal era after its myths were supposedly overcome by instrumental reason.[29]

As the utopia disappears with the end of the first chapter, feverish dreams and a sequence of nightmares follow. Entitled, as already noted, "The Third Man," the second chapter revolves around a father figure, gas chambers, and incest, linking the "father" to fascism and sexual violence. Bachmann scholars generally agree that the allegorical father represents the entirety of "masculinist" violence. The father "commands" and "imprisons" her, "blinds" her and "strips out her tongue," kills and tortures her in sequential nightmares. The "murder" originates in the oppressive realm of the bourgeois family and is a processual, gradually unfolding event characteristic of patriarchies. "The long journey" from the father to Ivan[30] runs a predetermined path of alternating dependencies, typical of traditionally heteronormative societies, from the "natural" subordination to the "father" to the later obedience to the husband. Bachmann's portrayal of gender or sex mirrors pre-"postmodern" middle-class norms and relations.

When Scholz speaks of the "hierarchische Geschlechterverhältnis im Kontext des modernen warenproduzierenden Patriarchats" (hierarchical gender/sex relations in the context of the modern, commodity-producing patriarchy), we must keep in mind that "Geschlecht" in German refers to both "sex" and "gender."[31] Bachmann's Undine and the protagonist of *Malina* were conceived in a time when a married woman in Austria needed her husband's permission if she wanted to work outside the home, thus naturalizing through law the subordination of women on the basis of their sex. This is reflected in their limited agency. In Bachmann's Austria, the differentiation between social and biological sex had not yet been theorized fully. Middle-class women, who had the "opportunity" to work during wartime, were again relegated to the domestic sphere, a development to which the second-wave feminist movement responded a couple of decades later. Scholz expands on the kind of work associated with and expected from women: besides reproductive work and other functions

---

Malina," *German Life and Letters* 67, no. 3 (2014): 320–40, here 320.

29 As Eva Revesz points out, Bachmann's poetry is imbued with a sense of utopia, embodied, for example, in the symbolic sphere of language or the divine. Revesz, "Poetry after Auschwitz," 206.

30 Bachmann, *Malina*, 129.

31 Scholz, *Geschlecht des Kapitalismus*, 21. In German, "biologisches Geschlecht" refers to sex, while "soziales Geschlecht" refers to gender—the Anglicism "gender" is well established meanwhile, however.

related to consumption, which the narrator in *Malina* rejects, Scholz includes care, nursing, eroticism, sexuality, and "love." "Love," in particular, is central to *Malina*.[32] Already in 1982, Charlotte Van Praag argued that Bachmann's figures do not personify individuals but rather "genres," as evidenced by Hans in "Undine Geht," Malina, Ivan, or the father in *Malina*, all of whom embody patriarchal violence per se. Yet at the same time, Van Praag herself recycles the modern gender dichotomy of loving, nature-bound (*naturgebunden*) feminine women and reasonable, down-to-earth men.[33] Targeting the "feminine," not the woman, patriarchal violence in *Malina* instrumentalizes love and sexuality as means to ensure masculine hegemony. As Scholz points out, some of the instruments that formerly served to confine middle-class women to the private sphere persist as tools of oppression, albeit in metamorphosed forms adjusted to the conditions of post-Fordism. Thus, according to Scholz, the traditional gender/sex division of modernity was overcome only superficially with the dawn of postmodernity and the concomitant era of "flexi" identities.

The Dawn of "Postmodernity": Female Agency or Just Another Web of Dependency?

Since the 1970s, the rather rigid sex and gender dualism of "modernity" transitioned along with the changing conditions of production, which include the breakdown of Fordism, increased outsourcing and global trade, and flexibilization in terms of time/hours and working conditions. While conceptions of masculinity or femininity are marked by geographical and temporal differences, and backlashes are not rare, advanced capitalism brings about distinctive material and social changes.[34] These changes are reflected in literature, though often not intentionally, but in the "unconscious" of the text. Early on, Elfriede Jelinek dismantled the false hopes associated with women's inclusion in the public sphere, particularly the job market, which proved to be exploitative, as working-class women had known for a long time.

Jelinek's works are no less remarkable than Bachmann's oeuvre: she wrote novels, plays, libretti, screenplays, essays, radio (audio) plays, and poems and translated various works from multiple languages. Born in Austria in 1946, the first year after the Second World War, Jelinek experienced firsthand the afterlife of Nazism and anti-Semitism in Austrian

---

32 Scholz, *Geschlecht des Kapitalismus*, 18.

33 Charlotte Van Praag, "'Malina' von Ingeborg Bachmann: Ein Verkannter Roman," *Neophilologus* 66, no. 1 (1982): 111.

34 Scholz refers to this transition as the "Verwilderung des warenproduzierenden Patriarchats" (barbarization of the commodity-producing patriarchy) in *Geschlecht des Kapitalismus*, 11.

society.[35] As in Bachmann's works, fascism, its legacies, and its repercussions on gender dynamics are among the central motifs in Jelinek's works. With the novel *Die Liebhaberinnen* (The Lovers) Jelinek achieved a literary breakthrough in 1975, which, coincidentally, was also the year when married women in Austria were legally declared to be "equal" to their husbands with the "Bundesgesetz über die Neuordnung der persönlichen Rechtswirkungen der Ehe (BGBI 412/1975)" (Federal Law on the Reorganization of the Personal Legal Effects of Marriage). Now, married women no longer had to ask for their husbands' permission in order to sell their labor power lawfully. In *Die Liebhaberinnen*, Jelinek describes the situation of two working-class women, one suburban and one from a rural area, who seek to liberate themselves from the hardships of labor by means of "love" or marriage. Jelinek dismantles the myth of love, as it is known from fairy tales, dime novels, and modern romances, with relish.[36] She unveils the subordination of women in the public as well as the private sphere: in factories, apprenticeships, and marriage. Similar motifs reappear in her play *Was geschah, nachdem Nora ihren Mann verlassen hatte oder Stützen der Gesellschaft* (1977; What Happened after Nora Left Her Husband; or, Pillars of Society). Here, bourgeois Nora leaves her husband and the restrictive realm of the family only to be exploited first in a factory (downward class mobility) and later by multiple men.[37] It appears as though her body and labor power function as interchangeable means to secure an existence; yet unlike her husband, the machines "kill": patriarchy does not necessarily murder its accomplices (subjects), but capitalism can and does.

With the 1970s feminist movement in Austria, which included autonomous, socialist organizations such as the AUF (Aktion Unabhängiger Frauen), the "social position" of female artists changed and new opportunities opened up. For example, as Wendelin Schmidt-Dengler points out, a number of new literary journals that supported female authors

35 Jelinek's father, who was Jewish, experienced and survived the Second World War. Verena Mayer and Roland Koberg, "Der Wanderer: Robert Walser als Vater-Imago im Werk von Elfriede Jelinek," *Autour de Jelinek: Regards croisés sur une artiste autrichienne*, May 5, 2014, https://jelinek.hypotheses.org/824.

36 Marlies Janz argues that Jelinek's work is strongly influenced by Roland Barthes's theory of myths and their deconstruction. See her *Elfriede Jelinek* (Stuttgart: Metzler, 1995), vii–viii. The volume examines trivial myths, myths of artistry and emancipation, and myths about "women, nature and sexuality" and emphasizes the critique of fascism in Jelinek's works.

37 The play is a sequel to Henrik Ibsen's play *A Doll's House* (1879). The original ending of the play was changed for its first staging in Germany in 1880, as it was feared that Nora's decision to leave her husband and family would cause an uproar. While Jelinek radicalizes Ibsen's play, a rather reactionary sequel to the play premiered in the US in 2017, directed by Lucas Hnath.

were founded.[38] Changes in social conditions along with the impact of the feminist movement brought about a radical shift in the literary arena. Jelinek's poetics diverge from Bachmann's, and yet, in an interview on her film adaptation of *Malina* (1991), Jelinek expresses high regard for Bachmann's prose and identifies her as an author who influenced her own writing. The film, however, a distorted version of Jelinek's reading of Bachmann—according to Jelinek, the director changed her script—earned predominantly negative responses. Feminist critics and scholars objected to its emphasis on a self-destructive, lunatic woman, while the sociohistorical background that motivates her state of mind is left out.[39]

Clara S.: Eine musikalische Tragödie is the second play published in *Theaterstücke* (1992), a compilation of four plays, including *Was geschah, nachdem Nora ihren Mann verlassen hatte oder Stützen der Gesellschaft*; *Burgtheater* (1985), a play about the rise and supposed "fall" of Nazism in Austria; and *Krankheit oder Moderne Frauen* (1987; Illness; or, Modern Women), the story of the vampiress and poet Emily. Nora, Clara, and Emily all illustrate the impossibility of combining career and motherhood: Nora fails to fulfill herself and ends up in the domestic sphere she had left; Clara dies after strangling her husband to death; and the artist Emily converges with the mother-figure Carmilla into a horrific mother-artist creature that drinks blood and is, in the end, shot dead.

Clara S. takes place in 1929 in Gabriele D'Annunzio's former residence and features almost exclusively historical figures: the Italian author D'Annunzio; his "mistress," Luisa Baccara; his housekeeper, Aélis Mazoyer; his wife, Donna Maria di Gallese; and Luisa's sister, Carlotta Barra.[40] The Nazis' rise to power and conquest of half of Europe is heralded in the first scene of the play, when Clara declares, "Wenn ich sage Inland, so meine ich natürlich Deutschland, wo ich zu Hause bin. Bald

---

38 For example, *wespennest, Asthma, Eselsohr, Aha, Frischfleisch, Podium*, and *Das Pult*. Wendelin Schmidt-Dengler, *Bruchlinien: Vorlesungen zur österreichischen Literatur 1945 bis 1990* (Vienna: Residenz, 2010), 221–22.

39 Elfriede Jelinek, Brenda L. Bethman, and Larson Powell, "Malina: A Film-script Based on the Novel by Ingeborg Bachmann, Scenes 116–123," *Women in German Yearbook* 16 (2000): 73–74.

40 As indicated in the 2008 *Theaterstücke* edition published by Rowohlt, Jelinek used multiple sources for the embedded quotes: the diaries and letters of Clara Schumann; the letters of Robert Schumann; novels by Gabriele D'Annunzio; Tamara de Lempicka and Gabriele D'Annunzio's correspondence; Aélis Mazoyer's diaries; and Ria Endres's thesis on Thomas Bernhard, *Am Ende angekommen* (1980). Except for Carlotta Barra, who represents a mixture of several people, all figures are based on real individuals. See Elisabeth Tunner, "Dem Starken die Herrschaft, dem Schwachen das Sklaventum?," In *Elfriede Jelinek: Sprache, Geschlecht und Herrschaft*, ed. Johann Sonnleitner (Würzburg: Königshausen & Neumann, 2008), 71.

wird die ganze Welt Inland werden."[41] ("When I say 'home' I mean of course Germany, which is where I live. Soon the whole world will be my home"[42]). Clearly, nationalism and patriotism coupled with megalomania also characterize female figures.

Clara's subordination first to her father, a piano teacher, then to Robert Schumann, the "genius" pianist, parallels Malina's "long journey" from father to Ivan. When Luisa asks Clara if something killed her sensuality, Clara's response stresses the interchangeability of male figures, both of whom are agents of masculinist violence: "Mein Vater, jener geliebte große Lehrer, und später mein Gatte Robert, der Teufel"[43] ("My father, that beloved master teacher, and later my husband Robert, the devil"[44]). According to Schmid-Bortenschlager, the cult of the genius (*Geniekult*) contributed to the undervaluation and underrepresentation of women authors in the German literary scene.[45] Jelinek unveils the Geniekult as a discourse designed to repress female artists, who could otherwise compete with their male contemporaries. Ironically, in one way or another all her female figures have internalized the (masculine) cult of genius along with other myths of patriarchal oppression. Aélis Mazoyer helps D'Annunzio to catch his prey; Luisa believes that she is not capable of composing, only of playing pieces composed by men; and Clara considers herself a "Symbiose" (symbiosis)[46] of artist and mother. In the end, this symbiosis leads to her death, just as it caused the demise of the double-creature of Emily and Carmilla. Clara refers to giving birth as "work," or even as "work for nothing"; that is, unpaid labor, while her other "work" as an undervalued female artist does not pay, either. Clara's revenge, her strangulation of Robert, is a response to the personified patriarchal oppressor,

41 Elfriede Jelinek, *Theaterstücke* (Hamburg: Rowohlt Taschenbuch Verlag, 2008), 81.

42 Elfriede Jelinek, *Clara S. (A Musical Tragedy)*, in *Women's Words, Women's Works: An Anthology of Contemporary Austrian Plays by Women*, ed. Udo H. D. Borgert, introd. Borgert and Andrea Bandhauer (Riverside, CA.: Ariadne, 2001), 53. Her longing for the homeland was interpreted as a satirical commentary on Goethe's *Kindfrau* (child-woman) "Mignon" in *Wilhelm Meisters Lehrjahre* (1795–96; *Wilhelm Meister's Apprenticeship*), who longs for Italy; for example, Jelinek mentions Mignon explicitly in the first scene, when Clara looks out of the window. Jelinek, *Clara S.*, in Borgert, *Women's Words*, 23.

43 Jelinek, *Clara S.*, in *Theaterstücke*, 82.

44 Jelinek, *Clara S.*, in Borgert, *Women's Words*, 54.

45 Sigrid Schmid-Bortenschlager, *Österreichische Schriftstellerinnen 1800–2000: Eine Literaturgeschichte* (Darmstadt: WBG, 2009), 18.

46 "In mir sehen sie die Künstlerschaft plus der Mutterschaft verkörpert. Eine Symbiose." Jelinek, *Clara S.*, in *Theaterstücke*, 84. "In me you see embodied artistic genius combined with motherhood. A symbiosis." Jelinek, *Clara S.*, in Borgert, *Women's Words*, 56.

her husband. In the end, Clara's complicity in her own oppression culminates in her death; as Janz points out, there is no place for the "utopia of female liberation"[47] in *Clara S.* The particularity of Clara's situation does not arise from her biological "sex" but from capitalism's specific reattribution of gender roles, which, paradoxically, Jelinek demonstrates through a figure that ought to belong to an earlier period. Women took on paid labor and domestic work simultaneously long before the late capitalist period and into Jelinek's present, the 1970s. Thus, the change consists not in the fact that women work but, rather, that late capitalist ideology touts the all-around woman, the target of the text's revenge.

Jelinek's figures do not embody individuals; rather, they are templates, or, as Udo Borgert and Andrea Bandhauer call them, "artificial constructs."[48] Similarly, the techniques of "montage and transposition of quotations"[49] disable mechanisms of identification, while the performance itself relies on the Brechtian alienation effect; Jelinek performances often take place on a bizarre stage where actors and actresses talk simultaneously with tones, actions, and gesticulations that do not match. Both D'Annunzio and Luisa accuse Clara of repressing her "female nature," a gender myth that Jelinek had already sought to break down in *Die Liebhaberinnen.* At the same time, Jelinek does not neglect the material base for the oppression of women but, rather, emphasizes it.[50] In her work, the cultural-symbolic space is embedded within the material base and vice versa, while the theater is revealed to be just another stage for a hyperbolic reflection of society's present state. Brigitte, the *homo economicus* in *Die Liebhaberinnen,* views her own and her husband's bodies as capital. Female figures in Jelinek's works are not victims but, rather, accomplices; they participate actively in the perpetuation of structures that oppress them: Clara believes in the genius of her husband, is proud of their "German" roots, and repeatedly reduces herself to her body ("mein Künstlerinnenkörperm" [my artist body]). Clara's revenge is directed toward the personified oppressor but also toward herself, as she recognizes her complicity.

47 Janz, *Elfriede Jelinek,* 58.
48 Borgert and Bandhauer, introduction to *Women's Words,* 21.
49 Borgert and Bandhauer, introduction to *Women's Words,* 22.
50 Jelinek considers herself a "communist," not a feminist; see Rebecca Thomas, "Subjectivity in Elfriede Jelinek's 'Clara S.': Resisting the Vanishing Point," *Modern Austrian Literature* 32, no. 1 (1999): 141–58, here 145. Thomas argues that the degeneration of male figures, and the murder of Robert, empowers female figures. In contrast, Janz claims that Clara's death symbolizes the impossibility of emancipation; similarly, Borgert and Bandhauer suggest that Clara's death expresses a critique of the status quo, as she does not know how to survive without her husband, whose genius she believed in.

The circus of desynchronized emotions, thoughts, words, and bodies in Jelinek's plays conveys an exaggerated portrayal of postwar society. As Jelinek points out in a filmed interview on *Malina*,[51] she paints an overall picture that is even more pessimistic than Bachmann's. To be sure, her figures show more resistance to their subjugation than Bachmann's, and they do not disappear into the walls; but they too die violently, either getting killed or mutilating and killing themselves, because they cannot see a way out. Jelinek also notes that during Bachmann's lifetime there may have been some hope that gender relations would change, that the discrimination of women based on their sex would end, that the walls of the private sphere would break down. In contrast, Jelinek shows that woman's oppression continues in the public sphere, and this is precisely what Scholz argues, in line with Becker-Schmidt. In the late twentieth and early twenty-first centuries, the simultaneously productive and reproductive woman[52] becomes the new ideal. This woman is expected to work but remains responsible for the spheres of reproduction and consumption as well. This can be seen as progress but also as an extension of her subjugation—as her twofold exploitation in the private and public spheres. In their analysis of *Clara S.*, Borgert and Bandhauer argue that "sexual transactions reduce the women and their bodies to mere commodities with a particular market value."[53] But it is not only women's bodies and sexuality that can be and are exploited, but their labor power as well. Whereas the former is central to critiques of patriarchies, women's exploitation as laborers receives less attention. Instead, their inclusion in the job market is often hailed as a step toward emancipation. Yet, it can also be read as just another relocation of women's exploitation, from the private to the public sphere, as the fluctuating market demands their (less worthy) labor power.

Instead of transhistoricizing "work" and prostitution, or the oppression of women in general, it is imperative to highlight the particularities of this oppression within capitalist society as well as in its various historical

---

51 *Der Fall Ingeborg Bachmann*, directed by Boris Manner (Munich: Kuchenreuther Film GmbH, 1990).

52 Or the "doppelte Vergesellschaftung" of women, as Regina Becker-Schmidt elaborates it in "Zur doppelten Vergesellschaftung von Frauen: Soziologische Grundlegung, empirische Rekonstruktion," *gender . . . politik . . . online*, July 2003, https://www.fu-berlin.de/sites/gpo/soz_eth/Geschlecht_als_Kategorie/Die_doppelte_Vergesellschaftung_von_Frauen/becker_schmidt_ohne.pdf. The term can roughly be translated as "twofold socialization," although Becker-Schmidt differentiates between "socialization" and "Vergesellschaftung," defined as a process that turns individuals into members of society. The lack of an accurate translation in English is perhaps related to the pronounced individualist ideology in the Anglo-Saxon world.

53 Borgert and Bandhauer, introduction to *Women's Words*, 23.

stages and cultural incarnations. Whereas Bachmann resists by critiquing the classic modern gender/sex dichotomy, which forces the "feminine" side of the androgynist artist to disappear into the walls, Jelinek shows that the wonder woman who combines a thriving career with mother-hood, responsibility for the household, and diverse nursing activities is just another product of advanced capitalism and the new demands of the market. Whereas male-penned "killer" vampiresses, murderesses, femmes fatales, etc., have often been projections of a fear of retribution, aris-ing from the guilt of subordinating the "feminine," the revenge motive does not appear as a means to overthrow capitalist patriarchy in either Bachmann's *Malina* or Jelinek's *Clara S.* Rather, the disappearance of the female narrator in Bachmann's novel and Clara S.'s revenge and death are consequences and symptoms of slightly diverging forms of patriar-chal oppression: first, the entrapment in the private sphere; second, the twofold subjugation in the public and private spheres. Contemporary #MeToo movements underline the continuity of women's oppression and show how access to the public sphere and the job market did not bring about its end. That this movement arose in the United States unveils once again the failure of advanced capitalism to ensure the mental and physical integrity of its subjects, whether in the "private" or the "public" realm, revealing the untenability of the dichotomy fundamental to this separation.

Bachmann's and Jelinek's works reveal the continuity, transformation, and adaptability of capitalist patriarchy. #MeToo is a discursive resurfac-ing of the omnipresent barbarity of capitalist patriarchies, but it does not consistently critique the objective, material conditions that perpetuate violence against women in the private as well as public spheres. While, as manifest in Bachmann's and Jelinek's works, capitalism's demands on women's work and bodies have changed, its gender-specific mechanism has remained unaltered. #MeToo reveals both the continuity of gender-specific violence and the shortcomings of our contemporary conception of critique: as long as the critique of patriarchal violence is limited to the discursive, hence symbolic, realm and does not target objective condi-tions, its impact is limited. The liberation of women is thinkable only alongside the liberation of humankind and nature and in tandem with the conception of alternatives that do not revision the revival of an illusory "past."

13: Staging Consent and Threatened Masculinity: The Debate on #MeToo in Contemporary German Theater

Daniele Vecchiato

"Hysteria," "totalitarian feminism," "witch hunt": the—in fact rather timid—response to the #MeToo movement in Germany was met with hostility by the mainstream public discourse, as these dismissively gendered retorts indicate. An unjustified and disproportionate reaction, one might argue, as Germany never witnessed a genuine wave of activism along the lines of the protests triggered by the launch of the famous hashtag in October 2017 in the United States. While in other European countries, such as France, Sweden, and Norway, national variants of #MeToo initiated an intense public debate over laissez-faire attitudes toward sexual misconduct that raised awareness about the scale of rape culture and structural sexism in our societies,[1] Germany has remained noticeably quiet. With the exception of only a few major accusations (e.g., against film director Dieter Wedel and the former president of the Munich Academy of Music, Siegfried Mauser), the German campaign against sexual harassment and sexual violence was quickly redirected into a broader—though certainly urgent—debate on inequities between the sexes and the gender pay gap.

Historian Jessica Gienow-Hecht has argued that two key factors may be responsible for the lukewarm reception of #MeToo in Germany: first, an increasing skepticism toward social and cultural trends coming from

---

1   For an overview of the contribution of the #MeToo movement to the reemergence of activism against sexual violence, see in particular Lori Perkins, ed., *#MeToo: Essays about How and Why This Happened, What It Means, and How to Make Sure It Never Happens Again* (New York: Riverdale Avenue, 2017); Bianca Fileborn and Rachel Loney-Howes, eds., *#MeToo and the Politics of Social Change* (Cham, Switzerland: Palgrave Macmillan, 2019); Karen Boyle, *#MeToo, Weinstein and Feminism* (Cham, Switzerland: Palgrave Macmillan, 2019); Birte C. Gnau and Eva L. Wyss, "Der #MeToo-Protest: Diskurswandel durch alternative Öffentlichkeiten," in *Alternative Öffentlichkeiten: Soziale Medien zwischen Partizipation, Sharing und Vergemeinschaftung*, ed. Stefan Hauser, Roman Opilowski, and Eva L. Wyss (Bielefeld: transcript, 2019), 131–65.

the United States, especially since Donald Trump's election in 2016; and second, the somewhat indolent character of some expressions of German feminism, which seem to have been "lagging behind for the last 40 or 50 years."[2] This stagnation is reflected in Germany's not always flattering position in European statistics when it comes to women's rights: it was not until 1997 that rape within marriage was recognized as a crime by the German Parliament; the number of *Frauenmorde* (femicides) continues to be worryingly high;[3] and polls indicate that an alarming "40% of women in Germany report having experienced sexual or physical abuse."[4] Furthermore, the number of German women in positions of power is still relatively low, despite the country having been led for sixteen years by a female chancellor.[5] Like other Western democracies, Germany seems to have failed to identify and foster positive models of female leadership, as evidenced by the disturbingly stereotyped—if not downright antifeminist—portrayals of career women and female political leaders not only in German public discourse[6] but also across a variety of cultural artefacts.[7]

Perhaps unsurprisingly, then, #MeToo has found little resonance in the German cultural scene when compared with more immediate

---

2   Quoted in Erik Kirschbaum, "Germany Had Seemed Immune to the #MeToo Movement. Then a Prominent Director Was Accused," *Los Angeles Times*, January 31, 2018, https://www.latimes.com/world/europe/la-fg-germany-sexual-harassment-20180130-story.html.

3   See a recent *Zeit* dossier with information about women who were murdered by their male partners: Elisabeth Raether and Michael Schlegel, "Von ihren Männern getötet," *Zeit Online*, December 4, 2018, https://www.zeit.de/2019/51/frauenmorde-gewalt-partnerschaft-bundeskriminalamt.

4   Kirschbaum, "Germany Had Seemed Immune."

5   The proportion of women in the German Parliament is currently just over 30 percent. On an international comparison, Germany is ranked 46th out of 190 countries, with Rwanda, Bolivia, and Cuba topping this ranking. See Friederike Bauer, "Equal Rights in Politics?," *deutschland.de*, October 16, 2018, https://www.deutschland.de/en/topicpolitics/this-is-the-proportion-of-women-in-german-politics. For a systematic, though slightly dated, analysis of the presence of women in German politics, see Beate Hoecker, "Frauen in der Politik," *Bundeszentrale für politische Bildung*, November 5, 2009, https://www.bpb.de/gesellschaft/gender/frauen-in-deutschland/49362/frauen-in-der-politik.

6   See Dorothee Beck, "Change, Persistence, and Contradiction: The Representation of Female Political Leadership in Gendered Media," and Patricia Anne Simpson, "'Mama Merkel' and 'Mutti-Multiculti': The Perils of Governing while Female," in *Realities and Fantasies of German Female Leadership: From Maria Antonia of Saxony to Angela Merkel*, ed. Elisabeth Krimmer and Patricia Anne Simpson (Rochester, NY: Camden House, 2019), 262–80 and 301–17.

7   See, for example, Helga Druxes, "'Leaning In': The Career Woman as Instrument of Neoliberal Critique," in Krimmer and Simpson, *Realities and Fantasies*, 243–61.

responses in other countries. The movement did, however, manage to permeate the theater—a medium that often serves as a seismograph for contemporary social trends and concerns. German theater in particular has a remarkable tradition of political engagement that dates back to the Enlightenment—notably to Friedrich Schiller's idea of the stage as a moral institution, aimed at educating as well as entertaining the spectators[8]—and that continues throughout the twentieth and twenty-first centuries. From Erwin Piscator's "political theatre"[9] to Bertolt Brecht's "epic theatre,"[10] from the documentarian and protest theater of the 1960s and '70s[11] to more recent forms of radical "postdramatic"[12] or "applied"[13] theater that seek direct intervention in the contemporary political debate, the German stage has continued to engage generations of spectators, making them aware of the social and power structures that shape the reality they live in.

Given the systemic discrimination and forms of abuse that all too often plague the theater profession,[14] performance spaces and theater

---

8   See Manfred Brauneck, *Die Deutschen und ihr Theater: Kleine Geschichte der "moralischen Anstalt" oder: Ist das Theater überfordert?* (Bielefeld: transcript, 2018).

9   Erwin Piscator, *The Political Theatre*, trans. Hugh Rorrison (London: Methuen, 1980).

10   Bertolt Brecht, "The Modern Theatre Is the Epic Theatre," in *Brecht on Theatre: The Development of an Aesthetic*, trans. John Willett (London: Methuen, 1964), 33–42.

11   Among others, see Laureen Nussbaum, "The German Documentary Theater of the Sixties: A Stereopsis of Contemporary History," *German Studies Review* 4, no. 2 (May 1981), 237–55; Brigitte Marschall, *Politisches Theater nach 1950* (Cologne: Böhlau, 2010); Ingrid Cilcher-Holtey, Dorothea Kraus, and Franziska Schößler, eds., *Politisches Theater nach 1968: Regie, Dramatik und Organisation* (Frankfurt am Main: Campus, 2006); Dorothea Kraus, *Theater-Proteste: Zur Politisierung von Straße und Bühne in den 1960er Jahren* (Frankfurt am Main: Campus, 2007).

12   See Hans-Thies Lehmann, "Wie politisch ist postdramatisches Theater? Warum das Politische im Theater nur die Unterbrechung des Politischen sein kann," in *Das Politische Schreiben: Essays zu Theatertexten* (Berlin: Theater der Zeit, 2002), 11–21.

13   See Matthias Warstat, Florian Evers, Kristin Flade, Fabian Lempa, and Lilian Seuberling, "Einleitung," in *Applied Theatre: Rahmen und Positionen*, ed. Matthias Warstat, Florian Evers, Kristin Flade, Fabian Lempa and Lilian Seuberling (Berlin: Theater der Zeit, 2017), 7–28.

14   Just a few months before the Harvey Weinstein case broke and #MeToo began, several playwrights and theater professionals published blog contributions to the journal *Der Merkur*, discussing their experiences of sexism, racism, and classism in Germany. In particular, see Darja Stocker, "Und was hat das mit Sexismus zu tun?" *Der Merkur*, August 11, 2017, https://www.merkur-zeitschrift.

organizations became particularly sensitive to #MeToo's advocacy of female empowerment and social change and were quick to proclaim solidarity with the campaign and its protagonists. The first reaction to the movement in German theater, however, was more pragmatic than political, consisting in a demand for better female representation and for equal pay for male and female performers and professionals.[15] Not unlike most economic sectors in Germany (and the rest of Europe), the performing arts in general are characterized by substantial gender-based inequities, as was demonstrated by the recent study *Frauen in Kultur und Medien* (Women in Culture and Media) published by the German Cultural Council.[16] Following in the footsteps of earlier successes by initiatives like Theater.Frauen (Theater.Women), which was launched in 2015, new campaigns—like the Pro Quote Bühne (Pro Gender Quota Stage) and the Initiative für Solidarität am Theater (Initiative for Solidarity in Theater)— were founded, each with its own specific aims, to help break repeating patterns of discrimination and paternalism in the theater profession.[17]

In a second phase, the core message of #MeToo has also begun to reverberate in theater programs, primarily via stage productions and event series that have addressed the issue of sexual violence with various aesthetic and discursive tools. The epicenter of this phenomenon was Berlin, where Freie Szene theaters associated with an independent performing arts community, such as Hebbel am Ufer, as well as major institutions, such as the Berliner Ensemble, organized lectures, debates, and performances

---

de/2017/08/11/und-was-hat-das-mit-sexismus-zu-tun. This article provoked an important debate on hierarchies and abusive structures in theater and academia that gained further relevance in the wake of #MeToo. See Azadeh Sharifi, "On Being Included: Eine intersektionale Perspektive auf deutsche Bühnen," in *Staging Gender: Reflexionen aus Theorie und Praxis der performativen Künste*, ed. Irene Lehmann, Katharina Rost, and Rainer Simon (Bielefeld: transcript, 2019), 167–73, here 169–70.

15 The February 2018 issue of *Theater heute* opened with an article with the telling title "Lasst Taten sehen!" (It Is Time to Act!), in which the author pushed for a 50 percent quota for female general managers (*Intendantinnen*), a 50 percent quota for plays by women, and a 50 percent quota for female in-house directors. Cf. Barbara Burckhardt, "Lasst Taten sehen! #MeToo ist im deutschen Theater angekommen—als Struktur-Debatte," *Theater heute* 59, no. 2 (February 2018): 1, https://www.der-theaterverlag.de/theater-heute/aktuelles-heft/artikel/lasst-taten-sehen.

16 Cf. Gabriele Schulz, Carolin Ries, and Olaf Zimmermann, *Frauen in Kultur und Medien: Ein Überblick über aktuelle Tendenzen, Entwicklungen und Lösungsvorschläge* (Berlin: Deutscher Kulturrat, 2016), 204–16.

17 Cf. https://www.facebook.com/theater.frauen/; https://www.proquote-buehne.de/; https://solidaritaet-am-theater.org/.

revolving around different aspects of gender justice.[18] Arguably, however, it was the Maxim Gorki Theater that offered the most prominent response to #MeToo on the German theater landscape by opening the 2018–19 season with two original plays that overtly address the aftermath of the movement:[19] *Yes but No* by Yael Ronen, a main stage production that premiered on September 7, 2018, and *You Are Not the Hero of This Story* by Suna Gürler and Lucien Haug, which was first staged on September 8, 2018, at Studio Я, a smaller Gorki venue.

The present contribution investigates the aesthetic strategies through which both productions represented gender conflict and sexual abuse onstage in order to reignite the relevance of the #MeToo movement in German cultural discourse almost a year after its inception. By highlighting the metareflective aspects of the plays—such as the Brechtian breaking of the fourth wall, the reflection on the representability of sexuality and sexual violence in the theater medium, and the performative nature of gender and social roles—the analysis will focus in particular on how the performances engage with a reflection on accepted patterns of harassment in both the theater world and society. At the same time, it will outline the extent to which both *Yes but No* and *You Are Not the Hero of This Story* attempt to thematize the transformative potential of #MeToo and, more generally, to promote the idea of theater as a space that can project and shape alternative social futures.[20]

Toward a Pedagogy of Consent:
Yael Ronen's *Yes but No*

Yes but No begins quite casually, with five actors appearing in white bathrobes and slippers—an irreverent allusion to predatory movie mogul Harvey Weinstein[21] that simultaneously creates intimacy between the actors

---

18 In April 2018, Hebbel am Ufer organized an evening on #MeToo called "Fearless Speech: Transgressing Transgression"; in October 2018 the Berliner Ensemble ran an event series under the title "Fokus: Gender," accompanied by a "feminist" two-play production that included *Revolt. She Said. Revolt Again* by Alice Birch and *Mar-a-lago. Oder. Neuschwanstein* by Marlene Streeruwitz (premiered on October 13, 2018).

19 Both productions were explicitly advertised as #MeToo plays in the theater program. Their respective webpages are https://www.gorki.de/en/yes-but-no and https://www.gorki.de/en/you-are-not-the-hero-of-this-story.

20 As neither script has been published to date, the discussion will be based exclusively on the productions. I am extremely grateful to the Maxim Gorki Theater for allowing me access to a recorded version of the plays and for providing me with additional materials. All quotations in the text are from these recordings.

21 For an investigation of the Weinstein case, see Jodi Kantor and Megan Twohey, *She Said: Breaking the Sexual Harassment Story That Helped Ignite a*

and spectators. Above the stage, an inclined screen displays the hexagonal pouffes, laid out in a vaguely phallic shape, upon which the actors sit.

In the prologue, actress Orit Nahmias, the director's alter ego and the show-stealer of the evening, introduces the topic with typical Gorki self-irony: after having performed a repertoire that was "actually based on Amnesty reports" and covered all sorts of politically charged themes, she states, it is time to talk about sexual violence and the abuse of power. Since Shermin Langhoff and Jens Hillje took up the artistic direction of the Maxim Gorki Theater in 2013, Berlin's smallest city theater—which was named by German critics *Theater des Jahres* (Theater of the Year) in 2014 and 2016—has systematically linked its productions with social justice issues. By staging both updated classics and new plays written and performed by professionals from different nationalities and migration histories, the Gorki Theater has extensively explored the question of otherness and belonging in contemporary German culture (continuing Langhoff's aesthetics of a "post-migrant theater"[22]) and addressed topics such as homophobia, Islamophobia, and past and present wars and conflicts, reaching out to audiences that go beyond the traditional white middle-class theatergoers.[23] In light of this track record of productions with a clear political stance, it is not surprising that the Gorki included relevant projects on #MeToo in its repertoire.

Instead of replicating a traditional dramaturgy based on conflict, Yael Ronen and the Gorki ensemble set out deliberately to offer a positive "vision" of a culture that moves "from domination to cooperation" and that is based on communication and consent. In order to realize this vision, Ronen worked in collaboration with the ensemble to shape the show as *Eine Diskussion mit Songs* (A Discussion with Songs), as the play's subtitle reveals. *Yes but No* must thus be read as a work in progress: as a theatrical project and as a source of stimuli for reflection, rather than as a polished play with a coherent plot and fully developed characters. In the style of previous works written by Ronen for the Gorki, such as

Movement (New York: Penguin, 2019).

22   See Azadeh Sharifi, "Postmigrantisches Theater: Eine neue Agenda für die Deutschen Bühnen," in *Theater und Migration: Herausforderungen für Kulturpolitik und Theaterpraxis*, ed. Wolfgang Schneider (Bielefeld: transcript, 2011), 35–45; Matt Cornish, "Migration: Common and Uncommon Grounds at Berlin's Gorki Theater," in *Postdramatic Theatre and Form*, ed. Michael Shane Boyle, Matt Cornish, Brandon Woolf, Enoch Brater and Mark Taylor-Batty (London: Bloomsbury, 2019), 179–95; Brangwen Stone, "Migration and Theatre in Berlin: The Maxim Gorki Theater and the Komische Oper," in *Theater and Internationalization: Perspectives from Australia, Germany, and Beyond*, ed. Ulrike Garde and John R. Severn (London: Routledge, 2020), 199–214.

23   See Till Briegleb, "A Stage for an Open Society," *DE Magazin Deutschland: Forum on Politics, Culture and Business* 4, no. 2 (2015): 66–69.

The Situation (2015) and *Roma Armee* (2017), the play combines post-dramatic techniques, such as the accumulation of monologues and anecdotes, with revue elements like sketches and songs. On the one hand, this is reminiscent of Brecht's *Verfremdungseffekt*, an "alienation" or distancing effect that prompts the audience to detach itself from the dramatic action in order to engage critically with the topics presented onstage.[24] On the other hand, the style and language of some sections of the play pay tribute to the tradition of feminist stand-up comedy and radical women's theater, whose goal was "to disseminate feminist issues more widely, to work on political issues and, close to an agitprop style, [to] raise awareness of those issues."[25]

The actors' monologues form the backbone of the play; it is unclear whether they are autobiographical or fully fictional. They emerge initially during a frivolous group therapy session as memories of childhood and youthful sexuality, of failed attempts at masturbation, and of clumsy first times. The mood changes rapidly, however, when stories of abuse begin to be recounted. These stories, which pile up successively at a higher and higher pace, reproduce onstage the online cascade of #MeToo threads. Simultaneously, they sensitize the audience to the feelings of disgust and shame behind each story, conferring a sense of "presentness" and tangibility to the victims' bodies and voices that cannot possibly be achieved in the immateriality of virtual space.

The most striking among these stories are those told by Svenja Liesau, who recalls being sexually abused by her stepfather and raped by a group of boys as a teenager. In an extremely powerful scene, the character dismantles the hexagonal brick flooring that covers the stage, symbolically losing the ground under her feet and unleashing her despair. Her description of the abuses is sober: Ronen chooses not to stage the violent acts themselves but to represent them verbally, so that the focus remains on the victim's account and her inner tribulations rather than on her violated body. By doing so, Ronen precludes the possibility of giving space to questionable forms of voyeurism—a topic much debated in the German theater industry during the months preceding the premiere of *Yes but No*, when critics accused the explicit representation of sexual violence in the Deutsches Theater adaptation of Björn SC Deigner's *In Stanniolpapier* (In Tin Foil) of being pornographic and objectifying.[26]

---

24 See Bertolt Brecht, "Alienation Effects in Chinese Acting," in *Brecht on Theatre*, 91–99.

25 Kim Wiltshire, "Women's Theatre," in *Scenes from the Revolution: Making Political Theatre 1968–2018*, ed. Kim Wiltshire and Billy Cowan (London: Pluto Press, 2018), 126–57, here 127.

26 See, for example, Anke Dürr, "Alles doch ganz geil? Frauenverachtung im Theater," *Spiegel Kultur*, June 23, 2018, https://www.spiegel.de/kultur/gesellschaft/frauenbild-im-theater-der-missbrauch-des-missbrauchs-a-1214593.

Ronen's more subtle and intimate mode of representation removes the play from the current trend of dramatic realism that, as Elin Diamond has pointed out, is not simply a mimetic reflection of reality but in fact constructs and "*produces* reality by positioning its spectator to recognize and verify its truth."[27] To re-create an episode of sexual violence onstage would be to reiterate the same violence before an audience at every performance, potentially reinforcing the same patriarchal truth claims that underlie sexual abuse and often shape female subjectivity.

Another noteworthy monologue from the first part of the play is spoken by Taner Şahintürk, who denounces the methods of a famous Volksbühne director he had worked with. The director (we later find out it is Johann Kresnik) called all actresses "Ilse" to disempower them; wanted the ensemble to rehearse naked; and forced members to simulate traumatizing sexual intercourse. This monologue is of particular interest because it opens a breach in the problematic use of certain acting methodologies in the theater profession that blur the lines between the real and the performed, often legitimizing abusive behavior. In a recent article, Emma Willis has analyzed different instances of sexual harassment and violence in which an actor, director, or coach exploited their role in order to exert power over others, transforming them into victims with the justification that theater has to "feel real," postulating that "practices that require sexual and emotional discomfort on the part of female actors are simply part and parcel of what professional acting entails."[28] In all cases, perpetrators described their exploitative behavior as simply the consequence of a commitment to the craft of acting, thereby calling into question the professionalism of the victims in addition to casting doubt on the veracity of their complaints.[29] By inserting Şahintürk's monologue into *Yes but No*, Ronen highlights one of the merits of the #MeToo movement: namely, that it exposed "behind-closed-doors" behaviors within (and beyond) the

---

html. See also the response by actress Linda Pöppel, who played the role of the protagonist, to such criticism in Esther Slevogt, "'Ich mache mich verletzlich': Wie Autonom ist die Kunst in Zeiten von #MeToo und Sexismusdebatten?," *Nachtkritik*, June 29, 2018, https://nachtkritik.de/index.php?option=com_con tent&view=article&id=15615:sex-und-gewalt-auf-der-buehne-wie-autonom-ist-die-kunst-in-zeiten-von-metoo-und-sexismusdebatten-interview-mit-schauspiel-erin-linda-poeppel-ueber-ihre-rolle-einer-prostiuierten-in-in-stanniolpapier-am-deutschen-theater-berlin&catid=101&Itemid=84.

27 Elin Diamond, "Realism and Hysteria: Toward a Feminist Mimesis," *Discourse* 13, no. 1 (Fall–Winter 1990–91): 59–92, here 61.

28 Emma Willis, "'Acting in the Real World': Acting Methodologies, Power and Gender," *Theatre Research International* 43, no. 3 (October 2018): 258–71, here 259.

29 Cf. Willis, "'Acting in the Real World,'" 266.

entertainment industries.[30] Embarking upon a metareflective process, she
used a prestigious stage, the Gorki Theater, to confront sexual harassment in her own profession, thus underlining the importance of speaking out when we hear about abuse in our surroundings in order that we
as spectators do not actively abet collaboration with rape culture. Very
much in line with Brechtian epic theater, *Yes but No* invites the audience
to take action: the performative character of the play is extended beyond
the stage, manifesting in visible action that is meant to change the direction of the issues posed by theater.

In the play overall, #MeToo is referenced as a moment of hope, a
"crack in the system" that allows the exploration of new possibilities:
"Endlich bricht dieses Männer-können-sich-wie-Arschlöcher-benehmen-
System zusammen; . . . endlich ändert sich was" (Finally, this system of
"men get to behave like assholes" is collapsing; . . . finally something is
changing). As Liesau points out, however, in Germany the movement has
had no repercussions for perpetrators:

> In Deutschland gab's über 200.000 #MeToo-Posts, aber es gab
> keine Skandale, keine Selbstmorde, keine Rücktrittsankündigungen,
> keiner musste sich dramatisch im Internet entschuldigen—wir hat-
> ten keinen Harvey. . . . Das waren alle Geschichten von anonymen
> Männern, da wurden keine Namen genannt. . . . Ohne Namen
> gibt's keine Wirkung.

> [There were over 200,000 #MeToo posts in Germany, but there
> were no scandals, no suicides, no resignations, nobody had to
> apologize dramatically on the internet—we had no Harvey. . . .
> These were all stories about anonymous men, no names were men-
> tioned. . . . Without names there is no real impact.]

In this passage, Ronen addresses a question that has been recurring in
public debates on sexism since the #MeToo hashtag went viral: namely,
whether it is effective to name names, or if talking about individual sexual predators reduces responsibility to a small group of people instead
of tackling the structural problem of rape culture and its underlying
societal patterns. The two positions are dialectically dissected by the
actors: Liesau insists that it is important to single out perpetrators,
whereas Şahintürk maintains that #MeToo is not a witch hunt but a

---

30   Although media coverage focused primarily on the film industry, the theater profession had to confront its own practices as well. In 2018, for example,
American Theatre magazine published a special section in its August issue entitled
"#TheatreToo," which examined systemic abuse in the US scene and described
how various theaters were addressing the issue. Cf. https://www.americantheatre.
org/category/special-section/theatretoo/.

movement born out of civil courage to empower victims and stop systemic power abuse:

> Ich will nicht, dass es um Einzeltäter oder irgendwelche perversen Einzelfälle geht, sondern um Verhaltensweisen und eine Kultur. Darüber, was als "normal" angesehen und akzeptiert wird. Ich will über existierende Machtstrukturen sprechen, deshalb macht es für mich mehr Sinn über Statistiken als über Namen zu sprechen.

> [I don't want this to be about individual perpetrators or some perverted individual cases, but about common behavior patterns and a culture. About what is viewed as "normal" and accepted. I want to talk about existing power structures, so it makes more sense for me to talk about statistics than about names.]

At this point, the actors turn to the audience, who are now being filmed so that they appear on a screen above the stage. Undertaking a show-of-hands statistical survey, the actors ask spectators to answer specific questions about their personal experiences with sexual harassment and violence, and their reporting of it:

> Wer hat schon jemanden direkt damit konfrontiert, dass er oder sie jemanden andern belästigt oder missbraucht hat? . . .—Wer wurde schon mal sexuell belästigt? . . .—Wer hat schon mal ein #Metoo-Post geschrieben? . . .—Wer kann sich an ein konkretes Erlebnis erinnern, hat aber kein #MeToo-Post geschrieben?

> [Who has ever directly confronted someone with the fact that he or she has molested or abused someone else? . . .—Who has ever been sexually harassed? . . .—Who has ever written a #MeToo post? . . .—Who remembers a specific experience, but didn't write a #MeToo post?]

These onstage reflections and moments of audience interaction are punctuated by musical intervals ranging from rock to soul, from R&B to operetta, that add layers of nuance to the contents of the play. Memorable examples include a hilarious duet in which a couple negotiates a "deal of consent" prior to intercourse, discussing their sexual desires and boundaries in detail; and the closing cabaret number, in which male penetration is evoked as a panacea for toxic masculinity ("every man / in every land / should try to be penetrated / at least once!").[31] These breezy, even comedic, insertions—which are effective in balancing serious moments with

---

31   All songs in the play are in English (with German supertitles). They were composed by Israeli singer-songwriter Shlomi Shaban.

lighter ones—help facilitate a frank discussion about the delicate subject of abuse, demonstrating that humor and laughter can be used cleverly as a means to stimulate reflection and critique.

Although the tragedy of sexual abuse and harassment is very much present throughout the play, the playwright's ultimate goal of promoting a positive "vision" remains paramount. To this end, after the play's conclusion, the ensemble breaks the fourth wall to demand a relevance that moves—literally—beyond the stage. The audience is divided into groups and invited to join impromptu workshops that explore distance and proximity; audience-member participants are shown how to recognize and accept a rejection. Some critics have raised their eyebrows at this interactive and pedagogical ending,[32] though it is fully in line with the practices of so-called applied drama, which, as Judith Ackroyd and others have pointed out, *requires* audience participation to act out its radical "intention to generate change (of awareness, attitude, behaviour etc.)."[33] Asking the audience to shape a performance by participating in it means making spectators aware of not only the transformative potential of (political) theater but also their own ability to have an impact on real life by ceasing to be passive bystanders and becoming responsible citizens. As Jacques Rancière has suggested in his essay *Le spectateur émancipé* (2008; The Emancipated Spectator), the state of passivity inscribed in the traditional role of the spectator can be revoked only by theater itself, whose primary aim should be to challenge the idea that viewing and acting are separate things.[34] The workshops at the end of *Yes but No* set out precisely to cultivate spectators' engagement, thus liberating "a form of consciousness, an intensity of feeling, an energy for action"[35] that can empower them, make them aware of the social reality in which they live, and foster their desire to transform social structures that are clearly dysfunctional.

32   See, for example, Ulrich Seidler, "Berliner Theater-Premieren: Die Tücken der Harmonie," *Berliner Zeitung*, September 10, 2018, https://www.berliner-zeitung.de/kultur-vergnuegen/berliner-theater-premieren-die-tuecken-der-harmonie-li.9407.

33   Judith Ackroyd, "Applied Theatre: Problems and Possibilities," *Applied Theatre Research* 1 (2000), https://www.intellectbooks.com/asset/755/atr-1.1-ackroyd.pdf.

34   Cf. Jacques Rancière, *The Emancipated Spectator*, trans. Gregory Elliott (London: Verso, 2011), 1–23.

35   Rancière, *Emancipated Spectator*, 14.

Threatened Masculinity: Suna Gürler and Lucien Haug's *You Are Not the Hero of This Story*

You Are Not the Hero of This Story constitutes a discursive continuation of *Yes but No* in its addressing of the male response to #MeToo. In particular, Gürler and Haug's work makes explicit reference to prominent figures from the cultural world who have expressed skepticism toward the movement, such as journalist Jens Jessen, who wrote of "totalitarian feminism" in a highly controversial text for *Die Zeit* entitled *Der bedrohte Mann* (The Threatened Man);[36] award-winning film director and screenwriter Michael Haneke, who called #MeToo a "[degoutante] Vorverurteilungshysterie" (disgusting prejudicial hysteria);[37] and theater director Frank Castorf, who compared women in theater to female football players, claiming that he struggled to find any woman in either field who was more skilled than her male colleagues.[38] Reactions from politicians across the ideological spectrum are mentioned as well, from representatives of the far-right Alternative für Deutschland (Alternative for Germany, AfD) and of the conservative Freie Demokratische Partei (Free Democratic Party, FDP), who evoke the bugbear of "Genderwahn" (gender madness),[39] to Gregor Gysi from Die Linke (The Left), a party

---

36 Jens Jessen, "Der bedrohte Mann: Seit einem halben Jahr tobt die #MeToo-Debatte. Es geht dabei längst nicht mehr um Gleichberechtigung, sondern um den Triumph eines totalitären Feminismus," *Zeit-Magazin*, April 4, 2018, https://www.zeit.de/2018/15/metoo-debatte-maenner-feminismus-gleichberechtigung.

37 Gabriele Flossmann, "Michael Haneke: 'Hexenjagd im Mittelalter belassen'; Der österreichische Oscar-Preisträger über seine kommende TV-Serie, Politikverdrossenheit und #MeToo," *Kurier*, February 2, 2018, https://kurier.at/kultur/michael-haneke-hexenjagd-im-mittelalter-belassen/310.169.980. It is no surprise that a particularly gendered word like "hysteria" was used to diminish the movement. Another prominent figure to use this term was controversial film director Roman Polanski, who notoriously fled from the US in 1978 in order to escape sentencing for a charge of statutory rape, and who labeled #MeToo "mass hysteria" before getting expelled from the US Film Academy. Cf. Yohana Desta, "Roman Polanski Thinks the #MeToo Movement Is Just 'Mass Hysteria,'" *Vanity Fair*, May 9, 2018, https://www.vanityfair.com/hollywood/2018/05/roman-polanski-opinion-me-too-movement.

38 Cf. Christine Dössel, "'Es ist so wie mit einer Liebe, die vorbei ist': Der ehemalige Volksbühne-Regisseur Frank Castorf über Theater und Frauen, über die Zukunft und sowieso das Leben," *Süddeutsche Zeitung*, June 28, 2018, https://www.sueddeutsche.de/kultur/frank-castorf-im-interview-es-ist-so-wie-mit-einer-liebe-die-vorbei-ist-1.4033924.

39 The Alternative for Germany even has a special section on its website devoted to the alleged "Genderwahn": https://afdkompakt.de/tag/genderwahn/. For an analysis of the political manipulation of gender politics in Germany, see Sabine Hark and Paula-Irene Villa, eds., *Anti-Genderismus: Sexualität*

that emerged from the former East German Socialist Unity Party in 2007, who stated that he still wishes to be able to compliment women on their outfits.[40]

The play, however, does not focus primarily on prominent figures. Instead, it draws attention to "average" men who were interviewed by the authors during their preparatory research. These men's voices play in the background during some scenes, as the interviewees try to define masculinity and discuss their insecurities about relationships with women, which seem to have been exacerbated by #MeToo: "Wenn det so weiterläuft," says one man with a strong Berlin accent, "wird et bald so sein, dass een Mann Angst haben muss, ne Frau anzusprechen" (If this goes on like this, soon men will be afraid even to speak to a woman). The collage of audio excerpts is intended to provoke hilarity and to expose the inappropriate, often risible ideas men come up with when they talk about women and women's issues. As Gürler has explained, the play is built on the "Paradox, dass wir einerseits den Mann zu Wort kommen lassen wollen, ihm andererseits nicht schon wieder zuhören wollen" (paradox that on the one hand we want to let the man have his say, and on the other hand we don't want to listen to him yet again).[41]

Curiously enough, the actors onstage are all female—with just one exception. They are all dressed in suits and sneakers, and they wear fake moustaches, as though to demonstrate how easily gender boundaries can be crossed. As Marjorie Garber, following Judith Butler, pointed out in *Vested Interests* (1991), drag is a cultural practice that displays the constructed and performative nature (as opposed to the innateness) of gender, questioning the age-old dichotomy of male vs. female—and, indeed, all forms of binary categorization by extension.[42] In *You Are Not the Hero of This Story*, the cross-dressing strategy allows the actresses to caricature and stereotype certain male habits and thought processes; simultaneously, it invites self-reflection on the part of its male audience members at a time of an alleged crisis of masculinity:

> Was ist nur los mit uns Männern? . . . Wollen wir nicht ein friedliches Geschlecht sein, wollen wir nicht wissen, was uns zu Gewalt treibt?

und Geschlecht als Schauplätze aktueller politischer Auseinandersetzungen (Bielefeld: transcript, 2015).

40   Cf. Belinda Grasnick, "'Sie dürfen alles anfassen': Sexismus im Bundestag," *taz*, December 12, 2017, https://taz.de/Sexismus-im-Bundestag/!5471433/.

41   Quoted in Anna Opel, "Penetration neu denken: Das Maxim Gorki Theater eröffnet die neue Spielzeit mit zwei Uraufführungen, die vom #MeToo und den Folgedebatten angestoßen worden sind," *Zitty*, September 3, 2018, https://www.zitty.de/metoo-am-gorki/.

42   Cf. Marjorie Garber, *Vested Interests: Cross-Dressing and Cultural Anxiety* (London: Routledge, 1991), 17.

Haben wir Angst davor, dass es in unseren Genen liegt, dass es nicht
zu ändern ist? Wo liegt das Problem?

[What's wrong with us men? . . . Do we not want to be a peaceful
gender, do we not want to know what drives us to violence? Are we
afraid that it's in our genes, that it cannot be changed? Where does
the problem lie?]

A steeply raised stage represents visually this sense of crisis and precarious-
ness. The play opens with the ensemble confidently marching—with choreographed, "macho" movements—up and down the slope. The group
singles out each performer in turn, always referring to him as "Adam,"
the biblical prototype of masculinity, and assigning him the role of protagonist, though with no apparent rhyme or reason. The question of male
privilege is central here: Adam has for centuries been the "hero of the
story," although each Adam in the play does not seem to claim power
openly for himself.

Because of the sedimentation of gender stereotypes, we tend to take
for granted that some are destined to play main roles while others will
always be extras, but no one can explain the reasons for this ancestral
inequality. The Adams' choreography rapidly turns into an oneiric dance
from which paranoid thoughts emerge:

Was wenn ihr mich einsperrt, was wenn ihr mir den Prozess macht?
Was wenn eine Horde extremistischer Frauen mich . . . foltert und
dann vergewaltigt? Was wenn sieben hundert Schäferhunde auf mich
losgelassen werden, um Jahrtausende Ungerechtigkeiten an Frauen
zu rächen? Was wenn die Frauen Männermassaker anrichten? . . .
Was wenn wir nicht mehr gebraucht werden?

[What if you imprison me, what if you put me on trial? What if a
horde of extremist women . . . tortures me and then rapes me? What
if seven hundred German shepherds are unleashed on me to avenge
thousands of years of injustice toward women? What if women exe-
cute massacres of men? . . . What if we are no longer needed?]

These fears, which derive from a potential loss of power in the wake of
#MeToo, are displayed in a parodistic way that voices the nightmares of
the "threatened men" and ridicules their concerns.[43]

---

43 On this aspect, see Paula Perschke, "'Wann ist ein Mann ein Mann?':
Zwischen Behauptungsdruck und der Angst vor der Rache der Frauen. Dieses Stück verhandelt Männlichkeit neu," *Missy Magazine*, September 14, 2018,
https://missy-magazine.de/blog/2018/09/14/wann-ist-ein-mann-ein-mann/.

As the play progresses, the Adams onstage grow more and more vulnerable: they slide down the slope and struggle to climb back to the top—a clear metaphor for the loss of certainties experienced by some men, and for the effort that will be required to rebalance power during the challenging times ahead. At the end, the actors sit in front of the stage, facing the ramp, and an offstage voice evokes the prospect of a new era in which differences between the sexes are finally erased: "Adam, es kommt eine neue Zeit. Versetz dich zurück in deine Anfänge. Das ist auch kein Paradies mehr, das musst du zugeben" (Adam, a new time is coming. Go back to your beginnings. You must admit that, too, is no longer a paradise). This open ending, however didascalic,[44] implies the possibility of a change that can occur only if Adam renounces playing the victim and begins to acknowledge his privileges.

The question of privilege is central to the play[45]—not just male privilege but also white privilege, as the different ethnicities of the members of the Exil Ensemble, who act in this production, seem to suggest. The choice to include three actors from this important Gorki project, which provides theater professionals who have been forced to flee their homelands with a platform from which to perform, expands the play's focus on equality from a gender-oriented perspective to a broader one that encompasses diversity more generally. This conceptual widening of the topic to questions of intersectionality and inclusivity is in line not only with the agenda of the Gorki Theater, which markets itself as "#contemporary #queer #radically #diverse"[46] in its social media and is, to date, the only state-funded playhouse in Germany led by a woman of color, but also with the general discourse in contemporary theater, where gender issues are increasingly associated with themes pertaining to race, class, ethnicity, age, and ability.[47] On a metareflective level, by asking who "the hero of the story" in theater currently is, Gürler and Haug also ask who has the privilege to be seen and heard onstage (and beyond, in society at large),

---

44 A reviewer lamented that the play was "zu viel Erklär-Seminar, zu wenig Theater" (too much explanatory seminar, too little theater). Cf. Barbara Behrendt, "Jezt geht's an die Schmutzwäsche: Das Maxim Gorki Theater startet mit zwei Regisseurinnen und ihren Stücken zur #MeToo-Debatte in die neue Spielzeit," *Taz Archiv*, 11 September 2018, https://taz.de/Jezt-gehts-an-die-Schmutz waesche/!5531394/.

45 "Es geht um Reibungen zwischen den privilegierten und weniger privilegierten Positionen" (It is about frictions between the privileged and less privileged positions), as Lucien Haug has pointed out. Cf. Opel, "Penetration neu denken."

46 Maxim Gorki Theater Instagram profile, https://www.instagram.com/maxim_gorki_theater/.

47 Cf. Jenny Schrödl, "Gender in Theater, Performance und Tanz der Gegenwart: Themen, Strategien, Diskurse," in Lehmann, Rost, and Simon, *Staging Gender*, 47– 64, here 48.

which social groups have the power to interpret and possibly shape reality by means of artistic representation, and how theater can make issues around underrepresentation relevant in public discourse.[48]

Theater as a Rehearsal Space for Social Change

Conceived with the aim of amplifying #MeToo's message through the medium of theatrical performance,[49] *Yes but No* and *You Are Not the Hero of This Story* offer two different perspectives on the movement and its aftermath. While Ronen stages well-defined stories of abuse, anchoring her dramaturgy to the narrative aspect of #MeToo and promoting a pedagogy of consent, Gürler and Haug use the highly gendered Genesis myth to analyze gender conflicts and stereotypes, shifting the perspective of #MeToo from victims to perpetrators in order to explore (and

---

48   The intersection of race and gender also appears in *Yes but No*, where the racial connotation of media reports on sexual violence in Germany is criticized in a monologue: "Wenn man 'Deutschland' in Zusammenhang mit 'sexuellen Übergriffen' googlet, dann vertauscht Google die Anfrage automatisch mit 'Flüchtlingen.' Soll uns das sagen, dass wir sexuelle Übergriffe importiert haben, oder dass deutsche Männer keine Frauen missbrauchen? Oder heißt es vielleicht am ehesten, dass deutsche Männer das Vorrecht haben, Frauen zu missbrauchen, und dass sie sich dieses Vorrecht nicht einfach wegnehmen lassen wollen von irgendwelchen Fremden?" (If one googles "Germany" in connection with "sexual assaults," Google automatically replaces the query with "refugees." Is this supposed to tell us that we have imported sexual assaults, or that German men don't abuse women? Or, most likely, does it perhaps mean that German men have the prerogative to abuse women, and that they don't want to have this prerogative taken away by strangers?). On the racialization of rape in contemporary German public discourse, see Beverly Weber, "'We Must Talk about Cologne': Race, Gender, and Reconfigurations of Europe," *German Politics and Society* 34, no. 4 (December 2016), 68–86.

49   The plays were also received by critics as complementary works and were often reviewed together as part of a single discourse on gendered social justice. See, for example, Georg Kasch, "Liebe in Zeiten von #MeToo und Chemnitz," *Berliner Morgenpost*, September 9, 2018, https://www.morgenpost.de/kultur/article215283131/Liebe-in-Zeiten-von-MeToo-und-Chemnitz.html; Mounia Meiborg, "Er, sie, ja, nein: Zum Saisonstart am Berliner Gorki-Theater befragen Regisseurinnen Männer, Frauen und das Publikum," *Süddeutsche Zeitung*, September 19, 2018, https://www.sueddeutsche.de/kultur/gorki-theater-berlin-er-sie-ja-nein-1.4123439; Patrick Wildermann, "#MeToo als Theaterstoff: Wie kann man heute noch Sex haben?," *Tagesspiegel*, September 13, 2018, https://www.tagesspiegel.de/kultur/metoo-als-theaterstoff-wie-kann-man-heute-noch-sex-haben/23013406.html; Christine Wahl, "Lasst uns über #MeToo reden: Doppelschlag am Maxim Gorki Theater," *Republik*, September 13, 2018, https://www.republik.ch/2018/09/13/lasst-uns-ueber-metoo-reden.

parody) models of masculinity that align with the social validation of toxic behavior. Ronen relies on the power of empirical testimonies, extending her practical interest to the workshops after the show; Gürler and Haug develop a more rarefied discourse on the dichotomy between feminine and masculine as well as on the origins of inequality.

Despite their differences, both texts converge in their metareflection on theater and the use of theatrical metaphors: in *Yes but No* the spectator is educated in the culture of consent via theatrical tools, while *You Are Not the Hero of This Story* explores the roles of main and supporting actors in the real-life drama between the sexes, also expanding the question of gender equality to the broader frames of racial and social justice. Both plays thematize harassment and discrimination in the theater profession, citing prominent cases of abuse and addressing the issue of the representability of sexuality and appeal onstage. At the same time, they propagate an idea of theater as a space that can project hopes and "visions" that may help build alternative social futures ("eine neue Zeit"). In their own specific ways, Ronen, Gürler, and Haug ask how we can think differently about existing power structures as well as consider what changes can be made and how to enact them.

By exploring the utopian potential of #MeToo almost a year after its inception, the Gorki Theater brought the debate on sexual misconduct back to the center of German cultural discourse, once again transforming performance spaces into a social laboratory where new ideas and attitudes for cultural change can be tested—not just in theory but in practice. Through reflection and confrontation both on- and offstage, the theater thus becomes a meeting place of the aesthetic and the social[50] that, in the best tradition of German political drama, reclaims the possibility of making an impact on real-world policy and behavior.

---

50 Cf. Benjamin Wihstutz, *Der andere Raum: Politiken sozialer Grenzverhandlung im Gegenwartstheater* (Zurich: Diaphanes, 2012).

Part V

#MeToo across Cultural and National Borders

14: Patriarchy, Male Violence, and Disadvantaged Women: Representations of Muslims in the Crime Television Series *Tatort*

Sascha Gerhards

O N DECEMBER 30, 2007, an estimated thirty thousand Alevi Muslims protested in Berlin against the *Tatort* (Crime Scene) episode "Wem Ehre gebührt" (To Whom Honor Is Due). The protestors argued that the episode, which revolved around a father raping and impregnating his youngest daughter and killing his older daughter because she planned to report the rape to the authorities, misrepresented Alevi Islam. Roughly ten years later, after the 2015/16 New Year's Eve celebrations in Cologne, when hundreds of women were sexually assaulted and several raped, news media were quick to report that most offenders were identified as Muslim immigrants.[1] These incidents frame a problematic perception of Muslim life in Germany, bolstered by a tendency in the media to exploit isolated negative incidents, such as abuse, rape, and honor killings, when reporting on Islam. This depiction of Muslim life has had an impact on German anti-immigration politics: it contributed to the success of right-wing movements like PEGIDA (Patriotische Europäer gegen die Islamisierung des Abendlandes; Patriotic Europeans against the Islamization of the West) and the rise of the political party Alternative für Deutschland (AfD; Alternative for Germany). In this chapter, I investigate the interrelationships between the representation of Muslim gender stereotypes in the media—specifically, in the popular *Tatort* series—and the criminalization of Islam in German society more generally. The instrumentalization of gender constructs and violence against women in the service of xenophobic discourses situates this investigation at the nexus of Muslim identity and the emergence of the #Metoo movement in the Federal Republic.

---

1   Jörg Diel, "Bilanz der Kölner Silvesternacht—Hunderte Opfer, fast keine Täter," *Spiegel Online*, March 2019, https://www.spiegel.de/panorama/justiz/koelner-silvesternacht-ernuechternde-bilanz-der-justiz-a-1257182.html#:~:text=Bilanz%20der%20K%C3%B6lner%20Silvesternacht%20Hunderte,f%C3%A4llt%20die%20Bilanz%20ern%C3%BCchternd%20aus.

When the #MeToo movement reached Germany in 2018 after the accusations against filmmaker Dieter Wedel,[2] it generated extensive media coverage and revived a public debate about Islam. It particularly refueled criticism of patriarchal structures, abuse, the objectification and lack of agency of women in traditional Muslim families, and, most controversially of all, honor killings. The latest public debates on this topic once again ask how well integrated Muslims really are into German society and what role the media has played through its coverage of Muslim life. Analyzing media representation of Muslims, Rod Gardner, Yasemin Karakaşoğlus, and Sigrid Luchtenberg conclude that

> the portrayal of migrants in the German media is mainly one in which their roles are those of victim or perpetrator, and far less often one of their relationship to German society or the state. In Germany, the media have great difficulty in finding adequate words to refer to both the people who have migrated into the country and to their descendants. . . . Thus, the gap between "us" and "them" is maintained in the media discourse.[3]

The media, one could argue, both shape and reflect public opinion, and the gap between German natives and immigrants occurs not only in the German news media but also in fictional television productions. Three *Tatort* episodes, "Wem Ehre gebührt," "Schatten der Angst" (2008; Shadow of Fear), and "Wacht am Rhein" (2017; Watch on the Rhine), which depict Muslim gender roles, had a visible impact on the media coverage of Muslim life in Germany. I argue that these episodes tend to portray Muslim women who lack agency, while Muslim men are associated with toxic masculinity. The portrayals in these fictional crime productions offer evidence of the prevalence of distorted, negatively charged representations of Muslim culture, customs, and religion in the genre of the German crime film, contributing to fearful "othering" of Muslims in some segments of German society.

In my analysis, I first provide a brief historical sketch of Muslim life in post–World War II Germany and its negotiation in the media, followed by a discussion of the tensions related to the portrayal of Muslims with gender-specific stereotypes. Finally, I offer close readings of the episodes "Wem Ehre gebührt," "Schatten der Angst," and "Wacht am Rhein." My analysis relies heavily on the official mandate of the producing television

---

2   Kathleen Hildebrandt, "Ein Skandal in grauen Aktenordnern," *Süddeutsche Zeitung*, March 2018, https://www.sueddeutsche.de/medien/metoo-und-dieter-wedel-ein-skandal-in-grauen-aktenordnern-1.3926711.

3   Rod Gardner, Yasemin Karakaşoğlus, and Sigrid Luchtenberg, "Islamophobia in the Media: A Response from Multicultural Education," *Intercultural Education* 19, no. 2 (2008): 119–36, here 123.

network ARD (Allgemeine Rundfunkanstalten Deutschlands) to educate and integrate its viewership, thus shaping and constructing cultural
knowledge and practices.[4] With more than a thousand episodes of fea-
ture-film length, twenty-four teams of detectives,[5] and more than fifty
years on the air, the *Tatort* series as a product of the ARD deserves attention as one of Germany's most important pop-cultural artifacts.

The (Mis-)Perception of Muslim Life in Germany

Germany has faced challenges integrating Muslims into society ever since
Turks were first invited to come to the country as guest workers. From
the start, the German government failed to offer adequate integrative
programs, such as language courses, and Germans, like their Western
European neighbors, were hesitant to accept Muslim culture, its customs,
and particularly its religion. Andreas Schmoller has shown that "coexistence with Muslims is a sensitive issue in Western societies, and is largely
dominated by a securitization approach by policy-makers."[6] As a result,
public and news media discourses in the 1960s and 1970s predominantly
revolved around patriarchal structures and distinct disadvantages for
Muslim women, while Germans remained reserved toward Muslims.

The second generation of Turks born in Germany faced a different
set of challenges in German society, a complex issue that can only be presented reductively here. A study conducted by the Bundesministerium
des Inneren (Federal Ministry of the Interior) in 2007 suggests that patriarchal family structures often remained intact. On the one hand, second-
generation Turkish immigrants often embrace a conservative, religious
outlook that the parent generation seemed to have left behind.[7] They
also tend to feel discriminated against, are more likely to regard democratic ideals skeptically, and tend to feel poorly integrated into German

---

4   *Bildungsauftrag* (education) and *Integrationsauftrag* (integration) are
integral parts of the mission statement of the public ARD network. See, for
instance, Hendrik Buhl, *Tatort—Gesellschaftspolitische Themen in der Krimireihe*
(Munich: UVK, 2013), 19–23.

5   Typically, a team of detectives investigates in *Tatort* episodes. The episodes
from Mainz and Wiesbaden are an exception, with only one investigator.

6   Andreas Schmoller, "'Now My Life in Syria Is Finished': Case Studies on
Religious Identity and Sectarianism in Narratives of Syrian Christian Refugees in
Austria," *Islam and Christian-Muslim Relations*, 27, no. 4 (2016): 419–37, here
433.

7   Katrin Brettfeld and Peter Wetzels, *Muslime in Deutschland—Integration,
Integrationsbarrieren, Religion und Einstellungen zu Demokratie, Rechtsstaat und
politisch-religiös motivierter Gewalt—Ergebnisse von Befragungen im Rahmen einer
multizentrischen Studie in städtischen Lebensräumen* (Hamburg: Bundesministerium des Inneren, 2007), 42.

society.[8] On the other hand, second-generation Turks are often character-ized as highly motivated and well educated, which would imply successful integration into German society. At the same time, xenophobic attacks against Turks and other foreign nationals have continued, especially but not exclusively after German reunification. The murders committed by the right-wing terrorist group NSU (Nationalsozialistischer Untergrund) come to mind here and will be discussed in the context of the episode "Schatten der Angst" below. Studies show that second-generation Turks respond to such racist attacks with more self-confidence than the parent generation. They tend to confront stereotypes actively, resist discrimina-tory integration politics, and are more likely to fight back verbally, both in the media and in direct confrontation.[9] Hence, the media's ambivalent role in both shaping and reflecting public opinion could have a nega-tive impact on the integration of Muslims into German society, prompt-ing them to contest negative coverage while also hesitating to adapt to German society.

The rhetoric of "crisis" in news coverage on the 2014 refugee wave further shaped public opinion in a negative way. After the attacks in Cologne on New Year's Eve 2015/16, attention in the news media once again shifted to the Muslim male gaze and the objectification of women in Muslim cultures. This, in turn, fueled the fires of those opposing Muslim immigration to Germany. According to Ipek A. Celik, "research on the representation of Islam in German media shows that the topics of terrorism and communal and domestic violence in Muslim countries con-stitute nearly 80 percent of the German news on Islam. Hence, perhaps the composition rather than the content in the German media's agenda creates an 'enlightened Islamophobia.'"[10] Christina Ortner also confirms that news media often trigger and amplify prejudice, xenophobia, and anti-immigrant behavior.[11]

Celik's and Ortner's analyses confirm a parallel between the news media's shaping and reflecting of public opinion and previous statistical data and survey results: As of 2015, only 5.4 percent to 5.7 percent of the 82.3 million people living in Germany were Muslims, a percentage that includes German Turks of the first and second generations, converts, and refugees. These numbers were presented after the Deutsche Islam

---

8   Brettfeld and Wetzels, *Muslime in Deutschland*, 146.

9   Brettfeld and Wetzels, *Muslime in Deutschland*, 36.

10   Ipek A. Celik, "Performing Veiled Women as Marketable Commodities: Representations of Muslim Minority Women in Germany," *Comparative Studies of South Asia, Africa and the Middle East* 32, no. 1 (2012): 116–29, here 116.

11   Christina Ortner, "Tatort: Migration—Das Thema Einwanderung in der Krimireihe Tatort," *Medien & Kommunikationswissenschaft*, no. 1 (2007): 5–23, here 12.

Konferenz (German Islam Conference), which also took place in 2015.[12] The next census was scheduled for 2021.[13] Recent research indicates that 3.6 million (80 percent) of the roughly 4.4 to 4.7 million Muslims in Germany consider themselves religious. Public perception, however, differs significantly. Surveys show that Germans tend to believe that 20 million religious Muslims live in Germany.[14] In other words, the number of devout Muslims is considerably lower than the average German assumes, indicating a crucial misperception of the "Other": the Muslim immigrant or refugee. The discrepancy shown here also sheds light on social and political developments in German society, such as the rise of PEGIDA and the extreme-right AfD, as well as the events in Cologne on New Year's Eve 2015, commonly labeled *Kölner Silvesternacht* (Cologne New Year's Eve).

Founded in October 2014, PEGIDA, a German nationalist, anti-Islam, far-right political movement, organizes weekly protests and rallies that have generated significant attendance, especially before the political success of the AfD in the 2016 regional elections and the 2017 Bundestag election, and again after the Kölner Silvesternacht.[15] From the beginning, PEGIDA officials populated various media with verbal attacks on refugees. Over the course of only a few weeks after their inception, PEGIDA protests grew in sophistication, while PEGIDA's xenophobic rhetoric lost any remaining inhibitions. Especially initiator and former figurehead Lutz Bachmann quickly radicalized PEGIDA's rhetoric, as Kate Connolly notes in *The Guardian*: "Bachmann's language has changed. He started off talking of 'asylum seekers,' which became 'asylum spongers,' and now he is frequently heard saying 'invaders.'"[16]

Like the PEGIDA movement, the extreme-right party AfD has been on a mission to denounce Muslims since its formation in 2013. With their

---

12 Bundesamt für Migration und Flüchtlinge, *Zahl der Muslime in Deutschland*, accessed June 1, 2020, http://www.bamf.de/SharedDocs/Anlagen/DE/Publikationen/WorkingPapers/wp71-zahl-muslime-deutschland.pdf?__blob=publicationFile. At the time of writing, these data are the most recent.

13 Zensus 2021, accessed July 28, 2020, https://www.zensus2021.de/DE/Was-ist-der-Zensus/_inhalt.html.

14 Christian Röther, "Zahl der Muslime in Deutschland—Wie viel Millionen sind es wirklich?," Deutschlandfunk, January 2017, http://www.deutschlandfunk.de/zahl-der-muslime-in-deutschland-wie-viel-millionen-sind-es.886.de.html?dram:article_id=375505.

15 Patricia Anne Simpson and Helga Druxes, "Plurals of Pegida: New Right Populism and the Rhetoric of the Refugee Crisis," *German Politics and Society* 34, no. 4 (2016): 1–125, here 3.

16 Kate Connolly, "'Like a Poison': How Anti-Immigrant Pegida Is Dividing Dresden," *Guardian*, October 2015, https://www.theguardian.com/world/2015/oct/27/pegida-germany-anti-immigrant-group-polarising-dresden.

anti-immigration, anti-Muslim policy, the AfD has elevated PEGIDA's mission to an institutional level. The political success of anti-Muslim sentiment can be seen in election results, fostering greater speculation about the connections between representation and reality. In the 2017 Bundestag elections, the party received 12.6 percent of the votes, which translates to 93 out of 709 total seats in the German parliament.[17] This confirms Michael Ignatieff's statement that "even in Germany, where refugees continued to arrive and be integrated, majority opinion is turning against a politics of generosity that only a year before seemed to be holding its ground."[18] The change from *Willkommenskultur* (culture of welcome) to an increasing rejection of Muslim refugees ties in with the events labeled Kölner Silvesternacht.

The reported massive sexual harassment during the 2015/16 New Year's celebrations occurred predominantly in the area between Cologne's main train station and its gothic cathedral. After staying silent about the incidents for an astounding two-day period, several media outlets, citing police officials, reported that Muslim refugees had committed the attacks. Although the police quickly backpedaled, the damage was done.[19] Blaming refugees for the crimes committed in Cologne fanned the flames of those who actively opposed Germany's refugee policy, especially PEGIDA and the AfD. The following year, the police prepared extensive security measures to prevent a similar situation from happening. Roadblocks were erected around the cathedral and the train station; seventeen hundred police officers were brought to Cologne in buses; and hundreds of private security personnel were hired. Consequently, no major incidents were reported. And yet, on New Year's Eve, the police issued a controversial tweet that coined a new term and initiated a public debate about racism: "Am HBF werden derzeit mehrere Hundert Nafris überprüft. Infos folgen" (Hundreds of Nafris are currently being checked at the main train station. More information to follow).[20] The term *Nafri*, an acronym for *NordAFRikanischer Intensivtäter*, was meant for internal use

---

17 Der Bundeswahlleiter, "Pressemitteilung Nr. 32/17 vom 25. September 2017–Bundestagswahl 2017: Vorläufiges Ergebnis," accessed July 28, 2020, https://www.bundeswahlleiter.de/info/presse/mitteilungen/bundestags wahl-2017/32_17_vorlaeufiges_ergebnis.html.

18 Michael Ignatieff, "The Refugee as Invasive Other," *Social Research* 84, no. 1 (Spring 2017): 223–31, here 226.

19 For more details on the Kölner Silvesternacht events, see the *Themenseite* (topic page) of *Die Zeit* magazine: http://www.zeit.de/thema/koeln-silvester-uebergriffe.

20 Justin Huggler, "German Police in Hot Water after 'Racial Slur' Tweet after New Year's Arrests," *Telegraph*, January 2017, http://www.telegraph.co.uk/news/2017/01/02/german-police-hot-water-racial-slur-tweet-new-years-arrests/.

only and refers to petty criminals from Morocco, Tunisia, and Algeria.[21] Once again, and only after harsh criticism for racial profiling, the police backpedaled and soon corrected the term *Nafri* to "nordafrikanisch beziehungsweise arabisch aussehende junge Männer" (North African or Arabic-looking young men, respectively).[22] Ultimately, it transpired that most of the young men who were checked and taken into custody were from Syria, Iraq, and Afghanistan, and there was no evidence that they had planned or committed any crimes.[23]

Anti-Muslim political developments and xenophobic sentiments in German society can be attributed to a variety of causes. For the purpose of this analysis, I highlight a combination of factors. First, the long history of mismanaging the integration of Muslims into German society created a problematic legacy that impacts the current crisis. Second, German politicians were largely unprepared for the refugee crisis. The failure to respond to the refugee crisis with a well-thought-out plan created an opening for the leaders of the AfD and the figureheads of PEGIDA, who promoted a position on refugees that directly opposed that of the coalition government of the Christlich Demokratische Union (Christian Democratic Union; CDU) and the Sozialdemokratische Partei Deutschlands (Social Democratic Party of Germany; SPD). The events in Cologne fueled fear and hatred of foreigners and turned refugees—especially male Muslim refugees—into a new sort of scapegoat. What has transpired in the current sociopolitical and socioreligious discourse is a new manifestation of "Us" versus "Them." The opponent is not primarily defined by his or her African or Arab descent but, rather, by religious affiliation: "Muslim or not?" At the same time, this renewed form of racism distinguishes between male perpetrators and women who lack agency, thus presenting all women as victims, while eliding the reality of Muslim women who fall victim to male aggression in modern-day Germany.

Furthermore, there is a media-political dimension at play here that is not to be underestimated. The poor handling of the refugee crisis in its initial weeks and months by politicians and government officials immediately affected the perception of Muslim refugees, as evidenced in Gaby Hinsliff's analysis of the Cologne attacks:

---

21 Anna Kröning, "'Jung und aggressiv'? Was hinter dem Wort 'Nafri' steckt," *Welt*, January 2017, https://www.welt.de/politik/deutschland/article160771061/Jung-und-aggressiv-Was-hinter-dem-Wort-Nafri-steckt.html.

22 Mely Kiyak, "Durchs wilde Nafristan," *Zeit Online*, January 2017, http://www.zeit.de/kultur/2017-01/silvesternacht-koeln-polizei-nafris-kiyaks-deutschstunde.

23 "Polizei korrigiert Angaben zu Nationalität der Kontrollierten," *Zeit Online*, January 2017, http://www.zeit.de/gesellschaft/zeitgeschehen/2017-01/silvester-koeln-polizei-neue-erkentnisse-kaum-nordafrikaner.

Too often anti-immigrant feeling stems from what's really a long-running failure of the state—to protect children at risk, to provide enough social housing or school places, to police what has reportedly been a rough area of Cologne for years—which becomes more visible as the population grows. And since that growth can't be turned on and off like a tap, whatever some politicians say, the answer is for governments to do what we elect them to do: rise to the challenge, calm the fear that breeds extremism by demonstrating they can cope.[24]

Calming the fear, however, requires carefully calibrated information politics and media strategies. For two consecutive years, politicians and German news outlets failed to inform the public objectively and comprehensively with respect to both the refugee crisis and the events in Cologne. Rather than clearly demarcating refugee-related problems that have persisted in Cologne for over two decades, politicians downplayed petty criminality by North African individuals in Cologne for too long.[25] At the same time, both the police and the media promoted prejudicial terminology, such as *Nafri*, and overemphasized crimes and misdemeanors committed by Muslim men rather than focusing on stories of successful integration.

Adding another dimension to the problematic reception of Islam, Beverly M. Weber argues that we need to rethink what defines humans and what constitutes human rights with respect to our idea of Europe: "The Syrian refugees, for example, who arrive in order to claim their right to be free of the violence they face in Syria, are simultaneously hypervisible—discussed as masses of non-European bodies, often masculinized—and invisible, as humans claiming the very human rights by which Europe often defines itself."[26] Tying our moral standards to what Europe is or should be bears the risk that we might create groups who are less valued—with respect to the Cologne incidents, those immigrants from the

24 Gaby Hinsliff, "Let's not shy away from asking hard questions about the Cologne attacks," *Guardian*, January 2016, https://www.theguardian.com/commentisfree/2016/jan/08/cologne-attacks-hard-questions-new-years-eve.
25 Ulrike Scheffer and Nils Wischmeyer, "Köln und die Folgen—Männer aus Nordafrika zieht es nach Deutschland," *Der Tagesspiegel*, January 13, 2016, https://www.tagesspiegel.de/politik/koeln-und-die-folgen-maenner-aus-nordafrika-zieht-es-nach-deutschland/12822844.html; Reiner Burger, "Taschendiebe schrecken vor Gewalt nicht zurück," *Der Tagesspiegel*, January 15, 2016, https://www.tagesspiegel.de/politik/koeln-und-die-folgen-maenner-aus-nordafrika-zieht-es-nach-deutschland/12822844.html.
26 Beverly M. Weber, "We Must Talk about Cologne—Race, Gender, and Reconfigurations of Europe," *German Politics and Society* 34, no. 4 (Winter 2016), 68–86, here 72.

Maghreb (Morocco, Tunisia, and Algeria)—and those who are more valued and deserving.

In sum, news media depictions of Muslim life in Germany have been extremely biased, as they tend to project "anxieties onto displaced people by morally delineating the deserving refugee from the undeserving migrant while casting both groups as outsiders threatening the well-being of an imagined homogenous Europe."[27] Migrants and refugees encounter difficulties when they attempt to integrate into German society, much like Turkish immigrants of the guest worker generation and their descendants. Then and now, processes of othering have contributed to an increasing Islamophobia, especially in conservative circles. Rod Gardner, Yasemin Karakaşoğlus, and Sigrid Luchtenberg argue that German media contribute to this Islamophobia in a variety of ways:

(1) Only rarely do they report on Muslim immigrants in a positive way;
(2) They tend to portray Muslims as traditional Muslims (headscarf, traditional clothing), neglecting their varied and often very individual expressions of religiosity and even the refusal of an affiliation to any religion by Muslim-born individuals;
(3) They often quote political pronouncements without comment or rectification of bias.[28]

Such negative representations appear in news media, TV shows, and feature films alike. The crime television series *Tatort*, however, might be unique in this regard. Traditionally, *Tatort* screenwriters have come from a rather progressive, left-wing background. Associating himself and other *Tatort* screenwriters with the 1968 student movement, author Felix Huby states, "Wir haben den Krimi als Vehikel benutzt, Dinge zu sagen, die wir sagen wollten, also Gesellschaftskritik anzubringen" (We used crime fiction as a vehicle for social critique; to say things that we wanted to say).[29] The multitude of *Tatort* screenwriters Huby mentions theoretically increases the likelihood of a more diversified depiction of Muslim life in Germany. With twenty-four teams of detectives, the series covers a broad range of regions and their socioeconomic and demographic idiosyncrasies. Consequently, it offers an extensive portfolio of topics, including those related to Islam. Since 2007, at least fourteen *Tatort* episodes

---

27 Seth M. Holmes and Heide Castañeda, "Representing the 'European Refugee Crisis' in Germany and Beyond: Deservingness and Difference, Life and Death," *American Ethnologist* 43, no. 1 (February 2016): 12–24, here 13.

28 Gardner, Karakaşoğluss, and Luchtenberg, "Islamophobia," 130.

29 Eike Wenzel, ed., *Tatort—Recherchen und Verhöre, Protokolle und Beweisfotos* (Berlin: Bertz, 2000), 216.

covered, in one way or another, Muslim life in Germany, Austria, and Switzerland. Of these fourteen episodes, six offer a largely negative depiction of Muslims and Islam or revolve explicitly around Islamist terrorism,[30] two depict Muslims as victims of right-wing radicals,[31] one does not take a stand and allows viewers to form their own opinions,[32] and five episodes with Muslim main characters do not explicitly address Islam.[33] The sheer number of episodes warrants a selective rather than a comprehensive analysis. In the following, I offer a close reading of three episodes that allow insight into the series' intended message and general direction. The episodes "Wem Ehre gebührt," "Schatten der Angst," and "Wacht am Rhein" are similar in their negative depictions of Muslim masculinity but differ significantly in their complexity of characters and plots. Only "Wem Ehre gebührt" and "Schatten der Angst" reference Muslim women as victims without agency, but all three depict toxic masculinity and foreshadow the discourse initiated by the German #MeToo movement in 2018. To be sure, the *Tatort* series does not directly engage with #MeToo discourses. The focus on toxic masculinity, however, and the continuous reiteration of images of Muslim women as victims without agency warrant a closer look, both with respect to #MeToo and potentially underlying xenophobia.

"Wem Ehre gebührt"

Set in and around Hannover, "Wem Ehre gebührt" aired in 2007 and induced massive protests targeting the ARD television network. The episode revolves around male domination, family disgrace, and the concept of honor in Turkish culture. At the beginning of the episode, Afife Kara is found dead in her apartment. Her husband, Erdal Kara, claims that he found her after coming home from working the third shift. Detective Charlotte Lindholm quickly associates Afife's death by hanging with an honor killing, but her colleague, Attila Aslan, disagrees. He is convinced

---

30 "Wem Ehre gebührt" (set in Hannover, 2007); 694: "Schatten der Angst" (Ludwigshafen, 2008); 821: "Der Weg ins Paradies" (Hamburg, 2011; The Way to Paradise); 980: "Zorn Gottes" (Hannover, 2016; God's Wrath); 999: "Borowski und das verlorene Mädchen" (Kiel, 2016; Borowski and the Lost Girl); 1019: "Sturm" (Dortmund, 2017; Storm).

31 "Zwischen den Fronten" (Vienna, 2013; Between the Front Lines); 957: "Verbrannt" (Hamburg, 2015; Burned).

32 "Wacht am Rhein" (Cologne, 2017).

33 "Land in dieser Zeit" (Frankfurt am Main, 2017; Land in These Times); 1013: "Kriegssplitter" (Lucerne, 2017; War Shrapnel); 1018: "Am Ende geht man nackt" (Bamberg, 2017; In the End, You Walk Naked); 1056: "Alles was sie sagen" (Lüneburg, 2018; Everything They Say); 1062: "Tschiller: Off Duty" (Hamburg, 2018; Tschiller: Off Duty).

that Afife committed suicide and insists on focusing on her brother's involvement in big-scale software bootlegging instead. Even Lindholm's police chief refuses to have Afife's body autopsied, stating, "Das Thema Islam ist aufgeladen. Wenn sich der Ehrenmord nicht bestätigt, ist das ein Politikum und der Staatsanwalt kann seinen Hut nehmen" (The topic of Islam is ideologically charged. If the honor killing is disproved, the topic will become political and the district attorney will have to resign). In conversations with Detective Lindholm, however, Afife's sister, Selda Özkan, keeps insisting that Afife fell victim to an honor killing. Selda turned away from the more liberal Alevi sect toward conservative Sunni Islam, telling Lindholm, "Die Sunniten sagen auch, die Alewiten sind eigentlich gar keine richtigen Moslems" (The Sunni too say that the Alevi aren't real Muslims).[34] Selda eventually admits to Lindholm that she is pregnant but refuses to reveal the identity of the baby's father or to consider abortion. She seems to be afraid of someone and may have been threatened with murder. Eventually, Selda tries to commit suicide by hanging herself; but her father, Aka Özkan, finds her just in time and accuses Erdal Kara of influencing her negatively. In the end, viewers learn that Aka Özkan raped and impregnated his own daughter Selda and killed his daughter Afife when she threatened to report the rape to the authorities.

Several factors complicated the public reception of "Wem Ehre gebührt." First, throughout, the episode plays with the concept of the abusive male Muslim, embodied by Aka Özkan and Attila Aslan, Charlotte Lindholm's new colleague. When Lindholm first speculates that Afife may have been the victim of an honor killing, Aslan responds, "Aha, die türkische Weltverschwörung. . . . Klar, eine junge Türkin stirbt, dann war es Ehrenmord" (Ah yes, the Turkish world conspiracy. . . . Sure, a young Turkish woman dies, it must be an honor killing). When further debating the potential honor killing, Aslan rebukes Charlotte's claim that "Sie wollen nicht sehen, was da nicht stimmt" (You don't want to admit that something's wrong), stating, "Doch, ich weiß es ganz genau, Sie sind xenophob" (But I do, I know very well that you are xenophobic).

Throughout, Aslan patronizes Lindholm, exemplifying male domination, strength, and power vis-à-vis the female detective while continuously criticizing anti-Islamic stereotypes. By having a dominant Muslim character point out xenophobia in Charlotte Lindholm, the German main character of the Hannover chapter of *Tatort*, while also having him patronize her, screenwriter and director Angelina Maccarone made a

---

34   There are three denominations of Islam: Sunni (75–90 percent), Shia (10–15 percent), and Alevi (a relatively small percentage, but the second largest group in Turkey). "Sunnis and Shia: Islam's Ancient Schism," BBC News, January 4, 2016, https://www.bbc.com/news/world-middle-east-16047709.

controversial move: she reproduces anti-Muslim male stereotypes, but she also points to the continued existence of xenophobia in Germany. It is questionable, however, whether the Lindholm character is indeed xenophobic. As one of the best-established and longest-running characters in the series, Charlotte Lindholm's vita has been developed as progressive and left-leaning as opposed to conservative and/or racist. Thus, Lindholm's character might lead viewers to discount the prevalence of xenophobia.

Second, the ARD television network aired the episode on Eid al-Adha [eed *uh*l-**ahd**-hah], the "Festival of the Sacrifice," one of the two most important religious holidays of Islam. The network ignored requests by the Alevi Muslim community to change the date for the episode's premiere, insisting on the fictional nature of the *Tatort* series. This move was as unfortunate as it was unusual, since the ARD frequently emphasizes the sociocultural relevance and topicality of the *Tatort* series and its mission to educate and integrate.

Unsurprisingly, the episode's plot, specifically the incest motif in direct connection with Alevism, caused outrage in Germany's Alevi community. Alevi Muslims also vehemently criticized the implied differences between Alevi and Sunni Islam, especially the fact that the episode leaves the impression that Sunni Islam is superior to the Alevi tradition. Combined, these factors caused a heated controversy, resulting in public protests by some three hundred people in Berlin on December 27, 2007, up to thirty thousand in Cologne on December 30, 2007, and a sedition lawsuit against the television network.[35]

In conclusion, "Wem Ehre gebührt" tends to confirm existing stereotypes against Muslims rather than questioning them. The biased presentation of Alevi and Sunni Islam reaffirms stereotypes, especially in audiences inclined to accept the series' depiction as fact. The incest motif likewise intensifies the negative depiction of Germany's Alevi community. Only the controversial dialogues between Detective Lindholm and her colleague Attila Aslan have the potential to trigger a more multifaceted discourse, which is, however, potentially foreclosed by the long-established probity of the Lindholm character. Moreover, the victimization of women remains a prop in the larger discourse about xenophobia and the treatment of Muslim men in German society.

---

35 Anne-Catherine Simon, "Inzest Tatort: Opfer einer Propagandalüge?," *Die Presse*, January 2, 2008, https://diepresse.com/home/kultur/news/351296/Inzest Tatort_Opfer-einer-Propagandaluege?_vl_backlink=/home/kultur/index.do.

"Schatten der Angst"

The ARD network's poor handling of "Wem Ehre gebührt" explains the much more proactive approach of episode 694, "Schatten der Angst," which first aired only four months later, on April 8, 2008. Via superimposed text, the audience was encouraged to discuss "Schatten der Angst" in a moderated chat forum after the premiere, fulfilling the need to shape and reflect public opinion. The ARD also moved the premiere to a later date out of respect for nine Turkish immigrants who died in a fire in a large apartment building on February 3, 2008. "Schatten der Angst" was originally scheduled for February 10, 2008, when authorities still believed that the fire was caused by xenophobic arson, an assumption that was later proven wrong.[36]

Set in Ludwigshafen, "Schatten der Angst" aired well before the European migration crisis, the Cologne New Year's events, and the #MeToo movement. The controversial subject matter in "Schatten der Angst" is relegated to the subplot, which revolves around the maltreatment of Turkish women, the concept of honor in Islam, and a potential honor killing ("Ehrenmord"). The crime that motivates the police investigations and provides the framework for the subplot occurs at the beginning of the episode. Ercan Celik, co-owner of a Turkish fast-food restaurant, is killed with his own truck when leaving work. Önder Sahin, German-born son of Turkish immigrants and the other co-owner of the restaurant, does not seem to be emotionally affected by the murder, arousing suspicion in police detective Lena Odenthal. In the course of the investigation, in which even the Landeskriminalamt (LKA; State Office of Criminal Investigation) gets involved, it becomes clear that Önder is spearheading a large-scale drug-trafficking ring. Over a couple of months, several Turkish owners of small businesses have been murdered, and LKA investigator Yilmaz, pointing out a recurring pattern in the crimes, is convinced that Önder is involved. The police suspect that he killed his business partner, Ercan, as well. Interestingly, Detective Yilmaz states early in the investigation, "Ein islamistischer oder rechtsradikaler Hintergrund ist ziemlich sicher auszuschließen" (It seems safe to rule out an Islamist or extreme-right background).

In retrospect, Yilmaz's analysis proves unfortunate, if not problematic, since the murders in "Schatten der Angst" closely resemble and are clearly inspired by the crimes of the Nationalsozialistischer Untergrund (NSU). Between the years 2000 and 2007, NSU-affiliated individuals killed nine small-business owners with a migration background and a female police

---

36 "Tatort-Krimi entwickelt sich zum Quotenhit," *Welt*, April 7, 2008, https://www.welt.de/fernsehen/article1877665/Tatort-Krimi-entwickelte-sich-zum-Quotenhit.html.

officer in major German cities; launched three bomb attacks (in 1999 in Nuremberg, 2001 and 2004 in Cologne); and attempted an additional forty-three murders.[37] As did the fictional investigators in "Schatten der Angst," the German police linked the crimes; but rather than investigating radical right-wing circles, they categorically ruled out neo-Nazi involvement and instead assumed that the Turkish mafia was responsible. This served as a further confirmation of a continuing stigmatization of Turks and Turkish businesses, although only some of the murder victims were of Turkish descent. The police investigated family members as potential suspects, which further added to the stigmatization,[38] and some prejudiced media outlets labeled the murder series *Dönermorde* (kebab murders).[39] The writers of "Schatten der Angst," it appears, included allusions to the NSU crimes, unwittingly contributing to this stigmatization and thus neglecting the mandate to educate and integrate. Once again, like "Wem Ehre gebührt," the episode "Schatten der Angst" ran the risk of shaping public opinion negatively.

Evidence for the existence of the NSU and its involvement in the series of murders was revealed only after the suicides of Uwe Mundlos and Uwe Böhnhardt and the arrest of Beate Zschäpe in 2011. In defense of the screenwriters, one should note that the LKA investigator who is sent to aid Odenthal and Kopper is a German citizen of Turkish descent, which helps to circumvent one-dimensional characterizations and national stereotypes. Further, the episode draws attention to prejudiced perceptions of Turkish immigrants in Germany and the continuing problem of enduring, open xenophobia in German society by having a witness state during a hearing, "Sie haben ja keine Ahnung wie das da ist mit den Türken. Wenn man sich in deren Angelegenheiten mischt, hat man doch gleich den ganzen Clan am Hals" (You have no idea what it's like with the Turks. If you get involved in their affairs, the entire clan will come for you).

As the investigation continues, "Schatten der Angst" introduces another subplot that revolves around the conservative religious values of Önder Sahin's family. Jill Walker Rettberg and Radhika Gajjala have argued that "the stereotypical image of Middle-Eastern men in contemporary times

37 "Eine Chronologie zu den Verbrechen des NSU," *Welt*, July 12, 2018, https://www.welt.de/print/welt_kompakt/print_politik/article179197972/Eine-Chronologie-zu-den-Verbrechen-des-NSU.html.

38 Susanne Güsten, "Türkische Reaktionen auf Nazi-Morde—Opferwitwe: 'Sogar mich hatte die Polizei im Verdacht,'" *Der Tagesspiegel*, November 15, 2011, https://www.tagesspiegel.de/politik/tuerkische-reaktionen-auf-nazi-morde-opferwitwe-sogar-mich-hatte-die-polizei-im-verdacht/5839006.html.

39 Christian Fuchs and John Goetz, *Die Zelle: Rechter Terror in Deutschland* (Reinbek bei Hamburg: Rowohlt, 2012), 182.

often suggests that they are dangerous."[40] This holds true for "Schatten der Angst." Ercan Celik, the murder victim, was married to Önder Sahin's sister, Derya. The Sahin family brought Ercan to Germany to supervise Önder in the fast-food business. As a Turkish citizen, Ercan needed papers to be able to stay in Germany, and Derya's father forced Derya to marry him. Derya, however, fell in love with Peter Bogner, a German man, and is pregnant with his child. Discussions about honor, moral beliefs, and disgrace dominate the plot going forward. Be it in the family's home, in discussions between Derya and her siblings, or in police hearings and interrogations, male members of the Sahin family are associated with toxic masculinity, while the women of the family are continuously deprived of agency. During a witness hearing at the gym, for instance, a coworker of Derya blames Önder when explaining to Detective Kopper why Derya quit her job:

Mitarbeiter:	Seine Schwester Derya hat hier gearbeitet, bis vor einigen Wochen. In der Buchhaltung. Sie hat natürlich auch am Tresen ausgeholfen, wenn viel los war. Da ist er beinahe ausgeflippt.
Kopper:	Und warum?
Mitarbeiter:	Sie soll sich nicht so in der Öffentlichkeit präsentieren, wie eine Hure, hat er gesagt. Die Männer würden sie angaffen. Ihren Mann hat er auch dauernd schlecht gemacht, weil er ihr soviel Freiheit lässt. Freiheit, weil jemand arbeiten geht. Der hat nicht kapiert, dass wir im 21. Jahrhundert leben.
[Coworker:	His sister Derya worked here, until a few weeks ago. In Bookkeeping. Of course, she also helped out at the front desk when we were busy. He almost flipped out about it.
Kopper:	And why?
Coworker:	He said she is not supposed to present herself in public like a whore. Men would gawk at her. He also constantly belittled her husband because he gave her so much freedom. Freedom because someone has a job. He did not understand that we live in the twenty-first century.]

This conversation reveals a number of important facts. First, Derya's family did not think very highly of her husband, Ercan Celik, which makes every family member a potential suspect for the murder. Second, the family does not approve of Derya's lifestyle: working a regular job and

---

40   Jill Walker Rettberg and Radhika Gajjala, "Terrorists or Cowards: Negative Portrayals of Male Syrian Refugees in Social Media," *Feminist Media Studies* 16, no. 1 (2016): 178–81, here 179.

appearing in public without a headscarf. Third, Derya is, in one way or another, receptive to their criticism, evidenced by the fact that she quit her job at the studio, returned home to live with her family, and, in a police hearing, blindly recites her family's moral guidelines. During this hearing, the audience realizes that Derya must be afraid of something or someone to have changed her lifestyle so drastically.

Detectives Odenthal and Kopper suspect that Önder might be the reason and confront him with his criminal record of aggravated assault. During the interrogation, the following conversation emerges:

Önder:	Egal, verstehste. Es ging um die Ehre.
Odenthal:	Aha. Um wessen Ehre ging's denn da?
Önder:	Um die Familie.
[Önder:	Whatever, you know. It was all about honor.
Odenthal:	Ah. So whose honor was it about?
Önder:	It was about the family.]

Önder here justifies violence as a means to defend a family's honor. Shortly after this scene, his brother Baris beats up Peter Bogner severely, warning him, "Wenn Du noch einmal mit ihr sprichst, dann erlebt ihr die Hölle" (If you talk to her again, I will give you [Peter and Derya] hell). While Baris brutalizes Peter, Derya, in another hearing conducted by Lena Odenthal, affirms her family's perception of honor—"Baris weiß, was Ehre ist" (Baris knows what honor means)—and blames herself for violating it. The episode's representation of a lack of agency among Muslim women points to an ongoing debate, as Beverly M. Weber has shown: "Since the so-called *Anwerbestopp* (end of labor recruitment) of 1973, dire warnings about the failed integration of immigrants in Germany increasingly have been linked to discussion of the oppression of women in Islam and Muslim communities."[41] Thus, there is a risk that gender is instrumentalized in support of xenophobic discourses. Moreover, the perceived lack of agency in Muslim women may be problematic in and of itself if "violence and agency are defined within liberal subjectivity," as Ipek A. Celik has shown. Consequently, Celik says,

> Muslim women are once again produced as sexualized bodies, this time liberalized through an added gist of agency defined by the freedom of choice. Difference is exoticized and eroticized within the frame of authentic experience, while it stays purely in cultural terms without an opening for alternative thinking that situates Muslim

41 Beverly M. Weber, "Freedom from Violence, Freedom to Make the World: Muslim Women's Memoirs, Gendered Violence, and Voices for Change in German," *Women in German Yearbook* 25 (2009): 199–222, here 201.

women in their social, political, and economic relation to German society.[42]

In "Schatten der Angst," Önder and Baris Sahin represent the second or maybe even third generation of male Turks in Germany who uphold the patriarchal, oppressive values taught by first-generation fathers who immigrated to Germany in the 1950s. Baris's antiemancipatory sentiments culminate in a final scene in which he prevents Derya from escaping from her family and running away with Peter. In this scene, Baris holds Derya at gunpoint and admits to her that he killed her husband, Ercan Celik. Like Önder in a previous scene, Baris justifies his violence with a reference to an honor code, stating that Ercan did not treat Derya with enough respect and consequently deserved to die. He then proceeds to blame Derya: "Und was machst Du, Du bringst Schande über unsere ganze Familie!" (And what do you do? You bring disgrace to our whole family!). Baris tells Derya to leave, but instead she approaches him and kisses him on the cheek. At this point, the audience expects an honor killing, but, in a last-minute twist, Detectives Odenthal and Kopper appear on the scene and prevent the murder. The episode ends with a remarkable statement by Baris: "Jetzt kann mich niemand mehr zwingen, ihr etwas anzutun" (Now, no one can force me to hurt her anymore). This ending, which keeps the fate of the main characters open, accords with a well-established tradition in the *Tatort* series. All the while, the producers of the episode intermittently superimposed an invitation to an online discussion forum during the last twenty-five minutes of the episode: "Diskutieren Sie nach dem Film in unserem Forum" (Join the discussion in our forum after the film). Rather than promoting passivity, this approach actively seeks to engage an audience whose country has struggled with its immigration policy for decades, as Rod Gardner, Yasemin Karakaşoğlus, and Sigrid Luchtenberg have demonstrated:

> As Germany only acknowledged its status as a country of immigration a few years ago, there is no strong acceptance of multiculturalism and diversity. Thus, contentious issues such as the building of mosques, special requirements of female Muslim students in schools or Muslim traditions for slaughtering animals have been part of the political, everyday, and media discourse for years.[43]

Maybe the head-on approach of "Schatten der Angst" enabled a more sophisticated discourse on this issue, depicting ongoing male-dominated

---

42 Ipek A. Celik, "Performing Veiled Women as Marketable Commodities: Representations of Muslim Minority Women in Germany," *Comparative Studies of South Asia, Africa and the Middle East* 32, no. 1 (2012): 116–29, here 119.

43 Gardner, Karakaşoğlus, and Luchtenberg, "Islamophobia," 122.

behavior in Muslim families, on the one hand, while facilitating an educated cultural discourse on Islam and its customs in German society via the moderated forum of the *Tatort* website, on the other. Unlike "Wem Ehre gebührt," "Schatten der Angst" addresses both Bildungsauftrag and Integrationsauftrag of the ARD network. In particular, the use of the moderated forum holds the potential to both reflect and shape public opinion. At the same time, the episode itself fails to strike a balance between the representation of #MeToo issues as they relate to Muslim women and an interrogation of xenophobia in German society. Derya, like the characters in "Wem Ehre gebührt," is depicted as a Muslim woman whose only agency consists in her complicity, a common perception of gender relations in Muslim families. German society, however, and its continuous problem with xenophobia, as described by Karakaşoğlus and Luchtenberg, is not the center of attention on "Schatten der Angst."

Both "Schatten der Angst" and "Wem Ehre gebührt" allude to the honor killing of Hatun Sürücü, who was murdered in Berlin by her brother on February 4, 2005. Ferda Ataman and Markus Ehrenberg wrote about the incident in *Der Tagesspiegel*: "Der Tod sorgte bundesweit für Entsetzen und löste eine Debatte über Zwangsehen und Wertvorstellungen von in Deutschland lebenden muslimischen Familien aus" (Her death instilled horror nationwide and jump-started a debate about forced marriage and moral concepts of Muslim families living in Germany).[44] In "Schatten der Angst," *Tatort* sought to negotiate topicality, social commentary, and public discourse on the controversial topics of patriarchy and male violence in Muslim families in Germany, years before the #MeToo movement and the Cologne New Years' incidents, even if it ultimately failed to do so successfully. In both episodes analyzed so far, the ARD offered a one-sided, biased depiction of Muslim customs, beliefs, and gender perceptions and thus can be said to have failed in its mission to educate and to facilitate integration. At the same time, the decentralized structure of the ARD television network results in an involvement of dozens of screenwriters. The network's plurality and the seriality of *Tatort* provide numerous opportunities to overcome generalized preconceptions against Muslims living in Germany while also raising awareness of Islamic customs and traditions that contradict the moral and ethical standards of modern German society.

---

44 Ferda Ataman and Markus Ehrenberg, "Tatort und Sürücü—Stolz und Vorurteil," *Der Tagesspiegel*, February 7, 2009, https://www.tagesspiegel.de/gesellschaft/medien/tatort-und-sueruecue-stolz-und-vorurteil/1438052.html; and Kathrin Buchner, "Wenn der Bruder die Schwester töten soll," *Stern*, April 7, 2008, https://www. stern.de/kultur/tv/tatort--kritik-wenn-der-bruder-die-schwester-toeten-soll-3085798.html.

"Wacht am Rhein"

While "Schatten der Angst" and "Wem Ehre gebührt" offer a biased view, other *Tatort* episodes contribute to a diversified, educated discourse on Muslims living in Germany. In the first half of 2017, two years after the Cologne attacks, *Tatort* premiered five episodes about Muslim refugees. Although a more positive negotiation of Muslim gender relations remains absent in the five episodes, "Wacht am Rhein," set in Cologne, offers a remarkable take on Muslim immigrants and extreme right movements such as PEGIDA, leaving the audience with a more multifaceted, more positive impression of male Muslims. This, in turn, may lead to different conclusions on gender relations. "Wacht am Rhein" premiered on January 15, 2017, a few days after the Nafri tweet of the public relations department of the Cologne police. The plot revolves around a robbery in a Cologne pet shop, during which the owner's son is shot and killed. The only description of the perpetrator indicates that he was wearing a hoodie and had a "migration background," a problematic yet official term commonly used in Germany to describe foreign nationals since the 1990s.[45] Critics such as journalist Sandro Mattioli claim that it is only used when negatively reporting on a person not born in Germany; for instance, when a crime has occurred.[46] Shortly after the robbery, Adil Faras, member of a neighborhood watch, is convinced that he identified the sweater in question during a walk and thus found the robber. Faras follows the suspect and eventually subdues him with a Taser. Faras then keeps the suspect hostage in the basement of his grocery store, torturing him frequently to force a confession. The audience quickly realizes that the suspect, Syrian exchange student Baz Barek, is not guilty when the true perpetrator, the young Moroccan Khalid Hamidi, is introduced. As the case unfolds, it turns out that Peter Deisböck, the owner of the pet shop and also a member of the neighborhood watch, accidentally killed his own son while defending his store against the robber. In the meantime, exchange student Barek has been reported missing. When the police investigators reach Faras's basement after receiving a tip, they find Faras dead and Barek gravely injured: Barek killed Faras with a screwdriver in self-defense.

The timeliness and topicality of "Wacht am Rhein" are remarkable. Filmed in between the incidents in Cologne on New Year's Eve 2015/16 and 2016/17 and aired only days after the police's infamous

---

45 Statistisches Bundesamt, "Migration und Integration—Personen mit Migrationshintergrund," accessed March 9, 2022, https://www.destatis.de/DE/Themen/Gesellschaft-Umwelt/Bevoelkerung/Migration-Integration/Methoden/Erlauterungen/migrationshintergrund.html.

46 Sandro Mattioli, "Die Deutschen erster und zweiter Klasse," *Stuttgarter Zeitung*, September 9, 2006.

Nafri tweet, it offers three main characters with a migration background: the Syrian exchange student Baz Barek; the asylum seeker Khalid Hamidi from Morocco, who has an extensive criminal record; and the Moroccan immigrant Adil Faras, who has lived and worked in Germany for decades. Unlike "Wem Ehre gebührt" and "Schatten der Angst," "Wacht am Rhein" strives to be honest with its audience, more so than politicians and the media. It portrays Muslims with a range of vitas. Several scenes and dialogues create opportunities for a critical public discourse on Islam.

Barely six minutes into the episode, a disapproving comment on the neighborhood watch by police detective Schenk references the events of the previous New Year's Eve: "Wacht am Rhein. Eine von diesen soge-nannten Bürgerwehren, die sich nach der Silvesternacht in Köln gegrün-det haben" (Watch on the Rhine. One of those so-called vigilante groups that were formed in Cologne after the New Year's events). Schenk notes the growing skepticism against Muslim refugees in German society and, at the same time, a growing distrust in politicians and the police. With contrasting perspectives presented, the audience is left to form its own opinion, although the sexual harassment of women in Cologne is not directly referenced.

The ambiguity of all characters, however—Muslims and non-Muslims—becomes apparent when the police detective's assistant, Tobias Reisser, an openly gay character with an implied migration background, interrogates Adil Faras:

Tobias:	Eine Frage noch, was macht einer wie Sie in der Bürgerwehr?
Adil:	Ist lustig, dass Sie das fragen. Was macht einer wie SIE eigentlich bei der Kölner Polizei?
[Tobias:	Just one more question, why is someone like you joining a neighborhood watch?
Adil:	Funny that you ask. Why does someone like YOU join the Cologne police force?]

In this scene, Adil Faras reverses Tobias Reisser's prejudiced approach—doubting a Moroccan immigrant as a member of a nationalistic neigh-borhood watch—with a counterquestion that could target either Reisser's sexual orientation or his supposed migration background, thereby both offering a gender discourse and exposing inherent underlying prejudice.

Discussions about moral imperatives, immigration politics, and the refugee crisis are interwoven throughout the plot. These conversations occur in various social circles: members of the police force, the neighbor-hood watch, and characters with or without migration backgrounds alike. Rather than imposing a single opinion and moral judgment, the show presents the audience with different options and thus gives it the chance to form its own. Interestingly, even characters in seemingly homogeneous groups are at odds. In one scene, Adil Faras gets involved in a verbal fight with Moroccans who offer him hashish, marijuana, and LSD. Faras grabs one of them by the collar and shouts at him in Arabic. Subtitles are not provided, but it is clear from the context that he is criticizing their social conduct. Similarly, during an anti-immigrant protest organized by Peter Deisböck and the neighborhood watch, the murder victim's mother, Katharina Deisböck, appears on scene and accuses the protesters of "propaganda, right where my child has died," pointing to the xenophobic nature of the protest.

The most disturbing scene by far is set in Adil Faras's basement. Adil threatens to beat up the already gravely injured Baz Barek with a crowbar. Long close-ups of victim and perpetrator followed by a long montage of teared-up faces on all sides make clear that there can be no winner in this situation. The ambiguity of the characters is painfully evident in the ensuing discussion between Barek and Faras, during which Barek questions the morality of Faras's actions. Faras's response, "Ich war mal stolz, aber Ihr [!] kommt hierher und macht das kaputt" (I used to be proud, but you all come here and destroy everything) reminds viewers of his own immigrant status even as it shows that black-and-white thinking fails to describe the complexity of the situation. In this scene, Faras replicates the notion of "us" versus "them" mentioned in the introduction to this chapter, even though he himself came to Germany as an immigrant.

My close reading of "Wacht am Rhein" offers snapshots of an episode that is laden with references to migration and otherness and with emotional discourses about reasoning and morality. "Wacht am Rhein" fulfills the self-imposed Bildungsauftrag of the public television network ARD, as it offers a more comprehensive, multifaceted, and less polarized approach to the refugee crisis and Muslim immigrants. This approach is, in many ways, less biased than that of many political debates and media representations. The episode shows how the media can approach controversial topics of human interest in a critical but unbiased manner. And yet, like "Schatten der Angst" and "Wem Ehre gebührt," it fails to tie its critical interrogation of xenophobic discourses to a representation of #MeToo-adjacent topics, even though the latter are referenced explicitly.

Conclusion

The mission of the ARD network to educate and integrate includes a commitment to represent the social, ethnic, and religious diversity of German society. This includes Muslims who immigrated when Turks were first asked to come to Germany as guest workers as well as recent immigrants from the Maghreb and from Iraq, Afghanistan, and Syria. Crime fiction, by definition, features at least some negatively portrayed characters as it contrasts the victim(s) of a crime with one or more perpetrators in a variety of different social milieus. The *Tatort* series follows the same recipe. Consequently, any time an immigrant is portrayed as the perpetrator, there is a chance that this negative portrayal could reinforce stereotypes about foreigners. One could argue that protests targeting the network whenever a Muslim is cast as a perpetrator are unjustified. At the same time, criminal acts perpetrated by immigrants, such as the Cologne incidents, contributed to the formation of the #MeToo movement in Germany, and one might argue that they too should be represented on television. For the ARD, these conflicting circumstances along with the self-imposed mission to educate require a tightrope walk. On the one hand, patriarchy, abuse, and isolated honor killings still occur in Muslim families living in Germany. On the other hand, as this chapter has shown, data suggest that Muslims are much more integrated into society than is depicted by the media, which contributes to a distorted public perception that fans the flames of movements such as PEGIDA and the AfD. While both news media and fictional media have contributed to the negative depiction of Muslims, #MeToo has not been negotiated in the *Tatort* series to this day (early 2022). This raises the question why the media avoid exploring possible connections between xenophobic representations of Muslims, on the one hand, and #MeToo discourses and the supposed maltreatment of Muslim women, on the other. Indeed, a negotiation of the connection between gender and xenophobia is absent not only from the *Tatort* series but from public discourses on Islam in general. More than forty years after the *Anwerbeabkommen* (recruitment agreement)[47] with Turkey went into effect in 1961, Germans, it seems, are still struggling with a meaningful discourse on Islam.[48]

* * *

---

47 In the *Anwerbeabkommen*, the German and Turkish governments agreed to have Turkish workers come to Germany as so-called guest workers. Some 867,000 Turkish workers came to Germany between 1961 and the end of the treaty in 1973. Stefan Luft, "Die Anwerbung türkischer Arbeitnehmer und ihre Folgen," bpb: Bundeszentrale für politische Bildung, August 5, 2014, https://www.bpb.de/themen/europa/tuerkei/184981/die-anwerbung-tuerkischer-arbeitnehmer-und-ihre-folgen/.

48 See, for instance, Andrea Dernbach, "Der lange Weg in die neue Heimat," *Der Tagesspiegel*, October 29, 2021, https://www.tagesspiegel.de/politik/60-jahre-deutsch-tuerkisches-anwerbeabkommen-der-lange-weg-in-die-neue-heimat/27752390.html.

The analyses of the *Tatort* episodes "Wem Ehre gebührt," "Schatten der Angst," and "Wacht am Rhein" show that *Tatort* screenwriters have produced biased depictions of Muslims. Often male Muslims are portrayed as patriarchal, invasive, and abusive, and as exhibiting little respect for women. Muslim women, on the other hand, are often characterized by a lack of agency; when they dare to dissent, they are either murdered, like Afife in "Wem Ehre gebührt," or they repent, like Derya in "Schatten der Angst." This leaves the *Tatort* audience with a distorted picture of Muslim life in Germany, suggesting that abuse and honor killings are frequent occurrences when, in reality, they are rare but highly publicized by sensationalist media. *Tatort* screenwriters must find a way to live up to the ARD's mission to educate and integrate: they must address important movements like #MeToo and broach the issue of male dominance, abuse, and honor killings while also promoting a multifaceted, unbiased depiction of Muslim life in Germany.

This raises the question why the relation between gender and xenophobia is not or is hardly addressed in the series, especially considering its multifaceted staff of screenwriters and teams of detectives. This warrants a look to France and even across the pond to the United States. In the United States, more and more Muslim women have come forward online in the #MosqueMeToo movement, revealing sexual exploitation, assaults, and rape in religious settings. Journalist and feminist commentator Mona Eltahawy started the movement almost thirty-five years after being sexually assaulted during the hajj,[49] and she argues that "we must make sure #MeToo breaks the race, class, gender, and faith lines that make it so hard for marginalized people to be heard."[50] Similarly, the #BalanceTonPorc (#ExposeYourPig) movement in France accuses Swiss-born Muslim scholar Tariq Ramadan of rape and sexual assault. In both movements, a problematic relation between gender and xenophobia or specifically Islamophobia transpires. Jalal Baig notes that "anti-Muslim sentiment has made Muslims balk at publicly airing their dirty laundry; nobody wants to fan the already raging flames of Islamophobia."[51] German public discourses are confronted with a similar situation, which would explain the absence of a discourse on the relation of gender and Islamophobia in the *Tatort* series.

---

49   The hajj is the annual pilgrimage to Mecca.

50   Jason Rezaian, "The #MeToo Movement Has Shaken the World. Can #MosqueMeToo Shake Islam?" *Washington Post*, March 8, 2008, https://www.washingtonpost.com/news/worldviews/wp/2018/03/08/the-metoo-movement-has-shaken-the-world-can-mosquemetoo-shake-islam/.

51   Jalal Baig, "The Perils of #MeToo as a Muslim," *Atlantic*, December 21, 2017, https://www.theatlantic.com/international/archive/2017/12/tariq-ramadan-metoo/548642/.

What's more, much like the #MeToo movement in the United States, which revealed predators in Hollywood, the media, politics, and business, the #MeToo movement in Germany has often focused on celebrities such as filmmaker Dieter Wedel or TV producer Gebhard Henke. Henke was accused of sexual assault by several women, among them author and television host Charlotte Roche,[52] and subsequently discharged by the WDR television station. As *Leiter des Programmbereichs Fernsehfilm, Kino und Serie* (head of programming for television film, cinema, and series), Henke was, among other WDR productions, responsible for the *Tatort* series.

I would suggest that, much like in the United States and France, Muslim women in Germany might not step forward or might do so only hesitantly out of fear of contributing to an increase of xenophobia or Islamophobia. And yet, while this hesitation might make it harder to learn their stories, the *Tatort* screenwriters are required to educate and integrate and should shed a light on the relation of xenophobia and gender. The German #MeToo movement can serve as a role model here: its spin-off #MeTwo has extended its criticism of discrimination past the gender debate, no longer focusing exclusively on the abuse and discrimination of women but also of other races and minorities, as well. The initiator of the #MeTwo debate on the discrimination of Turks is soccer player Mesut Özil, who was born in Germany and naturalized as a German citizen in 2007.[53] Much like #MosqueMeToo and #BalanceTonPorc, #MeTwo might have the ability to give a voice to minorities and marginalized people, including Muslim women. Maybe a *Tatort* episode revolving around #MeTwo could open a new chapter in the year of the series's fifty-second anniversary and initiate a more multifaceted public debate on Islamophobia and gender relations in Germany.

52 "Charlotte Roche wirft WDR-Programmchef Belästigung vor," *Welt*, May 4, 2018, https://www.welt.de/kultur/medien/article176062866/Charlotte-Roche-wirft-WDR-Programmchef-Gebhard-Henke-Belaestigung-vor.html.

53 Oliver Bilger, "#MeTwo dokumentiert die tägliche Diskriminierung," *Der Tagesspiegel*, July 27, 2018, https://www.tagesspiegel.de/politik/rassismus-in-deutschland-metwo-dokumentiert-die-taegliche-diskriminierung/22854940.html.

Filmography

Episode#	Title	City, Year
684	"Wem Ehre gebührt"	Hannover, 2007
694	"Schatten der Angst"	Ludwigshafen, 2008
821	"Der Weg ins Paradies"	Hamburg, 2011
863	"Zwischen den Fronten"	Wien, 2013
957	"Verbrannt"	Hamburg, 2015
980	"Zorn Gottes"	Hannover, 2016
999	"Borowski und das verlorene Mädchen"	Kiel, 2016
1006	"Land in dieser Zeit"	Frankfurt, 2017
1007	"Wacht am Rhein"	Köln, 2017
1013	"Kriegssplitter"	Luzern, 2017
1018	"Am Ende geht man nackt"	Bamberg, 2017
1019	"Sturm"	Dortmund, 2017
1056	"Alles was sie sagen"	Lüneburg, 2018
1062	"Tschiller: Off Duty"	Hamburg, 2018

15: Fatih Akin's *Head On*: Challenging Mythologies of German Social Work

Florian Gassner

FATIH AKIN'S FILM *Gegen die Wand* (2004, Against the Wall; *Head On*, 2004) follows the existential crisis and eventual stabilization of two second-generation Turkish Germans living in Hamburg. The female protagonist, Sibel Güner (Sibel Kekilli), who is around twenty years old when the film begins, drives the action. Having survived an attempted suicide to escape the confines of her patriarchal family, she proposes a marriage of convenience with Cahit Tomruk (Birol Ünel), who is almost twenty years older and also suicidal. After a period in which Sibel lives out her sexual fantasies with a series of lovers, she gradually develops a deep affection for Cahit. When a fatal, jealousy-induced altercation leaves him in prison, Sibel relocates to Istanbul, where she enters the world of substance abuse. The ensuing downward spiral ends in a gloomy bar where, during an alcohol- and drug-induced blackout, she is raped by her dealer. The sequence is not pornographic, but the camera does not spare the audience. We see Sibel from the side, from about four or five meters away, lying prostrate on the floor. Her assailant clumsily removes her trousers and rearranges her torso to enable his violent assault. The camera remains mercilessly static throughout the action; only a few cuts reduce our exposure to this agony. When he is done, the attacker coldly sends his victim into the Istanbul night, where her tragedy continues. On a dark street, she passes a group of men who start catcalling her. Sibel retaliates by insulting their manhood and physically assaulting the ringleader. Three times the men attack her, egged on by Sibel's unabating invectives, until one of them pulls a knife and stabs her. Taken aback by his own actions, the man retreats and calls out, "Is that what you wanted? Is it?,"[1] before the group flees the scene, apparently leaving its victim for dead. The sequence concludes with Sibel being discovered by the headlights of a cab. The film

---

1   Unless otherwise noted, the translations are taken from the subtitles provided in the DVD released for North American audiences: Fatih Akin, *Gegen Die Wand* (Strand, 2005). Whenever the characters speak Turkish, only the English translation is provided.

resumes after five years, when she reemerges on the screen as a middle-class mother in a committed relationship.

Considered in isolation, Sibel's character arc aligns with misogynist and orientalist traditions of Western cinema. The exposition evokes the motif of the Muslim woman as victim, "oppressed by her 'culture' and in need of liberation by enlightened Western saviors."[2] The denouement, however, "leaves the film open to a particular criticism often levelled at Hollywood's treatment of sexually promiscuous women, who typically are either punished by death or reformed by marriage. Arguably, Sibel undergoes both fates."[3] Moreover, *Head On* seems to invite victim blaming, as Sibel is continuously warned of the negative consequences of her actions. Her parents exhort her not to wed so rashly; Cahit, the prospective groom, and Sibel's cousin Selma (Meltem Cumbul) also caution against the sham marriage. Selma—a single and successful businesswoman from Turkey whom Sibel idolizes—in fact offers a viable alternative by inviting Sibel to join her in Istanbul. When, after the marriage and murder, Sibel indeed moves to Turkey, Selma supports her and urges her to stay the course toward an independent life. Even strangers push back as Sibel gradually turns away from her cousin and seeks access to Istanbul's drug scene. It appears that she repeatedly eschews the advantageous opportunities of her Western or Westernized environment, instead choosing a path that inexorably leads to disaster.

Ultimately, *Head On* brings the Western convention of representing the Muslim woman as victim into question by gradually alienating the representation of Sibel. Notably, her violent ordeal fades into one of six musical interludes that "not only lock the story into a structured frame"— the classical five-act drama—"but also function as an alienation effect to interrupt spectator identification with characters."[4] The contrastingly picturesque shots of a Romani band performing traditional Turkish songs in front of a postcard panorama of the Golden Horn[5] have been repeatedly linked to the dramaturgy of Bertolt Brecht by virtue of their interrupting

---

2   Katherine P. Ewing, "Between Cinema and Social Work: Diasporic Turkish Women and the (Dis)Pleasures of Hybridity," *Cultural Anthropology* 21, no. 2 (2006): 267.

3   Rob Burns, "On the Streets and on the Road: Identity in Transit in Turkish-German Travelogues on Screen," *New Cinemas: Journal of Contemporary Film* 7, no. 1 (2009): 11–26, here 16.

4   Mine Eren, "Breaking the Stigma? The Antiheroine in Fatih Akın's *Head On*," in *Muslim Women, Transnational Feminism and the Ethics of Pedagogy: Contested Imaginaries in Post-9/11 Cultural Practice*, ed. Lisa K. Taylor and Jasmin Zine (Hoboken, NJ: Taylor and Francis, 2014), 90.

5   Matthias Knopp, "Identität zwischen den Kulturen: *Gegen die Wand*," in *Kontext Film: Beiträge zu Film und Literatur*, ed. Michael Braun and Werner Kamp (Berlin: Schmidt, 2006), 63.

the narrative flow at pivotal plot developments.[6] Moreover, in its depiction of Sibel the film implements the chief object of Brecht's theory of *Verfremdung*. "Die neuen Verfremdungen sollten nur den gesellschaftlich beeinflußbaren Vorgängen den Stempel des Vertrauten wegnehmen, der sie heute vor dem Eingriff bewahrt" (The new alienations should only remove from socially-influenceable phenomena the stamp of familiarity which today protects them from intervention),[7] Brecht writes in his *A Short Organum for the Theatre* (1948). In *Head On*, the socially conditioned phenomena under scrutiny are the misogyny and orientalism that have long determined the representation of Turkish Germans, and Sibel serves as the lynchpin for this self-reflexive examination. Initially, the film encourages the audience to identify the heroine with familiar prejudices about Muslim women. But then, by drawing parallels to the male protagonist, *Head On* alienates and undermines these racist and sexist stereotypes, taking away the "stamp of familiarity which today protects them from intervention" and urging a critical review of the foundations of these prejudices.

Head On and the Mythologies of German Social Work

In the exposition of *Head On*, the character of Sibel is modeled after a crowd-pleasing trope that pervades German culture: the young Turkish German woman struggling to break free from her stifling, patriarchal community to live and love just like her German peers. As she puts it on her first date with Cahit, "Ich will leben Cahit. Ich will leben, ich will tanzen, ich will ficken, und nicht nur mit einem Typen. Verstehst du mich?" (I want to live, Cahit. To live and to dance and to fuck! And not just with one guy. Get it?). The religious studies scholar Katherine P. Ewing places this trope at the center of what she calls "mythologies of German social work" about Turkish German culture. She argues that these mythologies generate "polarized images of the Muslim woman as victim" that are then perpetuated "not only in the news media but also in the widely publicized writings of many experts, social activists, and those carrying out social policy such as social workers."[8] Mass culture reacts by prioritizing representations that correspond to these hegemonic

---

6   See, for example, Burns, "On the Streets," 18; Daniela Berghahn, "Seeing Everything with Different Eyes: The Diasporic Optic of Fatih Akin's *Head-on* (2004)," in *New Directions in German Cinema*, ed. Chris Homewood and Paul Cooke (New York: Tauris, 2011), 239–56, here 250.

7   Bertolt Brecht, "Kleines Organon für das Theater," in *Schriften zum Theater 2*, ed. Elisabeth Hauptmann (Frankfurt am Main: Suhrkamp, 1967), 681.

8   Ewing, "Between Cinema and Social Work," 267.

discourses. Ewing argues, "Cinematic images are particularly powerful when they are consistent with other forms of knowledge that are tied to governmentality."[9] Among other things, these mythologies of German social work perpetuate the notion of the female Muslim as victim and in response set "a normative goal of the total assimilation of the Turkish young woman into German society, defined in the most liberal terms of total freedom of choice."[10] In *Head On*, the character of Sibel in many ways conforms to this skewed image, leading some to accuse the film of "victimizing Turkish women and thus reinforcing cultural stereotypes."[11] And to a certain extent, *Head On* indeed reproduces the polarized images Ewing describes. On her date with Cahit, Sibel explains that her plan to elope serves the same purpose as her suicide attempt—to escape her conservative family: her parents would only accept a Turkish suitor, and her brother, Yilmaz (Cem Akin), once even broke her nose for holding hands with a boy. Once Cahit agrees to wed Sibel, he is required to navigate the traditional marriage negotiations, concluding with a kiss on the hand of his future father-in-law. Later, when Cahit inadvertently kills one of Sibel's former lovers, it is unclear how much the Güner family actually discovers about the sham marriage—they learn about the "Eifersuchtsdrama auf St. Pauli" (Jealousy Killing in St. Pauli) through a tabloid headline. The audience sees a montage in which the distraught family wordlessly sits at a table, the tearful father burns his daughter's pictures, and Yilmaz confronts Sibel on the street, causing her to take flight. Shortly after, she leaves for Istanbul. Years later, when Cahit is released from prison and tries to find Sibel's whereabouts, Yilmaz explains that he no longer has a sister: "Wir mussten unsere Ehre retten. Verstehst du doch?" (We had to save our honor. Don't you see?). Such a statement invites associations with the concept of honor killings, further corroborating the notion of Sibel as a victim of Turkish patriarchy.

Much of the scholarship on *Head On* has adopted Sibel's interpretation of her fate, including Ewing, for whom the plot "takes off from the conventional starting point of a young woman's flight from her family, complete with a conventional authoritarian Turkish father."[12] Polona Petek paints an equally dire picture, arguing that Sibel's family "is represented in exclusively negative terms, as irredeemably oppressive,

9   Ewing, "Between Cinema and Social Work," 267.
10   Ewing, "Between Cinema and Social Work," 272.
11   Karin Lornsen, "Where Have All the Guest Workers Gone? Transcultural Role-Play and Performative Identities in Fatih Akin's *Gegen die Wand* (2004)," in *Finding the Foreign*, ed. Robert Schechtman and Suin Roberts (Newcastle-upon-Tyne: Cambridge Scholars, 2009), 13–31, here 15.
12   Ewing, "Between Cinema and Social Work," 275.

inexorably patriarchal, and nothing short of fanatical at that."[13] Alexandra Ludewig similarly contends that "Sibel's hunger for life clashes with [her family's] concepts of Turkish tradition and patriarchy,"[14] and—without citing evidence—Ludewig even goes so far as to claim that Sibel's brother "would have killed her had she stayed in Hamburg."[15] Many more voices suggest that Sibel's move to Istanbul comes under "the threat from her own family for the . . . cause of honour,"[16] or that it is an escape from "the rage of her family."[17] From these discussions, Sibel indeed emerges as the prototype of the Turkish German woman as perennial victim of an overwhelming patriarchal order.

But in fact, *Head On* offers a far more ambiguous representation of Sibel's victimization and of her Turkish German family. This begins with the first appearance of her parents and brother, during a visit at the psychiatric ward where Sibel is recovering from her suicide attempt. "The shame you have brought upon us is unforgivable"; these are the first words her father (Demir Gökgöl) utters—tellingly, off camera, leaving it to the audience to imagine a grim and forbidding parent already plotting an honor killing. But once the camera cuts to the Güners sitting around a table in the cafeteria, a bright space rich in natural light, the situation appears tense but not menacing. Father Güner is an old, gray, and slightly stooped man speaking quietly and cautiously. Neither mother nor daughter is wearing a headscarf—the supposed epitome of female subjugation in Turkish culture[18]—and Mrs. Güner even has her hair dyed blond. The father continues his speech, measured, calm, and with pauses after each sentence: "Mankind's greatest gift is life. There is no greater gift than that. Who do you think you are to throw this gift away? You should be happy that you're still alive." When he gets up, he takes his leave with a rather cold "See you later," but nothing he says comes across as overbearing or even unreasonable; instead, he seems torn, tired, and resigned.

Subsequently, Sibel's brother, Yilmaz, does in fact threaten her, asking whether she cannot see how much pain she is causing their father, adding on his way out, "Wenn dem Alten was passiert, dann wisch ich dich weg"

---

13 Polona Petek, "Enabling Collisions: Re-Thinking Multiculturalism through Fatih Akin's *Gegen die Wand/Head on*," *Studies in European Cinema* 4, no. 3 (2007): 177–86, here 181.

14 Alexandra Ludewig, *Screening Nostalgia* (Bielefeld: Transcript, 2014), 400.

15 Ludewig, *Screening Nostalgia*, 404.

16 Arslan Savaş, "Head-On, Head-Off: How the Media Covered a Former Porn Actress's Rise to Stardom," *Film International* 6, no. 6 (2008): 62–71, here 67.

17 Lornsen, "Where Have All the Guest Workers Gone?," 26.

18 Ewing, "Between Cinema and Social Work," 280.

(If anything happens to the old man, I will wipe you aside).[19] It is remarkable that this grave threat goes unacknowledged, especially coming from the man who broke Sibel's nose when the two of them were children. Yet as Yilmaz pompously struts out of the hospital cafeteria, Sibel and her mother nonchalantly light up two cigarettes and coolly discuss the situation. Throughout the film, Yilmaz alone "seems to uphold his father's dream of a Turkish life in Germany—at the expense of Sibel's right to self-determination."[20] Sibel's unimpressed demeanor and the overall dramaturgy of *Head On* suggest, however, that "her brother is a somewhat laughable keeper of the family honor."[21] Much of this the film communicates through Yilmaz's physical traits. This is particularly evident when we compare *Head On* with another production starring Sibel Kekilli in which she plays a Turkish German woman who indeed becomes the target of an honor killing. *Die Fremde* (2010; *When We Leave*, 2011) unambiguously "represents both Turks and Germans through stereotypes that emphasize the oppression of young Turkish women by their families, epitomized by male violence based on traditional ideas of honor."[22] The film's vain and violent men, who otherwise lack any character development, are physically fit; their fashionable and often elegant wardrobes add definition to their bodies; and their stylish haircuts evidently require regular maintenance. The brother in *Head On*, in contrast, has shaggy hair; his clothes reveal his lower-middle-class standing; and he is so out of shape that Sibel will later outrun him while wearing heels. In this chase scene, Yilmaz does not appear a convincing "avenger of the family honor." He attempts to confront his sister on a populated street in broad daylight, and when she takes flight, he has to abort his pursuit after no more than two hundred meters—huffing and puffing, he throws his jacket to the ground. He does not wield a weapon, making an intended honor killing seem unlikely, and it appears that he immediately gives up for good. In view of this characterization, Yilmaz could be read as an almost comedic character, a distant relative of the bumbling Capitano from the Italian Commedia, "the loudmouth, but cowardly, soldier"[23] who in the end always undergoes "a complete final transformation from pride to humility, confidence to

---

19   My translation.

20   Ludewig, *Screening Nostalgia*, 401.

21   Lornsen, "Where Have All the Guest Workers Gone?," 28.

22   Katherine P. Ewing, "From German Bus Stop to Academy Award Nomination: The Honor Killing as Simulacrum," in *Gender, Violence, and Human Security: Critical Feminist Perspectives*, ed. Aili M. Tripp, Myra M. Ferree, and Christina Ewig (New York: NYU Press, 2013), 181.

23   Mace Perlman, "Reading and Interpreting the Capitano's Multiple Mask-Shapes," in *The Routledge Companion to Commedia Dell'arte*, ed. Judith Chaffee and Olly Crick (New York: Routledge, 2015), 82–90, here 82.

panic."[24] And in his final appearance, he is indeed humbled: when Yilmaz in conversation with Cahit asserts that the family had to save its honor by disowning Sibel, Cahit sardonically inquires, "Und? Habt ihr sie gerettet, eure Ehre?" (And? Did you save it, your honor?). The putative champion of Turkish patriarchy has no response and sheepishly averts his eyes. All this is not to say that the film glosses over the violence that indeed exists in Sibel's environment. But Akin clearly distances the male protagonists of *Head On* from canonical representations of the murderous male relatives of Turkish German women.

Even though *Head On* at first evokes the motif of the Turkish German woman as victim, the plot ultimately reveals a community of conflicted men with at best tenuous control over the women around them. Most notably, "Sibel's parents, while traditional, appear by no means as tyrannical as her reactions would indicate. Her family, while religious, is not fundamentalist in outlook and appears benign."[25] This becomes most evident during Cahit's courtship. In a telling scene preceding the in-person negotiations, Sibel's father, arms tightly folded, asks his wife (Aysel Iscan) about the potential son-in-law without ever removing his uneasy gaze from the television. "How can you give our daughter to a stranger?" he wants to know, and when she overrules his concerns, he has little resistance to offer: "When are they coming?" "Tomorrow, whether you like it or not." "So soon? Then let them come, damn it!" To be sure, Mrs. Güner has her own concerns about the match, and during Cahit's visit she asks her daughter in the kitchen: "Couldn't you find anyone better?" But in the end, both parents respect their daughter's wishes. After hearing the official proposal, Mr. Güner even asks Sibel whether her mind is made up and then, with a mournful expression and through several sighs, gives a short speech: "What can one do? When two young people have come together, and are in love with one another, what is left for us to say? God bless you both." His resignation is palpable and paradigmatic for the limited power of men in *Head On*.

The film at first invokes but in fact never plays out those mythologies of German social work that government policy, academic discourses, and popular media have cemented in public consciousness. *Head On* never forthrightly disavows these notions, but they gradually forfeit their cogency as the plot unfolds. This happens in a rather unconventional manner: there is no iconoclastic attempt on the image of the Turkish German woman as victim, nor does Sibel speak out against the normative

---

24 John Rudlin, *Commedia Dell'arte: An Actor's Handbook* (London: Routledge, 2015), 123.

25 Matthias Konzett, "Revisiting Fassbinder's Ali: The New Realism of Fatih Akin's German Turkish Cinema," *Excavatio: Nouvelle revue Émile Zola et le naturalisme international* 22, no. 1–2 (2007): 196–206, here 205.

goal of total assimilation to Western ideals of self-realization. Instead, Sibel embraces both these concepts in an exaggerated manner that successively exposes their respective absurdity (though without turning into parody). Initially, her character ideally embodies German stereotypes about Turkish culture and German hopes for Turkish women. But as the plot unfolds, her libertinage in fact ends up challenging Western morality. She thereby exposes the inconvenient truth that the Western ideal of individualism, as Ewing points out, "often smuggles the cultural particularities of the dominant group into a discourse of universal human rights and justifies forced assimilation to these norms."[26] In the case at hand, this means unequivocally equating Western modernity with freedom: "Moderne bedeutet Freiheit, alles andere ist Repression" (Modernity equals freedom, everything else is repression).[27] For the Turkish German woman, "freedom" thus becomes tantamount to internalizing gendered and sexual norms perpetuated by Western media, all of which are cloaked in the rhetoric of liberation: "The woman who wears a headscarf must be liberated so that she is free to expose her body to the male gaze or be free to engage in premarital sex."[28] In *Head On*, the character of Sibel exposes the hypocrisy of this demand by embracing individualism to a degree that challenges supposedly objective—that is, Western—notions of propriety. As Özkan Ezli has observed, Sibel "ist nicht nur ein Problem für die konservative 'türkische Community,' sondern ebenso für den modernen westlichen Emanzipationsdiskurs" (Sibel is a problem not just for the "Turkish community," but just as much for the Western discourse on emancipation).[29] Her character confronts the moral self-certainty of German audiences by stress-testing their "German freedoms."

Sibel and the Male Gaze

Sibel's assimilation to and subsequent exaggeration of Western ideals of female self-determination is particularly evident in her relationship with the male gaze. *Head On* first establishes the male gaze through Cahit's casual lover, Maren (Catrin Striebeck), whose naked body is exposed twice in the exposition during scenes of rough, consensual intimacy. Sibel takes on a job in Maren's hair salon and chooses her boss as a point of reference as she explores her femininity. She styles her hair in the same way,

---

26 Ewing, "Between Cinema and Social Work," 285.

27 Özkan Ezli, "Von der Identität zur Individuation: *Gegen Die Wand*—Eine Problematisierung kultureller Identitätszuschreibungen," in *Konfliktfeld Islam in Europa*, ed. Monika Wohlrab-Sahr and Levent Tezcan (Baden-Baden: Nomos, 2007), 283–301, here 291.

28 Ewing, "Between Cinema and Social Work," 285.

29 Ezli, "Von der Identität," 291.

adopts the same fashion, and—after expressing admiration for Maren's backside—arranges for the same type of tattoo to be placed on her lower back. The mise-en-scène buttresses this conflation of the two characters: during their first erotic encounter, the shot of Sibel leaning over Cahit is a mirror image of a previous frame involving Cahit and Maren. As she approximates her German idol, Sibel gradually moves to the focus of the male gaze. The camera first sexualizes her in the exposition when she jogs away from Cahit on the grounds of the psychiatric ward. Later, when she gives him a haircut, the camera moves in closely as Sibel presses Cahit against her lightly covered bosom. Their first abortive attempt at sexual intimacy in the third act is saturated with erotic shots of parts of Sibel's body, but it is not until the final act, when the two reconnect for a brief affair in Istanbul, that Sibel is repeatedly framed in the nude.

At this point, the sexist and racist traditions of Western cinema would suggest that Sibel's liberation is complete and that her integration into German society has been successful: by exposing her naked body, the Turkish German woman emphatically claims her freedom.[30] But *Head On* qualifies this logic at several key points, beginning with the fact that none of the Turkish German women in the story ever wear a headscarf, the iconic symbol of Turkish patriarchy in German public discourse.[31] Moreover, Sibel's Western savior is in fact a Turkish-born man (even if he has strongly assimilated to German culture, to the point that he speaks Turkish poorly but German with a local dialect). But most importantly, Sibel's spring awakening following her marriage to Cahit is also what leads to disaster rather than a happy ending.

Conflict first arises when Sibel and Cahit head to a nightclub, where he watches as she dances. The scene opens with a full-body shot of Sibel wearing high-heeled boots, hot pants, and a deep-cut, transparent white shirt with only the top button fastened, exposing parts of her bra as she moves in the style of a go-go dancer. A reverse shot reveals Cahit standing on the side of the dance floor drinking beer and smoking a cigarette. The handheld camera moves toward and around him, inviting the audience to interpret the next reverse shot of Sibel as his point of view, a notion that is corroborated when she makes frequent eye contact. This sequence perfectly embodies the principles of the male gaze, with the woman serving "as erotic object for the characters within the story, and as erotic object for the spectator within the auditorium."[32] The coincidence of perspectives invites the audience to vicariously enjoy control over the

---

30 Eren, "Breaking the Stigma?," 83.

31 Ewing, "Between Cinema and Social Work," 270.

32 Laura Mulvey, "Visual Pleasure and Narrative Cinema," in *Film Manifestos and Global Cinema Cultures: A Critical Anthology*, ed. Scott MacKenzie (Berkeley: University of California Press, 2014), 359–70, here 364.

woman via the male protagonist. "By means of identification with him, through participation in his power, the spectator can indirectly possess her too."[33] But in *Head On*, the male protagonist also is the male gaze's weak spot. As Laura Mulvey argues, the audience wishes to identify with a "more perfect, more complete, more powerful ideal ego,"[34] but Cahit, who calls himself a "Penner" (bum) and who is first introduced collecting empty glasses and drinking the dregs, does not fit this bill. This makes for a tenuous grip on the transformed Sibel, which becomes evident in the denouement of the nightclub scene. As Cahit and the audience observe Sibel dancing, the camera gradually brings into focus a competing male gaze from a tall, blond, athletic, and significantly younger man, with a tattoo sleeve and fashionable clothing rather than a dark long coat. To Cahit's obvious chagrin, the stranger and Sibel begin to move provocatively across the dance floor, and after they exchange a few words, she retrieves her coat and exclaims, "Cahit, ich geh' jetzt ficken!" (Cahit, I'm gonna go fuck now!).[35] As she pulls off her wedding ring, she enthusiastically adds, "Hast du den Typen gesehen?" (Did you see the guy?). Glumly, Cahit returns home, where he first trashes the shared apartment, then cleans it better than before, and eventually falls asleep while inhaling the scent of Sibel's clothes. This eruption of jealousy "marks the beginning of their passionate yet destructive love affair,"[36] but it also marks the departure from the mythologies of German social work. The heroine no longer fits the stereotype of the helpless Turkish German girl, grateful for her liberation. Instead, she becomes a provocation for Western patriarchy: "Presented as the libidinally unrestrained (Muslim) woman who is in control of the male gaze, Sibel's character soon emerges in the image of a seductive *femme fatale*."[37] Rather than fleeing her Muslim community to take shelter with a German savior, Sibel challenges the patriarchal order of her Western environment by uninhibitedly embracing her sexuality.

Head On thus aligns the character of Sibel with a form of pop feminism that entered German public discourse in the 2000s. A hybrid of second- and third-wave feminism, the movement "positively embraces the negatively coded female body, whether raunchy, pornographic, sick, injured, or otherwise unruly."[38] Authors associated with this movement

33 Mulvey, "Visual Pleasure," 366.
34 Mulvey, "Visual Pleasure," 365.
35 The subtitles use a less literal translation: "Cahit, I'm gonna get laid!"
36 Senta Siewert, "Soundtracks of Double Occupancy: Sampling Sounds and Cultures in Fatih Akin's Head On," in *Mind the Screen: Media Concepts according to Thomas Elsaesser*, ed. Jaap Kooijman, Patricia Pisters, and Wanda Strauven (Amsterdam: Amsterdam University Press, 2008), 198–208, 203.
37 Eren, "Breaking the Stigma?," 92.
38 Carrie Smith-Prei, "'Knaller-Sex Für Alle': Popfeminist Body Politics in Lady Bitch Ray, Charlotte Roche, and Sarah Kuttner," *Studies in 20th and 21st*

pushed the envelope for socially acceptable depictions of intimacy. One of its most striking exponents is the scholar and publicist Reyhan Şahin, better known by her stage name, Lady Bitch Ray. In this role, Şahin appropriated the misogynist language and stereotypes of hip-hop to challenge racist and sexist discourses prevalent in German society. Her intention was to provoke and offend, especially male politicians, music producers, and journalists, the guardians of "good taste" and "proper feminism," who questioned the propriety of her lyrics even though she simply copied the vocabulary frequently used by male artists.[39] Şahin's paramount concerns included reclaiming the epithet "bitch," which she defined as follows in an evening talk show on German public television: "Eine 'Bitch' ist eine selbstbewusste Frau, die sich nimmt, was sie braucht. Es steht dafür, dass—wenn die Möse juckt—man sich holt, was man braucht" (A "bitch" is a confident woman who takes what she needs. It means that, when your pussy itches, you get yourself what you need).[40] Her biography increased the shock value of "Lady Bitch Ray." Like Sibel in *Head On*, Şahin is a "Deutsche mit türkischem Migrationshintergrund," a second-generation Turkish immigrant, whose body "is marked as triply other."[41] By confounding German critics, who were aghast that a Turkish German woman would so blatantly overstep supposedly objective standards of decency, Şahin exposed the culturally and historically contingent limits of German notions of morality.

Incidentally, a media-hyped "scandal" surrounding the premiere of *Head On* elicited similarly revealing reactions from the German public. After a leading tabloid had discovered that Sibel Kekilli, the actress portraying Sibel Güner, had acted in a number of porn films, this "'scoop' was quickly exploited by both the German and the Turkish media and became a public issue about morality and Turkish immigrant life in Germany."[42] Kekilli's adamant defense of her work in adult entertainment once again confounded critics. As the journalist Jörg Lau observed at the time: "Sibel Kekilli passt niemandem so recht in den Kram. Ihr Selbstbewusstsein im Umgang mit einem inkorrekten Lebensweg ist eine Herausforderung für Feministinnen und Islamisten" (Sibel Kekilli rubs a lot of people the wrong way. Her confident manner of dealing with an

Century Literature 35, no. 1 (2011): 18–39, here 18.

39 Reyhan Şahin, Christina Scharff, Carrie Smith-Prei, and Maria Stehle, "Riot Grrrls, Bitchsm, and Pussy Power: Interview with Reyhan Şahin/Lady Bitch Ray," *Feminist Media Studies* 16, no. 1 (2016): 117–27, here 123–24.

40 Sandra Maischberger, "Menschen bei Maischberger: Keuschheit statt Porno—Brauchen wir eine neue Sexualmoral?," interview with Reyhan Şahin and Michaela May, December 4, 2007.

41 Smith-Prei, "'Knaller-Sex für alle,'" 27.

42 Savaş, "Head-on, Head-off," 62.

incorrect path through life is a challenge to feminists and Islamists).[43] It is notable that Lau, even though he sympathizes with Kekilli's position, remains committed to the misogynist framework that allows him to label the actress's choices about her body during her early career as "incorrect." This just goes to show how Kekilli, like Şahin, brought to light the sexist biases at the center of pop-feminist criticism. As far as the German public is concerned, the Turkish German woman is welcome to expose her body, but only if it can be controlled by the male gaze of Western audiences. In *Head On*, these control mechanisms break down by the end of the third act.

Alienating the Turkish German Woman

After Cahit is sent to prison for manslaughter, Sibel further distances herself from conventional expectations set out for Turkish German women by the mythologies of German social work. At the beginning of the fourth act, she relocates to Istanbul, "which is portrayed as a modern and open space in contrast to the old-world, claustrophobic Hamburg,"[44] calling into question the notion of Germany as a place of longing for freedom-seeking female Muslims. Moreover, she no longer embodies the ideal of the imprisoned oriental beauty inviting the male gaze of a German savior, having shed all patriarchal signifiers of femininity. By the time she arrives at the Istanbul airport, her "erotic allure" has given way "to an understated androgyny":[45] She has cut her hair, she no longer wears makeup, and her baggy clothes no longer accentuate her body. Her cousin, the independent Selma, climbing the ranks in the hotel business, provides her with a job in room services, but Sibel quickly tires of the menial work in this heavily gendered profession and instead focuses on exploring the masculine world of Istanbul's nightlife. She is warned that this is not a welcoming space for a woman: when without invitation she takes a seat at the table of two young men in a diner, they are taken aback and loath to include her in their conversation. "You are not from around here, are you?" one of them inquires. Sibel wants to know, "Where can I get some drugs?," to which the other man replies, "Are you out of your mind?" Ultimately, she breaks off all contact with Selma, insulting her as a careerist and a spinster, and joins the entourage of an opium dealer, the same man who will later rape her on the floor of his club. Sibel no longer appears the sympathetic, quasi-mythical figure of the exposition

---

43 Jörg Lau, "Die Türken sind da," *Die Zeit*, February 26, 2004.

44 Petra Fachinger, "A New Kind of Creative Energy: Yadé Kara's *Selam Berlin* und Fatih Akin's *Kurz und schmerzlos* and *Gegen die Wand*," *German Life and Letters* 60, no. 2 (2007): 243–60, here 258.

45 Burns, "On the Streets," 16.

358 ◆ FLORIAN GASSNER

but, rather, a recalcitrant and inconvenient character who acts on impulse without regard for the pain she causes herself and those close to her.

The manner in which the fourth act strings together unflattering observations about Sibel—in a self-indulgent letter to Cahit she even likens her new lower-class existence to his incarceration—seems like an invitation to sever all empathetic ties with the heroine and to partially blame her for becoming the victim of the violent assaults that conclude her abortive journey to "liberation." In fact, however, *Head On* opens this door only to immediately challenge the audience to question the premises for passing such a judgment. In other words: the story is designed to activate emotions linked to cultural biases and simultaneously to reframe these biases in a way that allows for a critical reflection of their foundations. The invitation to blame the victim sets up a critique of victim blaming. It is a textbook example of alienation in the Brechtian sense, an attempt to free a socially conditioned phenomenon—the victimization of Turkish German women—from "the stamp of familiarity which today protects them from intervention."

Previous discussions of alienation in *Head On* have focused on the musical interludes, connecting them to Brecht's vision of music, which should "emphasize the general gest of showing," which must "not accompany except in the form of comment," and which the director "should clearly mark . . . off from the rest of the text."[46] These studies have elucidated how the six interludes serve as counterpoints,[47] interrupt the storytelling,[48] anticipate key plot developments,[49] and provide commentary on the action; for example, by opening the film with a song about a tragic and unrequited love.[50] The conclusion of the fourth act combines all these elements when the image of Sibel's battered body fades into a mournful performance by the Sesler group, interrupting the dramatic flow while preempting the film's somber finale. Yet this is but the conclusion of the process of alienating the Turkish German woman in *Head On*, a process that revolves around gradually conflating the characters and the tragedies of Cahit and Sibel.

In the scene preceding the violent attacks on Sibel, all visual, acoustic, and cinematic choices evoke associations with the movie's opening

---

46 Bertolt Brecht, "A Short Organum for the Theatre," in *Brecht on Theatre: The Development of an Aesthetic*, trans. John Willett (London: Methuen, 1964), 203.

47 Deniz Göktürk, "Sound Bridges: Transnational Mobility as Ironic Drama," in *Shifting Landscapes: Film and Media in European Context*, ed. Nezih Erdoğan and Miyase Christensen (Newcastle: Cambridge Scholars Publishing, 2008), 153–71, here 159.

48 Berghahn, "Seeing Everything," 249.

49 Knopp, "Identität zwischen den Kulturen," 65.

50 Ezli, "Von der Identität," 299.

sequence, with the night Cahit attempts to end his own life. Both events take place in dark and gloomy spaces with black and red colors dominating, Sibel's clothes follow the same black-and-green color scheme as Cahit's, and her androgynous haircut is a near replica of his earlier appearance. Sibel has become Cahit's doppelgänger, and "like Cahit earlier, . . . she seeks release from the monotonous servitude in a hedonistic excess of alcohol and drugs that climaxes in a frenetic exhibition on the dancefloor."[51] The music playing as Sibel drunkenly staggers through the bar creates a further link between two people "who are both experiencing extreme physical pain and emotional despair."[52] The same Depeche Mode song plays while the severely intoxicated Cahit experiences a breakdown in his car and deliberately speeds into a wall. Even the camerawork singles these two scenes out, as they are the only instances in which the film works with jump cuts to reflect the characters' inner turmoil.[53] The imagery, the sound, and the dramaturgy all suggest that Sibel and Cahit are one in their suffering. What is more, they mirror each other's behavior as they approach disaster: both have pushed away those closest to them, both are aggressive and belligerent, and both are recklessly inebriated. This in turn means that if one were to judge Sibel with less sympathy than Cahit, the reason must lie in the only thing that distinguishes them: their gender.

As is evident from the pop-feminist work of Reyhan Şahin: the misogynist traditions of Western society reserve the epithet "bitch" for women who behave as carelessly and narcissistically as Cahit. Moreover, film conventions suggest punishing these "bitches" for their lewd and licentious behavior. *Head On* draws attention to this hypocrisy by unexpectedly emphasizing the similarities between the male lead and the unruly heroine, precisely in the moment when the plot enacts its self-righteous punishment. Sibel's and Cahit's "crimes" are the same, but only she gets caught up in the maelstrom of filmic and literary tradition that foresees a violent or humiliating ending for the female transgressor. Akin's film simultaneously confirms and subverts this tradition by conflating the protagonists and thus alienating the popular notion of the Turkish German woman.

One might therefore be tempted to say that Sibel has become unfamiliar by the end of the fourth act, that she no longer is the woman she was at the beginning of the film. But the fact of the matter is that she never was familiar, that she only seemed familiar because her character superficially corresponded to a "socially conditioned phenomenon," to use Brecht's formulation once more. The film certainly encourages the

---

51 Burns, "On the Streets," 16.
52 Siewert, "Soundtracks," 204.
53 Ezli, "Von der Identität," 296.

audience to situate Sibel in the tradition of the oppressed Turkish German woman who longs for integration into Western society, to interpret her actions and motivations by relying on the same tired cultural biases that have allowed generations of Germans to make sense of or, rather, gain power over first-, second-, and third-generation immigrants. But this is simply a very elegant sleight of hand that sets up a process in which an audience eager to follow this path is ultimately confronted with its own biases about Muslim women.

The most effective tool for misdirection in this process is Sibel herself. She is the narrative authority that introduces the mythologies of German social work into *Head On*, but these myths are immediately called into question by the nuanced representation of her family. The audience in effect receives no substantiated information about Sibel's personal history. Only two things are clear: when we meet her, she is being held in a psychiatric ward, and when her parents later discuss Cahit's marriage proposal, her mother adds for consideration, "She's already made so many mistakes. This could be a change for the better." The film never elaborates on these "many mistakes" she has made, but it alludes to a past that was complicated not just because of the protagonist's Turkish background.

This is another way in which Sibel's character resembles that of Cahit. Toward the end of the movie, in a conversation with her cousin, Cahit paints a very dark picture of his mental state at the beginning of their affair. "When I met Sibel first time," he explains in broken English, "I was dead. I was dead even long time before I met her. I'd lost myself." Once again, the audience knows little about the origins or the quality of this struggle, although it is likely connected to the untimely passing of his first wife. What distinguishes the portrayal of Cahit, however, is that there exists no comparable popular discourse about Turkish German men that would encourage making a connection between his self-destructive tendencies and certain aspects of his "culture." He is free to suffer like a Western man would suffer in his place. In the case of Sibel, however, *Head On* plays with the fact that a Western audience could comfortably rely on the popular mythologies of German social work to make sense of this complex character.

By gradually complicating and alienating the motif of the Turkish German woman as victim, the film exposes the extent to which the efficacy of this stereotype is rooted in racist and sexist traditions. *Head On* thus stages a critique of a public discourse still rife with xenophobia and misogyny. Remarkably, the film does this without appearing overly moralistic, without pointing the finger at and thus potentially cutting short the dialogue with the public. This allows the film to work on two levels. Audiences with no interest in a critical examination of cultural biases can still be educated and entertained by the story of an unconventional Turkish German character, a female character that defies expectations.

For those audiences, on the other hand, who already in the early 2000s were exploring the realities of systemic racism, the movie provides a platform to reflect on one's own expectations of a Turkish German heroine and how these expectations have been shaped by mythologies of German social work. *Head On* thus provides one possible blueprint for a socially conscious cinema that does more than preach to the choir.

16: Is a Prostitute Rapeable? Teresa Ruiz Rosas's Novel *Nada que declarar* in Dialogue with #MeToo

Kathrin Breuer

> *Nothing is more revolting than to fuck without being horny.*
> *. . . without passion, desire, attraction, or at least curiosity.*
>
> —Teresa Ruiz Rosas, *Nada que declarar*, 118

THE #MeToo MOVEMENT provides a powerful platform to collect and publicize the testimony of victims of sexual harassment and violence. It has provided a platform for formerly invisible victims of sexual assault, empowered women and young girls, and addressed persistent cultural blind spots about gendered violence. To date, #MeToo has supported white middle-class women, actresses, women of color, incarcerated women, female domestic workers, and female veterans. Yet #MeToo excludes accounts of sex workers, thereby implicitly discrediting their experiences of abuse and perpetuating the still widespread societal belief that prostitutes cannot be sexually harassed or raped since they are women who are always consenting.[1] The historical persuasiveness of that view is reflected in jurisdiction skewed against prostitutes, as legal scholar Barbara Sullivan documented.[2] Some argue that not only the exclusion of professional sex workers from the debate but also the #MeToo movement's explicit support of Survivor's Agenda, an organization that lobbies for the legalization of sex work, is alarming and antithetical to their proclaimed goal of strengthening women's rights. The fluid boundaries between voluntary and coerced sex work and life as a prostitute are subjects of Teresa Ruiz Rosas's 2013 novel, *Nada que declarar*,[3] which raises questions that substantially enrich the #MeToo discourse.

---

1   Melissa Farley, "#MeToo Must Include Prostitution," *Dignity: A Journal on Sexual Exploitation and Violence* 3, no. 1, article 9 (2018): 1–5, https://doi: 10.23860/dignity.2018.03.01.09.

2   Barbara Sullivan, "Rape, Prostitution and Consent," *Australian and New Zealand Journal of Criminology* 40, no. 2 (2007): 127–42.

3   Teresa Ruiz Rosas, *Nada que declarar* (Lima, Peru: Tribal, 2013), 118. All translations from the original Spanish text into English are mine.

Rosas's novel addresses the issue of legalized and allegedly well-regulated prostitution in Germany through the story of the eighteen-year-old protagonist, Diana Postigo, who was brought from Peru to Germany and forced into prostitution. While the story is fictional, Ruiz Rosas's work is well researched and reflects frequently employed recruitment methods and working conditions of some of those sex workers who offer their services in brothels. In the novel, the author draws on her intimate familiarity with her country of origin, Peru, and her knowledge of Germany, her country of residence since the early 1990s. In both places, Ruiz Rosas has been involved in raising awareness about gendered violence, human trafficking, and exploitation in the prostitution industry. Ruiz Rosas wrote *Nada que declarar* in the aftermath of the 2006 Soccer World Cup, which led to a drastic surge of prostitution and human trafficking with the goal of sexual exploitation. (She observed these developments firsthand in her then hometown of Cologne.)[4] The title of Ruiz Rosas's novel translates to "Nothing to Testify" or "Anmeldefreie Waren/Nothing to declare"[5] and conjures up the corresponding sign at every customs control point. This phrase points to an innate link between the crossing of borders in human trafficking and the discursive silencing of sex workers, which I will address below. It also highlights the transactional side of prostitution that turns intimately physical, erotic acts into merchandise and arguably commodifies humans themselves. This commodification is one of the major topics that Ruiz Rosas explores in her novel.

In this chapter, I contextualize my analysis of the novel with a discussion of the status quo of prostitution in Germany after the introduction of the Gesetz zur Regelung der Rechtsverhältnisse der Prostituierten (Law Regulating the Relationships of Prostitutes; ProstG; Prostitution Act) in 2002. In doing so, I shed light on how the novel's protagonist, who is forced into prostitution against her will, finds a way out by relying on the cornerstones of the #MeToo movement: free speech and forging alliances. In conclusion, I explore the potential for including sex workers in the movement to further women's rights.

Nada que declarar can be read as a coming-of-age narrative with all the traditional characteristics of a bildungsroman. It tells the story of Diana Postigo Dueñas, who was raised in the slums of Lima. As an eighteen-year-old, she chooses to follow Murat, a man she barely knows, to Germany, where she soon finds herself working in prostitution. After three years of forced sex work in a Düsseldorf brothel, in which Murat functions as her pimp, she manages to escape and return to her home country. Diana's story, I argue, exposes human trafficking and sexual violence as constitutive elements of the legalized prostitution industry in Germany

---

4   Gad J. Bensinger, "World Cup 2006: Sex Trafficking and Prostitution in Germany," *Crime & Justice International* 22, no. 95 (2006): 19–21.

5   Ruiz Rosas, *Nada que declarar*, 332.

and brings forth a forceful critique of the 2002 Prostitution Act. Ruiz Rosas offers a candid assessment of the gaping rift between an ambitious piece of legislation and a reality in which human rights violations and sexual abuse are normalized—or, rather, made invisible—through the legalization of sex work. The novel showcases how Diana liberates herself and turns from a young student pressured to prostitute herself and terrified to speak up against the physical and emotional abuse she experiences into a *mündige* (responsible; mature; of age) and self-determined free woman. In tracing Diana's progress, the text reveals a viable trajectory toward a more holistic empowerment of sex workers in Germany that exceeds the options laid out in current legislation.

To date, *Nada que declarar*, which was written in Spanish and first published in 2013 by the Peruvian publishing house Tribal, has not found a translator or publisher in Germany who is willing to disseminate this key work of social criticism among the German-speaking readership. This glaring absence quite possibly indicates a cultural preference for avoiding the painful and complex topic of prostitution. While Ruiz Rosas has been invited to speak about her novel on numerous occasions (some of these discussions are available on YouTube), her work has not yet met with a proper scholarly response in either Spanish, German, or English; there are no publications on the text nor is it included on course syllabi. This failure to engage with Teresa Ruiz Rosas's novel is not due to a lack of talent on the part of the author. Indeed, *Nada que declarar* was a finalist in El III Bienal internacional de Novela (The Third Biennial of Novels), in 2011.

Diana's Story

Diana's inexperience and desire to escape abject poverty and sexual abuse by her Uncle Eustaquio make her an easy prey for the attractive lover boy Murat. His courtship offers a respite from the violence and deprivations of her upbringing. He woos Diana by bringing her flowers and taking her to a restaurant she could never afford on her own and quickly impresses the high school graduate with the seductive powers of his olive-green eyes and outer signs of wealth that promise economic safety. When Murat asks her to return to Germany with him, Diana stands at a crossroads in her life: she feels discouraged by the lack of desirable employment in Peru despite her excellent grades in school. Furthermore, a happy and fulfilling romantic partnership seems next to impossible in her present environment. Consequently, Murat's designs on Diana prove successful. Anticipating marriage and job opportunities, Diana follows him willingly to Germany, where she soon becomes emotionally dependent on Murat and is coerced into prostitution. Her recruitment into prostitution through a lover at a moment of personal difficulties, his immediate removal of the young woman from her known environment and promise to help her improve her life circumstances through job opportunities and/or a romantic relationship, emotional support, and new socioeconomic mobility reflect routine recruitment tactics, as accounts of former sex workers substantiate.[6]

Diana, now refashioned into the prostitute Dianette Pöstges, enters a shadow world governed by the iron laws of psychological manipulation and physical subjugation, which force upon her a life that differs drastically from the vision that informed the progressive German legislature in early 2002 when it passed new prostitution laws. Diana endures commercialized sexual abuse for a three-year period that the auctorial narrator describes as "atrocious for her body of Dianette P. and her soul of Diana."[7] The use of an alias, rather common among sex workers, indicates dissociation as a psychological defense mechanism against traumatic physical abuse and emotional harm. It also underlines the annihilating corrosion of Diana's original sense of self as she lives through the daily degradations of prostitution.

Diana is exhibited in one of the hundred numbered windows of a street-view brothel near Düsseldorf's central station, where she is perpetually exposed to the gaze of travelers, covetous clients, and the musclemen who guard the women. The architecture of this building is based on the "Bahndamm," one of the oldest and best-known window brothels in Düsseldorf, which mirrors the structural principles of innumerous buildings in red-light districts from Hamburg's Reeperbahn to Amsterdam's De Wallen. Evoking such similarities, the novel suggests that Diana's experience reflects the greater structural degradation faced by sex workers in these establishments. The architecture not only displays human merchandise in highly visible form, even from afar, but also serves as a disciplinary device, as theorized by Michel Foucault in his analysis of the panopticon in *Discipline and Punish* (1975). In *Nada que declarar*, the ever-present policing gaze controls the commodified women and elicits their self-subjugation: they know of the ever-present risk of swift punishment, and this knowledge coerces their acquiescence in their own sexual enslavement. Cell-like rooms with single street-facing windows impede communication among sex workers and make them, arguably, even more compliant with the power structure that controls them. In this building, all sensory perceptions remind the women that they are under the power of their pimps. At the same time, the building undermines the women's

6   See, e.g., Ingeborg Kraus and Sandra Norak, "Never Again! Surviving Liberalized Prostitution in Germany," *Dignity: A Journal on Sexual Exploitation and Violence* 3, no. 3, article 5 (2018): 1–10, https://doi.org/10.23860/dignity.2018.03.03.05.

7   Ruiz Rosas, *Nada que declarar*, 333.

ability to draw strength from the community of fellow sex workers whom they cannot see or feel.

As Teresa Ruiz Rosas's novel describes Diana Postigo's unlikely path from subjected body silenced by the law of *nada que declarar* toward free agency, it becomes apparent that the central character is not the true protagonist. Rather, the spoken word is at the center of Ruiz Rosas's novel. Regaining the forbidden power of speech is the key to the heroine's freedom and emancipation: first, she learns the German language, then she gains a new understanding of her existence and begins to forge alliances—both imaginative ones with the radio speaker Lorena Marín and real ones with people in her surroundings, such as the Ukrainian prostitute Vika or Dániel A. Carrión, the only one of her clients whom she experienced as kind. Lastly, she records her experience to warn other young women. In doing so, Diana takes back control over her life, asserts her place in history, and becomes fully mündig.

Silence, Speech, and Abuse

The German concept of *Mündigkeit*, the leitmotif of the Enlightenment, is premised on the mouth (*Mund*) and thus on speech. Through speech, we access our rights, we call for justice, we enter history by relating our stories. We become seen and turn into fully actualized members of society whose very existence, rights, and duties deserve consideration. Through Mündigkeit we give consent, or we do not. Any form of abuse depends on the absence of speech; that is, on invisibility and silence. Silence is the always-present third player in the constellation of perpetrator and victim of crime. In the sex trade, the john's payment functions as compensation for two services: it buys access to the prostitute's body with the objective of receiving sexual relief by using her body for physically intimate and invasive acts; and it serves to ensure the prostitute's silence about their transaction. Consequently, the prostitute's acceptance of money is interpreted as a sign of her consent to what would otherwise be regarded as assault and rape. As sex-equality scholar and lawyer Catharine MacKinnon reminds us, however, "when fear and despair produce acquiescence and acquiescence is meant to mean consent, consent is not a meaningful concept."[8] While MacKinnon warns us not to confuse despair and consent, to proponents of the legalization of sex work the concept of consensual sex within prostitution is paramount. They concede that consent is absent if a woman is a victim of human trafficking and is likely undermined when she is controlled by a pimp, but they do not consider that the fear and despair caused by homelessness, poverty, prior sexual abuse, and

---

8   Catherine MacKinnon, *Women's Lives, Men's Laws* (Cambridge, MA: Harvard University Press 2005), 260.

a lack of economic choices also trouble the concept of consent. Clearly, the question whether prostitution occurs between consenting adults or whether it is commercialized sexual abuse hinges on the sex worker's uncompromised freedom of choice. I argue that, in order to determine the nature of this freedom, we need to consider that life circumstances can be as coercive as being forced by some*body*.

In *Nada que declarar*, Diana Postigo ran up against a prohibition to speak years before she was seduced by the lover boy Murat, who removed her from her social support network, brought her to a foreign country where he was the only person she knew, and prostituted her. While Murat forced her into prostitution, Diana's metamorphosis into Dianette the prostitute began when her Uncle Eustaquio abused her as a teenager and she stayed "silent, just as the violator had threatened her [to do . . . since] when you open your mouth, so he had said to her, you're not telling it because I will steal you and make you disappear." [9] Silence keeps the crime invisible and protects the reputation and freedom of the perpetrator, while it disempowers the victim, who remains cut off from help if she cannot relate her experience. In Germany, the harmful effect of silence manifests once more when Murat not only forbids Diana to speak about his role in prostituting her but also threatens her: "How dare you, Goddess of Darkness, [if you run away,] be sure that I find you and then, yes, you will never see the light again."[10] By alluding to Diana's dark skin color, Murat sets her apart racially, seemingly elevating her to a goddess. And yet, his words remind us harshly that it is Diana who is enslaved, in shackles, under his absolute control. Possibly without being aware of Diana's past trauma of rape and being coerced into silence, he inflicts the same physical and psychological abuse that Diana had suffered as a teenager.

Ausgang aus der Unmündigkeit—or the Liberation of Diana Postigo

The architectural surveillance system of the brothel that augments Murat's oppressive power over Diana functions as both a disciplinary and an educational tool. It generates knowledge that governs Diana's life in prostitution and determines what she does—that is, offering her body for sale—and how she does it, based on her current understanding of her surroundings. The process is reminiscent of Pierre Bourdieu's concept of habitus. According to Bourdieu, habitus shapes a person's behavior within a specific social context according to lessons acquired through lived experience. At the beginning of her life as a prostitute, Diana knows with

---

9   Ruiz Rosas, *Nada que declarar*, 332.
10   Ruiz Rosas, *Nada que declarar*, 336.

absolute certainty that she is completely and utterly at the mercy of Murat
and the system he represents. She is convinced that his power of domination over her is unlimited and that putting up any resistance could cost
her her life: "Would he lock her up for life in a dark cell? Would he scratch
her eyes out? Would he kill her and make every bone of her disappear?
She believed him capable of going that far."[11] According to Foucault,
exercising power means steering the behavior of others. Diana experiences seemingly limitless control by others over her life and is defenseless
against Murat and a tightly interlocking system of instigators, musclemen,
and johns. Consequently, she behaves in a self-subjugating manner and
complies with the people who prostitute her. Her lived reality exemplifies
the near impossibility of objecting to sexual abuse and protecting herself
under the given circumstances. Even though in theory Germany's 2002
Prostitution Act endows Diana with the right to dissent, she can neither
refuse a john nor protect herself from sexual assault in a brothel that constitutes a de facto legal vacuum. Thus, her liberation cannot unfold by
means of physical revolt or outright disobedience. Instead, Diana regains
her freedom and achieves her transformation back from the prostituted
Dianette Pöstges to Diana Postigo by constructing an alternative system
of knowledge.

As a first step, Diana learns the language of her environment through
German courses broadcast by Radio Multiculti. Her new skill allows
her to draw strength from participating in communities that are initially
abstract, such as the bond of friendship she forms with the radio modera-
tor Lorena Marín, "her best unknown voice friend," but become more
concrete over time. Months prior to escaping from the brothel, Diana
starts reclaiming her independence when she listens to Lorena's radio
program on March 8, International Women's Day, about "the practice of
commercial sex with girls, boys, and adolescents."[12] She learns about the
Rote Zora, a militant group that fought for women's rights, and she hears
the comments on prostitution of Alice Schwarzer, the activist and founder
of the feminist journal *Emma*: "What men buy here is not sex but power.
What excites the clients is their power of command and the servitude of
[the girls]."[13] These two sentences become the driving engine that motivates Diana to change her life. Schwarzer's words ignite a thought process
that leads to a reframing of her experience of prostitution and that helps
her obtain a new understanding of her own situation, and Diana refuses
to accept the status quo any longer. She withdraws mentally from Murat,
even though she continues to provide the same deeply humiliating sexual
services as a prostituted woman for a few more months. Quoting from

---

11 Ruiz Rosas, *Nada que declarar*, 336.
12 Ruiz Rosas, *Nada que declarar*, 333 and 24.
13 Ruiz Rosas, *Nada que declarar*, 22.

a recent study, the radio speaker Lorena Marín sums up the prevalent argument against the legalization of prostitution on grounds of viewing sex work as an inherent violation of human rights (the text suggests that this stance converges with Diana's newly formed viewpoint): "By virtue of this being a commercial transaction, one feels justified to dispose of that which had been bought, and they [the buyers of sex] do not consider that the situation might be violent and even less so that it would violate human rights, as obvious as that might be."[14]

Diana comes to understand prostitution as one of the crassest manifestations of gendered violence within a patriarchal society and starts questioning the system of knowledge and power that had forced her into compliance. At this point, Diana's escape becomes a certainty. She captures this moment with an affectionate term, a shortening of her birth name used by her family and close friends: "A gift that kills Dianette and revives Diani Posti."[15]

It is the transformative power of speech that leads the main character of *Nada que declarar* out of *Hörigkeit*, defined as listening to—that is, obedience toward—others, and into Mündigkeit, conceived as speaking and acting on behalf of oneself. The destabilization of knowledge and certainty about what life in the brothel allows and what it forbids propels the revolution in Diana's thinking and motivates her subsequent actions. It makes it possible for her to overcome victimhood and empowers her to decode the functional structure of the system that oppresses her. Furthermore, she now mobilizes her understanding of her own role within the system as a powerful instrument in her physical liberation.

The ruse the character Diana devises does not easily lend itself to imitation, but it is ripe with insightful, symbolic imagery and conveys deeper layers of truth about the control experienced by a woman in forced prostitution. It starts with Dániel A. Carrión, the only client who seems to genuinely care about Diana, recommending to her that she should carefully protect her eyes. Diana's eyes are her most prized possession since they remain out of reach for her tormentors even when her body is controlled and abused by others.[16] Shopping for eyeglasses, Diana overhears an optometrist who warns other customers against using a telescope to observe the sun since this would most certainly blind a naive viewer for life. Fascinated, Diana comes up with an ingenious plan. As a phallic symbol and expression of the desire to see beyond our normal range of view, the telescope embodies the nexus of *Sehen* (seeing), *Sehnen* (desiring), and control that perfectly captures the essence of Diana's life as a prostitute.

---

14 Ruiz Rosas, *Nada que declarar*, 24.
15 Ruiz Rosas, *Nada que declarar*, 24.
16 Ruiz Rosas, *Nada que declarar*, 334.

Thus, it is only fitting that it is the tool that ends the hold of Murat's seductive olive-green eyes over Diana along with his ability to exploit her.

With saved tips, Diana secretly purchases a small telescope and arranges for a special celebration with her pimp and lover, Murat. Murat, who keeps prostitutes compliant through occasional favors and demonstrations of his affection rather than through inflicting physical injuries (which would make them unable to earn money, at least temporarily), is willing to humor Diana on her birthday and thus takes the bait. They spend an evening together, as Murat gets high on cocaine, exchanging intimacies and looking at constellations. As the night leads into the morning, Murat, exasperated by Diana's enthusiasm for celestial bodies, relaxes his vigilance. "The great star, look at it. . . . Something like this you've never seen in your life!," Diana entices him once more."[17] As Murat looks through the telescope, he realizes in the throes of pain that his "Goddess of Darkness" blinded him.

Without his eyesight, Murat's power as a seducer, procurer, and enforcer is broken. Diana could kill the now helpless man who betrayed and enslaved her. The novel insinuates that the murder would be chalked up to self-defense, and she would walk free. But Diana chooses to let him live. She, whom Murat called his "Goddess of Darkness," brings him eternal darkness but also the promise of redemption. As Diana's last words to Murat explain, "[I] gave you the chance to be left with much time to reflect on and renounce, slowly and calmly, your depraved way of living."[18] Thus, she defines the punishment as an opportunity for Murat to learn and to change his life.

Later, Diana reflects on her life in prostitution. In a conversation with her friend Silvia Olazábal Ligur, the two discuss whether sex workers derive pleasure or a sense of satisfaction from their profession. This passage is significant because it speaks to the concept of voluntary (self-) prostitution, which would leave room for the notion of deriving gratification from the professional activity of selling one's body and thus allow for a vision of mostly happy, empowered, and self-actualized sex workers.

Silvia, who once successfully fought off a rapist, is accustomed to an emancipated, self-assertive, and self-determined enjoyment of her sexuality. Initially, she is open to the idea of sex work as a free choice and source of personal fulfillment. Thus, she asks Diana whether having access to quick money through selling one's body makes the experience of prostitution a positive one and whether some prostitutes enjoy a sense of dominance over their clients. In response, Diana paints a dismal picture of sex workers, who feel trapped and ultimately resign themselves to their work. When Diana casts prostitution as the result of coercion, even though she

17 Ruiz Rosas, *Nada que declarar*, 506.
18 Ruiz Rosas, *Nada que declarar*, 509.

does not go so far as to call it rape, Silvia interrupts in disbelief: "¿A nadie le gusta?" (Nobody liked doing it?).[19]

> There are those who feel completely contented and don't feel ashamed because they are as horny as they come, says Diana Postigo and gazes into the distance. . . . They get used to pretending that they like it, and by pretending so much, they come to believe it. But don't think that those are many, overall, they are few. Vika couldn't stand it, and I didn't like it either. For us, it was torture. The disgust that we felt afterwards often made us vomit the moment the guys left, right there, into the washbasin that these rooms have.[20]

The explanation Diana provides reveals the limits of solidarity among the women working in the brothel. Her solidarity extends exclusively to Vika, a barely nineteen-year-old prostitute from Kiev, whom she considers her "hermanita menor," her little sister,[21] while she degrades a group of sex workers as lewd women because she assumes that they find pleasure in doing their job. Tellingly, Diana insists that these women lie to themselves about their alleged enjoyment, because it enables them to provide the repulsive services they are asked to perform. While Diana is a fictional character, her statement is remarkably consistent with expert views. Psychotraumatologist Ingeborg Kraus speaks of trauma-bonding with one's offender and other significant forms of psychological damage among sex workers whose levels of post-traumatic stress syndrome (PTSD) exceed the severity of the condition among combat veterans. Defense mechanisms to keep the painful awareness of one's abuse at bay include not only resorting to emotional apathy in all areas of life but also physical numbness and even loss of the sense of smell, which functions as a survival strategy to withstand the repulsiveness of providing intimate services to strangers.[22]

When Silvia digs further and asks why such instances of forced prostitution and coercion to engage in certain sex practices are rarely reported, Diana echoes the testimony of former prostitutes:

> Many girls don't even think about going to the police, not only because they could be killed one day for denouncing these suckers. [The girls] would be deported if they were to run away because

---

19 Ruiz Rosas, *Nada que declarar*, 156.

20 Ruiz Rosas, *Nada que declarar*, 156.

21 Ruiz Rosas, *Nada que declarar*, 156.

22 Ingeborg Kraus, "Survivor Strategies to Deal with Traumatic Stress: Dissociation and Trauma Bonding," presentation given at the 2019 Coalition to End Sexual Exploitation Global Summit on 14 June 2019. *Vimeo*, uploaded by Center on Sexual Exploitation, 2019, vimeo.com/354289634.

372 ◆ KATHRIN BREUER

these jerks took their papers [and] it would be unimaginably humiliating to return to their families with such a stain on their reputation after they dedicated themselves to "the life."[23]

Diana's account addresses factors that do indeed prevent the reporting of a crime in the sex-trade industry. According to the International Committee on the Rights of Sex Workers in Europe, the threat of deportation counts among the top reasons why sex workers suffer violence without seeking justice.[24] It is also noteworthy that the German Ministry for Family, Senior Citizens, Women and Youth Affairs (Bundesministerium für Familie, Senioren, Frauen und Jugend) concluded in 2001 that 98 percent of female prostitutes had experienced at least one traumatic incident at work and 68 percent had been raped at least once. Margrit Brückner's and Christa Oppenheimer's research, published in 2006, found that 73 percent of all interviewed prostitutes had experienced violence (an additional 14 percent preferred not to answer), and more than a third of the individuals who had suffered such offences stated that they did not seek police intervention because they were afraid of additional violence and retribution from the perpetrators; a third stated that they were concerned about the safety of their families.[25]

Giving Testimony

After Diana escapes from the Düsseldorf brothel, she returns to Peru and completes her liberation by breaking the commandment of *nada que declarar* that had governed her life as a prostitute. Encouraged by Silvia, she shares her story as a warning to other girls "so that they may see the danger, not step into the trap every time [and] drown in the pot of honey like flies."[26] By giving testimony and warning other women about migration under false pretenses and sexual enslavement, Diana affirms herself anew as a free person and raises her voice to advocate for the protection of women's human rights. She fully owns her story and overcomes the

---

23 Ruiz Rosas, *Nada que declarar*, 155.
24 International Committee on the Rights of Sex Workers (ICRSE), "Policy Brief and Recommendations on the Rights of Migrant Sex Workers," *SexWorkEurope* (2006), www.sexworkeurope.org/sites/default/files/userfiles/files/ICRSE_Briefing%20paper_MIGRANTS%20RIGHTS_Policy%20brief_November2016_02%281%29.pdf.
25 Margrit Brückner and Christa Oppenheimer, "Gewalt in der Prostitution," in *Das Prostitutionsgesetz: Aktuelle Forschungsergebnisse, Umsetzung und Weiterentwicklung*, ed. Barbara Kavemann and Heike Rabe (Opladen: Verlag Barbara Budrich, 2009), 153–66.
26 Ruiz Rosas, *Nada que declarar*, 153.

psychologically harmful dissociation that marked her years as a prostitute. In doing so, she creates a firm foundation for her present and future self:

> Writing the story of Dianette Pöstges was an unresolved matter. . . . [Diana] needed to see it in print to believe herself, Silvia came to understand. As if the miracle of her present life did not hold any higher merit as long as the former one was not kept sealed in black over white, taking on an indelible quality withstanding the passing of time. An intact chapter to refer to whenever needed without mixing up details or leaving up to memory the tiniest propensity [weakness] toward forgetting of which Borges speaks.[27]

Diana comes to believe in the power of stories: "When you begin to read, there are things that sound familiar to you, you start to think, you get involved, you believe that they're telling you your own story."[28] Much in the same way, *Nada que declarar* challenges the reader to reflect on prostitution as work and life design and to undo the Othering of sex workers (an Othering that is also evident in #MeToo's exclusion of prostitutes from the movement). As the novel offers insights into a social sphere that all too often remains closed off from the lived experience of most readers, we start to wonder to what extent story and social reality correspond to each other. Thus, the text facilitates empathy, compassion, and identification with the Other, in this case the prostituted woman. Readers might reflect on the socioeconomic, educational, and other circumstances that prevented them from recognizing in Diana Postigo's story a fictional parallel to their own lives, or as Diana said, to believe that the novel is telling our own story. The novel does much more, however. It raises awareness that prostitution is an integral part of most societies and that we all live with it even if we have never actively bought or sold sex. Moreover, *Nada que declarar* illustrates that those who are outsiders to prostitution nonetheless have a moral responsibility to acknowledge its existence and the humanity of those who work in the trade under different degrees of volition.

Forging a bridge between the novel and the current state of affairs, I now turn to the status quo of legalized prostitution in Germany and reflect on a discrepancy between legislation that intends to protect sex workers from suffering harm in their profession, on the one hand, and ongoing human rights abuses, on the other.

---

27 Ruiz Rosas, *Nada que declarar*, 149–50.
28 Ruiz Rosas, *Nada que declarar*, 153.

Status quo

The Gesetz zur Regelung der Rechtsverhältnisse der Prostituierten, which was promulgated in 2001 and became law in 2002, further liberalized already liberal prostitution laws in Germany. Most significantly, it allowed for legal brothels and for procurement of sex workers (pimping). While the law aimed at destigmatizing and normalizing "the oldest profession" and at creating safer and more empowering working conditions for sex workers, it came to be regarded as a failure in the face of a substantial increase in human trafficking and the establishment of mega-brothels, such as the Pascha, Artemis, and Paradise chains that sell sex in Germany at a near-industrial scale. In many instances, these brothels neither provide the working conditions nor adhere to the business practices the legislation hoped to institute, as the prominent case of Paradise owner Jürgen Rudloff illustrates. Rudloff, once the poster child of "clean" prostitution in Germany and frequent talk show guest advocating for prostitution as a "health service for men," was sentenced in 2019 to five years in prison for human trafficking, forced prostitution, fraud, and involvement with criminal gangs such as the Hell's Angels and United Tribune in the daily operation of the brothels, including the recruitment of women. Rudloff's crimes exposed criminal operations of international reach at the core of the German prostitution business. Similar illegal practices led to long-term prison sentences for Paradise's head of marketing, Michaël Beretin, and Pascha's founder, Hermann Müller, and raise grave doubts about the effectiveness of the Prostitution Act.

In 2016, a key amendment was passed to improve the original ProstG. The revised Prostitution Act, called the Prostituiertenschutzgesetz (Prostitute Protection Act; ProstSchG), took effect on July 1, 2017. Its central contribution is the so-called *Anmeldepflicht* (Registration requirement), through which individuals can receive a *Prostitutionsausweis*, an ID card that qualifies the holder for legal work in the prostitution industry and for state benefits such as social welfare. It comes with obligations too, such as regular health checks, payment of taxes, and adherence to certain rules while on the job, including a requirement to use condoms. And a sex worker can now hold a john accountable if he fails to pay the agreed-on fees. She can also sue a client if he demands services that were not agreed upon or does not respect physical boundaries. There is, however, a fly in the ointment: to raise a legal claim, a sex worker needs to provide the name and address of the alleged perpetrator, along with witnesses of the breach of contract who can testify to the unfolding of the sexual act in question.

Tellingly, only 44 individuals registered as sex workers during the first year after the passage of this law. According to data provided by the Statistisches Bundesamt (Federal Bureau of Statistics), the number rose to

40,369 individuals by the end of 2019. Alice Schwarzer holds that these 40,369 registered prostitutes in Germany represent only a small fraction of an estimated 1 million sex workers in the country. Other sources cite 400,000, a number that has frequently been quoted in the literature since 1986 and is also used by the Federal Bureau of Statistics.[29] While a million might be too high, the much lower number disregards key factors such as the impact of the 2004 eastern expansion of the European Union and of more than a million refugees who arrived in Germany in 2015 and 2016. Both forms of mass migration have, as the work of anthropologists such as Heide Castañeda, has shown, drastically increased the number of prostitutes working in Germany. In 2006—that is, before the migrations mentioned above—the percentage of migrants among sex workers was 73 percent of all female and above 90 percent of all male prostitutes.[30] The situation was likely exacerbated by the influx of individuals who lived for years without access to a work permit and who were therefore motivated to seek illegal employment, including that available in illegal prostitution. Some additional benchmark data provide information about the gender and age of sex workers: approximately 90 percent of all sex workers in Germany are female, 7 percent male, and 3 percent trans; nearly 20 percent are assumed to be underage.[31]

In Germany, sex workers offer their services, forced or by choice and without protection, as streetwalkers; as high-end escorts; in brothels, saunas, and massage parlors; in private apartments; or in flat-rate and *tabulos* (tabooless) clubs where anything goes. Even advertisements for "sloshing parties" during which women are plied into submission with alcohol are not unheard-of.

While these clubs maintain a facade of legality, pictures of women with swollen and injured bodies hint at sexual practices and transgressions that cannot be promoted explicitly. In contrast, more-moderate advertisements—for example, for brothels such as Berlin's Artemis or Cologne's Pascha—appear on buses, in subway stations, and in department stores frequented by teenagers and families with young children. The liberalization and legalization of prostitution turned Germany into a *Schlaraffenland* (land of Cockaigne) and discount paradise for commercial sex buyers with starting prices on the streets as low as fifteen to twenty euros and average prices for intercourse in a brothel, as estimated by the Federal Bureau of Statistics, of fifty euros. With 1.2 million daily

---

29   Lars Marten Nagel, *Prostitution—Hier noch mehr Zahlen*, November 3, 2013, *Investigativ*, investigativ.welt.de/2013/11/03/black-box-prostitution/.

30   Brückner and Oppenheimer, *Lebenssituation*, 12.

31   TAMPEP, "National Mapping Reports 2010" (2010), https://tampep.eu/wp-content/uploads/2017/11/ANNEX-4-National-Reports.pdf and *Bordell Deutschland—Milliardengeschäft Prostitution*, ZDFinfo documentary (2017).

users of the services of sex workers, Germany has established itself firmly as the new destination for sex tourism in Europe.[32]

This paradise produces considerable tax revenue. At 6 billion euros within two years of the new law taking effect, annual profits from prostitution in Germany rivaled those of companies like Porsche or Adidas. For 2017, the Federal Bureau of Statistics cites a profit of 14.6 billion euros from prostitution in Germany and of nearly 25 billion from human trafficking in the European Union.[33] Petra Follmer-Otto of the German Institute of Human Rights in Berlin and lawyer Heike Rabe argue that the official numbers of investigated cases do not accurately reflect the actual number of victims of trafficking (THB) but, rather, mirror the allocation of resources within the police force.[34] Still, a look at these numbers reveals important tendencies, even if it severely underrepresents actual trafficking. From 2000 to 2019, the Bundeskriminalamt (Federal Criminal Police Office; BKA) investigated approximately 350 to 500 cases of THB with the purpose of sexual exploitation annually. Alarmingly, this number dropped to 287 cases in 2019, likely not because there was less THB but because the ProstSchG was implemented and drove more sex workers into illegality to avoid the Anmeldepflicht. Commenting on the issue, the BKA conceded that a shift in prostitution sites—for example, into private apartments—makes them harder to control and thus results in an increased dark figure.[35]

Illegal and forced migration with the goal of sexual exploitation, the economic recession of 2008, a discount marketplace where "Geiz ist geil" (greed is hot), and gimmicks such as punch cards with free service for every ten paid visits contribute to harsh working conditions. (The long-term impact of the COVID-19 pandemic remains to be seen.) Substance abuse and violence are widespread. As Rachel Moran, a former prostitute—who objects to the term "sex worker"[36]—explains, alcohol, valium,

---

32 Nagel, *Prostitution*.

33 Nagel, *Prostitution*.

34 Petra Follmer-Otto and Heike Rabe, *Menschenhandel in Deutschland: Die Menschenrechte der Betroffenen stärken* (Berlin: Institut für Menschenrechte, 2009), 61.

35 Bundeskriminalamt, "Bundeslagebild Menschenhandel 2000–2019," *BKA*, https://www.bka.de/DE/AktuelleInformationen/StatistikenLagebilder/Lagebilder/Menschenha ndel/menschenhandel_node.html.

36 Moran objects to the use of the term "sex worker" because, so she argues, the language of sex work was introduced to frame prostitution as ordinary work and to whitewash the mental imagery conjured up by the term "prostitution." Or, borrowing from Andrea Dworkin, "We are talking about the use of the mouth, the vagina, and the rectum. The circumstances don't mitigate or modify what prostitution is," and neither should euphemistic terminology sanitize an ugly reality. Rachel Moran, *Paid For: My Journey through Prostitution* (New York: W. W. Norton, 2015), 222 and 90.

prescription sedatives, and cocaine "are used to numb the simple awfulness of having sexual intercourse with reams of sexually repulsive strangers."[37] A comparison of the percentage of the general population who have experienced physical violence, 32 percent, with the percentage of prostitutes who have done so, 88 percent, reveals the prevalence of violence in the industry. Similarly, only 12 percent of the general population have experienced *sexual* violence, compared to 59 percent of prostitutes.[38]

The liberalization and legalization of prostitution successfully glossed over these alarming numbers and generated a sense of normalcy. This deceptive sense of normalcy marginalizes critics and promotes a mindset that allows intimacy, sexual acts, and ultimately women themselves, or in some cases men or trans individuals, to be regarded as objects of legitimate mercantile transactions. In so doing, it espouses gendered violence—violating Article 3 of the German Constitution (Grundgesetz) that postulates that "No person shall be favored or disfavored because of sex."

Gendered Violence or Tolerance?

The legalization of prostitution in Germany gives rise to a cognitive dissonance between the moral imperative to uphold and defend human dignity and human rights, on the one hand, and the desire to be progressive and tolerant of people's individual choices, on the other. As this article shows, the legalization of prostitution insinuates that prostitution could be regulated in such a manner that the mercantile exchange between prostitute and client occurs on an equal footing. In this mindset, prostitution is considered an inevitable fact of life (does it have to be so?). Through the existence of such legislation, a government signals that any illegal ancillary practices are controlled and persecuted. This sanitizes prostitution and allows citizens to deny or ignore the possibility of sexual abuse, human trafficking, and human-rights violations. Not thinking about the existence of these crimes and social grievances is a privilege available only to those who are not at the receiving end—much like the white privilege Peggy MacIntosh talks about, which allows a privileged group to ignore the life circumstances of the Other.

Legalization, I argue, promotes indifference and makes violations of human rights invisible, because these violations are no longer recognizable as systemic problems; if they occur at all, so this logic dictates, they must be absolute exceptions rather than recurring and foreseeable events inherent in the nature of the trade.

In *Nada que declarar*, Sylvia, who, unlike Diana, evinces historical consciousness, likens the indifference of mainstream society to prostitution

---

37 Moran, *Paid For*, 5.
38 Brückner and Oppenheimer, *Lebenssituation*, 198.

to the kind of national amnesia that has historically been employed by colonial powers to suppress memories of their crimes against humanity. Quoting W. Somerset Maugham, Silvia warns against the hubris of European nations that consider themselves enlightened and progressive, and concludes, "*Tolerance is another word for indifference.*"[39]

Until the introduction of the 2002 ProstG, legal standards were based on the premise that prostitutes violate their own human dignity and must be protected, even against their will, from engaging in prostitution. Such legislation categorically *entmündigte* all sex workers; that is, it deprived them of their right to self-determination. In contrast, the new legislation went to the opposite extreme, assuming that, barring human trafficking and forced prostitution, the reasons that motivate individuals to enter prostitution are expressive of their free choice and their consent to the lifestyle.[40]

But is this so? Poverty has been identified as the primary reason for entering prostitution. Thus, it cannot come as a surprise that the largest group of migrant prostitutes working in Germany comes from the poorest economies in the European Union: in 2017, 31 percent of all registered prostitutes were from Romania; other large groups came from Bulgaria, Hungary, Poland, Thailand, and Spain; only 22 percent were German nationals.[41] Yet economic deprivation alone does not account for the decision to enter prostitution. Often a prior experience of sexual violence in combination with economic despair tips the balance.

Conservative studies show that nearly 50 percent of all sex workers had experienced sexual violence before they started to work as prostitutes.[42] Their preprostitution experiences tended to cause negative self-assessment ("I do not deserve any better" or "I am only good for prostitution anyway") and severely compromised their ability to protect themselves in situations that triggered memories of past sexual trauma.[43] Josie, a sex worker featured in the 2015 documentary *The Mega-Brothel*, shares her story: "I was sexually abused when I was ten or eleven years old. After that . . . it's not a big deal to work as a prostitute." While such self-disparaging narratives of a woman's entry into prostitution characterize a

---

39 Ruiz Rosas, *Nada que declarar*, 68.

40 Doris Winter, "Arbeitsbedingungen in der Prostitution im Wandel von Zeit und Gesetz," in *Das Prostitutionsgesetz: Aktuelle Forschungsergebnisse, Umsetzung und Weiterentwicklung*, ed. Barbara Kavemann and Heike Rabe (Opladen: Verlag Barbara Budrich, 2009), 221.

41 Bundesministerium für Familie, Senioren, Frauen und Jugend (BMFSFJ), "Zwischenbericht zum Prostituiertenschutzgesetz," June 29, 2020, *BMFSFJ*, https://www.bmfsfj.de/blob/156998/bfc0e8295e1bcc04b08159e32e95281f/zwischenbericht-zum-prostituiertenschutzgesetz-data.pdf.

42 Brückner and Oppenheimer, "Gewalt," 156.

43 Kraus, "Survivor Strategies."

significant percentage of sex workers, their decisions are marked by different degrees of freedom. Thus, a stronger argument against the concept of "consenting adults" is the following: it is arguably not possible to comprehend prostitution fully and accurately—that is, to understand what one is consenting to—until one is already immersed in it.[44]

Holistic Empowerment

Nada que declarar presents a young woman's path into prostitution that is eerily realistic: an upbringing marked by physical and sexual violence, seduction by a lover boy, the tempting prospect of socioeconomic gains, subsequent extraction from the familiar environment and thus her support system, and emotional pressure and physical threats forcing her to consent—or rather, to acquiesce—to her own sexual abuse. Diana is a victim of human trafficking and sexual exploitation whose rights as a human being are violated while she is living in a buzzing German city yet remains completely invisible to her surroundings. Abundant data, some of which I presented above, suggests that both sets of sex workers, those who are coerced like Diana and those who enjoy a higher degree of free choice when entering the industry, are likely to encounter physical and psychological harm when they are offering their bodily orifices and their hands, tongue, and skin for the sexual relief of strangers.

Diana regains her freedom when she shares her story with others. Communication creates bridges between individuals. As the #MeToo movement has shown with respect to other groups who suffered gendered violence, sharing the specific history of prostituted women, men, or children allows an audience to relate on a personal level by recognizing each other's humanity and developing empathy. Authenticity in sharing one's story, as promoted in the #MeToo movement, leads to reciprocity. It encourages a sincere and honest response and a rethinking of one's own views, questioning assumptions one might have held previously, and redefining one's outlook on the issue in question.

What consequences might it have for our societal view on prostitution and for legislation if the cultural bubble of "you cannot rape a prostitute" were to pop? If we were to listen to the accounts of sex workers, such as the former prostitute Bell, who, trafficked and forced into prostitution at age seventeen, reminds us that "there are no jobs where 'choking, getting beaten, and sodomized' is the norm"?[45]

---

44 Moran, *Paid For*, 50.

45 Gabrielle Fonrouge, "Organizations Like Me Too Pledge Support for Legalizing Prostitution, Sex Buying, Pimping," *New York Post*, October 8, 2020, https://nypost.com/2020/10/08/orgs-like-me-too-support-legalizing-prostitution-and-pimping/.

What is tolerable, whether there is adequate payment for intimate physical services, and whether these transactions should be legal in the first place, depends on individual experiences and morals. Such experiences also determine whether human dignity and freedom of choice are intrinsically violated in prostitution. Strictly speaking, only sex workers themselves can answer these questions, and their responses might vary with each sexual transaction that is propositioned.

For this reason, it is imperative that we listen to *their* truth about *their* experiences in prostitution in the way the reader does when learning about the story of Diana in *Nada que declarar*. As the success of the #MeToo movement in other areas of gendered violence has shown, these testimonies possess the power to transform an existent culture, and such a transformation will ultimately offer better safeguards than any legislation against a reoccurrence of sexual abuse of all women, prostitutes included! Moreover, the collection of testimonies as an expression of mainstream concern for all members of a society has the potential to heal by purposefully reaffirming the dignity and humanity of everyone who experienced physical and emotional violation.

Contributors

AYLIN BADEMSOY is a PhD candidate in the German Department at UC Davis. Her dissertation project is a comparative study of genocide in literature and film, focusing on anti-Semitism and anti-Armenian ressentiments in early twentieth-century Turkish, Austrian, and German works, as well as their contemporary reverberations. She is the author of "Homeland, Nation and Gender in the Life Writing of German and Jewish Émigrés" in *Contested Selves: Life Writing and German Culture* (Camden House, 2021). Her research interests include Marxism, feminist theory, and the Frankfurt School.

SONJA BOOS, PhD, was associate professor of German at the University of Oregon, where she was also affiliated with the European Studies Program. Her research interests included the poetics of knowledge, film theory, feminism, psychoanalysis, narrative theory, nineteenth–twentieth-century literature, and critical thought. Her monograph, *In the Event of Speech: Postwar Germany, the Public Sphere and the Holocaust*, appeared in 2013 (Cornell University Press). At the time of her death in 2021, she had completed a book entitled *The Emergence of Neuroscience and the German Novel: Poetics of the Brain* (Palgrave Macmillan, 2021), which she described as a "systematic and comprehensive study of the historical emergence of neuroscience and the concurrent development of the novel in the German-speaking world." Additionally, she had embarked on a new research project about the cultural meaning of home movies and amateur film in Germany and Austria.

KATHRIN BREUER is an associate professor of German at Brandeis University, where she also serves as the director of the German Language Program. Her research interests have been in following the trajectories of myriad migration movements—including political refugees from Nazi Germany immigrating to South America, especially to Colombia, and human trafficking in present times from various nations into Germany. She has published on German Colombian intellectuals during the middle decades of the twentieth century, such as Erich Arendt (*Erich Arendt y su encuentro con el trópico: Serie Monografías Transatlánticas* [Del Centro Editores, 2015]) and Ernesto Volkening, a founding member of the first German Colombian cultural magazine, *Eco: Revista de la cultura de occidente,* and avant-garde translator of German literature into Spanish. She is currently preparing a book, tentatively titled "Ernesto Volkening: Intellektueller, Mittler deutscher Kultur, Exilant in Kolumbien, 1934–1983."

MAUREEN BURDOCK is an award-winning artist, writer, and teacher. Her creative and scholarly work examines topics of displacement, gender, memory, and trauma. Burdock is currently working on "The Queen of Snails," a graphic memoir that is slated to be published by Graphic Mundi in 2022. Burdock is also the creator of *Feminist Fables for the Twenty-First Century: The F Word Project,* a series of graphic fables that address forms of gender-based violence in various cultures, published by McFarland in 2015. She has also published a number of shorter graphic narratives and peer-reviewed essays about comics, life writing, and memory, including "Shapeshifters: Metamorphosing Transgenerational Trauma through Comics" in *Contested Selves: Life Writing and German Culture* (Camden House, 2021), "Desire Paths: PathoGraphics and Transgenerational Trauma" in *PathoGraphics: Narrative, Aesthetics, Contention, Community* (Penn State University Press, 2020), and "Walking Home: A Feminist Tracing of Home and Belonging," in *Sentient Performativities of Embodiment: Thinking alongside the Human* (Lexington Books, 2016).

JESSICA DAVIS is a PhD candidate majoring in modern/contemporary art with minors in African art and eighteenth-nineteenth century European art. She received her BA in art history with a minor in gender studies from Stephen F. Austin State University in 2012 and her MA in art history from Texas Tech University in 2014, where she was the first to graduate from their inaugural program. Davis's master's thesis, "Violence on Canvas: A Representation of Inner Turmoil, or, An Analysis of Otto Dix and his Lustmord Series," focuses on the German artist Otto Dix's gory postwar series of mutilated women. Her dissertation, "The 'Third Sex': Jeanne Mammen's Representations of the *Garçonne* and Lesbians in Print Media," explores connections between Weimar artist Mammen's queer art published in mainstream periodicals and Germany's reception of female homosexuality.

FLORIAN GASSNER received his PhD in Germanic studies from the University of British Columbia, followed by lectureship at Mount Allison University, postdoctoral fellowship at the New Europe College in Bucharest, and DAAD-Lektorat at the Donetsk National University. Associate professor of teaching at the University of British Columbia since 2018, guest professor at the University of Kassel, and collaborator for documenta 14 in 2016–17. Recent publications include "Lenka Reinerová's Uncanny Encounter with Theresienstadt" in *Austrian Studies* (2021),

"Martin Luther in Nineteenth-Century Music, Literature and Politics" in *Edinburgh German Yearbook 13* (Camden House, 2021), and "Garten Eden und Babylonisches Exil in Eginald Schlattners *Das Klavier im Nebel*" in *Spiegelungen* (2021).

SASCHA GERHARDS is a visiting assistant professor of German at Wittenberg University in Springfield, Ohio. He completed his dissertation, "Zeitgeist of Murder: The Krimi and Social Transformation in Post-1945 Germany," in 2012. Gerhards received his BA equivalent in English and social sciences from the University of Cologne and his MA in comparative literature from the University of Rochester. He has published an interview with acclaimed linguist Claire Kramsch on her book *The Multilingual Subject* (2012) and a chapter about the postwar Edgar Wallace films in Jaimey Fisher's *Generic Histories of German Cinema: Genre and Its Deviations* (Camden House, 2013) and contributed to Todd Herzog and Lynn Kutsch's volume *Tatort Germany: The Curious Case of German-Language Crime Fiction* (Camden House, 2014). In 2017 *German Quarterly* published Gerhards's essay "Tracing the Stasi in the Televised German Krimi: *Tatort* and *Polizeiruf 110* Episodes as Precursors to the Post-Reunification Stasi Debate."

LISA HAEGELE is assistant professor of German at Texas State University. Her research focuses on German and Austrian cinema from the postwar period to today. She has published essays in the edited volumes *Berlin School Glossary: An ABC of the New Wave in German Cinema* (Intellect, 2013), *The Berlin School and Its Global Contexts: A Transnational Art Cinema* (Wayne State University Press, 2018), *Celluloid Revolt: German Screen Cultures and the Long 1968* (Camden House, 2019), *Cold War Spy Stories from Eastern Europe* (University of Nebraska Press, 2019), and *New Critical Approaches to the Giallo Film* (University of Mississippi Press, 2022) and in a special issue of *The Sixties: A Journal of History, Politics, and Culture* (2017). She is currently working on a book, "From Pop to Punk: West German Genre Films in the Long 1968," which explores long-forgotten genre films in West Germany from the late 1960s to the early 1980s.

DEBORAH JANSON is an associate professor of German at West Virginia University. Her scholarly interests include national and personal identity in literature by minority and East German writers and issues of social justice, gender equality, and eco-criticism in works from the Enlightenment and Romantic periods through the present. Recent publications include "Unearthing a Post-Humanist Ecological Socialism in Christa Wolf's 'Selbstversuch,' *Kassandra* and *Störfall*" in *Christa Wolf: A Companion* (De Gruyter, 2018), "The Path Not (Yet) Taken: Bettina von Arnim's

Ecological Vision in Her Romantic Fairy Tale 'The Queen's Son'" in *Feminist German Studies* 34 (2019), and a forthcoming article titled "'To Follow the Trail of Pain': Coming to Terms with the Past in Christa Wolf's *In the Flesh*" in *What Remains: Responses to the Legacy of Christa Wolf*, volume 24 in the series Spektrum: Publications of the German Studies Association (Berghahn, June 2022).

Elisabeth Krimmer is professor of German at UC Davis. She is the author of *In the Company of Men: Cross-Dressed Women around 1800* (Wayne State University Press, 2004), *The Representation of War in German Literature: From 1800 to the Present* (Cambridge University Press, 2010), and *German Women's Life Writing and the Holocaust: Complicity and Gender in the Second World War* (Cambridge University Press, 2018). She has also coedited a number of books on German literature and culture for Boydell & Brewer/Camden House, including *Enlightened War: Theories and Cultures of Warfare in Eighteenth Century Germany* (2011), *Religion, Reason, and Culture in the Age of Goethe* (2013), *Realities and Fantasies of German Female Leadership: From Maria Antonia of Saxony to Angela Merkel* (2019), *Writing the Self, Creating Community: Germany Women Authors and the Literary Sphere 1750–1850* (2020), and *Contested Selves: Life Writing and German Culture* (2021).

Anna Sator is a doctoral candidate at the University of Freiburg. Her research project on gender in travel literature on the Soviet Union has an interdisciplinary and intersectional approach. Currently Anna is working at the Centre for Anthropology and Gender Studies Freiburg as the coordinator of the MA Gender Studies Program and as a teacher. Besides her research interest on the topic of the depiction of sexualized violence in children's and adolescent media, she is working in activist groups that aim, through theoretical and practical approaches, to create attention for the topic of sexualized violence. Her most recent publication is "Pucki, Quex und der Dackel am Wagenjoch: Eine Analyse zu Genderaspekten in nationalsozialistischer Kinder- und Jugendliteratur" in *Gender in der deutschsprachigen Kinder- und Jugendliteratur: Vom Mittelalter bis zur Gegenwart* (De Gruyter, 2022).

Melissa Ann Sheedy is a lecturer in the Department of German, Nordic, and Slavic at the University of Wisconsin—Madison. Her research interests center on German Romanticism, fairy tales, feminist theory and ecocriticism, GDR- and post-GDR literature, and intersections of violence and gender. Recent publications include "Flowers, Women, and Work in the Socialist Fairy Tale: Toward a Feminist, Materialist, and Ecocritical Approach" in a cross-issue of *German Quarterly* and *Die Unterrichtspraxis* (2021) and "Es war (noch) einmal: Grimm Versions of

New Fairytales in the GDR," coauthored with Brandy E. Wilcox, in a special issue of *Colloquia Germanica: New Perspectives on Young Adult GDR Literature and Film* (2019). She is also the author of "Feminine Paradigms and Fairy-tale Transformations in the Works of Kerstin Hensel: The Political Implications of Telling a Tale," which appeared in the volume *Protest und Verweigerung: Neue Tendenzen in der deutschen Literatur seit 1989/Protest and Refusal: New Tendencies in German Literature since 1989* (Brill, 2018).

Patricia Anne Simpson, PhD, is professor of German at the University of Nebraska—Lincoln, where she is also affiliate faculty in women's and gender studies. With a primary research focus on gender in the Age of Goethe, Simpson has published widely on German literature, philosophy, and culture from the early modern period to the present. Her monographs include *The Erotics of War in German Romanticism* (Bucknell University Press, 2007); *Cultures of Violence in the New German Street* (Rowman & Littlefield, 2011); and *Reimagining the European Family: Cultures of Immigration* (Palgrave Macmillan, 2013). *The Play World: Toys, Texts, and the Transatlantic German Childhood* (Penn State University Press, 2020) examines German theories and practices of play from 1631 to 1912. Currently serving as coeditor of the *Goethe Yearbook*, she has also coedited several volumes that focus on questions of gender, power, and nation. Simpson is completing a monograph on coloniality in German studies and working on a project about gender and community in early modern Europe.

Katherine Stone, PhD, is an associate professor in the School of Modern Languages and Cultures at the University of Warwick. Her research focuses on the intersections between gender and memory in contemporary Germany. She is the author of *Women and National Socialism in Postwar German Literature: Gender, Memory, and Subjectivity* (2017). Her next monograph will use cultural works to reconstruct how the collective memory of wartime rape evolved in post-1945 Germany, with a focus on the role played by emotion in the reception of difficult histories. Recent articles on the representation of sexual violence and contemporary debates about motherhood have appeared in journals including *Violence against Women, European Journal of Cultural Studies, Feminist Media Studies*, and *Signs: Journal of Women in Culture and Society.*

Niklas Straetker is a doctoral candidate in the Department of Germanic Languages at Columbia University. Working at the intersection of literature, law, and philosophy, he is completing a dissertation on the conceptual transformations of legal and moral guilt (and its imputation) in the eighteenth and nineteenth centuries, with particular emphasis on how narrative and aesthetic strategies were employed to gain access to the supposedly "criminal" or "nonstandard" (irrational, female, non-Western) mind. While, in his dissertation, he focuses on such authors as Rousseau, Lessing, Schiller, Kant, and Kleist, his further research interests include the ambivalent stances toward modernism found in the writings of Nietzsche, Simmel, Kafka, and Musil as well as, more generally, narratology and the Frankfurt School. His publications include "Vom Leben und Sterben der Werte: Relativistische Kantlektüren als Grundlage der Werttheorie in Georg Simmels Philosophie des Geldes" in *Jahrbuch für Interdisziplinäre Anthropologie 8* (2020).

Daniele Vecchiato is assistant professor of German and Translation Studies at the University of Padua. He has published extensively on German literature of the Age of Goethe and is the author of *Verhandlungen mit Schiller* (Wehrhahn, 2015), a monograph on the presentation of the Thirty Years' War in late eighteenth-century literature and historiography. He has also coedited the volume *Kreative Praktiken des literarischen Übersetzens um 1800* (De Gruyter, 2019) and a special issue of *Law and Literature* entitled "Legal Cultures in the Age of Goethe" (2022). His further research interests encompass contemporary German poetry and the aesthetics of political theater. Publications in this latter field include a companion to the work of Durs Grünbein, *Versi per dopodomani* (Mimesis, 2019); an edited volume entitled *#CoronaTheater: Der Wandel der performativen Künste in der Pandemie* (Theater der Zeit, 2022); and a special issue of *Colloquia Germanica* entitled "Staging Justice: Trials and the Law on the German Stage" (2022).

Lisa Wille earned an MA in German studies, art history, and philosophy, as well as a bachelor's degree in economics, at the University of Kassel. Since 2015 she has been a research associate in the Department of Modern German Literature at the Technical University of Darmstadt. Wille received her PhD in 2019 with a dissertation about identity problems in Heinrich Leopold Wagner's dramatic work. Further research interests include gender studies, intersectionality, eighteenth- and twentieth-century literature, and contemporary literature as well as the intersection of literature, economics, and culture. Among her publications are *Einführung in die Gender Studies* (De Gruyter, 2020), with Franziska Schößler; *Zwischen Autonomie und Heteronomie: Bürgerliche Identitätsproblematik in Heinrich Leopold Wagners dramatischem Werk* (Königshausen & Neumann, 2021); and *Heinrich Leopold Wagner: Neue Studien zu seinem Werk*, coedited with Matthias Luserke-Jaqui (Königshausen & Neumann, 2020).

Index

Printed and bound by CPI Group (UK) Ltd, Croydon, CR0 4YY
19/07/2022
03136864-0005

.